DOES NORTH AMERICA EXIST?
Governing the Continent after NAFTA and 9/11

In the wake of the North American Free Trade Agreement and the terrorist attacks of September 11, 2001, renowned public intellectual and scholar Stephen Clarkson asks whether North America 'exists' in the sense that the European Union has made Europe exist.

Clarkson's rigorous study of the many political and economic relationships that link Canada, the United States, and Mexico probes this curious question by looking at the institutions created by NAFTA, a broad selection of economic sectors, and the security policies put in place by the three neighbouring countries following 9/11. This detailed, meticulously researched, and up-to-date treatment of North America's transborder governance allows the reader to see to what extent the United States' dominance in the continent has been enhanced or mitigated by trilateral connections with its two continental partners.

The product of seven years' political research in the areas of economy, international relations, and policy, *Does North America Exist?* is an ambitious and path-breaking study that will be essential reading for those wanting to understand whether the continent containing the world's most powerful nation is holding its own as a global region.

STEPHEN CLARKSON is a Professor of Political Economy at the University of Toronto, Senior Fellow at the Centre for International Governance Innovation, and Fellow of the Royal Society of Canada.

DOES NORTH AMERICA EXIST?

Governing the Continent after NAFTA and 9/11

Stephen Clarkson

UNIVERSITY OF TORONTO PRESS
Toronto Buffalo London

and

WOODROW WILSON CENTER PRESS
Washington, DC

ISBN 978-0-8020-9712-5 (cloth)
ISBN 978-0-8020-9653-1 (paper)

∞

Printed on acid-free paper

Library and Archives Canada Cataloguing in Publication

Clarkson, Stephen, 1937–
    Does North America exist? : governing the continent after NAFTA
    and 9/11 / Stephen Clarkson.

    Includes bibliographical references and index.
    ISBN 978-0-8020-9712-5 (bound).   ISBN 978-0-8020-9653-1 (pbk.)

    1. North America – Economic integration.   2. North America – Economic
    policy.   3. Trade blocs – North America.   4. North America – Economic
    conditions – 21st century.   5. North America – Politics and government –
    21st century.   6. Free trade – North America.   7. National security –
    North America.   I. Title.

    HF1746.C53 2008   337.1'7   C2008-904277-8

University of Toronto Press acknowledges the financial assistance to its
publishing program of the Canada Council for the Arts and the Ontario
Arts Council.

University of Toronto Press acknowledges the financial support of its
publishing activities of the Government of Canada through the Book
Publishing Industry Development Program (BPIDP).

Contents

DOES NORTH AMERICA EXIST?
Governing the Continent after NAFTA and 9/11

Introduction: Framing the Question

'Does North American exist?' To anyone who has ever looked at the Western Hemisphere on a map of the world, this must seem like a silly question. As with South America, which can be seen on every globe hanging from the Panama Canal like an inverted, slightly off-centred pear, North America is obviously the great land mass below the North Pole and between the Pacific and Atlantic oceans.

But, even if North America can be located geographically, does it 'exist' in any meaningful way economically, politically, culturally, or sociologically? Between the Second World War and the end of the Cold War, this question could easily have been answered 'Yes,' although that affirmative would have meant something very different from what it would signify today, now that the North American Free Trade Agreement (NAFTA) has promoted Mexico to fully fledged membership in the continent. From the 1950s through the 1980s, 'North America' was understood to be just the capitalist world's colossal champion plus its northern neighbour – an entity of little moment to Americanists though of obsessive concern to Canadianists.

Analysts of the United States' role in the world scarcely gave Canada a minute's thought, which that country's absence from the index of almost every book on US foreign policy will confirm. For their part, analysts of Canada have always had great difficulty trying to define the nature of the entity that their country comprised with the United States. Already in the 1930s, Canada's leading political economist described the highly integrated dependency as a pair of Siamese twins – 'a very small twin and a very large one,' to be exact.[1] 'Partnership' suggested an equality belied by the huge power asymmetry between the two states. 'Protectorate' or 'empire' conjured up unacceptably pejorative images of Eastern Europe under Soviet control. 'Continental sub-systemic dominance' referred to the many sociological realities in which the Canadian presence was a mere appendage to the American dynamo, but it was a political-science mouthful that never caught on.[2]

However it was described, this unique dyad of free-market super-power and enthusiastic middle-power ally – what I will refer to as the 'old' North America – had become, by the early 1980s, so interdependent and the two governments' interactions so institutionalized that their relationship could be understood as having developed its own, largely unwritten, constitution[3] with a set of norms, rules, rights, and decision-making institutions, whether implicit or explicit, that guided the two governments' behaviour towards each other.[4]

Implicit were the norms, rules, and rights that had become accepted by the civil servants and politicians responsible for managing the relationship. According to the 1960s doctrine dubbed 'quiet diplomacy,' Canada was not to criticize American foreign policy overtly and, as quid pro quo, the United States was not to bully its neighbour. To keep conflict from escalating, issues were not to be linked but were to be dealt with separately, each on its merits. As a result, Canadian-US disputes were mediated to the extent feasible by bureaucrats behind closed doors in order to keep touchy politicians at bay.[5] Whenever Canadian governments tried to promote the interests of and increase the economic space for their domestic firms, the affected US corporations – backed up by Washington's muscle – insisted they had acquired rights not to have their assets' value diminished.

Explicit were the considerable number of institutions established by the two neighbours. The International Joint Commission (IJC) (1909), the St Lawrence Seaway legislation (1954), and the Columbia River Treaty (1961) set up structures for the management of shared rivers and lakes which were bisected by the international boundary. The Auto Pact (1965) offered the major US car assemblers' Canadian subsidiaries privileged conditions for expanding their share of the North American market.

The most consequential institutionalization of the Canadian-American relationship was in security matters. A Permanent Joint Board of Defence had advised the two federal governments on strategic planning since Franklin Delano Roosevelt and William Lyon Mackenzie King signed the Ogdensburg agreement of 1940. The Defence Production Sharing Agreement (1956) gave limited access to the Pentagon's military contracts for Canadian-based companies. In 1958, at the height of the Soviet nuclear threat, the North American Air Defence Command was set up, consummating an integration within the Pentagon's command structure in which Canada retained only nominal control over the deployment of its own air forces.

Canada's colonial economy had originally been controlled by its mother country in Europe and driven by that power centre's market demand, capital, and technology. Piloted along water routes, such abundant raw materials as furs and timber were shipped eastward across the Atlantic. During the first decades of the twentieth century, Canada's economy became progressively more integrated along a north-south axis owing to new networks of roads and railways. By 1950, when the British Empire was in both political and economic ruins, the United States had completely displaced Great Britain as the Canadian economy's chief investor, having provided an overwhelming 86 per cent of its stock of incoming foreign direct investment, taking 65 per cent of its exports, and supplying 67 per cent of its imports.[6]

The old North America's apparently irreversible integrative trend was put on hold from the late 1970s to the early 1980s by a complex concatenation of domestic developments in Canada, American actions, and Ottawa's reactions. Domestically, two decades of positive nation building were triggered by the enthusiasm that was unleashed in Expo '67, the country's centennial self-celebration, and culminated in the 1982 patriation of the Canadian constitution complete with its emblematic Charter of Rights and Freedoms. During this period, growing evidence of the Americans' military disaster in Vietnam was accompanied by such manifestations of social dysfunction in the United States as conflagrations in its racial ghettos and assassinations of its political leaders, phenomena that provoked among Canadians a strong desire to distance themselves from the US model. The Canadian government resisted responding to this new anti-Americanism until, in August 1971, President Richard Nixon unilaterally imposed a surcharge on all foreign imports. Unable to obtain an exemption from an action it feared would cripple Canadian exports, Pierre Trudeau's government belatedly began to consider whether its continental dependency was excessive.

The 'Third Option' of 1972 proposed to redirect Canadian foreign policy along more independent lines. The Foreign Investment Review Agency and the Canada Development Corporation were established to moderate and even try to reverse the steady growth of US ownership of the Canadian economy. In the context of Hollywood's overwhelming dominance of mass entertainment north of the 49th parallel, various measures were introduced to bolster Canadian writers' and artists' capacity to communicate with their readers, listeners, and viewers via books and magazines, radio and television. Finally, as the meteoric emblem of the Trudeau era's ineffectual nationalism, the controversial National Energy Program (NEP) of 1980 flamed over Canada's political space for a year and a half. Although the NEP failed to extract the petroleum industry from its continental integration, scholars agreed that Canada had become more autonomous by the early 1980s.[7]

Deeply worried during this same period about its apparent hegemonic decline, the United States launched a threefold strategy to change the rules by which its economic rivals favoured their corporate champions in order to outdo US transnational corporations. The US government aimed simultaneously to reduce the autonomy of its foreign competitors and increase the capacity of its own corporate champions on a globally levelled playing field. Washington's preferred option, multilateral negotiations under the aegis of the General Agreement on Tariffs and Trade (GATT), proved agonizingly slow because of resistance by the other major players – the European Union (EU), Japan, Brazil, and India – which wanted to nurture their economic autonomy and feared that their own corporations would succumb under Washington's proposed rules. The US fallback position – individual arm-twisting with its global competitors – used denial of access to the US market to lever reductions in their discriminatory practices. But extensive economic force exerted unilaterally against its Cold War allies tended to be counterproductive, generating ill will and increasing resistance.

With multilateralism blocked and unilateralism backfiring, the US government realized that successfully negotiating new bilateral agreements would increase pressure on its more recalcitrant competitors to come to the bargaining table lest they face exclusion from a new US-led system. Bilaterally negotiating comprehensive agreements with compliant countries might also yield important precedents for the rules that Washington wanted to universalize. Two of its most potentially compliant interlocutors lived next door.

The United States applied its new bilateralism to its North American neighbourhood with a combination of tactical and strategic aims. Tactically, it had a direct interest in resolving what it liked to call specific trade and investment 'irritants' with its two neighbours, particularly industrial policies that favoured domestic over US companies. The US agenda also included obtaining more secure supplies of Canada's abundant resources and better access to Mexico's cheap labour, as well as expanding its consumer market in both economies.

At the same time, the United States' neighbourhood was responding to the pressures of neoconservative globalization, with Canada first off the blocks. The influential 1985 Royal Commission Report on Canada's Economic Prospects judged that the Trudeau-era attempt to engineer more national economic autonomy had failed. By this time, Canada's economic reliance on trade had reached the point that its total exports and imports had grown from 43 per cent of its GDP in 1950 to 54 per cent. That trade reliance was sustained by a bilateral commercial dependency: by 1986, Canada was getting 70 per cent of its imports from United States and sending 78 per cent of its exports there. For the commission, this meant that the future depended on fostering, not resisting, the economic relationship with the United States. Its report converted the recently elected Prime Minister Brian Mulroney from a sworn enemy to an eloquent advocate of an economic-integration agreement with the United States.

Canada's tariffs were already extremely low, and its economy had historically been one of the most receptive to foreign investment, so Canadian concessions on energy and investment in the economic negotiations with Washington were more formal than transformative. Nevertheless, the controversial Canada-United States Free Trade Agreement (CUFTA) was bitterly contested among Canadians during the 1988 federal election campaign, which turned into a quasi-referendum on the agreement. The voting public was deeply polarized over whether the limitations on their federal and provincial governments' policy autonomy – which Brian Mulroney's government had conceded in order to gain what it claimed was 'secure access' to the vast American market – heralded the end of Canada's two-century-long struggle to maintain its sovereignty. Even if CUFTA did not precipitate Canada's demise when it came into effect on January 1, 1989 – as many had feared – it represented both the apogee of the old North America's integration and the prelude to its demise.

From the Old to the New North America

Given their settlement history and Hispanic culture, Mexicans had traditionally considered that they belonged to both Latin and North America. Although its parallels with Canadian economic development during the nineteenth century were striking,[8] Mexico's relationship with the United States had developed in a completely different manner, following the humiliating US military occupation of Mexico City in 1847 and the loss of more than half its territory to what became Texas, California, Nevada, Utah, and parts of New Mexico, Arizona, Wyoming, and Colorado. Just as the Dominion of Canada's resource exploitation and industrial development had taken place under the auspices of both British and American capital, Mexico's economic expansion in the late nineteenth century was fuelled by American and British capital, owing to the welcome mat extended by President Porfirio Díaz to foreign investors. Whereas in the first decades of the twentieth century, Canada had shifted from autonomy within the declining British Empire towards dependence within the United States' rising imperium, Mexico did the reverse by shifting from dependence to autarchy. Its prolonged and violent revolution culminated in the socially progressive constitution of 1917, whose rhetorical radicalism generated political substance over the next two decades through an ever-expanding socialization of farms and nationalization of resources, a campaign that eventually led to the expulsion of foreign enterprise from the energy sector in 1938 during the presidency of Lázaro Cárdenas.

Although Mexicans' nationalism identified with a Latin American development model and nourished strong anti-'gringo' sensitivities, it was deeply ambivalent. Because of the US need for agricultural labour and because of the large numbers of Chicanos who remained in the southern US states a hundred years after their annexation, transborder familial and economic networks developed to the point that the southern American and northern Mexican states took on some characteristics of a border region. These social relations supported a quiet economic integration with the United States, which continued to supply a growing share of Mexico's capital, imports, and export market, the rhetoric of the 1917 revolution notwithstanding.

Over the years, the two countries worked out a modus vivendi in which Mexico's political leaders would denounce US imperialism in public but make backroom deals with Washington in private. This informally constituted set of norms and practices was regularized in a few institutions, most importantly those set up by the 1944 Treaty relating to the Utilization of Waters of the Colorado and Tijuana Rivers and of the Rio Grande between the United States and Mexico.

During the Second World War, Mexico cooperated militarily with the Pentagon in monitoring its western shores for Japanese incursions and in watching the Caribbean for German naval threats. In response to its acute, draft-induced labour shortages in 1942, Washington initiated the Bracero ('arm') guest-worker program, which authorized some 300,000 agricultural and railroad workers to work in the United States until the end of the war.

To accommodate the inflow of returning contract workers after 1964, when the program was terminated by the United States, the Mexican government initiated the Border Industrialization (maquiladora) program, which allowed US corporations unique concessions if they located assembly plants in northern border states and re-exported their entire output back to the United States.[9] The broad American public did not realize how much social integration these labour flows were creating on both sides of its southern border, still less how much economic integration. Nor did most Mexicans understand how dependent they had become on the economic relationship with their historic enemy-cum-partner. By 1977, the United States held an astounding $3.2 billion or 70 per cent of Mexico's foreign direct investment and, by 1980, it accounted for 70 per cent of its foreign trade.[10]

Canada's shift from a policy paradigm promoting national autonomy to one pursuing continental integration had required a change of government. Mexico's experience was different. While CUFTA was being negotiated in the mid-1980s, the economic controls that for decades had shored up Mexico's stubborn experiment in industrial autarchy were already losing their effectiveness. Mexico City executed a more radical, if parallel, transformation than that of Canada but without replacing its ruling party. Under pressure in the early 1980s from a devastating currency crisis and the failure of its banking system, which it had nationalized in order to fend off further economic disaster, the ruling Partido Revolucionario Institucional (PRI) carried out an internal paradigm putsch against itself.

Within the PRI, a new generation of young technocrats, who had been largely educated in American graduate schools, performed a strategic volte-face by abandoning the party's autonomist, almost autarchic development strategy in favour of rapidly opening the economy to the world and drastically dismantling the interventionist state which their authoritarian one-party-government mentors had constructed over the previous decades. Joining the world's best two economic clubs – GATT (1986) and the Organization for Economic Cooperation and Development (OECD) (1992) – required Mexico to commit to deregulating its elaborate systems of trade controls, to liberalizing the marketplace, and to privatizing its myriad state-owned entities. Other changes such as abandoning its agricultural controls were made on President Carlos Salinas de Gortari's own initiative without support by the World Bank and were regarded as ill-conceived from the beginning. The need to democratize its political institutions was accepted in theory but resisted in practice by a presidency ever more centralized in its decision-making process.

Spaniards may have settled Mexico long before the French sailed up the St Lawrence, but relations between the United States' two neighbouring states were minimal. Distant if amicable in their consciousness of each other, Ottawa and Mexico City had inhabited separate worlds, the one focused in the North Atlantic community, the other looking southward to Iberian America. They shared few common interests. Formal diplomatic relations were established only in 1944 and for twenty-five years did not generate even the hint of a close relationship.

Despite Prime Minister Pierre Trudeau's prowess in Spanish and his easy relationship with President Miguel de la Madrid, his government paid Mexico scant attention. A Canada-Mexico Joint Ministerial Committee created in 1968 to provide a forum for discussion held its first meeting only in 1971. Mexico remained just as remote as the whole of Latin America from the Canadian government's prime concerns even when, in 1972, Ottawa announced its 'Third Option' strategy of international diversification. Conscious of shared economic interests in the energy sectors, however, the two countries drew closer in their foreign-policy thinking during the later 1970s and early 1980s as a result of their objections to the United States' policies. Both opposed US sponsorship of right-wing militarism in Chile, both supported the Contadora peace process against the Contras' atrocities in Central America, and both resisted Cuba's ostracism from the hemisphere's governance, helping it survive the United States' economic embargo.

Whatever the affinities between the two members of the continental periphery may have been, Mexico was long a negligible factor in Canada's trade, representing its sixteenth export market and ninth supplier of imports. Ottawa's consciousness of the United States' other neighbour was still minimal when Minister Brian Mulroney decided in 1990 to occupy the chair that had been reserved for Canada in the Organization of American States (OAS) and announced yet another new Canadian strategy for Latin America.

Although these two countries' relationships with Washington were routinized in many formal and informal ways, virtually nothing linked the three states at a political level in the governance of the entire trinational space. The economy was an entirely different matter, because an increasing number of transnational corporations (TNCs) had been forming cross-border networks and were already treating North America as a single production, distribution, and marketing zone. With operations, shareholders, and alliances in all three economies, these firms' boundaries and nationalities began to blur. By 1989, TNCs based in the United States accounted for 69 per cent of total US exports to Canada, 65 per cent of which were shipped to the TNCs' affiliates. The analogous figures for exports to Mexico were 46 per cent and 52 per cent.[11] Such high levels of intra-firm trade set the stage for CUFTA and NAFTA, whose rules helped these corporate networks further intensify their transborder linkages.

Notwithstanding this evidence of a deepening, continent-wide capital accumulation, the gulf between the three polities remained deep. Mexico had an authoritarian, non-aligned, Third World political economy which had entered a prolonged exchange and debt crisis in 1982. For its part, Canada had an industrialized economy and, as a liberal parliamentary democracy, was deeply committed to NATO's confrontation with the Soviet bloc. The countries did not compete directly in the American market where each had created niches in complementary export areas – Canada with natural resources, semi-finished products, and other producer goods; Mexico with low-wage, labour-intensive manufacturing. Nevertheless, by the end of the decade, the idea of free trade with Mexico loomed as a threat to the Canadian understanding of the old North America, a concept towards which Ottawa felt highly possessive. In June 1990, when the Mexican and American governments announced that they were negotiating a commercial agreement, Ottawa reacted coolly. It worried that the Mexicans would intrude into its special economic relationship with the United States, fearing that a Mexico-US treaty might dilute whatever advantages CUFTA had won for Canadian exporters. Specifically, Ottawa fretted that Canada might become less attractive to foreign investors as a platform where they could locate in order then to gain access to the American market. So it was in order to limit its losses – not to welcome a new ally – that Canada sought admission to the Mexico-US talks.

With support from presidents George H.W. Bush (who agreed to Canada's participation in the Mexico-US economic negotiations in return for Ottawa's naval support for the US fleet in his attack on Iraq) and Salinas (who thought that Ottawa could help Mexico City offset its negotiating disadvantage), Canada was duly admitted to the negotiations that began in June 1991. What would have become another bilateral US investment treaty morphed at the negotiating table into the controversial three-way NAFTA.

The idea of free trade with Mexico was hotly contested within the US labour and environmental movements. Sensing an opportunity in his 1992 presidential campaign against President Bush, the Democratic Party nominee, Bill Clinton, promised to amend the deal. From the right, third-party candidate Ross Perot railed against the 'giant sucking sound' that would drain jobs to the barely regulated maquiladora assembly plants south of the Rio Grande. In Mexico, where the PRI still remained in near total political control, few outside the ranks of academic specialists and government policy makers debated the issues. NAFTA was peddled through the state-manipulated media as a giant, triumphant step towards Mexico's opening to the world.

Thus, it was literally with the stroke of a pen that Mexico became the third member of what I call the 'new' North America, whose territorial boundary suddenly jumped southward to the Mexico-Guatemala border on January 1, 1994 when, slightly enlarged by President Clinton to include two trilateral commissions on labour and the environment, NAFTA came into effect.

Restraining the interventionist capacities of the Canadian and Mexican governments was tactically important to the United States but secondary to achieving its broader strategic objective. It used one of the breakthroughs in its North American negotiations – the inclusion of services in trade law – as a bargaining lever to have these norms integrated in the new General Agreement on Trade in Services (GATS) of the World Trade Organization (WTO). The Americans also used the precedent of incorporating intellectual property rights in NAFTA to achieve the WTO's agreement on Trade-Related Aspects of Intellectual Property Rights.

Whereas CUFTA had been commonly dismissed abroad as merely consolidating the United States' dominance over its northern fiefdom that had been a century in the making, NAFTA burst into the global consciousness as further evidence that regionalizing forces were reshaping the post-Cold War world's economic geography. It was commonly understood that a continuing revolution in information technology had been liberating corporations from regulation by the nation-state so that they could manufacture and market transnationally. In the double movement associated with the new interdependencies called globaliza-

Figure 1: GDP of the EU and NAFTA, 1960–99 (current US$ million)

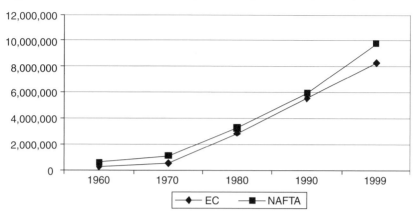

Source: Pastor, *Towards a North American Community*, 34–6 (see n.13).

tion,[12] some governments reacted to losing control over their domestic market by aligning themselves with their former neighbour-competitors in order to create bigger, more efficient markets that could be regulated by supra-state forms in continental groupings – a strategy designed to enhance the ability of these countries' corporations to compete in the global arena against other regional economies' firms. NAFTA's innovation was to incorporate the world's only superpower and leading industrialized economy in a continentally integrated regime that included a Third World country.

As I explain in more detail in the next chapter, by 1990, North America's three economies constituted the world's largest world region, slightly exceeding the European Union's twelve states in both population and gross domestic product. Whereas North America's 361 million inhabitants constituted roughly 7 per cent of the world's population and produced 30 per cent of global gross domestic product (US$6.6 trillion) at the time NAFTA was formed, the EU's 345 million people represented a slightly smaller 6.5 per cent of total world population and produced 29 per cent of world GDP (US $6.5 trillion).[13] The figure above graphs the growth of these regions' GDPs from 1960 to 1999. As can be seen from the chart, NAFTA's gross domestic product was not only higher than that of the EU, its growth was also faster, especially from 1990 to 1999, when Mexico was joining the North American community. Whereas EU GDP grew by $8.1 billion (from $200 billion to $8.3 trillion) between 1960 and 1999, the three economies of North America together grew by $9.2 billion (from $565 billion to $9.8 trillion).[14]

So the question 'Does North America exist?' turns out not to be as frivolous as it may have appeared at first. This book's nineteen chapters propose answers to this question by probing a range of distinct problems. But, before launching into these detailed studies, I need to reframe the basic issues and clarify the analytical tools I will use.

Reframing the Question

In textbook-simple terms, markets need states to provide the legal and regulatory framework within which enterprises can pursue their profit-seeking activities. In the classroom, political institutions also enjoy a perfect geographical fit with the markets they direct. In fact, when the Keynesian nation-state was at its apogee during the first decades after the Second World War, markets actually did mainly coincide with the territorial boundaries of the states that regulated them. In this period, the production processes, market organization, distribution systems, and division of labour fitted within economies whose regulatory institutions were provided by the national or federal government and its subcentral provincial, state, or municipal units.[15] Problems developed when the economic-production and capital-accumulation regimes became disconnected from the political systems' regulatory mode.

A massive disjuncture from this model developed when the accelerating technological and organizational interconnections we call globalization started to undermine nation-states' regulatory capacity, with the result that transnational corporations increasingly raised their capital, installed their production operations, and pursued their marketing strategies beyond the boundaries of the states where their head offices were located. When their operations' scope became regional or even global, TNCs pressed for types and sites of regulation more supportive of their expanding entrepreneurial objectives. State governments responded domestically by deregulating themselves and internationally by creating new regulatory regimes – whether in regions (the European Union), at the global level (the World Trade Organization), or in functional policy regimes with no specific territorial base (the Internet). In the old North America, this realignment between the economic and the political was signalled with CUFTA's norms, rules, rights, and institutions, which were designed to establish a mode of regulation for an economic zone in which TNCs would be empowered to operate across the international boundary free of many of the Canadian and US government regulations that had previously constrained them.

When the University of Alberta's Julian Castro-Rea wrote that 'in January 1994, North America formally entered the club of world regions, launching the project of an integrated economic space,'[16] he was venturing the idea that NAFTA had reconstituted this three-member territory as a post-EU, second-generation political economy belonging to the same global phenomenon as Mercosur in South America or ASEAN – the Association of South-East Asian Nations – in Southeast Asia.[17] Touted as fostering the three economies' integration into one continental marketplace, NAFTA heralded higher rates of cross-border TNC expansion through mergers, acquisitions, and new investment, as well as greater trade flows through intra-firm transactions. Whether these transborder economic interactions indicated the birth of a distinct 'world region' with its own mode of regulation for a self-contained political economy, or were merely manifestations at the regional level of globalization's integrative processes, is a central concern in this book. If, as in one case, NAFTA pushed General Motors, for which Mexico had previously been part of its Latin America marketing region, to turn the trinationalized North America into a separate region within its global production system, and if similar restructuring was typical of most major market players' response to this 'integrated economic space,' it would suggest that the new North America did exist in a significant political-economy sense.

Answering the Question

This study is not primarily focused on the normative question whether North America *should* advance along the lines established by the oldest, most institutionally mature world region, the European Union. This view is certainly attractive, has such eloquent academic advocates as Robert Pastor,[18] and has been promoted by none other than Mexican President Vicente Fox (2000–6) and his first foreign minister, Jorge Castañeda. The three-member region unquestionably shares deep historical roots with Europe. But whether North America under NAFTA 'exists' in any way similar to the EU, with its increasing political, economic, sociological, and cultural integration, is the empirical question I propose to investigate.

The European Community was a political project first and foremost.

The integration of the former belligerents' economies was the means chosen to achieve the visionary objective of ending centuries of internecine war. 'To make Europe is to make peace,' the Community's founding father, Jean Monnet, famously said. Its highly complex system was designed to constrain the region's largest power, Germany, from abusing its economic clout. At the same time, its institutions would empower the smaller members by offsetting their low political weight. Established at a time when social-democratic ideas held sway, the European Community developed solidarity programs that helped raise the poorer members to the economic level of the richer. Since its foundations were laid during the Keynesian era, Europe's regional institutions – particularly its Commission and Court of Justice – mimicked those of a strong state.

It is risky to assume that North America is an embryonic version of this ambitious model. Its membership is small – three compared to the EU's twelve member states in 1990 – but its asymmetries are much starker. The United States overpowers its neighbours to the north and south economically. In 1990 US GDP of $5.8 trillion was ten times Canada's $574 billion and twenty-two times Mexico's $262 billion. It represented 87 per cent of North American GDP, of which the neighbour economies accounted for only 9 and 4 per cent respectively. The United States' citizens were also richer, enjoying a gross national income per capita of $24,000 – which, while just 18 per cent higher than the Canadian GNI per capita of $20,000, was over eight times higher than the Mexican GNI per capita of only $2,800. This imbalance compared strikingly with the relative symmetry in Europe, where the largest economy, Germany, at $1.7 trillion, represented 27 per cent of the European Union's GDP and was merely two-fifths larger than the second and third largest markets – France ($1.2 trillion) and Italy ($ 1.1 trillion) – which each produced 19 per cent of the EU's GDP. (At $0.99 trillion, the United Kingdom– the fourth-largest EU economy – produced 15 per cent of EU GDP in 1990.) The EU's wealth disparities were also considerably smaller: Germany's gross national income per capita in 1990 ($20,560) was some three times higher than that of Portugal ($6,810), the EU's poorest member state at the time.[19]

No multi-state region can any longer be understood without considering its global context, least of all North America. As the United States of America's home base, the northern continent of the western hemisphere is the platform from which the world's only superpower engages with the rest of the planet. With its political energies consumed by its geopolitical strategic challenges and its ongoing domestic political drama, the United States government has little time to spare for what appears to it to be the pettier, day-to-day problems of dealing with its immediate periphery. For these two neighbour states, the opposite is true: huge, disproportionate amounts of energy are spent obsessing about their relationship with the United States. Our task is to develop a clearer understanding of the transborder governance that ties these three countries together.

At this point, I wish to clarify the meaning of a number of concepts that weave through my analysis, concepts whose connotations vary considerably from author to author or from one academic discipline to another. Sometimes categories simply attempt to describe a reality, like so many labels affixed to objects in a museum. But static situations change over time, so many concepts raise questions concerning how relationships are evolving. The notions in question here concern the power system in North America, the relationships between its individual states, the types of power they enjoy, and the main spaces in which they operate.

The Power System in North America

Although the new North America has only three members, its central state has such superior clout vis-à-vis the two neighbour states that I use three categories to describe the power system that they form together.

Imperium: When a state imposes its will over states in its sphere of influence through the use of coercion – typically the threat to use physical force or impose severe economic penalties – I see an imperial system.

Hegemony: When the same state achieves its goals by generating a willing consensus with the system's other, weaker members about how the system should operate, I consider it hegemonic. Of course, such a project as NAFTA may be hegemonic for those in a neighbour state who support it (its economic elites) but appear imperial to those who strenuously oppose it (the labour and environmental movements). While situations described by these labels may appear static, they can quickly become dynamic. If we see a shift towards Canadians accepting US norms and rules, we may see a process of hegemonification taking place. However, if the United States is exerting its muscle more coercively than consensually with respect to its immediate neighbours,

North America would have become more imperial than hegemonic. ('Periphery' is used in this text in a purely territorial sense to refer to Canada and Mexico's continental location on either side of the United States. It will not connect with world-systems theory.)

Autarchy: At the opposite end of the spectrum from imperium, we have situations where a state is disconnected from the other members of its system. Instead, it may simply want to control what is going on within its own space in any way it pleases and, to that effect, may erect barriers at its border to prevent the passage across it, for instance, of diseased cows from Canada. Mexico's approach to economic development in the mid-twentieth century was largely autarchic, and the United States continues to assert autarchy in certain economic sectors, such as its coastal shipping.

Relations between the System's Individual States

Bilateral: In a three-member system, inter-member relationships are either bilateral or trilateral. Because of its history, most of North America's transborder relationships have been bilateral, taking place within the US-Canada or the US-Mexico dyad. Since most transborder interactions remain bilateral, I include these in my discussions of transborder governance.

Trilateral: Only with the advent of NAFTA have trilateral relations emerged in various sectors, particularly among the three governments. Following September 11, 2001, trilateral inter-governmental relations developed on border-security matters and have deepened since the inauguration of the Security and Prosperity Partnership of North America (SPP) in March 2005.

Asymmetry: Because of the huge power discrepancies between the United States and its two neighbours, the principal two dyads are strongly asymmetrical. I assess whether these asymmetries have become more acute or less so.

Imbalance: Because Mexico's political economy is so different from Canada's, there is also a discrepancy between the US-Canada relationship and the US-Mexico relationship. I call this effect 'imbalance' and try to identify in what respects the disproportion is diminishing as the two peripheral countries become more similar in their US relations. Related to this question, I particularly wish to assess whether the development of the third North American bilateral has helped Mexico to become more like its northern counterpart and so reduce the imbalance with Canada of its periphery-centre relationship. Furthermore, I want to determine whether, and in what ways, the North American 'world region' has evolved from simply two separate bilateral relationships to a more trilateral space, be it through new institutions such as the SPP or through the workings of corporations across the continental marketplace.

The Types of Capacity Enjoyed by Individual States

A state's ability to do what it wants within its territory and outside it is the subject of much international-relations and political-economy analysis. Several concepts tend to describe this phenomenon. Here, I use the terms 'sovereignty,' 'autonomy,' and 'capacity' but not 'independence' to address three separate aspects of this subtle question.

Sovereignty: This term is reserved for the formal, legal notion designating a state as a legitimate member of the world community if it is recognized as such by its international peers and if it has a properly constituted political system. It may concede elements of its sovereign powers when it signs and implements an international treaty. The treaty's other signatories also give up parts of their sovereignty in order to achieve the ends defined in the agreement.

Autonomy: I use this term to refer to the ability of a state to act as it wishes *within* its own territory.

Capacity: This refers to the ability of the state to achieve its objectives *outside* its own territory. By giving up some sovereignty, a state or its stakeholders may lose domestic autonomy but gain the international capacity to achieve what they want beyond their borders. By asserting autarchy, the opposite may occur: a state may lose capacity beyond its borders but gain autonomy within them.

The Spaces in Which States Operate

Given the centrality of state groupings in this study, we have to be careful how we use the ambiguous notion of 'region.' For the category of multi-state collectivities such as the European Union and NAFTA, I talk about 'world regions.' The notion of 'region' is restricted to the phenomenon known mainly in North America as border regions – areas such as the Great Lakes states and provinces which share common interests but are divided by a national boundary. As adjectives, 'continental' is reserved for describing North America as a whole, 'regional' for smaller, cross-boundary areas, and 'local' for areas within countries.

To raise the question of transborder governance in North America suggests that I am addressing a purely continental problem. However, many global transformations affect North America just as they affect Europe or Asia. In this work, I try to distinguish governance phenomena that are continental from those that are actually global even though they are occurring in the space of North America.

In sum, this book's goal is to assess whether and in what sense the new North America, created by NAFTA in 1994, reconfigured in the wake of the September 11, 2001 attack, and reanimated by the 2005 SPP, actually 'exists.'

Instead of proceeding deductively from a priori assumptions about the nature of world regions, it adopts a more inductive approach in order to take the reader through a dozen and a half probes whose purpose is to describe the continent's institutions, many of its economic sectors, and its inter-governmental security relations. I present the results of more than seven years' research on these issues in five political and economic modes:

- state re-regulation through regional institutionalization;
- market reconfiguration at the continental level;
- the transition from embryonic continental to more mature global governance;
- market reconfiguration at the global level; and
- persistent state dominance through inter-governmental relations.

Most of the politically significant institutions on North America's vast territory continue to operate within its three countries' national boundaries. Nevertheless, their frontiers are far from impermeable. Indeed, the people, goods, services, energy, information, and natural resources that are constantly moving across the Canada-US and Mexico-US frontiers (and to a lesser degree between Mexico and Canada) create a multitude of social, cultural, economic, and political transboundary relations whose characteristics I define under the rubric of governance, a notion whose use in this work needs some further explanation.

Two Key Concepts: Government and Governance

Since much of North America's transborder reality is driven by the independent actions of non-state economic, cultural, or social actors, these non-governmental players need to be included in our study. Nevertheless, relations among the three states remain of central importance on the continent. To help readers work their way through these generally complex issues, I need to explain the distinction between *government* and *governance* that runs throughout my analysis.

Not so many years ago, political science did perfectly well with the notion of 'government,' which denoted the institutions and processes of legitimately sanctioned (that is, constitutionally established and/or internationally recognized) public policy making, regulation, adjudication, and enforcement. Understood in this traditional way, government was the prerogative, responsibility, and monopoly of the nation-state's political institutions and of those in its subcentral and municipal components. Typically, its functions and processes included the activity of legislatures, of executives, of bureaucracies, of courts, and of the enforcement mechanisms assigned to the state's police and armed forces.

This is not to say that politics outside the narrow confines of government was ignored. Political parties were studied as the prime democratic link between the citizenry and its government. No analyst was naive enough to assume that the connection between government and society was cut off the moment an election's results were announced. Considerable research was devoted to interest groups, which championed the positions of business in the marketplace and lobbied to influence government policies. Studied as well were citizens' organizations, which campaigned for legislation to ameliorate various societal causes such as the plight of pensioners, natives, or the handicapped.[20]

Until a few decades ago, domestic and international politics were understood to occur in separate, watertight compartments. Accordingly, the academic discipline of international relations (IR) dealt with the efforts of nation-states' diplomats or generals to achieve their goals beyond their borders. Institutionally, IR focused on the inter-governmental organizations that states established to manage certain collective issues, such as war (the North Atlantic Treaty Organization), peace (the United Nations), commerce (the WTO), or culture (the United Nations

Educational, Scientific, and Cultural Organization [UNESCO]). These organizations varied in their relative power – the International Monetary Fund (IMF) was strong (in the sense that it could impose policies on countries suffering economic crises), while the International Labour Organization was weak (since its conventions prescribing workers' rights could not be enforced on recalcitrant regimes) – but they all operated at the behest of their member governments.[21]

This text diverges from much current writing pertaining to the international domain, which tends simply to replace the notion of government with that of governance. For instance, discourse on the European Union generally refers to all continental-level politics as governance, despite the fact that some of the EU's institutions and processes exhibit such authoritative characteristics of government as the binding directives made by the European Commission or the judgments issued by the European Court of Justice, which have direct effect in the legal systems of the member states. Even in domestic political analysis, one finds the notion of governance defined in a way that could equally well explain government: 'The institutions, processes, and traditions by which power is exercised and directions are set for society.'[22] The now mothballed Law Commission of Canada explicitly viewed governance as a normative issue of quality – transparency, legitimacy, accountability – and so considered governance to be an integral and coexisting aspect of the more mechanical workings of government.

Adopting a conceptually conservative position, I propose keeping both the baby (government) and the bath water in which it sits (governance) while distinguishing between them in terms of causal effectiveness. I call governance those activities of extra-parliamentary parties and interest groups that take place on the boundary of formally constituted government. The boundary between the two concepts is necessarily difficult to determine. Extra-parliamentary activities such as business lobbying and citizen-group pressures are considered governance. Parliament's debates and hearings involving its successfully elected representatives are seen as part of government.

Since my aim is to understand whether North America exists beyond the internal operations of the continent's three nation-states, I am asking whether transborder governance – economic exchanges of goods, services, and capital; political arrangements to regulate these interactions; social movements that contest these arrangements or support them – constitutes a significant reality. To understand transborder politics in North America, we need to unpack the nuances of how policies are made and how politics are conducted in issues that play out binationally or trinationally both *inside* and *outside* formally constituted legislatures, executives, bureaucracies, courts, and security forces.

Across national boundaries, new forms of political decision making are emerging as TNCs and civil-society organizations (CSOs) negotiate directly with governments.[23] This new transborder governance manifested itself dramatically in the WTO's decision regarding the pricing and production of pharmaceuticals to treat pandemics in low- and middle-income countries. In this case, Médecins sans frontières negotiated with both governments and the pharmaceutical TNCs to bring down the price of drugs for HIV/AIDS patients in the global South.[24] Much government aid – whether financed directly by individual states or collectively by government-funded international organizations – is actually delivered in the field by such CSOs as the International Red Cross, which are treated in this study as elements of governance.

In some cases, market or civil-society actors take responsibility for implementing the policies that are formulated in their sector. Here, the former hierarchical superiority of government has been replaced by a heterarchical relationship in which government interacts more cooperatively than authoritatively with other entities in the marketplace or civil society to generate governance. Although it is not new that nongovernmental players take the initiative in pushing an issue onto the governmental agenda, it is new that government has become not just accustomed to living with this kind of governance but sometimes even reliant on it.

While the bulk of public policy making is still the preserve of the various federal, subcentral, or municipal levels of government, governance affects this traditional government activity when domestic and foreign TNCs and CSOs impinge on the state's decision making. To sum up, *government* involves the exercise of power with constitutional legitimacy and binding effect, while *governance* is the exercise of influence outside or on the boundary of government structures through interactions among various political, social, and economic actors. Transborder governance is our concern when the traditional government institutions – legislatures, bureaucracies, or executives – are not exercising power exclusively but are engaged in partnerships with networks, coalitions, agencies, TNCs, and CSOs or when a company or its business association or a trade union or a citizens' group interacts with a municipal, provincial, or federal government official.[25]

In making the distinction between government and governance, I recognize that the boundaries between the two concepts are contestable and variable. Analysts will disagree in their definitions of what reality fits which category. Indeed, as political circumstances change, some phenomena may shift from one category to another. A specific government activity becomes governance every time a public-sector entity is privatized. Alternatively, what may once have been market government can become public government, as was the case when the Hudson's Bay Company, having earlier ruled a vast territory across British North America, lost these political functions to the newly constituted Dominion of Canada in the latter half of the nineteenth century. Throughout the second half of the twentieth century, the European Community has been erecting a system of institutions which began as governance and progressively approached government in their heft.

In short, I identify *government* first by its structures' and its actors' formal legitimacy (which comes externally from a state's recognition by the international community and internally from its legally legitimate constitution) and, second, by the directly authoritative and inherently coercive force of its decisions, regulations, norms, and judgments. The structures and actors that I consider *governance* also contribute to the generation of a government's norms, rules, goals, and processes of decision making, but the scope of governance is generally narrower and rarely territorially fixed. Both can involve very specific issues or a whole system. In general, government has more permanence and stability, while governance is more transient: what is here today may be gone tomorrow.

Recognizing that the member governments of NAFTA operate on a range of at least five planes from the local, provincial, and federal through to the continental and global, I focus in this book on the fourth level to ask what kind of continental government or governance exists in North America. There is continental *government* if any legitimate institutions can make decisions that have direct effects on the member states. Alternatively, if there are binational or trinational actors or institutions that can take actions influencing the behaviour of the member states, there is transborder or continental *governance* in North America.

An Editorial Note

The *Canadian Oxford Dictionary* has been used as the authority for spelling: labour, Department of National Defence. However, when US institutions are mentioned or American documents are cited directly, their US spelling is left intact: labor, Department of Defense.

Since I refer to some of NAFTA's chapters in the course of this analysis, and since I also cross-reference material in other chapters of this text as I proceed, I have adopted the following convention. NAFTA's sections are referenced, as in the literature on the subject, in upper case with Arabic numerals: Chapter 11. The chapters in this book are referred to in lower case with an upper-case Roman numeral: what follows is chapter I.

I North America as Market and Community

Part of the discourse about world regions involves the development of a common identity. This chapter reflects on whether a North American community has developed and, if so, who belongs to it, whether consciously or unconsciously.

Most of the eighteen studies in this book focus on the details of transborder governance in order to tease out the extent to which a North American political economy 'exists' in any meaningful sense. But, as background for a detailed study of North America's political economy, it is important to identify what general characteristics – whether objective or subjective – were displayed by the North American space that was reinvented when the governments of Canada, Mexico, and the United States implemented NAFTA and how these traits evolved.

Objectively speaking, the first two parts of this chapter look at data that can tell us something about the economy in North America. Reflecting on the latest bald statistics, I report on what can be said about the continent's economic reality compared with other regions and in the context of global growth trends. I then consider the cross-border flows of workers and migrants in order to assess whether population movements in North America are in any way defined by the new regional space.

Even if we find that North America objectively looks more like a world region than it did before NAFTA, its citizens may not behave, *subjectively* speaking, like members of a community. The chapter's third section considers the extent to which the citizenry in Mexico, the United States, and Canada consider themselves to be members of a continental entity which transcends their national territory and exists as a conscious community.

The Objective Economic Reality of North America

For an analyst of the three neighbouring countries' aggregate economic data, the issue is less whether the North American region exists politically than what is the nature of its economic interactions. This section introduces the reader to North America by presenting an overview of the basic statistics on trade and investment and comparing them with those of other world regions such as the European Union, Mercosur, and ASEAN. As outlined here, the economic data do show that North America became more robustly integrated after NAFTA was signed.

Measured by adding together the *gross domestic product* of the three economies in 2005, the new North America was actually – by a whisker – the largest regional trading area in the world, representing 32 per cent of world GDP (US$14.3 trillion). The twenty-five EU states then accounted for 31.2 per cent of world GDP (US$13.7 trillion).[1] Measured by *trade value*, however, the European Union reigned supreme. North America's intraregional trade in 2004 ($742 billion) was decidedly small compared to the EU's $2,973 billion, though still very large compared to Mercosur's $17 billion and ASEAN's $128 billion.[2] While NAFTA countries trade with each other forty-three times more than the four-member MERCOSUR and six times more than the ten-member ASEAN, its internal commerce is only one-fourth of the intra-EU figure.

By the standard measure of *regional economic integration* – the region's internal trade as a share of its members' total world trade – the NAFTA partners' share of 56 per cent was high compared to ASEAN (23 per cent) or MERCOSUR (19 per cent) but much lower than the European Union's 74 per cent. This can be explained by North America's stark asymmetries compared with the better balanced EU. The United States produces a massive 87 per cent of North American GDP, so that most commerce – that is, the exchange of goods – inside North America takes place within the United States' own borders.[3] Moreover, the United States accounts for 62 per cent of North America's total merchandise exports.[4] By comparison, Germany's merchandise exports constitute only 23 per cent of the EU total.[5] Given EU members' more equally distributed share of European GDP, intraregional trade is naturally much higher there than it is between the three very unequal North American partners. This explains why North America's intraregional trade is lower than the European Union's both as an absolute figure and as a percentage of NAFTA members' total world trade.

That said, North America's integration has been deepening. Exports

Figure 1.1: FDI inward stocks in the EU and North America (US$ million)

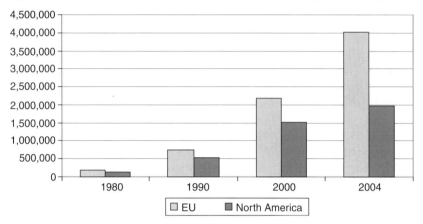

Figure 1.2: FDI outward stocks in the EU and North America (US$ million)

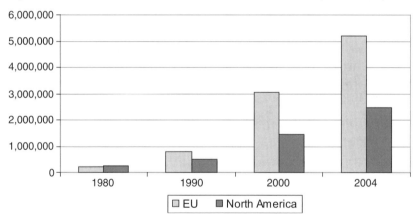

Figure 1.1 through 1.5 use hybridized data sets from the following sources. For FDI stocks 1990–2004 and FDI flows 2002–5: UNCTAD, 'World Investment Report (WIR) 2005 – TNCs and the Internationalization of R & D,' Annex B, http://www.unctad.org/Templates/ WebFlyer.asp?intItemID=3489&lang=1 (accessed on April 20, 2008), 303–12. For FDI flows 1988–93 average and 1994: UNCTAD, 'World Investment Report (WIR) 2000 – Cross Border M & A Development, Annex B, http://www.unctad.org/Templates/WebFlyer.asp? intItemID=2435&lang=1 (accessed on April 20, 2008), 283–93. For FDI flows 1995–2000 and FDI stocks 1980: UNCTAD, 'World Investment Report (WIR) 2001 – Promoting Link- ages,' Annex B, http://www.unctad.org/Templates/WebFlyer.asp?intItemID=2434&lang=1 (accessed on April 20, 2008), 291–311.

and imports among the three NAFTA partners increased by 455 per cent between 1980 and 2004. Intraregional imports increased from US$133 billion in 1980 to US$705 billion by 2004. The greatest change occurred between 1990 and 1999, the period that includes NAFTA's implementation: intraregional imports rose by 574 per cent.

However, *investment statistics* paint a picture of relative regional failure. Measured by foreign direct investment (FDI) flows, North America has ranked behind the European Union since 1980 for both inward and outward flows of FDI stocks. While North America's stock of incoming FDI rose sharply in the two and a half decades between 1980 and 2004, Europe did considerably better (Figures 1.1 and 1.2).[6]

Furthermore, North America's share of world FDI inflows declined drastically from 28 per cent in 1990 to 18 per cent in 2004. Within North America, the data suggest greater convergence among the three NAFTA players. The United States declined marginally and Canada lost significantly as hosts for inward FDI, while Mexico received by far the largest inflow of the three economies. (See Figure 1.3.)

That the North American economy suffered reverses in the 2000s was a legitimate concern. Between 2000 and 2005, North American gross domestic product increased from US$11.1 trillion to US$14.3 trillion, concealing major setbacks in trade growth.[7] Following the 2001 recession, intraregional trade declined from US$421 billion in 2000 to US$382 billion in 2002, corresponding to a drop in the share of internal NAFTA trade as a percentage of world merchandise exports from 6.8 per cent in 2001 to 6.1 per cent in 2002. From 2003, intraregional trade recuperated, reaching an all-time high of US$824 billion in 2005, or 8.1 per cent of world merchandise exports. Intra-NAFTA trade as a percentage of total NAFTA trade rose from 40 per cent in 2001 to 56 per cent in 2005, suggesting that the three North American players sold most of their merchandise goods to their continental partners after the events of 9/11.[8] After 2001, North America's share of both imports and exports declined sharply to below those of 1995 when the effects of NAFTA began to materialize.

If flows of capital more accurately measure a region's competitiveness, the news was less rosy. As Figures 1.4 and 1.5 show, North America's FDI inflows and outflows continued to decline compared to the European Union in the years following the events of 9/11 – most likely in response to the US recession, although in 2004 FDI inflows gradually recovered from their low in 2003. Sluggish FDI flows gave North American TNCs valid concerns about correcting what they perceived as their

Figure 1.3: Per country share of NAFTA FDI inflows, 1990 and 2004

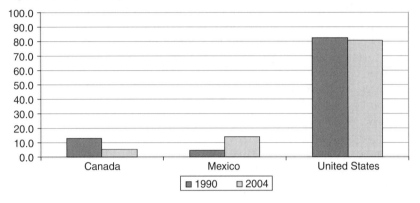

Figure 1.4: FDI inflows in the EU and North America (US$ million), 1988–2005

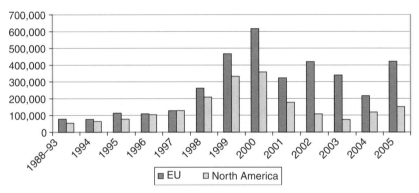

Figure 1.5: FDI outflows in the EU and North America (US$ million), 1988–2005

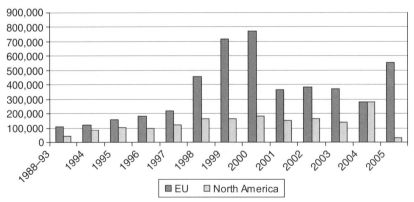

declining competitiveness in the global marketplace and preserving whatever advances they had made through North American market integration.

North America as a Common Market for Labour

Just as a country's population is the base for its economy, a regional economic space is defined by its population. Geographic proximity, interlocked histories, and cross-border economic links have created unique population mobility between the United States and each of its North American neighbours. Mexican and Canadian migratory flows to the United States have followed two distinct patterns. Whether these patterns signify that connections among the three national labour markets are fostering a continent-wide economic integration is the question addressed by this section.

Canada-United States

The absence of linguistic and cultural barriers facilitated virtually unrestricted early anglophone migration patterns from Canada to the United States.[9] Largely driven by work opportunities in the United States' burgeoning industrial economy, Canadian emigration grew significantly from the mid-nineteenth century through the 1920s, often within cross-border regions such as Quebec-New England.[10] Between 1840 and 1930, an estimated net total of 2.8 million Canadians left for the United States, making Canadians the period's third-largest immigrant group to the United States.[11] (American demographers have generally ignored these flows, focusing instead on the much smaller subset of French Canadian migrants whose cultural distinctiveness made their impact on American society more interesting.)[12] By the 1920s, up to 2 per cent of the Canadian population left for the United States every year.[13]

Mexico-United States

Mexican labourers in the United States have always been a more contested problem. Upon their military conquest and annexation by the United States, much of the scattered Mexican population in the states of California, Nevada, Utah, Arizona, Colorado, Texas, New Mexico, and Wyoming remained in place. Their ranks were strengthened immediately when a gold boom induced a mass immigration into southern California between 1848 and 1856.[14] Otherwise, general migrant flows remained minimal until the 1870s, when American employers began to recruit Mexicans to do heavy labour on farms and in railroad construction. Throughout this early period, movement across the Mexico-US border was as unrestricted as with Canada: US immigration law allowed unlimited immigration of qualified aspirants from the Western hemisphere until well into the twentieth century.[15] Despite this accessibility, Mexicans only constituted 1 per cent of total immigration flows to the United States by 1910.

The outbreak of civil war in 1910 precipitated the first major outflow of Mexicans, which reached 713,000 people by mid-decade. This politically driven Mexican emigration was increased by the United States' economically driven demand for labour: in 1917, 73,000 contract labourers were hired to supplement the US wartime workforce. Overall, at least 459,000 legal Mexican migrants moved to the United States in the 1920s, with another half-million entering illegally.[16] Some of this flow reversed in the 1930s, as the Great Depression eliminated jobs in the American southwest, causing an estimated 400,000 Mexicans to return home.[17]

When the United States entered the Second World War and drafted large numbers of working-age men to fight abroad, it faced both a general labour shortage throughout the economy and particular pressure from industry in the southwest, which had been lobbying for more Mexican labour since the 1930s. Accordingly, Washington negotiated a contract-labour program with the government of Mexico, the first cohort arriving in September 1942 to assist with the American beet harvest. By the end of the war, 215,000 agricultural workers and 75,000 railroad workers had been authorized for contract employment under this Bracero program. Eventually, about 200,000 braceros a year working in twenty-six states were granted contracts by the US government. While they constituted only 2 per cent of the country's total farm labour force, they made up 20 per cent of its seasonal migrant workforce.[18]

This legal employment framework sprouted a parallel immigration of many 'wetbacks' who typically swam across the Rio Grande in search of work. Employers hired many such illegal workers and lobbied US authorities vigorously to allow them to remain in the country. Consequently, by the early 1950s, many of the braceros were illegal wetbacks who had been legalized by American authorities to simplify their recruitment.[19]

Modern Migration

These two distinct labour relationships carry over into the present day, with the Canadian-US relationship rooted in supplies of brain and the Mexican-US relationship based on the supply of brawn to the US economy. In 2007 North America's population was slightly over 443 million, with some 301 million in the United States, 33 million in Canada, and 109 million in Mexico. The corresponding labour force totalled 214 million people, with 151 million in the United States, 18 million in Canada, and 45 million in Mexico.[20]

Canada-United States

Permanent flows of people between Canada and the United States remain small. Yearly migrations of Canadians comprise less than 3 per cent of the approximately 915,000 immigrants admitted each year to the United States, or generally under 30,000.[21] For example, legal immigration to the United States from Canada has rarely risen above 20,000, though numbers have been increasing since the early 1990s.[22]

Some estimates suggest that significant numbers of Canadians illegally enter the United States each year. Many may be workers who continue their stay even after their official visa has expired, people who extend trips, or students who fail to return to Canada after studies. A more recent estimate has put the total number of unauthorized Canadians residing in the United States at 122,000.[23]

For their part, Americans have flowed in only minimal numbers to Canada. Figures ranged between 4,000 and 6,000 annually between 1990 and 2004, constituting no more then 3 per cent of total inflows into Canada.[24]

Mexico-United States

Migration between the United States and Mexico has been similarly one-sided, with insignificant numbers of Americans moving south of the border. Mexicans, however, have migrated to the United States under radically different circumstances than those prevailing on the northern border, becoming the dominant immigrant and demographic group in many parts of the country.

Since 1952, the McCarren-Walter Act's 'Texas proviso' has made 'harboring' unauthorized workers illegal. However, following the 1965 demise of the Bracero program, the legal context for immigration from Mexico became exceedingly complex. Under the 1965 amendments to the Immigration and Nationality Act, the United States established a quota system for immigration with an annual limit of 120,000 for the Western hemisphere. In 1976 per-country limits (20,000 annually) were added.[25] Legal immigration numbers into the 1980s were thus quite stable, fluctuating between 10 and 15 per cent of total immigration.[26] Overall, 454,000 Mexicans are estimated to have entered in the 1960s (14 per cent) and 637,000 in the 1970s (also 14 per cent).[27] At the same time, the basis for US immigration policy shifted. While Canadian immigration policy favoured individuals who had skills needed by the economy, family reunification became the main rationale for legal entry into the United States.[28]

Under the 1986 Immigration Reform and Control Act (IRCA), which was designed to address the United States' complex legal and illegal migration patterns, 2.7 million people applied for permanent resident status. Since the majority of IRCA legalizations were for Mexicans, Mexican immigration numbers relative to other nationalities spiked in the late 1980s and early 1990s, cresting at 52 per cent of all immigrants in 1991; the million Mexican immigrants that year were almost double the entire flow of Mexicans to the United States in the 1960s. By 1994, the Mexican share of immigration had stabilized at 13 to 14 per cent, with absolute levels of immigration at about 100,000 Mexicans annually.[29]

During the 1990s, legal migration of Mexicans to the United States grew four times faster than other immigrant flows owing to legislative changes that gave further preference to family members of US citizens.[30] All the families of Mexicans legalized under the IRCA were eligible for American citizenship, which generated momentum for further immigration.[31] Currently, Mexicans make up one-third of the foreign-born population in the United States, the highest fraction of any immigrant group since 1830, when Germans constituted 30 per cent of the country's foreign-born. In absolute terms, there were 21 million Mexican-born in the United States in 2000[32] – a figure that represented 15 per cent of Mexico's domestic workforce.[33]

Growing numbers of American retirees go in the opposite direction and settle in Mexico. In 2001 the US Embassy in Mexico reported 600,000 retired US citizens living in the country; by 2007, this number was estimated as closer to 1 million[34] – some 25 per cent of the total number of Americans living abroad.[35] At the same time, because few formally immigrate and assume Mexican citizenship, many remain there illegally without even registering as foreign citizens.

Tightened border controls under NAFTA and since September 11, 2001 have changed illegal migration patterns from Mexico. In the quarter-century from the end of the Bracero program until 1990, some 56 million undocumented workers entered the United States, but 86 per cent of these are thought to have done so on a temporary basis, resulting in a net inflow of about 5 million Mexicans. After the first round of IRCA legalizations, the number of undocumented Mexicans in the United States was estimated at between 2.5 and 3.0 million.[36] Unauthorized entries into the United States are thought to have begun exceeding legal immigrants by 1995.[37] In 2004 nearly 500,000 unauthorized Mexicans went to the United States, compared to approximately 90,000 who immigrated legally.[38] Between 2000 and 2004, 2.4 million unauthorized Mexicans are believed to have entered the United States.

Since September 11, 2001 and the concurrent politicization of the debate about Mexican immigration, increased border security has shifted patterns of illegal entry. One of the key reasons explaining the dramatic increase in undocumented Mexicans residing permanently in the United States is the greater risk of being caught when returning across the border. More permanent migration patterns entail further secondary migration of families, replacing the seasonal circulation of single labourers from a family base in Mexico. The 'border crackdown' and the family reunification associated with IRCA legalizations are considered the main factors driving increased Mexican population growth in the United States.[39]

The first implication for our analysis of these two narratives is that, despite some similarities, the scale and politics of US-Mexican and US-Canadian migration remain worlds apart. Both have evolved from distinct historical circumstances and from different policy attempts by the United States to manage flows of people across its borders. While much Mexican labour is low-wage and serves as the backbone for the US economy in its southwestern states, Canada-US flows are dominated by highly skilled professionals making the most of their opportunities in two closely linked developed markets. This picture of two dissimilar migration relationships was not much altered by NAFTA's modest labour-market effects.

NAFTA

NAFTA did not create a common labour market, although some policy makers have proposed creating one as a radical measure to reanimate NAFTA's region-building project. The agreement nevertheless did contain one uniquely North American labour provision – a professional 'TN' visa – which was heralded as the foundation for a regional labour market in certain professional occupations.

Although US immigration law does not require migrants to meet US labour needs,[40] temporary workers have been allowed ever since the McCarren-Walter Act of 1952 legalized their entry and began the differentiation between skilled and unskilled entrants.[41] Generally, temporary workers must come to the United States under visa arrangements, but only when American employers can certify that no native workers are available who meet their job description. The H1–B visa has become the primary means for skilled foreigners to work in the United States for stays of up to six years. While simplifying the red tape, the Immigration Act of 1990 introduced an annual cap of 65,000 for H1–B visas.[42] Strong demand in the late 1990s and early 2000s resulted in the annual quota being reached before the US fiscal year even began.[43]

CUFTA created an additional TN visa that was extended to Mexicans by NAFTA. Seen as a 'a primary instrument to facilitate trade' by increasing labour mobility in North America through the cross-border flow of human capital,[44] the TN visa, which has no quotas for Canadians, can be issued directly at a border crossing if the applicant can provide a passport, proof of a bachelor's degree, and an offer of temporary employment from a US employer. An annual cap of 5,000 TN visas for Mexican nationals has since been phased out, as originally specified in the NAFTA text. TN visas are issued for a one-year period but can be renewed an unlimited number of times subject to certain legal requirements. TN visas thus enable a form of labour mobility that allows skilled labour from Canada and Mexico to move with few restrictions into the United States and, in principle, between Mexico and Canada.

The absolute number of TN visas granted to Canadians has increased dramatically, so that, by 2000–1, up to 90,000 were being issued annually.[45] This represents a temporary migration about 2.5 times as large as the estimated labour-related permanent immigration flows from Canada and was more than half the total number of H1–B visas issued for all foreign workers in 2000–1.

Since September 11, 2001, TN-issuing officers at US border crossings have been replaced by officers often untrained in TN visa procedures and more concerned with border security. Applications by individuals for TN visas are 'subject to the whim of the guards' and rejection rates have increased to over 50 per cent at high-traffic crossings.[46] Migrants may thus be increasingly attempting to use H1–B visas that, although scarce and more complicated to obtain, are issued in advance and are not subject to uncertainties and arbitrary decisions at the US-Canadian border.

Some analysts contend that this apparent increase in labour flows is artificial, and that TN visa use is not an indicator of increased labour mobility but instead merely reflects substitution of TN-visas for H1–B visas and other working arrangements.[47] Others note that the TN visa program partially restricts labour mobility because it is very inflexible about what constitutes a 'skilled professional' compared to the H1–B visa.[48]

Mexican TN visa use never reached its cap, peaking at 3,341 visas issued in 2001.[49] Mexicans are subject to the same process as Canadians, except that they must have a US consulate pre-approve their visa before travelling to a border crossing. Since the quota for Mexican TN visa use has been removed, there is some evidence that Mexicans have increasingly become comfortable with TN visa use: numbers of TN visas trended slightly upwards through 2005.[50] Regardless, Mexican visa-use numbers remain modest and a fraction of the dramatic flows evident between Canada and the United States.

While NAFTA's TN visa might have been an impressive driver for regional integration, it has failed to produce a shared labour market even in skilled human capital. Instead, it merely perpetuates the existing bifurcated character of population movements across the United States' two land boundaries. In short, the objective reality of population movements in North American is very much less than what it seems.

These data tell us how much North America exists as a world region in an *objective* economic sense and how little it exists in a demographic sense. They cannot tell us whether those who live in the United States, Canada, and Mexico share a *subjective* sense that they belong to a North American community, a question to which we now turn.

North America as a Subjective Community

Theorists of integration argue that increasing degrees of economic interdependence, social interaction, and interpersonal communication among countries can raise levels of knowledge about and confidence in formerly mistrusted foreigners, gradually replacing differing national identities with a collective regional one.[51] Applied to Europe, integration theory predicted that French lambs and Germans lions would lie down together as happy members of a broader communal zoo if only they could interact and communicate more together.[52] In this perspective, the question of North America as community must be addressed on two levels. We must first define what 'North America' means interactively so that we can know what groups are considered to belong to it. Then we need to know how much importance its members attach to belonging to the continental community.

Defining North America

World regions are notoriously unstable in their geographic definition. For the past half-century, the European community has been progressively extending its borders, starting with five members and growing to its present twenty-seven. Because of its economic, political, and social success, neighbouring states clamour to join a commonwealth that may one day accept Turkey, Ukraine, and even Russia. But there is a price to pay in identity terms for success in economic and political terms: as membership in a community becomes less exclusive, identifying with it becomes less compelling.

When CUFTA was signed, the notion of the old North America was extended far into the Pacific Ocean, since the state of Hawaii was constitutionally part of the United States, and deep into the Caribbean, owing to the agreement's provisions applying to the US territory of Puerto Rico.[53] When NAFTA created a new North America by incorporating Mexico, an accession provision anticipated other countries – not necessarily restricted to the same hemisphere – joining the putatively 'North American' economic area.[54] If North America's boundaries are not fixed, developing a sense of belonging to it becomes more difficult.

Belonging to the Community

Objectively finding oneself in a region does not automatically create a subjective sense of belonging to it. This tension is most obvious in Mexico, where 'norte americano' was the polite word for 'gringo' – the dangerous, white, English-speaking Americans to the north. Even Mexican scholars of NAFTA still use 'norte americano' to denote a culturally and geographically demarcated reality distinct from themselves, rather than inclusively to recognize their own membership in the new common entity. In general, Mexicans are ambivalent about the notion of 'norte americano.' On the one hand, they know they are North Americans: by virtue of their geography and demography, they look north towards the continent to which they belong economically. On the other hand, they are Latin Americans: by virtue of their geography and demography, they look south towards the hemisphere to which they feel they belong culturally.

Far from NAFTA creating positive attitudes between Mexico and the United States, a mutual alienation has been nurtured by the United States' continuing political uproar over undocumented immigrants. President Bush's authorizing the construction of a 1,100-km anti-migrant wall along the border was a metaphor for the United States' rejection of Mexicans as members of the same political community.[55] When CNN's Lou Dobbs talked of undocumented Mexicans as 'illegal aliens' or when Samuel Huntington provocatively claimed that Hispanic immigrants who had successfully located in the United States were subverting the country's Anglo-Saxon political culture,[56] they were reinforcing Americans' distance from their continental partners. On the other side of the border, the wall and the chauvinism that had built it strengthened a sense of exclusion from the United States and, ipso facto, weakened any putative community-like feeling of belonging to the new North America.

In Canada, culturally embedded notions continued to have their traditional valence even within its political and diplomatic elites. Canadian foreign-policy analysts talking about a 'continental' foreign policy are typically referring to the Canada-US relationship, not a trilateralism that involves Mexico.[57] For its part, the Canadian government is so fixated on its special relationship with the United States that it still prefers to deal bilaterally with its neighbour, rather than act in concert with Mexico – despite evidence suggesting that Canada enjoys greater capacity when acting trilaterally.[58] When George W. Bush made his first official trip abroad to visit Vicente Fox and proclaimed that 'the United States has no more important relationship in the world than the one we have with Mexico,' Canadian diplomats interpreted this as an alarming portent that Canada's influence on the White House was growing weaker, not as a positive sign that the North American community was growing stronger.[59]

Some scholars argue that the public is ahead of the politicians in identifying with an integrated North American political community.[60] A decade ago, the World Values Surveys pointed to a convergence among citizens in the United States, Canada, and Mexico across a wide range of issues, from beliefs about the importance of economic growth to attitudes towards government, and even in patterns of church attendance.[61] A later iteration of this research confirmed the increasing homogeneity of the three populations' values without going so far as to affirm that a specifically North American consciousness had evolved.[62]

But different data produce different conclusions. One analyst has argued that, although Canada and the United States are converging in their economic integration, the two countries' publics are as divergent as 'fire and ice' on social issues.[63] Another survey of attitudinal clusters suggests that, where value similarities cross the national frontier, they draw together binational border regions. For instance, the populations of the Atlantic provinces and the New England states have more in common with each other than they do with their fellow citizens in the prairie provinces and western states where cross-border attitudes converge along different lines.[64] These border-regional similarities help account for the high levels of friendship between Canadians and Americans, but they underline the bleak prospects of a continental community consciousness emerging.

Different questions, of course, produce different answers. When asked in 1990 whether they favoured erasing the border, only a minority was supportive. When the same question was framed more positively (Would you support political union 'if it meant that you would enjoy a higher standard of living?'), a majority approved.[65] These numbers have declined to more moderate levels in recent years.[66] Here, too, the implications are negative. Since Americans identify NAFTA with causing a lower standard of living and job losses and since Mexican public opinion remains highly anti-'gringo,' North America's prospects for developing a positive identity appear slim.

Unique among world regions, all three members of North America are federations whose provinces and states engage in bilateral or multilateral relations independently of their national governments. Subfederal relations across the US-Mexico border are typically bilateral, with one US state having an agreement with its neighbouring Mexican state. There are bilateral Canadian-American subfederal relationships as well, dealing with such functional issues as water management, road maintenance, and firefighting. Often more consequential are the multilateral interrelationships, which include such major initiatives as the Pacific Northwest Economic Region and the Conference of New England Governors and Eastern Canadian Premiers.[67] This kind of governance involves many issues where there is common jurisdiction (agricultural or immigration) or common responsibilities (environment, natural-resource management, policing, and transportation).[68]

Regular cooperation between political leaders, senior government officials, and stakeholders from the private sector and civil society may generate positive regional identities for these borderlands. However, conflictual linkages between subfederal governments may shatter more than they foster transborder identities. When North Dakota, for instance, created inspection processes designed to impede flows of Canadian farm goods across the border, it was not buttressing sentiments of North American solidarity. When Albany briefly excluded Ontario and Quebec companies from bidding on state contracts because of alleged procurement discrimination against New York firms in those two provinces, it was helping preserve cross-border attitudinal differences, not erasing them.[69]

If a North American community were emerging, the news media might report on the continent as an entity and an increasing proportion of Americans, Mexicans, and Canadians would conceive their identities not just along local and national lines but along North American ones as well. For instance, Eurobarometer data from 1999 indicate that, on average, 56 per cent of European respondents reported feeling 'very' or 'fairly' attached to Europe, compared to 40 per cent of respondents who felt 'not very' attached or 'unattached.' Similarly, when asked the extent to which they felt European – as opposed to having exclusively national ties – 52 per cent of respondents chose the former, compared to 45 per cent preferring their national identity.[70] In contrast, between 1981 and 2002, the percentage of Canadians who said that their primary identity was 'North American' rose from a mere 3 to 6 per cent. Although it may have doubled, this figure underlines the North American identity's strikingly low salience.

Because the three countries' business elites have the least to lose from globalization, it is not surprising that their attitudes towards a continental community have become the most positive. When the US House of Representatives endorsed NAFTA in 1993, the final vote broke not along party lines but rather by the socio-economic background of the congressional districts – 'the wealthier, more educated, more white-collar a district was, the more likely was its representative to vote in favour of NAFTA.'[71] In Canada, the strongest advocacy of North America as an integrated community without internal borders comes from big business. Following September 2001, when the corporate-financed C.D. Howe Institute proposed the 'Big Idea' of deep integration, it was still talking about the old bilateral North America. Other suggested variants of a 'NAFTA-Plus' became increasingly trilateral. The neoconservative Fraser Institute was far from alone in advocating a North American monetary union – the subject of periodically intense debates among economists in Canada.[72] Responding to Washington's disinterest in further continentalization, the Canadian Council of Chief Executives' 2003 North American Security and Prosperity Initiative (NASPI) made a far less extensive proposal for trinational integration.[73]

The groups calling for a common currency and erasing the border are doing so for the same self-interested reasons that led to the development of NAFTA – not because of any communitarian self-conception. The influential 2005 task force report titled *Building a North American Community* was a trinational effort sponsored by the US Council on Foreign Relations, but it focused on the objective policy components of community, proposing a common front on economic and security issues rather than measures that would build a common consciousness.[74] The closest the report came to identifying what this community would look like was negative: its deepened North America would be structured in a way that avoided creating a European-style 'bureaucracy.' The public that is ahead of the politicians in its support for an integrated continental community is a transnational elite of influential public servants, academics, and representatives from the corporate sector – a powerful but highly unrepresentative cross-section of North America's society.

Of course, the fact that the North American faith is nurtured by an elite does not mean it will not spread, particularly if spillover effects from deepening material integration cause national chauvinisms to soften and transborder trust to grow. The European Union was itself born of technocrats, and support for it still varies greatly along socioeconomic and national lines. The obstacles it encountered during the 2000s in ratifying a collective constitution showed that it was still riven by deeply rooted parochial sentiments, although the material and symbolic gains from closer integration appear greater to Europeans than they do to North Americans.

The Security and Prosperity Partnership of North America – which is analysed at the end of this book – evoked strong reactions from nationalists in all three countries. In Mexico, the Red Mexicana de Acción Frente al Libre Comercio (RMALC, Mexican Action Network on Free Trade) was a leading organization unalterably opposed to the SPP for fear it would lead to much deeper integration. The negative reaction to the SPP from Canadian civil-society groups had everything to do with similar fears of American domination and little to do with Mexico. The Council of Canadians presented the issue as a choice between Canada as 'country' or 'colony.'[75] Extreme anxiety in the United States about American sovereignty was whipped up by the Minutemen Project – a group virulently opposed to illegal Mexican immigration – which erected a 'Stop the Security and Prosperity Partnership' website complete with a silhouette of the North American continent engulfed in flames.[76] In response to these fears, the US government established a website with 'SPP Myths and Facts' designed to make clear that many of the supranational implications attributed to it by outside voices were not present in its actual agenda.[77] The fact that Washington felt compelled to explain that the SPP did not undermine the American constitution, was not being undertaken without the knowledge of Congress, and, most intriguingly, was not an 'agreement' or 'treaty' but rather a mere 'dialogue' shows that there are major divisions and deep doubts within the United States itself about the value of a stronger North American community.

The persistence of this nationalist, sometimes xenophobic sentiment does not negate the possibility of a North American community emerging. Still, it is noteworthy that, outside a limited number of business associations, there are few entities that consider the new North America as a political, cultural, or social reality. Even if Europe is not a united political community, there is a symbolic and functional reality to the rhetoric of its integration in which the EU narrative and European policy function reciprocally, each one bolstering the other. Some policies are implemented there in order to reinforce the narrative of a collective endeavour: the Erasmus education-exchange program sends undergraduates in their thousands to study in universities across the continent with the specific intent of helping them develop a European consciousness. The common passport design, the EU flag, the Euro currency notes, even the European anthem constantly remind citizens in the European Union's twenty-seven member states that they are also members of a transnational community. North America boasts none of these symbols – let alone the political will and policies that created them.

The European narrative mandated such flagship policies as the structural-development programs that offered economic assistance to bring poor countries up to the level of the EU's general welfare. When President Fox proposed a deepening of NAFTA to build Mexico's infrastructure and help reduce horrendous, emigration-inducing levels of poverty there, prime ministers Jean Chrétien and Paul Martin successively gave him the back of their hand. Regional equalization may be proclaimed in the Canadian constitution but it is not a norm that Ottawa wanted to practise for North America as a whole. The United States was still less responsive, never having warmed to the idea of equalization even within its own boundaries.

European integration was launched with an overriding political raison d'être: to prevent a resurgence of its centuries-long civil war.[78] In the absence of a similar political telos, North American integration was undertaken for narrowly economic reasons.[79] Consequently, its political face has little continental salience, and there is nothing resembling a coherent North American narrative. Although NAFTA's provisions function along with the World Trade Organization as part of the supra-constitution reframing the legal environment in which Canada, Mexico, and the United States operate, their scope is much more modest than that of its transatlantic counterpart.

Given Mexican and Canadian fears about US domination and given the Americans' anxieties about defending their own sovereignty, the prospects are bleak for the three countries moving towards a more formalized North American community – short of a major crisis in which the United States was forced to confront its own weakness, as in the early 1980s when its two neighbours found themselves thinking that they had no alternative to further integration. The present North American identity amounts to little more than trinational business interests operating in functional groupings. As long as North American integration speaks the language of corporate self-interest rather than continental identity, material factors will prevail without building the subjective consciousness needed to form a political community. Compared to the European Union, NAFTA's members are not attached to a social contract as a community, having never known what a social contract is.[80] Without a broader vision, the North American community will continue to 'exist' only as political fiction.

Conclusion

This preliminary review of the objective and subjective indicators of North American integration began with the presumption that the European Community was the prototype for the regionalism of the post–Second World War era. We can now conclude that, although aggregate economic statistics suggest continuing integration is occurring among the three economies, the United States' rising barriers against migration since the signing of NAFTA and increased obstacles to trade since September 2001 have made North America look *less* like the EU than it was expected to be at birth. Conscious though they may be of their neighbours, the three countries' citizenries have made little progress towards feeling like members of a continental community.

As a space mediating between the centrifugal forces of globalization and the centripetal needs of its three states for economic well-being and domestic security, however, North America can be presumed to play some role.[81] Because this world region houses the global hegemon which relates to other regions and countries independently of the needs of its periphery, this role is likely to vary considerably from field to field.[82] The detailed probes that follow in the next chapters will explore the nature and dynamics at play within this North American space.

PART ONE

Less Than Meets the Eye:

State Re-regulation via Regional Institutionalization

Given the intensity of the economic and social relations between the United States and Canada and between the United States and Mexico, particularly along their originally quite porous international boundaries, various kinds of transborder governance have existed in North America for many decades. Since it was NAFTA that reframed North America as a world region alongside the European Union, Mercosur, and ASEAN, it is logically – if not chronologically – appropriate to start our study by looking at what institutional substance NAFTA created.

In chapter II, I explain that, to the surprise of non-specialists, most of the institutions that came into being under NAFTA are weak. Then, in chapter III, I turn to one element of NAFTA's institutional structure, its dispute-settlement mechanisms, which were supposed to give the new continental governance real clout. In chapters IV and V the focus shifts to later additions to the NAFTA agreement. As a result of their fierce political engagement in contesting free trade with Mexico, US labour and environmental organizations obtained an apparently significant concession in 1992 from the newly elected Clinton administration, which insisted on adding to NAFTA separate trilateral commissions for labour (chapter IV) and the environment (chapter V), with the mandate of warding off that race to the bottom so feared by US civil-society activists. Chapter VI analyses the original and most important version of the continent's transborder governance, the management of the lakes and rivers bisected by the US-Canada and US-Mexico boundaries.

The argument linking these analyses is that, although NAFTA may have created impressive-sounding organizations, they turn out to be much less than meets the eye. Far from supporting any global trend in which new forms of transborder governance have re-regulated the nation state by diminishing it, they leave the governments of North America with their principal powers – or inherent weaknesses – largely intact.

II NAFTA's Institutional Vacuum

The North American Free Trade Agreement's negotiations were distinguished by each partner's extreme reluctance to institutionalize its continental relationship. Understandably, the global superpower had little interest in tying its hands with provisions that might concede some decision-making parity to its two smaller neighbours. For Canada's part, even when it negotiated the Canada-United States Free Trade Agreement in 1988, its main – if contradictory – aim was to avoid organizational entanglements while nevertheless constraining the US government's unilateral acts of trade protectionism. More surprisingly, President Salinas de Gortari accepted CUFTA's weak-institution model as the organizational premise for his trade negotiations. Having had to comply with the prescriptions of the International Monetary Fund and World Bank in the wake of its severe financial crisis in the early 1980s, the Mexican government felt that it had been on the receiving end of enough US-directed multilateral institutions' dictates.

In the fifteen months when the American, Mexican, and Canadian negotiators were finalizing this agreement to enhance their three economies' integration, they seemed to be haunted by the spectre of the European Union. However admirable it might be with its supranational commission (whose funding had raised Portugal, Greece, and Ireland out of poverty), its weighted decision-making formulae (which offset some of the power asymmetry between small countries like Denmark and big ones like Germany), its ambitious Parliament (which gave citizens in each country direct representation in European-level policy making), and its Court of Justice (which could force member states to redress injustices suffered by their citizens), the EU presented the institutional antithesis of what NAFTA's founding fathers had in mind.

In each of these respects – executive, legislative, and judicial – NAFTA was to be a world region with a major difference. No supranational commissioners were going to issue directives instructing what sovereign Mexico, sovereign Canada, or still less the sovereign United States should or should not do. North America's power structure was not to be reconfigured to bulk up the weak periphery vis-à-vis the overpowering centre. No future cohort of radical politicians would be able to give the continent's citizenry a meddling voice in proposing policies for the continent as a whole. No transborder court with pre-eminence over the judicial systems of the three federal states was to hear cases on behalf of aggrieved citizens and businesses.

NAFTA embodied a vision of continental economic integration by setting limits on what would constitute legitimate policy in the three parties' systems. Unlike previous agreements that dealt exclusively with such border barriers as tariffs and quotas imposed on goods physically crossing national boundaries, NAFTA extended its normative reach from the three members' boundaries to their internal policy regimes. In addition to tariff elimination, it contained provisions on such potential non-tariff barriers to trade or foreign investment as health or environmental standards and introduced rules with respect to services, intellectual property rights, and international trade law.

The agreement's wide-ranging norms asserted so much intrusive authority over its members' domestic policy and regulatory capacities that it could be considered part of the signatories' external constitution.[1] For instance, Canada was required to amend the Special Import Measures Act, the Federal Court Act, the Trademark Act, and the Patent Act. The United States amended its Customs Court Act of 1980. Mexico committed itself to introduce many new provisions to let American and Canadian companies launch appeals against antidumping measures (AD) and countervailing duties (CVD). But, to keep its NAFTA obligations consistent with its domestic constitution, it refused to exempt AD and CVD procedures from Mexican nationals' treasured right to appeal, the *juicio de amparo*.[2]

As the *rule maker* during the negotiations in which the prize was meant to be greater access to its market, the United States made the fewest concessions in this continental accord, which turned out mainly to increase US access to its neighbours' markets. As the much weaker *demandeurs* at the bargaining table, Mexico and Canada were the *rule takers*, finding themselves under extreme pressure to make concessions in order to resolve the legion 'irritants' – especially regulations that impeded US transnational corporations' unhampered operation in their economies – on whose resolution Washington insisted as the quid pro quo for opening up its market to more Mexican and Canadian imports. NAFTA had the greatest impact on the Mexican state, which had to make the most radical changes to conform to its new obligations. Canada, which had already made significant adaptations to its legal order when implementing CUFTA, was less drastically affected by this second agreement.

Although subsequent parts of this book examine how these external constitutions along with other pertinent political-economy factors have affected transnational decision making in specific sectors of North America's political economy, this chapter and the next three consider the formal institutions that NAFTA established in terms of continental governance. I start by analysing the NAFTA system as if it were a traditional government manifesting the typical characteristics of:

1 a *constitution*, which defines the system's norms, lays down its rules, and establishes its institutions;
2 an *executive*, which makes decisions and policies to sustain the government's operation;
3 a *legislature*, whose function is to adapt the system to changing conditions by writing new rules;
4 a *judiciary*, which resolves conflicts among constituents by interpreting the constitution's norms;
5 a *bureaucracy*, which makes the whole system actually function by implementing legislation and administering programs; and
6 a *coercive branch*, which enforces public law, administrative regulations, and judicial rulings.

In the following sections, I delineate the paradox in which the transnational economic regime defined by NAFTA's strong rulebook was structured by weak institutions without the capability to adapt North America to changing conditions. To explore how this 'reluctant trinity'[3] of states had *not* created an effective new mode of regulation, I examine North America's government under the six rubrics set out above.

Constitution

If a polity's constitution is the rulebook that defines its institutions and establishes the norms by which they are run, then the complex transnational jigsaw puzzle in North America already had various constitutionalizing elements before 1994. For sixty years, binational military cooperation between the United States and Canada had generated an elaborate structure of reciprocal defence obligations that were in effect constitutionalized by over eighty treaty-level agreements such as the North American Air Defence Command, 250 memoranda of understanding (MOUs), and 145 bilateral defence-discussion forums. CUFTA created a more general constitutional framework for the US-Canada relationship with strong rules but weak administration.

Though more conflictual and often antagonistic, the US-Mexico relationship had also developed constitutionalizing elements over the twentieth century. Various treaties and agreements defined explicit modalities for managing flows of all kinds across the common border. Informally, American officials knew that politicians' fierce anti-'gringo' denunciations of American imperialism would coexist with Mexican officials carrying on bilateral business as usual behind closed doors.

NAFTA was the first North American accord with trinational scope. But, compared with the multidimensional set of rules embedded in the European Union's treaties, it contained a strong but unidimensional set of economic *norms*, national treatment being of prime importance. These principles had supra-legislative weight in the sense that they could trump acts of the member states' legislatures. The agreement also contained hundreds of pages of *rules* directing member states' legislative and regulatory actions, whether negative, 'thou shalt not' injunctions (Canada was forbidden to price oil exported to the United States higher than its domestic prices), or positive, 'thou shalt' commandments (Mexico had to legislate new intellectual property rights). These measures applied to a wide range of policy fields such as telecommunications, agriculture, government procurement, energy, cultural development, and industrial promotion.

Whether NAFTA's norms and rules reduced the power asymmetries in North America or enhanced its hegemonification is a central question running through this study. Canada's trade-liberalization advocates argue that a middle power does much better in a rules-based than in a power-based environment. However, much depends on what the rules say, which raises the question of how they are made. Produced in a power-based process in which Canadian prime minister made it clear he was desperate for a deal, thereby leaving the United States in control of the negotiations, CUFTA's rules achieved a major breakthrough for Washington when Canada accepted that the norm of national treatment be extended from goods to investment. This long-resisted but little understood concession meant that no federal or provincial government in an economy dominated by US capital could any longer promote its domestically owned firms without extending the same benefits to the American branch plants with which they were competing. With the government of Canada committed to maintaining its free-trade agreement, the subsequent trilateral talks were even more one-sided, Mexico having to accept CUFTA's rules as the basic negotiating template.

By comparison, the World Trade Organization's rules were made in a multilateral negotiation in which the United States' interests were balanced by those of the EU and Japan. While the latter two shared the US desire to strengthen the overseas rights of their transnational corporations, they also wanted to preserve some scope for their governments' programs. As a result, a subsidy code – which Washington had refused to incorporate in CUFTA or NAFTA – was a central feature of the WTO's rules, clarifying what government supports for national industry were acceptable and what ones would be deemed illegal subsidies for export.

Beyond these norms and rules, the constitution that NAFTA created for North America had a weak executive, an even weaker legislative capacity, a set of uneven adjudicatory mechanisms, an ineffectual bureaucracy, and almost no coercive capacity – subjects to which we now turn.

Executive

The functions of the North American Free Trade Commission (NAFTC) were specified in Article 2001 as supervising the implementation of NAFTA, overseeing its further elaboration, resolving disputes that arise from interpretations of the agreement, and supervising the work of the committees and working groups it established. Its powers were also to:

a establish and delegate responsibilities to ad hoc or standing committees, working groups, or expert groups;
b seek the advice of non-governmental persons or groups; and
c take such other action in the exercise of its functions as the parties may agree to.

This apparently weighty mandate notwithstanding, the NAFTC turned out not to be a functioning institution at all. It has been allocated neither headquarters nor address. Nor does it have a staff or secretariat to call its own. 'Trade Commission' is just a label for meetings of the signatory states' three trade ministers. According to the Office of the United States Trade Representative (USTR), these get-togethers are 'intended to assess the implementation of the agreement, resolve any new disputes, and oversee the work of numerous committees established to address specific issues described in each chapter in the agreement.'[4] It convenes only as required, or for annual meetings, at which it supposedly:

- receives and adopts reports regarding the work of the agreement's several dozen committees, working groups, and subsidiary bodies;
- instructs officials on how to address a broad range of NAFTA implementation issues;
- approves agreements on unresolved issues;
- discusses pending issues that require ministerial level attention; and
- implements trade-facilitating technical modifications to the NAFTA rules for determining which products receive the favourable tariff treatment afforded by NAFTA.

This last role suggests that, as an executive, the NAFTC potentially has some legislative capacity because, in principle, the three ministers could make determinations that substantially transform the North American rulebook. In practice, they have shown no taste for such leadership. In sum, NAFTA's central institution has never actually been constituted and so has been unable to exercise its potentially considerable powers.[5]

Legislature

Constitutions cannot be the only source of a polity's norms and rules, because no single document can anticipate future conditions which might require adjustments to the existing legal framework. In liberal-democratic societies, it is the legislature that is the most visible and publicly legitimate source of making new rules and changing old ones. At the transnational level, legislators may confer in inter-parliamentary associations, but they do not get together to legislate. NAFTA has no institution such as the European Parliament through which representatives from the three countries can adapt its rules to changing circumstances or respond to new public concerns. The closest it comes to this is the NAFTC, which can issue interpretive instructions for the arbitration by investor-state dispute panels. When in 2001, after some years of lobbying by Ottawa, the three trade ministers did agree to issue an interpretation, this opinion was challenged by a NAFTA panel as an amendment of NAFTA and so beyond the commission's power.[6]

NAFTA's legislative incapacity leaves to other negotiating forums the evolution of more formal, continentally applicable economic rules. For instance, a rule stipulating that, when tariffs on a good have fallen to zero, its cross-border commerce may not be subjected to AD or CVD resulted from the bilateral negotiations between Canada and Chile. To adopt this rule for NAFTA's internal governance, its three signatory states would have to agree to alter the agreement – risking their legislatures' involvement in the question. The resistance of the US Congress to giving up its AD or CVD powers makes this possibility unfeasible. Similarly, new trade norms were expected to emerge in the Western hemisphere through the negotiation of a Free Trade Area of the Americas (FTAA), which, had it not been blocked by Brazil, would presumably have trumped those of NAFTA, once ratified by its signatories. Norms with trilateral impact can also emerge from the WTO's negotiating rounds in which the member-states' trade delegations constitute a type of continuing global legislature. Other norms may also evolve in such forums as UNESCO, whose 2005 convention on the protection of cultural diversity could affect the three North American states. But NAFTA itself is in legislative spasm. What normative evolution that does take place is through the workings of its adjudicatory processes.

Judiciary

No constitution is effective unless it has some means by which to resolve the disputes that inevitably surface when opposing interests take differing positions on the meanings of its clauses. Although NAFTA was established without an actual court and judges, it does have provisions for resolving general disputes about the agreement's implementation (Chapter 20), for mitigating disputes over trade harassment through AD or CVD (Chapter 19), for empowering aggrieved companies to sue member governments (Chapter 11), for settling conflicts concerning energy (Chapter 6) and financial institutions (Chapter 14), and for addressing certain environmental- and labour-law issues by using the complex procedures established in two supplementary agreements.

Because its judicial system comprises the most substantial part of NAFTA's institutional reality, the next chapter will be devoted to exploring it. Suffice it for the moment to affirm that Chapter 20 failed to provide an arbitral process superior to previous government-to-government arm-twisting; that Chapter 19 did not manage to induce the Americans to comply with its specially constituted binational panels' putatively binding rulings; that Chapter 11 provided NAFTA investors substantial new arbitral means with which to prevail over domestic governments; that the environmental and labour commissions' dispute-settlement processes proved unusable; and that the dispute-settlement processes envisaged for the energy and banking sectors remain unused to this day. As we shall see in greater detail in the next chapter, NAFTA's judicial realities were considerably less than met the eye.

Bureaucracy[7]

Just as constitutions create judicial organs to interpret them, they also set up administrative institutions to manage legislated programs. The NAFTA text established a 'Secretariat [which] administers the NAFTA dispute resolution processes under Chapters 14, 19, and 20 of the NAFTA, and has certain responsibilities related to Chapter 11 dispute settlement provisions.' In their anti-institutional wisdom, the three governments not only failed to set up the Free Trade Commission but did not create this secretariat either. Instead, each contented itself with opening a small office within its trade department and giving it such minor record-keeping responsibilities as maintaining a court-like registry of panel, committee, and tribunal proceedings.

Bereft of its intended secretariat, some twenty committees and working groups (CWGs) were mandated by NAFTA to monitor and direct the implementation of its various chapters' provisions.[8] Since these groups had the potential to become instruments for a genuine, coordinated, and transnational decision-making authority within the new continental structure created by NAFTA, I will compare their official purposes with their actual performance.

Official Purposes

The CWGs were officially set up to be not supranational but rather intergovernmental and explicitly *professional* forums in which civil servants from the three countries' pertinent ministries could exchange relevant information, resolve minor disputes, and discuss further liberalization. Their structure and composition were intended to favour objective analysis and pre-emptively to achieve the resolution of conflicts through the ministrations of small networks of experts. It was hoped that such epistemic communities would be inclined to treat issues impartially and focus on the long-term, mutually rewarding benefits of increased economic activity, rather than worrying about the short-term costs of immediate dislocations that might be politically contentious.[9]

Indeed, the implicit connotation of professional was *apolitical*. The thinking behind the CWGs was grounded in a desire to create forums where all three member states could voice and transmit their interests in a depoliticized arena. While political direction for the CWGs' work was to be by ministers through the Free Trade Commission, the groups were to be insulated from direct political pressures in their day-to-day activities.[10] The basis for having specialized groups staffed by civil servants who were selected for their detailed knowledge of the issue at hand – whether pesticides, trucking standards, or customs issues – was the belief that NAFTA's rules were more likely to work if their operation was at least partly removed from domestic politics and placed in new, problem-solving transnational institutions.[11]

Central to the working groups' professional make-up was their *trilateral* nature. In the spirit of the new continentalism, these CWGs were created with a view to trilateralizing relations by evaluating and even helping direct trade-related public policy making within all three member states. The groups were supposed to meet from one to four times a year or as issues arose and to produce reports for the Free Trade Commission. Meetings were to take place in Canada, the United States, and Mexico in rotation.[12] Trilateral forums were expected to defuse bilateral conflicts and so provide a means to transcend the two traditional bilateralisms of North American trade politics.

Trilateralism had its own implicit corollary – *symmetry* – a step in the direction of a new continental relationship founded on the legal equality of its constituents. There was to be approximately equal representation of the three countries on each group, which was to be co-chaired by an official from each member state. The mere existence of such trilateral institutions could be expected to offset the asymmetry in power that existed between the United States and its neighbour-partners, ensuring that all three states were given 'voice opportunities' with which to make their views known and possibly give them effect.[13]

The CWGs' trilateral, professional, and symmetrical mission marked a significant innovation for North American relations. Whether this novelty had any substance was another matter entirely. Just as the CWGs' mandates varied, so did their actual processes and functions.

Actual Performance

Most committees and working groups were engaged in a combination of activities that fell into the following five categories:

Implementing or Overseeing the Implementation of the Agreement. The majority of the CWGs were involved in the oversight of NAFTA's implementation. The most successful was the Committee on Trade in Goods (CTG). Having completed all four rounds of its tariff-acceleration mandate, it ceased to meet.[14]

Exchanging Information. All groups acted as information forums. This included tracking each country's administration or implementation of its chapter of the agreement, formulating understandings around various problems, laying the groundwork necessary for achieving further integration, and, more generally, understanding the needs and concerns of each member state. This information exchange sometimes resulted in the production of trilateral statements or reports and in some cases became the groups' primary function.[15]

Resolving Conflicts. The groups worked on low-level disputes concerning, for example, the appropriate classification of goods (Customs Subgroup of the Working Group on Rules of Origin),[16] the increased Mexican duties on the importation of frozen Canadian geese and US ducks (Committee on Trade in Goods), and the application of a merchandise-processing fee by the United States on imports of some Canadian textile products (Committee on Trade in Goods).[17]

Harmonizing Regulations. Some CWGs had explicit instructions to harmonize rules or to generate new regulations that would directly affect how NAFTA was to be implemented and administered. For example, in 2002 the Working Group on Rules of Origin was very active in reconfiguring and realigning seven NAFTA rules of origin in order to ensure their conformity with changes in the Worldwide Harmonized System promulgated by the WTO in January 2002.[18]

Forums for Relaying Information between the Governments and Interested Parties. The CWGs' final function was to facilitate the exchange of ideas between interested non-governmental players in the private sector. In this mission, they were to encourage a high level of private-sector participation and so create new and more explicit access points for these interests. For instance, the key responsibility of the Telecommunications Standards Sub-Committee (TSSC) was the coordination of efforts and the exchange of information with the Consultative Committee for Telecommunications (CCT), an organization that represented the interests of the telecommunications industry in North America. The TSSC's membership consisted of two to three government officials from each of the NAFTA member states, but since 1999 the chair and the vice-chairs of the CCT have been invited to all of the committee's meetings in order to enhance the feedback coming from the pertinent business communities of the three countries.[19]

Although the involvement of private-sector interests was appropriate in the context of a free-trade agreement, the CWGs blurred the lines between the consultant and the consulted. Despite the fact that the level of consultation was 'nothing beyond the usual day-to-day interaction' for an administrative entity such as the US Department of Commerce,[20] their almost total lack of transparency prevented individual citizens, civil-society organizations, or researchers from having any knowledge about the nature of privileged private-sector access, let alone its influence on whatever regulatory changes might result. In this way, the administrative side of NAFTA's implementation created a deficit in the new continental governance's democratic legitimacy.

That said, the threat to democracy is minuscule. Rather than become agents of a muscular new continental government, the CWGs have proven largely inconsequential even as instruments of governance. Those with too politically sensitive a mandate first became deadlocked and then inactive; by 2002, two-thirds of the CWGs were dormant. In the case of the Committee on Trade in Goods, inactivity signified success, because implementing its final round of tariff acceleration ahead of schedule left it without an agenda. However, the CTG stands out as the only example of a working group that has, to the satisfaction of all three member states, completed its NAFTA mandate.[21]

Some groups such as the Committee on Trade in Worn Clothing and the Working Group on Emergency Action were born out of the NAFTA negotiators' inability to reach agreement on certain controversial issues. To forestall delay in signing the agreement, some unresolved but still contentious issues were assigned to working groups as a way to erase the impression of failure.[22] In these cases, establishing the groups was simply a cover-up – a 'graceful way of pretending there would be more discussion' after a failed negotiation.[23] These CWGs encountered insuperable difficulties in operating, since issues that were too contentious prior to 1994 did not subsequently become easier to navigate. For instance, the Chapter 19 Working Group on Trade Remedies was established in 1993 as a face-saving device for Ottawa, which had targeted the elimination of US anti-dumping and countervailing duties on Canadian exports as its prime negotiating objective when it first solicited a trade agreement with Washington. The group was mandated to seek solutions that reduce the possibility of disputes over subsidies, dumping, and the operation of trade-remedy laws regarding such practices. The exceptionally controversial nature of these issues ensured that the group quickly became moribund.[24] Two particularly instructive cases of contentious bilateral issues that defied resolution through NAFTA's bureaucratic frameworks are energy and trucking.

NORTH AMERICAN ENERGY WORKING GROUP

On April 22, 2001 in Quebec City, the three countries' energy ministers set up the North American Energy Working Group (NAEWG) to build a deeper continental consensus regarding energy,[25] to foster communication and cooperation among the governments and energy sectors of the three countries on energy-related matters of common interest, and to enhance North American energy trade and interconnections consistent with the goal of sustainable development, for the benefit of all.[26]

Since its creation, the NAEWG has been quite successful in carrying out meaningful but politically unrisky tasks.[27] Most of Canada's members come from its Department of Natural Resources, although a small number work for the Department of Foreign Affairs and International Trade or serve on the National Energy Board.[28] In the same spirit as that of NAFTA's CWGs, the NAEWG operates informally and by consensus as a trilateral forum performing a range of low-key functions such as information exchange and the harmonization of statistical methodologies among the three member states so that their data are comparable. For Canada, the NAEWG also served as an effective tool through which the Paul Martin government could have Alberta's vast tar sands reclassified as part of North America's petroleum reserves.[29]

The question arises why a trilateral group of energy officials, who are chiefly exploring issues around continental energy supply and the harmonization of energy practices, was not set up under NAFTA. The answer lies in energy's controversial yet central status in each of the three member states. The fact that the NAEWG was created on an ad hoc basis supports the argument that highly politicized issues involving powerful interests, long-term national-security concerns, and billions of dollars do not get channelled through transnational institutions that might exert a political authority compromising the member states' autonomy. Continental government? No. Continental governance? Only if this means consultation.

THE MEXICO-US TRUCKING DISPUTE

In the NAFTA negotiations, the United States agreed to end long-standing restrictions against Mexican trucking companies and allow them to operate in the US market in a staged process that was to have been completed by January 1, 2000.[30] Although the Canadian and Mexican ministers of transportation signed MOUs permitting Canadian and Mexican truckers equal access within both countries, the US restrictions were maintained by the Clinton administration because of strong domestic pressure from interest groups benefiting from the status quo.[31] Financial stakes were substantial: the cross-border trucking industry carried US$250 billion in Mexican-US trade. If American truckers were to be transporting fewer goods, the US insurance companies' market share and profits would also fall.[32] For their part, US trucking unions argued that Mexican trucks would not meet American safety standards. In 1995 the Salinas government requested that a dispute-resolution process be activated under the aegis of NAFTA's Chapter 20, whose arbitral inadequacies will be addressed in the next chapter. American manoeuvring managed to drag out the adjudicatory process, but finally, in February 2001, the panel ruled that the US moratorium violated NAFTA and ordered the US Department of Transportation to begin processing all Mexican applications.[33]

Beyond confirming the impoverished justice offered by Chapter 20, this long and unhappy episode illustrated a failure of NAFTA's working-group system. The Land Transportation Sub-Committee (LTSC) had been established under NAFTA's Chapter 9 to achieve 'more compatible standards related to truck, bus, and rail operations and the transport of hazardous materials among the United States, Mexico, and Canada.'[34] Within this general mandate, the LTSC established a Cross-Border Operations and Facilitation Consultative Working Group (TCG #1) to deal with the Mexican-US border issue. Since its inception, however, its most significant activity has been merely to arrange for 'a meeting of the trilateral ad hoc government-industry insurance group formed by TCG #1.'[35] The LTSC primarily functioned to exchange information and study national regulatory systems, despite NAFTA's Annex 913.5.a-1 explicitly directing that 'the Subcommittee shall implement the following work program for making compatible the Parties' relevant standards-related measures. No later than three years after the date of entry into force of the Agreement, [it shall determine] standards-related measures respecting vehicles, including measures relating to weights and dimensions, tires, brakes, parts, and accessories, securement of cargo, maintenance and repair, inspections, and emissions and environmental pollution levels.'[36]

This list identified many of the safety concerns subsequently expressed by the US government as its rationale for non-compliance. The task of harmonizing weight standards for bus and truck operations fell within the mandate of the LTSC as an issue that was meant to be resolved in a trilateral, professional fashion by a group of experts. The bilateral nature of the dispute was one reason why the LTSC did not function well in the trilateral framework. Canada remained involved only to the extent that it kept itself informed of developments and wanted to see the dispute resolved. Despite formally being a NAFTA issue, trucking confirmed that much of the trade agreement dealt with particular bilateral issues that were irritants for one party or another.[37]

Politics played a contradictory but illuminating role both in provoking and in resolving this dispute. On the one hand, it was its highly politicized nature that prevented the LTSC from dealing with the issue in any meaningful way. On the other, the 'Mexicanization' through immigration of the United States' southern states gave Mexico more clout than it had had before NAFTA. The increasing importance of Mexican-Americans in US presidential and Congressional politics built up pressure for a politically negotiated solution. Since the issue was the US government's refusal to act in the face of powerful domestic interests which were opposed to granting national treatment to Mexican trucks, a solution was required that would allow Mexican trucks into the United States while also taking into account domestic political sensitivities. This issue was only provisionally resolved by high-level negotiations between presidents Bush and Fox a few days before September 11, 2001.

The LTSC was reinvigorated as a result of the Bush administration's eventual decision to honour the Chapter 20 panel's ruling. The procedures for implementing the dispute panel's ruling were defined when the US Congress set specific guidelines that the Department of Transportation (DOT) was to follow. In November 2002 President Bush modified the moratorium on granting operating authority to Mexican motor carriers and enabled the DOT to review the 130 applications already received from Mexico-domiciled truck and bus companies. Ultimately, the LTSC had little to do with the resolution of this dispute. Washington's agreement to comply with its obligation was primarily determined by executive will, but even then implementation was obstructed by the US trucking interests' use of the courts.

The story of NAFTA's committee and working groups is not only about decline; it is also about revival. Certain groups have been revitalized as a result of the continued bilateralism of North American relations. Some of the more active trilateral committees are those that deal with bilateral issues, such as the Committee on Standards Related Measures, the Temporary Entry Working Group, and the Committee on Sanitary and Phytosanitary Measures, as well as the technical working groups set up to deal, for example, with pesticides and animal health. That these groups maintain fruitful information exchanges and meet more regularly than some of their more exclusively trilateral counterparts confirms that bilateral realities continue to drive the North American relationship.

Higher levels of working-group activity can result from political leaders redirecting activity from other, but related, areas of government policy. Since the negotiation and implementation of 'smart border' initiatives between the United States and Canada and Mexico following September 11, 2001, the Customs Subgroup of the Working Group on Rules of Origin has been largely concerned with issues of border security.[38] That extraneous political motivations recharged this CWG's mandate suggests that the existence of a latent structure has the potential to generate an active function.

In sum, because of the incongruity between the CWGs' trilateral, professional, and symmetrical nature and the bilateral, political, and asymmetrical reality which continues to characterize the power relations of the continental periphery with its common behemoth, the committees and working groups set up under NAFTA have turned out to be largely insignificant. In practice, purportedly continental issues play out bilaterally and therefore are of little interest to the uninvolved government, thus rendering the CWGs an inappropriate mechanism for the resolution of most disputes or the discussion of emerging issues. Furthermore, the stakes in these relations are generally too high for discussions and disputes to be channeled through technocratic institutions built on the assumption of formal legal equality. It appears that NAFTA-style CWGs can deal only with low-level and low-interest disputes. More politically sensitive controversies require a legislative forum with appropriate representation of the interests involved and flexible processes that provide room for compromise and trade-offs between one issue area and another.

Enforcement

No executive, no bureaucracy, and no judiciary can have a meaningful existence without there being some means by which the decisions of those in command, the determinations of the bureaucrats, and the rulings of the judges can be given effect. Not having coercive power at their disposal is generally the Achilles' heel of regimes established by inter-governmental agreements, but many a system operates effectively nonetheless because its members find it in their interest to participate in the new institutions and play by their rules. In these cases, even when they suffer some losses along the way, the members feel they gain in the long run.

In a transnational regime as unbalanced as NAFTA, the problem of compliance is constantly on the agenda. 'Trucking' is a word that evokes for Mexicans, just as does 'softwood lumber' for Canadians (as we see in the next chapter), the problem of unabashed US non-compliance. Washington may get its way in the short term, but, in the long term, it undermines the legitimacy of a system of which it may nevertheless be the prime beneficiary. Asymmetrical compliance produces asymmetrical justice. With the United States willing to flout both NAFTA's letter and spirit on these major issues, its two neighbours have had reason to reconsider how to defend their interests.

Conclusion

NAFTA's patent failure to generate the transnational government that was predicted by its more optimistic defenders (and feared by its most vociferous opponents) generated a search for solutions in both theory and practice. In an interesting example of transnational epistemic co-operation, the American political scientist Robert Pastor developed a strong case for reforming NAFTA's institutions by shunting them along the trail blazed by the European Union.[39] His thesis persuaded his Mexican colleague Jorge Castañeda who, as policy adviser to Vicente Fox, induced the presidential candidate to adopt these ideas for his 2000 campaign platform. Following his victory, President Fox made Castañeda his foreign minister and promptly proposed these reforms to his NAFTA partners. Prime Minister Jean Chrétien responded unenthusiastically. Once Fox fell from grace with the White House following September 11, 2001 and after Castañeda resigned in frustration over US resistance to immigration reform, these proposals to bolster NAFTA's institutions disappeared from Mexico's agenda as well.

In practice, the three governments voted with their feet and turned to broader levels of governance. When trying to generate new transnational economic norms and rules, they ignored NAFTA's stillborn Free Trade Commission and spent their efforts negotiating globally in the WTO's Doha Round and hemispherically in what turned out to be a failed attempt to extend NAFTA into a Free Trade Area of the Americas.

To evaluate the paradox of NAFTA's strong rules and weak institutions, we need, first, to assess their differing valence for the three states' sovereignty, internal autonomy, and external capacity. Once we have appraised NAFTA's institutional impact on the balance of power within the continent, we can consider what it implied for the management of this 'world region.' NAFTA's proponents argued that its members had not lost sovereignty because they could unilaterally abrogate the agreement by giving six months' notice. In practice, only the United States could abrogate without taking a significant risk. The Canadian and Mexican economies have had to make such major structural adjustments in deepening their cross-border integration that the commercial and political costs of abrogation would be too high to contemplate. If the availability of abrogation is the test of continuing sovereignty, the two peripheral states' actual loss of legal sovereignty needs to be recognized as substantial.

NAFTA's effects on governmental autonomy were also asymmetrical. As the overwhelmingly powerful negotiator, the United States rebuffed Canada's original demand to be exempted from US anti-dumping and countervailing duty legislation. Washington not only preserved Congress' autonomy to apply its protectionist measures against goods imported from its periphery; it could even strengthen them provided it adhered to some minor conditions. In effect, its only loss of internal autonomy was accepting review of AD and CVD trade determinations by binational panels under Chapter 19 – a loss it has been able to negate by refusing to comply with adverse rulings. On the other hand, by causing Canada, then Mexico, to internalize some of its norms in their systems, the United States extended its corporations' external capacity throughout the continental periphery – a considerable gain given that, in 1990, US foreign direct investment abroad totalled $431 billion, of which $70 billion or 16.1 per cent was in Canada and $10 billion or 2.3 per cent was in Mexico.[40] By 2005, this had increased to $2.07 trillion, of which $235 billion or 11.3 per cent was in Canada and $71 billion or 3.5 per cent was in Mexico.[41]

For the two members of the continental periphery, the significance of this negligible reconstitutionalization of the United States was not to increase their capacity there – a failure that was not offset by gaining voice through workable new continental institutions. At the same time, by ingesting in their own legal orders constraints on the scope of their policy making that were designed to further the interests of US companies operating across North American borders, the two peripheral states curtailed their own internal autonomy.

In Ottawa, this represented less a loss of its sovereign monopoly over decision making – a condition Canada had never achieved in its evolution from a British colony to an American dependency – than a reduction in form and degree of an already deeply constrained autonomy. NAFTA expanded the scope of old North America's basic dynamic in which Washington played *rule maker* and the periphery *rule taker*. The expansion of American norms in its political domain represented only a change in degree for Canada, intensifying and formalizing a relationship of asymmetrical integration with the United States that, having deepened throughout the twentieth century, had been ratcheted up by the Canada-United States Free Trade Agreement. (Because diminishing the interventionist capacity of the Canadian state was a prime ideological goal for the Mulroney government, constraining the industrial-policy reach of the federal government was no loss in the eyes of the Conservative leader. In this way, free trade provided a useful external pressure helping to impel Canada's shift to a neoconservative paradigm.) That said, Canada continued to enjoy considerable internal policy autonomy – far greater, for instance, than Norway, which, despite only having an associate relationship with the European Union, has to implement most of the European Commission's often highly intrusive directives.

By the same token, since Canada exported more direct investment capital than it imported, NAFTA's autonomy-reducing rules increased its corporate community's capacity in the US market, where Canadian companies had placed 61 per cent of their total $98 billion invested abroad by 1990. In 2006 this number had fallen to 43 per cent of their total $423 billion invested abroad – presumably because Canadian companies could operate in the US market without having to relocate there. Notionally, NAFTA also increased these corporations' capacity in Mexico, but, by 2006, only $4 billion (0.8 per cent of Canadian direct investment abroad) was located in Mexico. By comparison, $224 billion of Canadian direct investment abroad is located in the United States.[42]

By contrast, adopting NAFTA was a decisive move for Mexico City in its attempt to transform the country's whole system by abandoning much of the state's monopoly controls. Having exerted titanic efforts throughout most of the twentieth century to forge its own identity independent of its intrusive neighbour to the north, the PRI made an abrupt change in ideological direction in the 1980s when it opted for a radical, neoconservative solution to transform the structure it had itself created. Making a bold leap of faith based on highly optimistic political-economy assumptions, the governing party abruptly abandoned substantial aspects of a sovereignty that its previous leadership had zealously defended for decades. Entering the new North America required it to accept norms, rules, and rights for US and Canadian investors that substantially reduced its policy-making autonomy. As with the Mulroney Conservatives, having NAFTA diminish its own governing powers was a convenient external pressure to help the PRI rationalize its radical, state-shrinking goal.

As a minor exporter of corporate capital, Mexico's external capacity was increased the least. Despite quadrupling during the last decade (from $0.6 billion dollars in 1990 to $2.5 billion in 2000), Mexican direct investment in the United States continued to be an insignificant 0.2 per cent of the United States' total FDI stock. Mexican direct investment was even tinier in Canada, where little changed between 1990 and 2006. Since its $277 million makes Mexico twenty-fifth on the list of global investors in Canada, Chapter 11's investor-state dispute-settlement mechanism brought it little new capacity in Canada.[43]

Nevertheless, NAFTA's formal trilateral parity was of some significance for Mexico, since its participation in regular meetings of the trade secretaries/ministers and various working groups helped offset the severe asymmetry of its dyadic relationship with Washington and opened the prospect of strengthening its negotiating capacity through alliances with Canada. To the extent that it is practised, trinational governance also helps make Mexico's dominant bilateral relationship more similar to Ottawa's somewhat less unequal US relationship. Overall, the periphery's far greater loss of internal autonomy than gain of external capacity suggested that, normatively and institutionally speaking, NAFTA represented a significant increase for US power within the new North America, where it acquired considerable capacity while surrendering minimal autonomy. This did not mean that NAFTA created an instrument for managing this new world region.

A brief glance at the European Union is enough to confirm that NAFTA created no viable framework for North American *governance*, let alone continental *government*. The EU provides both governance and government for its whole region. While its policy-making capacity is strong enough to promote the development of an integrated continental economy, it also offsets market-liberating norms with some instruments for democratic participation. It can develop new norms as changing circumstances require. In establishing powerful economic rules for a putative continental community in 1994, the United States, Canada, and Mexico adopted a grand bargain to make a trinational North America more economically integrated through the increase of cross-border investment and the spread of cross-border production processes. Endowing this new North America with the weakest possible political structure to oversee its evolution left it unable to manage its increased interdependence and so it remains institutionally impaired.

NAFTA broke down some of the periphery's barriers to a continental regime of production and capital accumulation without constructing an alternative mode for regulating this expanded economy. This disconnect between the economic and the political was exacerbated by the asymmetry between the centre and the periphery, since NAFTA did not offset the diminution of Canada's and Mexico's regulatory autonomy by creating an overarching regime to regulate the more continentalized economy in which they were so largely integrated.

NAFTA created a further disequilibrium by strengthening transborder corporate powers without balancing them with institutions subject to democratic controls. With North America having no viable forum for deliberation and decision, new norms had to be negotiated outside the continent at the WTO or during the efforts to create the FTAA. Subsequent proposals responding to business associations' and continental visionaries' dissatisfaction with the continent's integration confirmed that inadequate institutions were central to the new North America's failed governance. In the United States, Robert Pastor remained the champion of deeper institutionalization. In 2000 his ally, the newly elected Mexican president, Vicente Fox, eagerly presented proposals for new institutions to achieve continental solidarity. In Canada, Wendy Dobson[44] and Allan Gotlieb were but two of the many voices expressing the business community's recognition that integration without institutions was a recipe for stalemate. Trilaterally, the Council on Foreign Relations sponsored a major review of the continent's institutional limitations and offered suggestions in 2005 to rectify them. Advocacy for a continental competition law and tribunal (to replace the partners' trade-remedy legislation), a common external tariff (to eliminate rules of origin and the need for customs agents at the Canadian-American border), a continental energy policy, a common market for labour, a North America Monetary Union, and even a common security perimeter (to alleviate American concern about Canada's and Mexico's anti-terrorism capacities) underlined how deficient had been the structures put in place on January 1, 1994.

A final imbalance was the favouring of investment and commerce over other public-policy issues, whether national security, environmental quality, or macroeconomic management. NAFTA set up no institutional mechanisms to cope with these necessarily connected issues should its consequences differ from the rosy forecasts that celebrated its birth. True, it did create two other institutional elements. But the commissions on labour and the environment have proven largely ineffectual, whether to deal with the labour market and environmental effects of greater trade and investment or to give civil-society organizations greater voice in these issues, as chapters IV and V explain. In short, the new North America's made-by-NAFTA institutions amounted to much less than they appeared on the surface – even in their judicial processes, a subject explored in the next chapter.

III NAFTA's Uneven Judicial Capacity

Since it had been negotiated within the context of increasingly politicized commercial conflicts between the United States and its two neighbours, the North American Free Trade Agreement was intended to provide mechanisms through which the parties could resolve their recurrent disputes. Because of the differing problems each faced, the three signatories had different objectives for the various dispute-resolution procedures to which they finally agreed. Canada's prime negotiating objective was to shelter itself from harassment by the torturous procedures of Congress-mandated trade protectionism, which often used anti-dumping and countervailing duties aggressively to block imports from Canada. Mexico sought to position itself as a stable and attractive destination for foreign investment. For its part, the United States wanted to resist abandoning any of its trade-remedy powers while securing greater rights in the periphery for its exporters and investors, particularly in the face of Mexico's perennial antipathy to foreign capital and its less-than-transparent legal system.

In examining to what extent the various NAFTA dispute-resolution provisions met each of these objectives, this chapter investigates whether the accord's three principal dispute-settlement processes actually achieved the breakthrough to a new continental judicial order that its negotiators had so triumphantly claimed. The argument proceeds in the following stages:

- The supranational panels provided for in the agreement's Chapter 20 to resolve disputes over the meaning of NAFTA clauses can be viewed as legal *governance*, because of the non-binding nature of their rulings, which amount to mere recommendations for consideration by the North American Free Trade Commission.

- NAFTA's Chapter 19 specified how binational panels can be formed to review a member's imposition of anti-dumping or countervailing duties and remand the protectionist ruling for reconsideration.
- Chapter 11 provided access to international commercial tribunals for NAFTA's transnational corporations seeking to protect their investments against the regulatory measures of host governments.
- Chapter 11 tribunals and Chapter 19 panels were supposed to set up elements of continental *government*, because of the explicitly binding nature of panel or tribunal decisions and the resulting constraints they were to place on domestic protectionist actions.
- NAFTA's judicial procedures, when compared to the World Trade Organization's dispute-settlement mechanisms, fall short of the continental judicial governance in North America that the public had been led to expect.

The Old North America: Canada and the United States

Disputes between the Canadian and US governments in the old North America were historically addressed through actions ranging from diplomatic consultations and bureaucratic cooperation to threats of economic retaliation and, at earlier periods in their not-so-tranquil history, military force. In 1909 a chronically contentious issue – the management of rivers and lakes shared by the two countries – was devolved to a supranational institution, the International Joint Commission, whose remit I examine in chapter VI. Commercial disputes often involved the application of domestic laws that constrained unwanted imports. During the Cold War, the informal closeness between Canada and the United States developed into a 'special relationship' characterized not only by further economic integration but also by multiple levels of interdependencies that served as a restraint whenever interests between the two countries became misaligned.[1] With the US administration in firm control over foreign relations, Canada's Department of External Affairs managed conflict in the relationship by dealing with fellow diplomats in the US Department of State.

But, when the disaster of the Vietnam War and the scandal of Watergate shattered the presidency's pre-eminence, Congress recaptured some of its authority over foreign policy. As the United States started to experience trade deficits in 1970 – having enjoyed almost a century of surpluses – Congress went on vigorously to reassert its constitutional prerogative over trade policy. While Americans debated how to reverse the apparent decline of their global dominance, politicians tightened

Congress' trade legislation in order to give the United States' now-beleaguered industries sharper weapons with which to protect themselves against foreign competitors on a contingency basis.[2]

Growing harassment of its exports sparked by this new US protectionism caused Canadian business enormous concern. Particularly aggravating for the federal government were its struggles within the American political, legal, and administrative system to overcome punitive duties levied against its exporters. Such bitter disputes as the softwood-lumber case, which was based on the American complaint that provinces gave unfair subsidies to their logging companies, led Canadian policy makers to argue for a Canadian-American tribunal which could take commercial conflicts out of the highly politicized trade courts administered by the US Department of Commerce. When the Mulroney government requested economic-integration negotiations with Washington, it naively expected that the Nirvana of free trade would give it a complete exemption from US protectionism.

Specifically, Canada sought exemption from countervailing duties (which were often levied on Canadian exports to offset government subsidies the exporters had allegedly received) or anti-dumping duties (which were imposed on exports on the grounds that they were allegedly being dumped at predatory prices below their domestic level). Ottawa hoped that binational dispute settlement, based on a subsidy code specifying what kinds of government assistance to exporters were acceptable, would mitigate inter-governmental conflicts and provide unrestricted access for Canadian exporters to the world's biggest market. Alas for Ottawa, the American negotiators brushed off the Canadian demand as a non-starter, affirming that Congress would never waive its constitutional sovereignty over US commerce. When the Canadian negotiators ultimately staged a walkout over this issue, a hastily drafted compromise established the basis for what became the Canada-US Free Trade Agreement's putatively binding binational review panels for domestic CVD and AD duties, a unique system that was transposed into NAFTA's Chapter 19.

Mexico and the United States

The notion of 'manifest destiny' rationalized not just the United States' push to the west and the north in the nineteenth century but its southward expansion as well. After the Mexican-US hostilities from 1845–8 forced Mexico's surrender of approximately half its territory, significant tensions persisted. Mexico-US agreements signed during the latter half of the nineteenth century reflected Washington's domineering approach to its Latino neighbour. After France's brief installation of Maximilian as emperor in Mexico City, tensions softened between Mexican liberals and the United States, and relations warmed considerably when Porfirio Díaz opened Mexico to foreign investment. However, the revolutionary years' violence after 1910, the radical 1917 constitution, and the 1938 expropriation of foreign oil companies under President Lázaro Cárdenas kept bilateral conflicts simmering until military threats from Germany and Japan induced the two countries to cooperate again. After the Second World War, disputes between Mexico and the United States focused largely on labour migration and the drug trade. The regulation of both was handled by the US Immigration Service, which tended unilaterally to impose its directives on Mexico.

Prior to its entry into the General Agreement on Tariffs and Trade in 1986, the Mexican government did not have the legal infrastructure to deal with trade-related questions. Foreign trade was managed through a convoluted system of subsidies and import licences that was tainted by rampant governmental corruption.[3] Derived from Spain's social and legal culture, Mexico's civil law system was incompatible with US-style dispute settlement, which was rooted in Anglo-Saxon common law traditions. Instead, Mexico relied on the Calvo Doctrine, which stipulated that only Mexicans by birth or naturalization and Mexican corporations had the right to acquire land, water, and mineral resources or obtain concessions to exploit them. It further specified that 'the state can offer the same right to foreigners as long as they agree before the Department of Foreign Relations to consider themselves as nationals as far as the said property is concerned and not invoke the protection of their government subject, in case of breaking this agreement, to losing the goods they had acquired.'[4] The insistence that foreign investors complaining of unfair regulation come under the rule of domestic Mexican – rather than international commercial – law was a major irritant that Washington was bent on resolving.

During its economic negotiations with the United States and Canada, Mexico agreed in Chapter 19 to introduce special procedures that would create a separate domestic forum for dealing with trade disputes. Through its 1993 Foreign Trade Law,[5] it hoped that, by transforming its domestic trade-dispute system through the creation of impartial, transparent, and fair best practices for settling conflicts over anti-dumping and countervailing duties, it would achieve its objective of secure access to the US market.[6] Pursuing the parallel objective of attracting investment from abroad, Mexico abandoned the Calvo Doctrine and, in Chapter 11, agreed to let foreign investors have their claims against government regulations be heard by international commercial tribunals.

Transborder Adjudication

As a means to understanding the nature of North America's transborder adjudicatory reality, this section evaluates NAFTA's judicial institutions by moving from the least to the most effective. Within the broader context of global trade law, I then consider the impact of the dispute-settlement mechanisms on the continent's transborder legal governance.

Ineffectual: Chapter 20

Built on a solid tradition of international trade agreements, NAFTA established two levels for dealing with disputes over its provisions. Through the mechanism of the North American Free Trade Commission, the trade ministers from the three member countries consult about the proper interpretation and application of NAFTA articles and review pertinent changes in domestic trade policy. When such consultations fail to satisfy an aggrieved party, Chapter 20 mandates ad hoc bilateral panels to arbitrate formal inter-governmental disputes. Once a panel's decision is rendered, the NAFTC is responsible for recommending a resolution to the three governments.

Chapter 20's binational panel system cannot be considered transnational *government* since it has no enforcement mechanism to punish a party that refuses to correct its offending behaviour. It has been ineffective even as transnational governance, since it focuses on 'consultations, good offices, conciliation, and mediation over arbitration.'[7] Furthermore, because it lacks binding effect, Chapter 20 arbitration offers little reason for an offending country to comply with a panel's ruling. Of a handful of cases initiated in NAFTA's first decade, only three progressed to the stage of actual deliberations.[8] In one dispute dealing with agricultural tariffs, the United States lost its case against Canada.[9] In the second case, the panel found in favour of Mexico in its dispute with the United States relating to corn brooms,[10] but Washington chose not to comply with the unanimous panel ruling against it for almost a year.[11] In the most contentious and drawn-out dispute, the United States denied Mexican trucks access to its roads.

Introduced in the US Bus Regulatory Reform Act of 1982, a moratorium on foreign trucks transporting goods across the US border initially applied to both Canadian and Mexican truckers. While a presidential MOU later lifted the restriction against Canadian trucks, the moratorium against Mexico persisted. As a result, truckloads from Mexico were required to offload their cargo at the US border. In turn, these border trucks had to reload the same cargo onto other US trucks once they got through the border zone. These two operations added some $160 per load to the cost of shipment and prevented Mexican transport companies from enjoying the fruits of market liberalization.

Although Washington agreed in NAFTA to permit Mexican trucks to operate in the United States by gradually lifting the moratorium, strong political pressures caused the Clinton administration to postpone compliance. Financial considerations were substantial: if US truckers were to transport fewer goods, the American insurance companies' profits would decrease.[12] US trucking unions put up a bitter resistance to the NAFTA commitment, since many of their members' jobs were at stake.

In 1995 the Mexican government requested that a dispute panel be struck under the auspices of Chapter 20. The United States stalled the discussion while attempting to negotiate with domestic lobby groups. President Clinton was extremely wary of displeasing angry trucking unions seeking to avoid competition from Mexican trucks, which, they claimed, did not meet US safety standards. This was a questionable charge, since some Mexican trucks had better long-distance safety records than their US counterparts.[13] In 2001, after years of protracted discussions between the two parties, the binational Chapter 20 panel called for an end to the moratorium and for Mexican truckers' applications to enter the United States to be evaluated solely on relevant safety and economic considerations.[14] The issue was ostensibly settled for good later that year at a meeting between President Bush and President Fox, but continuing obstruction was rationalized on the basis of NAFTA's Article 2101, which required Mexico to establish the same security measures as the United States and Canada in order to attain cross-border transit for Mexican trucks.[15]

In June 2004 the United States Supreme Court overturned a 9th Circuit Court of Appeal's ruling in favour of various interest groups seeking to keep the border closed to Mexican trucks.[16] Even after multiple court rulings and further negotiations between presidents Fox and Bush, it took until March 2007 – thirteen years after the dispute had first arisen – before the United States agreed to a partial lifting of the suspension and opened its border. Even then, the suspension was on a probationary basis and limited to 100 Mexican trucking firms.[17] The Chapter 20 arbitral process had played a negligible role compared to the hurly-burly of US politics and rulings by US courts.[18]

Domestic US politics and law had easily thumbed its nose at the continental legal governance enshrined in what had turned out to be a patently ineffectual Chapter 20 dispute-settlement process.[19] Bound only by national interest – as opposed to a more tangible financial or political penalty – the United States had made a mockery of the Chapter 20 process, rendering it unable to settle conflicts. Instead, as the situation now stands, the parties resort to power politics and direct diplomatic negotiation, which nullifies the original goal of neutral arbitration.[20] Interestingly, the 2006 Softwood Lumber Agreement between Canada and the United States specifically rules out resort to Chapter 20 dispute-settlement procedures.[21]

Effective Except Where It Mattered: Chapter 19

In 1987 Ottawa's negotiators of the Canada-US Free Trade Agreement waxed eloquent about what they considered their triumph in overcoming resistance by Congress to any infringement of its sovereignty over the administration of US trade law. The Chapter 19 binational panels, which are selected from national rosters of trade-law experts, were expected to produce binding reviews of US (or Canadian) trade-protectionist actions. Once a domestic anti-dumping or countervailing duty determination was 'remanded' – referred back as deficient – the trade department in question was obligated to rectify its erroneous decision. Thus, to the Canadian negotiators, Chapter 19 represented an important breakthrough towards continental judicial government.

It was one thing for Americans to tolerate Canadian trade lawyers and academics participating in judgment over the determinations of the US Court of International Trade. It was something else for them to swallow the idea that Mexicans with little training in Anglo-American law should enjoy such powers. Nor was it plausible for Mexicans that American or Canadian trade experts would be knowledgeable enough about the intricacies of Mexican administrative law to be able to judge whether an AD determination had been correctly made. The most contentious result of the NAFTA negotiations was CUFTA's trade-law dispute settlement being pasted into NAFTA's Chapter 19, incorporating

Mexico into a now trilateral system designed to let exporters challenge the imposition of countervailing or anti-dumping duties.

Had CUFTA and NAFTA really established free trade as does the European Union or the Australia-New Zealand Closer Economic Relations Trade Agreement, the signatories would have given up their capacity to apply anti-dumping or countervailing duties to imported goods coming from their trade-accord partners. Problems associated with the unfair pricing of exported products would have been addressed by a continental anti-trust policy designed to punish predatory dumping practices. The question of governments subsidizing domestic firms to give them an unfair competitive advantage in their partners' markets would have been dealt with by rules distinguishing legitimate from illegitimate types of export-promoting state aids, as does the WTO's subsidy code. Such provisions would have introduced genuine transborder government, but they had been dismissed out of hand as unacceptable by the US negotiators in both negotiations. Ironically, Chapter 19 enshrined the very protectionism that the free-trade agreements were supposed to eliminate. Indeed, Article 1902 explicitly accepted the entrenchment of domestic protectionism: 'Each Party reserves the right to apply its antidumping law and countervailing duty law to goods imported from the territory of any other Party.'

Chapter 19 created a judicial mongrel – an international panel system to apply domestic law. In effect, it provided a binational appeal process which could replace a NAFTA member's own judicial appeal process in order to determine whether it had fairly applied its national trade-remedy laws to products imported from a NAFTA partner. Instead of launching appeals on their exporters' behalf through the importing country's national courts – their only previous recourse – Chapter 19 allowed parties to challenge another NAFTA member's AD or CVD determinations before ad hoc binational panels.[22]

This ad hoc composition of Chapter 19 panels produced a number of problems. First, the transience of panellists led to a lack of continuity and consistency in panel judgments. Given prevailing criteria for impartiality and expertise, recommended panellists have often been forced to withdraw because of conflict-of-interest concerns expressed by the other party. Finding alternative panellists has slowed down the adjudicatory process tremendously. Although NAFTA specified a two-month time limit for parties to establish panels, the average time taken to set up Chapter 19 panels has turned out to be almost a full year – 301 days.[23]

Other problems have significantly weakened the binding arbitration process originally envisioned by the NAFTA negotiators. Of particular note, Chapter 19 does not provide the opportunity for the participation of stakeholders who are not formally parties to the dispute, including provincial and state governments, non-governmental organizations (NGOs), private companies, civil organizations, and concerned citizens.[24] This exclusion of important interests and sometimes relevant sources of testimony throws into question the soundness of panel judgments. Their legitimacy is further jeopardized because the arbitration proceedings are conducted in virtual secrecy. Judgments made in this vacuum may lack an accurate gauge of political reality if they are based solely on the testimony of parties to the dispute, with little consideration given to other important social, environmental, or political interests.

Notwithstanding these problems, Chapter 19 reviews of AD and CVD determinations have had the general effect of reducing power asymmetries in North America. The United States is the world's most active user of trade-remedy duties, but Chapter 19 panels have disciplined their application to the continental periphery. Of the first forty-five cases in which panellists issued a decision under NAFTA's Chapter 19, they remanded 83 per cent of the American, 75 per cent of the Mexican, and 36 per cent of the Canadian AD or CVD determinations. It appears that even anti-dumping measures themselves have had an asymmetry-reducing effect. Of the 172 anti-dumping cases initiated among the three North American countries from 1987 to 1999, Mexico initiated seventy (41 per cent), followed by the United States with fifty-three (31 per cent). Moreover, US exports were the most affected of those from the three economies, with 111 determinations (65 per cent) against them, followed by Canada with thirty-eight (22 per cent).[25] The fact that Mexico City is as energetic an initiator of AD and CVD measures as Ottawa (both ranked fourth in the world) suggests that its conversion to trade-remedy politics and its use of Chapter 19 have acted to reduce the imbalance between its US relationship and Canada's.

Chapter 19 panels appear on the whole to have increased the capacity of all three states. American corporations have had some success using Chapter 19's arbitrations to discipline Mexico's and Canada's imposition of anti-dumping and countervailing duties. Compared to the previous alternative of pursuing claims in the US judicial system, Chapter 19 represented an improvement. In the majority of cases when the shoe was on the other foot, the US International Trade Commission

(ITC) and the International Trade Administration have complied with the binational panel remands. To this extent, Chapter 19 created a more symmetrical transborder arbitral space. However, the devil lurked in two massive exceptions.

Although Washington has a solid record of compliance with Chapter 19 panel decisions when it experienced little resistance from domestic interests, binational panel rulings have not managed to discipline American governmental behaviour on issues of major political salience. In a crucial test, Chapter 19 proved unable to resolve a sixteen-year-long conflict in which Washington imposed anti-dumping duties against imports of Mexican cement. Even a ruling in favour of Mexico under GATT did not induce Washington's compliance. It was only in the wake of the devastating Hurricane Katrina in August 2005 that a national cement shortage precipitated a political deal which, on April 3, 2006, finally led the US government to accept the annual importation of 3 million tons of Mexican cement.[26] It was continental weather, not continental government, that brought this protracted trade dispute to a provisional end.

While Chapter 19 institutes a binding judicial mechanism and therefore a small measure of continental *government* for low-profile cases, in practice it has proven unable to overcome the power of determined US lobbies to protect their interests using Congress' complex trade-remedy mechanisms. This impotence of NAFTA's judical government has been confirmed by the denouement of four rounds of the long-standing dispute involving the United States' imposition of anti-dumping and countervailing duties on billions of dollars' worth of Canadian softwood-lumber exports that are used largely by the US home-building industry. The dispute was rooted in a profound political-economy asymmetry. Canada's vast forests are mostly administered by provincial governments, which charge stumpage fees in exchange for granting lumber companies the right to harvest the trees from Crown land. Whenever Canadian softwood-lumber imports have threatened to capture more than one-third of the US market, the American softwood industry has cried 'Unfair!' and mobilized huge lobbying resources to get Congress to protect it from the Canadian competition.

A first round of protectionism in the early 1980s took the form of countervailing duties imposed because the United States alleged that the stumpage fees unfairly subsidized Canadian logging companies. These duties were ultimately disallowed through the domestic procedures set up by US trade law. However, when Congress amended the law to suit the US Coalition for Fair Lumber Imports so that new countervailing duties could be imposed, Ottawa agreed in 1986 to tax Canadian softwood exports while the provinces increased their stumpage fees. A third episode began in 1991 when Ottawa used CUFTA's new dispute-settlement mechanism to challenge another US round of countervailing duties. When the Chapter 19 panel twice remanded the US determination, the Office of the United States Trade Representative appealed the remand by requesting an Extraordinary Challenge Committee, an option provided for in the NAFTA chapter. When this appeal was lost, and Round 3 had clearly gone to Canada, Washington complied. The countervailing duties were removed, and the Canadian exporters were reimbursed for those they had already paid.[27]

By 1996, when Congress changed the law again to make provincial stumpage fees qualify more easily as subsidies, Ottawa signed a new five-year agreement to restrict Canadian lumber exports. On the agreement's expiry in 2001, when the Coalition for Fair Lumber Imports obtained another round of significant AD duties (some 10 per cent) and CVDs (some 19 per cent) on Canadian softwood lumber,[28] Ottawa adopted a two-level strategy, initiating actions both in Geneva and through NAFTA. It obtained mixed, though largely favourable, rulings from no less than three WTO panels and three NAFTA Chapter 19 panels on various highly legalistic issues involved in the bafflingly complex case. In an extraordinary sequence, the US ITC thrice refused to accept the NAFTA panel remands, though it ultimately and with great reluctance conceded.

Ottawa was also victorious in a parallel action, participating with other countries in winning a WTO ruling against the United States that invalidated the infamous Byrd Amendment, which, by funneling the CVD and AD duties collected by the US government directly into the pockets of the industries that had petitioned for protection, provided further incentives for trade harassment.[29] However, Washington refused to repeal the Byrd Amendment, and Canada announced retaliatory measures against imports from the United States.[30]

Along with the Mexican cement case, softwood lumber was unique in its depth and breadth owing to its economic importance (by 2006, Canadian annual softwood-lumber exports amounted to C$10 billion)[31] and length (twenty-four years). The protracted dispute showed that, despite its positive achievements, Chapter 19 had failed its crucial test as judicial government, having had virtually no effect on the US Department of Commerce's approach to trade-remedy legislation, which has actually hardened since NAFTA was signed.[32] Rather than abide by the Chapter 19 remands, Washington kept changing its laws to suit the harassment strategy of an entrenched industrial lobby. For its part, Canada acted as though its interests were not in fact protected by NAFTA and the WTO.[33] Instead, it aggravated the asymmetrical bilateral power relationship by submitting to an adamant United States even in the face of rulings favouring Canada's position by both NAFTA and WTO panels.

Despite winning most of these battles using the mechanisms of continental and global trade governance, Canada lost the war. In 2006, after Washington had kept refusing to reimburse the $5 billion of duties that both WTO and NAFTA panels had deemed illegal, the Stephen Harper government capitulated, accepting reimbursement for only 80 per cent of the duties which had been imposed and further agreeing that Washington would – in the spirit of the Byrd Amendment, by then ruled illegal by the WTO – distribute much of the remaining $1 billion in tariffs to the lumber lobby. For all Canada's rhetorical commitment to rules-based trade, it had succumbed to Washington's power-based tactics. Thus, Ottawa made itself complicit in legitimating Washington's defiance of WTO dispute judgments (on the Byrd Amendment and softwood lumber) and NAFTA panel rulings. In this way Canada helped undermine both regimes as instruments of transnational judicial government.[34] This cavalier behaviour made the Harper government's apparently bold 2007 WTO challenge of the United States' farm-subsidy program appear quixotic, an ill-considered effort to appear to be standing up to the Americans.[35]

The Most Effective: Chapter 11

If the government-to-government dispute-settlement processes contained in Chapters 20 and 19, which were based on international and national trade law, are weak as institutions of continental governance, the investor-to-government dispute mechanism established by NAFTA's Chapter 11 is markedly strong. Derived from the processes of international private commercial arbitration, Chapter 11 aims to let NAFTA investors hold member governments directly to account through the arbitration of international tribunals set up under the auspices of the United Nations or the World Bank.[36] Prior to NAFTA, investors who claimed that their investment in North America was expropriated or otherwise discriminated against owing to the actions of a host government had to plead their case within the courts of that state[37] or appeal to their home government either to submit the dispute to arbitration at GATT or to exert diplomatic pressure on the host state.[38] Because the Calvo Doctrine rejected foreign-government intervention in foreign investors' domestic cases and because the Mexican justice system was still blighted with corruption, the United States had insisted that internationally adjudicated investor-state dispute settlement be incorporated in NAFTA.

Reprising the many previous bilateral investment treaties that the United States had negotiated to ensure that Third World governments did not jeopardize its transnational corporations' interests, Chapter 11 defines very broadly the obligations that each NAFTA party assumed towards investors and investments of one of the other two parties. It also lays out the mechanisms enabling an investor to pursue a claim that a host government violated obligations arbitrated under the procedures set up by the World Bank's International Centre for Settlement of Investment Disputes (ICSID) or the United Nations Commission on International Trade Law.[39]

In addition to extending very broad rights to NAFTA corporations, Chapter 11 stipulates that foreign investments be treated according to the principles of international law.[40] Since the possible interpretations of 'international law' are legion, this proviso can easily be adapted to accommodate the US interpretation of a contested concept – a prospect made more likely by the predominance of American legal thinking among experts on international commercial law. For instance, NAFTA's Article 1110(2), which requires compensation for the expropriation of foreign assets by member governments, has been widely regarded as the most threatening because of the very broad meaning that 'expropriation' has acquired in US jurisprudence. The concern is that investors may arbitrarily allege violation of their property rights and make extravagant claims for remuneration.

Chapter 11's potential supra-constitutional effects are particularly significant because this section of the agreement is genuinely binding, the three signatory states having amended their legislation to make Chapter 11 arbitration rulings enforceable in their domestic courts. As a part of a process driven by transnational corporate interests in the Third World, Chapter 11 had its greatest impact in the old North America, whose activists were astonished to be governed by such a powerful yet democratically inaccessible form of adjudication. In a first phase, the initial Chapter 11 cases seemed to justify the worst fears of the original free-trade opponents, particularly in Canada. The American experience of Chapter 11 cases raised a different kind of nationalist furore in US politics, although more recent arbitrations went some way to alleviating these anxieties in both countries.

Ethyl Corporation of Virginia launched a suit against Ottawa's Bill C-94, which banned the gasoline additive and suspected neurotoxin MMT. Unsuccessful in requesting Washington to launch a dispute-settlement panel under Chapter 20, Ethyl used Chapter 11's investor-state arbitration to bypass its government's reluctance – because MMT had been banned by the US Environmental Protection Agency – to fight on its behalf. Chapter 11 empowered Ethyl to launch a case claiming that Ottawa's legislated ban on this putatively toxic fuel component had cost it US$250 million in lost business and future profits and that the Canadian government had failed to provide adequate and convincing evidence that MMT released harmful amounts of manganese into the air.[41] Although the Canadian government denied all accusations made by Ethyl Corporation, it opened the floodgates for other cases of alleged expropriation by settling out of court, paying US$13 million in damages, and issuing a formal apology.

S.D. Myers, an Ohio-based hazardous-waste disposal company, also filed a successful suit under Chapter 11, claiming that Environment Minister Sheila Copps's order to block the transport across the border of the known carcinogen PCB violated NAFTA Articles 1102, 1105, and 1110. In this action, Canada was honouring the commitments it had made when signing the Basel Convention on the Trans-Boundary Movement of Hazardous Waste, a treaty that NAFTA's preamble explicitly stated had precedence over its own rules. Notwithstanding this environmental imperative, the ICSID tribunal judged that the Canadian government had violated its national-treatment obligations (Article 1102) and minimum standards of treatment under international law (Article 1105). Ottawa had to pay US$6 million in damages for failing to allow the export of the hazardous waste.[42]

The implications of this case were explosive. The award illustrated that an ad hoc tribunal, with no basis in the legal system of Canada, the United States, or Mexico, and using flimsy legal reasoning, could force a change in domestic legislation and overturn the directives of an internationally recognized treaty that had been implemented in domestic Canadian law.

A similar problem occurred in Mexico when Metalclad, an American hazardous-waste disposal company, demanded over US$43 million plus damages in a Chapter 11 expropriation claim against the state of San Luis Potosí for refusing to permit the opening of a hazardous-waste disposal site in an area designated for ecological protection. The Mexican government insisted that it was following the Ecological Decree of September 1997, which called for the creation of an ecological preserve that included the disputed landfill area. The ICSID tribunal decided that Mexico had indirectly expropriated Metalclad's investment without providing the compensation required by NAFTA's Article 1110. It further ruled that 'the Tribunal need not decide or consider the motivation or intent of the adoption of the Ecological Decree' when determining the final award.[43] In other words, other public-policy considerations – in this instance, protecting the environment – were irrelevant to the case: Metalclad was awarded more than US$16 million in damages.

Mexican technocrats felt the Metalclad fine was money worth paying as a signal to global corporations that NAFTA had made their investments in Mexico safe.[44] The Mexican environmental movement was too weak to turn Metalclad into a domestic political issue, but in Canada environmental NGOs were deeply disturbed by its implications, which, along with those of the Ethyl and S.D. Myers cases, were seen to constitute serious threats to the three countries' environmental policy-making autonomy. Chapter 11's power to expand the reach of NAFTA in ways not intended by its negotiators[45] was understood as a threat that could extend NAFTA's dominion over areas such as water exports, public services, and Crown corporations that had been excluded from the original trilateral agreement. More immediately, Chapter 11 cases threatened to circumscribe the three governments' regulatory jurisdiction. Activists also heard from their allies in environmental ministries that the threat of Chapter 11 litigation had started to inhibit federal and provincial governments from regulating in the public interest. For instance, the threat of a Chapter 11 case dissuaded federal policy makers from imposing a ban on cigarette advertising and the government of New Brunswick from adopting public auto insurance. This 'regulatory chill' among policy makers was linked to the enormity of the expropriation claims that Chapter 11 tribunals were being asked to award – some as high as US$14 billion.[46]

As a result of environmentalists' lobbying, the Canadian government urged NAFTA's Free Trade Commission to alter Chapter 11's investor-state dispute mechanism. In 2001 the NAFTC attempted to narrow the range of possible claims by issuing an interpretation of the term 'international law' in Article 1105. This was to serve as guidance for future

Chapter 11 tribunals by limiting them to the consideration of only 'customary international law.'[47]

It was a wider and angrier constituency that reacted to three Canadian Chapter 11 claims against US state governments. Loewen, a Canadian funeral-home business, filed a Chapter 11 claim against the United States alleging that a Mississippi jury verdict had engendered its expropriation without adequate compensation. Mondev, a Quebec development company, brought a $50–million claim alleging expropriation without compensation following a Massachusetts Supreme Judicial Court decision that had denied Mondev the right to purchase a property in Boston. Arbitration by foreigners able to overturn US court decisions raised the flag of judicial sovereignty – an extremely sensitive issue for Americans. Environmentalists joined the ranks of outraged constitutionalists when Methanex, a Canadian company producing the methanol feedstock for the gasoline additive MTBE, launched a claim following the governor of California's ban of gasoline containing the additive. Accusations that Chapter 11's secretive arbitral proceedings gave foreign investors greater investment protections than domestic investors, undermined governmental regulations, threatened the environment and public health, and violated US sovereignty echoed the Canadian debate.[48]

The United States was hoist on its own petard. Having long demanded full protection and security for the foreign assets of its nationals in Mexico and other countries of the globe, Washington found itself arguing in these cases for more restrictive rules that would circumscribe foreign claimants' judicial prerogatives in its own territory.[49] However, a series of investor-state panel rulings has taken the steam out of the protests against Chapter 11.

In *Methanex v. United States*, the Canadian corporation lost its claim for $970 million in damages against the Californian regulation. The tribunal upheld the state government's right to regulate the use of MTBE, which California proved had contaminated drinking water supplies. In its decision, the panel restated the general international-law principle that 'a non-discriminatory regulation for a public purpose, which is enacted in accordance with due process and, which affects, inter alios, a foreign investor or investment is not deemed expropriatory and compensable.'[50] The Methanex ruling suggested that Chapter 11 could not be misused to override a government's legitimate right to regulate in the public interest.

Another landmark Chapter 11 ruling dismissed United Parcel Service's claim against Canada Post for unfair competition. Legal experts responded with a collective sigh of relief, inferring that this judgment would avert a flood of similar claims by foreign corporations protesting unfair competition from such government-run services as water treatment, highway operations, health institutions, and public universities, or a vast range of other Crown corporations with which Canadian companies had always had to coexist.[51]

As with Chapter 19 panels, Chapter 11 tribunals are not bound by precedent, so it cannot be known how future panels may rule on similar issues. Furthermore, judicial reviews by domestic judges are inconsistent and remain unpredictable. For the moment, we can see that – ironically – NAFTA's investor-state dispute-settlement mechanism has reduced North America's juridical asymmetry, albeit by applying equally to Mexico as to the United States and Canada the same international arbitration formerly imposed by the US government on Third World states. By 2007, Chapter 11's investor-state dispute mechanism had been applied four times unsuccessfully to the United States, three times successfully and once unsuccessfully to Canada, and twice successfully and five times unsuccessfully to Mexico.[52] The record illustrates how NAFTA has created a hegemony in North America, with the dominant power's norms having been accepted and applied by its weaker neighbours.

NAFTA has transformed investor-state commercial arbitration into an institution controlling the exercise of the three states' regulatory authority over foreign investors.[53] This means that the North American states have had their powers reorganized and their autonomy limited in a number of dimensions. The discretion to pass legislation is more limited. The ability to issue regulations is constrained. The three governments have lost to the World Bank's arbitral tribunals the adjudicatory power to review regulatory behaviour affecting domestic operations of foreign corporations, although they took on the obligation to enforce these tribunals' rulings. The effect of the Metalclad award and similar cases in Mexico has been to shift public policy towards privatization and contracting out public services so that federal, state, or municipal governments can avoid the risk of foreign investor claims.[54]

While North American states have lost autonomy because of Chapter 11, their transnational corporations have gained capacity. Bypassing the need for their home government's diplomatic protection and eliminating the uncertainties of government-to-government dispute settlement, they can engage in aggressive and direct legal action against host governments – even the mighty United States – in an international forum where legal norms and arbitrators' professional norms favour investment freedoms over such other public-policy values as environmental sustainability or social justice.[55] This increased capacity is not restricted to NAFTA-based corporations, since any global company with a branch in a North American country can have its property rights enhanced by Chapter 11's protections. Nevertheless, the time and costs associated with these claims act as a constraint on TNCs' abuse of this weapon.

This capacity-building effect makes NAFTA Chapter 11's judicial government part of three global trends. First, domestic law is becoming de-territorialized as functions are devolved from national courts to international bodies. The judicial sphere of international commercial law is also becoming privatized, as corporate arbitration increasingly prevails over state-to-state dispute settlement.[56] Furthermore, Chapter 11 tribunals help marginalize public interests by increasing corporations' judicial ascendancy and decreasing civil society's access to – and even information about – the secretive processes typical of commercial arbitration. As a result, Chapter 11 remains a wildcard in the future of North America's transborder government – as binding in application as it is unpredictable in direction.

The Global Trade-Law Context

The coexistence of a continental with a global judicial regime raises the problem common to all situations of legal pluralism: the overlap and tension between competing and potentially conflicting norms and institutions. For instance, NAFTA's Chapter 19 appeals displaced the Federal Court of Canada as the route for appealing the anti-dumping or countervailing-duties determinations made by the Canadian International Trade Tribunal. Since corporations from non-NAFTA countries can appeal this tribunal's determinations only before the Federal Court of Canada, the potential for confusion and conflict is introduced should NAFTA panels and Federal Court rulings differ when judging the same anti-dumping or countervailing duty.

The legal profession in North America was just contemplating such implications of NAFTA's mechanisms for settling trade and investment disputes when the World Trade Organization's system for resolving economic conflicts was set up in Geneva. The juridical relationship between NAFTA and the WTO remains particularly unclear. Whether NAFTA or WTO rules will prevail in the event of a discrepancy could have serious implications for the development of regional legal norms. For example, if arbitral panels were to accord legal priority to NAFTA over WTO rules, this would give the regional system superior standing compared to the multilateral system. Uncertainty regarding the boundaries between the two levels continues to prevail, because no such hierarchy has been established.[57]

NAFTA's Article 2005 requires that the complaining party choose between NAFTA and the WTO to resolve a dispute.[58] Now that Chapter 20 is seen to be little more than an avenue for discussion,[59] many continental conflicts are in fact pursued through the WTO's dispute-settlement process because it obviates many problems that exist in NAFTA's system.[60] First, it has greater institutional clout and offers binding arbitration. Whereas NAFTA panel members are selected from a roster of nationals chosen by the disputing governments, WTO panellists cannot be citizens of a party involved in a dispute, thus ensuring a greater degree of perceived fairness in the arbitration. Furthermore, the WTO Agreements on Subsidies and Dumping define the meanings of 'subsidies' and 'dumping' more specifically, thus making cases less vulnerable to the capricious interpretation of key terms – a characteristic for which Chapter 19 cases have been criticized. In addition, WTO dispute panels use international norms and not domestic laws when arbitrating disputes. As a result, the US Congress cannot arbitrarily change a law to reverse a WTO panel decision, as it famously did to overturn the effect of Chapter 19 rulings in the softwood-lumber saga.[61] Furthermore, WTO dispute settlement is more disciplined than NAFTA panels have proven to be and has a more extensive roster of panelists, rendering it less vulnerable to US business-lobby politics.[62] The penalties for non-compliance with the decisions of an international panel are much greater than those for ignoring the decisions of a NAFTA panel. More important still, the WTO process has greater automaticity: a WTO case can proceed without requiring the defendant government's consent. By contrast, if the defendant NAFTA party does not agree to convening a panel, there is nothing the plaintiff can do to get judicial satisfaction.[63]

Problems arise when NAFTA's rules conflict with the WTO's. In 1995 the United States launched a NAFTA Chapter 20 challenge against Canada for astronomically increasing its agricultural tariffs, arguing that Ottawa had violated NAFTA's injunction against raising tariffs. Canada countered that it was simply complying with its obligation under the WTO's Agreement on Agriculture to replace all quantitative barriers to imports of such supply-managed produce as milk and poultry by 'tariffying' them. This conflict between the global and the continental legal regimes was stark but confusing. While NAFTA required that all tariffs be eliminated by January 1, 2008,[64] Article 710 of the Canada-US Free Trade Agreement, which was incorporated into NAFTA by Annex 702.1, stipulated that Canada retained its rights and obligations with respect to agricultural goods under GATT. The panel found that the Agreement on Agriculture was a GATT agreement and, on this basis, ruled – unanimously – that the WTO's norms prevailed over NAFTA's.[65]

Whether NAFTA's – and indeed the WTO's – dispute-settlement processes reduced the power asymmetries in North America or enhanced them can be debated both in theory and in practice. Conceptually speaking, placing the weaker peripheral countries on a level, judicial playing field with the central power has de-asymmetric implications. Indeed, Mexico and Canada have used Chapter 19 with some success, although this effect has been offset by the Washington's non-compliance with adverse judgments on major issues.

Although Mexico quickly learned how to play the new game, the United States has had a massive advantage applying its huge legal power – with but 5 per cent of the world's population, it harbours 50 per cent of its lawyers – in a system that it has designed for itself. For instance, in 2004 the United States requested that the WTO establish a panel to examine Mexico's special tax on soft drinks and fructose sugar.[66] Mexico protested that the dispute should be heard by a NAFTA panel rather than the WTO, because the tax was imposed in retaliation against what it considered was Washington's non-compliance with a side deal made during the NAFTA negotiations which granted increased access for Mexican sugar to the US market.[67] Nevertheless, when the United States took the dispute to Geneva, the panel found that it could not decline its jurisdiction over the case[68] and, disregarding the NAFTA context, ruled in favour of the United States on the grounds that the tax discriminated against US sugar products.

Canada does not suffer the disadvantage of being a latecomer to trade-law adjudication, but the socio-psychology of the trade-law community favours the United States' mercantile values over the periphery's concerns for social solidarity or cultural diversity. The global trade regime's profound bias against non-economic values was dramatically illustrated in the *Sports Illustrated* case, in which Canada's effort to defend its magazine industry fell victim to the WTO's goddess of culturally blind justice. When Time Warner evaded Canadian tariff barriers that had excluded 'split-run' magazines (which reproduce American editorial content but splice in Canadian ads) and Canada responded by imposing a drastic excise tax on split-run magazines' advertising, the United States launched a case at Geneva. Canada thought it would win because advertising was a service and its obligations under the General Agreement on Trade in Services did not extend to advertising. However, Washington successfully argued not only that magazines were a 'good' (so deserving no special treatment as vehicles for cultural expression) but that the American *Time Magazine* and the Canadian *Maclean's* were 'like products' – which meant that the norm of national treatment forbade discriminating against foreign magazines. The WTO judgment struck down the excise tax along with other Canadian policies that had been in place for decades and had successfully fostered a burgeoning domestic magazine industry.[69]

When, in response, Canada proposed to criminalize Canadian advertising in split-run editions, the United States then invoked CUFTA's Article 2005(2)[70] in order to threaten the retaliatory imposition of duties on some $1 billion of Canadian exports. With this flexing of its commercial muscle, the Americans brought Ottawa to its knees, having masterfully played both the WTO and CUFTA/NAFTA to their advantage. The United States had long protested against Canadian cultural policies which tried to create space for Canadian cultural expression in the mass-entertainment industries. The *Sports Illustrated* case showed that, however impartially and with whatever integrity the WTO's panellists may have exercised their best professional judgment, their own biases favouring economic liberalization and the system of values embedded in the rules they were applying successfully helped the United States extend its power over its periphery.

Conclusion

A North American Court on Trade and Investment[71] along with a permanent legal secretariat has been proposed to help rectify the many deficiencies inherent in NAFTA's ad hoc panel system. If it served as a permanent appellate body to hear appeals to Chapter 11 rulings, it could ensure some uniformity and predictability in investor-state cases.[72] Such a body could confer a more equal status on Mexico if a wider array of judges were employed and the discrimination against the use of Spanish were eliminated. This proposal to build transborder legal governance implicitly confirms my argument that the continental arbitral regime established by NAFTA amounts to only weak governance, characterized by both tenuous legitimacy and limited effectiveness.

Dispute settlement also lies at the heart of the labour-market regime established by one of NAFTA's two side agreements, but – unlike Chapter 11 – the Byzantine processes for resolving NAFTA labour cases are notable for their ineffectiveness, as we will see in chapter IV.

IV Transborder Labour Governance

Just because the transborder 'governance from above' created by NAFTA turned out to be toothless – with the important exception of Chapter 11 endowing transnational corporations with a hard-law capacity to discipline governments in the three countries – it does not follow that NAFTA failed to generate any 'governance from below.' Indeed, its two landmark side agreements, which created formal trinational commissions in response to pressure from the labour and environmental movements, appeared to give the lie to those critics who alleged that neoconservative globalism was liberating transnational corporations from constraints on their ability to exploit workers and despoil the environment. After all, did not these NAFTA commissions for labour and environmental cooperation give civil society a role, inviting labour unions and environmentalists to participate in governance on a more level public-policy playing field at the continental level?

In the case of organized labour, governance 'from below' had originally involved attempts by workers trying to ameliorate their grim living conditions in politically parlous circumstances. Defying the anti-labour laws of their Dickensian times, they organized illegally in order to defend themselves against exploitation by owners, who were openly supported by complicit governments. As they battled against their repressive work conditions in the late-nineteenth-century industrializing economies, defiant trade unions were actively involved in workplace struggles regardless of where they were located. Their mission was to reduce the dog-eat-dog competition for jobs of isolated individuals by generating solidarities that could mobilize the large numbers of their politically weak comrades – wherever they might be employed – against the small number of politically powerful industrialists who employed them.

By this logic, the craft unions within the American Federation of Labor (AFL) organized Canadian workers within their respective jurisdictions and intervened regularly in the Canadian and Mexican labour movements. The anarcho-syndicalist Industrial Workers of the World gloried in the fact that it organized mineworkers in Colorado along with lumberjacks in British Columbia and oil workers in Mexico. In the same spirit, the first Mexican labour union saw itself as continental in scope, taking the name Confederación Regional Obrera Mexicana (Regional Confederation of Mexican Workers). So a hundred years ago, when national borders mattered little in North America, transborder labour governance from below 'existed' more than it does today, when labour markets are highly regulated by federal and state governments and continent-wide labour solidarity is far easier to preach than to practise.

This chapter examines the complex issues of industrial relations – which is primarily an enterprise- or industry-based phenomenon mainly regulated by federal or subfederal jurisdictions – from a continental perspective, asking whether the North American entity created by NAFTA includes any significant component of labour-market governance. After an outline of the three countries' labour movements' origins, a second section reviews how neoconservative free trade and its associated policies affected labour in the three states so that, in the third section, NAFTA's labour commission can be assessed. Finally, the chapter examines what potential there may be for continental labour solidarity at a time and in a context when most unions' energies are focused on challenging domestic labour legislation and protecting their own interests – which often conflict with those of their continental neighbours.

National Roots: North American Labour Movements before Free Trade

With revolutionary nationalism's emergence in Mexico in the 1910s and Keynesian social democracy's much later ascendance in the United States and Canada in the 1940s, the federal governments and their provincial/state components became the somewhat irresolute guarantors of trade unions' powers and workers' rights. The industrial-relations compromises struck between labour leaders, corporate interests, and the state varied in the three countries, but in each country relatively stable collective-bargaining regimes emerged.[1] By the end of the first decade after the Second World War, labour governance 'from above' came to predominate as the three federal states enforced laws that brought labour policy more effectively under government control. As a result, the labour movements in each country concentrated on their domestic political battles for most of the twentieth century.

Mexico

After the First World War, North America's labour-union visage changed dramatically. Ties between Hispanic and anglophone labour disintegrated, as Mexican industrialization proceeded along an autonomous path behind tariff and regulatory walls designed to discourage US investment and promote Mexican capitalism. The product of extensive workers' struggles, the continent's most powerful labour-rights code was legislated in Mexico, whose 1917 constitution was among the most progressive in the world. Five fundamental labour laws[2] guaranteed the right to association, strike, and bargain collectively; required that wages meet the material, social, and cultural needs of the workers' families; regulated safety and hygiene; and provided for federal inspection of working conditions. It also established tripartite boards of business, labour, and state representatives to oversee the justice and functioning of industrial relations.[3]

In practice, labour organizations became more restricted than these provisions suggested. For example, in order to be recognized by the state, a union was required to register with the local labour tribunal, which took almost full control of union activities. Under the corporatist direction of the authoritarian Partido Revolucionario Institucional, the Mexican labour movement was co-opted through the Confederación de Trabajadores de México (CTM, Confederation of Mexican Workers), which exerted almost complete, but soon corrupt, control over the country's industrial labour force. State dominance over the labour movement led to the emergence of unofficial unions,[4] which the government has alternatively repressed or declared non-existent.

Canada and the United States

Mexican unions' withdrawal from a continental operational sphere left labour in the old North America as an almost completely integrated 'international' movement in which Canadian unions operated as dependent branches of their American parents. The virtual monopoly that Samuel Gompers's business-friendly AFL had already achieved over Canadian trade unions in 1902[5] was divided in the late 1930s by Canada's industrial unions' integration in the far more radical US Congress of Industrial Organizations (CIO).[6]

In this period, American workers won protection under the 1935 Wagner Act, which forced employers to negotiate with unions and promoted the view that 'informed consent' at work would promote productivity by dampening rebellion and reducing alienation.[7] By the mid-1940s, the AFL and CIO had merged, causing their Canadian affiliates also to come together under one umbrella organization, the Canadian Labour Congress (CLC). The support provided US labour by the Wagner Act, which had fostered a spectacular growth in American union organization and activities, was undermined in 1947 with the Taft-Hartley Law – a measure that, by permitting employer intervention in the strike-voting process and by banning boycotts and the unionization of supervisory workers, set the tone for tumultuously contentious labour politics in the post-war United States.[8]

In Canada, the Mackenzie King government of the 1940s adopted an ambivalent position. On the one hand, it belatedly gave workers the right to form unions, required employers to negotiate with them, and established a tribunal to rule on 'unfair' labour practices.[9] On the other, the legislation outlawed some of labour's most effective bargaining tactics, such as boycotts and solidarity strikes. Nevertheless, the organized labour movement in Canada enjoyed enough influence in policy making to win important social and labour-market reforms.[10] Through the 1960s and into the early 1970s, labour reached the peak of its powers in the two countries, having made a tacit compromise with management, which agreed to give workers a share (in the form of higher wages) of the greater profits that resulted from the increased productivity generated by mass-production technologies.

Although the old North America was becoming an increasingly integrated space for capital accumulation, the labour movement paradoxically became more nationally fragmented. Within Canada, unions in Quebec grew autonomous from their anglophone comrades. Across the country, the labour movement received thousands of new members and an enormous boost of political energy when public-service employees won the right to unionize. Many Canadian industrial unions pushed for more autonomy from their US parents. In 1984 the Canadian Auto Workers (CAW) declared themselves independent of their erstwhile Detroit parent, the United Auto Workers (UAW). Even within the United Steelworkers of America (USWA), the Canadian section became functionally autonomous. Transborder governance from below was decreasing at the very moment that Canada was becoming more economically integrated with the United States.

Trade Liberalization and the Restructuring of the Labour Market

Beginning in the 1970s, domestic production processes became increasingly disaggregated and restructured along continental and even global lines. Growing penetration of domestic markets by imports and increased mobility of capital seeking cheap production sites in low-wage jurisdictions pushed governments to be more aggressive towards their own labour movements. As neoconservatism became the new orthodoxy with the election of Margaret Thatcher in 1979 and Ronald Reagan in 1980, trade unions found their demands greeted with wage controls and restrictive monetary policies that raised unemployment rates. The rights of workers to associate and organize were curtailed or revoked through legislation.[11] By the time that the turn to neoconservative globalism had culminated in the Canada–United States Free Trade Agreement, the North American Free Trade Agreement, and the World Trade Organization, government priorities had shifted from protecting workers' rights and raising labour standards to promoting foreign investment and cutting social programs. Organized labour was now forced to fight a rearguard action of resistance against the erosion of its hard-won labour-law protections.[12]

More continental integration in the form of CUFTA did not bring greater transborder solidarity: the American labour movement remained cool to its Canadian comrades' desperate fight against the agreement. In its turn, when the AFL-CIO mobilized protests against the economic-integration negotiations leading up to NAFTA, its Mexican counterpart, the CTM, showed scant sympathy for its 'gringo' comrades because it believed that the agreement would boost both job numbers and wages by attracting foreign investment to Mexico.

Because of the political pressure brought to bear by the AFL-CIO's mobilization within the United States, the North American Agreement on Labour Cooperation (NAALC) explicitly addressed the US movement's fear that free trade would provoke a 'race to the bottom' with

Mexico in wages and working conditions.[13] This section examines how free trade helped undermine labour standards in all three countries, while the next explores how the NAFTA labour commission failed to offset the degradation of working conditions that trade liberalization and the technological displacement of labour had exacerbated in all three countries.

CUFTA and NAFTA constituted only one of the thrusts in the three federal governments' efforts to promote their corporations' competitiveness by diminishing labour's political influence. To be sure, the *lowering of tariff barriers* weakened organized labour by displacing jobs to other countries, but so did *wage stagnation* under conditions of growing productivity, as did *punitive labour laws* which gave expression to governments' volte-face from their former defence of workers' rights.

Tariff Reduction and Job Destruction

In all three countries, tariff liberalization exacerbated other trends that were eroding jobs and causing sharp sectoral changes in the balance of trade.[14] Although Canada was running a trade surplus, more jobs were displaced than export growth added.[15] Between 1989 and 1997, 870,000 jobs were created because of an increase in exports, but 1,150,000 jobs were destroyed, resulting in a net loss of about 280,000.[16] Typically, the jobs lost tended to be secure and unionized, while the work created was precarious and non-unionized. Free trade was responsible for a 4 per cent reduction in total manufacturing employment in the period between 1988 and 1996, with an 18 per cent reduction in those industries particularly exposed to tariff reduction.[17]

Labour market trends in the United States followed a similar pattern. The trade deficit aggravated by NAFTA displaced millions of jobs in manufacturing and trade-related sectors of the American economy. A net loss of one million manufacturing jobs could be attributed to the United States' trade deficit with its NAFTA partners over a ten-year period following the agreement's passage. While this number may be small in comparison with the total number of jobs created and eliminated in the US economy every year, the new jobs tended to be less well paid and less secure than those that had been displaced.[18] Workers fired because of free trade lost pensions, health coverage, and seniority and were typically re-employed at lower wages in more insecure jobs or, if they could not find work, dropped out of the labour market altogether.

A much stronger link can be made between tariff reduction and deteriorating working conditions in Mexico, where NAFTA-induced labour-market transformations led to a marked deterioration in the quality of employment starting with the abandonment of the *ejido* communal landholding system. By the 1980s, ejidos covered two-fifths of Mexico's territory and provided work for three million families. With an eye to a future trade deal with the United States, President Carlos Salinas's neoconservative administration passed an amendment to Article 27 of the constitution which removed the communal-property protection that ejidos enjoyed under the law. With their capacity to scratch out a livelihood shattered by massive NAFTA-sanctioned imports of subsidized US corn and with the amendment facilitating the privatization and consolidation of ejido plots, hundreds of thousands of ejidatarios were pushed into an already flooded labour market.[19]

Tariff elimination also caused the bankruptcy of many small-and medium-sized businesses that tended to be in the more highly unionized sectors of the economy. The informal economy absorbed much of the resulting surplus labour both domestically and in the United States. By 2006, some 26 million people – a quarter of the population – worked in Mexico's unregulated economy, causing the quality of employment in the formal sector to decline in turn.[20] Of new formal-sector jobs, 62 per cent no longer pay any social benefits.[21] In manufacturing, almost all post-NAFTA job creation occurred in the non-unionized maquiladora assembly plants located along the US border. Any downturn in US manufacturing is experienced as a full recession in Mexico's northern industrial centres, where precarious workforces expand and contract in response to the fluctuations of the US economy. The auto-parts manufacturers, which account for the most employment, are particularly vulnerable owing to their reliance on Americans' demand for vehicles. At the same time, the rise of China as an industrial power has undercut one of the advantages – low wages – upon which the maquiladora model is premised. A sharp decline in employment in the 2001–2 recession was later reversed, but the subsequent rate of job growth did not return to the 1990 level.[22]

Productivity Increases and Wage Stagnation

The closure of less productive plants coupled with wage stagnation creates labour crises. In Canada, free trade brought an increase in productivity in the manufacturing sector, but average wages in 1999 still remained at 1983 levels.[23] As economic modelling predicted, free trade promoted a polarization of incomes. While average earnings remained constant in real terms since the mid-1980s, the top 1 per cent share of the nation's income doubled, from 5.3 per cent to 10.5 per cent.[24] After the United States, Canada had the lowest wages in the advanced industrialized world.[25] Since NAFTA was implemented, the wage gap in the United States has grown even wider. In 2004 alone, the shift of 1 million jobs from traded- into non-traded-goods industries reduced wage payments to US workers by $7.6 billion.[26]

Mexico experienced the widest increase in the gap between productivity increases and remuneration. While productivity increased by 138 per cent, wages fell 62 per cent between 1993 and 1999. The state-decreed minimum salary earned by many workers in the border zone declined from 16 to 11 pesos per day in the period between 1994 and 2000. Manufacturing wages declined from 22 per cent of the US level in 1980 to 8 per cent in 1996, rebounding to only 10 per cent in 2000, where they have remained.[27] Despite a small increase under NAFTA, wages in the maquiladoras still remained 40 per cent below manufacturing wages as a whole.[28] By 2004, average family labour income in Mexico was still 15 per cent below 1994 levels.[29]

Far from lifting millions out of poverty, as the Mexican government and its allies in the labour movement had predicted, NAFTA did nothing to mitigate the growing income gap and failed to strengthen the middle class. While the top 10 per cent of Mexicans have seen their part of the nation's wealth increase since 1994, the other 90 per cent lost income share or have seen no change.[30] These downward pressures kept Mexico attractive for US and Canadian manufacturers wanting to locate their labour-intensive activities in a low-wage environment situated close to their principal markets. In the automotive sector, for example, American and Canadian workers compete with Mexicans who are equally skilled and disciplined, who work in plants under similar conditions with the equivalent technology, and who make identical products to be sold in the same market but for one-fourteenth of the pay and – depending on the number of years worked in the same enterprise – with only six to twelve days of annual vacation.[31]

Toughened Labour Laws

The pattern of change in labour law and regulatory standards is one of continual pressure towards deterioration, not convergence towards higher norms. Laws ensuring workers' rights to associate, to bargain collectively, and to strike have been labelled unfriendly to business and retrenched across the continent.

Canada came under pressure to harmonize labour legislation down to the lower US common denominator in order to stay attractive to investors.[32] Workplace laws were under-enforced as new, more precarious, and unregulated forms of employment become prevalent. Throughout the 1980s and 1990s, the imperative of competitiveness inspired provincial legislatures, which had jurisdiction over 90 per cent of the country's employment relations, to pass amendments to their industrial-relations statutes in order to make it harder to establish unions. Rates of success in unionization drives under the new rules declined significantly owing to employers' new opportunities to intervene in certification elections.[33] Reducing the organizing rate in newer sectors and industries slowly lowered the overall union density rate.

American labour laws are the most hostile to unions in the industrialized world. Many categories of workers are denied coverage of protective laws, employers are granted rights of interference commonly prohibited elsewhere, and standard forms of labour solidarity, such as secondary pickets, are prohibited. Although US labour-law statutes have not been substantively revised in the free-trade period, the legal environment nevertheless worsened appreciably. A 2001 report commissioned by Human Rights Watch documented a 'culture of near impunity' which 'has taken hold in much US labour law and practice.'[34] Employers commonly fire union supporters during organizing drives, preferring to pay fines when these are awarded by the National Labor Relations Board (NLRB), whose cutbacks have caused increased delays in hearings and thereby further undermined the unions' organizing efforts. As in the rest of North America, US labour law has not evolved to cover the variety of casual, part-time, and subcontracted forms of precarious employment characteristic of the post-industrial economy.[35]

Research on union-certification elections suggests a direct link between NAFTA and the deterioration of legal protections afforded American workers who try to unionize. In securing protections for foreign investment in Mexico, NAFTA increased the credibility of (illegal) US employer threats to relocate their plant when they face a union-organizing campaign. Data compiled from union-certification elections between 1993 and 1995 revealed that employers threatened to close their factory in 50 per cent of all cases. Of a sample of 400 NLRB filings between 1998 and 1999, employers in the especially mobile industries of manufacturing, communications, and wholesale distribution threatened to move their plants in 68 per cent of cases. The next year, a full 70 per cent of corporations used the threat of relocation to frustrate union drives. [36] By 2005, relocation rates from both the United States and Canada, which had tripled since NAFTA, were reflected in the 450 per cent increase in US foreign direct investment in Mexico.

Despite claiming that it wanted to raise labour standards in Mexico, the PRI restricted core labour rights in the hope of maintaining Mexico's advantage as North America's provider of a cheap, highly flexible workforce. Less anticipated was the Fox government's determination to bolster the official, still corrupt labour movement in order to suppress the activities of the independent unions. A draft labour-law reform negotiated under the Fox administration proposed to loosen the protective aspects of Mexican labour law while reinforcing the power of the official labour movement and creating new hurdles for independent organizing.[37] As currently constituted, the machinery of Mexican labour law effectively prevents the establishment of independent unions in the maquiladora industry.

Caught between the disaggregation of its industrial strongholds and a hostile legal environmental which has stymied new organizing, union representation across North America has continued to decline. In Canada, it peaked in 1984 at 42 per cent of the workforce and has fallen slowly since then.[38] The current union density rate of 32 per cent in both the public and private sectors compares favourably with other industrialized countries; however, density in the private sector alone is considerably lower, at 18 per cent.[39] Notwithstanding the AFL-CIO's decade of efforts to reverse a long decline by pouring extra resources into organizing, the rate of union density in the United States has fallen to 12.5 per cent overall and just 7.4 per cent in the private sector, the lowest figure in over a century.[40] In Mexico, levels of union representation are likewise at historical lows. Although union-density rates, which are not recorded by any government agency, are difficult to calculate, it is estimated to be approximately 11 per cent of the economically active population.[41] This figure would of course include a large number of workers covered by the official labour movement and fake contracts.

Given neoconservatism's triple union-reducing pressures of tariff reductions, wage stagnation, and toughened labour laws, it must have given some cause for hope to labour activists to hear that NAFTA had created a new institution dedicated to improving the worker's lot throughout North America. They were to be disappointed.

NAALC's Ineffectiveness as Continental Governance

Negotiated following President Clinton's election in the first months of 1993 with a highly reluctant Mexico and a dubious Canada, the North American Agreement on Labour Cooperation was born in hypocrisy. Trumpeting it as the only institutional means of regulating industrial relations across North America, Human Rights Watch enthusiastically called it 'the most ambitious link between labor rights and trade ever implemented.'[42] More sceptical critics asserted that the NAALC was a necessary payoff through which Clinton could mollify his supporters in the AFL-CIO and gain Congress' support for NAFTA without ever being intended to work.[43]

The agreement was both deliberately deceptive in its rhetoric and weak in its institutionalization. Its explicit aim was to 'improve working conditions and living standards in each member country'[44] according to eleven core principles which included the freedom of association and the rights to strike, to organize, and to bargain collectively. To put these principles into practice, the agreement established an autonomous and trilateral North American Commission for Labour Cooperation (NACLC). Financed by a small budget allocated by each federal government and first located in Dallas before moving to Washington, the NACLC quickly found itself hamstrung in its two principal functions, monitoring labour policy in the three countries and administering disputes about their labour practices.

Since none of the three federal states was inclined to have a supranational entity sit in judgment over its statutory or regulatory performance regarding workers' rights, NACLC's monitoring of labour policy in the three jurisdictions was quickly reduced to small research projects of a quasi-academic nature on related issues. Managing the more tortuous but equally innocuous dispute-settlement process set up by the agreement was a more complicated responsibility but no less ineffectual in its implementation.

The NACLC is supported by a National Administrative Office (NAO) established by each of the three countries in their labour departments to manage dispute-settlement procedures. These NAOs receive complaints from individuals, union leaders, and human-rights defenders against violators of labour standards in one of the *other* NAFTA countries and convene working groups and relevant experts to discuss possible solutions. While this process is informational rather than adversarial, if a party shows a persistent failure to enforce its occupational, safety and health, child labour, or minimum-wage labour standards, the disputing parties may agree on a mutually satisfactory action plan. However, of the first twenty-five complaints filed with the NACLC, none reached this stage. In other words, the agreement set up a 'soft-law' approach designed to induce virtuous government behaviour through moral persuasion. And, like its far more substantial global counterpart, the International Labour Organization (ILO), whose interventions in domestic labour issues are basically hortatory, its actual impact has been negligible. While the NACLC has made many requests of Canada, the United States, and Mexico not to loosen their labour regulations in order to undercut their NAFTA competitors, words have not prevented competitive deregulation of labour standards.

From a high of ten complaints filed in 1998, NAALC's caseload has dropped off dramatically, with an average of one per year since 2000. The decline was due not to the member governments having improved their behaviour but to the inadequacies of the NAALC's dispute-settlement mechanism. The high costs involved in filing complaints as well as the dim prospects of success have made unions increasingly reluctant to bother with it. The Canadian division of the United Steelworkers, reporting on its experience with filing a complaint, noted that the process is a 'resource intensive dead end.'[45] The American United Electrical Workers (UE) and the Frente Autentico del Trabajo (FAT, Authentic Workers' Front) have used the NACLC only to publicize labour-rights issues and to expose the inadequacy of the agreement. The CAW flatly refuses to have anything to do with the institution.[46]

A case frequently cited to illustrate the agreement's failure is the 1997 incident concerning unaffiliated workers at the Hyundai Workers in Metal, Steel, Iron and Allied Industries in Tijuana, where union organizers were fired after leading a strike over health and working conditions that had been ignored by their government-controlled unions.[47] The plant manager maintained that in Mexico 'if you want to strike, you must get permission first. Their work stoppage was illegal, so we fired them.'[48] After the Mexican labour board refused to recognize the worker's union-certification vote, a cross-border alliance was set up between FAT, the San Diego Support Committee for Maquiladora Workers, and Mexico's National Association of Democratic Lawyers. Although the American NAO ruled eight months later in favour of the workers, the Mexican labour board refused to accept the results, fearing that the precedent would encourage the drive for independent unions across the sector. The NAO had no authority to enforce its decision.

Enrique Hernandez, a union representative, summed up his experience with the NAALC, saying: 'There is no question that the purpose of free trade is to create favourable conditions for foreign investment. On the border, those conditions include low wages and company unions, so it's hard to give any credibility to the labour side agreement, which was just window dressing to get us to accept NAFTA to begin with.'[49]

While the labour agreement's proponents asserted that its soft-law approach was necessary in order to respect sensitive domestic issues, critics pointed out that NAFTA Chapter 11's hard-law approach (discussed in chapter III) was deliberately designed to override such delicate domestic feelings. Because of its non-enforceability, the agreement has failed to provide the labour sector with 'governance from above,' confirming the inherent incompatibility between neoconservative free trade and such social-democratic values as labour rights. No less an authority than the *Wall Street Journal* reported that, under the NAALC, 'not a single worker was ever reinstated, not a single employer was ever sanctioned, no union was ever recognized.'[50]

Governance from Below: Evidence of Continental Labour Solidarity

Unions in Canada and the United States had argued that the absence of core labour standards in Mexico's workplace and in the 'right-to-work' American states condoned practices that constituted 'social dumping.'[51] Further erosion of workers rights under free trade did generate some attempts at transborder grassroots union activity. In February 2005 an alliance of North American unions and labour federations filed a complaint before the US National Administrative Office claiming that Mexico was violating the agreement's Article 2, which obligated each party to 'ensure that its labour laws and regulations provide for high labour standards, consistent with high quality and productivity workplaces, and [that it] shall continue to strive to improve those standards in that light.'[52] When, a year later, the American NAO determined that a review of this complaint 'would not further the objectives of the NAALC' and declined to review it further, the signal was clear: efforts to give effect to cross-border solidarity could not pass through NAFTA's institutions, which were actually operating to protect the governments against labour.

Trinational cooperation among labour unions has ranged from broad educational and mobilization coalitions to industry-based alliances that confront common employers. Typically, the broad coalitions that were formed to oppose NAFTA fostered some links between unions that later matured into formal agreements to cooperate in collective bargaining and organizing campaigns. The process is best exemplified by the activities of the Red Mexicana de Acción Frente al Libre Comercio, formed by the independent FAT along with environmentalists and other social-justice NGOs in 1991.[53] RMALC conferences established contacts between Canadian and US unions and FAT, which, prior to the threat of NAFTA, had experienced difficulty in interesting its northern counterparts in trinational cooperation. When the United Electrical Workers lost ten thousand US manufacturing jobs to Mexico during the 1980s, it decided to forge an alliance with FAT to bargain collectively with common employers, particularly in the burgeoning maquiladora industries.[54] According to an RMALC statement, 'the best way to defend jobs in the United States is to work together to elevate the level of salaries and workplace and environmental conditions in Mexico.'[55] A UE statement concurred, predicting that 'if we succeed, workers will be able to unite in their demands for decent wages and working conditions on both sides of the border.'[56] FAT organizers and projects were financed with the help of several US and Canadian national unions and locals.[57]

While the UE and FAT have always stressed internationalist perspectives and strategies, NAFTA helped increase the interest in continental solidarity among other national labour unions. In Canada, public-sector unions, including the Canadian Union of Public Employees, the Public Service Alliance of Canada, and the Canadian Union of Postal Workers, built links with their American and Mexican counterparts, sharing research about NAFTA's impact on the privatization of public services.[58] A trinational Coalition to Defend Public Education was formed in 1995 out of the fear that NAFTA would open public education to commercialization. The alliance represented half a million mostly Canadian and Mexican teachers and showed itself 'able, in moments of conflict, to pressure the governments of the three countries to avoid further impoverishment of the education sector.'[59]

One of the more productive cross-border alliances within the broader labour movement involved the Sindicato de Telefonistas de la República Mexicana (STRM, Telephone Workers' Union of the Mexican Republic) cooperating with the Communications Workers of America and the Communications, Energy, and Paperworkers of Canada in order to combat Nortel's anti-union activities. The STRM was also asked to send organizers to a Sprint call centre in San Francisco, where most of the workers were Mexican-Americans. The organizing drive was successful, but Sprint closed the plant before a contract could be signed. In 1995 the alliance filed a complaint with the NACLC, alleging a violation of the right to association. The complaint was successful: the US National Labor Relations Board found that the plant closure was indeed motivated by anti-union animus and ordered it to reopen. Sprint successfully appealed the ruling in the US Court of Appeals, and the NLRB decision was overturned. Disappointed with the outcome of the proceeding – which demonstrated the superior muscle of domestic government over continental governance – the alliance decided to focus its energy on independent strategizing.[60]

The explicit goal of the alliance is wage parity, understood as equal pay for work of equal value. Proposals for concrete cooperative tactics have included Canadian and US unions putting pressure on employers with operations in Mexico not to sign agreements with the corrupt CTM. This transborder cooperation has helped the STRM learn how to deal with the technology and productivity changes which anglophone unions had already confronted in their collective bargaining. More broadly, international labour cooperation in the telecom sector has helped to develop a common understanding of global and regional challenges and a common approach to resistance. The participation of a large delegation from the STRM in the 2001 World Social Forum in Porto Alegre, Brazil, was instrumental in formulating the union's opposition to the proposed Free Trade Area of the Americas.[61]

The changing composition of the US working class resulting from legal and illegal immigration has generated a new form of transborder labour militancy from below. In particular, the growing population of Latino and especially Mexican workers has impelled Mexican unions to offer increasing support to US labour campaigns. In addition to the Sprint plant drive, FAT organizers were sent to a plant in Milwaukee to mobilize predominantly Mexican workers. The Teamsters and the United Fruit and Commercial Workers organized apple workers in the state of Washington with the assistance of organizers from independent unions in Mexico. These cross-border alliances of Hispanic workers in Mexico and the United States boosted the prospects for binational – if not continental – labour solidarity.[62]

This experience with NAFTA's labour commission also led the AFL-CIO to reassess its relationship with the official Mexican labour movement. The CTM's support for NAFTA, its corruption, and its ineffectiveness in raising Mexican wages and improving working conditions strained its ties with the AFL-CIO. An agreement between the two federations committing the CTM to discontinue the use of 'protection contracts' had no effect. Referring to these negotiations, one of the CTM signatories stated that 'we do not make agreements with American unions.'[63] Originally, FAT was rebuffed when it sent a delegation to the AFL-CIO in 1991 to propose an anti-NAFTA coalition. However, while still working with the CTM, the AFL-CIO leadership subsequently supported the efforts of FAT and other independent organizations in Mexico, sending a delegation to the foundation of the independent Union Nacional de Trabajadores (National Workers' Union) in 1997.[64] Under the leadership of John Sweezy, the AFL-CIO's international activity shifted. Its Cold War institutes were dismantled, and the federation's members and southern allies were promised a new era of openness and solidarity in foreign relations.[65]

The Limits to Solidarity: Contradictions in the New Labour Continentalism

Despite this kind of limited transborder engagement, national, state, and provincial labour organizations remain focused on their domestic concerns.[66] Most of organized labour's political resources continue to be directed towards the federal and state/provincial governments which decide whether or not to raise interest rates, to legislate strikers back to work, to enforce existing labour standards, or to privatize public institutions. Even in the European Union, where continental integration has involved a greater degree of institutionalization in the sphere of industrial relations, the European labour movements remain largely national in scale and scope. For varying reasons, transborder organizing coalitions almost always fail. The US labour movement has not been able to organize South Carolina, let alone significantly assist workers in Chihuahua, Mexico.[67] Until 2007, the unions in the Canadian auto and manufacturing industry had consistently failed in their many efforts to organize their own auto-parts sector, which employs workers in the same jurisdictions as the car-assembly plants. The most ambitious continental labour coalition yet formed, the DANA alliance, fell apart when the United Electrical Workers lost representation at the one DANA plant that it had organized.

The closest continental labour cooperation occurred in the late 1990s when the US labour movement was gaining some momentum. But this incipient solidarity broke down following the demonstrations against the WTO in Seattle in 1999 and the subsequent protests against the World Bank and International Monetary Fund in Washington. Dissatisfaction with the movement's leadership tore the AFL-CIO apart at its July 2005 national conference, which was celebrating the 60th anniversary of the two unions' amalgamation. A series of major defeats – concessions totalling tens of billions of dollars in wages, forgone retirees' pensions in several industries, and the failure of several high-profile strikes to prevent the introduction of reduced wage and benefits structures – were body blows to the labour movement.

Many unions, including the United Steelworkers of America and the Canadian Autoworkers, supported continental forms of cooperation in the wake of NAFTA by participating in NACLC proceedings. They experimented with independent forms of cooperation and established some productive relations with their Mexican counterparts. But this solidarity was undermined by their primary set of concerns, which is to lobby against the negative impacts of free trade on the domestic labour market. These same unions that attempt to offer each other moral support and establish continental solidarity pressed their home governments for higher tariffs and domestic investment subsidies, in other words, for protection against the products made by comrades in the other NAFTA countries.

Conclusion

The pressures caused by NAFTA have contributed to the many other factors altering the way organized workers in Canada, the United States, and Mexico relate to their respective governments, their employers, and to each other. One of the weaker trends among the labour movements in North America has been confronting new globalist continentalism with a parallel continentalization of solidarity through cross-border governance and union-to-union cooperation in political campaigns, lobbying, organizing drives, and collective bargaining. At the same time, industrial unions have remained strongly committed to protecting domestic markets with traditional trade-policy protectionism. In instances where both corporate and union structures are closely integrated across the borders, as in the steel industry, lobbying for trade remedies has adopted a distinctly binational approach, but even this has not succeeded in preventing competitive pressures from undermining the unions' bargaining power.

Labour movements everywhere remain on the defensive and cautious about pursuing international strategies. Although solutions at the national level no longer provide the protections that they once did, the nature of North America's integration, which is characterized by transborder labour-market immobility (with the exception of massive legal and illegal Mexican migration to the United States), poses considerable barriers to continental labour cooperation. The stark differences in the relationship between labour regulation in the United States and Mexico mean that North America 'exists' much less – whether in the sense of substantial transborder labour solidarity or in the sense of a trinational policy harmonization to protect labour rights against trade liberalization – than the much ballyhooed North American Commission for Labour Cooperation had made it appear in 1993.

A century ago, North America's transborder labour governance from below reflected the continent's open borders and the US labour movement's participation in the expansionist momentum we now identify with Teddy Roosevelt's progressive imperialism. Domestic labour governance from above was then responding only grudgingly to workers' demands for legal protections. At the end of the twentieth century, corporate restructuring on a continental basis had not brought about a consolidation of the three states' labour movements. Mexico remained largely autarchic, with transborder cooperation developing only at the edges. The Canadian labour movement had become more autonomous by the time CUFTA was signed and remained largely self-directed.

Labour governance from above had come full circle during this period, with governments more inclined to use the law to impede workers' efforts to organize unions than support efforts to foster wage increases and employment security. NAFTA's genuflection before the altar of workers' rights proved to be what its sceptics alleged – a deceptive sop to the AFL-CIO cunningly designed to be ineffective. In this aspect of its civil-society effects, NAFTA did not replace the autonomy resulting from Canadian unions' separation from American parents with a new kind of more symmetrical working-class solidarity. Nor did it greatly diminish the skewed quality of North America's two main bilateral relationships, since the Mexican labour movement remained largely under the CTM's autarchic control. Its main – though definitely minor – consequence has been to develop a cooperative relationship between some major Canadian labour unions and some Mexican independent unions and their progressive allies in Mexico's civil society.

Even though trade unions are civil society's most strongly organized element because of their independent power base and income from members' fees, the North America created by the NAALC remains pro-foundly weak, even illusory. If observers were looking at NAFTA to find evidence that it had generated greater social-movement solidarity, they would have to shift their focus from labour to the environment, the subject of chapter V.

V Transborder Environmental Governance

As we could have assumed, a putatively pro-labour institution established by three neoconservative governments bent on liberating North American business from regulatory constraints was designed to fail. Sceptics about a parallel, environment-friendly institution had less obvious grounds for a priori despair. Whereas the corporate community and its political associates had little reason to care about the condition of the working class, they could not ignore the environment with equal impunity. Plunging wages and weakened labour rights may be positive for the bottom line, but environmental degradation can be bad for business. To the extent that green is good for the economy, there were obvious economic and political reasons for the three governments and their business allies to have NAFTA take the environment seriously.

Aware though they are of dying lakes, contaminated land, and polluted air, citizens in all countries have reacted intermittently to the implications of environmental neglect. By the 1960s, it was clear that the destructive behaviour of individuals, corporations, and governments had already affected local environments in alarming ways. By the 1970s, scientific research on the universal, toxifying impacts of atmospheric warming, ozone depletion, and resource exploitation on water, soil, and air had given ecology an increasingly global face. With the public's consciousness starting to link concerns about their own children's well-being with that of their planet, environmental NGOs (ENGOs) pressured their governments to sign many international agreements.[1] From 'Stockholm' (1972) to 'Kyoto' (1997), the arduous job of convincing governments to regulate their economies' environmental effects went from reducing the production of gases that warmed the atmosphere to producing protocols for emissions trading.

Although these environmental accords transformed the international agenda, their success in changing governments' behaviour was generally more symbolic than substantial, in large measure because they came up against a different, more powerful set of international agreements dedicated to expanding transborder trade and investment. As an epicentre of the clash between economic logic (which preaches corporate liberation) and environmental logic (which favours government regulations to deal with the 'externalities' caused by business and human misbehaviour), North America presented a contradictory eco-visage to the world. The United States was home both to the most vocal, well-funded, and dynamic environmental non-government organizations (ENGOs), which were raising eco-consciousness throughout the world, and to some of the globe's most toxic energy and chemical corporations. Like Canadians, American citizens endorsed progressive new measures to protect the environment but resisted paying for them. Meanwhile, their neighbours in Mexico appeared immune to developing a green consciousness, let alone a serious environmental regulatory regime.

Along with the ill-fated labour commission, a trinational North American Commission for Environmental Cooperation (NACEC) was appended to NAFTA in an effort to deal with US environmentalists' concerns that trade and investment would expand across North America to the detriment of the environment. The NACEC is the prime subject for this chapter's analysis, but, to assess its significance as transborder governance, I need to cast my analytical net more broadly.

I first examine the domestic context of environmental politics in the three countries and then the transborder environmental governance generated by the individual US-Canada and US-Mexico relationships before NAFTA. The third and fourth sections address NACEC and the ENGO politics it was meant to promote. After examining NAFTA's incapacity to reconcile the tension between expanding trade and protecting the environment, the chapter concludes that the failures of the loose networks of ENGOs fostered by the NACEC to develop significant transborder governance have been only partly offset by the cross-border efforts of American, Mexican, and Canadian states and provinces to deal directly with their common environmental challenges.

The Emergence of Domestic Environmentalism

While the three governments adopted similar regulatory approaches to command (setting maximum levels of permissible pollution) and control (monitoring and enforcing these standards)[2] instruments, there were significant differences in the scope and content of their legislation as well as in the three political systems' ability to implement effective regulatory measures. Responding to successive waves of public alarm throughout the twentieth century, environmental-protection legislation in the two countries of the old North America followed similar trajectories, with Mexico following behind at a considerable distance.

United States

By the 1970s, governments had started placing environmental restrictions on industrial processes. In Washington, President Richard Nixon introduced 'a period of environmental transformation,' in which he raised national air-quality standards, created strict guidelines for vehicle emissions, proposed legislative environmental-policy changes, and put a tax on gasoline additives. Congress' National Air Pollution Control Administration required every project with potential environmental consequences to submit an environmental-impact statement and instructed the president to establish a Council on Environmental Quality in his cabinet.[3] Nixon established the independent Environmental Protection Agency (EPA), which proceeded to bring together all environmental initiatives under a single set of national regulatory measures concerning air, water quality, waste, toxics, and pesticide management.[4]

Through its lobbying for the Clean Air Act of 1970 and its 1977 amendment, the US environmental movement demonstrated to US politicians that it had substantial scientific knowledge of ecological issues and the ability to mobilize successful political pressure.[5] But this environmental mobilization proved short-lived. The 1980s shift to neoconservatism reversed the trend, with the federal government devolving regulatory responsibility to states, municipalities, and the private sector, even though the EPA remained the central environmental regulator.[6] In 1990 amendments to the Clean Air Act introduced greater market-based initiatives through emission-trading measures for sulphur dioxide and low automobile-emissions standards, which reduced the pressures on industries for air-quality compliance. Enforcement was to be achieved through administrative penalties and citizen lawsuits against individuals and organizations within their state jurisdiction. Consequently, states became important players in US environmental policy because they implemented the EPA's standards and could be held accountable should these targets not be attained.

Canada

At a time when they were still inspired by a social-democratic faith in government activism, Canadian politicians proved eager to respond to green pressures. Invoking its jurisdiction over interprovincial and international trade, navigation and shipping, fisheries, criminal law, and the ownership of federal lands, Ottawa stepped in to establish a regulatory framework by creating a new ministry, Environment Canada, and legislating elaborate marine safety standards and eco-toxicity restrictions. The provinces addressed economic activities within the broad domains of their own jurisdiction – agriculture, forestry, mining, and hydro-electric generation – and signed a series of federal-provincial accords to implement their own standards and incorporate federal ones through parallel laws and institutions. The Canadian Environmental Protection Act of 1988 expanded the role of the federal government in setting environment-related regulations, and the Canadian Environmental Assessment Act of 1990 went so far as to create a quasi-judicial process that made sustainable development a basic norm.

Further legislation extended the federal government's regulatory role and declared sustainable development a fundamental objective. In 1990 came the announcement of a dramatic Green Plan that would spend $3 billion in five years on over one hundred government policy initiatives to clean up air, water, and land as far north as the Arctic Ocean and foster global environmental security, environmentally responsible decision making, ecological initiatives, and preparation for environmental emergencies.[7] A series of judicial rulings supported Ottawa's assertion of environmental leadership, with the Supreme Court of Canada giving jurisdiction to the federal government in cases where a province's inability to deal effectively with intraprovincial matters could have adverse effects beyond its borders.[8] Ironically, just as Ottawa's environmental authority was expanding, its neoconservative leaders started bailing out. They hamstrung their own environmental capacity by reducing Environment Canada's scientific, policy-making, and enforcement capacities, shifting many of its responsibilities to the provinces, deregulating its remaining powers, and negotiating international agreements such as CUFTA and the WTO that further limited its capacity to protect the public domain.

Mexico

Influenced by the need to embellish its image in the international community, the presidency of Luís Echeverría (1970–6) inserted the environment into its agenda, though it remained at the margins of policy-making priorities.[9] Rhetorically committed to addressing such issues as rapid urbanization, social neglect, weak infrastructure, and poor air quality, Mexico's first environmental legislation was more effective in impressing the international community than satisfying a nascent domestic environmental movement,[10] which had more success in preventing projected developments than it did in persuading the government to accept sustainable development as an overarching norm to guide its policy making.[11]

A growing international consciousness about the environment in the 1980s increased pressure on the de la Madrid administration to strengthen environmental policy making, implementation, and enforcement.[12] Domestically, pressure increased with public outrage over an explosion of a Pemex gas plant.[13] Reforms to the 1917 constitution and a deepening environmentalist vision led to federal environmental authorities having the strongest legal basis for taking action, as well as the political authority to do so, but their effectiveness was limited by crippling budgetary constraints.[14] Imbued with the political culture of the PRI's authoritarianism, the Under-Secretariat of Ecology, which had the power to set regulatory standards and fine environmental violators, was both unwilling to use its authority to discipline corporate misdemeanours and even more reluctant to empower non-governmental groups. Environmental violations were often dealt with weakly through temporary closures or agreements that did little to control industrial contamination.[15]

Emerging ENGOs pushed for regulations on vehicle emissions and landfills as well as other measures for pollution control. They succeeded mainly in Mexico City,[16] where in 1984 a network for eco-communication was incorporated, representing over 130 organizations. Soon after, a first national meeting of ecologists took place, generating cooperation among ENGOs under the Pacto de Grupos Ecologicos (PGE, Pact of Ecologist Groups).[17] The PGE worked primarily within RMALC, the largest network against free trade, which combined unions, social-justice collectives, human-rights organizations, and women's groups.[18] These groups cooperated with American and other international agencies, increasing the leverage of some ENGOs in their demands for environmental responsibility.[19]

North American Environmental Governance before NAFTA

When *national* borders are not *natural* borders, the political barriers to regulating environmental degradation increase significantly, since the polluting jurisdiction generally resists paying for any remediation which benefits the neighbour it is contaminating more than itself. Consequently, with the United States sharing so many watersheds and airsheds with Canada and Mexico, transborder pollution inevitably presented serious, often intractable, governance challenges.

Before NAFTA, it was only rarely that an environmental or natural-resource problem was addressed by the three countries together: the North American Forestry Commission and the Trilateral Agreement for the Protection of Migratory Birds are two examples of such continental cooperation. Because most other environmental challenges, which could not be fully addressed through domestic initiatives in one country alone, had to do with specific border regions, transborder environmental governance had been overwhelmingly bilateral, involving formal agreements or informal arrangements between the United States and one or other of its neighbours. We need first to understand the asymmetries driving or constraining the two US-Canada and US-Mexico environmental relationships and the imbalance between them if we are to grasp NAFTA's eventual impact on North American environmental governance.[20]

The United States and Canada

Once ecologists proved in the late 1970s that the prevailing winds were carrying sulphur dioxide and nitrogen oxide across the US-Canada boundary and acidifying the aquatic ecosystems in Ontario and Quebec, air pollution became a binational issue. In the ensuing negotiations, industry lobbyists representing companies in the Ohio valley, which burned coal to generate electricity, blocked progress in Congress because, although Canada was predominantly affected by acid rain, the clean-up costs would be borne within the United States.[21] With half of their province's acid deposition coming from the United States, Ontario activists decided to go transnational, creating the Canadian Coalition against Acid Rain that lobbied in the United States for Congressional action alongside the Canadian Embassy. It was only when New York residents found dying lakes in their Adirondack mountains and joined the Canadian environmentalists' cause that Congress seriously considered toughening its air-quality standards. The Canada-United States treaty of 1990 gave Canadians the impression that their personal outrage about acid rain and their government's and citizens' pressure had caused the American government to rein in the electrical industry, but the desired changes to the US Clean Air Act, which the Agreement between the Government of the United States of America and the Government of Canada on Air Quality merely formalized, had in fact resulted from the mobilization of domestic American interests.

The United States and Mexico

The Mexico-US border region includes many of the most prosperous and densely populated Mexican states and some of the poorest, most thinly populated US communities. Pollution is a by-product of industrialization on both sides of the border. With over 11.8 million people living in the border area and unplanned developments projected to continue well into the future,[22] the border has become the meeting place for many economic interests that have created nearly insuperable social and environmental challenges. In the run-up to the NAFTA negotiations, the border region's environmental crisis was worsening because of the population growth that accompanied its industrial and commercial expansion. When presidents de la Madrid and Reagan met in Washington in 1983 to discuss transboundary environmental issues, the central US concern was pollution caused by Mexican copper smelters and maquiladoras. By 1990, 12 million gallons of raw sewage were being dumped into the Tijuana River daily, and dust-churning traffic on unpaved roads added to the high levels of particulates in the air. Every day Mexico's border cities produced over 3,000 metric tonnes of solid waste, of which only 46 per cent was collected by municipal authorities.[23] For its part, the United States had major problems of its own on its side of the border owing to poor sewage systems, lack of clean water, and weak housing infrastructure.[24]

By 1992, urbanization in the border region had increased to such a degree that neither country was able to cope on its own with the new environmental pressures.[25] Mexico's scarce government funding for sewer and water-treatment infrastructure, its civil service's weak administrative muscle, and local politicians' term-limited tenures impeded the development of the facilities needed to sustain the growing urban population.[26] The PRI government moved to improve its environmental profile only when it understood this to be the price of admission if it wanted the US Congress to support an economic deal that would increase Mexico's access to the American market.

The PRI administration centralized the country's environmental policy making and research into a single agency with a cabinet-level position, creating the Secretaría de Medio Ambiente, Recursos Naturales y Pesca (Secretariat for the Environment, Natural Resources, and Fisheries)[27] along with a standard-setting agency, the Instituto Nacional de Ecología (National Institute of Ecology), and an environmental law-enforcement agency, the Procuraduría Federal de Protección al Medio Ambiente (Federal Attorney General for Environmental Protection). The environmental budget shot up from US$6.6 million in 1989 to $570 million by 1995, while the budget for environmental research rose from $4.2 million in 1992 to $7.2 million by 1994.[28] The government also enacted five environmental statutes and eighty-seven regulations specifying various environmental standards, all of which were modelled on US environmental laws.[29] While these actions demonstrated Mexico City's greater commitment to environmental protection, it also showed how Mexican environmental policy making was evolving within the bilateral power relationship.

The US and Mexican environmental authorities worked out the Integrated Environmental Plan for the Mexican-US Border Area (IBEP), which focused mainly on infrastructure improvements to sewage-treatment plants but extended to strengthening environmental law, expanding cooperative planning, and developing an electronic system to track transboundary hazardous waste.[30] Improvements to the plan in 1993 included projects that focused on environmental sustainability. By then, the Mexican government evinced a new commitment to impose controls, because the debate over NAFTA had brought with it substantial pressure to address the environmental issues raised by freer trade.

NAFTA and the Environment-Trade Nexus

During the 1980s, the publication of scientific research about climate change, stratospheric ozone depletion, desertification, and deforestation revived environmental consciousness. By the time the three governments became involved in negotiating trade and investment liberalization, environmental groups created oppositional fronts first in Canada, then in the United States,[31] and ultimately in Mexico. Their concerns included the alarming connection between increased trade on the one hand and, on the other, the role of greenhouse-gas emissions in climate change, the reduction of the protective stratospheric ozone layer, and the long-range transport of such Persistent Organic Pollut-ants as DDT. Public anxieties about the Mulroney government's trade negotiations with Washington spurred the interest of otherwise com-placent ENGOs, some of whose more moderate leaders were even appointed to the government's Sectoral Advisory Groups on Interna-tional Trade and its International Trade Advisory Committee, which I analyse in chapter VII.[32]

Although government spokesmen claimed that the Canada-US Free Trade Agreement had no ecological implications because it did not include clauses mentioning the environment, a number of ENGOs sounded the alarm during the 1987–8 debate over free trade. Their rhet-oric was intense and passionate, addressing such issues at the heart of Canadian identity as sovereignty, public health care, and control over natural resources.

Three main problems were identified. First of all, CUFTA's bias towards growth made it inherently hostile to environmental regulation. Next, it aimed to stimulate resource depletion, making *un*sustainable development CUFTA's subtext. This was clearest in the energy chapter, which entrenched the United States' desire to accelerate the delivery of Canada's non-renewable petroleum reserves at the lowest possible prices. Lastly, Canadian environmentalists claimed that CUFTA created a legal route to massive water exports. The argument was that the agreement deprived the Canadian state of its capacity to protect the country's water by not specifically exempting water from the protocols concerning national treatment and market access to goods. Once the tap was turned on, CUFTA would prevent it being turned off.[33]

During this intense debate, Canadian environmentalists had great difficulty interesting their American counterparts – even within the same transnational ENGOs – who found the connection between eco-nomic growth and environmental degradation difficult to comprehend. Once free trade with Mexico appeared on the horizon, however, the same American ENGOs finally found that this connection had become alarmingly comprehensible. In its basic text, NAFTA did indeed follow the CUFTA template. Focused on maximizing trade and investment growth, it was explicitly designed to ensure a stable supply of non-renewable resources from the periphery to the United States rather than to achieve conservation or foster new energy technologies.[34] For US environmentalists, NAFTA heralded a 'race to the bottom' in which investment would flood towards the eco-catastrophic maquiladoras just across the Texas, New Mexico, Arizona, and California borders. At the time, the American public's environmental consciousness was at a cyclical low, and promises of jobs and prosperity resulting from free trade won the day politically.

For their part, Mexican environmental NGOs were interested but passive. Weak in organization, poor in finances, small in numbers, and nervous in the face of the systematic political violence meted out to critics of the PRI regime, the Mexican environmental movement had little traction in the run-up to NAFTA. Constrained by limited information and debilitated by puny resources as well as discordant views, Mexican environmental opposition to NAFTA came mainly from ENGOs along the border with the United States, which teamed up with their US counterparts and were supported by experts in such universities as the Colegio de Sonora and the Colegio de la Frontera Norte in Tijuana. ENGOs in central Mexico had different concerns but had neither the incentives nor the resources to cooperate with border organizations, while those in such southern states as Chiapas continued to suffer from a severe deficit of political influence compared to their northern colleagues.

Trilateralism among environmentalists in the three countries revolved mostly around the politics of US ENGOs, which were split between those opposing the trade agreement entirely and those supporting it on the condition that certain environmental provisions were included. In 1992 fifty-one moderate organizations from all three countries signed a joint letter asking for 'specific language in the NAFTA to ensure increased public participation and oversight, improved enforcement of environmental laws, increased funding for environmental programs, and protection of national, state, and local standards intended to protect the environment and health.'[35] The more moderate ENGOs were won over by government assurances that these demands had indeed been met and accepted the claim that NAFTA was eco-friendly. After all, NAFTA's preamble asserted that, with sustainable development and environmental-law enforcement as two of its central goals, increased trade was to be achieved 'in a manner consistent with environmental protection and conservation.'[36] In addition, Chapter 7B on sanitary and phytosanitary measures allowed the signatories to implement more restrictive regulations than specified by other international norms, albeit Chapter 9 stated that such protective measures would be 'considered appropriate' only as long they did not discriminate or create unnecessary barriers to trade. With this language in the agreement, the anti-NAFTA movement lost its most powerful demographic, middle-class North America.[37]

As with the labour movement, one of NAFTA's side effects was to mobilize a momentary continental solidarity among more radical ENGOs. US environmentalists opposing the agreement cooperated with such Canadian and Mexican organizations as the Action Canada Network and the RMALC which linked the environment to other social-justice issues in developing a multi-level critique. They noted, for instance, that, although NAFTA gave the environment considerable soft-law precedence over trade, Chapter 11 gave transnational corporations hard-law powers to punish governments for enacting 'unfair' environmental measures. As we already saw in chapter III, legislation promoting environmental stewardship remained vulnerable to Chapter 11 legal suits being arbitrated by international commercial tribunals designed to promote and protect the interests of foreign investors.

Furthermore, national-treatment obligations prohibited NAFTA members from discriminating between 'like' products sold by domestic firms and foreign exporters in the domestic market. This meant that, if a product produced abroad in an environmentally damaging manner was sufficiently 'like' a safely produced domestic good, a trade restriction could not legitimately be imposed on the foreign item. As a result of the prohibition against states' discriminating on the basis of process and production methods, domestic industries facing foreign competitors that did not internalize their environmental costs would inevitably lobby for regulatory relief. Others pointed out that NAFTA's economic-expansion priorities paid no heed to such related questions affecting environmental sustainability as energy efficiency and greenhouse-gas emissions.

A less tangible side of the NAFTA debate focused on the regulatory climate that made environmental standards subject to the subtle pressures of regulatory chill and competitive deregulation. Competitive deregulation was evident in Canada where environment ministries at federal, provincial, and municipal levels underwent drastic financial cutbacks. In the name of competition, environmental responsibilities were offloaded onto other jurisdictions, the marketplace, or the citizen.[38] Regulatory chill occurs when regulators do not strengthen or enforce their environmental laws for fear of losing potential business investment or being litigated against under Chapter 11. When added to such other factors as the global South's lower labour costs, the threat of corporate relocation provided powerful pressure for crushing any fledgling environmental legislation in the bud.[39]

The economic-integration negotiations raised similar public concerns in Mexico, where activists pointed out the already horrific environmental crisis caused by rapid industrialization along the border.[40] Because increased trade would entail further degradation, Mexican environmentalists looked to colleagues in Canada and the United States for enlightenment about NAFTA's implications. Coincidentally, funding by international agencies, especially from the United States, increased tremendously, helping to consolidate various Mexican ENGOs which established offices in Mexico for international cooperation. Trilateral cooperation among anti-NAFTA ENGOs climaxed in the final negotiation phase with a joint proposed alternative to NAFTA.[41]

NAFTA's Environmental Commission

Finally exercised about the problems that were lurking in the negotiators' text, American ENGOs put up a spirited resistance to NAFTA on Capitol Hill. NAFTA's strongest environmental critics were US-based Friends of the Earth, Sierra Club, and Greenpeace. Together with three hundred grass-roots organizations, the Sierra Club declared its opposition to the 'NAFTA package.'[42] Some of the fiercest opposition voices came from the border region: the Arizona Toxins Information, the Border Ecology Project, the Environmental Health Coalition, and the Texas Center for Policy Studies each voiced trenchant criticisms of the agreement and proposed sustainable alternatives.[43]

Capitalizing on organized civil society's animosity to NAFTA, Governor Bill Clinton courted its support in his 1992 presidential campaign by promising to renegotiate the deal in order to prevent the dreaded environmental race to the bottom. Once elected, President Clinton delivered part of his promise.[44] Although Mexico had resisted more environmental safeguards, which it saw as another form of American trade protectionism that would prevent it from penetrating US markets,[45] it understood that the North American Agreement on Environmental Cooperation was one of President Clinton's two conditions for accepting NAFTA. Canada also had misgivings, arguing that, since much of its environmental jurisdiction was provincial, environmental violations could be disciplined internally.[46] Whether the North American Commission for Environmental Cooperation could effectively mitigate the environmental damage generated by economic expansion was the question.

The NACEC was a trilateral environmental body characterized by a strong mandate but weak mechanisms. The Canadian Environmental Law Association immediately reported that nothing in the 'proposed

North American environmental commission can fix the environmental problems that will flow from NAFTA.'[47] As it turned out, public authorities were reluctant to push industry by launching public lawsuits under the NACEC, and no government has invoked its dispute-resolution process.[48]

Each party contributed equally to the NACEC's US$9 million total budget, a rare instance of continental symmetry resented in Mexico since its $3 million represented 0.34 per cent of its environmental budget, a levy that was, relatively speaking, eight times more than the 0.04 per cent that $3 million took out of the US EPA's annual allocation.[49] Although better financed than the parallel NAFTA labour commission, the NACEC has experienced worsening budgetary constraints. The North American Fund for Environmental Cooperation, a NACEC granting program for local communities, saw its budget cut from $1 million to $755,000 in 2003[50] and then completely closed down, disrupting local community environmental projects.[51] Such niggardly financial support silently signalled the three governments' ambivalence about sponsoring this continental institution.

Composed of a Council, a Secretariat, and an innovative Joint Public Advisory Committee (JPAC), the NACEC depended not just on its three member governments' financial contributions but on their political support. While the Secretariat's functions were autonomous in principle, its activities had little independence from the Council, which was controlled by the three countries' environmental ministers. It could bring environmental issues into the trade debate,[52] but its recommendations would be non-binding and therefore ineffective. While a proficient producer of reports, the NACEC has been shown not to have the legal or political power to deal with the core issues of the trade-environment nexus. In short, its ability to deliver the wide range of functions promised in its charter was limited.[53]

The most promising aspect of the NACEC process was its potential through the JPAC to create public pressure on the three governments concerning environmental matters.[54] But, under the agreement, the public and ENGOs can only complain. Far from issuing powerful sanctions that would remediate the environmental damage resulting from increased trade, the Secretariat, which must rely on the voluntary disclosure of information by industry, merely prepares 'factual records' of alleged environmental misdemeanours. It can call in experts, make recommendations, and communicate with the disputing parties. In turn, industries can lodge a complaint with the Council if they feel that the Secretariat's request for information is unwarranted or difficult to comply with. By a two-thirds vote, the Council – which has the right to intervene in the formal dispute process and impose a solution before the issue moves to a tribunal – can apply restrictions to the Secretariat's investigation.[55]

Articles 14 and 15 of the side agreement established the Joint Public Advisory Committee as a unique citizen-dispute process within the NACEC to enable civil society's participation in North American environmental governance by providing information to the Council on various issues related to the agreement. While the JPAC chooses its own chair, its rules and procedures are set by the Council. Because its members are themselves appointed by the three governments, the range of its opinions on environmental issues is limited to mainstream thinking. In practice, its panels turned out to suffer from problems that paralleled those of disputes launched under the NAFTA labour commission – an inability to render judgments in a timely manner and the absence of enforcement mechanisms. Besides, once a complaint has been launched, citizens groups can no longer engage in the review process, which increasingly – but ineffectually – has targeted provinces, including those that refused to commit to the environmental side deal.

As a result of these weaknesses, the NACEC has become less a regulatory body than a research institute which gathers knowledge, coordinates projects, and works as a continental agency for sharing information among governments on North American environmental issues.[56] As part of its monitoring efforts, NACEC's yearly 'Taking Stock' reports name the worst industrial offenders in North America, but it cannot assess total pollution, especially from non-point sources like cars. Further, depending as the organization does on data supplied by the individual countries' statistical monitoring programs, its documents may be misleading, since reporting pollutant emissions in Canada and the United States is mandatory only if facilities produce toxic substances above a certain threshold. That said, though the data exclude Mexico, they have given some sense of emissions in the old North America and have been used to shame industry and governments into taking some action to reduce pollution levels there.

The NACEC also acts as a regional node for the Persistent Organic Pollutants convention and works with the International Joint Commission and other transborder programs in devising research and implementation plans for reducing toxin levels. However, its insufficient funding combined with the member governments' own antipathy to it inhibits it from exercising its mandate.[57] Nor can it address standards or enforcement explicitly, since these are the responsibility of the national governments.

The NACEC's data have served to facilitate public challenges to some government policies and so have had a mildly positive effect on the development of trinational civil-society networks,[58] but the NACEC does not generate enough pressure to justify the investment of time and energy required for most ENGOs to raise an issue with JPAC or initiate a dispute process. It remains little more than a forum for discussing, researching, and advising agencies, industries, and governments.[59] Lacking teeth to standardize and enforce environmental norms and policy continentally, it ends up 'greenwashing' the environmental effects of trade liberalization.

As a continental institution, the NACEC has had some limited influence on Mexican policy capacity. According to Mexico's environmental ministry, it affected five separate trends: 'identifying consumer demand and markets for "green" products that can be produced in Mexico for export with minimal environmental costs; enhancing Mexico's ability to conserve threatened or endangered species; strengthening public participation in environmental decision-making; strengthening Mexico's institutional capacity to manage toxic chemicals; and establishing an environmental technology fund for small- and medium-sized industries in Mexico.'[60] By supporting a program to strengthen domestic laws and environmental management, the NACEC has also helped increase transparency in government operations and citizen participation in environmental decision making, even though this is mostly limited to a few elite ENGOs. As well, by facilitating the downward flow of environmental information and technical expertise and by supplementing the funding for NGOs, the NACEC has contributed to the promotion of various facets of Mexico's environmental movement.

At the ministerial level, the NACEC has functioned in complete isolation from NAFTA's Free Trade Commission. Despite language in the agreement requiring the two bodies to interact, they have never met. After over a decade, it is clear that the continental environmental effects of trade liberalization are not taken seriously by any of the three governments.[61] Nevertheless, although the NACEC confirms that – institutionally speaking – North America is considerably less than meets the eye, its marginal role does not prevent other forms of civil-society governance from attempting to address critical ecological questions.

ENGO Responses to NAFTA

The trilateralism-from-below that had arisen in opposition to NAFTA lost its strength over the years, as ENGOs preferred to work bilaterally or globally. For example, Greenpeace and the Sierra Club soon considered Mexico merely to be part of a larger international program rather than a privileged continental partner. In general, unless they were working explicitly on salient transboundary environmental issues with groups across the border, there was little incentive for American or Canadian ENGOs to devote their limited funds to working in other jurisdictions.

Transnational ENGOs play an important role in monitoring government and industry compliance with environmental regulations and agreements, including NAFTA.[62] With the support of the Canadian Alliance on Trade and the Environment, the Sierra Club has done extensive monitoring of the environmental effects of trade and has achieved some citizen access to trade-policy developments while adding substantially to research networks and information sharing.[63]

Once NAFTA had been implemented, transborder discourse among environmentalists in the three countries revolved mostly around the activities and interests of American-based ENGOs. The principal groups that worked to develop environmental policies complementing NAFTA were the National Audubon Society, the Natural Resources Defense Council, the National Wildlife Federation, the World Wildlife Fund, the Nature Conservancy, Defenders of Wildlife, and the Environmental Defense Fund.[64] These groups became influential political actors because they enjoyed legitimacy in the US Congress.

Moderate ENGOs, which helped develop public support for NAFTA, received more funding from foundations and more media attention and were generally regarded with more favour than groups that opposed NAFTA even with its NACEC. Critics accused these moderate organizations of toeing the government line, but the anti-NAFTA environmental movement lost steam once the agreement came into effect.

While growing at a remarkable pace, environmentalism in Mexico remained very weak and extremely heterogeneous.[65] In fact, continental links actually increased disparities within the movement, because only some Mexican groups benefited financially and organizationally by cooperating with their larger and richer American ENGO counterparts.[66] ENGOs were able to rally against the construction of a toxic-waste treatment site in the central state of San Luis Potosí, successfully pressuring the municipality to deny it a construction permit, even after the Californian company, Metalclad, bought over 94 per cent of the firm's stock.[67] However, as we saw in chapter III, Metalclad used NAFTA's Chapter 11 to appeal this action to an international tribunal which ruled it illegal and fined the Mexican government $16 million.

As for the corporate sector, it has taken no unified continental position on environmental issues. Different industries adopt differing stances, depending on the associated costs and benefits of proposed measures, with the US sector tending to guide the views of its corresponding Mexican and Canadian players. Exceptionally, some work has been done trilaterally on automobile-emissions standards through a NAFTA working group dominated by the Detroit Three.[68] Normally, Mexican and Canadian business lobbyists do not combine to act bilaterally or trilaterally on environmental issues, since foreign corporations have little clout in US politics. They become involved when their interests are directly affected, which is most often the case in border zones.

US-Mexican Environmental Relations under NAFTA

While cooperation between the Mexican and US governments in border regions strengthened after NAFTA, these relationships remained asymmetrical because of the discrepancy between Washington's economic clout and the meagre funding available for local communities on the Mexican side of the border.[69] Cooperation was made even more difficult because of the two sides' differing environmental priorities and their unequal abilities – suggested by Table 5.1 – to address their respective problems.[70]

Far from creating a transborder government structure, the La Paz Agreement for the Protection and Improvement of the Environment in the Border Area was a non-binding executive agreement serving as a framework to establish environmental cooperation at the border, to which some annexes were added to deal with more specific problems. But it had no enforcement capacity,[71] and both sides subsequently took only limited steps towards combating pollution. The agreement included in its targeted areas the improvement of human health, the protection of natural resources, and the development of state and local government capacity through technical support, training, funding, and partnerships.[72] The program envisaged various federal agencies in both the United States and Mexico working together on issues of sustainable development.

Table 5.1: Economic and environmental disparities in North America

	USA	Canada	Mexico
Population (millions)	299	33	104
GDP (US$ billion)	13,164	1,271	839
Agricultural land (1,000 sq km)	4123	637	1069
Forest area (1,000 sq km)	3023	3101	642
CO^2 emissions per capita (metric tons)	20.6	20.0	4.3
Renewable freshwater resource per capita (m^3)	9,443	88,203	3,967

Source: World Bank, The Little Green Data Book: 2008 (Washington, DC: World Bank, 2008); http://siteresources.worldbank.org/ENVIRONMENT/Resources/LGDB2008.pdf

In 1996 the two governments signed the final version of the Border XXI Agreement for cooperation on the environment in the border region, with plans to strengthen the enforcement of environmental laws, increase cooperative planning, expand waste-water treatment facilities, and track the movement of transboundary hazardous waste.[73] Border XXI proceeded to establish nine binational working groups bringing together representatives of federal agencies with responsibilities in environmental and public-health matters. Although this program established an important transboundary liaison mechanism, it was still criticized for being federally controlled and unresponsive to local needs. Communication and cooperation increased between the two countries, but the agreement was criticized because large federal agencies dominated the deliberation processes and negotiations, leaving little room for actual citizen participation at the local level.[74]

In 2003, three years after Border XXI ended, the US and Mexican governments extended their cooperation in the Border 2012 Program, which sought to expand the involvement of state government agencies by taking a bottom-up, border-region approach to decision making and project implementation. The program was broken down into subregions and subissues and involved other agencies apart from the US EPA and Mexico's Secretariat for the Environment, including the International Boundary and Water Commission. The governments aimed to harmonize methods, systems, and protocols to facilitate information transfer.[75] One effect of this institutionalized but asymmetrical cooperation is that new Mexican policies and regulations tend to be modelled after those in the United States.

Air quality was also addressed through a series of projects, primarily focusing on reducing particulates in the air by paving city roads, but actual infrastructure projects for air quality were limited, because such causes of air pollution as urban sprawl or increased personal vehicle use are largely intractable. A further constraint impeding progress has been the legal restriction preventing Mexican communities, which receive little governmental support by way of funding or infrastructure, from acquiring debt in a foreign currency or with a foreign institution.[76]

Further changes resulted from NAFTA's two new border institutions. The Border Environment Cooperation Commission (BECC)[77] is a binational, autonomous organization that supports local communities and agencies in developing environmental-infrastructure projects related to water, waste water, and management of solid waste. It certifies projects that it then recommends for project loans and loan guarantees to its sister organization, the North American Development Bank (NADBank). Surprisingly, these two bilateral institutions have not reduced prevailing high levels of Mexico-US asymmetry. Even though there is an equal participation by both sides, the BECC and NADBank have demonstrated asymmetry in their approval and allocation of funds, as will be explained in chapter VI.

Looking at successful experiments in participatory water-infrastructure planning carried out by the BECC/NADBank, Border XXI program managers agreed to rely more heavily on the participation of local and regional agencies, state governments, and indigenous authorities in order to flesh out the program's goals, objectives, and activities.

The successor program, Border 2012, more adequately represented the interests of local and regional actors and also created four binational regional forums linking program participants to a place-based venue for cooperative regional environmental planning. Studies and recommendations were one thing; concrete results and regulatory mechanisms were another. Encouraging public participation did not oblige federal or binational authorities to respond to local demands. How good intentions would translate into specific reforms and how the various levels of government would cooperate to finance projected activities remained to be seen.

Eco-degradation produced by economic growth provoked increased efforts at environmental protection. Although regulatory standards rose as a result of information sharing, coordination, and pressures from civil society,[78] pollution worsened in the US-Mexican border regions because of their increased volumes of manufacturing and sprawling urbanization.

Transborder solidarity at the civil-society level is an important feature of the bilateral relationship. Mexican ENGOs have gained greater
autonomy through receiving support from US counterparts whose collaboration on both a formal and informal basis has helped build their
capabilities and infrastructure. The US Sierra Club offers funds, trains
personnel, and organizes Mexican ENGO grassroots activities through
its Beyond the Borders program.[79] It also protests human-rights violations in Mexico, including intimidation and illegal arrests of Mexican
environmentalists. Part of its mandate is to foster connections between
grass-roots initiatives in the United States and Mexico on environmental issues in order to raise awareness, increase public participation, and
collaborate on primary-research projects. Valuable though it is at one
level, critics worry that this solidarity may result in policies that address American rather than Mexican environmental priorities.

Civil society is still a young player in Mexican politics. Nevertheless,
ENGOs have been growing exponentially: by 1997, there were over five
hundred registered in Mexico. The upsurge of environmentalism in
Mexico also increased the heterogeneity of the movement, with only
some, predominantly urban, groups benefiting financially or otherwise
from transborder cooperation.[80] Reliance on external funding breeds a
culture of dependency among Mexican ENGOs and increases Washington's dominance in environmental policy making and regulations,
since most policy changes result from pressure exerted by US-backed
ENGOs.

NAFTA's Uneven Domestic Effects

NAFTA engendered a number of contradictory environmental results.
Although the United States increased its own output of pollution, it
demanded that the Mexican government improve its environmental
administration and enforcement standards. Yet Mexico was the main
victim of NAFTA's negative environmental effects, since the maquiladoras' poorly regulated production escalated and the Mexican state
had less ability than the other two countries to take remedial or adaptive measures. Besides air quality, the most affected sectors were agriculture (transgenic maize contamination) and water (receiving polluted
water from California).[81]

Mexico's inadequate infrastructure and its politicians' unwillingness
to treat environmental degradation as a genuine priority were reflected

in the country's poor record in implementing environmental regulations. Even though progress has been made, industries' lack of transparency and accountability, public agencies' insufficient expertise and weak regulatory capacity, and government's budgetary constraints prevented environmental sustainability from being integrated into Mexico's economic-development paradigm.

NAFTA's domestic impact on environmental policy has been least significant in the old North America, which took the initiative in lowering environmental standards. In Canada, although the Mulroney Conservatives had already reduced their ambitious Green Plan's initial budget and postponed much of its proposed action by 1993, the Liberals under Jean Chrétien terminated the plan entirely in 1995, by which point less than 30 per cent of the originally budgeted $3 billion had been spent.[82] Following two program reviews, the Department of the Environment's budget was cut by almost a third and its staff by a quarter.[83] Parallel cutbacks by the provinces saw governments such as Ontario cut their budgets for enforcing environmental regulations in half.

Similarly, after George W. Bush took office in Washington, the Environmental Protection Agency underwent a series of leadership shake-ups, budget cuts, and changes to internal policy which neutered its capacity to enforce environmental regulation. The EPA was roundly criticized for cozying up to industry, stacking panels with industry lobbyists, and letting industry dictate its mercury policy. The Bush administration was able to undo years of environmental progress. To reduce the costs of compliance for industry, Washington allowed the new source-review measures of the Clean Air Act to be waived and provided more lenient deadlines to industry. Investigations into companies for non-compliance were suspended indefinitely. These changes sparked indignation among ENGOs, policy makers, and all but the most conservative politicians and industry groups. Several key EPA officials resigned in protest.

The US Department of Energy (DOE) was also criticized by environmentalists for giving a lower priority to environmental protection than to favouring industry, whose regulatory requests passed through the federal policy process virtually intact. Since the DOE sets much of the energy sector's policies in the United States, its strong deregulatory push also put government priorities at odds with high environmental standards. NAFTA's rules and the NACEC played a negligible role in resisting this sad saga.

Border Region Environmental Governance

The three federal governments' failure collectively to achieve any significant regulatory progress to reverse environmental degradation is only one part of the story, because North America's transborder environmental governance includes a complex set of subfederal relationships that have developed as provinces and states from all three countries directly engaged with each other to address common challenges. Indeed, more environmental action is generated by some of North America's ninety-four other governments – Mexico's thirty-two states, the forty-nine continental American states, and the thirteen Canadian provinces and territories – than the NACEC could ever contemplate.

Subfederal environmental linkages develop[84] because individual states' or provinces' shared geography makes them vulnerable to the behaviour of their neighbours. US-Mexican partnerships, which have multiplied since 1995, are overwhelmingly bilateral and have been largely concentrated along the border in the form of separate agreements between one Mexican state and the US state next door. Some of the seventeen agreements that have been negotiated include joint environmental strategies, notably the one between the Texas Commission on Environmental Quality and Neuvo Leon's Natural Resources and Environmental Protection Agency.[85]

Some of these transborder interactions are so intense that the notion of 'borderlands' has been coined to describe the physical, ideological, and geographical regions that both integrate and differentiate areas on both sides of the boundary line – in short, communities that have more in common with each other in certain respects than they have with other parts of their national jurisdiction.[86] The shared culture, history, and economic integration characterizing many North American borderlands facilitate these subfederal governments' capacity to address the localized, cross-border nature of common environmental challenges.

US-Canadian subfederal partnerships are increasingly multilateral, in that they are often joint initiatives by clusters of neighbouring states and provinces. For instance, the establishment of the Pacific Northwest Economic Region brings together stakeholders from the provinces of Alberta, British Columbia, and the Yukon Territory with the states of Alaska, Idaho, Montana, Oregon, and Washington in varying forums to address numerous issues of common concern. The New England governors (Connecticut, Maine, Massachusetts, New Hampshire, Rhode Island, and Vermont) and eastern Canadian premiers (Quebec, New Brunswick, Newfound and Labrador, Nova Scotia, and Prince Edward Island) have convened an annual summit for over three decades.[87] These manifestations of border-region governance feature environmental questions prominently in their broad agendas.

More recently, subfederal regions have become involved in climate-change initiatives in reaction to perceived inaction by the three federal governments. Thus, the Conference of New England Governors and Eastern Canadian Premiers has adopted a regional greenhouse-gas reduction target.[88] Likewise, British Columbia partnered with a group of western states to form the Western Regional Climate Change Initiative (WRCI), comprising Arizona, British Columbia, California, New Mexico, Oregon, and Washington, which ultimately seeks to develop a regional carbon-trading market.[89] Along the Mexican border in 2005, Arizona and Sonora formulated a Regional Climate Change Initiative committing the two states to reduce levels of greenhouse gases emitted in the region.[90] With such a globalized issue, environmental partnerships themselves appear to be expanding beyond the borderlands. British Columbia and New Mexico are both party to the WRCI. In 2006 the government of Manitoba signed an MOU to partner on climate-change initiatives with distant California.[91] In 2007 Ontario and California signed an agreement to coordinate fuel-policy standards.[92]

It is not clear whether these climate-change partnerships are constructing a new type of regulatory governance in North America. While the number of US-Canadian linkages has increased over time, the regions do not appear to be integrating or even harmonizing their environmental policies. Partnerships are not becoming functionally closer but instead are generating more formalized information sharing.[93] Clearly, domestic politics still matter most, and, despite an overarching sense of shared stewardship, there is no transcendent trend to cross-border cohesion. On the contrary, increased border security since 2001 has reduced cross-border integration even in the putative borderlands.[94]

Although it has not produced a cohesive continental framework, this rich set of subfederal linkages constitutes the core of environmental governance in North America. Indeed, independently of NAFTA, such linkages are injecting what little substance can be found in the shared stewardship of the continent's natural environment.

Conclusion

NAFTA and its environmental side agreement have produced mixed results for North America. Although environmental degradation cannot be said to be caused by the trilateral trade agreement, the agreement's rules and its environmental institution have failed to live up to their misleading promise that the increased economic activity that it was designed to stimulate would be environmentally sustainable.

NAFTA's rulebook was intended to weaken the three governments' regulatory grip on economic issues directly. The governments' regulatory powers over environmental issues were indirectly weakened through investor-state arbitration targeting the allegedly expropriatory consequences of some environmental measures. Because the NACEC did not create an offsetting continental regulatory regime, environmental regulation remained a domestic matter to be supplemented by ad hoc cooperation on border issues. This non-development of transborder governance can be confirmed by the fact that, having lost the battle against NAFTA, most ENGOs proceeded to lobby nationally. Only in particular circumstances have they extended their lobbying across the border.

Asymmetries in environmental politics have as much to do with negative polluting power as with positive governing capacity. Between the United States and Canada, NAFTA and the NACEC seem neither to have increased nor diminished the asymmetry, doing nothing to stop governments from weakening their environmental protection as they see fit. At the same time, the imbalance between Canada and Mexico's relationships with Washington has been reduced by raising the Mexican government's environment-policy autonomy and by supporting Mexican civil society's environmental movement. Notwithstanding these improvements, which occurred mainly in Mexico City, agreements between the US and Mexican governments and various border states have institutionalized and sometimes even enhanced the bilateral relationship's stark asymmetry, while their shared border-regions remain on the brink of ecological catastrophe.

Following the ephemeral continentalism-from-below engendered by the debate over NAFTA, the NACEC buttressed mainstream Mexican civil society's increased role. Paradoxically, while a stronger activism in Mexico attenuated its overwhelming weakness vis-à-vis its neighbour, Mexico's more effective ENGOs became an instrument in broadening the capacity in Mexico of US ENGOs on whose support they depended.

In the borderlands, Mexican civil-society organizations remained crippled by desperate financial needs as they faced near-insuperable conditions.

During the years of the George W. Bush administration, a yawning gap emerged between continental and global environmental governance. Its rhetorical support of environmental sustainability notwithstanding, the US government abstained from signing three major global conventions on biodiversity, climate change, and desertification or their associated protocols.[95] Washington's disconnect from multilateral environmental globalism exerted strong pressure on Canada and Mexico to evade keeping their own international environmental commitments or making new ones. Canada's behaviour clearly illustrated this dilemma. Ottawa signed the Kyoto Accord but did nothing to fulfil its commitments because its corporate community rejected paying for higher standards – a resistance to ecological prudence with which the Canadian public was complicit.

Blocked continentally, ENGO efforts shifted from the continental to the global or local levels. The same trend was evident in the specific area of border-water management, as chapter VI explains.

VI Transboundary Water Governance

The previous four chapters evaluated NAFTA institutions' capacity to provide governance in the various domains to which they were assigned. This chapter takes a different tack. It addresses the question of boundary waters to see how this aspect of North American trans-border management had long preceded – but was subsequently affected by – trade and investment liberalization.

In North America's two sets of borderlands, shared water has become the lifeblood not just for the human existence of over a hundred million residents in the three countries but for the economic activity in which these people engage. The waters in the two binational zones enable cities to exist, allow crops to grow, provide power for manufacturing, facilitate transportation, and make a multi-billion-dollar tourist economy possible. Beyond the multitudinous uses they afford to humans, North America's transboundary waters are also vital to the functioning of the areas' various ecosystems. Essential ecological diversity is sustained by hydrological cycling that connects visible lakes and rivers with subterranean water in invisible aquifers that spread across huge areas bisected by one or other of the two international borders.

The immense scope for conflicting uses of this resource and the long-term repercussions that could result from undermining its capacity for replenishment make the creation of successful governance frameworks for managing shared waters essential to the human use and ecological integrity of North America's border regions. Essential does not mean inevitable: what may seem necessary for global survival to armchair analysts may be rejected by pragmatic politicians seeking political survival at the hands of citizens with narrowly self-interested mental horizons. Since water is such a vital commodity, short-term parochial interests can easily negate what may in the longer term be rational and equitable solutions.

Water treaties governing the use and allocation of North American transboundary water resources have facilitated binational cooperation by helping to resolve disputes regarding shared lakes or river systems. Yet to restore ecological integrity by mitigating biological, physical, and chemical threats to water quality and quantity in territorially divided waters and, at the same time, to promote more balanced regional economic development requires a greater level of both political cooperation and integration of management processes than has existed historically.

Until the mid-twentieth century, policy making for transboundary waters was a diplomatic prerogative of the federal governments, with local stakeholders involved peripherally, if at all. However, rapid economic development, the industrialization of agriculture, and proliferating urbanization in the latter half of the twentieth century transformed border regions into highly dynamic spaces in which government officials, private actors, and organized civil-society groups communicated and pursued cross-border synergies outside formal diplomatic frameworks. This process was related to North American transboundary water management because – as a consequence of changing political and scientific approaches to governing hydrologically connected border regions – significant shifts occurred among levels of government, in the power relations between the public and the private sectors, and in the engagement of civil society.

The de-territorialization of politics associated with globalization – both the cause and consequence of deeper economic integration between neighbouring states – is also a context for the process whereby socio-economically interdependent borderlands caused the federal governments to lose their policy-making monopoly over bilateral relations.[1] On each side of the border, governments retained the final say in issuing, financing, and enforcing new rules and regulations. However, the process by which new rules and regulations emerged became strongly influenced by relevant scientific experts and affected businesses, as well as by public stakeholders in civil society.

This chapter also explores what impact NAFTA has had – if any – on North American transboundary water management. More generally, it assesses whether NAFTA's associated policy paradigm – the neo-conservative toolkit – helped bolster the United States' dominance over its neighbours or reduced the continent's bilateral power asymmetries.

The comparison of water management along the United States' two land boundaries reveals that it is misleading to speak of 'North American' transboundary water management as if it were a single, continent-wide phenomenon. The two sets of water-control regimes along the US-Canada and the US-Mexico borders are not just geographically remote from each other but politically distinct. Each was shaped by specific regional bio-geophysical characteristics, varying degrees of socio-economic integration, dissimilarity in the scale and quantity of its shared resource, differing political systems, contrasting cultural values, and different bilateral treaties governing the use of transboundary waters. It would even be incorrect to assert that there is a single transboundary water regime for the United States with Canada and another one for the United States with Mexico, because management systems for specific basins along each border display a significant amount of diversity among themselves. This chapter contrasts two of these regimes to demonstrate their unique characteristics and to illustrate how widely the governance of the shared transboundary water resources can vary across North America.

The Tijuana/San Diego watershed's extreme vulnerability to floods and landslides and its chronic water scarcity made that border region a potential beneficiary of NAFTA's only two binational institutions, the Border Environment Cooperation Commission (BECC) and its sister organization, the North American Development Bank (NADBank). Cooperation through these institutions and through various other governance arrangements at the local and state levels, however, failed to prevent unilateral local action in California that is threatening what had been for half a century a relatively conflict-free shared river system.

By contrast, continental economic integration has had less direct impact on the management of the Great Lakes, where developments over the past quarter-century present a curious contradiction. Binational efforts to restore water quality in the Great Lakes have been frustrated by the US and Canadian governments each adopting more autonomous, less cooperative stances. While binational cooperation on *quality* issues at the federal-government level was disintegrating, inter-governmental cooperation at the state/provincial level triumphed on the *quantity* question of water diversions.

North America's transboundary water-management regimes are in flux as they face ecological crises. The political instability that is their central feature makes the creation of resilient and adaptive governing systems capable of protecting water resources without placing undue constraints on economic activity an enormous challenge. In addition, as a result of major differences between engineers' and ecologists' recommendations, the political will necessary for their implementation often cannot solidify even when the politicians are disposed to act.[2] Some international lawyers detect a gradual normative evolution towards ecosystem-based regimes in international arrangements which favour long-term environmental security over competing sovereign interests and can promote common interests through binding international norms.[3] Yet, while there is considerable public support in the United States and Canada for far-sighted solutions, authorities and decision makers on the Mexican side evince little concern for environmental questions as a whole.[4]

This analysis assesses the progress that has been made towards water-management integration across the two boundaries. In the old North America of Canada and the United States, the considerable harmonization that had developed over a century was rooted in normative similarities between the two countries' legal systems. This context of low levels of conflict in dealing with common problems contrasted radically with the gulf separating the political cultures of the United States and Mexico. Despite these basic differences, harmony prevails between the three federal governments. When conflicts break out, they tend to be at lower political levels.

The chapter's two sections discuss the evolution of the transboundary water-management regimes in the Great Lakes and Tijuana River basins before and after NAFTA in order to illustrate the complexities of regional institution building and to determine the effects of continental economic integration on this aspect of transboundary cooperation. The analysis focuses on the contentious issue of water diversion in these two disparate watersheds, which are distinguished by, among such other factors as culture and scarcity, the imbalance in the power asymmetry between the United States and its two disparate neighbours.

Governance of the Great Lakes Basin

Quality Control

The Great Lakes basin is the world's largest freshwater ecosystem, containing 20 per cent of the planet's fresh surface water and supplying drinking water to forty-five million people. The region's agriculture, manufacturing sectors, and urban centres have long enjoyed access to this cheap and seemingly boundless resource, often without incurring the true cost of the ecological damage they have caused. Over the past forty years, Canadian and US legislative mandates have helped curb significant sources of pollutants, but the restoration of the Great Lakes' quality has been a halting process.

The legal foundation for cooperative management of the Great Lakes basin lies in the 1909 Boundary Waters Treaty concluded between Great Britain (on behalf of its quasi-colonial dominion) and the United States. The treaty established what for its time was an extraordinary institution. The International Joint Commission was a weak but supranational agency that offset the power asymmetry between the United States and Canada by being run as a binational organization on the basis of the two partners' equality. The Great Lakes' apparent abundance of water resources shaped the way that the IJC addressed its responsibilities in their regard. Until the mid-twentieth century, it focused on conducting joint studies of such physical issues as how to facilitate navigation or hydropower generation in fulfilment of the treaty's agreement that planned obstructions or diversions on either side of the boundary affecting the level and flow of water would not be made without the joint authorization of both countries. The IJC offered a governance venue to the two governments which could issue a 'reference' to it in order to obtain independent scientific advice on such quantitative issues as fluctuating lake levels or, more recently, qualitative problems of water contamination. Over the lifetime of the Boundary Waters Treaty, observers have credited the peaceful and almost dispute-free management of US-Canadian transboundary waters both to the IJC's supranational ability to render authoritative, politically neutral decisions on proposed water projects and to the two federal governments' crucial willingness to take this advice.

Reform in Great Lakes governance began in the mid-1960s when the IJC advised the two states that excessive dumping of phosphorus and toxic chemicals was degrading water quality and harming sensitive ecosystems in Lakes Ontario and Erie.[5] In the face of public alarm that Lake Erie was 'dying,' the United States and Canada signed the Great Lakes Water Quality Agreement (GLWQA) of 1979, which led to the establishment of two binational boards – the Water Quality Board (WQB) and the Science Advisory Board – to help the IJC meet its important new coordinating responsibilities in data collection and analysis, research, and program evaluation. At this point in the regime's evolution, binational cooperation and collaboration took place within the

IJC, where national representatives were expected to work independently of governments whose progress towards meeting the commitments made under the 1979 agreement they assessed. For Canadian agency representatives, this was an important, basically symmetrical forum for influencing the Great Lakes agenda.[6]

The GLWQA was subsequently amended in 1987 by a protocol transferring the WQB's responsibilities to Environment Canada and the Environmental Protection Agency, which assumed the responsibility for gathering and analysing information and reporting progress to the public and to the IJC. Because the Water Quality Board now meets only to provide advice on policy coordination, there has been much less participation of national representatives in the IJC. With this parity-based forum reduced in significance, Canada's influence over the Great Lakes agenda also declined.

In combination with the IJC's reduced influence, the new, more informal arrangements allowed the two parties more flexibility in pursuing their respective interests. As a result, emphasis focused more on developing separate domestic programs and less on creating cooperative binational approaches, a process that had a profound impact on the effectiveness of the Great Lakes' governance regime and its accountability.

Meanwhile, as neoconservative deficit-trimming and small-government values took hold within each country, Washington and Ottawa offloaded program responsibilities to their states and provinces. The amended GLWQA formally recognized the eight Great Lakes states' and the province of Ontario's new responsibilities in implementing the programs necessary to achieve the agreement's restoration goals so that, by the time NAFTA was implemented in 1994, the eight states and Ontario were resenting these obligations since neither federal government had provided them the funding commensurate with their new duties. The stage was set during this period for the increasing disintegration of binational Great Lakes governance.

Although NAFTA had no direct impact on the Great Lakes' water-governance regime, one of its corollaries – a neoconservative approach to government budgeting in the shadow of intensified continental and global competition – resulted in pared-back levels of funding for environmental science and restoration projects. Moreover, what resources were devoted to Great Lakes restoration and management were invested mainly in domestic programs, leaving international agreements to be implemented as a secondary concern. During this period, the US government initiated a departure from the binational guideline-setting embodied in the GLWQA by developing domestic water-quality guidelines and criteria known as the 'Great Lakes Initiative.'

In contrast to the United States, Canada's Great Lakes programs entered a period of regression. Despite the tabling of a federal water policy in 1987 which was to have been a framework for addressing issues such as drinking-water safety, water exports, research, and intergovernmental arrangements, Ottawa did an about-face, slowly de-emphasizing water in Canadian environmental policy.[7] A major cut to Environment Canada in the federal government's 1994 budget and another to Ontario's Ministry of the Environment in 1995 further weakened Canada's ability to meet water-quality standards and fulfil the GLWQA's terms. Federal-provincial relations became strained: between 1991 and 1994, the Canada-Ontario Agreement, which outlined the federal and provincial responsibilities under the GLWQA, was actually suspended.

While inter-governmental disputes grew and Great Lakes science confirmed the need for higher levels of investment to protect human and ecosystem health, the GLWQA's binational vision faded away, becoming a source of intermittent embarrassment to Canadian and US officials who were unable, when challenged, to report making significant progress towards the agreement's goals.

Paradoxically and pregnantly, while federal organizational and budgetary constraints stalled progress towards ecosystem integrity, Great Lakes environmental NGOs remained as vocal and active as they had been when the environment movement had begun. Incorporated non-profit, watershed-based groups worked collaboratively with local, state/provincial, and federal agencies to develop watershed plans for restoration and protection. This emerging informal water-management regime was held together by a matrix of transborder governance energized by well-organized citizen groups' efforts in restoration.[8] Along with the silent power of shared legal norms, this variegated web of civil-society networks explains how the management of the highly contentious water-diversion issue ultimately engendered more integrated binational governance – if only at the province/state level.

Quantity Control

Without effective transboundary institutions dedicated to their sustainability, concerns about possible diversions in massive quantities cannot be laid to rest now that scientists have shown the lakes' precious liquid to be non-renewable. Although the Great Lakes are so vast that they are sometimes referred to as inland seas, they are now known to be filled with what is known as glacial water, which is left over from the melting of the continental ice sheets.[9] Only 1 per cent is replenished by rainfall or snowmelt, with the result that, once water is removed from the basin, it is gone forever. This non-renewable nature of the lakes' contents has made proposals for massive withdrawals or diversions highly contentious: thirsty regions beyond the watershed covet a resource which the watershed's inhabitants insist must be husbanded in principle but used in practice by themselves alone.

Despite the asymmetry in economic power and institutional might between the two countries, an almost hundred-year-old history of common legal norms and binational cooperation prevailed over significant constitutional obstacles. Under the English common law from which both American and Canadian legal norms derived, riparians – people who own or occupy land beside lakes and rivers – have the right to the natural flow of water beside or through their property, providing it remains unchanged in quantity or quality.[10] Although riparian law evolved differently in the United States and Canada, Article 8 of the Boundary Waters Treaty asserted that no water use 'shall be permitted which tends materially to conflict with or restrain any other use.' Canadian and American riparian law also shares the requirement that water must be used in connection with the riparian land and be returned to the watershed of origin. This principle was established to maintain the level of flow for downstream riparians and has been interpreted in the United States to mean that the water must be used on land that drains into streams below the place of diversion,[11] a notion that is echoed in Canadian jurisprudence.

Under the US constitution, the constituent states have the right to manage water withdrawals, diversions, and consumptive uses by virtue of their police power but are limited in their right to control interstate diversions by the interstate commerce clause (Art. 1, 8: 3), which endows the federal government with the right to regulate a large variety of interstate commercial activities, including navigation and water diversion.[12] Since the late 1800s, the US government has authorized the construction of several projects to divert large bodies of water, including the Chicago Diversion to carry the city's sewage into the Mississippi River. This pre-emptive federal power over diversions has been the cause of much anxiety in the Great Lakes region lest the growing population in the water-scarce American southwest prevail in Congress and impose massive water diversions. These fears are not unfounded, since the Great Lakes states formally lack the constitutional authority to stop water being taken for use outside their basin.

In contrast, the Constitution Act of Canada gives the provinces massive legislative authority to regulate the use of surface and groundwater. Provincial authority in property and civil rights, matters of a local or private nature, non-renewable natural resources, forestry, and electrical energy is exercised subject to the federal government's constitutional jurisdiction over trade and commerce, navigation, seacoast and inland fisheries, treaty making, and 'peace, order, and good government.' This division of powers gives the provinces enormous bargaining leverage over the implementation of international agreements.

During a regional water-management conference in Toronto in 1984, when Ontario committed its support for a cooperative jurisdictional approach to the basin's management, the Great Lakes Governors' Task Force on Water Diversion and Great Lakes Institutions was established to develop a set of principles to guide the management of Great Lakes water resources.[13] The task force, formed by representatives of the eight Great Lakes governors plus the Ontario and Quebec premiers, delivered its report on February 11, 1985, the same day that the governors and premiers signed the Great Lakes Charter. This non-binding, good-faith agreement committed the signatories to develop cooperative regional water management, to share information among jurisdictions, and, most important, to give prior notice and consult on any new or increased diversion or consumptive use exceeding five million gallons (nineteen million litres) per day.[14] The charter also created a decision-making 'Water Resources Management Committee,' which became the negotiating forum for successive water agreements and was staffed by water-policy and technical advisers appointed by the governors and premiers.

At the time the charter was signed, considerable uncertainty prevailed about the states' legislative authority to regulate diversions and consumptive uses of interstate waters lest any intended measures be deemed to interfere with interstate commerce. Jurisprudence had clarified that, although it could regulate water use by exercising its police power, no state could ban out-of-state diversions unless it treated in-state and out-of-state applications similarly.[15] The Great Lakes Charter successfully incorporated these rulings by applying the same non-discriminatory regulatory standards to all users of Great Lakes water, whether in-state or out-of-state. The US government brought this part of the charter under federal law through the 1986 Water Resources Development Act (WRDA), which prohibited any diversion of water from the Great Lakes basin without the permission of the governors of each Great Lakes state. For Canada, the WRDA seemed a double-edged sword since the veto power accorded to the state governors excluded Ontario and so reduced the ability of Canadian provinces to influence Great Lakes diversion issues in Lake Michigan.[16]

The galvanizing event that triggered the regional resolve to revisit the Great Lakes Charter occurred in 1998, when Canada inadvertently demonstrated its unilateral capacity to inflict environmental damage on its neighbour. Without notifying or seeking the consent of its charter partners, the government of Ontario issued a permit to the Nova Corporation, a water exporting company, to take up to 600 million litres of water a year out of Lake Superior. A public outcry on both sides of the border forced Ontario to withdraw its permit and, as regional hydrologic unity was evidently dissolving, generated political support for revising the charter to reflect the changing reality of water consumption in the basin. The process for arriving at a strengthened agreement was structured to maximize the knowledge and input from a wide range of government representatives, citizen groups, and industrial stakeholders. Openness in decision making had long been the practice in the Great Lakes policy domain, and policy makers regularly consulted with stakeholders, scientists, and professional consultants on new initiatives or problems. The public was often invited to voice its opinion on proposed projects, and the basin's NGOs routinely contributed their intellectual and human resources to ecological-restoration initiatives and to policy development. The process to negotiate the charter annex was consequently structured to benefit from this large diversity of perspectives.

In 2001 the Great Lakes governors and premiers signed the Great Lakes Charter Annex, a document to guide the development and implementation of a new decision-making standard to be used when reviewing new or expanded proposals for water withdrawals. It also provided a role for the public's input in the preparation and implementation of new binding agreements and set a deadline of three years from the signing of the annex to reach a conclusion.

Over the four years of the agreements' development, the cooperative approach of the Council of Great Lakes Governors' Water Management Working Group's lent a high level of legitimacy to the process and fostered the view that the council had made a serious effort to ensure fair access to the decision makers. But, because of urban sprawl, an outright ban on water diversions was rejected in favour of regulating diversions by imposing minimum standards of ecosystem protection. (Ontario and Ohio maintained throughout the drafting process that, considering future threats, new diversions should be banned.)

For the first three years, the negotiations were driven by the pressure on many states to provide drinking water to urbanizing communities whose territorial limits lay outside the watershed. The result was a first draft that sought to facilitate, not restrict, new diversions. On July 19, 2004 the 'compact' and the agreement were released to the public for commentary. The vast majority of the commentators expressed opposition to their vague standards for diversions and condemned the lack of clarity regarding conservation measures. Following this public-comment period, further drafting was shaped by the Canadian negotiators' refusal to accept anything less than a prohibition on all new diversions from the basin on the grounds that they could not sign an agreement that violated Canadian legal prohibitions against such practices. The Canadian government and environmental organizations considered the agreements to be too far below recently revised Canadian standards. (The federal government had been sufficiently alarmed by the Nova Corporation export permit that it had amended the Boundary Waters Treaty Act to prohibit the bulk removal of boundary waters from Canadian basins, and Ontario had subsequently passed a mirror law to ban exports or diversions from boundary waters.) The Canadian consensus considered the agreements insufficiently respectful of the Boundary Waters Treaty or the IJC's role.[17] Reports that Americans would be able to take 'Canadian' water aroused nationalist sentiments, giving political support for the official anti-diversion position. Since many of Ontario's objections were echoed by the American public and by anti-diversion states, the texts were revised.

Canadian intransigence on this principle consequently forced the negotiators to review years' worth of arguments that had been used to explain the impossibility of adopting a blanket prohibition on diversions. Until this point, legal opinion had stressed that an all-out ban on diversions would run afoul of US inter-state commerce laws. Yet, after several more months of negotiations, a second draft adopted the Canadian-backed prohibition. It banned new diversions with the exception of strictly regulated ones for communities straddling the basin boundary and for within-basin transfers.[18] The second draft also gave fuller recognition to the role of the federal governments and the Boundary Waters Treaty, accepting Canada's equal rights and particularly its equal decision-making authority. Although intense business lobbying managed to reinstate some of the vagueness of the first draft, the final text was considered an acceptable compromise.

On December 13, 2005, after four years of intense negotiations, the governors of the eight states bordering the Great Lakes and the premiers of Ontario and Quebec signed two parallel landmark water-management agreements: the Great Lakes Sustainable Water Resources Compact (a legally binding interstate compact among the Great Lakes states) and the Great Lakes-St Lawrence River Basin Sustainable Water Resources Agreement (a good-faith agreement between the states and the two provinces). The new parallel documents definitively established the political authority of the states and provinces over Great Lakes water usage and placed clear prohibitions on large-scale diversions of water outside the bounds of the hydrologic basin. It was an astonishing outcome, given the considerable power asymmetry between Canada and the United States, where vociferous interests outside the Great Lakes basin pressed for opening, rather than closing, the tap.

In this dramatic episode of binational water-quantity governance, Canada's power asymmetry at the federal level had been offset by common legal-political norms, its capacity to authorize diversions as damaging as its neighbour's, and the effects of the considerable transborder civil-society integration that had taken place within the border region itself.

Governance of the Tijuana River Basin

Pre-NAFTA

While many decades of cross-border human integration between the two politically, culturally, and economically similar countries sharing Great Lakes water may have prevailed over the two federal governments' distinct disinterest in serious cooperation, an even longer experience of integration between two politically, culturally, and economically dissimilar nations struggling against overwhelming water scarcity has had opposite effects. Although Washington and Mexico City have talked the talk of sustainable development and signed documents promising ever-greater binational cooperation, recent action has shown how local self-interest and immediate political needs have prevailed over ecosystem thinking to the serious detriment of the weaker partner.

The Tijuana River basin covers an area of approximately 4,500 square kilometres, with its upper third in southern California and the rest in Baja California. The rapidly burgeoning twin cities of San Diego and Tijuana are situated within the basin, but, owing to the region's desert climate (which is among the driest in North America, with rainfall averaging less than 250 mm per year), these municipalities must transport the bulk of their water via lengthy aqueducts from the Colorado River, the dominant river system in the US southwest whose natural course drains through northwestern Mexico into the Gulf of California. Because of multiple water needs stemming from agricultural, industrial, and urban expansion on both sides of the international boundary, there is tremendous competition for – and therefore conflict over – the Colorado's limited supplies. A different legal culture for water in the southwestern American states, favouring the first user over the interests of downstream users, has led to over-allocation and pollution. Inadequate treatment of upstream agricultural run-offs results in serious contamination, with noxious effects on those who have to reuse the polluted liquid downstream. Tijuana's and the Mexicali valley's problems in receiving the smallest share and the most contaminated water are compounded by Mexico's serious infrastructure deficit: less than one-half of its waste water is treated, one half of its piped water disappears through leakage, and one- half of its irrigated water is lost through evaporation or seepage.[19]

The legal basis for the cooperative international management of the Tijuana River basin lies in the 1889 convention that created the International Boundary Commission (IBC) and the 1944 Treaty Relating to the Utilization of Waters of the Colorado and Tijuana Rivers and of the Rio Grande between the United States and Mexico, which gave Mexico the right to 1.85 billion cubic metres of water from the Colorado and converted the IBC into the International Boundary and Water Commission (IBWC, or CILA in Spanish), a joint commission with national sections, each dependent on its respective federal government's agencies.[20] The very limited surface-water resources in the arid US-Mexico border region required bilateral water-management arrangements to focus originally on allocating agricultural water-use rights to the inadequate quantities available in the shared river. Later agreements dealt with allocating waters for urban and industrial use as well.

The treaty was concerned with the municipal, industrial, and agricultural use of scarce surface water resources but did not address the more demanding issues of water quality, groundwater, or conservation. The IBWC role was to assure the delivery of the national entitlements specified in the treaty. To this end, it was mandated to build and operate dams and water reservoirs in order to control and deliver the flow of the apportioned waters of the Colorado, Río Grande, and Tijuana rivers. Anticipating future disputes, the 1944 treaty also empowered the IBWC to address problems not envisioned in the treaty through the subsequent negotiation of binational amendments or 'minutes.' Consequently, the IBWC's mandate has more recently expanded to include hydropower generation and the construction, operation, and maintenance of waste-water treatment plants on both sides of the border. It also developed information sharing and risk-management practices in periods of drought, particularly for the Rio Grande.

Until the 1960s, the commission fulfilled the technical requirements of these mandates and played a central role in influencing the management of the transboundary water resources.[21] When the impact of the shared waters' unregulated pollution became apparent, a paradigmatic shift from the idea of resource *development* to that of resource *management* began to affect the IBWC's operations. In the latter half of the twentieth century, new institutions and organizations with new powers and rights to influence the control of transboundary waters increasingly eroded the commission's traditional authority. The vertical layering of new mandates and actors within the two countries on top of a horizontally managed diplomatic relationship between the two federal governments had a transformative effect on transboundary water control. Whatever the motivation – often thought to include the federal governments' offloading onto local authorities such responsibilities as the monitoring of water quality in order to reduce expenditures – this paradigm shift in the overarching management regime began to lead local governments and non-state actors to participate more meaningfully in water governance.

The dramatic post-war transformation of the region's economy from its largely agricultural orientation to a mushrooming industrial area created pressures on the IBWC. Restricted by its purely quantitative mandate to protect the two countries' respective water entitlements, it was unable to address issues of water quality unforeseen in the 1944 treaty. By 1973, after more than a decade's piecemeal negotiations of various accords, the Mexican and US governments signed Minute No.

242 to regulate the salinity of the Colorado River. Minute 242 established limits to the annual average salinity of the water received at the Morelos Dam, where water provided to Mexico was kept at the border between the states of Sonora and Baja California. According to the agreement, these limits were to be related to the levels observed at the Imperial Dam in California, where water was stored for American use.

Chemical wastes are present in water that has already been used for agriculture and in urban centres in the United States. Despite the bilateral agreement to raise the quality of water shared by the two countries, some 200 of the 1,850 million cubic metres to which Mexico is entitled through the treaty and which the United States delivers to Mexico remain too polluted as run-off waters from the Wellton-Mohawk Irrigation and Drainage District at Yuma, Arizona, to be used for irrigation.[22] There is nothing that Mexico can do about this polluted water as long as the minimum pollutant concentrations averaged over five-year periods are respected. The water's poor quality forces farmers in the Mexicali valley to mix it with water pumped from aquifers in order to be able to use it for irrigation.[23] The contaminated water received from the United States as well as the pollution generated by local industry is aggravated by the inefficient processing of the vital liquid: just 20 per cent of the water is treated.[24]

Before NAFTA was negotiated, several development schemes stimulated Mexican migration to the twin-city region and precipitated grave transboundary sanitation problems owing to the paucity of sewage-treatment infrastructure in Tijuana. The maquiladora program – which attracted foreign-owned assembly plants employing low-wage Mexican labour on the assumption that environmental regulations would not be enforced – multiplied the unregulated dumping of hazardous chemical wastes and untreated industrial waste water into river beds in urban centres and in the industrial corridors along the frontier. These issues caused grave concerns among citizens of the two countries, but, because they were not covered by the 1944 treaty, they could not be addressed by the IBWC.

By the early 1980s, it was becoming clear that Mexico and the United States lacked a decision-making structure to address environmental management in the border region. As a first step, the La Paz Agreement for the Protection and Improvement of the Environment in the Border Area, signed by presidents Ronald Reagan and Miguel de la Madrid in 1983, established binational working groups to formulate policy recommendations regarding sanitation problems in the San Diego/Tijuana area, hazardous material spills, transboundary shipments of hazardous waste, air pollution by copper smelters, and urban air pollution along the border.[25] The new agreement addressed some long-standing transboundary issues but was still heavily criticized as being federally conceived, lacking mechanisms for public participation, committing no funds, and delegating no financial power to local authorities. Industry and high-income householders benefited, while the environment, the agricultural sector, and low-income people remained negatively affected.

After a decade of mounting environmental pressures and new transborder civil-society concerns about increased trade liberalization creating additional stress on the border environment, the La Paz Agreement was transformed into the Integrated Environmental Plan for the Mexican-U.S. Border Area. The 1992 IBEP proposed to strengthen environmental-law enforcement, increase planning cooperation, and expand treatment facilities for waste water, but it did not establish an institutional framework able to achieve its goals.[26]

At the same time that these binational negotiations were proceeding continentally, the domestic water-management system was being transformed in Mexico both because of the country's early involvement with multilateral institutions committed to Third World development and because of its subsequent obligations, as a member of the Organization for Economic Co-operation and Development (OECD), to accelerate certain environmental reforms. In the early 1990s, a major restructuring of Mexico's water-management regime implemented a complex program of decentralization and privatization prescribed by the World Bank and the Inter-American Development Bank, which financed almost half its $1-billion budget.[27] In step with the Washington consensus, the new policies offloaded many federal water-management functions to the state and municipal levels of government and opened water services to private-sector participation.[28] The National Water Law of 1992 gave states and municipalities responsibility for monitoring and enforcing regulations on pollution from municipal sewage systems and the disposal of solid waste.[29] However, the federal treasury (Secretaría de Hacienda) retained its control as the source of funds for the states and municipalities, which, unable to finance the obligations that had been thrust upon them, found themselves forced to resort to the private sector to find the money required to run public-sector water programs. The other side of the decentralization coin was a lack of coordination, which resulted in adjacent jurisdictions having completely opposing policies on these issues.[30] The Comisión Nacional de Agua (CONAGUA, National Water Commission) had also been established to draft a water policy and formulate regional and national water-management plans, but it was widely felt to be just as closed in its process of decision making and resource allocation as the IBWC.

Despite their pronounced socio-economic asymmetries, the US and Mexican border communities in the Tijuana region shared a long history of informal cross-border linkages between economic actors, citizen-based volunteer organizations, and academic institutes.[31] In the lead-up to NAFTA, local governments and binational, citizen-based environmental coalitions seeking a stronger position in infrastructure planning and decision making called for an increased formalization of cross-border relationships.[32] With protests highlighting the already severe environmental and public-health issues generated by unplanned and under-regulated urban and economic growth, the United States and Mexico agreed to the NAFTA environmental side agreement creating regional institutions for the development and financing of border environmental infrastructure. Given the significant and relatively long experience with transborder water governance, negotiators developed new institutional channels, paying greater attention to local problems and to the concerns expressed by NGOs, scientists, and academics on both sides of the border.[33]

Post-NAFTA

In sharp contrast with NAFTA's negligible impact on the Great Lakes' governance, the environmental side agreement created new structures affecting the institutionalization of binational cooperation on water management and environmental issues in the Tijuana River basin and throughout the border region in general. The Border Environment Cooperation Commission was established expressly for these purposes, and the North American Development Bank was set up to finance the BECC's water-infrastructure projects.[34] As explained in the previous chapter, the BECC[35] is a binational, autonomous organization that supports environmental-infrastructure projects related to water, waste water, and management of solid waste. It certifies projects which it then recommends to its sister organization, NADBank, for loans and loan guarantees. It is remarkable that, their mandate notwithstanding, these bilateral institutions did not reduce prevailing high levels of Mexico-US asymmetry. Even though their governance is run on the basis of parity, the BECC and NADBank have demonstrated asymmetry in their approval and allocation of funds.

Of the twenty-seven projects that had *not* been approved by 2003, twenty were Mexican. And, of the projects that were approved, over forty-one were built in the United States and only twenty-nine in Mexico. Considering that Mexican communities have minimal access to the capital market for loans and state grants compared with their US counterparts, the asymmetry is more drastic than these figures make it appear.[36] By March 2005, over eighty-five projects were completed under the BECC and another thirteen were under design. Although 50 per cent of the funding comes from each party, of the first US$1,287 billion in project value that was approved, only $496 million was used for projects in Mexico, compared to $792 million for projects in the United States.[37] This discrepancy in project financing derives in part from Mexico lacking the human and financial capability to deal with the long, complex process involved in securing a BECC/NAD-Bank loan. A further problem with those loans that are granted relates to their being used to buy US technology which does not necessarily suit Mexican needs.

Cross-border networks linking academic institutions, volunteer organizations, and government agencies have worked to share knowledge and to overcome sectoral and jurisdictional boundaries, although both federal governments actually cut back their funding for border programs. These instances of cross-border cooperation took place in the context of the administrative decentralization that accompanied Mexico's neoconservative transition. But offloading such new responsibilities as water and sanitation services without providing the necessary financial resources left beleaguered local authorities unable to cope. Their financial straits worsened every time that Mexico City granted local water concessions to big investors as an incentive to establish job-creating maquiladoras, commercial developments, or tourist centres. The resulting spread of municipal water-service privatization generated a strong reaction from various NGOs, which protested against the ensuing higher prices and demanded that water be retained within the public domain. As pointed out by one of these NGOs – Movimiento Urbano Popular – the spreading dominion of both domestic and transnational water companies threatened the public's access to this vital resource. It proposed making access to water an entrenched constitutional right.[38] (At the same time, some analysts argue that higher prices are necessary as incentives for better consumption patterns.)

While still the most important binational agency in the area of trans-boundary water management, the IBWC has nevertheless had little influence over the new agenda for decentralized environmental protection in the border area. The changed political context demanding a more intense focus on water-quality issues and procedural transparency has forced the IBWC to reassess its mandate and to use the 1944 treaty's minute process to establish binational technical groups, but its diplomatic culture of secrecy has been criticized by public forums organized by local citizens groups and agencies.[39]

At the local level, new transborder water-governance strategies were pioneered. The San Diego Association of Governments' Committee on Binational Regional Opportunities (COBRO) convened a Border Water Council in 1998 to facilitate cooperation on the distribution of raw and finished water, the provision of potable water, and the achievement of cross-border water-infrastructure improvements.[40] Though the council had no planning or regulatory authority, it was considered a valuable forum in which regional perspectives on water-supply issues might be explored and elevated to the federal level where binational policy is made.

Supplementing governmental efforts to adopt more regional approaches to water-management issues, universities on both sides of the border have combined their efforts to advance the scientific study of the Tijuana River basin's ecology. In 1994 the San Diego State University and the Colegio de la Frontera Norte coordinated the development of a watershed Geographic Information System to integrate binational multimedia ecological and socio-demographic data. The universities' watershed-based approach was a major departure from the long-standing governmental approaches which have tended to use political jurisdictions or agency mandates as sources of authority for water-management activities. The watershed approach is gradually being embraced throughout the United States, and funding has been made available through various sections of the Clean Water Act.[41]

For its part, Mexico has been working on its commitment to reform its water-management institutions along watershed boundary lines ever since it adopted the international water-use principles advocated at the UN Conference on Environment and Development in Rio in 1992, but debates continue about whether jurisdictional boundaries should not be retained for planning and policy purposes. Today, river basin councils (consejos de cuenca) operate in thirteen separate regions and assist CONAGUA in developing water projects and managing water use with the input of local water stakeholders. CONAGUA proposes to decentralize more of its water-management responsibilities to the local level and claims to be developing local capacity to ensure a successful transition. Unfortunately, there is a serious coordination problem in Mexican institutions: the Ministry of the Environment, which is responsible for aquifer management, cannot control the autonomous CONAGUA, which issues new licences for groundwater extraction.[42] Notwithstanding pressure from such transnational actors as the OECD, Mexico's national institutions have done little to implement ecosystem management or establish indicators to evaluate what actions have been taken.

At one level, the institutional reform of transboundary water management in the US-Mexico borderlands seems to be trending towards more integrated binational management practices. Analysts of US-Mexico transboundary water politics judge that liaison mechanisms like COBRO have facilitated collaborative and binational regional solutions to shared water-resource challenges that would have been thought impossible only a few years ago. However, it seems unlikely that something as integrated as a binational watershed council will be created.

Despite these promising prospects based on good-faith cooperation between the federal governments, transborder water governance in the Tijuana River basin has been blighted by US unilateralism at the border-region level. A 2003 agreement between the San Diego County Water Authority and the Imperial Valley Irrigation District to transfer water along a newly paved All-America Canal will have a severe impact on the environment and the agricultural economy in the Colorado River basin. Although seepage over the decades from the canal, which runs just inside American territory along the Mexican border, has been a significant source of replenishment for the Mexicali aquifer, the San Diego-Imperial agreement was made without studying its environmental implications for Mexico – which are expected to be a 20–30 per cent decline in agricultural production.[43] Already in February 2006, some farmers were forced to sell some 20,000 of their livestock at prices well below their value, a phenomenon that was repeated all along the boundary.[44]

Conclusion

The contrast between the recent evolution of the Great Lakes' and the Tijuana River basins' governance regimes reveals several interesting parallels. The ongoing paradigm shift from an engineering attitude to water management caused fundamental transformations within the domestic politics of the continent's three countries. Despite the distinct institutional, political, and cultural characteristics that mark the use of North America's various water basins, a new common approach reflects recent developments in scientific knowledge of ecosystems and an aroused public's concerns for environmental health, water quality, and habitat. Resource management has shifted from sectoral and compartmentalized decision making towards a holistic, more integrated search for balance between the priorities of economic growth and a healthy environment.

The conventional diplomatic means by which transboundary water quality/quantity issues were addressed in government structures designed to protect sovereign interests proved inadequate for managing the enormously complex problems of restoring ecosystems. Subfederal challenges to the existing diplomatic framework by organizations that introduced innovative transboundary water-governance arrangements reduced but did not replace the federal governments' influence over transboundary water-management decision making. Federal agencies and commissions still continue to provide important leadership in formulating, facilitating, and financing transboundary water-management policy, but top-down policy making has been supplanted. The devolution of environmental-protection responsibilities to the state/provincial and municipal levels acknowledges the local nature of transboundary environmental problems and the need to temper the defence of national interests with cooperative information gathering and binational policy making.

Greater participation by local governments in transboundary water governance is subtly changing inter-governmental power dynamics. On the one hand, it is widely believed that policy networks that incorporate agencies and actors with relevant decision-making ability reduce the chance that different orders of government will adopt conflicting strategies. On the other, empowering local levels of government can lead to more conflict when higher levels provoke overuse or insist they have ultimate control over resources without actually monitoring and enforcing their regulations.[45]

Related to the changing role of the federal vis-à-vis other levels of government, non-state actors have featured more prominently in policy-specific decision-making networks in which public officials collaborate, learn, and are challenged by varying viewpoints on specific policy options. In the case of transboundary water governance, scientists, academics, and environmental non-profit organizations supplement government agencies by providing independent research, initiating citizen-education programs, and generating a higher level of accountability and transparency in the formulation and implementation of government policy. Cross-border networks formed around a single issue area can work unconstrained by jurisdictional or partisan priorities as depoliticized forums for independent information gathering. Governments are often members of these networks but do not necessarily dominate the process or determine its outcome. Though the decision process is lengthened by the addition of a larger range of civil-society stakeholders, it is thought to result in greater acceptance of collaboratively generated management plans and, as a consequence, greater compliance with measures once enacted.

In sum, the gradual paradigm shift towards resource-sustainable development is displacing the state-centric approach to transboundary water governance with a multilayered, sometimes binational governance framework in which the strategic interests of the territorially defined federal state are being reformulated to accommodate cross-border, regionally defined needs and goals.[46] In this sense, the case of the Great Lakes water-management regime supports the argument that progress is being made towards transboundary water governance based on common interests. However, the unilateral action taken within the state of California respecting the paving of the All-America Canal shows how rhetorical endorsements of ecosystem-based approaches to policy regimes are meaningless in the face of the gross asymmetry in power between the strong nation and the weak one.

Water management today must be viewed in the context of general changes to territorial organization in the era of globalization, when frontiers have grown into regions that present enormous opportunities for resource development, production, and urban growth. Innovations in communication technology have made international borders more porous and regional economies more interdependent. In this political-economic context, hierarchical federal governments' command-and-control structures lose their effectiveness as socio-economic patterns of interaction and consensus building come to depend on negotiated agreement among regional stakeholders. Though the three federal governments of North America retain responsibility for transboundary resources, their role and activity have changed dramatically since continental economic integration began strengthening socio-economic linkages connecting non-state actors in border regions.

By comparing the evolution of the Great Lakes and the Tijuana River systems, we can witness the effects of deeper continental economic integration on transboundary water governance. The paradigmatic shift towards liberal trade changed the function of North America's border zones and consequently the nature of relations between the continent's governments. Cooperation, binational planning, and meaningful public participation in the Tijuana River basin during a phase of intense binational socio-economic integration appeared to underscore the benefits of such integration, although the paving of the All-America Canal did not. In the Great Lakes, the gradual disintegration of binational governance during the same period suggests that cooperative transboundary resource management is driven as much by socio-economic factors as by political leaders' and policy makers' ability to commit to a process of binational decision making for the shared resource.

Reframing the analysis more graphically, the old transborder governance model featured vertical power relations driven from above within each state and supplemented by horizontal, federal-state-to-federal-state relations institutionalized through binational treaties. Two more complex models have emerged in which government-from-above sustained by federal financial muscle has been shoved aside by a proliferation of governance-from-below pressures involving experts and diverse non-state stakeholders. In the Tijuana basin, horizontal links, which had developed and been maintained at the federal level through NAFTA's enabling specialized institutions, have been unable to prevent local unilateralism from undoing years of gradual progress. The Great Lakes ecosystem shows a different, but also contradictory, mix of increased horizontal linkages among non-state actors coupled with a disengagement of the two federal governments from the border-region's governance that almost allowed a ruinous unilateral US-states-driven regime to come into effect.

The harmonization of water-quality standards may offset power asymmetries because water levels and water pollution are experienced equally by riparians, whichever national flag they may salute. When Canada inadvertently showed its capacity to damage US interests by withdrawing water in bulk from the Great Lakes, interested Americans felt an urgent need to find a cooperative solution to water diversion. A compromise that reflected a more symmetrical power relationship was achieved. To the extent that environmental degradation in Mexico threatens the quality of American life north of the border and arouses civil society there, the two countries' interdependence raises Mexico's bargaining power. But on questions of water quality and quantity, with Mexico unable to deliver more water to the United States than it receives and unable to do more damage to its neighbour than it suffers itself, this hydrological asymmetry perpetuates the basic political asymmetry between the two countries. This asymmetry was only nominally offset by NAFTA's bilateral institutions, which have in practice failed to remediate Mexico's debilitating financial incapacity.

The institutionalization of cooperation through transboundary water-management integration may be the most promising means by which to moderate the unilateral exercise of superior power, whether by the US government, by border states, or by such other actors as agro-industry and urban water corporations. However, the Bush administration's refusal to intervene in North Dakota's unilateral decision to divert Devil's Lake's waters into the Lake Winnipeg ecosystem (it would not agree to refer the issue to the IJC) confirmed its increasing disregard for the Boundary Waters Treaty in particular and its unilateral attitude towards its international commitments in general. The All-American Canal's paving reminds Mexicans of the same problem in the sense that unilateral subfederal action by American states can contravene the spirit and practice of a century's worth of water-management cooperation along the two US borders.

This present disaster-in-the-making in the Colorado/Tijuana basin underlines how weakly institutionalized is North American governance in the border regions. Not only did NAFTA fail to remedy this situation, it did not help reduce the disparity between the two bilateral relationships. To the south, the local manifestation of overwhelming power superiority in California set back the cause of more equitable binational water governance, perhaps irremediably. To the north, a federally led trend to disintegration in border-waters governance was overcome by enhanced, asymmetry-offsetting subfederal cooperation. Since September 2001, when migration and security issues have dominated the binational agenda for the two international borders, the federal governments have been notably uninterested in giving priority to environmental concerns.

Border-region cooperation also gives voice to civil-society actors and raises the hope that transboundary water-resource security can be achieved for future generations. Tangible progress towards this goal on the US-Mexico border has been less than had been hoped when NAFTA's environmental institutions were established. While NAFTA's asymmetry-offsetting institutions were generally less than met the eye, they proved to be an optical illusion in the Tijuana basin, where NAD-Bank actually provided less funding for border projects in Mexico than in California. Because they have no established governance institutions of their own, both water basins' transborder governance remains highly vulnerable to future shifts in domestic politics.

It is now time to leave behind the consideration of overt structures of North American governance in order to examine, in the three chapters of Part Two, some of the many forms of transborder governance that characterize specific sectors of the continent's economy.

PART TWO

More Than Meets the Eye:

Market Reconfiguration at the
Continental Level

As we have just seen in Part One, the world region created by NAFTA hardly demonstrates much institutional substance, because its formal instruments of continental government and governance are so ineffectual. But to say that NAFTA produced weak structures – whether intentionally or not – is not to say that North America has no transborder governance, if the notion is understood as those interactions among various government, business, and civil-society actors which steer the continent's political, economic, and social systems towards collective goals and decisions. Since the North American economy's US$6.3 trillion in estimated annual product demonstrates high degrees of economic interdependence and social interactions, the apparent contra-diction between inadequate institutions and a powerfully integrating market raises the possibility that, to have focused on new continental political processes in Part One was – if not misguided – at the very least inadequate.

Rather than parsing official NAFTA documents or international treaties that committed the signatory governments to create formal structures, the search for North America's essence may be more fruitful if we look at real-world economic systems in order to determine how the market's many sectors are managed. To do this, I take my cue from the marketplace itself by investigating in the first chapter of Part Two the role that big business played in negotiating CUFTA and NAFTA. The two other chapters in this section begin the process of examining transborder governance in the context of specific economic sectors by focusing on energy and agriculture. That approach continues in Parts Three and Four with an analysis of other economic sectors.

Clearly, all economic sectors involve government in the sense that international, federal, subfederal, and municipal statutes and regulations play a role in directing entrepreneurial decisions. But, just as clearly, businesses are involved in pressuring government to produce the regulatory framework they want so they can prosper, whether at home or abroad. The resulting interactions between corporate soliciting and government responses constitute the more nebulous – but sometimes more consequential – domain that I label 'transborder governance.'

VII   The Role of Big Business in Negotiating Free Trade

To introduce the subject of transborder governance, whose workings in a variety of economic sectors I explore in Parts Two and Three, this chapter addresses the general issue of how business-government interactions occur at the level of national economic policy making. A case in point is the negotiation of the Canada-US Free Trade Agreement and the North American Free Trade Agreement – the framework that re-constitutionalized the three countries' economic interrelationships.

The analysis highlights how transborder governance was both a consequence of earlier and a cause of further North American integration. Indeed, the contemporary dynamics of transborder governance in North America have not only evolved from traditional inter-governmental relations but have actually reshaped them. Trends creating a continental market have expanded corporations' role from determining their countries' national policy agendas to participating directly in continental rule making – in this chapter's case, the negotiation of two significant deep-integration agreements. (In Part Five, I examine how the corporate community interacted with their governments some years later in another effort to mould national policy during the three countries' response to the border-security crisis resulting from the September 11, 2001 terrorist attacks in New York and Washington.)

It is well established that American transnational corporations play a direct and decisive role in shaping US foreign economic policy – whether multilaterally in global institutions or bilaterally when dealing with individual countries. Washington's consultative structures require that the voice of business be heard clearly by US trade negotiators, and the famous business-government revolving door ensures that the senior ranks of US officialdom are recruited from the senior ranks of big corporations. Here, I focus on the part that corporate lobby groups play in the periphery. First I report on Canadian business' role in creating the bilateral Canada-US Free Trade Agreement. Then I look at how business organizations in Mexico helped produce its trilateral successor, the North American Free Trade Agreement. As we will see, the initiation of the CUFTA and then the NAFTA negotiations as well as their implementation are not fully comprehensible without understanding the private sector's central role in these three stages.

The talks leading to CUFTA and NAFTA were extraordinary events which brought together political and economic actors – while marginalizing protesting civil-society groups – to establish new norms governing trade and investment first for the old North America, then for the new one created by the inclusion of Mexico. In the process, they revealed North American governance in action.

The Corporate Sector in Canada and Mexico

When examining North America's non-structured governance, it becomes evident that, of all non-state actors, corporations play the dominant role through business associations that exercise power both internally and externally.[1] Internally, these organizations are involved in providing such services to members as collecting and disseminating crucial information (management services) and establishing regulations for members (setting product standards and codes for self-regulation). In these ways, associations exert internal *government* power over members directly inside their own sectors. Externally, business associations engage in government relations, which enable their members to influence public policy. In their external *governance* activities, associations representing the interests of their members monitor events in the corridors of government and disseminate information about government programs to members. These groups can be involved in lobbying domestic, and sometimes foreign, governments to influence public policy.

For the purposes of this chapter, lobbying includes any activity or strategy aimed at influencing government decisions either directly (arranging meetings with ministers or bureaucrats, submitting briefs to royal commissions or congressional committees) or indirectly (mobilizing interests through communications technologies, advertising in the media to stimulate public awareness, or funding think tanks). More exceptionally for Canada and Mexico, if not for the United States, business associations are sometimes called upon to participate directly in the actual formulation of a country's economic and trade policies. This was the case for both CUFTA and NAFTA.

Because an actor's power is related to its economic strength or strategic position within a political system and because big business commands a disproportionate amount of resources and enjoys a credible reputation for expertise in its sector of the economy, this chapter concentrates on big business associations' role in the trade-liberalization negotiations.[2] Civil-society groups were excluded from the two actual trade-negotiation processes although they were much more visible and vocal in the partisan debates following the agreements' signature and preceding their implementation.

For much of the post-Second World War era, Canadian and Mexican economic-development strategies were based on the logic of import-substitution industrialization (ISI) – a strategy that sought to encourage the development of domestic industries through trade and investment protection. By the early 1980s, however, import substitution had become unpopular for both political and economic reasons. Politically, a dramatic decline in the world price for oil in 1982 placed significant budgetary constraints on the Canadian and Mexican governments, foreclosing the possibility of continuing such controversially interventionist policies as Pierre Elliott Trudeau's National Energy Program and López Portillo's bank nationalization.[3] Economically, the global economic slowdown of 1981–2, which was the most severe since the Great Depression of the 1930s, and the increase in global competition that resulted from GATT-related tariff reductions forced corporations to restructure both their internal and external operations.[4]

In their efforts to reduce costs and increase the efficiency of production, North American TNCs began large-scale downsizing, which involved the removal of middle layers of management from corporate headquarters. In addition, increased global competition in an era of severe economic crisis forced firms to abandon the low-output, high-cost branch-plant operations that were sheltered behind high Mexican and Canadian tariffs. Instead of operating these miniature replicas of their parent firms' large-scale operations, North American TNCs began reducing production costs by implementing two key changes in strategy and structure. They integrated their subsidiaries into more or less coherent systems of regional production and rationalized their productive capacity and workforces.[5] Within this general framework, new methods of production management, including 'lean production' and 'flexible manufacturing,' which relied on intra-firm trade and 'just-in-time' inventory systems, further integrated the three formerly protected, geographically contiguous, and culturally converging markets.[6]

Though systematic quantitative analysis of corporate restructuring cannot be documented owing to the governments' inadequate production of statistics, changes in the cross-border stocks of FDI among NAFTA partners in the 1980s support the qualitative evidence of structural change within transnational capital. Between 1981 and 1990, stocks of Canadian direct investment in the United States grew by an annual average of over 12 per cent per year, and nearly doubled between 1981 and 1985, the year the Canadian government decided to request trade negotiations with the United States. Similarly, though much smaller in absolute terms, the stock of Mexican FDI in the United States increased sevenfold between 1981 and 1989.[7]

The political significance of these changed investment patterns was profound. In conjunction with the well-documented intra-firm, trade-creating effects of FDI,[8] increases in intraregional FDI were responsible for shifting Canadian and Mexican business preferences towards economic liberalization. A chicken-and-egg process ensued. First, investors – mostly from the United States and increasingly from Canada – sought more business-friendly, lower-wage environments in which to outsource their labour-intensive operations without fear of nationalization. For its part, Mexico was desperately seeking incoming FDI which it hoped would increase employment and productivity. Already high levels of economic integration had revealed a number of regulatory incongruities, a situation that led firms and their industry associations to lobby governments for a harmonization which could 'secure access' to a larger market (desired by Canadian firms), increase 'competitiveness' by realizing economies of scale (expected by Canadian and US firms), control inflation (wanted by Mexican firms), and decrease other transaction costs (needed by all companies).

The negotiation of CUFTA and NAFTA surprised many analysts because it contradicted both peripheral countries' long-standing traditions of state activism, trade protection, and public fears about and hostility towards US domination. When, during his 1980 presidential campaign, Ronald Reagan proposed a 'North American accord' in response to heightened American economic insecurity amidst the oil shocks of the time, ballooning balance of payments deficits, slumping productivity growth rates, and the rise of the highly competitive German and Japanese economies, Canada and Mexico had rejected the idea.[9] Since such powerful economic interests as the Canadian Manufacturers' Association (CMA) in Canada and the Cámara Nacional de la Industria de Transformación (CANCINTRA, National Industrial Chamber) in Mexico were fearful of US competition, benefited from state protection, and opposed free trade, Canadian and Mexican political elites opted for the status quo.[10] Brian Mulroney, for example, had opposed the free-trade idea in his successful 1983 campaign to become leader of the Progressive Conservative Party, and, once elected prime minister, several of his key cabinet ministers (notably James Kelleher, minister for international trade, and Joe Clark, minister for foreign affairs) were publicly cautious about the idea. Similarly, newly elected Mexican President Carlos Salinas de Gortari had declared in 1988 that a NAFTA-style arrangement was 'not feasible' because it was contrary to Mexico's short- and medium-term interests.

That the idea of free trade came to dominate the Canadian and Mexican political agendas a few years later was the result of the respective business communities' structural and strategic pressure on government. Without the reversal of business's historic position – especially that of the CMA – on the issue of free trade, CUFTA would not have happened. The Tory government faced a vigorous lobbying effort from Canadian business organizations for a comprehensive free-trade arrangement.[11] Similarly, support for NAFTA originated in the Mexican private sector, so that various business-government free-trade coalitions played an essential part in Mexico's paradigm shift.[12] A close look at the lobbying behaviour of specific business groups and at the actual timing of the decision to negotiate free trade sheds much light on the heterarchical nature of North American governance and on whether the state led or followed during the pre-negotiation phase. To be sure, the market reforms embodied in CUFTA and NAFTA marked historic turning points in the evolution of business-government relations in Canada (which had been largely antagonistic under Liberal Party Keynesians) and Mexico (which, under the PRI, can be described as corporatist, government-dominant, and business-subservient). Change began in both countries in the mid-1980s when business-government relations converged towards the neoconservative model.[13]

The Role of Business Groups in Setting the Free-Trade Agenda

As business preferences began to shift in the mid-1980s amidst changing economic conditions, certain factions within the Canadian and

Mexican business communities provided the governments of Brian Mulroney in Canada and Carlos Salinas de Gortari in Mexico – both receptive to neoconservative notions of laissez-faire – with decisive political support. Exemplifying North American transborder governance, business interests forged a consensus domestically and engaged in lobbying binationally in order to implement a series of economic reforms designed to restructure their national economies through continental market integration.

In Canada, the Business Council on National Issues (BCNI) is widely acknowledged to have been the key political actor that placed the free-trade initiative on the political agenda and drove it to fruition.[14] Indeed, the BCNI took the lead during the first stage of the pre-negotiation process by identifying Canada's economically urgent challenges as 'contingent protectionism' (US anti-dumping and countervailing duties) and its consequent lack of 'secure access' to the US market.[15] In the words of the BCNI president and chief executive, Thomas D'Aquino: 'When we first floated the idea [of a free trade agreement with the United States] early in the decade, no government in Canada favoured outright free trade and there was intense scepticism even in parts of the business community. Massive amounts of homework, extensive consultations, and six years of advocacy helped to deliver a wide-ranging deal with our most important trading partner.'[16]

As a powerful business lobby composed of the chief executive officers of some 150 of Canada's largest – mostly US transnational – firms, the BCNI played the important roles of forging consensus within the domestic Canadian business community concerning the benefits of free trade, persuading the Canadian government and population that a comprehensive free-trade deal with the United States was necessary, and even generating interest among US political and economic elites.[17] In 1983, for example, BCNI members met with US Vice-President George Bush, who 'seemed almost stunned' by their free-trade proposal. Later, they persuaded a 'distinctly uninterested' US Business Roundtable to lobby the US government for a deal.[18] At home, the BCNI had played an instrumental role in forging consensus within the Canadian business community by pitching slogans of increased 'competitiveness' through free trade to other business groups – notably the CMA. Finally, in what has been called the 'biggest public relations campaign in Canadian corporate history,'[19] the BCNI persuaded its members to contribute enormous amounts of resources to the Canadian Alliance for Trade and Job Opportunities for a massive third-party advertising campaign during the 1988 federal election campaign.[20] The BCNI was thus engaged in both domestic and transborder governance activities.

Although the CMA's support for free trade had lagged behind that of D'Aquino's group,[21] it was more decisive in helping to construct a business-government free-trade coalition. Indeed, the Canadian government did not formally announce its intention to negotiate with the United States until after the CMA came out in support of a free-trade deal in 1984[22] and after the Macdonald Commission, whose report adopted the big business (but not the more negative medium- and small-business) position,[23] formally endorsed the free-trade option with the publication of its report in 1985. The CMA's reversal was significant because its membership included the rank and file of the Canadian business community and not just major transnational firms. This deepened support leant legitimacy to the initiative.[24]

Given that the CMA had been created in 1911 specifically to militate against free trade and for measures that would protect Canadian industry,[25] its volte-face in favour of an economic-integration deal was dramatic. As late as 1984, a survey found that only one-third of its members thought that a free-trade agreement with the United States would benefit them, yet the association's executive came out in support of the idea anyway.[26] During the course of the 1970s and 1980s, the proportion of CMA members involved in export had risen from 15 to 40 per cent.[27] The fact that the CMA eventually abandoned import substitution as a means to increase Canadian manufacturing competitiveness, even if a majority of its members did not stand to benefit directly from the deal, demonstrated the consensus-forming role played by the BCNI and the persuasive power of the 'strength through integration'[28] argument articulated by the pro-free-trade forces. By the time the CMA climbed aboard the free-trade bandwagon, the BCNI had already done much of the groundwork, thus preparing the way for Prime Minister Mulroney's announcement on September 26, 1985 that he intended to negotiate with Washington.[29]

If the role of the BCNI in setting Canada on the path to free trade is clear, understanding the role of the Mexican private sector is more complicated, if only because the Mexican political system is less transparent than Canada's. Indeed, most explanations of Mexico's economic liberalization in the 1980s downplay the role of business.[30] Where the private sector is acknowledged to have played a role, most would credit the US Business Roundtable as instrumental in promoting NAFTA in

Mexico.[31] In contrast to its secondary role during the CUFTA process, and much like the BCNI visit to Bush in 1983, the Roundtable took the initiative, visiting Mexico in 1989 to drum up support for continental free trade. By that time, when the European Union had already re-buffed his advances, it was not difficult to convince President Salinas de Gortari, a Harvard PhD, of the desirability of a US-Mexico eco-nomic-integration agreement. In line with Salinas's personal belief in the need to cut back the Mexican government's sweeping controls over the economy, the US-Mexico Business Committee started to promote trade liberalization by providing much of the intellectual rationale for an agreement.

In addition to American business's role in leading Mexico's govern-ment towards free trade, activism within its business community was also significant. Despite US protectionism and pressure from the United States on Mexico to eliminate its export subsidies, Mexican manufac-tured exports rose in the 1980s, surpassing oil.[32] The period beginning in the late 1980s initiated a transformative economic opening triggered by Mexico's accession to GATT in 1986.[33] Indeed, initial support for the economy's 'apertura' had begun by 1985, as certain potentially compet-itive national and transnational firms realized that liberalization could help reduce their input costs and improve their competitiveness.[34] As a result of the reforms required by accession to GATT, export-oriented firms prospered, while smaller firms serving the domestic market started to decline.[35]

Beyond demanding more economic liberalization, Mexican big busi-ness lobbied against populist policies that hurt their interests. The much despised bank-nationalization program in 1982 had motivated the Mex-ican business community to exert more influence on public policy, par-ticularly through its Consejo Coordinador Empresarial (CCE, Business Coordinating Council), an umbrella group.[36] The Mexican private sec-tor's double transformation had begun: medium and small business interests were marginalized in favour of the corporate community's upper echelon, which sought greater flexibility in rationalizing its oper-ations. It was willing to exchange reduced protection against import competition for US business's demand: more favourable conditions for incoming foreign investment.

Politically, the Mexican equivalent to the BCNI was the Consejo Mex-icano de Hombres de Negocios (Mexican Council of Businessmen), a powerful member of the CCE. Beginning with President de la Madrid and continuing with Salinas, the CMHN met regularly with the presidency, lobbying hard for economic reforms. The announcement in early 1990 that Mexico would pursue a free-trade agreement with the United States[37] reflected a fundamental shift in the PRI's political base towards an explicit, largely exclusive alliance with the most elite segments of big business.[38] Accordingly, when Salinas travelled to the United States and Canada in April 1991 to promote NAFTA, he brought with him eight members of the CMHN.[39] As was the case in Canada, Mexico's pro-free trade business interests were not just instrumental in forming a business-government coalition in favour of free trade; they were directly included in the subsequent decision-making process.

Negotiating CUFTA and NAFTA

Once business had placed the free-trade initiative on the agenda and the respective decisions were made in both Canada and Mexico to negotiate CUFTA and NAFTA, the two periphery governments set up similar institutional structures linking corporate interests to governmental officialdom in order to facilitate the latter's negotiations. A system of trade-advisory groups provided mechanisms through which business could be involved in creating new rules to govern the North American economic space. No longer lobbying from outside the formal mechanisms of the state and so participating in *governance*, these selected business representatives were acting from the inside as part of the policy-making process – if only for a time-limited agenda – within the actual negotiating structure set up by their governments.

This consultative machinery was first developed in the United States. Growing out of the 1974 Trade Act, which gave the US executive the authority to conduct commercial negotiations, spelled out congressional procedures for implementing trade agreements into US law, and established the advisory committees designed to integrate the private sector directly into the decision-making process,[40] the consultative machinery consisted of a presidentially appointed Advisory Committee on Trade Negotiations presiding over twenty-seven Industry Sector Advisory Committees.[41] At a general level, these advisory groups played three important roles.[42] They provided negotiators with industry-specific requests for changes in international rules, information regarding potential effects of alternative deals, and advice to Congress on whether the final outcomes were in the broad national interest. The groups also acted as buffer-and-control mechanisms to channel and contain domestic pressures by helping to manage public opinion.

Finally, they bolstered the negotiations' legitimacy in the corporate world by creating an avenue through which business constituents could articulate their needs.[43] In performing these functions, the trade-advisory groups proved to be indispensable structures within the US government that served as models for Canada and Mexico.

Canada's consultative machinery used for negotiating CUFTA (1986–7) was a product of its experience during the Tokyo Round of GATT negotiations, when business had felt that the broad-based consultations set up through the International Trade Advisory Committee had blurred industry-specific concerns.[44] For the CUFTA negotiations, Ottawa proceeded to adopt a two-tier structure modelled directly on the American system.[45] While the thirty-eight-member ITAC continued to provide the minister of international trade with business's general view on the conduct of the negotiations, fifteen Sectoral Advisory Groups on International Trade (SAGITs) provided negotiators with advice specific to each industry.[46] This design allowed the Canadian advisory groups to fill three main functions. The formal and non-partisan business support embodied in the ITAC helped foster free trade's legitimacy in the Canadian business community. The SAGITs generated the required information that allowed negotiators to assess the potential implications of alternative negotiation outcomes. And, together, ITAC and the SAGITs acted as a buffer against particularly vulnerable sectors' pleas for special treatment.

The broader representation of business in the SAGITs made conflicts inevitable, both among and within the various advisory groups. Despite a common public front, conflicts occurred between SAGITs representing different interests (auto parts versus services) and within SAGITs representing internally conflicting needs (food producers and food processors in different regions).[47] These conflicts were muffled by Ottawa's controlling role in appointing and financing the advisory groups, as well as by the closed-door consultations, which ensured secrecy and facilitated government control of the process.[48] Overall, the Canadian advisory groups' two-tier structure successfully balanced the need to represent the various, often conflicting, factions of Canadian business and the need to achieve a consensus.

While Canadian business interests were broadly represented in the trade-advisory groups, the same cannot be said of other important stakeholders. Organized labour leaders' hostility to the very idea of trade liberalization conditioned their fear of being co-opted by a process in which their voice would have been drowned out. The Canadian Labour Congress refused the one place it was offered in the SAGIT structure, so the labour movement was almost completely absent from the process. The one exception was the Canadian Federation of Labour, a dissident union in the construction industry that had broken away from the CLC; it participated initially. This ensured that the trade-advisory groups would be a consultative mechanism giving voice almost exclusively to business.[49]

The provinces' involvement in the negotiation process fell somewhere between the complete exclusion of civil society and the direct participation of business. The earliest GATT negotiations had focused on tariffs, which were the responsibility of the federal government alone. As the GATT agenda expanded to touch on areas of domestic policy, Ottawa recognized the need to bring the provinces into these negotiations to monitor the constitutionality of any commitments it made and ensure their implementation. In several cases, the federal government also came to rely on its provincial counterparts for expertise and information on specific economic sectors.

In 1977 a Canadian Coordinator for Trade Negotiations (CCTN) had been appointed with the mandate to gather relevant information from the provinces, the federal bureaucracy, industry, and NGOs. During the CUFTA negotiations, Ottawa and the provinces agreed that the CCTN would remain their main forum of consultation. Issues such as the Auto Pact, energy, culture, and agriculture had received a great deal of attention in earlier federal-provincial consultations, but, as the CUFTA negotiations proceeded, the provinces complained that they were being kept at arms' length. Ultimately they were shut out from the final, decisive phase of the negotiations, as had been the provinces' own structures of interest-group consultation.[50]

Business participation in the CUFTA negotiations provided the government's trade initiative with a consultative mechanism and partial legitimacy, but, in the absence of formal power to tender public advice or opinion (as in the US system), the influence of particular businesses on negotiation outcomes through this process was limited. Indeed, according to some observers, the CMA and the BCNI exerted much more influence outside the government's institutions during the trade negotiations than other groups within them by shoring up their alliance with US business counterparts at strategic moments when their respective governments appeared to have 'dropped the ball.'[51] In effect, business provided the bilateral process with legitimacy by manifesting general support and articulating its views on specific dossiers under negotiation.

Unlike the Canadian case, the Mexicans had no prior experience with incorporating business into international economic negotiations, although a trend to increasing certain business groups' participation (especially those not wedded to state protection) in policy making had begun in the 1980s.[52] When asked by the Mexican equivalent of Ottawa's Trade Negotiation Office, the Secretaría de Comercio y Formento Industrial (SECOFI, Secretariat for Commerce and Development) to prepare assessments of the impact of a potential agreement on the different sectors of the Mexican economy, the CCE created the Coordinación de Organismos Empresariales de Comercio Exterior (COECE, Coordinator for Foreign Trade and Business Organizations) in 1990.[53] As Mexico's first trade-advisory group, COECE's primary purpose was to present a single position to the Mexican negotiating team.[54] To achieve this unity, it adopted a horizontal structure[55] patterned after the Canadian ITAC. It struck some twenty working groups that corresponded to the subject areas covered by the negotiations (market access, rules of origin, textiles and clothing, and so on), which paralleled the structure of the Mexican negotiating team. Although COECE's executive director affirmed, 'We copied it from the Canadians!'[56] closer analysis reveals that the Canadian and Mexican consultative machinery differed substantially in terms of their structure, functions, relationship with government, and impact on outcomes.

In contrast to Canada's two-tier structure, COECE mirrored the Canadian ITAC but without the SAGIT components. The Mexican government apparently thought it more important for COECE to develop a single view from the business community's disparate and conflicting interests than receive the expression of divergent sectoral concerns. Indeed, COECE's single-tier structure ensured that, notwithstanding the working groups' broad, horizontal representation, the concerns of small- and medium-sized enterprises (SMEs) would be ignored.

Despite their enormous importance for job creation and the special needs they have in government policy, the SMEs in the trade-advisory groups were clustered together with large firms and treated as members of separate industry groups, for example, textiles, apparel, or furniture. In this institutional framework, SMEs and large firms were assumed to have similar needs because both were dependent on the characteristics of the particular economic sector to which they belonged.

By over-representing large firms and minimizing the SMEs' influence within COECE, the Mexican government avoided internal conflict in its negotiation process. Moreover, the self-appointed, privately funded nature of COECE contrasted sharply with the Canadians' government-appointed and funded system and served further to exclude SMEs from the negotiation process because they simply could not assign full-time staff to the negotiations and could not afford the high costs of hiring private consulting firms to produce the sectoral studies that COECE required in the preparatory phase.[57]

Paradoxically, while COECE was meant to create a united business front, its exclusion of broad economic strata had the unintended consequence of fomenting conflict among different business sectors, between small and large firms, and between certain sectors and the government.[58] Little opposition was voiced at the time, because the still-authoritarian government would tolerate no opposition[59] and because most of the relevant information was closely held at the summit of Mexico's corporate community.[60] In the absence of perfect information regarding the free-trade deal's projected effects on different sectors of the Mexican economy, leaders of Mexican SMEs embraced the official discourse linking free trade with macro-economic stabilization and so supported NAFTA, although – as their subsequent suffering showed – it was objectively against their interests to do so.

If COECE was much less representative than the Canadian advisory groups, it was also substantially more decisive in influencing government negotiation positions and eventual outcomes. There is broad consensus within Mexico that 'the participation of the private sector in the NAFTA negotiations was extensive, intensive, and effective.'[61] COECE's representatives participated actively and directly in the formulation and revision of Mexico's negotiating positions.[62] In addition to meeting with negotiators in Mexico City after every negotiation round, Mexican private-sector representatives travelled with the government's team, reserved hotel rooms close by, met with them at the beginning and end of each day's negotiations, and made themselves available during the talks in the so-called *cuarto de junto* (room next door).[63] Although COECE did not have the research capability of the Canadian ITAC or SAGITs to define private-sector positions,[64] its representatives maintained a continuous presence in the negotiations and had *immediate* access to members of the SECOFI team, who worked enthusiastically with their private-sector partners. In sum, whereas the two-tier, publicly funded and appointed Canadian advisory groups were more representative of Canadian business interests and provided greater legitimacy, the horizontal, privately appointed, and self-financed Mexican advisory groups were more influential and provided a stronger political buffer against opposition from the smaller domestic firms which were most likely to be driven out of business by the concessions being made at the negotiating table.

Conclusion

The decisions to negotiate the CUFTA and NAFTA agreements and the actual negotiations themselves constituted an important moment in North America's governance. Before negotiations began, lobbying highlighted the key role of business's domestic and transborder *governance* activities, which helped place free trade on the Canadian and Mexican political agendas.

The use of the trade-advisory groups by both Canada and Mexico demonstrated the way that business actors were included in their governments' actual negotiation process. This experience also showed the extent to which governance structures in North America were converging, with business playing a direct role in economic policy making not only in the United States but also in Canada and Mexico. Compared to previous decades, when governments had negotiated trade agreements largely on their own, the greater equality of business and government actors in the agenda-setting and negotiation stages reflected a shift from hierarchical towards more heterarchical government in North America. Nevertheless, the combination of politically appointed and sectorally loaded representation on committees which met behind closed doors confirmed that the three governments continued to dominate North America's transborder relations.

The several strategies employed by business suggest the following four reflections. Although nothing in theory prevents civil-society groups from participating in processes of governance (and chapters IV and V demonstrated their importance in labour and environmental issues), business associations along with their associated networks, coalitions, and lobbies have proven the most powerful societal force in practice when setting the broad agenda for North America's political economy. As players in the domestic arena, business associations and business-funded think tanks facilitate communication between business and government officials; produce research in conjunction with like-minded academics; present business's view on national issues at public conferences, parliamentary/congressional committees, and other consultative fora; and participate in public-private partnerships of various sorts. As actors in the international sphere, business associations engage in cross-border lobbying, build transnational alliances, and meet with foreign government officials in order to press their case. Through such activity, business performs several important functions central to government, including setting the agenda, providing information, proposing alternatives, building consensus, generating legitimacy, and, ultimately, effecting policy change.

We can also see that Mexico's decision to emerge from economic autarchy and enter the new North America was both cause and effect of its business community's learning from and adapting to the governance processes pioneered in the old North America. Adopting the Canadian advisory-group model signalled how radically the skewed quality of its relationship with the United States has diminished compared to Canada's. When firms' production has been transnationalized,[65] their preferences for protection begin to change as they adjust to open borders and come to favour a liberal environment more generally. Though Canadian manufacturers continue to compete with Mexico for foreign investment and access to the US market, this rivalry in the marketplace has started to give way to cooperation in the public sphere.

Finally, the business-government nexus demonstrated that North America contains elements of transborder governance, at the same time as the absence of strong institutions prevents any form of supranational governance. Negotiating CUFTA and NAFTA showed that trilateral transborder governance in North America actually can take place at the macro level, if only during the episodic and ad hoc assemblage of national participants to make a grand continental bargain (NAFTA) or respond to a catastrophic crisis (September 11, 2001).

The exceptional character of big business's direct involvement in negotiating transformative treaties tells us by implication that the corporate community does not continuously occupy the 'room next door' in everyday public policy making. For their part, governments are continuously engaged in stimulating and steering, cajoling and obliging, regulating and responding to business in their efforts to generate the economic results required to create jobs and – with luck – deliver votes. In the rest of Part Two, and also in Part Three, I probe eight sectors of the North American economy in order better to understand how and to what extent they are managed through transborder governance.

VIII Continental Energy (In)security

North America has only 7 per cent of the world's population but accounts for nearly one-third of global energy production and consumes over four times more energy per capita than the global average.[1] With energy providing the lifeblood of its three economies, there can hardly be a sector more central to North America's 'existence' yet more complex in its transborder governance challenges.

The importance of energy to each of the three countries is manifested in strikingly different ways. Having been a measure of Mexico's exploitation by British and American capital in the early twentieth century, oil became a potent symbol of the country's national sovereignty in the 1930s, a prime tool for its autonomous, near-autarchic, capitalist development by the 1940s, its essential export and foreign-currency earner in later decades, and now such an inchoate mix of all these functions that it has become a bottleneck unable either to drive national economic development or support Mexico's continental integration within the neoconservative policy paradigm.

Unlike its neighbour to the south, the United States is not confused: energy is the essential ingredient determining its position at the top of the global hierarchy – including its military might. Although it has large oil and coal reserves of its own, the United States consumes far more energy than it can supply itself. Since conservation is not a politically palatable option, Washington pursues ever larger supplies from other countries – preferably stable ones that can offer secure delivery routes – of which none are better candidates than Canada and Mexico.

Whereas the United States is an energy introvert concerned about satisfying its own needs and looking to others for supplies, Canada is an energy extrovert. With supply generally exceeding domestic demand, most citizens consider energy less as a depleting, non-renewable resource that, if carefully husbanded, can give their economy a competitive edge than as just another staple to be extracted and exported – as rapidly as possible and preferably southward – for immediate profits.

The supply and pricing of energy contribute to determining each country's level of economic competitiveness, social welfare, and environmental health. Its population's attitude towards energy helps define its national identity. Its national interest is often contested and ultimately constructed around the question of energy security. In public policy, energy decisions involve balancing public-sector against private-sector actors, the needs of producers against those of consumers, and national against local priorities. Looking at the North American continent as a whole, additional complexities result when state boundaries intersect flows of energy from their sources to their markets. Yet another complication stems from the disconnect between regulatory processes, which are made domestically, and energy prices, which are ultimately determined in the global marketplace. Because negligible amounts of energy flow among all three countries together, we need to approach the two prime bilateral relationships separately if we are to understand transborder energy governance in North America. Accordingly, I begin by looking at oil, natural gas, and electricity governance in the old North America, then continue with the special characteristics that make Mexico's integration in the new North America so difficult, NAFTA notwithstanding. I end by considering the formal institutions of trinational governance that were launched in the new century.

The Old North America and Petroleum

The energy relationship between Canada and the United States is one of entrenched interdependence. From the discovery of large oil reserves in Alberta in the late 1940s, the Canadian oil and gas sector developed as a northern extension of the Midwestern United States' petroleum economy, which provided much of the investment capital, technology, managerial expertise, and, not least important, public-policy models for regulating the exploration, development, refining, and transportation of this liquid gold. Exploration and development was subsidized both by Ottawa's tax stimuli and by incentives designed in Washington to encourage US transnational corporations' exploration and development of foreign supplies. As a result, early provincial oil and gas policy was based on the recommendations of US parent firms invoking their experience in such states as Texas and Oklahoma.[2]

American advice did not simply determine the domestic regulatory system for petroleum production. It structured Canada's petroleum sector to service the United States' needs directly. Following recommendations from the US petroleum giants and the State Department, Prime Minister John Diefenbaker's misnamed National Oil Policy of 1961 integrated Alberta's oil and natural gas sector in the hemispheric market by splitting Canada's petroleum market into two parts. Prairie oil and natural gas were to flow southward to supply the United States, while central and eastern Canada would be supplied with oil that US TNCs shipped from their properties in Venezuela. As a reward for not developing a self-sufficient national market by extending pipelines from Alberta to service Ontario, Quebec, and the Atlantic provinces, Canada was exempted from US oil-import quotas and was able to offset the cost of importing oil for eastern Canada by selling to the locked-in market of the US Midwest the maximum possible volume of what was promoted as its everlasting surpluses.

Through the 1960s, Canada's petroleum industry became increasingly integrated continentally as it responded to US demand. The National Energy Board (NEB), the body responsible for enforcing tariffs, approving the construction and operation of pipelines, and regulating imports and exports of oil, gas, and electricity,[3] developed a close relationship with its US counterpart, the Federal Power Commission (FPC), and facilitated the proposals of oil and gas exporters as the FPC relaxed its protectionism.[4]

Following the 1970 Shultz Report's recommendation that the United States secure its continental energy supplies by recognizing Canada as a low-risk, reliable, strategically important energy partner, President Richard Nixon declared that imports of oil, natural gas, hydropower, and water from Canada would save the United States from its looming energy crisis. But, much to the Americans' dismay, Ottawa added an export tax to the price of oil exported to the United States in the wake of the energy crisis induced by the Organization of Petroleum Exporting countries (OPEC) in 1973, when world oil prices quadrupled and eastern Canada experienced energy insecurity not just as a hostage to global price increases but as the victim of supply interruptions like any other oil-importing country. Ottawa's revenue from the export tax paid by US importers would help offset the higher prices paid by central Canadian consumers of offshore oil. After years of growing concern about Canada's energy scarcity, the Trudeau government launched the National Energy Program in 1980 to foster a self-contained petroleum market that would shelter eastern Canada's economy from supply and price vulnerability. The US oil and gas industry – which had generously funded Ronald Reagan's 1980 election campaign – exerted strong pressure on the newly elected president to have Canada rescind the NEP.[5]

Canada's NEP was a short-lived experiment in government intervention and partial withdrawal from extensive north-south integration: during its eighteen months' existence, Canadian ownership of the energy industry jumped from 7 per cent to 34 per cent.[6] Because the NEP was crafted with almost no provincial or private-sector consultation, it also created a venomous backlash from the oil and gas industry and the provinces of Alberta and Saskatchewan, whose interests it was seen as sacrificing for the benefit of central and eastern Canada.[7] In the end, collapsing world oil prices caused the NEP to unravel and left the country's oil producers in the west securely integrated in the US market and its oil consumers in the east insecurely dependent on overseas markets.

The consequent re-regulation of transborder energy flows and pricing was constitutionalized in the Canada-United States Free Trade Agreement, which prohibited export taxes, required trade to be governed by corporate forces, and proscribed Canadian government interference with the industry's exports – although it expressly blessed Canadian subsidies promoting the petroleum sector's development. These provisions effectively castrated federal government powers so as to give US energy needs and Alberta producers' concerns priority over any pan-Canadian interest in directing long-term energy supplies towards domestic economic ends under conditions of environmental sustainability.[8] NAFTA's energy chapter reiterated the same norms, confirming Canada's commitments made under CUFTA to a government-constrained free-market economy. Although CUFTA and NAFTA allowed export restrictions for the conservation of exhaustible resources, supply shortages, price stabilization, and national security,[9] the Canadian government has not chosen to invoke these conditions, preferring instead the maximum deregulation of trade in petroleum products.

Canada-US Natural Gas Integration

In natural gas, the US-Canada relationship is a similar combination of freewheeling corporate leadership and weakened government regulations. The US Energy Policy Act of 1992 served as the fountainhead for the sector's liberalization through Order 636 of the Federal Energy Regulatory Commission (FERC), which mandated the unbundling of the United States' vertically integrated gas utilities to allow more private-sector participation in the wholesale market, access to pipeline infrastructure, and market-based pricing.[10] In this spirit, CUFTA and NAFTA entrenched the full integration of Canada's 'upstream' exploration and production with the United States' downstream market.[11]

Even though Canada's National Energy Board is still supposed to allow only surplus gas to be exported, in practice it lets sales be governed by market demand. NAFTA's Article 609(1) – which defines an energy regulatory measure as behaviour by 'federal or sub-federal entities that directly affects the transportation, transmission, distribution, purchases, or sales of an energy or basic petrochemical good'[12] – brings the provinces under the aegis of continental government,[13] thus compromising provincial autonomy over energy resources even in areas outside the federal government's powers. With Canadian resources coming under provincial jurisdiction and with Alberta as the major energy-producing province championing the deregulation of the distribution and pricing side of the market,[14] this loss of autonomy is moot. Alberta produces 80 per cent of Canada's natural gas and issues licences for all gas that is removed from the province without distinguishing between the US and Canadian markets.[15]

In the natural gas sector, Canadian and American TNCs have demonstrated an impressive ability to plan and invest cooperatively. One example is the massive Alliance Pipeline, a bilateral venture that stretches 3,600 kilometres from western Canada to Chicago.[16] Current gas-pipeline infrastructure reflects this integration: the border between the United States and Canada is effectively seamless, with pipelines criss-crossing the 49th parallel.[17] As FERC's chairman puts it, 'You look at a pipeline map of [the old] North America and it's just no boundaries.'[18]

Oil and gas flows in this old North America since the 1980s have mostly been southbound from Canada to the United States. As indicated in Table 8.1, the United States does export energy to Canada, its natural gas exports having reached 10 per cent of its total exports to Canada and its petroleum exports 7 per cent. However, Canada remains an overall energy exporter to the United States, having increased its petroleum exports from 455,000 barrels per day in 1980 to 2,353,000 in 2006, and its natural gas exports from 797 billion cubic feet in 1980 to

Table 8.1: Canada-United States oil and gas trade, selected years, 1980–2006

	Imports to US from Canada					US Exports to Canada				
	1980	1990	2000	2005	2006	1980	1990	2000	2005	2006
Crude oil and petroleum products (thousand barrels per day)	455	934	1,807	2,181	2,353	108	91	110	181	159
Natural gas (MMcf)	797	1448	3544	3,700	3,500	0.1	17	73	358	341

Sources: Energy Information Administration, Official Energy Statistics from the U.S. Government, 'Crude Oil and Total Petroleum Imports Top 15 Countries,' October 2006, http://www.eia.doe.gov/pub/oil_gas/petroleum/data_publications/company_level_imports /current /import.html; and 'Table 6.3: Natural Gas Imports, Exports, and Net Imports,' http://www.eia.doe.gov/emeu/aer/txt/ptb0603.html (both accessed Dec. 17, 2006). United States Energy Information Administration, *Annual Energy Review 2003, Natural Gas Navigator and Petroleum Supply Annual 2003*, http://tonto.eia.doe.gov/dnav/pet/pet _move_expc_a_EP00_EEX_mbblpd_a.htm (accessed April 15, 2008). The updated figures are from the updated websites of the same source.

3,500,000 in 2006. This leaves the United States dependent on Canada for over 33 per cent of its net energy imports.[19] Indeed, by 2006, Canada had become the single largest external source of petroleum to the United States.

The increasing energy flows between Canada and the United States (see Table 8.1), encouraged by the liberalization of trade policies, and concerns for US – but, curiously, not Canadian – energy security have intensified bilateral energy relations at various levels of governance. While the role of federal and state/provincial governments over energy practices is weakening, they still play a prominent role. The regulatory boards in both countries – FERC and the NEB – cooperate so intimately that they hold joint hearings on proposed cross-border projects. Because of this close relationship, it is almost as straightforward to seek approval for a transborder pipeline as it is for a domestic interstate or interprovincial one. Further indication of energy-policy coordination between Canada and the United States came with the May 2004 memorandum of understanding between the NEB and FERC, which promised coordination in decision making and the application of joint procedures.[20] 'Sharing information and timely decision-making are the two critical elements for the siting and construction of a natural gas pipeline across

Canada to bring natural gas stranded in Alaska to the lower 48 states' is one of the memorandum's main affirmations. [21]

The Electricity Sector: Deregulation and De Facto Transborder US Government

The connections between the Canadian and US electricity sectors are complex and rapidly expanding (see Figure 8.1). Even though Canada exported only about 10 per cent of its electricity in 2000 – a figure almost unchanged from 1980 – and Canadian exports made up only 1 per cent of US consumption,[22] interconnections between Canadian and US transmission and distribution systems began to grow in the mid-1990s. In a 2001 report on trade and development, the United States Energy Association noted that the geographic arrangement and the variance of peak demand times across the continent created extensive opportunities for two-way exchanges across the border.[23]

Originally, electricity was a government-regulated industry, because its generation required massive initial investments and its transmission lines and grids presented a natural monopoly: only one system was needed to service a given area efficiently. The United States relied principally on coal to generate electricity for a market comprised of non-competitive publicly, privately, or jointly owned utilities whose prices

Figure 8.1: US electricity imports from and electricity exports to Canada, 2000–5

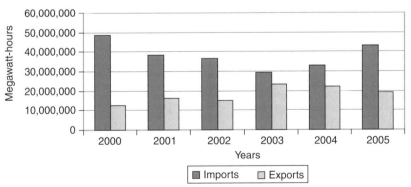

Source: Data for figures 8.1 and 8.2 from US Energy Information Administration, 'United States Electricity Imports from and Electricity Exports to Canada and Mexico,' http://www.eia.doe.gov/cneaf/electricity/epa/epat6p3.html.

were then regulated by government.[24] In the 1970s the United States began a process of deregulation by unbundling electricity's transmission from its generation and distribution.

The Canadian sector also consisted of public, vertically integrated utility monopolies, but they were regulated provincially.[25] Unlike their US counterparts, provincial utilities did not face supply scarcity and high prices, because most of their electricity was generated by abundant hydropower, requiring huge initial investments but proving much more cost-effective than thermal or nuclear generation.[26] With constitutional jurisdiction over resource management, royalties, and the economic development of their electricity sector, each province, with the exception of Alberta, had a publicly owned Crown electric utility, so that supply and pricing were firmly under provincial governmental control. As a result, the liberalization of electricity markets happened unevenly and on a province-by-province basis, less in response to CUFTA or NAFTA than to regulatory pressures coming directly from the US government.[27]

CUFTA's significance for energy deregulation came into play as the deregulation process unfolded. Once a province introduced competition into the market, its public utilities became subject to norms requiring a state enterprise to act solely in accordance with commercial considerations in its purchase or sale of the monopoly good or service in the relevant market, including with regard to price, quality, availability, marketability, transportation, and other terms and conditions of purchase or sale. In other words, CUFTA required that the public utility act as any other competitive player, which meant that government could no longer use energy for such public-policy purposes as supporting its industries or its poor with lower prices.

CUFTA did not address electricity explicitly except to clarify its status as a commodity, but it did reinforce the deregulatory pressure that was driving the trend towards market governance in the sector. The free-trade norm of national treatment should have offered Canadian utilities the same right to compete in the United States as American utilities had. On the other hand, with little private-sector activity in Canadian electricity markets, national treatment gave US utilities little scope to move northward. As a result, they lobbied hard to get Canada to copy the United States' deregulation policy and even accept the principle of 'reciprocity,' which would give them the same rights in Canada as they enjoyed at home.[28] (The United States had vigorously resisted the principle of reciprocity being applied to banking since this would have given Canadian banks an advantage over the US banks in the

American market because of their long-established ability to operate across provincial/state borders.)

This pressure bore fruit in the 1992 US Energy Act, which had significant implications for Canada. Although FERC had no legitimate jurisdiction over Canadian utilities, it made reciprocity a condition for their continuing export of electricity to the United States. It simply required exporting provinces – British Columbia, Manitoba, Ontario, and Quebec – to provide US operators equal access to their transmission networks as the sine qua non for selling electricity through the US transmission systems.[29] Because of these provinces' desire to export, a key driver of provincial electricity restructuring was their attempt to conform to these unilateral policy stipulations made in Washington regarding importers' market access.

In 1996 FERC issued its landmark Order 888, which removed US utilities' monopoly power and required the unbundling of vertically integrated electricity suppliers, so that private generators and distributors could have open access to the utilities' transmission and distribution systems.[30] As a result, utilities could compete with each other if they wanted to expand their markets.[31]

To break down the US states' monopolies, FERC aggressively promoted larger regional operation and control for transmission by establishing Independent System Operators (ISOs). To encourage open access into wholesale markets, these ISOs consolidated the existing mid-Atlantic and eastern power pools and required that they operate the transmission system in their region independently, preventing the vertically integrated companies from giving their own generators preferential access to their transmission lines. To consolidate market control over the sector, FERC issued Order 2000 at the end of the decade, encouraging the formation of Regional Transmission Organizations (RTOs), which are larger ISOs charged with the same responsibility of ensuring independent access to transmission lines. [32] These RTOs were all subject to what FERC called 'a standard market design,' an operational template to ensure compatibility and similarity in all regions, even where they had not been initiated under Order 888.[33]

While non-exporting provinces had little incentive to liberalize their electricity markets[34] and no need to subscribe to US regulations, the exporting provincial utilities opened their markets to the private sector in order to conform with FERC standards.[35] For example, Manitoba joined the Midwest Independent System Operator in 2001, and Quebec tied itself into the grid linking New York and New England.[36]

Quebec, Manitoba, Saskatchewan, New Brunswick, and British Columbia deregulated their wholesale markets as well.[37] In order to enter the RTO-Pacific North West, the grid that covers the northwestern United States, British Columbia Hydro complied with FERC regulations on reciprocity, unbundling, market design, and generator-interconnection agreements by establishing the BC Transmission Corporation as a separate, private company.[38]

Alberta, which has no direct transmission links to the United States and routes its power for export through British Columbia to the US grid, followed close behind.[39] In 1995 the provincial government passed its Electric Utility Act, which established a competitive market in generation, eased pricing regulations, and created a power pool to trade electricity[40] in order to help its utilities comply with US policies and gain access to the US market. Alberta went on to establish retail competition in the sector[41] in which it allowed some US utility participation.[42]

Ontario is an exception, since it is large enough to have established an all-Canadian version of an RTO called the Independent Electricity Market Operator (IEMO). The IEMO works cooperatively with its neighbouring RTOs, with which its operation standards are compatible.[43] The province launched an aggressive restructuring plan in which further integration with US markets played a key motivating role.[44] Meeting FERC's reciprocity requirements allowed US generators to sell power in its market. To the extent that American RTOs have become regulatory bodies whose remits cross the national border, transborder electricity regulation is 'governed' in Washington. But, with little room for Canadian input, the imposition of reciprocity has been more a matter of imperial government from the United States than hegemonic governance.[45]

In April 2002 FERC issued a proposal to standardize generator-interconnection agreements, integrating north-south electricity flows between Canada and the United States and allowing Canadian utilities to market directly to US customers. [46] Quickly, two private Canadian utilities from Alberta and British Columbia gained FERC's approval, and Ontario and Quebec pursued the same path.[47] However, there is some US reluctance to grant Ontario Hydro and Hydro-Québec continued direct access to US customers, because of their continuing monopoly in their home markets.[48]

Because electricity requires substantial infrastructure, there is an increasing need for joint Canadian and US governance of system improvements to keep pace with rising demand.[49] In response to the need for greater cooperation in planning, development, and operation of the electricity sector, the North American Electricity Reliability Council (NERC) gained more clout. But, because complying with NERC standards was voluntary, firms competing against each other to use transmission grids could neglect compliance.[50] For example, the violation of NERC standards on the part of the Ohio-based utility First-Energy provoked a colossal blackout on August 14, 2003,[51] proving that self-imposed standards were insufficient to ensure reliable and secure operation of North American power systems.[52] A bilateral US-Canada Power System Outage Task Force recommended enforceable standards to prevent mismanagement by utilities that could result in the destabilization of the entire system.[53] The US Energy Association has suggested that FERC be given the authority to enforce NERC standards through the RTOs, effectively transforming electricity governance into electricity government.

In sum, the Canadian government's lack of an agenda for a national energy market and its abstention from regulating exports to the United States has served to facilitate individual provinces' compliance with FERC standards, so that changes in the entire sector have resulted from US policy directives rather than from the pursuit of Canadian-defined interests.[54] American policy also drove the restructuring of provincial utilities because their small regulatory boards lacked the clout that Ottawa's National Energy Board would have had in dealing with FERC.[55] Given the provinces' constitutional autonomy in energy matters and their differing interests, the electricity market is becoming bilaterally integrated on a province-by-province basis and driven by US policy, with only embryonic transborder governance institutions such as the North American Energy Standards Board (NAESB), which became operational in 2002.

The Evolution of Mexico's Energy Policy

For the most part, Mexico's oil and gas sector has been government-owned and -operated and has had limited integration with the US market. The importance of energy in Mexican politics can be traced back to the 1917 constitution's Article 27, which declared the exploration, exploitation, development, and sale of oil and gas, and the generation, transmission, and distribution of electricity, to be exclusively under the federal government's aegis. Mexico's nationalist approach to its energy sector was further strengthened in what was seen as its second declaration of independence, the 1938 nationalization of foreign oil and gas properties and the establishment of the state-owned oil and gas company, Petróleos Mexicanos (Pemex), by President Lázaro Cárdenas.

Pemex explores and develops Mexico's petrochemical reserves, including the management of the downstream facilities needed to refine and market them.[56] It is the country's biggest corporation, with one of the largest unions in the country, and it is a vital source of tax revenue since it is legally required to transfer up to 30 per cent of its earnings to the federal government. [57]

Pemex's political-economy orientation has passed through three distinct stages corresponding to the governing party's prevailing social project. From 1938 to 1976, when Mexico protected its energy sector from the United States and resisted its privatization, it was administered as a service enterprise with the mandate to support the country's economic development and to meet its energy needs. A second stage began when new oil fields were discovered and President José López Portillo decided that an aggressive oil-export policy should provide the revenue necessary to finance his ambitious, state-led industrialization process. Under pressure to take on this new export role, Pemex abandoned the husbanding of its hydrocarbons for the nation's domestic needs. Management guidelines were made more flexible so that Pemex could accelerate drilling and development by signing contracts with private operators.[58] During the debt crisis (1982–8), Pemex's exports remained an indispensable source of foreign revenues, making it a cash cow through which the government could service the public debt.

A third stage found Pemex being used for macro-economic stabilization. As the Mexican economy liberalized, successive governments attempted to encourage greater private-sector participation. Through a gradual process, direct state control of the oil, natural gas, and petrochemical sectors was loosened. Instead, a series of theoretically competitive markets put more of the petroleum industry in the hands of private national and foreign firms, which operate through a system of contracts and permits. Under this new logic, the state limits itself to playing the role of ultimate guardian of natural resources and regulator of the emerging competitive market.[59] This piecemeal privatization can be measured by the contraction of Pemex's workforce from 210,000 to 100,000 between 1989 and 1995.[60]

With the government draining off its profits, Pemex has not devel-

Table 8.2: US-Mexico natural gas and petroleum trade, 1980–2006

	Imports to US from Mexico					US exports to Mexico				
	1980	1990	2000	2005	2006	1980	1990	2000	2005	2006
Crude oil and petroleum products (thousand barrels per day)	533	755	1,373	1,662	1,705	28	9	358	268	255
Natural gas (billion cubic feet)	102	0	12	9	13	4	16	105	305	321

oped the capacity to refine its petroleum into the derivatives needed by the economy. As a result, Mexico is a net importer of natural gas from the United States (see Table 8.2) and also imports gasoline because it lacks the financial capacity and/or technical expertise to develop the facilities needed for refining its own crude oil. The electric sector also requires the importation of natural gas for power generation.[61] These limitations, coupled with increasing demand, create strong pressure for greater deregulation in general and more private and foreign investment in particular.

Although NAFTA put a veneer of common control over the continent's petroleum sector, it actually sanctioned the perpetuation of two separate bilateralisms. Chapter 6 reiterated Canada's CUFTA commitments to a deregulated, integrated, free-market economy,[62] but the national-security exception, which is recognized as an appropriate reason for export restrictions, is defined in NAFTA differently for US-Canada relations than for Mexico. Canada negotiated a narrow definition of national security to protect itself against arbitrary US import restrictions justified in the name of national security, but Article 605 gave Mexico the right to restrict exports or imports any time it is deemed necessary to protect what is broadly defined as the country's 'essential security interests.' Beyond the distinct interpretations of national security in each relationship, the skewed nature of these two bilateral relationships can also be seen in the proportionality provision, which, to assure Washington that Canadian supplies would not be interrupted by another NEP, prohibits Canada from reducing the percentage of its production that it exports to the United States, a restraint to which Mexico refused to be bound.

In the 1980s Mexico had instituted a limitation on the amount of oil that could be exported, but after the implementation of NAFTA this changed: 75 per cent of its petroleum is exported directly to the United States, with another 10 per cent flowing via Haiti or the Bahamas. This put Pemex in an insoluble bind. On the one hand, it laboured under an enormous debt. On the other, it could not prosper from its high foreign income because the politicians' failure to bring in an effective fiscal reform made them dependent on appropriating Pemex's foreign earnings. Indeed, Pemex's oil-export earnings increased from 7 per cent of GDP in 2001 to 9 per cent in 2005, representing 30 and 38 per cent of the federal budget respectively. This growth was due partly to the increase in oil prices, partly to an increase in the volume of exports, and partly to an increase in the demand for various oil products and petrochemicals in the domestic market.[63] Most of Pemex's limited disposable revenues were spent on extracting crude oil rather than on modernizing its infrastructure. As a result, Mexico has reverted to the classic Third World position, exporting its unprocessed, lower-cost raw material and importing the value-added, higher-cost refined products.

During the NAFTA negotiations, it seemed that the United States failed to loosen Pemex's dominance over the country's oil and gas sectors.[64] It is true that Mexico made fewer energy-policy concessions in NAFTA than had Canada. For instance, the first article of Chapter 6 stated that 'the Parties confirm their full respect for their Constitutions'[65] – implicitly recognizing that Mexico retained the right to control the exploration and exploitation of its oil and gas, along with associated activities such as refining and foreign trade.[66] In fact, private participation in cross-border trade was accepted, subject to the Mexican government's approval: 'Where end-users and suppliers find cross border trade may be in their interests [they] shall be permitted to negotiate supply contracts ... [with] the state enterprise.'[67] NAFTA reduced Mexico's tariff on natural gas imports to 10 per cent in 1993, with a 1 per cent reduction scheduled for every subsequent year. By 1998, the Interstate Natural Gas Association of America successfully lobbied the US government to accept Mexico's proposal to hasten the complete elimination of the tariff on natural gas in exchange for decreases in US tariffs on Mexican chemicals,[68] a reduction that promoted the development of cross-border pipelines. Furthermore, the Mexican government has actually gone a long way down the road to privatization and deregulation of its energy monopoly, encouraging Pemex to purchase services from foreign corporations, particularly Halliburton.

Natural gas is the most deregulated part of the Mexican energy sector.

Efforts to privatize Pemex's gas operations began in 1995, when the regulatory law applying to Article 27 of the constitution was reformed to put natural gas outside the publicly controlled petroleum industry. In preparation for opening the natural gas sector, the government created a special commission to establish regulations for the new market.[69] Federal legislation opened natural gas transportation, storage, and distribution to private and foreign investment and allowed private companies to export and import this fuel. Shortly afterwards, the distribution networks were sold to private companies, and, in open defiance of the constitution's mandate, explicit prohibitions were put in place to prevent the public sector from participating in the distribution of natural gas.[70] As a result, the gas-pipeline infrastructure between Mexico and the United States has a small number of private pipelines crossing the Mexican-US border.

In 2003 two pipelines began service, with export-to-Mexico-only capability.[71] In 2004 the Del-Rio-Acuna pipeline was completed, with two other border-crossing pipeline projects proposed by the Tidelands Oil and Gas Company for 2007.[72] There were thirteen gas pipelines running across the US-Mexico border – mostly to export gas from the United States to Mexico – that connected with both Pemex's supply pipelines (which account for 85 per cent of current capacity) and a few privately owned connections into northwestern Mexico.[73] Pemex still controls the upstream gas sector, but midstream and downstream activities are fully open to private competition, subject to the limitation that private companies can be involved in only one function.

Mexican President Ernesto Zedillo set up a program called Pidiregas (an acronym for 'productive infrastructure projects with deferred impact on expenditures'), which permitted two different types of private investment. Under 'direct investment,' a contractor could develop the infrastructure and then transfer it to the government corporation, which incurred public debt to pay for it. Under 'conditioned investment,' the contractor built and operated the plant and then sold the energy to the state – electricity to the Comisión Federal de Electricidad (CFE, Federal Electricity Commission) and nitrogen for boosting oil extraction to Pemex, which paid for it from current revenues.[74] As such, Pidiregas represented an alternative for financing public infrastructure after the financial crisis of 1994–5, but it also presented a risk when used excessively – as has been the case since its implementation – given that it increases the level of public indebtedness and displaces self-financed investment in the public sector.

For economic and environmental reasons, Mexico's current energy policy commits it to increase its use of natural gas over other fuels, putting even more pressure on the government to seek private and foreign investments. Currently, under the Regulatory Act on Petroleum, exploration, extraction, production activities, and direct sales are considered strategic and thus protected, whereas only construction, operation, transportation, storage, and distribution are open to private participation. Under these restrictions, Pemex has made efforts to ally itself with international private oil and gas corporations, such as a joint-venture refinery with Royal Dutch/Shell.[75] Under President Vicente Fox's administration, increasing numbers of contracts were opened to private-sector participation, including areas that are constitutionally reserved for the state. This resulted in the involvement of TNCs in the whole cycle – from exploration to production – leaving only retail distribution under Pemex's exclusive control.[76] In 2005 it signed seventy-seven contracts with Mexican firms, while only twenty-two were signed with foreign firms. Still, foreign contracts brought in more than double the revenue of the Mexican firms. Of Mexico's total revenue from exploration, development, refining, and petrochemicals in 2005, US$1,054 million came from foreign firms while only US$462 million came from Mexican firms.[77]

Mexico's march towards natural gas liberalization was boosted by the first ever meeting between FERC and Mexico's Comisión Reguladora de Energía (CRE, Energy Regulatory Commission) in February 2003.[78] A second indication of Mexico's liberalization was the government's reduction of the number of 'basic' petrochemicals (which are constitutionally reserved for state control) by reclassifying many of them as secondary (and therefore opening them to private participation), thus shrinking the number of primary petrochemicals from fifty to eight.[79]

Large US firms wanting to invest in oil and gas exploration and development in Mexico are still deterred by the political risks they associate with the Mexican energy sectors.[80] For example, at the beginning of March 2004, Marathon Oil cancelled its US$1.5-billion investment plans to build a regional energy centre near Tijuana because the Mexican government had expropriated its land without warning or reason.[81]

Despite the Fox administration's willingness to comply with US demands, public opposition limited how far the Mexican government could go in selling off one of its few remaining national industries. Some Mexican critics allege that Pemex has been deliberately driven towards bankruptcy by the government draining off its profits in order then to justify opening it up to private investment.[82] Most analysts share President Felipe Calderón's vision of the need for further reform in the energy sector in order to attract greater investment and modernize the petroleum infrastructure, expand the production of gas and refined oil products, and exploit the country's reserves' full potential.[83] Yet most agree that a basic cause of the sorry state of Pemex's infrastructure is the result of the Mexican government leeching its profits.[84] In 2006 the federal government took 54 billion pesos from Pemex, which constituted 40 per cent of federal tax receipts, while depriving Pemex of the capacity to develop its exploration, development, and refining capacities. In 2007 President Calderón finally negotiated what had eluded Vicente Fox for six years: Congressional approval for a fiscal reform designed to address the country's high levels of tax evasion and so reduce its appropriation of Pemex's profits.[85]

Privatization and deregulation have reached their constitutional limits, still leaving Mexico's oil and gas sector the most nationally contained and strictly governed of the three NAFTA partners. In the National Congress in 2005, PRI delegates actually called for the expansion of state-ownership and governance over the energy sector,[86] affirming the need to strengthen Mexico's autonomy in the face of an attempt by the president's party, Partido Acción Nacional (PAN), to introduce private-sector control. Absent the political will to restructure Pemex's ability to expand exploration and development and increase its revenues, Mexico will not be able to satisfy either increasing domestic demand or insatiable federal budgetary needs.[87]

Mexico's Electricity Regulation: The Road to Market Management

Originally, electricity in Mexico was supplied by hundreds of local utilities. Throughout the 1940s and 1950s, these small regional monopolies began to consolidate in order to capture economies of scale. Recognizing that generation facilities could be vertically integrated with transmission and distribution systems, thus improving efficiency, the Mexican government nationalized and consolidated the electricity sector in 1960, creating a vertical monopoly. As a result, Mexico's electricity sector came under state ownership, being regulated and administered through the Comisión Federal de Electricidad (CFE, Federal Electricity Commission), which is the second-largest Mexican public corporation, owning over 83 per cent of the country's generating capacity.[88]

Technological improvements in generation processes by the 1980s meant that the advantages of scale had lessened and that smaller generators could operate efficiently as competitive players.[89] However, Mexico was much slower than Canada and the United States to allow private competition. In 1992 recognition that electricity demand in Mexico was growing faster than the CFE's capacity to generate adequate supply[90] led to Mexico's Ley del Servicio Público de Energía Eléctrica (Public Electricity Service Act) being amended by sidestepping the constitution to allow limited private participation in the generation of electricity. The Comisión Reguladora de Energía (CRE, Energy Regulatory Commission) was created as an autonomous agency to regulate electricity. In 1997 the CFE's decision to increase rates by 6.2 per cent and reduce consumer electricity subsidies was a further attempt to improve its financial situation and enable much needed investment.[91]

NAFTA's Article 602.3 acknowledged that Mexico's generation, transmission, distribution, and sale of electricity were under public control. However, generation projects, co-generation, imports and exports, small-scale generation, and independent power production have been opened up to private investment and participation on the condition that surplus power must then be sold to the CRE, which is still the only entity allowed to distribute electricity to Mexican consumers.[92] As a result, various foreign firms have entered the Mexican market, some functioning as independent producers and developers of CRE's new plants. The CRE regulates public electricity supply, private electricity generation, public electricity acquisitions, private exports and imports, and transmission services between private generators and the public suppliers in a new governance setting of public, private, and civic actors.

As late as 2002, Mexico was a net importer of electricity, because many of the northern-border communities relied on US power in emergency situations.[93] Allowing for limited private and foreign involvement in the electricity sector, the CRE has stimulated a flurry of investments and an increase in the transmission lines running between Mexico and the United States in cross-border grids. But these limited changes have not met the need for greater investment in generation, transmission, distribution, and infrastructure, as is demonstrated by frequent blackouts across the country.[94] In the mid-2000s, Mexico demonstrated the most rapid growth in net electricity generation on the continent, averaging 5.8 per cent per year in both the residential and commercial sectors, and now exports more electricity than it imports.[95] However, in order to produce electricity, Mexico has to import 700 billions of BTUs of natural gas every day from the United States costing $3.5 million per day.[96] In this way, Mexico is not autonomous in electricity despite its growing exports to the United States (see Figure 8.2).

President Fox fully supported this reading of the situation and pushed for further opening of the sector to private investment by issuing a decree in 2002 which would have allowed electricity generation by all interested parties.[97] Yet the Supreme Court ruled that Fox's electricity-privatization reforms were unconstitutional. For its part, the Senate's rejection of the same proposals reaffirmed Mexico's will to maintain public ownership of its electricity resources. This popular opposition in Mexico's Congress and by the electricity unions to regulatory reform and incentives for private investment has slowed the development of the country's electricity sector.

In order to strengthen the electricity sector in Mexico, various specialists have suggested the installation of nuclear plants, which, together with natural gas generators, would help reduce dependency on fossil fuel resources. The plan is to construct them on the coastline, where the nuclear-electric plant Laguna Verde is already located.[98]

With regard to bilateral and trilateral cooperation in the energy sector, critics have warned about the risk of Mexico becoming an energy *maquiladora*. For example, the proposed installation of three new facilities to receive liquefied natural gas from South America has been announced as a means to supply the Mexican market, but 75 per cent of their volume is earmarked for California. The United States prefers to keep these plants outside its territory, because the possibility of massive explosions makes them environmentally hazardous and possible targets for terrorists.[99] Since there have already been accidents in Mexico, various organizations such as Oil Watch en Tabasco, Organización Pueblo, and the Unión Nacional de Trabajadores de Confianza de Pemex, which are studying the impact of the energy sector on the environment, have opposed this development.[100]

The US-Mexican border is becoming increasingly porous in terms of private-sector trade in natural gas and electricity. Despite differences between the two countries' environmental goals and socio-economic agendas, there has nonetheless been a proliferation of pipelines and power lines crossing the border.[101] Yet Mexican integration in the North American oil, gas, and electricity system remains truncated. Even though it is inching towards the privatization and liberalization that prevails in the United States and Canada, Mexico remains largely self-contained, having exempted itself under NAFTA from CUFTA's energy

Figure 8.2: US electricity imports from and electricity exports to Mexico, 2000–5

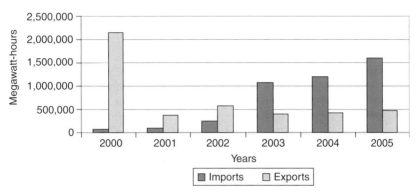

rules. As long as Mexicans stay committed to their constitutionally nationalized energy sector, further integration and greater US involvement in the Mexican energy sector will be limited.

Continental Energy Governance: The NAEWG and the SPP

Although the US government systematically resists trans-border institutions lest they give its neighbours greater clout in pressing their case in Washington, energy presents a different challenge because the United States is the *demandeur*, seeking greater access to its periphery's resources.

Vice-President Dick Cheney's 2001 National Energy Policy was just the latest in a long series of US government reports which advocated expanding and accelerating 'cross-border energy investment, oil and gas pipelines, and electricity grid connections.'[102] Emphasizing the vulnerability of the United States to disruptions in foreign energy supplies, the Cheney Report took the major step of officially recognizing Alberta's tar-sands reserve base of 176 billion barrels as a 'pillar of sustained North American energy and economic security.'[103] When the September 11, 2001 terrorist attacks placed homeland security at the forefront of its agenda, Washington's strategy of maximizing continental energy security was already in place in order to take advantage of its neighbours' energy riches.[104]

With 'North American energy security' a euphemism for *American* energy security, Washington pressed Mexico City and Ottawa to formalize cross-border energy integration and establish a clear regulatory framework for making infrastructure-investment decisions. North American energy governance was advanced in 2001 when Jean Chrétien and Vicente Fox agreed with George Bush's proposal to create the trilateral North American Energy Working Group. Expanding the pre-existing bilateral yearly energy consultations between American and Canadian officials,[105] the NAEWG was given a mandate to 'foster communication and co-operation among the governments and energy sectors of the three countries on energy-related matters of common interest and to enhance the North American energy trade interconnections, consistent with the goal of sustainable development, for the benefit of all.'[106]

The September 11, 2001 terrorist attacks and the August 14, 2003 power blackout added new urgency to the United States' search for secure access to continentally located sources and intensified its pressure on its two neighbours to increase their supply capabilities.[107] Action beyond symbolism was taken in March 2005, when the three heads of government announced their Security and Prosperity Partnership. The three countries agreed to continued cooperation on the energy file, by folding the NAEWG into an SPP working group mandated to continue fostering better communication and closer relationships. In addition, it was to work on removing barriers, enhancing infrastructure interconnections and overall energy trade, and facilitating more efficient energy distribution throughout the continent.

With no legislative, executive, administrative, or budgetary powers of its own, the trilateral group can have only a hortatory role. Nevertheless, three months later, the SPP's *Report to Leaders* energy chapter contained nine commitments: 'expand science and technology collaboration, increase energy efficiency collaboration, increase regulatory co-operation, enhance electricity collaboration, greater economic production from oil sands, increase natural gas collaboration, enhance nuclear collaboration, enhance co-operation on hydrocarbons, improve transparency and coordination in energy information, statistics, and projections.'[108] This comprehensive wish list reflected the strategy behind the SPP: promoting continental integration through incremental bureaucratic actions, given that political paralysis in the Mexican legislature prevented a major move towards further energy deregulation or any privatization of Pemex that might divest it of its dominion over the country's petroleum industry.[109]

When the SPP's North American Competitiveness Council (NACC) issued its first report in February 2007, its strongly deregulatory recommendations concerning Mexico's energy market appeared to be the result of pressure exerted by Canadian and American TNCs. In fact, the energy text had been written by the NACC's Mexican secretariat, the Instituto Mexicano para la Competitividad (Mexican Institute for Competitiveness), which was using this big-business forum to provide international legitimacy for its own, home-grown muscularly conservative program.[110]

Conclusion

The integration characterizing the US-Canada energy relationship, which started with oil and gas and is advancing in the electricity sector, continues to expand as liberalization proceeds. Currently, the governance of oil and natural gas is largely integrated between Canada and the United States. Although NAFTA enshrined these neoconservative values, the agreement changed little in terms of energy integration, because Canadian policy makers had already subscribed to the US vision of free-market-led transborder integration, making north-south links in the old North America both more extensive and more intensive than east-west connections within them.

While Mexican involvement in the market paradigm has been slow, it is growing. For the first time, in May 2003, Mexico's CRE attended a meeting with the NEB and FERC (which had been meeting bilaterally to discuss gas policy since the mid-1980s). The meetings are designed to respect the sovereignty of each participant while coordinating with and learning from each other to increase efficiency.[111] Mexico's participation in the meeting was symbolically important, marking a step towards harmonization with its North American partners.

In electricity, continental cooperation in planning, development, and operation has enhanced the North American Electricity Reliability Council, whose ten regional councils account for almost all of the electricity generation in Canada and the United States and some in the Baja California region. Continental cooperation has also resulted in the establishment of the North American Energy Standards Board, an industry governance group focused on the 'development and promotion of standards which will lead to a seamless marketplace for wholesale and retail natural gas and electricity.'[112] The NERC and the NAESB are well-established, functional entities that have full involvement from the energy sectors, even though observing standards is voluntary.

These trilateral organizations demonstrate relatively high levels of private-sector integration and cooperation through a continental governance that is more than initially meets the eye and is more advanced than that of formal government regulators.

Still, North America is far from being governed as a single energy system. Strongly nationalistic in its oil, gas, and electricity regulation, Mexico's political sensitivities make major and rapid deregulation unlikely. Within the framework of the US need for its neighbour's petroleum supplies, it seems less appropriate to talk of a power asymmetry between Canada and the United States than of a virtual absorption of the Alberta petroleum sector within the Americas. In electricity, Washington managed to turn a previous Canadian policy autonomy into a regulatory dependency. Consequently, the North American energy sector remains skewed between a highly integrated bilateral Canadian-US system that operates under a mix of hegemonic (for petroleum) and imperial (for electricity) governance and a very partially integrated one between the United States and Mexico.

With the public-policy agenda crowded by the need to address global warming, the uncontrolled expansion of highly polluting tar-sands production in Alberta, more plans for pipelines along the Mackenzie River, schemes for biofuels, and proposals for a network of liquefied natural gas terminals, it is unclear how Mexico will participate in the trilateral transborder governance that is advancing through the Security and Prosperity Partnership. What also remains unclear is whether US success in harnessing its continental periphery to increase its energy security will engender greater energy insecurity in Mexico and Canada.

So much for energy. Another sector – agriculture – presents a somewhat different picture. Whereas there is a geographical necessity driving much energy integration owing to supplies being separated from nearby markets by national boundaries, the continental integration of most agriculture is a product of the industrial and transportation revolutions that have replaced domestic family farming with globalizing agribusiness, a subject to which we now turn.

IX Agriculture: Beef, Wheat, and Corn

Ever since coal made possible the first industrial revolution, most forms of energy have been transportable across national boundaries, making them early candidates for transborder governance. In contrast, farming had been historically a local activity, regulated autarchically within each national jurisdiction. Agricultural sectors became internationally significant only when farmers produced more than could be consumed domestically and when their produce could be transported over long distances – two conditions that first applied to grains, which extended Canada's staple-export integration in Great Britain's imperial economy. With the development of refrigeration and air transport, global markets developed for even the most perishable foodstuffs. Under pressure from their farmers, governments either generated barriers to protect local producers from imports or, when they had surpluses of their own, pressed for international standards to limit others' domestic protectionism. If their economies had both uncompetitive and export sectors, they could unashamedly take both protectionist and liberal positions simultaneously – as did both Canada and the United States.

North America offers us a fascinating locale for looking at transborder agricultural governance, since it contains the three basic levels of the international power hierarchy. At the centre is the United States, the global superpower. At the margin is Mexico, feeble in state capacity and low in rural productivity. And in the middle is Canada, generally on the receiving end of international rule making but able on occasion to wield power of its own. The huge imbalance in the relationship between prosperous Canada and the United States on the one hand and poor Mexico on the other starts with differences in their comparative natural endowments. Although Mexico contains territories as vast as

Table 9.1: Availability of land per agricultural worker in the United States, Mexico, and Canada

	Hectares of arable land	Proportion that is irrigated	Hectares of pasture	Hectares of forest
USA	59.1	7.4%	79	58.5
Mexico	3	0.7%	9.2	2.8
Canada	97.4	1.9%	74.4	116.8

Source: Calva Tellez, 'Efectos del TLCAN,' 230–1 (see n.1).

those in the United States and Canada, the quality of its agricultural land, much of which is mountainous, does not match that of its plains-rich neighbours to the north. The drastic difference in the quantity of land available for each agricultural worker in the three countries is summarized in Table 9.1 above.[1]

Differences in fiscal capacity, demographic make-up, and governing ideology have resulted in major asymmetries in agricultural capacity between Mexico and its two continental partners. The cumulative polit-ical-economy effects of over a century's agricultural policies applied to these differing resource endowments can be gleaned from a single technological index of agrarian competitiveness, the number of tractors each economy has per rural worker: Canada: 1.8; United States: 1.6; Mexico: 0.02 – that is, two tractors for every 100 campesinos.[1]

Prior to trade liberalization, tariffs, quotas, and other barriers were imposed when producers felt threatened by imports. In each country, these programs had evolved out of a desire to cosset the family farm and its voters, insulate domestic agriculture from the turbulence of the world market, and ensure long-term food security. Farmers were con-sistently strong enough to frustrate governments' attempts to liberalize agricultural trade in the GATT era. Meanwhile, processing industries remained primarily in the hands of domestic companies. Yet the pres-sures of global change has been relentless, so this chapter attempts to determine to what extent transborder governance has affected how the three national governments' juggle the often conflicting needs of their various farming sectors, some of which demand support for exporting surpluses while others seek protection from the importation of other countries' excess produce.

Because of the liberalization of specific sectors and the security that NAFTA provided for increasing cross-border investments in food-processing facilities, agricultural trade within North America increased rapidly from the 1980s on. Transnational corporations began consolidating processing facilities and rationalizing their location on a continental basis. As a consequence, marketing and food-processing TNCs started to pressure farmers to ensure the consistency and predictability of supply without regard for national boundary or season.

Of the many sectors whose regulatory problematic cast light on the governance issues that concern us, this chapter addresses two that reveal different tensions in US-Canada relations and a third that brings out in stark relief the US-Mexico asymmetry: wheat, beef, and corn. Wheat involves a dynamic in which Canada's power as a surplus exporter is substantial, while beef is a sector in which US health considerations have marginalized Canadian producers. Corn shows how Mexico has chosen to adopt the neoconservative paradigm, moving rapidly and radically from autarchy to joining the American hegemony – with catastrophic consequences.

The beef, wheat, and corn markets had achieved different levels of integration and domestic competitiveness prior to NAFTA. As trade in these products increased, different forms of conflict resulted. The manner in which national governments responded – or failed to respond – to the ensuing outcry from their domestic producers forms a central element of this analysis. In the already highly integrated Canadian-American beef sector, further integration gave rise to distinctly continental issues necessitating harmonized policy responses jointly crafted by government and sector representatives across borders. Increases in wheat flows from Canada to the United States spawned battles between producer and industry groups sparring for control over the US policy-making process. At the same time, increased exports of corn from the United States to Mexico provoked political struggles there by grass-roots activists championing redistributive and cultural concerns. In all three sectors, NAFTA's constraints on national governments allowed TNCs active on the domestic political scene to offset the traditional influence of farmers' lobbies. The overall result has been to weaken government support for domestic producers to the benefit of transnational agri-processors.

This analysis shows how these differences developed and how political actors managing the transition to NAFTA's regime failed to mitigate their impact once protective trade measures were removed. The chapter begins with a historical review of agricultural policy within the United States in order to explain how conflicts within Washington's regulatory system determined outcomes affecting the political economy of Canadian beef.

The US Agricultural Welfare State

Until the passage of the Agricultural Adjustment Act (AAA) of 1933, US government support for agriculture had been provided indirectly through tariffs, research grants, and credit assistance. Part of the New Deal's activist response to the Great Depression, the AAA represented the first major US effort at direct market intervention. Its acreage controls to reduce supply, minimum-price guarantees, demand-expansion measures, and stock holdings in the Commodity Credit Corporation dominated US farm policy for the next forty years.[2] In addition to protecting farmers against low-price imports, the AAA's infamous Section 22 authorized the secretary of agriculture to 'use import quotas and/or other quantitative restrictions to isolate domestic markets.'[3] The farming industry's chronic instability was resolved and the viability of both family farms and larger farm businesses enhanced. Subsequent measures saw to it that US government resources were used not only to provide such support for farming as research and conservation but also to subsidize specific crops: wheat, corn, rice, peanuts, milk, lentils, even honey. As a result, many US farmers were assured adequate returns on various basic farm products and were insulated from the oscillations of world market prices.[4]

Although this protectionist system was threatened by the 1947 GATT agreement, Washington took advantage of its global dominance by having the liberal global-trade hegemony that it was constructing exempt it from constraints on its agricultural protectionism. Three waivers from GATT's General Elimination of Quantitative Restrictions allowed it to protect any domestic farm program. Beginning in the 1960s, the US government shifted to direct subsidies that encouraged productivity. By the end of the 1970s, exports comprised 30 per cent of total US farm production.[5]

In the early 1980s, when European exports[6] were eroding the US share of the world market for grains and oilseeds, American agricultural lobbyists successfully pressed for more support. Productivity increased, but the cost of agricultural subsidization had risen by 1986 to over US$88 billion.[7] Limiting supply on the US market raised domestic prices, while encouraging exports ensured grain-handling and food-processing TNCs greater profits.

Table 9.2: US Agricultural Output and Export, 1998–2002

Product	US output as per cent of global output	US exports as per cent of global exports
Corn	41	67
Soya	22	54
Wheat	10	26
Sorghum	23	80
Cotton	19	27

Source: Calva Tellez, 'Efectos del TLCAN,' 227 (see n.1).

Although subsidies increased, the number of beneficiaries declined. By 1982, 2.5 per cent of the US population lived on the land. Of the surviving farms, only 1 per cent generated sales of over $500,000 but these took in 60 per cent of total farm income.[8] Government action to address the chronic problems of the family farm had evolved into the sponsorship of large agri-businesses in sectors that were either highly protected to preserve domestic markets or highly subsidized to promote export competitiveness.

The United States' global supremacy in agriculture by the turn of the century was impressive, as shown in Table 9.2. Given their electoral importance within states where they are concentrated, even relatively small rural sectors such as dairy and sugar wield remarkable influence over agriculture spending and trade commitments. US producer groups have also proven themselves adept at protecting themselves against imports by launching countervail and anti-dumping investigations through the Department of Commerce (DOC). The meagre burden of proof necessary to trigger 'temporary' duties through the DOC, when coupled with the extended process of litigation required to reverse DOC rulings at the International Trade Commission, has provided added protection for threatened producers. The long adjustment period provided by the DOC/ITC bureaucratic process is extended by the judicial system because policy changes by the Department of Agriculture (USDA) are enacted only after allowing for the policy's contestation through the often-biased forum of district courts in the various agricultural heartlands.

In a political climate in which US farmers and agricultural bureaucracies have been fighting hard to maintain their traditional political dominance, the mad cow (BSE) crisis in the highly integrated beef sector provides a timely case for evaluating the governance implications of the trend towards market continentalism. While initially appearing to herald a new era of protectionism in response to citizen and producer concerns, the crisis served ultimately to boost the impetus towards the continental coordination of food security necessary for maintaining the transnational agri-processors' supply lines and export markets.

Beef: Continental Interdependence

The trade in beef and live cattle attracted little political attention under NAFTA prior to the discovery of mad cow disease in a Canadian bovine. Canada-US tariff barriers, which had been relatively low, were removed soon after CUFTA was implemented, and NAFTA did the same for the beef trade among the three nations as a whole.[9]

The subsequent rationalization of beef-processing facilities led to distinct trade patterns across North America. Feeder cattle from Mexico, where they are raised more cheaply using imported US yellow corn, are increasingly exported to the United States where they are exchanged as needed with Canada. Differences persisting in meat-grading standards restricted US imports of packaged meat from Canada. Since slaughtered carcasses could be imported from Canada and still receive USDA grading, meat-processing capacity increased in the United States to handle Canadian exports. At the same time, the US beef-processing industry rapidly increased its exports to Mexico and Canada, both of which accept USDA grading. US feed-lot operators focused on delivering higher value cuts, as leaner Canadian-fed cattle serviced the US ground-beef market. This shows an industry taking advantage of comparative advantage in each country and adapting to fluctuations in market conditions across the continent.[10]

Industry associations across borders have made concerted efforts to lead the process of harmonizing sanitary requirements. The Restricted Feeder Program, a joint pilot project from 1997 in Alberta and Montana, sought to reduce testing requirements for brucellosis and tuberculosis on a reciprocal basis for cattle exchanged between specific regions in order to eliminate problems at border crossings and further reduce overall testing costs. The same year, the Canadian Cattlemen's Association launched an initiative of its own to track cattle through their lifetime using computer chips embedded in animals destined for human consumption.

The US Animal and Plant Health Inspection Service also urged that sanitary restrictions focus increasingly on setting standards for the whole of North America so that diseases could be better contained within continentally integrated markets.[11] The sanitary and phytosanitary provisions within NAFTA and the WTO's Agreement on Agriculture reinforced this view by confirming the need to base border measures on an objective scientific basis.[12]

Nevertheless, when the BSE crisis broke out, this emerging North American governance was swept aside as the United States closed its borders and separate national review processes were initiated to determine the extent of the outbreak. However irrational scientifically – cattle that could have been contaminated continued to be exchanged within national boundaries – this reaction was both a reassertion of the US government's traditionally strong regulatory power over agriculture and a seeming reversal of the NAFTA-accelerated continental-integration process.

Yet the February 2004 report issued by the USDA's Foreign Animal and Poultry Disease Advisory Committee's subcommittee investigating the BSE outbreak showed that a US-led transborder regulatory response was emerging. Staffed by international experts with experience in previous BSE crises (although, tellingly, with no representation from Canada), the subcommittee recommended policy actions for a continental hegemony which could minimize the risk of BSE spreading further. The subcommittee's comments on implementation bear quoting at length.

> The objectives cannot be successfully achieved by government alone. Effective implementation of measures requires a shared commitment and action on the part of national and state governments, producers, consumers, private industry, and veterinary professionals. *Extensive national coordination and cooperation is imperative, and should be extended to include the continent of North America.* We suggest that a BSE task force, which includes governmental and non-governmental stakeholders, be established under the leadership of the USDA in order to assure that policies are developed and implemented in a consistent, scientifically valid manner.[13]

The report stressed the importance of involving industry in developing these standards, which should be continental and would hence require some supranational governance. The sensitivity of markets to these issues would also demand the constant reinforcement and adaptation of standards over time. For harmonization to remain effective, some form of permanent supranational committee would need to oversee the maintenance and execution of shared standards across the continent's national boundaries. The Office of International Epizootics (OIE), an inter-governmental organization in Paris that provides guidance on animal-health issues, came to fill this role, introducing an element of global governance to the management of North America's transborder agricultural trade.

Since May 2003, when the ban on Canadian beef was implemented, the USDA and national cattle associations like the National Cattlemen's Beef Association actively sought measures that could accommodate the reopening of both US-Canada trade and US export markets. These efforts were consistently opposed by the Ranchers-Cattlemen Action Legal Fund (R-CALF), which represented local producers who benefited from the closed Canadian border. Although, in response to Canadian representations, the USDA announced a partial reopening of the border to Canadian boneless beef under thirty months of age in August 2003, R-CALF successfully sidetracked the USDA's efforts, preventing it from reopening the Canadian border in May 2004 and again in January 2005. In both cases, the ranchers' lobby argued before a Montana district court that the USDA had failed to justify its decision to reopen the border in scientific terms consistent with international standards as defined by the OIE.

In response, the USDA lobbied hard during the OIE's annual meeting in 2005 for a simplification of BSE risk categories. The OIE consequently approved a reduction in the number of risk categories from five to three and recast the criteria used to classify countries under each category. Canada and the United States were then put within the 'Controlled BSE Risk' category as countries that posed a negligible risk of transmitting BSE because of their risk-mitigation measures. In July 2005 the Court of Appeals for the Montana district reversed the earlier injunction and took specific exception to the district court's interpretation of the scientific standards for reopening the border by making eight specific references to the new OIE guidelines.[14]

The BSE crisis revealed two characteristics of integrated agricultural sectors under NAFTA. First, geographically concentrated US producers continue to exploit their protectionist mechanisms to prolong trade disruptions that favour their interests. The beef case underscored how the abundant avenues for litigation provided by the US judicial system can be manipulated to the temporary advantage of trade-vulnerable producers. However, national producer associations and the USDA have tended to support efforts to resolve trade disputes in order to minimize their impact on the larger issue of maintaining US export access to foreign markets.[15] The USDA's Animal and Plant Health Inspection Service stated this goal unequivocally in its response to R-CALF's continued litigation: 'Unless USDA takes the lead to establish the concept of Minimal-Risk Regions, based on risk analysis, for animal pests and diseases – especially for BSE – the United States (which has multiple effective mitigation measures in place) will be vulnerable to having its exports treated no differently than those of countries with rampant levels of pests and diseases ... By any measure, the United States presents a minimal risk of transmitting BSE. Likewise, we are convinced that Canada poses a minimal risk to trading partners.'[16] Rather than reverse course and oversee the weakening of the beef and cattle sector's continental integration, the export-oriented large producers and processors urged their government to redefine and raise the supranational standards governing trade so as to minimize the impact of isolated cases of BSE.

Given the USDA's support for the new OIE code, it seems unlikely that the border, once opened, will be closed again in response to the discovery of isolated cases of BSE in the future. To do so would negate US efforts to maintain stable world demand for its own beef and cattle. The crisis accelerated a process to harmonize sanitary measures by extending them to cover BSE. The new reliance on OIE standards provides the basis for avoiding further reversals. Given the dependence of Canadian exporters on US markets, fully harmonized standards premised on a US-backed version of the OIE code seem imminent. Of course, many variables could alter this scenario, including citizen response to a bigger outbreak.

As far as governance of the North American beef industry is concerned, the mad cow episode showed NAFTA to be irrelevant. The United States alternated between unilateral and imperial positions. Canada was partly peripheralized as it waited for the contradictions within the US political economy to be played out while defending its positions in Paris on the OIE and in Geneva on the WTO's Agreement on the Application of Sanitary and Phytosanitary Measures. Because of American TNC interests, transborder norms were ultimately strengthened but at the global not continental level. This picture of Canadian impotence shifts when we turn our attention to wheat, a sector in which Canada has been a major player, having developed its own institutional power on the international stage, in the form of the Canadian Wheat Board (CWB).

The Canadian Wheat Board in the Continental Grain Economy

During the Great Depression, Conservative Prime Minister R.B. Bennett rejected a comprehensive and interventionist program similar to the AAA. Instead, he negotiated preferred access to the British import market and resurrected the Canadian Wheat Board to help farmers to market their grain overseas. As part of an extensive effort in the Second World War to regulate agricultural production, prices, and exports, the CWB was given monopoly powers that were retained after the war. Gaining control of oats and barley in 1949, the CWB continued to grow in influence in export markets, becoming the single largest seller of wheat and barley in the world.

Canada then put extensive market-supply systems in place to shield central Canada's uncompetitive eggs, dairy, and poultry farmers from foreign imports. Domestic food-processing companies remained largely protected and Canadian-owned. Other forms of domestic support, such as freight subsidies for grain exports, were minor compared to those provided by the US government to its farm sector.[17]

The post-war period was a boon for Canada-US agricultural trade. While both countries protected sensitive sectors and subsidized those in which they competed in export markets, trade in livestock, fruits and vegetables, corn, durum, and hard red spring (HRS) wheat expanded steadily so that, by the 1970s, the United States had become Canada's main trading partner in agriculture. Although they rarely acted in unison, the two countries constituted the most powerful trading bloc in the global food regime.[18]

The bilateral free-trade negotiations of the mid-1980s did not bring major changes to Canadian agriculture. Canadian negotiators refused to make concessions on quota protections for the egg, dairy, and poultry industries.[19] The most significant agricultural item in CUFTA was the elimination of US tariffs on Canadian grains. Since US prices routinely exceeded the world price after 1989, the CWB shifted exports from third-country markets to the United States in order to take advantage of the price premium created by US domestic-supply programs which CUFTA now made available to Canadian wheat.[20] The increase in Canadian wheat exports directly affected North Dakota farmers who produced the same durum and HRS varieties that the Wheat Board was marketing. Despite multiple efforts by North Dakota wheat producers to restrict Canadian imports, NAFTA nevertheless reinforced the US commitment to a continental grain market.[21] American TNCs responded by increasing their investment in Canadian grain handling and processing operations from US$1.8 billion in 1989 to $5.0 billion in 1999,[22] a structural shift that would have important consequences for wheat's transborder governance.

The resistance of North Dakota farmers to agricultural continentalization illuminates the forces at play in this sector under free trade. No sooner had CUFTA come into effect in 1989 than the North Dakota wheat producers initiated a series of three legal challenges to block imports of Canadian durum,[23] which, they argued, the CWB was dumping in US markets. The first case claimed a violation under CUFTA Article 701.2 related to freight subsidies, the second sought to examine the 'conditions of competition' through the ITC, and the third utilized the binational panel process provided by CUFTA. By the time NAFTA was being debated, none of these cases had produced any convincing evidence of dumping, and no trade restricting actions had been recommended.

To persuade key lawmakers from wheat-producing states to support NAFTA's ratification, President Clinton committed himself to initiate an investigation under Section 22 of the AAA, but after NAFTA had passed through Congress, no Section 22 action was taken. The inadequacy of the free-trade agreements' judicial governance was confirmed when a truce in the conflict was achieved only by Washington and Ottawa hammering out a negotiated solution (the so-called 'Wheat Peace' agreement) which required Canada to limit its exports under fairly generous quotas for twelve months.[24]

By 1995, the United States had given up its Section 22 rights as part of the compromise reached in the Uruguay Round negotiations that launched the WTO. This further limited the North Dakota farmers' ability to challenge the CWB on questions related to discriminatory pricing or dumping, because the United States could no longer build a trade case simply to protect domestic supply. In this respect, global governance reinforced NAFTA's continental governance.

For its part, Canada's concessions within the Uruguay process included the elimination of the Western Grain Transportation Assistance (WGTA), which gave farmers subsidies for transporting wheat by rail. Ironically, market pricing undistorted by the WGTA rail subsidy made selling in US markets to the south even more attractive than hauling it by rail to ocean ports for export overseas. Propped up by export sales via the Export Enhancement Program (EEP), US prices provided a premium over the world market. Without Section 22 to protect the program, Washington implemented an End-Use Certificate program to track Canadian grain shipments in the United States and ensure that they did not end up as subsidized exports. This process was ineffective, since Canadian grain simply replaced the US grain that was exported. Washington soon responded by drastically reducing EEP expenditures after 1996.

While the Wheat Board was increasing shipments to the United States, American TNCs were investing heavily in Canadian grain-handling facilities. Prior to CUFTA, these facilities were primarily owned by provincial co-op pools and a few private Canadian firms.[25] After 1990, Con-Agra and Archer Daniels Midland (ADM) began building new elevators and forming joint ventures with provincial pools to improve handling facilities at US border points. Agricore, which had been created out of the Manitoba and Alberta wheat pools under ADM's control, was taken over by a resurgent Saskatchewan Wheat Pool, which itself went public, while Cargill became increasingly dominant in western grain handling. In the processing industry, the changes were equally radical. Prior to 1990, virtually all flour-milling plants had been Canadian-owned. By 2002, domestic ownership had fallen to 12 per cent of a milling industry in which ADM had acquired over 50 per cent of total capacity.[26]

The failure of US trade actions, combined with the consolidation of North American processing capacity in the hands of the same TNCs that handled US exports, supported the development of continent-wide procurement strategies which further reinforced export volumes. The Wheat Board began to make longer-term supply arrangements with the large-scale mills – especially for distinct crops earmarked for specific milling applications such as barley for malting, HRS wheat for bread, and durum for pasta.

While the barley trade presented only a few issues, American durum and HRS wheat producers pursued their quest to eliminate the Canadian Wheat Board. The Washington lawyer for the North Dakota Wheat Commission (NDWC) summed up the resilience of some US producers in the face of repeated defeats suffered in domestic, NAFTA, and WTO investigations: 'This will not go away, no matter who wins any of these individual decisions, until we achieve fundamental reform of the Canadian Wheat Board,' specifically the elimination of the

CWB's price guarantees to Canadian producers and its removal as the single-desk seller of Canadian wheat.

In 2001 the period of relative calm initiated by the 'Wheat Peace' agreement broke down once Washington agreed to the NDWC's demand for a Section 301 investigation of the Wheat Board. When the Office of the United States Trade Representative issued its report in 2002, it launched a four-pronged attack, including another anti-dumping and countervailing-duty investigation as well as three other cases that were routed through the WTO. The ITC investigation again found no material cause for action in the case of durum-wheat imports but ruled the opposite way for HRS wheat.

Significantly, the North American Millers Association (NAMA), which counted ADM and ConAgra among its members, sided with the Wheat Board in the hearings and lobbied against taking action against wheat imports from Canada. NAMA claimed that the CWB was an important source of supply at times when domestic stocks were low. Its members were especially well represented within the deliberations on durum when virtually every major milling organization steadfastly refuted any claim that the CWB was dumping grain into the US market.

During the investigation, the Commerce Department had levied duties on both HRS and durum wheat from Canada pending the ITC's findings. The durum duty was reversed and the HRS duty maintained pending the board's appeal of the final report. In February 2005 a WTO dispute panel confirmed that the CWB did not serve as an agent of the government in its export sales but rather acted in the interests of producers since its revised board structure was weighted towards producer representatives. In 2005 the ITC finally reversed its original decision on HRS in response to a NAFTA panel ruling in the board's favour. NAMA figured prominently, supporting the Wheat Board in both the NAFTA panel and ITC review process.

The issues in durum and HRS wheat reflected the reordering of political influence in the liberalized grain market. By opening up its domestic market to Canadian wheat, the United States had undermined its supply programs. Its concession to the WTO of Section 22 rights further weakened these programs by removing the protection they had relied on for sixty years. These changes in the United States' external constitution encouraged the rapid consolidation of its TNCs in processing. When American producers responded to the ensuing price pressures, any protectionist action by the US government was now subject to the

TNCs' offsetting Congressional influence as well as concern for the possible rulings of WTO/NAFTA dispute panels.

Conflicts over HRS and durum wheat reflected the turbulence among American domestic actors adjusting to a new policy paradigm in which integration continued as TNCs capitalized on their continent-wide procurement capacity. Nevertheless, locally concentrated producer groups like the North Dakota Wheat Commission persisted in their efforts to reconstruct protective trade barriers, if only temporarily. The numerous veto opportunities available to vulnerable American producers in both the legislative and the judicial process continued to provide them periodic respite, but they were now fighting an uphill battle.

Both NAFTA and the WTO had served to tip the long-term balance in favour of the US agro-industry's drive to continental dominance. Because of Canada's large, efficient, and high-quality production and the Canadian Wheat Board's global clout, the Canadian-American wheat relationship is the least asymmetrical of all North America's agricultural hegemonies.

While the CWB has successfully used global and continental trade norms to resist all attacks launched by Washington, it may ultimately be eliminated by Canada's own Conservative government because of Prime Minister Stephen Harper's Alberta-supported commitment to free-market solutions. An even more powerful example of the neoconservative paradigm in action is the contentious story of corn governance in Mexico under NAFTA.

Corn and Mexican Agrarian Reform

Mexico's agricultural industry developed throughout the twentieth century under the revolutionary rhetoric of the anarchistic Emiliano Zapata and the authoritarian reality of the PRI's corporatist control. Zapata's call for agrarian reform had mobilized peasants in the south of Mexico during the revolution by blaming some 300 powerful families' control of 70 per cent of the country's land for rural poverty.[27] Although Zapata never became president, his program for redistributing these lands to peasants and native campesinos was incorporated in the 1917 constitution. Soon after, the government began dismantling the country's haciendas and portioning them out into *ejidos* and other forms of communal landholdings that could not be sold because individual property ownership did not exist.

Prior to President Lázaro Cárdenas's election in 1934, ejidos were viewed by the state as a transitory instrument to placate peasant demands, but, believing that they were the key to the country's development, Cárdenas wanted them to become 'the central politico-economic actor in the countryside.'[28] By 1934, 7 million hectares had been allocated to 800,000 campesinos. During his six years as president, Cárdenas distributed to another million campesinos 18 million more hectares expropriated from large American, Italian, and German agricultural estates.[29]

In 1935 Cárdenas created the Confederación Nacional Campesina, which incorporated various elements of the peasant movement within the ruling party. Agrarian agencies of every variety and an agricultural bank were also set up – ostensibly to make the ejidos self-reliant but practically to extend the government's control over virtually all their production and marketing decisions.[30] Cárdenas's sweeping reforms provided a framework for his party and its long-lived successor, the Partido Revolucionario Institucional, to forestall unrest among the peasant population, a process that was centred on the president as mediator between interests, deriving his strength from holding together a set of constantly changing forces. The PRI and its presidents became adept at mitigating rural poverty just enough to keep renewing their lease on political legitimacy.

While some large irrigated ejidos prospered, most remained at the level of subsistence farming and focused on growing the traditional varieties of white corn used in making the staple of the campesino diet, tortillas. These varieties had evolved over thousands of years and were uniquely adapted to the growing conditions in the difficult terrain making up much of Mexico's rural farmland.[31] Meanwhile, owing to easier access to credit, better-quality land, investments in irrigation, and targeted subsidies for farm equipment, private landholders and ranchers were producing coffee, tomatoes, and livestock for export, thus providing critical foreign exchange to the Mexican economy.[32]

Successive presidents swung from declaring an end to land-reform policies (Díaz, 1964–70) to introducing sweeping new nationalist programs like the Sistema Alimentario Mexicano (SAM, Mexican Food System) under José López Portillo (1976–82). SAM promised to use oil-export revenues to subsidize efficiency improvements in smaller ejidos as a key element of a drive to food self-sufficiency for all of Mexico. But, when global oil prices collapsed in 1982, the foreign debt López Portillo had assumed to finance increased oil production triggered a banking crisis.

In order to meet debt-repayment guidelines, newly elected President Miguel de la Madrid began Mexico's counter-revolutionary transformation. He cut back heavily on social expenditures, began to wind down Mexico's import-substitution regime, and prepared the nation to join GATT in 1986. In 1987 the government signed a Pacto de Solidaridad Económica (Economic Solidarity Pact) with organizations representing business, labour, and agriculture. This was a somewhat less brutal version of the neoconservative anti-inflationary shock treatments prescribed by the International Monetary Fund for the other Latin countries of the hemisphere.[33]

Until then, the state had subsidized each link in the maize market chain through its Compañía Nacional de Subsistencias Populares (CONASUPO, National Company for Public Provisions), which provided a guaranteed price to producers, subsidized imports to meet any shortages in supply, and made cash transfers to compensate the milling and flour industries for selling their outputs at prices below cost. When subsidies at all levels were drastically reduced in the mid-1980s, various attempts to provide the poor with low cost or free tortillas failed to alleviate the deepening rural poverty.[34]

Despite de la Madrid's commitment to liberalizing the import-substitution regime, Mexico's protocol with GATT reaffirmed its right to manage its agricultural policy in accordance with the 'national interest' and, as a developing economy, afforded it continued latitude to protect its agricultural sector. But its attempts at targeting the needs of the rural poor remained ineffective.

By 1991, a census registered over three million campesinos in ejidos and indigenous communities that covered close to 60 per cent of rural land. The other 40 per cent was held privately by just over one million landowners.[35] These figures convinced President Carlos Salinas de Gortari (1988–94) to reinvent the rural economy through trade liberalization. 'Opening' the economy would fight inflation through the downward price pressure of cheaper imports and trigger the reallocation of resources to areas where Mexico enjoyed a comparative advantage.

Given what Salinas believed to be the failed promise of land distribution, he enacted a reform of the constitution's Article 27 in 1992 aimed at transforming the ejido property regime. These measures, which were meant to create more legal certitude in resolving disputes over tenancy and eliminate prohibitions on profit-making enterprises in order to attract investment and stimulate agricultural production, allowed members of ejidos and communes to gain legal title to their land and decide how to go about increasing its productivity – including mortgaging or selling it.[36]

Salinas hoped that resources going into inefficient maize production would be reallocated to investment in irrigation or machinery that would increase production in such lucrative export sectors as horticulture to supply the US and Canadian markets. Overall, the objective was drastically to reduce the rural population and channel its surplus labour power to low-cost export-oriented maquiladora manufacturing and assembly industries for American TNCs. Boldly, if recklessly, Mexico's import-substitution regime was replaced by an export-oriented growth policy that sought the efficiencies promised by free trade as a springboard for the modernization of Mexican agriculture.

To soften the blow most campesinos would suffer from these reforms, Salinas set up income subsidies through the Programa de Apoyos Directos al Campo (PROCAMPO, Program for Direct Support for the Country), which sought to achieve more equitable rural-income distribution by decoupling support payments made to campesinos from their planting decisions. In 1994 PROCAMPO provided one-quarter of the income for some 3.4 million campesinos through payments of $100 per hectare,[37] yet these payments lost 40 per cent of their real value as a result of inflation, so that Mexico's campesinos were ill-prepared for the next shock which came from the United States as a result of NAFTA.[38]

NAFTA Negotiations and the Grand US-Mexico Bargain

In the trilateral negotiations, Canada refused to re-open CUFTA's provisions on agriculture and so these were pasted virtually unchanged into NAFTA's text. Ottawa and Washington were content to leave such contentious issues as the role of the Canadian Wheat Board for discussion at WTO-driven multilateral negotiations. Meanwhile, protracted US-Mexico haggling focused on corn, horticulture, and sugar. The obvious trade-off was for Mexico to open its grain markets in return for getting its producers' access to US fruit and vegetable markets,[39] but both countries faced significant domestic obstacles to making concessions in these areas. Few believed that Mexico would subject millions of campesinos to competition from the efficient, industrialized, and heavily subsidized US corn industry.[40] For their part, American negotiators were well aware of Florida-, California-, and Texas-based fruit growers' influence in Congress and were loath to provoke a political storm by making concessions to Mexico's horticultural exporters that might hold up the entire NAFTA deal.

Supported by little more than a few orthodox studies predicting export-oriented growth following free trade,[41] Salinas signalled his willingness to open up the grain market, linking US access to the Mexican corn market to Mexican access to the US fruit and vegetable markets.[42] Aware of the domestic political costs on both sides of the border, negotiators mitigated their impact by granting an extended, fifteen-year phasing- out period for tariffs and quota restrictions. Rather than rely, as North Dakota farmers had to, on the Department of Commerce's countervail and anti-dumping investigations to prop up regionally vulnerable producers, Florida and California growers had their protective mechanisms written directly into NAFTA. Playing on Salinas's weakness once he revealed how desperate he was to close a deal, Washington obtained safeguard provisions allowing temporary trade barriers to block spikes in horticultural imports from Mexico.

On sugar, Mexico fought hard for concessions, but US negotiators were not willing to confront their powerful domestic lobby. The subsequently disputed compromise offered only limited access in the first six years, with later allowances designed to prevent Mexico from transshipping sugar to the United States from Caribbean states like Cuba. Well aware of low-cost High Fructose Corn Syrup (HFCS) replacing sugar in many sweetener markets, US sugar producers also wanted to avoid Mexico importing cheap HFCS from other countries and thereby creating a domestic sugar surplus that could be sold in the United States at the artificially high prices that government subsidies provided there.[43] The interpretation of this part of the deal hung on a letter US Trade Representative Mickey Kantor negotiated at the last minute when sugar interests formed a block that threatened to hold up NAFTA in Congress. Both the validity and the US interpretation of the letter were disputed by the Mexican government, which relied on a different version of the letter that their own trade negotiator had drafted. Neither text was ever signed by both parties, and the terms of the agreement remain at the centre of continuing disputes concerning trade in HFCS.

While the transition periods for sensitive industries were long, they were not endless. Despite their conflicts, both negotiating teams dreamed of the year 2008 ushering in continent-wide agricultural markets for all but a few farm products. With regard to corn, nightmares would have been more appropriate.

Corn: US-Mexico Trade with Low Tariffs and High Subsidies

Taking up 60 per cent of the arable land and employing 8 per cent of the country's total workforce when NAFTA went into effect, corn cultivation plays as big a cultural role in Mexican life as an economic one.[44] Fully 80 per cent of the land cultivated for corn is rain-fed, mostly broken into small plots that are managed by ejidos. Nearly half of these are subsistence operations, with campesinos supplementing household income with off-farm labour; the other half produces small surpluses for the purchase of necessities.[45] Opening up this marginal economy to imports of industrially produced American corn benefiting from massive US government subsidies jeopardized the livelihoods of millions of campesinos, disrupting a deeply entrenched way of life.

The Salinas administration's plan to deal with the social-welfare issues caused by liberalizing trade in corn centred on offsetting campesinos' income losses by direct income supports provided through PROCAMPO. Traditional price supports furnished by CONASUPO would be gradually reduced in tandem with the tariff declines negotiated in NAFTA. This decoupling of income support from the production of specific commodities was meant to liberate farmers' planting decisions and induce them to respond to the market's price signals. Increased technical assistance and greater expenditure on research would help increase yields. At the same time, cheaper staple costs through the reduction of price supports and duty-free imports would check inflation and attract foreign investment in the food-processing industries, resulting in more efficient production of profitable agricultural exports and a migration of farm workers to jobs provided by export-oriented manufacturing sectors in the cities.[46]

Virtually all these assumptions proved faulty. Import-enhancing policies resulted in an unsustainable current account deficit. In December 1994 the peso fell drastically, pushing the Mexican economy into its worst recession since the 1930s. PROCAMPO payments did not keep pace with inflation (which ran as high as 52 per cent) and consequently lost much of their real value to campesinos already beset by a slump in prices resulting from the market's abrupt opening. Rural producers' income fell as the state reduced its agricultural supports. Planned increases in spending on research and technical assistance were also cut and, in any case, could have little impact on the most destitute. With the fall in the peso, the volume of bad loans in the agricultural sector increased, shrinking credit available to ejidos, few of which had abandoned their traditional land-holding practices or privatized their land rights and so were unable to pledge their land as collateral. Credit available for corn producers fell 76 per cent between 1994 and 2000.[47]

While the reduction in credit and income support had a direct impact on small white-corn farmers, the Mexican authorities' decision not to apply permissible tariff rate quotas (TRQs) on yellow-corn imports was highly contested.[48] The government assumed that, because most imported corn was yellow and so destined for industrial or feed use, it would have no impact on the supply or price of domestic white corn, which is used for human consumption. By not implementing the TRQs, the government was deciding to encourage the growth of its livestock, HFCS processing, and industrial flour industries in order to create export opportunities and attract foreign investment. In the wake of the 1994 peso crisis, Salinas needed to encourage these FDI flows. What better way to show his commitment to the new spirit of NAFTA than by foregoing his right to impose tariffs on over-quota US corn exports?

Despite the government's optimism, domestic white-corn prices plummeted and, instead of being slowly reduced over the fifteen-year transition period that had been negotiated, converged with the US domestic price within thirty months of NAFTA's implementation.[49] At the same time, the billions in revenue that were lost by the government not implementing the TRQs limited the resources available to provide PROCAMPO-based income support to marginal farmers and encouraged even the most resilient to consider exchanging their livelihood for salaried employment.

Confronted with the stringent fiscal constraints imposed by Washington and the International Monetary Fund as a precondition of their 1995 peso bailout, the Zedillo administration accelerated cuts in CONASUPO by reducing the price floor CONASUPO provided to farmers. CONASUPO also redirected its reduced funds, helping states where corn farming was more efficient and abandoning those where smaller, less efficient, ejidos prevailed. With no access to credit, virtually no storage capability, and little experience with an open market, the small white-corn campesinos' already desperate position deteriorated further.

The overall impact of these economic changes also provoked new environmental problems. As mechanized farms responded to import challenges, they increased fertilizer and water use, leading to reductions in the levels in Mexican aquifers and to concerns about soil degradation.[50] In addition, while planting genetically engineered crops was officially illegal, increased use of US hybrid varieties as feed prompted concerns about the threat that transgenic varieties posed to Mexico's rich heritage of wild-corn varieties.[51] The expansion of rain-fed cultivation areas increased deforestation while existing land deteriorated for lack of the resources to maintain its long-term quality.[52]

The remaining elements of Salinas's plan met with mixed success. Horticultural production did increase, as did exports to the United States, but these increases satiated the US market long before they created enough opportunity to draw significant labour from corn cultivation. In addition, most ejidos' land was unsuited to horticultural production. Having used NAFTA-mandated import restrictions to reduce Mexican imports in peak growing seasons, US growers increased their efficiency, forcing Mexican producers to reduce their costs and negating the possibility of significant job gains.[53]

While exports of horticultural products more than doubled in the 1990s, productivity gains accounted for much of this increase. The number of hectares cultivated increased by only 19 per cent during this period and less than 5 per cent of the newly cultivated land grew corn.[54] Overall, the number of agricultural producers within Mexico decreased dramatically – by 21 per cent between 1991 and 2000. Among over 900,000 who left the industry, more than 85 per cent were either communal farmers (*ejidatarios*) or other peasant farmers (sharecroppers/renters) working marginal land in lower-yield areas.[55] While 9.3 million entered the workforce between 1994 and 2003, only 3 million new jobs were created in the formal sector.[56] Some campesinos may have been attracted to new job opportunities created by NAFTA in other sectors, but these employment data suggest that most left the land hoping in desperation to reach the United States.

The liberalization of the corn trade coincided with an increase in rural poverty, continuing the trend precipitated by the 1982 debt crisis: Mexico's index of income inequality, the GINI coefficient, increased steadily, rising from 42.5 in 1984 to 50 in 2000.[57] As a result, increased feelings of cultural displacement fostered rural rebellions inspired by the original hero of agrarian reform, Emiliano Zapata, most notably the insurrection that was launched in Chiapas by subcomandante Marcos on January 1, 1994, the day that NAFTA came into effect.

Explaining the Mexican government's failure to resolve the social-welfare issues exacerbated by liberalized corn trade requires an analysis of what factors, beyond its steadfast commitment to neoconservative ideology, helped to shape Mexico's trade-negotiation position and subsequent policy (non-)decisions. When Salinas and his negotiators consulted some business chambers concerning NAFTA, they virtually ignored maize producer groups. In contrast, representatives of the Mexican food-processing industry (industrial flour processing, meat/poultry processing, soft-drink bottling) were in close contact with Mexican negotiators through their representation within the private-sector consultation group, the Coordinación de Organismos Empresariales de Comercio Exterior, which, as we saw in chapter VII, enjoyed direct access to the negotiations in the 'room next door.'[58] Among other potential benefits of liberalized trade, processors of industrialized food were eager to gain access to the United States' large Mexican immigrant market.

Tortilla prices, which should have benefited from the fall in corn prices and the downward trend in real wages, increased at a rate more than double that of inflation.[59] While generalized subsidies were removed, subsidies to the two largest companies (GIMSA and MINSA) that accounted for 97 per cent of the market for industrial corn flour actually increased.[60] The government was subsidizing two firms which acted as a cartel, extracting monopoly profits.[61]

Other forces were at play. With the break-up of the Soviet Union, one of the United States' main export markets for corn disappeared. A possible ban on imports of genetically modified corn in the EU, Japan, and South Korea, which would eliminate three other big markets, made Mexico the largest remaining untapped corn market and so extremely attractive to American exporters.[62] US agri-business was equally eager to locate processing facilities in Mexico, taking advantage of lower labour costs. Under NAFTA, American TNCs rapidly stepped up their investment in Mexican food-processing facilities made economically attractive by the newly liberalized domestic Mexican market.[63]

Salinas was aware of the danger that opening up trade in corn represented for campesinos, but he was more attuned to the potential benefits it offered to corporate interests. Rather than continue previous presidential patterns, alternatively supporting and stifling the demands of the rural poor in order to play them off against corporate interests, Salinas chose sides. Having used NAFTA to pre-commit future administrations to his market-based agrarian reform,[64] he made decisions that drastically increased the costs future administrations would face if they tried to reverse this agenda.

Subsequently, the campesinos' worsening plight demanded attention by President Vicente Fox as corn imports continued to grow. Rising unrest finally prompted Fox to allocate $267 million more to rural-development programs, but in doing so he flatly refused farmers' demands to renegotiate NAFTA.[65] Fox's 2002 'Armour Package' – a range of non-tariff border measures that could slow down imports crossing the border into Mexico – promised to increase trade actions in order to give Mexico's agricultural industries the 'breathing space' necessary to develop into competitive players in world export markets. Far from addressing the welfare needs of smaller producers, Fox defended corporate trade interests.

In 2004 the Mexican Congress finally implemented the maximum bound tariff on above-quota white-corn imports (72.5 per cent as opposed to the token 2–3 per cent that had become the norm under NAFTA). Yet many marginal farmers had already been driven from their plots. Tariffs on yellow corn meanwhile remained low, while import levels were expected to remain high, with the one-third for human consumption competing with domestic white-corn production.[66]

Presidents Salinas, Zedillo, and Fox made decisions benefiting American TNCs and domestic corporate interests based on their faith that the market provided a better adjustment process than state intervention. In this process, the Mexican government became more responsive to the need for FDI and foreign exchange than to its own rural constituency.

Both the letter and spirit of NAFTA prevent any significant policy reversal. Mexico's need for FDI has not decreased, and to raise input prices for industries that have already chosen to invest in Mexico would send a bad signal to those considering new investments. To make the investments necessary to improve the competitiveness and viability of marginal campesinos would require a nationalist program of heroic proportions – given the policy framework established by NAFTA and the choices made by Mexican governments during its first ten years. It would also run counter to the rationale behind negotiating NAFTA in the first place. The campesinos have suffered swings in fortune before, but the current environment suggests that the best they can hope for is some mitigation of their utter impoverishment.

The corn story shows how US hegemony was extended in one sector through the power of its neoconservative ideology in the periphery. Adherents to that ideology in Mexico deliberately rejected national autarchy in favour of moving into the American economic sphere of influence.

Conclusion

National governments interested in liberalizing trade often face hurdles in advancing their agenda when protected industries command powerful domestic assets. Through their historical importance to both national culture and national security and their unique geographic dispersion within the liberal democracies that make up North America, farmers have historically wielded enough political power to ensure their continued protection in the face of trade liberalization.

Having approached the limits of liberalization in less contentious areas, some trading nations have sought to overcome the interests of protected domestic producers in favour of those that – whether owing to government subsidization or true comparative advantage – are competitive internationally. CUFTA and NAFTA provided an opportunity for North American nations to overcome domestic protectionist interests by negotiating a broad agenda and by divisive trade-offs within the agricultural sector.

In short, the executive branches of the US and Mexican governments used NAFTA as a way to trade agricultural producers' interests for gains in other areas. NAFTA's agricultural concessions would almost certainly have failed to pass either the US or the Mexican legislature had they not been bundled within the larger deal. The same was true for US concessions on agriculture during the Uruguay Round. The resulting trade rules in NAFTA and the WTO have caused the policy options of national governments to become increasingly constrained, while at the same time facilitating the investment strategies of American TNCs whose interests these agreements fostered.

The North American beef industry showed that integration created shared risks when a food-safety crisis like BSE emerged. The likelihood of similar crises in the future will cause transnational meat processors and export-oriented agri-businesses to continue to press for revisions to OIE-based standards that support both the viability of export markets and the continued exploitation of comparative advantage within the continent.

In wheat, where competitive sectors existed across the border, liberalization rendered domestic supply-control programs ineffective. Transnational agri-processors responded to the elimination of barriers by consolidating ownership and rationalizing facilities on a North American basis. NAFTA provided security for TNCs to pursue this continental-procurement strategy in the face of numerous trade disruptions by local domestic producer groups which continued to flex their considerable, if declining, political and judicial muscle. The emergence of powerful agri-business interests benefiting from increased trade buttressed the traditionally weak voices of opposition to protectionist producers in Congress. The resolution of the wheat disputes under NAFTA promises TNCs that the halting trend towards US-led cross-border market governance will continue. In this sector, we can see a less asymmetrical form of hegemonification in which the US corporate takeover of grain processing and transport in Canada has enabled the country's farmers to sell their wheat in the hegemon's formerly protected market.

US-Mexico free trade in corn heavily favoured the industrialized trading partner, suggesting that hegemonification in this sector has had a strongly asymmetrical character. The social-welfare crisis provoked among smaller Mexican producers was not easily alleviated by opportunities in other sectors, whether industrial or agricultural. The largely indigenous campesino population did not relocate to new forms of employment in different regions. To have subjected millions of its citizens to the market's violence was a harsh position for the Mexican government to have taken. To have exacerbated the adjustment pain by going beyond the treaty terms to promote narrow corporate interests was extraordinary. The pre-commitment of future regimes to NAFTA's disciplines has perpetuated these tragic consequences for marginal farmers across Mexico.

As revealed by these three sectors' distinct issues, the governance of agriculture in North America appears considerably more than meets the non-expert eye. Apart from the implementation of its rules, NAFTA's role as continental government has proven negligible. Instead, transborder governance turned out to be a mix of ideological clashes and internal conflicts within the US and Mexican political systems, structural shifts caused by massive transnational corporate investments in the periphery, and the occasional resort to global norm making – a confusing, ever-shifting scenario in which the United States government still plays the central role.

Intergovernmental power relationships differed significantly from sector to sector. In beef, the three federal governments seemed content to let the industry define itself on a North American basis. Handling the mad cow crisis, the United States was imperial, not hegemonic, since it did not include Canada and Mexico in working out a normative regime. In wheat, a rapid hegemonification of the grain handling and processing sectors through the extension of US corporate control in Canada coexisted with a persisting, more equal relationship between the American grain producers and their Canadian competitors, whose Wheat Board gave them substantial organizational clout. In the other bilateral relationship, NAFTA precipitated a massive extension of US hegemony into Mexico, which had willingly subscribed to the Washington consensus by rashly opening its gates to subsidized American surpluses. Mexico's voluntary self-insertion in the US agricultural economy marked an abrupt abandonment of its autarchy and so a reduction of the structural imbalance between its relationship with the United States and Canada's. On the other hand, its substantially increased rural destitution suggested that the demographic imbalance had increased between the two peripheries and their hegemon. Reframed in terms of the global hierarchy of power, Canada remained solidly in the middle, while Mexico split in two: its industrialized, export-oriented agriculture brought it into competitive play while its surviving ejido agriculture remained stubbornly marginalized, declining into deeper misery.

There are other economic sectors that appeared to show that North America was much more than met the eye. Yet, as we will see in the three chapters of Part Three, even the North American steel industry, with all its trilateral solidarity, textiles and apparels, and capital markets are experiencing severely globalizing pressures.

PART THREE

The Continent in Transition:

Further Reconfiguration under
Globalizing Pressures

Some sectors that presented themselves as decidedly North American just a decade ago are being transformed by strong globalizing pressures. The steel industry along with textiles and apparel developed a stronger North American character after NAFTA but have since begun to lose their continental coherence. Similarly, the continent's capital markets had developed a strong North American integration but are now losing their continental character as stock exchanges merge and acquire each other on the global stage.

This trend is explored in three separate chapters in Part Three. Chapter X focuses on steel, chapter XI on textiles and apparel, and chapter XII on capital markets, each analysing a sector with its own distinctive history and present-day challenges. Together, however, they illustrate the commonality that binds these sectors together, in particular their declining North American character in the face of globalization, NAFTA notwithstanding. Here again, the pattern is the same. So-called free trade among the continent's three constituent countries did not create a cohesive North American market, let alone a continental entity with shared interests, values, and political and economic strategies.

X The Steel Industry

As one of the most regionally integrated industries in North America, steel should be an excellent example of transborder governance. In the fallout from NAFTA and in the face of an increasingly globalized steel market, the United States, Canada, and Mexico did indeed band together continentally to an unusual degree. Since 2001, the North American steel sector has appeared to be functioning as a regional bloc in such international forums as the WTO and the OECD, where it proposed combined and cohesive international-trade strategies. In 2003 the North American Steel Trade Committee (NASTC) was created to institutionalize the already strong economic and political bonds that had developed among the three North American industries.

But these developments did not suffice to ward off the structural pressures of globalization, so that the steel industry's cohesion in North America is being eroded as significant portions of it have fallen under the ownership of companies from other continents. While all three steel industries have grown and play significant roles in their national economies, integration between the United States, Canada, and Mexico is highly unequal and so are the benefits of NAFTA. As in energy and agriculture, the US market tends to function hegemonically as the decision maker, with its two neighbours the decision takers who nevertheless participate actively in this steel regime. There are only marginal direct connections between the steel industries of Canada and Mexico.

This chapter first shows how the three national steel sectors had developed by the mid-1990s and then examines the change in their level of integration under NAFTA. Next, in the context of the steel industry's globalization, it discusses the difficulties and threats that drove the three sectors to seek safety in trilateral solidarity. This is followed by an analysis of the trinational cooperation in global and hemispheric policy formulation that occurred at both the industry and government levels and the resulting imbalance that emerged between the United States and the periphery. Finally, the chapter addresses the implications for continental industrial solidarity of the Mexican labour movement's inability to ally with its North American counterparts.

The Post-Second World War Boom and the Effects of American Protectionism

As the driver of their construction, transportation, and manufacturing sectors, steel has long constituted the highly prized and carefully protected core of the three North American industrial economies. Post-Second World War reconstruction was a major boon for steel companies in the United States, Canada, and Mexico, where new technologies and consolidated smaller producers fostered a significant increase in production.

By 1947, the United States controlled more than half of the world's steelmaking potential as a result of a huge expansion in its production capacity and the wartime destruction of its competitors' infrastructure. US steelmakers wanted to roll back labour-union gains that the Franklin D. Roosevelt administration had forced the industry to accept, but the United Steelworkers of America (USWA) – established in 1942[1] – was too powerful to be contained. Between 1946 and 1959, the USWA declared five strikes, each time shutting down the industry. American steelworkers emerged from these conflicts among the highest paid manufacturing employees in the world, but the burden of their gains in wages, health insurance, and pension entitlements – which became known as legacy costs – set up the industry for its subsequent collapse.

By the 1970s, such competitors as Japan and Germany had profited from government support to achieve technological breakthroughs and win back large parts of the global steel market in which the US share necessarily shrank. The only players in the American industry that expanded in the period between the 1960s and 1980s were the mini-mills, which had lower start-up costs, greater locational diversity, and more flexible job profiles as a consequence of using electric furnaces to melt and rework scrap steel. With mini-mill competition increasing and a decline in demand, the giant integrated US steel firms saw their market share plummet by 1985.[2] Several factors contributed to the decline of American steel, including stagnant technology in a protected industrial structure and a vertically integrated system that propped up the inefficient domestic mining industry and resisted importing cheaper Latin American ore.[3]

In the wake of the resulting bankruptcies and closures, labour groups pressured 'big steel' to mobilize politically and demand ever-greater government protection. By 1984, President Reagan had ordered voluntary restraint agreements (VRAs) to be negotiated with the twenty-eight countries that were perceived to be unfairly exporting to the United States. By 1989, imports had sunk from 27 to 18 per cent of total consumption.[4] Still, neither government support for new technology nor protection from more competitive international prices was sufficient to sustain the declining industry.

The combination of a deep economic recession in the early 1980s and the impact of US protectionism produced a crisis for the Canadian steel industry, whose only significant export market was the United States. Neither CUFTA nor NAFTA served as constraints on the US industry's litigious approach. As tariffs declined and trade pressures increased, so did US harassment of Canadian exports with anti-dumping and countervailing duties. Despite its big firms' membership in the American Iron and Steel Institute (AISI), Canada's status as the largest exporter to the neighbouring market only exacerbated US aggressiveness. Although Canada was not coerced into a VRA, American companies continually pressed for more trade-blocking sanctions. To defuse this pressure, Ottawa set up the Canadian Export Monitoring System in 1987. The next year the Canadian Steel Producers Association (CSPA) was formed in response to the AISI's failure to manage trade tensions between the United States and Canada.

Mexico's Steel Industry and the Crisis of the 1980s

As in the United States and Canada, Mexico's steel history is rooted in nineteenth-century railroad construction, when thousands of miles of track gave effect to President Porfirio Díaz's dual effort to create a nation state by industrializing the economy and linking the republic's disparate states. After the Second World War, the Mexican market was protected by import-substitution industrialization policies so that, by the 1960s, four companies dominated the market: Compañía Fundidora de Fierro y Acero de Monterrey (Fundidora), Hojalata y Lámina (Hylsa), Altos Hornos de México (AHMSA), and Siderúrgica Lázaro Cárdenas-Las Truchas (Sicartsa). During the 1970s, ISI fostered the expansion of national production, which reached more than 24 million tons by the end of the decade.[5] By 1980, Mexico's steel industry was able to meet the country's needs but was not internationally competitive in either price or quality.[6]

In the turmoil of the debt crisis in the early 1980s, Mexico's steel industry faced its own crisis when the collapse of global oil prices brought about a sharp decline in demand. The industry was also constrained by a system of strict price controls along with bottlenecks that kept production well below capacity and impeded specialization. This crisis was severely aggravated by the United States' own protectionism, which prevented Mexico from exporting its surplus northward.[7]

Even though the industry modernized in the 1980s, Latin America's external debt, which reached about US$300 billion and whose servicing amounted to more than half the region's total exports, led to severely decreased demand for Mexican steel in the hemisphere. The crisis continued even after Mexico embraced World Bank-enforced neoconservative reforms aimed at encouraging economic growth, attracting foreign investment, privatizing state industries, opening the market to foreign products, and joining GATT – in short, abandoning ISI. No longer protected by import permits, quotas, and high tariffs, Mexican steel producers found themselves unable to cope with rapidly increasing imports.

In the late 1980s, President Carlos Salinas de Gortari attempted to combat the effects of globalization on the Mexican steel industry by privatizing Mexico's steel mills, which had been nationalized. Although the new companies were profitable, they were sold at bargain prices and only after significant downsizing.[8] In most cases, the new owners had little or no knowledge of the steel industry. For example, the group that acquired Altos Hornos, the largest steel-mining corporation in Mexico, was formed only a few months before the takeover; later, it used the steelmaker as security for buying other state enterprises.[9]

NAFTA and the Roots of Continental Imbalance

NAFTA, and CUFTA before it, caused both Canada and Mexico to reorient their steel industries towards exporting to the United States. The removal of US tariff barriers made it possible for Canada and Mexico to export but also opened the floodgates for American steel exports to the periphery, introducing a high level of dependency and asymmetry between its two industries and the US hub.

Coinciding with CUFTA's implementation in the late 1980s, the United States experienced an import surge that provoked a new burst of protectionism. As hot-rolled steel imports surged by 70 per cent, prices declined by nearly 20 per cent, capacity-utilization rates fell, and six steel companies declared bankruptcy, a total of sixty anti-dumping cases were filed against foreign steel suppliers in 1999.[10] Further market-share loss to such international steel giants as Arcelor (Luxembourg), Mittal (India), and POSCO (South Korea) occurred, and continuing bankruptcies at the beginning of the twenty-first century led to American industry and union pressures for still more protection.

US-Canadian Integration

Following CUFTA and NAFTA, total Canadian steel production increased from 13 million net tons in 1985 to roughly 16 million in 2000. Total revenues rose from $8 billion to $11 billion in the same period and profits from $400 to $900 million.[11] This increase was largely due to penetrating the US market: during this period, Canadian steel exports to the United States increased from 3 to 4.9 million tons. In order to maintain a politically manageable share of the US market and to avoid the imposition by Washington of a VRA, Canadian steel companies were careful not to offend the American steel lobby. Despite the declaration of a free trade regime in 1989, the Canadian industry felt it prudent to limit its exports to its largest market.[12]

In a further attempt to evade continuing US harassment at the border, Canadian steel producers entered strategic alliances with American producers and consumers. By 2004, all of Canada's major steel producers operated in the United States. For example, Dofasco owned a plant in Ohio producing high-quality tubing for the automotive industry. The Saskatchewan-based IPSCO greatly increased its presence in the United States, operating plants in Minnesota, Arkansas, Iowa, Nebraska, Texas, and Alabama, so that the vast majority of the company's steel production took place in the United States. Stelco also partially owned and operated a variety of US-based businesses, focusing on iron-ore extraction.[13] By 2006, every major Canadian steel company had interests in the United States. Together, Canadian firms accounted for some 8,000 out of 100,000 US steel jobs with a total value of US$1.3 billion in an industry valued at approximately $50 billion.[14]

The Canadians' presence in the United States was not matched by American investment in Canada. Indeed, the only US steelmaker with a major stake in a Canadian plant was Oregon Steel, which owned 60 per cent of the Camrose Pipe Company of Alberta.[15]

US-Mexican Cooperation

After NAFTA, the Mexican and American steel markets became increasingly integrated. Mexican steel producers invested more than $4 billion in their steel sector, which allowed them to double their production from 10 million tons in 1991 to 19 million in 1999 (see Figure 10.1). Production lines expanded across the border, while strategic alliances, firm consolidations, and outsourcing became central to the industry's functioning. Grupo Villacero acquired a Texas-based mini-mill called Border Steel, becoming the first Mexican company to provide steel rods and wire to the US construction industry. In 1998 American AK Steel and Mexico's second largest steel producer, Hylsa, reached an agreement jointly to commercialize products in high demand by the Mexican automotive and appliance industries. In another instance, Altos Hornos established its most important alliance when it partnered with Ryerson Tull, a subsidiary of Inland Steel, to provide products for clients requiring high value-added steel and technical services. During this time, Mexico became the third-largest supplier of steel to the United States after Canada and Brazil.[16]

Growth in Mexico's steel capacity followed demand by the appliance and automotive industries. Between 1990 and 2001, the production of automobiles grew from 800,000 to 1,800,000 units.[17] Mini-steel produc-

Figure 10.1: Mexican national steel production, 1949–99 (millions of tons)

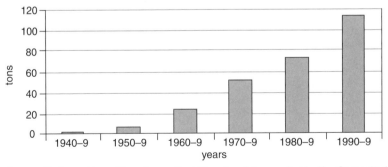

Source: Espinosa Vega, 'Transformación,' 58, using data supplied by the Gerencia de Análisis y Evaluación Económica de Canacero.

ers proliferated because they were more profitable than integrated companies. The inputs for finished steel products in Mexico are more expensive than in the United States, so low wages are necessary to achieve lower production costs.[18] In 1999 alone, the Mexican automobile industry consumed some 1.6 million tons of steel at the rate of one ton per vehicle. The development of high value-added steel products in Mexico depended on the demand from these two industries, but the domestic industry was still not developing adequate capacity, requiring most auto assemblers to import between 60 and 70 per cent of their steel needs, while truck assemblers imported between 30 and 50 per cent of theirs. Behind Brazil, Turkey, France, Taiwan, and Spain, Mexico produces 16.3 million tons of steel each year, exporting 5.6 million tons and importing 8.8 million tons.[19]

Because of the decreased demand for steel resulting from the Asian financial crisis during the late 1990s, when many manufacturing giants such as Daimler Chrysler and Samsung looked for new places to invest, Mexico became an attractive location because of its geographical proximity to the United States, its low labour costs, and its investment-friendly environment. This, and the sustained need for higher-grade steel by the automobile industry, pushed Mexico to improve the still comparatively low quality of its steel.[20]

A more aggressive, outward-looking steel industry, which has benefited from technology transfers, has made Mexican industrialists more self-confident and willing to approach the US market.[21] But, even with a free-trade agreement in place, the United States showed little continental solidarity, stepping up its anti-dumping cases against Mexico.[22] Despite NAFTA's putative border-lowering benefits, Mexico, as an exporter, became the target of many American trade actions. According to the US Commerce Department, out of the 250 trade cases being reviewed in 1999, 37 per cent were related to the steel industry.

The Emergence of a North American Steel Bloc

Despite the increase of intraregional trade (see Table 10.1), North American steel producers have been unable to improve their competitiveness vis-à-vis their Asian and European counterparts. As a result, less than 20 million of the more than 1 billion tons of steel traded in 1998 around the world were North American, compared to the more than 90 million and 60 million tons traded by the European Union and Asia, respectively.[23]

Table 10.1: North America's internal steel trade (thousands of tons/year)

	2002	2003	2004	2005	2006
Total Canadian steel imports from the US	3,275	3,758	4,657	5,204	5204
Total Canadian steel imports from Mexico	117	113	172	131	80
Total	3,392	3,871	4,829	5,335	5,284
Total Mexican steel imports from Canada	297	381	390	394	415
Total Mexican steel imports from the US	2,061	2,920	2,395	2,403	2,816
Total	2,358	3,301	2,785	2,797	3,231
Total US steel imports from Canada	2,766	2,668	3,670	23,463	31,467
Total US steel imports from Mexico	1,205	1,192	2,351	2,536	2,385
Total	3,971	3,860	6,021	25,999	33,852

Source: NASTC, 'Results of Search for Tombstone Information on the U.S., Mexican and Canadian Steel Sectors,' http://www.nastc.org/nasteel-index.html (accessed on April 14, 2008).

Between 2000 and 2005, China's production increased by 176 per cent, making it the largest steel producer in the world and the consumer of one-third of the world's output.[24] The seventh-largest producer of steel in the world, India, will double its steel capacity by 2019, when it will reach 100 million tons per year.[25] Brazil intended to use government loans to increase its total steel capacity by 30 per cent by 2008. Indonesia and South Korea were constructing one new steel-producing plant each every year with the help of their governments.[26]

This gigantic expansion of global capacity had direct and significant impacts on North America's three steel industries, causing them to consider new modes of cooperation. For the United States, the Chinese phenomenon was the latest symptom of a fundamental global imbalance. A 2000 report by the US Department of Commerce painted the familiar picture of fair-market-oriented US corporations beset by subsidized and unfairly traded foreign steel. The US industry had restructured itself in the 1980s and early 1990s by reducing production capacity 30 per cent and investing some $50 billion in new technology, but its rejuvenation was thwarted by the global financial crisis of 1997–8, when world steel demand collapsed and subsidized Russian, Japanese, Korean, and Brazilian steel flooded its market.[27]

The main institution through which the North American industry unified against the global steel market's pressure was the American Iron and Steel Institute. The AISI represented the largest and most important of North American steel industry's more than thirty special-interest groups. Its membership of thirty-one steel producers (including four in Canada and six in Mexico) together produce 75 per cent of North America's steel. Along with its counterpart in Mexico, the Cámara Nacional de la Industria del Hierro y del Acero (CANACERO, Mexican Iron and Steel Industry Association), and Canada, the Canadian Steel Producers Association – which boast solely national memberships – the AISI led a continental offensive against foreign steel producers.

The three associations' blamed their own weaknesses on their competitors' unfair systems. At the fourth WTO Ministerial meeting in Doha in 2001, the emerging North American alliance published a joint policy paper defending their governments' right to use anti-dumping and countervailing duties and advocating not just the elimination of all direct and indirect subsidies to steel industries but the liberalization of foreign steel markets, particularly in Asia, and the reform of the WTO dispute-resolution process.[28] These proposals were reiterated in their joint statement after the fifth WTO Ministerial meeting in Cancún in September 2003, which focused on the deleterious effect that currency manipulation by Asian governments was allegedly having on the global steel market.[29] As these positions showed, the global steel market was perceived by the North American industry as biased in favour of Asian producers. The insistence on the nation-state's right to use AD and CVD measures demonstrated the reactive and even antagonistic posture adopted by the North American steel industry towards its foreign competitors. Significantly, these proposals recommended reform of only foreign steel regimes; the North American status quo was implicitly supported as appropriate.

The North American steel alliance was much more open to its South American than to its Asian competitors. The US, Canadian, and Mexican industries were advocating the extension of their own economic-integration regime southward in order to create a hemispheric trade bloc that would stem trans-Atlantic and trans-Pacific steel imports.[30] A list of priorities was presented to each South American country's trade representative in the months before the November 2003 Free Trade Area of the Americas ministerial meeting in Miami. These included reaffirming the value of trade-remedy measures, eliminating subsidies, and defending open markets. The North Americans also argued for the maintenance of strong customs enforcement, the elimination of all steel tariffs, the creation of uniform national steel standards, and the extension of NAFTA's rules-of-origin criteria to the proposed free-trade zone.

The three North American industries also cooperated in various attempts to influence the international steel-trading system through the OECD's High Level steel process. The triad of AISI, CANACERO, and CSPA developed a direct relationship with the OECD secretariat when it solicited comments on its proposed Steel Subsidies Agreement, a controversial effort to develop a global consensus on disciplining state steel subsidies and limiting excess capacity. The North American steel alliance issued a formal commentary on the proposed agreement which offered suggestions on multilateral ways to 'balance' the steel trade by strengthening government measures.[31] Expressing enthusiasm for the OECD's desire to limit excess capacity in the global steel industry, it defended the North American countries' right to protect their domestic industries. The alliance maintained this position in its comments on the OECD's 'Elements of an Agreement to Reduce or Eliminate Trade-distorting Subsidies in Steel,' in which it rejected any moves to weaken domestic trade laws and give preferential treatment to developing countries.

Compliance by the Periphery with US Protectionism

To stem the import of allegedly unfairly traded foreign steel, the Bush administration introduced 'safeguard' tariffs under Section 203 of the 1974 Trade Act. Following extensive lobbying within the AISI by the CSPA and CANACERO along with their two governments, Canada and Mexico were exempted from the US safeguard action even though some Canadian and Mexican steel producers had been named as causes of the US industry's problems. By not challenging the new tariffs, Canada and Mexico preferred the special status they obtained through the exemption and entered a new hegemonic relationship with Washington.

The periphery's attempt to comply with the United States' safeguard tariffs is an unusual example of continental steel-industry cooperation. In June 2002 the AISI, CANACERO, and the CSPA released an analysis that listed techniques used to avoid the US tariffs put in place three months before. It stated that Mexican, American, and Canadian companies agreed that the US steel industry needed the protective tariffs to renew itself and outlined specific areas in which enforcement needed to be strengthened.[32] In this list were such tariff-avoidance tactics as 'transshipment' (when steel from overseas is shipped through a NAFTA country in order to claim being a product of that country) and 'substantial transformation' (when imported steel is allegedly 'transformed' in one NAFTA country in order to pass tariff-free across the border into another party's market). The analysis also justified Mexican and Canadian support for the tariffs in such circumstances by arguing that these evasive measures distorted statistics attempting to document market flows throughout the whole North American market.

While this collaboration illustrated the economic connections within the continental steel industry, it also brought to light an interesting paradox within the emerging system of continental steel governance: transnational cooperation by the periphery can strengthen protectionist tariffs imposed by the regime's leader. In the safeguards case, cooperation by Canada and Mexico legitimated measures that the US industry could later use against its two neighbours. Short-term policy collaboration seemed a second-best option since the safeguards were challenged by other trade partners and soon declared WTO-inconsistent.

North American Steel Trade Committee

At a meeting of the OECD High Level Group on Steel in December 2002, the three governments agreed to create the North American Steel Trade Committee, which would link their governments in a trilateral forum. The NASTC came into existence in Mexico City the following November, with the goal of promoting further openness within the North American steel market through the creation of an inter-governmental forum in which the three-capitals' positions could be coordinated.[33] The AISI, CANACERO, the CSPA, and the Steel Manufacturers Association, a second industry group headquartered in Washington, were the sole participants – apart from representatives of the three governments – at this inaugural meeting. Further developments occurred at the second NASTC meeting in May 2004, when discussions addressed the challenge of cheap foreign steel and the destructive impact of an eventual Chinese economic slowdown. At that time, the three industrial associations presented the three governments with their analysis *Challenges and Opportunities for the NAFTA Steel Industry and Governments.*[34]

While still in its infancy, the NASTC's mandate evolved from reacting to foreign and international developments to actively stimulating growth within the continental industry. In its mission statement released in 2004, the industry suggested that the governments also stress steel-market growth and competitiveness along with international trade-policy coordination.[35] As of 2008, it was impossible to know what effect these exhortations would have, but at the very least they were evidence of pressure for further government harmonization in steel policy.

Under the 2005 Security and Prosperity Partnership of North America, the NASTC advocated sectoral cooperation between the three countries' governments and industries.[36] With this goal in mind, the SPP directed the NASTC to develop a North American steel strategy to help articulate the policies it hoped the industry would pursue.[37] In June 2005 Canada, Mexico, and the United States coordinated their comments on the OECD 'Blueprint' for a steel-subsidies agreement. In it they praised the OECD for its efforts to forge an agreement to limit government subsidies but heavily critiqued the proposal itself, accusing the blueprint of being 'WTO-minus' and weakening existing trade disciplines. With a single voice, steel executives from Canada, the United States, and Mexico reported that 'unfortunately, the latest "blueprint" document prepared by the OECD secretariat falls far short of the objectives that are essential to any meaningful agreement ... As such, *North American* steel producers cannot accept it as a basis for further negotiations.'[38]

Since the creation of the SPP, movement towards further integration has been negligible apart from the creation of the North American Steel Trade Monitor website. This site presents consolidated trilateral information about the steel trade on the continent but does not give any analysis of the statistics.[39]

North America's governments are currently examining other ways of jointly addressing dumped and subsidized imports. The NASTC has successfully instituted a productive information exchange between the three governments which has laid the groundwork for a unified strategy to address distortions in the global steel sector, particularly government-supported capacity-expansion initiatives in large countries that have the potential to cause significant distortions in the global steel economy.[40]

The Influx of Foreign Capital: Decontinentalizing the North American Steel Industry?

Even as protectionist labour and government forces grappled with policies within the North American space, ownership of the steel industry has been shifting rapidly, as overseas steel giants established significant positions on the continent. In the United States, Arcelor Mittal acquired the large International Steel Group (a company that itself had taken over competitors Acme Steel, LTV, Bethlehem Steel, Weirton Steel, and Georgeton Steel). Since 2005, the Canadian steel industry that was once touted as a national success story has been completely hollowed out. Algoma was taken over by Essar (India), Dofasco by Arcelor Mittal (India), Ipsco by Svenskt Stal (Sweden), and, finally, Stelco by US Steel.[41]

At face value, these takeovers heralded a sharp shift away from a continentally focused steel policy, since in each case but one a North American producer was acquired by a globally competitive company controlled by non-North American capital. Indeed, only two of the top thirty global steel producers are owned in North America.[42] On the other hand, geography still plays a powerful role in steel production. Even under foreign ownership, steel producers located in North America are subject to unique continental circumstances. Arcelor Mittal, for instance, has been in the unusual position of having its North American subsidiaries defend – in US Congressional hearings – the maintenance of protectionist duties while representatives of its European subsidiary argue against these very same measures. Time will tell whether these new foreign owners continue progressing towards continental harmonization or, instead, integrate their North American operations within the larger global steel economy.

Labour: The Missing Link

A significant obstacle to transborder industrial and governmental steel-policy cooperation across North America is the isolation of Mexican labour unions, which have been less willing than industry to operate continentally. Mexican steel unions refrained from joining their counterparts within the NAFTA framework, because Mexico's labour code, its radically different labour history, and its weakening from neoconservative restructuring prevented the development of labour solidarity across North America.

In the early 1990s, when Mexican steel companies modernized, their needs for labour decreased and the resulting massive layoffs within the industry left thousands of workers virtually penniless. At the same time, programs of total quality control requiring that every step of the production process meet the highest standards forced steel manufacturers to be more vigilant. The automobile industry, for instance, demanded compliance with meticulous standards.

Workers who could not adapt to the new working conditions were considered superfluous and fired. Large firms split up their functions, services, and productive processes, subcontracting elements to smaller firms with the aim of reducing the number of contracted workers and so weakening the unions. When their national union accepted this radical downsizing, the steelworkers lost much of their power.[43]

Local unions were virtually powerless to support unemployed workers because the effect of the 1990s reform of the Ley Federal del Trabajo (LFT, the Federal Labour Law) facilitated direct links between employers and their workers. One of the LFT's most notorious features that had survived since the law came into effect nine decades earlier was the Exclusion Clause, which allowed a worker expelled from his or her union to be automatically fired by the employer.[44] Under this amended LFT, neither workers nor their local unions have any influence in the production process at any level. This lets a company hire only temporary workers and extend working hours at its sole discretion.[45] Services that used to be distributed through the local union such as continuing education for workers and their families can now be offered directly by the company using personnel from the Instituto Nacional de Educación para Adultos (National Institute for Adult Education), a federal government agency. The steel union leaders' concern to preserve their personal positions in the face of these reforms explained their disinterest in establishing links with their counterpart Canadian and US steel unions, which they saw as threats rather than sources of support. They had no interest in using NAFTA to recruit new members or to influence policy because doing so might mean relinquishing some of the personal privileges they enjoyed. Participation in a new level of governance would mean having to establish a working relationship with new actors whose language, interests, and motivations were foreign to them, and they were not prepared to risk this step.

Meanwhile, labour in Canada and the United States could agree on the issues facing the two steel industries, because the United Steelworkers of America was the dominant union in both. The Canadian and US branches of the Steelworkers were addressing the same two priorities: legacy costs and protection from foreign steel imports. The Steelworkers' US division actively lobbied Washington to guarantee the legacy costs resulting from failing steel companies' huge unfunded pension liabilities, which totalled $13 billion, so that pensions be paid to both active and already retired steel employees.[46] In Canada, the Steelworkers addressed the same issue, as both industry actors and government attempted to restructure Stelco, which had operated under bankruptcy protection since January 2004. The Canadian union's key demand was that any potential buyer of Stelco finance the company's $1.3-billion pension deficit.[47] Looking at the industry as a whole, the union proposed amendments to Canada's bankruptcy and insolvency laws that would strengthen Canadian workers' capacity to claim wages and benefits owed and retain existing collective agreements when a company enters bankruptcy protection. Like its US counterpart, it called on the government to guarantee pension benefits to steel workers.[48]

While the US and Canadian Steelworkers branches have often been in disagreement, since protectionist measures blocking imports of steel from Canada have generally had the support of the US union, they are for the most part aligned on significant issues. The self-isolation of the Mexican steel union restricts transborder labour solidarity, which might support the development of a coherent continental steel community, to the old North America

Conclusion

The failure of Canadian and US labour groups to achieve solidarity from below with their Mexican counterparts raises a broader question about the ambiguities of transborder governance in the North American steel industry. Since 2000, American, Canadian, and Mexican steel producers have indeed initiated a productive relationship with their industry organizations and governments in order to address common international problems, creating an embryonic transborder form of governance. The three governments have responded to the new co-operation among the continental steel producers by working with them in international negotiations.

Although trilateral governance in the steel industry arose as a reaction to a threatening imbalances in the international trade system, the North American attitude towards 'foreign' steel is ambivalent. While it has been decidedly hostile to imports, many industry actors have welcomed the rapidly increasing foreign ownership of the continent's major steel companies. In Canada, the Steelworkers chose to support the early bid of the Russian OAO Severstal for control of Stelco, even though Canadian and US companies were also engaged in the bidding process.[49] Similarly, in the United States, the Steelworkers welcomed the 2004 announcement that the International Steel Group (ISG) would be absorbed by the Indian giant, Mittal Steel, with President Leo Gerard tying the Steelworkers' support for the foreign acquisition to the purchasing company's ability to meet its legacy obligations to its workers. In both these examples, a foreign takeover was presented as a positive factor for the survival of steel production and its related pension obligations. The result is a strange dynamic in which major players in the North American industry rail against foreign steel *products* but invite their *producers* into the domestic marketplace with open arms.

During the debate over the Bush administration's safeguard program, private-sector actors largely supplanted government in providing a vision for the evolution of the North American steel industry vis-à-vis world markets. With the emergence of the NASTC, it appeared that the US, Canadian, and Mexican steel sectors were forging a new continental policy-making community, even though the organization supported a protectionism that was as old as industrial policy itself. Yet, while this trilateral steel governance was developing, European, South American, and Asian companies were acquiring steel operations in North America. The continent's restructuring by massive new foreign acquisitions suggests that the future of transborder governance in North America is much less certain than it had appeared for this sector just a few years ago. Continental steel governance is now becoming less important as global capital and global interests restructure transoceanically what – merely twenty-five years ago – were national and largely autarchic industries.

Steel was not unique, for, like it, the textile and apparel industry appeared to be continentalizing as a result of NAFTA's rules of origin. But chapter XI will show that such exogenous shocks as global regulatory change and China's emergence as the dominant world player broke down North America's incipient solidarity, leaving this sector's governance to its member governments' go-it-alone devices.

XI Textiles and Apparel

When NAFTA entered into force in 1994, a pair of industries expected to be shielded from global competition by a carapace of new regional rules: the auto sector was one, textiles and apparel the other. As it turned out, the combination of the three countries' textiles and apparel industries' under a single protection system unleashed dramatic changes in the relations between governments, private manufacturers, and labour unions across the continent. This chapter investigates the nature of these interactions and analyses the extent to which they make North America exist. It argues that the textiles and apparel sectors on the continent have generated a hub-and-spoke regime in which the US industry sets the rules, Mexico plays in inferior positions, and Canada participates, largely marginalized, along the sidelines.

If North America exists in this sector less than NAFTA's rules would have led one to expect, it is because of two subsequent seismic global events: the WTO's phase-out of the Multi-Fibre Arrangement (MFA) and China's ascendance as the world's textile superpower. Of the four parts to the analysis in this chapter, the first addresses the nature and structure of North America's three original textile and apparel industries. The next section gives a historical overview of the two bilateral relationships in the North American textile industry, while the third shows how NAFTA's rules of origin created a common North American production system in which the interests of US and Mexican companies meshed more closely than did those of US and Canadian firms. Finally, I evaluate how the relevant actors from industry, government, and labour across the continent responded to global adversities. It will ultimately become clear that, while the North American sector is more integrated than might have been thought, the prospect of a new continental governance of textiles and apparel in North America has dissipated under the linked forces of globalization and nationalism.

The History of North America's Textile Industry

In the multi-staged process of creating a garment, the textile industry produces fibres, spins yarns, then weaves, dyes, and finishes the fabrics. For their part, apparel manufacturers cut and sew the textile into garments. Lastly, retail chains market and sell the garments. North America's apparel chain has become a buyer-driven process in which the large US retailers play the pivotal role not just by setting the fashion trends and designing the garments but by directing production networks in a variety of exporting countries generally located in low-labour-cost economies in the global South.[1]

Textile manufacturing is capital intensive, so the barriers to entry in the industry are high. By contrast, fabricating apparel is a low-tech, labour-intensive, and very portable industry with few barriers to entry. The apparel sector is divided between producers of standardized clothes, who compete on the basis of price through economies of scale and low wages, and makers of garments for the fashion industry, who compete by proximity to the retailers and just-in-time manufacturing.[2] Although North America can be seen as one single production zone, Canada and Mexico are differentiated by their roles as fashion and standardized producers, respectively. As a result, the continent's governance in the sector consists of two bilateral relationships connected to the United States' large retail market. A brief profile of each national industry clarifies this picture.

The United States

The US textile industry first emerged when Samuel Slater, a gifted mechanic from England, established a water-powered cotton mill on Rhode Island in 1789. Over the course of a century, the industry gradually migrated south, consolidating its presence in the Carolinas, Georgia, Alabama, and Virginia, where it currently resides. Apparel manufacturing emerged much later in New York and Los Angeles.

The textile industry flourished in the twentieth century, profiting largely from economies of scale and extensive technological investments. Textile firms produced large runs of limited products to maximize efficiency.[3] Apparel prospered too. Singer's perfection of the sewing machine gave the industry some degree of automation, while standardized sizing propelled a ready-to-wear revolution in clothing. In 1879, 40 per cent of men's suits were ready-made; by 1920, factories produced nearly every suit.[4] The industry employed 1.15 million workers nationwide by 1960.[5] Intensely competitive, the apparel industry was also unusually lucrative.

Expansion in both industries came to an abrupt halt in 1958, when the import share of cotton goods largely made in an industrializing Japan escalated to 36 per cent of domestic production.[6] This trend politicized the entire industry, which promptly inserted itself into the corridors of American power, where it has remained ever since as a potent protectionist force.

The industry's grandest exercise of influence came with the Multi-Fibre Arrangement in 1974. Richard Nixon, whose blithe indifference to the textile industry's demands had cost him his bid for the presidency in 1960, vowed in his 1968 election campaign to negotiate an international arrangement for quotas on cotton, wool, and artificial fibre products.[7] The resulting MFA extended the Short-Term and Long-Term Arrangements negotiated by President John Kennedy, which had authorized one-year quotas for sixty-four categories of cotton textiles and provided an automatic limit of 5 per cent of the US market annually for all cotton textile and apparel imports to the United States. Violating the principles of free trade as outlined by GATT, the Arrangement established norms for bilateral-restraint agreements covering textiles and apparel. By 1986, Washington had signed bilateral quantitative-restriction agreements with thirty-four countries under the MFA, which, with other industrialized countries' quotas, imposed limits on fully 80 per cent of textile and apparel exports from developing countries.[8] A non-tariff shield for the US textile industry, the MFA constituted the international framework for the managed trade of textiles and apparel for over thirty years.

Subsequently, the United States cultivated separate bilateral trade relationships with the continental periphery to buttress its dominant position. To the south, Clause 807 (now 9802) of US trade law allowed garments assembled abroad with American fabrics to be reimported nearly duty free, thereby providing trade preferences to American textile firms in Mexico's nascent export-oriented, maquiladora sector. To the north, the Canada-US Free Trade Agreement similarly opened the

Canadian market to American industry by requiring that garments be manufactured from continentally manufactured – that is US-made – fabric to qualify for duty-free access. By 1992, two distinct bilateral relationships had emerged on the continent.

Mexico

Mexico's foray into modern textile production began when Estevan de Antunano established the first water-powered mill in Puebla in the 1830s.[9] The industry expanded steadily, numbering 120 mills by 1898. To be sure, many of these firms were small, but larger conglomerates like the Compañía Industrial Veracruzana S.A. also developed. Indeed, Mexico's early textile mills were comparatively modern, with production technology on a par with that of Great Britain and the United States.[10] Financed by the government's Banco de Avio and encouraged by President Porfirio Díaz's determined pursuit of modernization, Mexico's textile industry thrived until the 1910 revolution.

It then deteriorated because, unlike those in Canada and the United States, Mexican textile firms could not afford the investment necessary to adopt labour-saving automatic looms, one-process pickers, and high-speed warping devices during the 1920s.[11] Having little incentive and few resources with which to upgrade its productive capacity, the industry became outdated, a problem that proved increasingly difficult to resolve.[12]

The Mexican industry underwent a profound transformation with the government's 1965 Border Industrial Program, which actively encouraged American investors to combine the advantages of cheap labour with the US 807/9802 trade preferences by establishing 'in-bond' plants that assembled products from US components for re-export.[13] These maquiladoras were taxed only on their value added, not on the imports used for assembly, but garments had to be of American fabric, design, or tailoring.[14] Confined to assembly activities, the maquiladoras did not connect to the domestic Mexican textile sector which – protected by an import-substitution strategy – employed 18 per cent of Mexico's industrial workforce and produced 15 per cent of the economy's manufactured products by 1970.[15]

In the late 1970s, the domestic textile industry borrowed heavily to modernize using microelectronics to introduce open-end and continuous spinning. By the beginning of the 1980s, it was the most modern and second-largest in Latin America measured by spindles and looms.

Despite these advances, the domestic market was shrinking, the industry laboured under an enormous debt from buying machinery and equipment abroad, and its products were expensive while of poor quality.[16]

Maquiladoras transformed Mexico's apparel industry by refocusing it on the export market. By 1994, there were 83,000 Mexicans working in over 400 apparel maquiladoras, and 80 per cent of Mexico's apparel sales in the US market were exported under the 807/9802 regime, with an estimated 98 per cent of the inputs still being imported from the United States in 2002.[17] This commitment to re-exported manufacturing severed the economic linkage between Mexico's textile and apparel firms, thus condemning the former to technological backwardness. Small, technologically deficient, and labour-intensive, many mills were already on the brink of bankruptcy by 1990.[18]

Canada

A Canadian textile industry first materialized when Mahlon Willette, a young French industrialist, established a woollen mill in Lower Canada in 1826.[19] As Canada's population grew, so did textile manufacturing. Consequently, employment in the textile and apparel industry increased by 218 per cent over the first half of the twentieth century, eventually peaking at 205,000 in 1966.[20] Key firms like Dominion Textiles, Canada Cotton Manufacturing, and Peerless Clothing emerged during this period, settling in Quebec and Ontario. Montreal had the third-largest garment district in North America after Los Angeles and New York.

By the 1970s, distress had become the hallmark of an ailing Canadian industry. Foreign competition from the newly industrializing economies of Japan, South Korea, and Taiwan caused textile and apparel imports to increase one hundredfold during the 1960s.[21] The Canadian firms' share of their own market fell from 68 per cent in 1954 to 60 per cent in 1967, with job losses in the thousands.[22] Overwhelmed by this downturn, the apparel unions and the trade association, the Canadian Textiles Institute (CTI), sought assistance from a government whose aims were 'to provide a sense of direction, a framework, and conditions within which the textile and clothing industries can plan, invest, and develop with a greater degree of confidence' and 'to create conditions in which the Canadian textile and clothing industries continue to move progressively towards viable lines of production on an increasingly competitive basis.'[23] While the policy failed to protect Canadian interests, it successfully transformed the industry into one of the most modern in the world.

Support for the textile and apparel industries dwindled in the late 1980s, as neoconservatism became the dominant ethos for economic policy. Protection for the sector had historically been maintained through tariffs, duty-drawback measures, anti-dumping and countervailing duties, and twenty-nine bilateral import restraints negotiated under the MFA.[24] But, with the lowering of tariffs under CUFTA, Canada's textile and apparel industries faced stiffer competition from American firms. In particular, CUFTA contained a fabric-forward rule of origin, which required garments to be manufactured from Canadian or American fabric to qualify for duty-free access to the US market. This provision, which was inserted to expand the US textile industry's market in Canada, hurt Canadian apparel makers, whose fabrics were mainly imported from Europe. To mollify the more powerful Canadian textile industry, the agreement included special Tariff Rate Quotas, which allowed Canada to export certain fabrics duty-free without having to qualify under CUFTA's rules of origin. Canada used 98 per cent of its TRQs in 1990, thus preserving some of its competitive advantage vis-à-vis the United States under this special provision.[25] The textile sector therefore supported Canada's movement towards freer trade, parting ways with its counterparts in the apparel industry.

The Canadian industry's autonomy was further undermined by the NAFTA negotiations. When it lobbied to exempt apparel from the new free-trade agreement because of its even more protectionist, yarn-forward rules-of-origin (requiring fabric to be woven from North American – read US – yarn), Canada was told it would have to exempt textiles as well.[26] But Canadian textile firms had done well as a result of CUFTA's TRQs, which were due to expire at the end of 1992 along with Canada's special access to the US market. Hence, the more powerful textile industry's need for NAFTA motivated Canada's falling into line with the deal at the expense of its apparel makers.

Textile exports to the United States as a proportion of total exports increased from 55 per cent in 1989 to 70 per cent by 1992, although the total value of shipments fell from an estimated $7.7 billion to $6.9 billion in the same period.[27] Canadian apparel manufacturers eventually changed their production strategies to service the US market in light of the new rules of origin, shipping 86 per cent of their exports to the

Figure 11.1: Canadian textile and apparel exports to the United States and Mexico (thousands of US dollars)

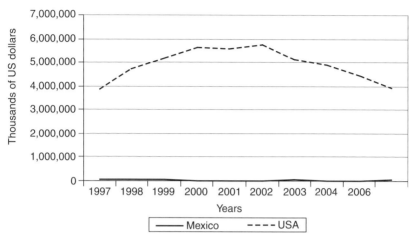

Source: Industry Canada, 'Apparel Industry of Canada,' http://strategis.ic.gc.ca/ sc_mrkti/tdst/tdo/tdo.php#tag (accessed on April 18, 2007).

United States in 1991.[28] This integration fastened Canada to the US market.

NAFTA and the North American Supply Chain

On January 1, 1994, when NAFTA entered into force, the pressures of import penetration, though stymied by the MFA, showed little promise of abating, as a growing number of countries were making garment exports the cornerstone of their economic-development strategies.

In theory, NAFTA signalled a new agenda to promote and protect the industry by creating a continental production zone and market whose rules of origin constituted the regulatory centrepiece. Whereas CUFTA specified only a fabric-forward rule, NAFTA's provision for apparel trade included the fibre spun into yarn and the yarn woven into fabric. In response to the American industry's demand during NAFTA's nego-tiation, the 'yarn-forward' rule prevented offshore apparel imports from penetrating the continental market via the country with the low-est tariff. It also ensured the US textile firms' viability by requiring

Canadian and Mexican apparel companies to manufacture garments from US materials.

As far as the North American industry's governance was concerned, only one apparel-related institution was created by NAFTA, and it was without significance. The NAFTA Committee on Trade in Worn Clothing met just once for informational purposes in 1996 and then gave up the ghost, never to convene again.[29]

The United States

The US textile sector employed approximately 350,000 workers in 2006 compared to 600,000 in 1992.[30] Yet the new rules of origin it had worked so fervently to engineer helped it survive. Nearly 36 per cent of United States' total fabric exports was shipped to Mexico, 17 per cent to Canada. Several textile firms established production-sharing operations with apparel factories in Mexico. Burlington Industries' interest there was underscored by the US$250 million it invested between 1996 and 2000.[31] These figures reflected the industry's efforts to augment its technological capabilities and improve productivity. American textile companies invested approximately US$2 billion per annum to maintain modern manufacturing technologies, such as shuttleless looms and open-end spinners, which operate at higher speeds than older variants, raising output capacity.[32] Meanwhile, the Canadian textile industry reoriented production away from staple fabrics for garments towards industrial textile products, including automotive and fire-retardant fabrics.[33]

Apparel production in the United States restructured dramatically through downsizing. Totalling 960,000 workers at more than 21,000 firms in 1992, the apparel sector employed a mere 313,000 workers in almost 17,000 firms across the country by 2006.[34] Those firms still operating in the United States took advantage of NAFTA's sourcing rules. For example, US apparel exports to Canada and Mexico accounted for 7 and 18 per cent of total exports in 1992, respectively, but, by 2003, 13 per cent of total US apparel exports went to Canada and 31 per cent to Mexico.[35] Nevertheless, while technological advances helped link American apparel firms with textile suppliers and retailers in the continental periphery, the US apparel industry's productive capacity continued to decline. Between 2001 and 2005, its manufacturing fell from 4.5 to 2.2 billion garments, with values falling 43 per cent from US$32 billion to $18 billion.[36]

During its first decade, NAFTA's rules of origin proved a lifesaver for the US textile and apparel industry taken as a whole. Total exports of American textiles and apparel rose 51 per cent between 1993 and 2003, increasing in value from US$10 billion to $15 billion over that period. From 1993 to 2002, US exports of textiles and apparel to Canada increased by 48 per cent, from $2 to $3 billion. For the same period, exports to Mexico jumped from $2 to $5 billion – an expansion of 173 per cent. US investment within the continent also grew from $376 million in 1993 to $626 million in 2004, much of this concentrated in Mexico.[37]

Mexico

NAFTA did not have a significant impact on the Mexican textile industry. Of 2,500 new textile and apparel companies created between 1993 and 2000, only 200 were in the textile sector.[38] Job growth for textiles was also less dramatic, increasing from 164,400 in 1992 to 166,500 in 1997.[39] Notwithstanding these limited gains, most of Mexico's textile firms remained unconnected to the apparel sector. Fully half the fabric in Mexican exports is still sourced from the United States,[40] a reflection of the domestic textile industry's historic problems of cost and quality.

Mexico's most dramatic reconfiguration under NAFTA occurred in the apparel sector. Between 1993 and 2000, apparel production increased 41 per cent and the number of workers by 120 per cent.[41] Significantly, most of this expansion occurred in the export-oriented maquiladoras, not in factories producing for the domestic market. Mexico's apparel maquiladoras expanded from 412 plants in 1993 to 1,119 in 2000,[42] as shipments from Mexico to the United States swelled 713 per cent.[43] By 2001, Mexico temporarily surpassed China as the number one apparel supplier to the United States,[44] but apparel manufacturing for the internal market used textiles imported mainly from Korea and the United States. By 2000, domestic inputs accounted for only 4 per cent of total consumption.[45] Full-package production networks in garment centres like Torreon and Puebla became the bedrock for the small yet ambitious industry. US clients were looking at Mexico to increase efficiencies in apparel manufacturing and shipping. This is the story of Torreon, dubbed 'blue jeans capital of the world' on account of its vivacious denim industry.

In short, NAFTA had integrated the Mexican industry with the American textile and apparel industries, supplying the US market with cheap clothing cut from US-made fabric. It was a good deal for the American retailing chains, which organized producers and suppliers and controlled the whole productive process in different countries without owning a single plant.

Canada

Modest in size and narrow in scope, Canada's textile and apparel industries were reduced to filling niche roles within the North American supply chain, with the United States being the primary destination for their exports. Canada's textile sector has undergone the more profound restructuring. In 2006 the industry comprised 1,417 firms employing 41,515 workers, but there were few Canadian-owned multinational textile companies. Textile production in Canada is capital-intensive; the industry invested $148 million in 2005 and is one of six manufacturing sectors to report higher levels of research and development than their counterparts in the United States. Indeed, Canada's textile industry is world-renowned for its technological competence and higher value-added commodities like household, consumer, and industrial textile products. Exports accounted for 48.3 per cent of total production, the majority of which was shipped to the United States. Textile exports swelled under NAFTA from US$1 billion in 1990 to a high of $3.5 billion in 2002. With increasing global competition, this trend has reversed.[46]

Many Canadian apparel operations, such as Peerless Clothing, have moved offshore as global competition continuously reshapes sourcing patterns. By 2006, the industry consisted of 2,150 small-scale establishments employing approximately 70,000 workers. The majority of these companies were domestically owned and 55 per cent were concentrated in the province of Quebec. Foreign-owned firms, mainly subsidiaries of American TNCs, accounted for under 2 per cent of the total. Canada's apparel industry engages in several high-value-added activities including product design and innovation, labelling, marketing, and just-in-time logistics and distribution. In 2005 the industry invested $100 million for new machinery, equipment, and facilities. At first, as with Mexico and the United States, Canada's apparel industry registered strong annual increases in exports following NAFTA's inception. Between 1994 and 2000, exports increased by 63 per cent while imports supplied 70 per cent of the domestic market. From 2000 to 2005, however, Canada's apparel exports declined precipitously – by 27 per cent.[47]

The apparel industry exploited its advantages under NAFTA to maintain its position, manufacturing $5.6 billion worth of apparel in 2005, 40 per cent of which was shipped to the United States which, in turn, is the largest supplier of textiles for Canadian apparel producers.[48] In vivid contrast, Canada-Mexico linkages are negligible, with Canadian shipments to Mexico nudging up from a trifling $28 million in 1994 to a mere $30 million in 2003.[49] (See Figure 11.1.)

Instead of a single production system connecting the three industries, North America consists of two distinct markets: niche fashion apparel and high-value-added textile manufacturing in Canada and standard-apparel assembly with nascent textile capacities in Mexico, with the United States' large consumer market and powerful textile industry remaining at the continent's epicentre. Within this newly integrated market, combined textile and apparel export trade among the NAFTA partners increased 260 per cent between 1993 and 2000, to US$23 billion.[50]

The End of the MFA and the New Global Competitiveness

Since 2005, international trade in textiles and apparel has undergone a vast and volatile transformation. The WTO Agreement on Textiles and Clothing terminated the MFA's four decades of quota-controlled trade on January 1, 2005, provoking an increase in competition for the United States and Canada as well as Mexico, because China, India, and Bangladesh gained unrestricted access to markets in the North.

China posed an immense challenge. With upward of ten million workers, its textile and apparel sectors' production capacity was unprecedented in scale. In 2003 some 3,800 textile plants were under construction in China, which had become the world's largest exporter, commanding 22 per cent of the world's apparel market and 30 per cent of its textile market. This directly threatened Mexico:[51] although its geographical proximity gives it an advantage in the production of upscale items for the US fashion market, its production remains concentrated in down-market apparel for which timing is less important.[52]

China became the dominant supplier of textiles and apparel to the US market by 2003, capturing 22 per cent of total US textile and apparel imports and supplanting both Mexico and Canada as the leading exporters to the United States.[53] In the first quarter of 2005 alone, US imports of textile and apparel products from China increased 52 per cent.[54] Canada's and Mexico's dilemmas are compounded by their dependency on the American market for export-led growth. From 2006 to 2007, Canada's exports of textiles and apparel to the United States declined 10 per cent, and Mexico's by 11 per cent.[55] Because the textile and apparel industry in North American is a regionally based commodity process, increased competition anywhere along the chain has a direct impact on all its parts.

Industry's Response

The North American textile industry has no governance per se, that is, no regional trade associations that cooperate to articulate collective goals, as in the steel sector.[56] The North American Textile Council, which provided a framework for cohesive policy building in the industry for a short period between 1995 and 1996, was abandoned. Without such a forum, policy setting in the industry is steered by US trade associations that wield considerable power in Congress and the Administration. Canada and Mexico took steps to protect their domestic markets from US dominance through filing domestic-safeguard petitions, lobbying for a separate sectoral negotiation for textiles and apparel within the WTO's Non-Agricultural Market Access talks, and unsuccessfully supporting the expansion of free trade from the continental to the hemispheric levels through the ill-fated Free-Trade Area of the Americas.

IMPLEMENTING DOMESTIC SAFEGUARDS

The US and Mexican textile industries first responded to global trade woes by filing domestic-safeguard petitions. Originally negotiated when China became a member of the WTO, the safeguard measure allowed any member country to impose temporary quotas on textile and apparel products from China if these goods were causing 'market disruption.' China was required to limit export shipments of the targeted good to 7.5 per cent of the previous year's shipment. The claimant country was expected to consult with China to negotiate a mutually satisfactory solution, a provision that was especially crucial since the safeguard provision was to expire at the end of 2008.[57]

In the immediate aftermath of the MFA's expiration, the National Council of Textile Organizations (NCTO) and the American Manufacturing Trade Action Coalition (AMTAC) – the two major US textile-sector associations – demanded safeguard protection. They argued to the

Committee for the Implementation of Textiles Agreements (CITA) that surging imports from China had caused major market disruption in several vulnerable sectors. CITA concurred, and in May 2005 it implemented China-specific safeguards on imports of cotton-knit shirts and blouses, cotton trousers, and cotton/man-made-fibre (MMF) underwear. The same month, quotas were extended to cotton/MMF non-knit shirts, MMF knit shirts, MMF trousers, and combed cotton yarn.[58]

Mexico's textile and apparel industries urged similar policy prescriptions. The Cámara Nacional de la Industria Textil (CANAINTEX, the National Chamber of the Textile Industry), Mexico's largest textile trade association, pleaded with the government to apply WTO safeguards and maintain current compensatory duties of 533 per cent on apparel and textile imports from China.[59] CANAINTEX also supported its 'colleagues in the US textile industry in asserting that the vigorous use of safeguard actions to combat unfair Chinese competition is essential to preserving a competitive textile and apparel industry in the United States and in Mexico.'[60] This statement, made in support of the NCTO's testimony before the Ways and Means Committee, illustrated the coordinated effort by the two industries to secure the US market with WTO-mandated safeguards.

By way of contrast, Canada's industries did not request safeguard measures domestically. For the Canadian Apparel Federation and the Canadian Textiles Institute, 'safeguards are really a temporary measure. What we're looking for is something much more substantial, much more long-term, committed, and strategic.'[61] The CTI acknowledged that it 'cannot survive without the United States market.'[62] Similarly, the apparel industry claimed that its 'big, unique, competitive advantage is our proximity to the US marketplace.'[63] Canada's ambivalence towards safeguard measures did not represent a challenge to the principles of protecting the North American market. Rather, it was a reflection of the Canadian industry's search for a more holistic remedy.

AGENDA-SETTING AT THE WTO

North America's three textile industries have made a concerted effort to achieve their objectives within international fora. This became apparent in 2002, when CANAINTEX, the CTI, and the American Textile Manufacturers Institute (ATMI, predecessor of the NCTO), in concert with textile associations in Europe and Turkey, developed a unified policy position with their governments at the WTO.[64] The coalition advanced five specific objectives: open the developing world's fabric markets by lowering tariffs and non-tariff barriers; reject the request by developing nations to abolish the quota regime before 2005; strengthen the effectiveness of WTO safeguards; cease allowing developing nations to violate intellectual property rights; and halt the proliferation of illegal trans-shipments and smuggling of textiles and apparel. Though neither explicitly nor exclusively North American, the cooperation between the CTI, ATMI, and CANAINTEX revealed substantial policy congruity among North American actors at the international level.

Since 2004, ties among North America's textile associations at the international level have both tightened and loosened. The focal point of this enigma is the Istanbul Declaration, an agreement spearheaded by American and Turkish textile associations to halt the dissolution of the global quota regime. The declaration calls upon governments to carry out three tasks: convene an emergency meeting of the WTO to address the post-quota environment; 'effectively and seamlessly' use safeguard measures in response to China; and 'vigorously' attack unfair trade practices within the WTO. The NCTO, AMTAC, and CANAINTEX immediately endorsed the declaration, but Canada's CTI did not. Despite its reticence, the CTI remained in contact with its continental counterparts. But, as Cass Johnson, president of the NCTO, noted, contacts have become less frequent and less strategic than in previous years. When the associations do converse, the exchange is primarily informational and decreasingly tactical.[65]

The Istanbul Declaration evolved into a transnational coalition of ninety-six trade associations from fifty-four countries called the Global Alliance for Fair Textile Trade (GAFTT). Along with the objectives outlined in the Istanbul Declaration, GAFTT was particularly concerned with setting the global agenda. For example, it called for a special textile negotiation at GATT's Doha Round to address the issue of market access. The US textile industry also used GAFTT as moral leverage in testimony before Congress. The NCTO's international policy activities were consequently conducted in tandem with CANAINTEX, as the survival of each after NAFTA has become inextricably linked.

Canada was absent from GAFTT for two reasons. The intense rationalization of Canada's textile industry had diverted the industry away from manufacturing clothing fabrics towards producing industrial fibres of increasing sophistication, so it did not compete directly with firms in China, Bangladesh, and India. Secondly, the Canadian government has typically been the least responsive of the three nations to its textile industry. Given its marginalization domestically, the CTI has little political (and likely financial) capital to expend internationally.

While domestic and international governance received considerable attention from the NCTO and CANAINTEX, all three industries concentrated on expanding free trade within the hemisphere. At the Fifth Western Hemisphere Trade Ministerial in Toronto in 1999, the American textile industry outlined its vision, positing NAFTA as the model for textile and apparel issues in the Free Trade Area of the Americas. Specific policy recommendations included strict yarn-forward rules of origin, tighter cross-country customs-enforcement provisions modelled on those in NAFTA, and reciprocal phase-out schedules for tariffs within the region.[66] Cumulatively, the policies proposed a hemispheric trade bloc in which rules of origin would establish seamless sourcing.

For its part, the Mexican textile industry engaged in multiple acts of transborder governance to press the importance of the FTAA on policy makers in Washington. At the Sourcing USA Summit in Scottsdale, Arizona, in November 2002, Adolfo Kalach, then general manager of Kaltex and chairman of CANAINTEX, presented an overview of Mexico's long-term strategies. Of these, the consolidation of a regional trading bloc of the Americas was considered vital.[67] As he said: 'Market based regional integration will allow suppliers in the hemisphere to deliver a "total package" regional product to our apparel customers in the United States at competitive prices, delivery times, and quality standards. We believe this is ultimately the only basis on which Western Hemisphere textile producers will be able to successfully compete with Asian suppliers.'[68] Endowed with locational comparative advantages, yet beset with illegally imported trans-shipments, Mexico's textile industry looked to the FTAA as a panacea to resolve its accumulating woes.

This sentiment permeated the minds of Canadian textile executives as well. The FTAA offered the 'long-term, committed, and strategic' remedy the CTI was looking for: 'Our industry has pinned its hope on the early implementation of the FTAA to provide for the seamless movement of goods within the hemisphere. It is the best prospect for resolving the inequities we now face vis-à-vis our United States' competitors.'[69] For Canada, as for Mexico and the United States, the southward expansion of NAFTA to include the rest of the Americas offered North America's textile and apparel firms a beacon of hope.

When negotiations succumbed to irreconcilable differences between the United States and Brazil, industry cooperation among NAFTA's textile associations fractured, as the American contingent focused on President Bush's immensely divisive Dominican Republic-Central American Free Trade Agreement (DR-CAFTA). The agreement occasioned a row within the US textile industry, AMTAC vociferously opposing the agreement on the grounds that DR-CAFTA's rules of origin – similar to those of NAFTA – would allow fabric produced in the Dominican Republic or Central America to qualify for duty-free entry into the United States and thus undermine the domestic industry. On the other side of the debate, the NCTO supported the agreement because its members held, and wished to further, close ties with apparel firms in the Central American region. DR-CAFTA represented 'a very important part of the domestic industry's supply chain' that would be necessary to 'ensure that the US textile industry remains competitive against China.'[70] In short, DR-CAFTA offered the NCTO a mini-FTAA.

More dramatic, as far as North American governance was concerned, DR-CAFTA was a bilateral deal made by the United States, which secured trade preferences for its own textile industry *at the expense of* Canada and Mexico. Only after aggressive lobbying did Mexico's CANAINTEX succeed in obtaining the addition of a 'cumulation' clause, which allowed for woven goods made in Canada or Mexico to qualify as 'originating' in the region and so be eligible for duty-free entry into the US market. However, 'cumulation' was subject to quantity limitations and a two-part proviso. First, Canada and Mexico had to provide reciprocal treatment for US-produced inputs under any free-trade agreements with other DR-CAFTA countries; and, second, both countries had to meet enforcement standards determined by US customs, a stipulation that denied Mexico 'cumulation' for at least two years.[71]

DR-CAFTA confirmed the weakness of North America's transborder governance. To Mexico's and Canada's consternation, the NCTO fought aggressively to forge exclusive preferences for itself in Central America. Ultimately, 'cumulation' ensured that American and Mexican textile firms would further integrate with new regional partners against their global competitors. When the NCTO and CANAINTEX discussed plans for establishing a new textile council for trade associations throughout the hemisphere,[72] it was unclear what role the Canadian Textiles Institute would play in these new efforts at regional coordination. Continued southward migration of the textiles and apparel industries would likely leave the CTI further adrift.

Government's Response

As North America's textile industries confront the need for policy cohesion and a common vision in a new era of global competition, so do their governments. Indeed, transborder governance, particularly on the part of CANAINTEX and the NCTO, is steering each government in the direction of increased, albeit modest, cooperation. The first visible signs of this trend appeared in the creation of NAFTA's ad hoc Working Group on Textiles and Apparel (WGTA).

The WGTA initially received its mandate in 2003, when NAFTA's Free Trade Commission met in Montreal and voiced the need for a careful review of the rules of origin pertaining to textiles and apparel. The directive quickly expanded, as the participants discovered a mutual need for dialogue on issues that had emerged following the end of the MFA in 2005. Accordingly, North America's trade ministers asked the working group to elaborate on 'areas where further trilateral work would be beneficial to the goal of strengthening the NAFTA textiles and apparel industries and promoting regional trade in light of the increasing competition from outside NAFTA as well as the elimination of quantitative restrictions.'[73]

The WGTA consulted with industry representatives from trade associations in each country. Predictably, the issues outlined by the group as particularly salient closely mirrored the industries' qualms: perceived imbalances in post-MFA trade, diminished availability of yarns within the region, and rising trans-shipments of illicit textile and apparel products being smuggled into the North American market.

To address these issues, the group reviewed six policy mechanisms for deepening integration and streamlining cooperation. These consisted of: modifying rules of origin to reflect the varying availability of supplies of particular fibres, yarns, or fabrics; further use of 'cumulation' for linking NAFTA's rules of origin to bilateral trade agreements; creating a customs union; expanding Tariff Preference Levels for Mexico and Canada; harmonizing and tightening common procedures for customs verification; and increasing collaboration within WTO's committees to address third-party compliance matters. Taken together, these policies suggested a concerted effort to deepen governance in North America with respect to textile and apparel policy.

A provisional agreement on six modifications to the NAFTA textile and apparel rules of origin was reached early in 2005.[74] These modifications exempted from the rules of origin certain fibres, like acrylic, that are no longer manufactured in North America. More significantly, the WGTA established a Textile Enforcement Subgroup chaired by US Customs to deal with deficiencies in customs enforcement, especially along the Mexican border.[75]

The WGTA is an ad hoc committee, neither permanent nor institutionalized, which will survive only so long as needed. Its mandate is constrained to fact finding, since its purpose is primarily informational. Though it puts forward policy options, agreement about and implementation of any policy must be undertaken through governmental channels in the three countries.

The fragility of transborder governance affecting textiles and apparel is readily apparent when considering how the US Congress has ratified several bilateral trade agreements to stimulate development in the sub-Saharan, Caribbean, and Andean regions. These agreements deliberately provide textile and apparel trade preferences to each region to encourage their industrial development, but each bilateral accord also favours US textiles to the exclusion of Canada and Mexico, causing North America to cease to exist as a trade bloc. For sub-Saharan Africa, the African Growth and Opportunity Act allowed apparel sewn from fabrics wholly formed and cut in the United States to be admitted duty- and quota-free. The Caribbean Basin Trade Preference Agreement extended the same terms to Central America in 2000, as did the Andean Trade Preference Act in 2002 for Bolivia, Colombia, Ecuador, and Peru. Together, these separate agreements favour the United States at the expense of its two neighbours and undermine the North American trilateral community so loudly trumpeted at NAFTA's inception.

Thus, while the WGTA and its recent work suggest that traces of some North American solidarity still survive in the textiles and apparel industries, the bilateral negotiation of separate preferential trade networks by the United States reveals how shallow is this continental governance.

Labour's Response

The end of the MFA posed greater challenges to workers than to manufacturers, who could always outsource their production overseas, shopping for the lowest wages, taxes, and regulations. Where the costs are too high, manufacturers can simply switch contractors, fomenting a race to the bottom by countries that try to attract foreign direct investment by maintaining the lowest standards possible. Because global capital is nomadic while people are largely confined within the boundaries of their states, labour unions are losing their capacity to protect their members, let alone to enhance their welfare.

As NAFTA's only developing country, Mexico is especially vulnerable to the caprice of capital. For example, when 200,000 maquiladora workers lost their jobs in 2002 from increased competition with China, the Bank of Mexico reacted by calling for a *reduction* of wages in 2003.[76] Within apparel maquiladoras, common problems include lower than minimum wages, compulsory but unpaid overtime, discrimination against pregnant women by requiring pregnancy testing before hiring, exposure to toxic chemicals in jeans laundries, and no freedom of association.[77] As one researcher concludes, 'of all the *maquila* workers, garment workers face the worst conditions.'[78] Pay for maquiladora workers has not increased despite greater complexity in the work required.[79] Managers threaten to move their plants abroad if they do not get unions' acceptance of lower salaries than what the law mandates.[80] For some employers, the only way to survive in Mexico is to close their plants and contract work out to be done at home for desperately low, sweatshop pay.[81]

The United States and Canada have experienced the competitive pressure from East Asia in the form of their own sweatshops, which typically violate wage, child-labour, safety, and health laws.[82] For instance, Toronto's garment industry is in widespread violation of the Employment Standards Act concerning its home workers, who, in some cases, make as little as $2 per hour.[83] The situation is worse in the United States, where there has been a decrease in the government's regulatory capacity. In 1995, for instance, each investigator at the US Department of Labor's Wage and Hours Division was responsible for investigating 8,600 workplaces accounting for 153,100 workers.[84]

Efforts by labour unions and civil-society actors concerned with protecting the rights of garment workers throughout North America are inhibited by such impediments as the ineffectiveness of the North American Agreement on Labour Cooperation and the power of Mexico's corporatist unions. As discussed in chapter IV, President Clinton managed to propitiate labour activists without disturbing NAFTA's neoconservative mission by drafting a labour accord that was vigorous in tone but impotent in practice. Only three cases in the NAALC's history involved the apparel industry. One complaint, filed with Mexico's National Administrative Office (NAO) by several workers' associations, alleged that the United States failed to enforce workers' compensation and occupational safety and health laws in New York's garment district. In response, the Mexican NAO simply urged 'the US Department of Labor to take appropriate action to allay the concerns of the petitioners and the public.'[85] Another two complaints were filed jointly with the NAOs in Canada and the United States. The Maquila Solidarity Network of Canada, the Worker Assistance Centre of Mexico, and the University Students against Sweatshops (USAS) submitted a petition in 2003 documenting various problems – failure to pay wages owing or overtime supplements, long hours, persistent health and safety violations – in two garment factories in Puebla, Mexico.[86] Both the Canadian and American NAOs recommended ministerial consultations, but the process ended there. In sum, after thirteen years, the NAALC had failed to balance the continental sector's industry-weighted governance with muscular labour governance.

The greatest barrier to labour cooperation in North America's textile and apparel industries is, as we saw with steel, Mexico's corporatist union structure. Union leaders continue to enjoy vast power, especially at the state level, where many actively subvert those garment workers who attempt to form independent trade unions. Many workers are unaware they even have a union. Collective-bargaining agreements are usually signed between foreign investors and corporate unions before a maquiladora opens. Such agreements are laden with 'exclusion clauses,' which require workers to be union members, thus rendering the union a 'hiring agent for the company,'[87] and oblige employers to fire any dissident workers expelled from union membership. As a result, incumbent unions can forcibly remove any worker before he or she is able to organize independent unions in opposition.[88] Although the Mexican Supreme Court ruled in April 2001 that using such exclusion clauses against dissidents violated the worker's right to freedom of association, such firings remain routine in practice. This is attributable to the privileged position occupied by corporatist unions in local Conciliation and Arbitration Boards, which are tripartite entities consisting of representatives from government, management, and labour unions and serve as the principal mechanism for enforcing labour laws. They can, and often do, deny legal recognition to independent unions. In cases where recognition is awarded, independent unions are then required to compete against official unions in elections in which workers must vote publicly in front of management, official union representatives, and government authorities.

By contrast, garment workers in the United States and Canada belong to a single organ, the Union of Needletrades, Industrial, and Textile Employees (UNITE), which is an active participant in the political decision-making process in both countries. Its current focus is competition in a post-quota world. Each branch played a crucial role in lobbying for the implementation of WTO safeguards against China. UNITE's American arm successfully worked with the powerful US textile lobby in filing seven China safeguard petitions with the Committee for the Implementation of Textiles Agreements. For its part, UNITE Canada filed a petition with the Canadian International Trade Tribunal in 2005 requesting Canadian action on safeguards as well. The Canadian effort, however, fell on less responsive ears. As a party to the Global Alliance for Fair Textile Trade, UNITE contributed to the international push for a special textile agreement in the Doha Round, hoping that the garment industry's woes and its workers' afflictions would receive more concerted attention from policy makers.

Yet, with only 25,000 members in Canada and 200,000 in the United States, UNITE is now but a shadow of its former self. The continual decline of union membership within the garment industry and the difficulties facing collective bargaining resulted in the merger in 2003 of UNITE with the Hotel and Restaurant Employees to form UNITE-HERE. The vicissitudes of an increasingly borderless world require that UNITE develop new strategies more amenable to flexible production patterns. One approach includes supporting the global anti-sweatshop movement.

Civil Society's Response

The governance of labour in North America's garment industry is rapidly becoming a multi-stakeholder affair. Without active enforcement by government and without union solidarity throughout the continent, UNITE and others recognize the need to work outside traditional labour organs and engage with civil society to hold retailers and manufacturers accountable for their contractors' production practices – a phenomenon labelled 'non-state market-driven governance' (NSMD).[89]

Under NSMD, the state's traditional authority is not granted (or ceded) by the state to other parties and is not used to force compliance. Rather, under NSMD governance, the relatively narrow institution of the market and its supply chain provide the institutional setting within which governing authority is granted and through which broadly based political struggles occur. When NSMD conditions exist, compliance results from market incentives and involves an evaluation on the part of those audiences the NSMD systems seek to rule.[90]

NSMD regulation is based on voluntary standards, generally outlined in corporate codes of conduct, which identify the norms and regulations factories must follow. When violations occur, civil-society actors use negative publicity against lead firms, like Nike or Wal-Mart, whose marketing success depends heavily on positive brand identities. It is expected that brand sensitivity will force lead firms to ensure factory compliance with their stated codes of conduct.[91] Of particular note is the Worker Rights Consortium (WRC), a third-party monitoring system developed by USAS in coordination with UNITE, the AFL-CIO, and an array of human-rights NGOs. A coalition of labour-rights experts, students, and 147 colleges and universities, the overwhelming majority of which are North American, the WRC tries to ensure that factories around the world producing clothing and other goods that bear college and university names comply with the WRC's basic codes of conduct, which include a living wage, respect for women, and rights to freedom of association and collective bargaining. The WRC is generally considered a verification system; it investigates factories whose workers have submitted a grievance. Accordingly, the WRC also operates locally to educate workers about its codes so they can report violations to local NGOs, worker-support centres, or the WRC itself. Unlike other monitoring systems, the WRC does not bestow upon corporations the epithet of sweat-free certification. Instead, the WRC simply collaborates with its university and college members in proposing remedial action where rights abuses are identified.

The NSMD model of governance has become a galvanizing force for North American labour-rights activists. Brand-sensitive retailers concentrated in the United States provide a focal point for local NGOs and activists in Canada and Mexico. For instance, in 2001 at Kukdong, a clothing factory in Puebla,[92] five supervisors were illegally fired for protesting poor working conditions. When they went to their company union, the Revolutionary Confederation of Workers and Farmers, it refused to help. The workers occupied the plant for three days in protest until paramilitary police units violently evicted them from the premises. David Alvarado, working for the American Center for International Labor Solidarity (AFL-CIO), contacted US student organs, which helped to identify Nike as Kukdong's primary customer. American students in the WRC put pressure on Nike, whose stated code of conduct was in direct contradiction with Puebla's reality. Local civil-society actors, notably the Centro de Apoyo para los Trabajadores (CAT, Workers' Support Centre), helped support workers during their suspension. After three months of cross-border participation, the workers succeeded in establishing an independent union, SITEMEX, which collectively bargained for a fairer contract with the plant's management.

The case of Kukdong suggests a growing tenacity in governance from below. The bonds between Mexico's CAT and America's NGO-labour coalition strengthened in the wake of this victory. CAT receives grants from the AFL-CIO and the Phoenix Foundation. In addition, USAS sends students to intern in the CAT office, which has links to UNITE in the United States and the Maquiladora Solidarity Network in Canada.[93] These groups also belong to the Coalition for Justice in the Maquiladoras, an explicitly North American non-profit initiative for organizing, educating, and protecting maquiladora workers. The coalition consists of more than a hundred labour, religious, environmental, community, and women's groups from Canada, Mexico, and the United States. Slowly, yet resolutely, transnational labour governance among North American civil-society actors is emerging. But, because many of these actors are also global in scope or hemispheric in orientation, North America's anti-sweatshop movement remains without a specifically continental identity, being instead just a subset of various global campaigns.

Conclusion

While NAFTA's rules of origin helped integrate the region economically, continental governance of textiles and apparel in North America remained weak and underdeveloped at all three levels of analysis. At the industry-level, US trade associations tended to develop and implement their own policies unilaterally, as they did with safeguards against China and the negotiation of DR-CAFTA. The US and Mexican industries engaged in bilateral cooperation as part of global initiatives directed towards confronting the common threat of China's competitiveness. At the same time, the Canadian industry's transborder participation declined owing to its marginalization as production migrated south. Somewhat deeper cooperation of a trilateral nature is emerging at the government level. However, policy coordination is weakened by the United States' proclivity for negotiating trade preferences favouring its own industry with states outside North America. Finally, there is virtually no cooperation among textile and apparel labour unions in the three countries. The only labour-governance programs emerging in North America are non-state market-driven initiatives among civil-society actors, but this movement is part of a broader anti-sweatshop campaign at the global level and thus not specifically North American. Taken together, continental governance in textiles and apparel remains weak even though the industry's consolidation is more than meets the eye. The following reflections emerge from this analysis.

NAFTA consolidated US dominance notwithstanding the trilateral and continental oratory routinely employed by the 'tres amigos.' North America remains a hub-and-spoke set of two bilateral relationships, of which, in textiles and apparel, the US-Mexican one is the more intense. Continental governance in textiles and apparel exhibits a tenuous, informal quality, with trilateral consultation fostered by NAFTA's Working Group on Textiles and Apparel.

Recent US unilateralism, succeeding dashed hopes for a new hemispheric trade association for textiles, suggests that governance arrangements among the three industries are unlikely to thicken. In the wake of exogenous adversities, industry and government actors have recognized the need for a more robust regulatory apparatus. The Textile Enforcement Subgroup exemplifies this post-quota consciousness. NAFTA's customs-enforcement rules are weak: there are no penalties for circumvention, no textile-specific verification procedures, and no provision allowing US Customs and Border Protection to conduct unannounced factory inspections. With the removal of quotas and the dawn of DR-CAFTA, textile-enforcement efforts have become matters of immense importance to both Mexico and the United States. China's increasing competitiveness and the end of the Multi-Fibre Arrangement assures that more routinized cooperation will be required if textile and apparel manufacturing are to survive in the Western Hemisphere.

Still, it would be folly to extrapolate from this a vision of NAFTA converging towards an institutional semblance of the European Union, especially with respect to textiles and apparel. To the extent that the 2005 Security and Prosperity Partnership of North America can be perceived as deeper institutionalization, it is noteworthy that textiles and apparel are not included among its working groups. NAFTA remains a set of increasingly out-of-date economic rules. Thus, further increments in governance will continue to be driven by such market actors as the NCTO and CANAINTEX, but only in areas where mutual benefits obtain.

Central America's rising importance in the region raises important questions about the extent to which the textile and apparel industries support a North American political economy. American and Mexican firms already share common interests in customs enforcement, in full-package production networks, and in the sheer volume of cross-border trade in textiles and apparel. As the locus of the textiles and apparel industry drifts southward, so too does the locus of its unstable governance. Indeed, with DR-CAFTA, governance at the industry-level involves the Caribbean more than Canada. Increasing competitiveness and the importance of market proximity portend an incremental movement towards hemispheric consolidation, away from an exclusively North American community.

While NAFTA's implementation suggested that a new continental hegemony had been established in which the United States led and the periphery consented to a new transborder regime, Washington's more recent and unilaterally negotiated trade deals with third countries heralded a move back from US hegemony to old-fashioned US dominance. At the same time, the imbalance between Canada and Mexico has shifted. Whereas Canada's textile and apparel industries were once more developed than Mexico's, the Canadian sector has been specializing and shrinking while the Mexican industry has expanded, making the Mexico-US dyad more substantial than the Canada-US relationship.

In textiles and apparel, then, North America's existence seemed to acquire substance when NAFTA's rules of origin offered the continent's industries a measure of protection, leading the textile/apparel sectors in the three countries to restructure within a US-centred production system. But, once the end of the Multi-Fibre Arrangement's constraints exposed the three markets to massive imports from Asia's textile giants, North America's NAFTA-induced corporate solidarity dissipated, leaving little transborder governance that was specifically continental and exposing the three industries to more pressures from overseas. As we will now see in chapter XII, another sector that was once North American but is increasingly global is the continent's capital markets.

XII The Governance of Capital Markets

As the chief source of financing for business (apart from bank loans, venture capital, and private sources), stock markets are crucial to a capitalist economy's functioning. Because the capital markets in Canada and Mexico have long been closely connected to those of the United States, this review of transborder governance in North America starts by examining how private markets and public regulators have interacted both within and between the continent's national boundaries.

When a business raises capital for its operations, it sells shares of its ownership known as stocks, or equity. A company may also offer bonds, which obligate it to repay the money over a stated period at a specified rate of interest. Governments can borrow money by offering bonds and treasury bills that are also traded in the market. Individuals participate either directly or through holding assets in mutual funds, pension funds, and such savings instruments as life insurance.

A stock market brings together the buyers and sellers of capital mainly through such financial institutions as insurance companies, investment corporations, or stock brokerages which issue and trade stocks, bonds, and other securities. Along with banks and credit unions, capital markets channel savings from individuals to firms and governments for investment. Although these transactions can also occur in the unregulated over-the-counter market that brokers create for unlisted securities, it is the organized security exchanges that this chapter analyses.

Stock markets are rooted in the private sector, but their economic role is too important for governments to allow them to regulate themselves without any state oversight. Corporate scandals have the power to shake investor confidence in the market and affect investment in other corporations trading on the same market or even in distant economies. The collapse of the US giant firms Enron and WorldCom in 2003 demonstrated the shock made possible by poor corporate governance and inadequate government regulation. Such scandals reinforce the view that both individual corporations and national exchanges need to be governed by public law and government regulators. To guarantee their integrity, regulation attempts to ensure fair and orderly markets that prevent managers from absconding with shareholders' funds and/or liquidating their savings by investing in excessively risky projects.[1] To this end, complex corporate-governance systems have evolved with economic and legal institutions to protect investors and establish conditions for a fair return on investments.

Each of North America's three countries has a different set of legal systems, regulatory structures, corporate cultures, and capital markets. The rules and standards that govern a national securities industry stem from each exchange's rules for making a stock listing, from laws regulating individual corporations' governance, and from the oversight of each government's commissions that regulate stock exchanges.[2]

The process of raising investment capital is further complicated when it flows across borders. If transnational corporations raise capital by cross-listing on stock exchanges in different countries, they must comply with each state's laws and with each exchange's rules. At the same time as they enjoy getting access to distant pools of capital, corporations dislike the expense incurred by having to comply with varying sets of rules. Instead, they prefer standards to be uniform. When the harmonization of regulations is on the agenda, the rules of the game naturally converge with those of the state within which most play. A state with a higher concentration of capital wields greater influence when suggesting regulatory change than less financially powerful states with a lower concentration of capital. Nevertheless, the dominant country's standards may not fit the needs of another country and may have to be adapted to serve unique environments.

Stock exchanges are themselves businesses, which earn profits from trading and so compete with one another both inside and between economies to attract the corporate listings from which they derive their income. As a result of the loosening of capital controls that took place towards the end of the twentieth century and accelerated the transborder integration of markets, companies' accessibility to capital increased, thereby encouraging more competition among stock markets.

As financial markets deregulated, the immense flow of capital across borders affected how North America's capital markets were governed. In the United States, Canada, and Mexico, the system of securities regulation underwent a period of re-regulation through corporate-governance reforms. This chapter examines the degree of stock-market integration in North America in order to consider how transborder forces are shaping the interrelated governance of the continent's capital markets.

Beginning with an overview of stock-market integration in the continent, it then outlines each national framework for securities regulation. The impact of deepening integration, cross-listings, recent regulatory reforms, competition between stock exchanges, and pressures for strong corporate-governance practices to contain scandals and increase stock share value are examined in turn. The chapter argues that securities regulation in North America is converging as Canada and Mexico conform to US standards, thus accentuating the continent's power asymmetries at the same time as US markets are losing their global dominance and becoming integrated with those of Europe and Asia.

Capital-Market Integration in North America

Competition among capital markets in the two peripheral economies of North America makes government regulators there very sensitive to the regulatory policies of their overwhelming neighbour as they compete to attract capital. If Canadian and Mexican companies list on an American exchange, they must comply with US regulations unless acceptably compatible regulations prevail in their national jurisdiction. Large Canadian and Mexican corporations lobby their home governments to adopt legislation similar to US laws so that compliance is uniform and cost-efficient. Otherwise, these companies threaten to bypass their home markets altogether. Furthermore, the North American market demands strong investor protection since investors are willing to pay more on average for the equity of a US corporation adhering to strong corporate-governance practices than for a corporation in the periphery with qualitatively weaker codes.[3] Consequently, Canadian and Mexican regulators are renewing their emphasis on good corporate governance both to match the United States' standards and to create more efficient market conditions for listings at home.

US capital market dominance in North America is substantial. At the end of 2003, Americans held $12 trillion in US and foreign equities, constituting 38 per cent of the market capitalization traded in the world's major exchanges.[4] On a per-capita basis, US GDP was US$39,500 in 2004, which was five times more than Mexico's and about 30 per cent higher than Canada's.[5]

Though capital trading and regulating is continentally interdependent, the direction of influence is a one-way street from the United States to the periphery. For Canada, the imperative for reform stems from domestic business pressures for a regulatory profile that mirrors US regulations and eases capital flows. In Mexico, the impetus comes from the government's desire for the securities industry to attract investment and become competitive. Despite the absence of formal mechanisms to govern North America's capital markets, the convergence of the three national regulatory systems governing securities signals that the US market is exerting de facto governance for securities regulation throughout the continent.

Stock-Market Integration

As part of the global trend towards the liberalization of international financial markets, North American stock exchanges became increasingly integrated in the 1980s owing both to new information technology that enabled the lightning-fast transmission of complex data and the instantaneous transfer of funds and to policies that lowered barriers to cross-border capital flows. These changes gave North American companies the opportunity to select the stock markets on which they chose to raise finance capital. Investors could also choose to buy and sell on one exchange rather than another and trade where the market seemed most attractive.

As home to the world's two largest stock exchanges, the New York Stock Exchange (NYSE) and NASDAQ (the National Association of Securities Dealers Automated Quotation System), New York remains the world's leading centre for capital trading. The NYSE boasts the highest concentration of investment capital in the world, trading over $14,100 billion in 2005.[6] Coming second with $10,100 billion traded in 2005, NASDAQ is the world's largest electronic stock market, listing more firms than the NYSE because it accepts smaller value companies. High-tech companies tend to gravitate towards the NASDAQ for listing, while large world players in every industry issue through the NYSE. There are also substantial exchanges elsewhere in the United States including the Boston Stock Exchange, the mutual fund capital of the world; the regionally based Pacific Exchange in San Francisco, catering to west coast corporations; and the Chicago Stock Exchange, serving smaller companies in the Midwest which may not qualify to list on the large New York exchanges. All of these exchanges also trade interlisted stocks from national and international corporations and other stock exchanges. The Chicago Mercantile Exchange is the world's second-largest futures exchange, which facilitates the trading of commodities. Although they are public companies, American stock exchanges are self-regulating organizations operating under the oversight of the US Securities and Exchange Commission (SEC) and the fifty states' own regulatory commissions.

Canadian companies have a more limited number of domestic exchanges available to them. The biggest Canadian corporations often issue on the nation's largest capital market, the Toronto Stock Exchange (TSX), which traded approximately US$9,002 billion[7] in 2005, roughly one-fifth of the NYSE's turnover. The Montreal Exchange (ME) is the oldest Canadian market. Having fallen behind the TSX over the past thirty years, it remains substantial by Canadian standards. Mining and forestry companies typically list on the Canadian Venture Exchange, a merger of the Vancouver Stock Exchange, the Alberta Stock Exchange, and the Winnipeg Stock Exchange. Canada has fewer public companies and these have smaller market capitalizations than their US competitors, but, because minimum-capitalization requirements are not as high, junior companies go public much sooner in Canada.

Companies have limited options for raising capital in Mexico, because it only has one organized national exchange, the Bolsa Mexicana de Valores (BMV, Mexican Stock Exchange), which has a smaller volume than the Canadian markets and had a trading value of only US$57 billion in 2005.[8] This figure is small because the stock market represents less than 10 per cent of the total internal financial market in Mexico[9] and most companies prefer to raise capital from family or friends' savings or use the banks. Nevertheless, larger Mexican companies are turning towards the BMV, because the new generation taking over family companies has been trained in top US business schools to use market mechanisms.

Cross-listing in the US market allows firms to raise cheap capital and enhances their stocks' liquidity.[10] With US markets' qualitatively higher disclosure standards and enforcement mechanisms, cross-listing there increases investor confidence.[11] The US capital markets' attractiveness was reflected in the 400 per cent increase from 1990 to 2000 in foreign cross-listings to US exchanges.[12] Large companies in North America increasingly register on multiple exchanges in different countries, seeking the greatest liquidity and market value for their stocks and the lowest trading costs. In addition to listing on their national or regional stock exchanges, corporations overwhelmingly favour the NYSE, which opens up access to sources of capital from Europe and Asia and is a mark of prestige demonstrating their success. Foreign listings on the NYSE and NASDAQ grew from 170 in 1990 to over 750 in 2000. In 2006 about 15 per cent of all companies listed on the NYSE were not American; of the 3,653 total, 192 were European, 87 were Asian/Pacific, 88 were Canadian, and 16 were Mexican.[13]

Though London and Frankfurt cater largely to European firms and Tokyo provides for Asian corporations, New York services both continental and global traders. Not only is it the global epicentre, with over 50 per cent of the world's capital trading, but it is also located in close geographical proximity to Canada and Mexico. Not surprisingly, larger Canadian and Mexican companies are drawn to New York when raising capital.

US-Canadian Stock-Market Integration

Canadian capital markets have long been partially integrated with their US counterparts. The Toronto and Montreal stock exchanges connected themselves with the New York Stock Exchange in 1882 when Canadian companies sought financing there. Following the Great Crash of 1929, stricter capital controls introduced in the 1930s separated the Canadian markets from their American counterparts. Further barriers to capital flows were created by the Keynesian welfare state's attempt to channel Canadian savings into the national economy, offering, for example, preferential tax treatment for dividends from Canadian firms and limiting the foreign content of pension funds.[14] By the 1980s, when neoconservatism replaced Keynesian thinking, regulatory barriers fell dramatically not just within countries but also between them.

In 1991 substantial capital-market integration followed the implementation of the Canada-US Multi-jurisdictional Disclosure System (MJDS), under which each country's securities regulator recognized the prospectus and registration statements of established companies prepared according to the other country's disclosure requirements. This mutual-recognition system permitted eligible Canadian firms to issue securities in the United States using Canadian disclosure requirements. Further integration occurred after 1994, when the MJDS was made available for a larger number of Canadian firms and the SEC harmonized Canadian and US disclosure requirements for firms issuing cross-border securities or listing in the United States.[15]

Between 1980 and 1998, the number of Canadian stocks interlisted on US exchanges increased by 198 per cent, from 82 to 244.[16] From 1990 to 2000, Canadian listings on the NYSE alone rose about 150 per cent.[17] By 2003, Canadian firms remained the largest national group of foreign firms listed on US exchanges, with over 180 firms cross-listing.[18] In contrast, only half of this number of Canadian firms cross-list on the London Stock Exchange.[19] Indeed, the 'market capitalization of all TSX-listed companies that are cross-listed on US exchanges or otherwise trade in US markets constitutes just over 50 per cent of the TSX's total market capitalization.'[20] US rules and practices therefore have a profound impact on large Canadian firms. Although the TSX is Canada's largest capital market, it is no longer the principal exchange for most of Canada's largest companies.[21] Failing to attract Canadian corporations, the TSX faces a severe challenge because 'only 30 percent of the total trading value for Canadian securities is now done on the regular Toronto market.'[22] Furthermore, more than one-third of heavily traded Canadian stocks are now traded in the United States rather than Canada.[23]

Cross-listing by Canadian issuers on the US market is one thing. Another is the 'hollowing-out' of corporate Canada, which refers to the loss of head offices in Canada as a result of the acquisitions of Canadian by foreign companies.[24] The extent of foreign control and ownership of Canadian companies is distinctive among advanced economies.[25] From 2000 to 2002, sixty-two of Canada's largest companies were acquired by foreign firms – the majority of which were American.[26] One of the many potential repercussions this has for capital markets is the de-listing of companies from Canadian exchanges in favour of foreign exchanges once those companies have been acquired. The years 2005 and 2006 witnessed record-breaking levels of foreign acquisitions of Canadian companies, most notably Inco and Falconbridge. While these efforts are led by the United States, China and other countries are playing an increasing role.[27] For example, Inco was acquired by a Brazilian company, Falconbridge by a Swiss-based company. We saw in chapter X that in 2006–7 all the large Canadian integrated steel corporations were taken over, mainly by firms from Asia and Latin America. The growing number of Canadian companies disappearing owing to mergers and acquisitions results in fewer companies involved both in trading on the TSX and in interlisting.

With Canadian corporations raising more capital on the US markets than they do domestically, a vicious circle has been established: the increased capitalization of US markets reinforces their financial power, erodes the Canadian capital markets, and makes Canadian corporations depend on their performance in the US stock market. The growing continental integration of capital markets means that, even when Canadian exchanges try to compete with their US competitors, their survival remains threatened.

US-Mexican Stock-Market Integration

The interconnectedness of the Mexican and US markets became obvious during the October 1987 stock market crash, when the sharp fall in the BMV's leading index tracked that of the US market. By the end of the 1980s, President José López Portillo's large-scale privatization and deregulation policies, including the reprivatization of the banks, which had been nationalized in 1982, led to the liberalization of Mexico's capital markets and, initially at least, a spectacular growth of Mexico's now internationalized stock market.[28] From 1982 to 1997, market capitalization of the BMV rose from US$12 billion to US$156 billion.[29] Almost a decade later, however, it had grown only to US$176 billion.[30] Subsequently, a process of elimination has reduced the quantity of the BMV's participants. Compared to 1987, when there were 354,000 accounts, twenty years later there are fewer investors (184,352). Fewer than 130 industrial, commercial, and service companies participate in the BMV.[31]

Foreign investors can trade on the BMV through Mexican brokerage firms but they can also buy American Depository Receipts (ADRs)[32] from major US banks which hold the Mexican shares and issue ADRs to US investors, who thereby enjoy the security of dollar-denominated trading. The Mexican issuer can list the depository receipts on a US exchange. Since transactions on the BMV involve US brokerage companies trading ADRs, Mexico is linked to the US market through the very act of buying and selling shares there. As in other emerging economies, the Mexican stock market has been plagued with the instability and volatility associated with such macroeconomic shocks as the 1994 peso crisis. Consequently, the BMV has been losing ground as Mexican firms go directly to New York to raise their capital. Trading follows listings:

already by the mid-1990s, stocks amounting to 87 per cent of the Mexican stock market were listed in the United States through ADRs.[33]

In 2001 the value of Mexican firms traded in foreign markets was more than nine times the value traded in the BMV. More than 24 per cent of the capital raised from 1990 to 2001 was from foreign markets.[34] In 2002 twenty-four Mexican companies raised US$30 billion worth of investment capital from trading on the NYSE alone.[35] Between 2002 and 2005, only six new companies listed on the BMV while another twenty stopped quoting.[36] Making the picture more ambiguous, however, is the fact that those companies that are listed on the BMV have performed well.[37] In 2006 there were some 123 million stocks of Mexican and foreign firms listed there, with a value of approximately US$180 million.[38] Though foreign listings enable Mexican firms to raise larger amounts of equity capital, they represent a loss to the local securities industry, constraining its market's liquidity.[39]

There is no commonly recognized criterion to measure stock-market integration, but loose capital controls and the dramatic increase in cross-listings reveal a deepening integration of the continent's capital markets as firms are freed from such national, market-segmenting regulations as taxation policies, limits on foreign content in certain types of savings, and restrictions on foreign ownership in certain sectors.

Though Canada's and Mexico's stock exchanges can never rival their American counterparts in depth and breadth, they are trying to regain their competitiveness by catering mainly to domestic investors and local specialties. By harmonizing their national regulations with US norms, by raising the standards they require for their members' corporate governance, and by adopting the standards of the International Organization of Securities Commissions (IOSCO), they hope to reclaim their national prominence while gaining international recognition as viable capital markets.[40]

This competitive quest could be seen in Mexico at the end of 1997 when Circular 11-29 concerning the registration of stocks and the authorization of public offerings committed the regulatory regime to full disclosure by, for the first time, specifying the content of stock-offering prospectuses and defining the issues that they had to address. In the same way, the so-called principle of relevance was established under which listing companies were obliged to include in their prospectuses all information that might be relevant for investors' decision making. These listing standards were based on the still unpublished International Principles for Disclosure in Multinational Listings developed by the Technical Committee of IOSCO, making Mexico the first country to adopt them. As a result, prospectuses used by Mexican companies in their own market can be used with minor modifications for public offerings both in the United States and abroad.

The adoption of corporate-governance measures in 2001 and 2002 is one of the clearest examples of high standards originating in the United States being adopted by Mexico to raise confidence abroad in Mexican corporations. Mexican regulators insist that they are applying universal principles and adopting best international practices – not copying US regulations. For instance, the 2001 stock market law – Ley del Mercado de Valores – brought in stringent requirements for corporate governance well before the Sarbanes-Oxley (SOX) law was promulgated in the United States.[41] In 2003 a Circular for Listing Companies, which consolidated in one document all regulations applying to listing companies, exemplified the way that Mexican law is adapting to international and American standards by considering such regulations as Sarbanes-Oxley in other countries.[42]

The Regulatory Frameworks Governing Capital Markets in North America

Securities regulation is the linchpin to investor confidence and so to the vitality of North America's stock markets. Since investors' pessimism reflecting their apprehension about the security or profitability of their investments can lead to a fall in stock prices, which would then trigger a downturn in the economy with falling output and employment, policing the capital markets is crucial to protecting investor confidence.[43] In North America, the capital market is policed by three distinct national regulatory frameworks.

US Securities Regulation

The protection of individual investors through the regulation of corporations and securities trading by the US government has its roots in the 1929 stock market crash which led Washington to pass laws that prohibited banks from owning corporate equity and required shareholders owning 5 per cent of a firm's stock to disclose this information.[44] In 1934 it also created the powerful, independent, quasi-judicial Securities and Exchange Commission to regulate the US securities market and administer federal securities laws.

As the United States' primary securities-industry regulator, the SEC's mandate is to maintain the market's regulatory integrity by ensuring that a company's dealings with shareholders are fair and transparent and that its board of directors is held accountable. The principle governing SEC rules is that investors, whether large institutions or private individuals, should have access to all appropriate information about an investment. Accordingly, the SEC requires companies trading on the US market to publish meaningful financial information; oversees stock exchanges and such key participants as investment firms, brokers, and public holding companies; and enforces these regulations by prosecuting insider trading and accounting fraud.[45]

Though the SEC has primary supervisory power over the exchanges where firms list their stocks, the fifty states' laws of incorporation dictate the fundamental duties of corporations and the fiduciary duties of directors for the United States' 15,000 publicly listed companies. By the end of the twentieth century, its apparently stringent rules made the US market, particularly the NYSE, the leader in requiring high disclosure standards and market transparency. This made it increasingly attractive to foreign companies.[46]

However, the US regulatory framework's actual failure to protect investors from corporate fraud motivated urgent calls for further reform. Public outrage in 2002 over the massive failures of Tyco, World-Com, and Adelphia, along with the additional accounting fraud by Arthur Anderson which concealed Enron's gigantic conspiracy to report imaginary profits, triggered calls for tough changes in securities and accounting standards. In order to restore investor confidence, Congress passed the Public Accounting Reform and Investor Protection Act of 2002, commonly known as the Sarbanes-Oxley Act, the most intrusive securities-law reform since the securities acts of the 1930s.[47]

In an attempt to improve the quality and transparency of financial statements issued by corporations, the new statute imposed myriad governance standards on all companies (concerning their boards of directors, corporate management, and audit firms) listed in US exchanges. Section 404 was the most controversial provision because it made managers responsible for their companies' financial reporting.[48]

SOX also created the Public Company Accounting Oversight Board (PCAOB) to monitor auditors, strengthen auditor independence, increase CEO accountability for financial statements, make CEOs and CFOs sign off on financial statements, ease private- securities litigation, and give the SEC more resources and authority to enforce its toughened securities law.[49] A strong board independent of the accounting profession and with quasi-governmental authority to determine auditing standards, the PCAOB is appointed by the SEC following consultation with the Federal Reserve Board and the secretary of the treasury.

Sarbanes-Oxley has been extremely controversial. Holding managers accountable to shareholders was necessary to quell the confidence crisis in US capitalism, but companies have vehemently complained that SOX imposes excessive costs and has set back the US market vis-à-vis its foreign competitors. Though widespread consensus supports the separation that SOX imposed between a company's auditors and its managers, many claim that the statute's restrictions are excessive.

SOX imposes direct and heavy compliance costs estimated to be $1.4 trillion on corporate operations, a burden that is particularly heavy for small firms.[50] Indirect costs include the danger that managers will take fewer business risks fearing that an ordinary mistake could be criminalized. The statute's heavy compliance costs induced many US companies to go private or seek less regulated markets[51] and drove foreign firms away from the US market.[52] An increasing number of American firms decided not to go public in order to avoid compliance costs. Moreover, the NYSE was dramatically superseded for five years by London and Hong Kong in the market for initial public offerings (IPOs). In 2000 nine out of every ten dollars in the world's IPOs were made in the United States; in 2005, nine out of every ten dollars were made in other countries.[53]

SOX put Mexican and Canadian corporations in a series of dilemmas, causing their regulators to respond with complementary, but not identical, policies. Mexican firms that use American Depositary Receipts and had reported annually to the SEC were faced with an extremely – and for some impossibly – expensive adjustment to comply with SOX's requirements for a technological capacity that can generate digitalized information on a rapid and current basis.[54] Even some very strong corporations such as Televisión Azteca, along with its subsidiaries Iusacell and Elektra, applied to withdraw from the NYSE.[55]

Large transnational corporations use sophisticated control systems to integrate suppliers, manufacturers, and warehouses so they can produce and distribute merchandise in the required quantities to the desired locations.[56] However, many Mexican participants in US production chains lack the necessary technological control systems. They are also affected by SOX's Article 409, which requires them to announce in real time or in less than forty-eight hours if an event compromises the organization's financial status.[57] For example, a maquiladora that had a production crisis would not have time to correct the situation before the publicity caused the American outsourcing firm's shares to fall.[58] This SOX-made situation, which can lead to the contract being cancelled, the maquiladora closing down, and its workers being fired, is obliging Mexican companies to secure their processes and certify them according to various international norms such as ISO 9000, 14,000, and 17799 so that information can be accessible at any moment while remaining confidential and secure. [59]

Securities Regulation in Canada

Fierce competitive pressures resulting from open financial markets and cross-border investment flows are pressuring Canadian capital-market regulators to modify their securities regulations in their struggle to retain a viable market. Intense debates focus on centralizing Canadian securities regulators and raising corporate-governance standards.

Unlike the US framework, in which the SEC sets national standards and oversees securities regulation, Canada's regulatory framework is highly decentralized because the provinces have constitutional jurisdiction over non-bank financial institutions. Judicial interpretations of the constitution's property and civil rights clause have also conferred jurisdiction on the provinces in the fields of economic development, business licensing and regulation, labour markets and collective bargaining, financial institutions, and the process of issuing and marketing securities.[60] With securities regulation a provincial responsibility, there are thirteen provincial and territorial commissions overseeing the country's stock markets: the Ontario Securities Commission (OSC) governs the TSX, the Commission des valeurs mobilières du Québec (CVMQ) regulates the Montreal Exchange, and so forth. The thirteen commissions cooperate through the umbrella Association of Canadian Securities Administrators (ACSA) but issue their own rules for capital-market activity within their jurisdiction.

The lack of a uniform national-securities regulation creates a complicated, confusing, inefficient, and costly system for corporations listing on Canadian markets. Arguing that the current system impedes domestic companies as they try to raise money, the industry has been pressing for a single national-security regulator and one set of securities law in order to ensure that firms can access markets all across Canada by dealing with and complying with one authority. The proponents of centralizing securities regulation note that Canada is the only indus-trialized country in the world, with the exception of Bosnia-Herzegov-ina, to have fragmented securities law and a different set of rules for each province or territory.

On the other side of the regulatory debate, the chief opponents of a national securities regulator – primarily the governments of British Columbia, Alberta, and Quebec – maintain that one national regulator would create a regulatory monopoly and thereby deprive Canada of the benefits derived from competition between the provincial and terri-torial regulators. These three provinces' opposition has frustrated action in the face of years of studies, reports, and exhortations, the latter including one by the governor of the Bank of Canada, who referred to Canada's regulatory system as the 'Wild West' and called on Canada to have uniform securities laws and regulations.[61]

The issue of national regulation came on the heels of demands by cross-listing domestic and foreign firms for regulatory convergence towards one standard for protecting investors consistent with Sar-banes-Oxley requirements.[62] Unlike earlier US securities laws, SOX treated national and foreign issuers alike, so any Canadian company listing in the United States had to be audited by a public accounting firm in good standing with the PCAOB. Concerned with SOX's impli-cations for Canadian financial-service providers operating in the United States, Ottawa enacted measures to strengthen corporate gover-nance, improve financial accounting, make management more account-able, and enhance the transparency of the audit process. While the changes were justified in terms of Enron-style corporate villainy, they were really designed to foster US regulators' confidence in Canadian practices and helped to persuade the SEC to exempt Canadian compa-nies – including banks – operating in the United States from complying with SOX's onerous corporate-governance and accounting rules.

Although Canadian regulators cannot adopt a regulatory framework that is identical with that of the United States, they must adopt a com-plementary system to avoid cutting Canadian companies off from the US market. The problem is that, while large Canadian companies do not deviate from the US regulations, smaller Canadian companies cannot comply with some of the US rules. Canadian regulators, therefore, have had to make rules similar and complementary to avoid inconsistencies, but also be conscious that the rules accommodate local conditions.

Since the Canadian legislative changes did not replicate Sarbanes-Oxley, they are not a literal example of regulatory harmonization.

Rather, the Canadian-US interaction demonstrates how, in order to retain Canada's place within the US hegemony, adjustments are made between the dominant and the dependent in order to implement US standards in a way that still permits the Canadian regulatory system to function. In practice, this involves accepting the premises of American reforms while both countries recognize each other's regulatory practices. The fear of Canada being perceived as lagging behind new US regulatory requirements[63] made market regulators, the Department of Finance, lawyers, and industry spokespersons discuss reforms to corporate governance, accounting standards, and criminal prosecutions for fraud. While some focused on retaining US confidence in the quality of Canada's capital markets and its overall regulatory framework, many expressed strong disagreement with the new US rules, which, although designed to attract investors, were actually scaring away companies.[64]

In 2002 federal and provincial financial and securities regulators created the Canadian Public Accountability Board (CPAB), an independent watchdog body (similar to the PCAOB) to oversee auditors of public companies. The board was to work in conjunction with provincial accounting boards and be held accountable both to the federal government and to provincial securities regulators. Under Rule 52-108, publicly traded companies in Canada must be audited by accounting firms in good standing with the CPAB. In addition, after years of acting as an informal umbrella group for Canadian securities regulators, the ACSA adopted many provisions similar to those contained in SOX, including requirements for outside auditor certification by the Canadian Public Accountability Board, independent internal audit committees (Rule 52-110), and CEO and CFO certification of financial statements (Rule 58-109).[65] Many large Canadian conglomerates operating in the United States are audited by Canadian accounting firms. Without the CPAB, Canada would have had no jurisdiction over its accounting firms. Parallel audit boards foster a good relationship between Canadian and American regulators, allowing capital flows to continue.

The PCAOB and the CPAB increased their cooperation to avoid a double overseeing of Canadian firms. The chairs of each, William McDonough and Gordon Theissen, communicated constantly, and the PCAOB sent advanced drafts of rules to the CPAB for input. Under SOX's Section 106, registration with the PCAOB is mandatory but who does the actual oversight is open for discussion. Accordingly, the PCAOB issued a proposal that would allow non-US auditing regulators to assist in the oversight of their own accounting firms if those regulators can demonstrate their independence from the accounting profession and competence to complete the necessary regulatory work. Canada's new audit-oversight board and new corporate-governance legislation reflect the power asymmetry between the United States, which has overwhelming influence on the Canadian system, and Canada, which has virtually no influence on US capital markets. Thus, the self-regulated NYSE has played a major role in determining regulations for Canada by setting the industry standard.

In 2004 the OSC proposed corporate-governance regulations similar in substance to NYSE and SOX rules.[66] Provincial regulators have not unanimously supported nationwide corporate-governance uniformity. The provinces and territories supported the OSC guidelines, while the CVMQ and the British Columbia Securities Commission (BCSC) objected to the standards and elected to publish their own principles.

The Canadian exchanges have adopted several measures to remain competitive, focusing their resources on niche markets and consolidating major securities exchanges. Equities trading has been consolidated in the TSX for senior equities with a minimum market capitalization of $50 million and in the TSX Venture Exchange for junior equities (many of which formerly traded on the Montreal, Alberta, and Vancouver exchanges). The Montreal Exchange specializes in derivative trading and the Winnipeg Commodities Exchange in trading agricultural commodities and options.[67]

The CVMQ and BCSC securities commissions have taken other initiatives to promote the continental integration of their financial sectors, with varying degrees of success. In 2001 the Quebec government lured NASDAQ to Montreal with special legislative permission to operate directly in the province and a generous incentive package.[68] In 2003 the BCSC made a decision to allow investors to trade directly with NASDAQ. The TSX complained that this policy created 'an unfair advantage for [the NASDAQ] and allows the US giant to operate in Canada without being domestically regulated.'[69] However, after only three years, NASDAQ Canada closed its Montreal office, officially to 'integrate its strategic efforts in the US and Canadian markets'[70] but also for a range of other reasons including regulatory barriers and a general lack of interest from the Canadian financial industry.[71] Given changes in the market environment since 2000 and NASDAQ's overall strategic decision to refocus on the US market rather than on a number of different markets, this tempest did not increase US market control in Canada.[72]

However, loss of brokerage services to the US houses can already be witnessed through cross-listing, which has become a phenomenon captured by foreign brokers. As more firms list on US exchanges, fewer shares are traded in the Canadian markets, leaving Canadian brokers less business in Canada. The loss has not been offset by increased Canadian trading in the United States because investors trading on the US exchanges use US brokerage firms even to trade Canadian stocks. The result is that 'the global houses do far more trading in cross listed Canadian stocks on US exchanges'[73] than do their Canadian counterparts. In short, cross-listing has diminished the provinces' exchanges and their brokerage houses.

Bilaterally, the SEC has a close relationship with the BCSC and the CVMQ and an even closer one with the OSC since the Ontario market is by far the largest in Canada. The SEC has memoranda of understanding with the OSC, the CVMQ, and the BCSC to facilitate enforcement assistance between them.[74] Furthermore, in an effort not to reinvent the wheel, the OSC frequently looks to the SEC to determine what is appropriate for Ontario markets. Thus, though the SEC and OSC do not formally collaborate to set rules, they are conscious of each other and of having jurisdiction over some of the same companies.

There is no formal continental governance in the shape of a centralized agency overseeing North American stock-market regulation. Nor has there been direct pressure from Washington. Political pressure takes the form of the SEC requiring that, if Canada wants it to fast-track Canadian companies accessing the US capital markets, then Canadian regulations have to meet its minimum standards.

In sum, external pressures from the US market and internal pressures from domestic business interests have generated policy convergence between US and Canadian securities regulation. Competition does not only lead to greater convergence but may also result in such greater specialization as the 2007 move towards an alliance between the Montreal and Toronto stock exchanges. On the other hand, pressures to protect regional interests, the federal-provincial distribution of power, and bureaucratic interests limit regulatory harmonization.

Mexican Securities Regulation

Historically, Mexico has had very weak legal protection for investors largely because its corporate structures are characterized by family ownership. Considering that countries with a French and Spanish legal tradition tend to have firms with community or family ownership patterns, it is not surprising that, in Mexico's highly concentrated economy, five companies constitute 60 per cent of the BMV's assets.[75] Traditionally, this system of 'family-run empires'[76] has focused on the owners' welfare and neglected to protect their shareholders.

The Mexican government regulates listed corporations on the BMV through the Comisión Nacional Bancaria y de Valores (CNBV, Mexican National Banking and Securities Commission).[77] The principal legislation is the Ley General de Sociedades Mercantiles (General Law of Corporations). Enacted in 1934 and amended several times since, the law provides for the basic rights of shareholders including the appointment of directors and auditors, access to financial information, and rules for conflicts of interest.[78] It does not protect minority shareholders, however, and so creates a disincentive for the middle class to invest in the Mexican stock market.

In recent years, the trend of Mexican firms cross-listing and migrating to the NYSE has decreased the Mexican stock market's liquidity and, consequently, prompted legislative reforms in Mexico after decades of inaction. As part of an ongoing process since the late 1990s, Mexico has enacted substantial corporate-governance reforms to attract investors. In 1999 the Committee for Better Business Practices (including government, industry, finance, and service-sector representatives) developed a code for best corporate practices which, though not legally mandatory, served as the benchmark for corporate governance, providing for the disclosure of information to shareholders and the independence of board directors. Based on US standards adapted to Mexico's corporate culture, these principles were intended to facilitate the creation of clear rules for its stock market.

Other Mexican laws building on this code and constituting Mexico's national securities framework include the 2001 amendments to the Ley del Mercado de Valores (Securities Market Law). The amendments improved accountability, transparency, and corporate governance and encouraged the development of Mexico's financial market. In particular, they addressed the need to eliminate conflicts of interest within the governing organizations of the BMV and required 25 per cent of board directors to be independent.[79] No executive down to three ranks below the top management could have a vote at a company's board meetings, and CEOs themselves were prohibited from voting. The law also included requirements for audit committees, insider-trading restrictions, and measures aimed at the protection of minority shareholders.[80] Minimum three-year prison sentences were introduced for such abuses of privileged information as insider trading. Distributing corporate information to the public became mandatory three times annually and this information had to be published in the government's official bulletin, the Diario Oficial de la Federación.[81]

In more recent years, the Mexican market continued to reform its corporate-governance practices by providing increased protection for minority shareholders similar to the US rules. For example, in 2002 the CNBV and the BMV drastically tightened the rules on tender offers to protect minority shareholders by enhancing their voting rights. The move pushed Mexican companies to 'abandon their highly complex multiple share classes, as non-voting shares will enjoy full "tag along" rights in the event of takeover offers.'[82] In addition, in March 2003, the CNBV added provisions to its rules which raised listed companies' disclosure standards.[83] Beyond serving as a benchmark, these new rules made complying with the code's corporate-governance standards obligatory for firms, which must regularly report to the CNBV on their degree of compliance.

A new stock-market law passed in December 2005 was designed to encourage medium-sized, family-owned enterprises to become more professional and enter the stock market. It promoted better corporate-governance practices, the protection of minority shareholders, and public disclosure. Another of this law's innovations was the Anonymous Company for Promoting Investment, which aims to promote Mexican enterprise by giving young companies three years to comply with standards for listing companies.

The recent reforms and discussions have revised Mexican 'rules on tender offers in order to strengthen the rights of minority shareholders and accord them a proportionate share of control.'[84] Interestingly, the impetus for securities-regulation reform has not come from Mexican corporations or from the US government, but rather from the Mexican securities industry – including the CNBV and the BMV – in response to the loss of firms cross-listing in the US market. Their rationale is that adopting standards similar to the NYSE rules will increase the attractiveness of the Mexican market since, in theory, firms will be able to raise more equity, and at a lower cost, with the improved governance standards.

Thus, the corporate-governance reform movement in Mexico stems from the effect of Mexican firms' integration through cross-listing and the efforts by BMV in collaboration with the CNBV to bolster the vitality of its securities markets. Since reform may reduce the benefits flowing from their personal control, Mexican business leaders have reacted angrily to these new governance reforms, denouncing them as an intrusion of Anglo-American-style policies into the Mexican business culture. What reformers call the protection of small investors, the founding families consider their expropriation.[85]

The relationship between the SEC and the CNBV, though new within the last decade, is positive. Its cooperative nature is evident in the fallout from the TV Azteca scandal, which prompted the SEC to launch its first lawsuit under SOX against an executive of a foreign company, the president, Ricardo Salinas Pliego, for fraud. The SEC has jurisdiction on account of accusations against TV Azteca's cellphone company, Unefon, and its involvement in questionable dealings while it was listed on the NYSE. Rather than resenting the SEC investigation, and following its own failed investigative attempts, the CNBV has offered its support. A senior Mexican official commented, 'We aren't getting nationalistic about this one at all. We welcome the outside help.'[86] Integrated capital markets enabling the SEC-led investigation have forced changes to Mexican business practices that the local authorities had been unable to achieve. Following the Enron and WorldCom scandals and the corresponding Canadian and US responses, Mexico has also established an audit-oversight board. In effect, Mexico has realized that, if, in the interests of autarchy, it does not converge with North American standards to protect investor confidence, it jeopardizes the opportunity to develop its markets, banking, and stock exchange.[87]

As Mexican companies continue to migrate, the US market's importance for equity finance cannot be disputed. In the last decade, Mexican companies trading in the United States have nearly doubled from thirteen to twenty-three, representing a significant loss to Mexico's market.[88] As in Canada, the CNBV's rules indicate movement towards adopting the NYSE's and US standards. As in Canada too, Mexico's securities market is consolidating its national framework, and regulators are maintaining ongoing discussions on securities reform in harmony with the US system. Although Mexican securities reforms have been impressive on paper, the outcome for Mexico's capital markets will depend on their enforcement. Mexico's history of corruption and concentrated family ownership is not likely to bend easily to a rules-based system of strict rules protecting minority shareholders. Furthermore, according to the Mexican securities industry itself, the future of Mexico's markets depends on further harmonization of its new corporate-governance reforms.[89]

Conclusion

Securities regulation in the United States, Canada, and Mexico demonstrates that each country is undertaking reform initiatives to improve the quality and competitiveness of its capital markets, with the periphery moving towards the system defined in the Sarbanes-Oxley Act.

To an extent, the harmonization of Canadian and Mexican standards to complement the US market constrains the autonomy of Canadian and Mexican regulators. The more the US stock market is accessible to Canada's and Mexico's firms and investors, the more unfeasible it is for the continental periphery to ignore changes in US regulation. At the same time, in Canada, such local forces as small companies, the BCSC, and the CVMQ are constraining the level of binational convergence. Similarly, in Mexico, corporations and the Mexican corporate culture of concentrated family ownership are tempering the pace of reform.

North America is part of a larger trend towards the internationalization of standards. As the EU considers establishing independent audit boards, it is clear that corporate convergence and transparency are on the international agenda. Major securities regulators around the world meet regularly through the International Organization of Securities Commissions to exchange information and develop policy standards, and North American regulators also meet through the North American Securities Administrators Association. However, as illustrated in the North American context, with different national heritages, political systems, and business traditions, national regulators' policies are converging but not becoming a one-size-fits-all continental securities framework.

The ability to secure exemptions in each other's jurisdictions within a high degree of convergence seems to be the preferred route of regulators in North America, rather than a complete trilateral harmonization of regulatory structures. Apart from such bilateral arrangements as the MJDS, the PCAOB/CPAB, and MOUs for recognizing and accepting standards, there is no formal continental institution governing North

America's capital markets. But the complementary content of Canada's and Mexico's regulatory frameworks with the US market facilitates these arrangements and enhances the flow of capital in the continent, demonstrating that, however invisible to the naked eye, the market itself acts as an informal institution of continental governance operating on the basis of a hegemony in which the dominant power collaborates with its much weaker but generally willing partners. Likewise, as capital flows across borders and issuers and investors migrate to New York, the SEC and US statutes are establishing de facto continental industry standards for securities regulation. North America's convergence towards US securities standards enhances regulatory hegemonification in a continent characterized by two asymmetrical and unbalanced power relationships.

Ten years ago, this analysis would have shown that North America did exist as a largely integrated capital market. But, because of integrating factors at the global level, Canada and Mexico are becoming part of a system of world governance. Ever since US exchanges began going public themselves, thereby subjecting themselves to the demands of shareholders, competitive pressures have been encouraging them to consolidate and globalize.[90] Motivated by the desire to give listing companies an option for avoiding high American regulatory standards, and also by the desire to cut costs by, for example, consolidating trading technology, American exchanges are turning their attention across the Atlantic Ocean. The merger of the NYSE with Euronext, a large pan-European stock exchange, created the world's largest exchange group, with a market capitalization of about $US27 billion.[91] While the NASDAQ similarly has expanded into Europe, the NYSE is also exploring its expansion into Asia.[92]

Many European business interests feared that NYSE-Euronext marked the extension of US dominance and regulatory creep into Europe,[93] but this expansion is in part defensive, indicating the end of the United States' autonomy in regulatory autarky. After the shift in the market for foreign IPOs to London, the SEC has become more aware not only of increasing competition to US stock markets from alternative venues for raising capital, but also of the sensitivity of foreign issuers to regulatory environments. As a result, it is actively seeking global regulatory harmonization through bilateral agreements and engagement in such global governance as the IOSC to improve efficiency and prevent global regulatory competition where undesired.[94] In this sense, North

America, which was more than met the eye in its capital markets during the twentieth century, looks more and more like an example of the region coming under the sway of global governance.

The story of North American capital markets and securities regulation, then, provides clear evidence of globalization trumping continentalization. Even clearer evidence of the same phenomenon can be found in the three chapters of Part Four.

PART FOUR

Not What Meets the Eye:

Global Governance in North America

North America's existence was intuitively obvious in the case of the capital markets, where, as we have noted, Canada and Mexico aligned their regulatory standards to approximate those prevailing over American stock exchanges. In other cases, however, the appearance of a North American regulatory reality may be deceptive. Just because standards are becoming more similar between the United States, Canada, and Mexico does not mean that this policy homogenization is a product of continental governance. With banking in chapter XIII, we can see that, despite NAFTA addressing financial services in a separate chapter, transborder governance is a matter of the three countries' central banks participating in global governance regimes dealing with the regulation of financial institutions.

Even the appearance of continental corporate governance may not be what it seems. Just because US biotech corporations have pressed the Mexican and Canadian governments to introduce the same policies favouring the use of genetically modified plants does not necessarily imply that this is a matter of continental governance, as we see in chapter XIV.

NAFTA also boasts a large chapter on intellectual property rights. Nevertheless, as explained in chapter XV, governance issues connecting US TNCs and Canada or Mexico have been played out within the global governance provided by the WTO. In all these sectors, therefore, we find that North America does not exist as a genuine governance zone.

XIII The Banking Sector

Anyone would be forgiven for having expected banking to rank with energy, agriculture, and the capital markets as a sector in which transborder governance and a pre-eminently North American character prevails. After all, proximity is a major facilitator of business, and banks could have been assumed to be driven by the continent's transnationalization. But banking in North America is not what it seems for two main reasons. Structurally, ownership patterns did not become integrated across the two US borders after the inauguration of free trade. And institutionally, NAFTA created neither norms nor mechanisms that could establish a transborder continental governance for financial services superior to already-existing global governance bodies.

There are three major types of banks: commercial, investment, and central. Commercial banks make loans and offer a range of other financial services to individuals, companies, and other organizations. Investment banks originate, underwrite, and distribute new security issues of corporations and government agencies and are therefore closely connected to the securities industry, which was explored in chapter XII. Central banks are governmental institutions regulating the money supply, manipulating interest rates, and trying to stabilize each currency's exchange rates. Since central banks are mostly apolitical governmental institutions, this chapter focuses on commercial and investment banks, which play an integral role in North America's political economy. The government and governance of these institutions have evolved in distinct ways in each country, providing a sharp counterpoint to the convergence we observed in the US-dominated, continentally integrated capital markets.

Banks across North America operate according to the policies formulated in each jurisdiction. This is not to say that the impetus behind these policies is always endogenous. Far from being determined internally, the room for policy manoeuvre and the governments' policies in North America's financial-services sector are significantly influenced by such external factors as the nature and nationality of the investment that arrives in each country. This vulnerability to exogenous forces is particularly true in Mexico, as we shall see. Additionally, its economy's sheer size gives the United States tremendous influence over the banking policies of its neighbours – which, though ranking among the dozen largest economies in the world, are only a fraction of the size of the US economy – while giving Canada and Mexico negligible political leverage over the US banking sector.[1]

For all of the talk about an emerging North American banking system, market integration varies according to each sector, with commercial banks more internationalized and retail banking more local in nature. While US influence in the periphery is strong, investment patterns are also affected by European and Asian influences. Indeed, activity in the NAFTA countries' banking systems confirms that, while Canadian banks remain heavily centred on the American market, the investment focus of US firms tends to be trans-oceanic in nature, with Japan being an important location for their investment.

For its part, Mexico's banking industry being mainly in foreign hands, firm strategies there are beginning to identify as a source of revenue the growing importance of remittances which Mexican labourers send home to their families from the United States. Many foreign banks took advantage of NAFTA's regulations – particularly Chapter 11's more substantial protection for foreign investors – to enter the Mexican market through their subsidiaries in the United States.[2]

The power pattern in North American banking cannot be understood in terms of the regional hegemony we saw in beef or energy. Instead, Canada and Mexico maintain partially autonomous banking policies, but their relationships to the United States are distinct and skewed. As branches of Spanish and US corporations, Mexican banks have ventured only recently into the American market, where Canadian banks have penetrated much further than have US banks in Canada.

This chapter begins by examining the distinct evolution of North America's three national banking sectors in order then to explain how little they are affected by NAFTA mechanisms when compared with the greater influence of global regulatory bodies. Lastly, the text explores the governance efforts of banking-sector associations, which have failed to organize transnationally or engage in continental governance.

Banking in North America

The United States

Because US banks focus mainly on the domestic market, they rank only sixth in total foreign loans behind the banks of Germany, the United Kingdom, Switzerland, Japan, and France. When they do operate abroad, they tend to look to the large European and British markets for clients. Over 40 per cent of US banks' loans abroad are across the Atlantic. Borrowers in the North American periphery account for just over 10 per cent of US banks' foreign loans. Switzerland has the leading amount of foreign bank claims in the United States ($1,055 billion), followed by the United Kingdom ($1,025 billion), Japan ($625 billion), France ($516 billion), Germany ($597 billion), the Netherlands ($503 billion), and finally Canada ($335 billion).[3]

The traditional openness of the US market in financial services has not led to any significant growth in the influence of foreign interests on US banking policy. Foreign countries have important investments in the United States, but the US economy is too large for any externally driven governance to be of major consequence. Nevertheless, financial-services firms based in other countries hire lobbyists to represent their interests in Washington. A common concern among foreign banks operating there had long been the anti-competitive restriction on interstate branching found in the McFadden Act of 1927 and the separation of commercial banking from investment banking required by the Glass-Steagall Act of 1933. Both of these restrictions also affected Canadian and Mexican banks, which did not face similar constraints in their own jurisdictions where they could operate from sea to sea. During the NAFTA negotiations, Canadian and Mexican negotiators pressed their US counterparts to eliminate these restrictions, but to no avail. Eventually, they were dismantled, though not as a result of foreign pressure.

Restrictions on interstate branching were officially lifted in the Riegle-Neal Interstate Banking and Branching Efficiency Act of 1994 and in many state jurisdictions throughout the 1990s. In effect, the 1990s legislation was the culmination of a long process during which the domestic industry's desire to dismantle the McFadden Act's restrictions on inter-

state branching in order to expand and be more internationally competitive was supported by bank regulators' leniency and judicial rulings.[4]
Years of whittling away the Glass-Steagall restrictions through technological innovation and piecemeal decisions by courts led to their final
dismantling in the Gramm-Leach-Bliley Act of 1999. Support for reform
came from the US banking sector, which wanted to adjust to the rapidly
changing landscape of the financial-services industry.[5] Though the
deregulation of US banking was welcomed abroad, the only role played
by the international arena in this development was to animate US
banks' concern for their international competitiveness.

Canada

Fuelled by their core nineteenth-century business of servicing the
export industry in such staple products as timber and wheat, Canadian
chartered banks developed under federal regulations as a handful of
widely held, domestically controlled, technologically sophisticated,
and managerially efficient firms operating in all provinces from coast
to coast. While this oligopoly of six large chartered Canadian banks
expanded abroad, it continued to dominate the domestic market, holding over 90 per cent of the country's banking assets.[6] An unusually low
level of US and other foreign bank investment in Canada was in large
part due to significant regulatory and market barriers. The requirement
that the chartered banks be widely held (no legal person could own
more than 10 per cent of any bank) prevented any single corporation
getting control of a large Canadian bank. Although not aimed at foreign
suitors, this rule dissuaded foreign banks from acquiring their Canadian counterparts. The relatively thin Canadian interest-rate spread
(the difference between what a financial institution charges on loans
and the interest it pays to its depositors) was an indicator of the chartered banks' considerable efficiency, proof of the system's high level of
competition, and a significant disincentive for foreign banks to enter
the market.[7] But it is the oligopolistic dominance of the large domestic
banks in their retail sector that remains the primary – and self-reinforc-
ing – barrier to transborder corporate integration.

   As a result, foreign corporations' share of Canada's banking sector is
atypically small. International – particularly American – complaints
about the restrictions of the 1967 Bank Act (which prohibited foreign
banks from entering Canada through branches and effectively blocked
foreigners from owning the chartered banks) ultimately led the Cana-

dian government to make significant amendments to the act in 1980, when it finally permitted foreign banks to enter the marketplace by setting up a subsidiary.[8] However, since subsidiaries could not use their parent banks' assets as the reserves on which they could base their lending, their operations were limited.

The American government had long pressed Canada to allow foreign banks to enter its market on a branching basis (so that US banks in Canada could use their parents' assets as their own reserves). The branching issue came up during the CUFTA and NAFTA negotiations as well as GATT's Uruguay Round. During the NAFTA negotiations, Canada stated that it would allow cross-border branching only when the restrictions on nation-wide branching in the United States were lifted – in effect, refusing national treatment for US banks in Canada but demanding reciprocity for Canadian banks in the United States. After the Riegle-Neal Act of 1994 permitted nation-wide branching in the United States, Canada's position became much harder to defend. Moreover, the fact that Canada had been the only member of the OECD not to permit cross-border branching made the government's position all the more untenable. This international pressure was an important element in the eventual legislative changes that were enacted in 1999. However, the changes also respected Canada's long-standing concerns about foreign banks, since their branches were permitted to accept only commercial deposits and not to engage in retail banking, which has typically been much more profitable.

In time, the Canadian chartered banks, which wanted to consolidate into two or three super banks, came to see cross-border branching as a support rather than a threat to their political strategy. Foreign branching would bring more competition to the market, thereby alleviating Ottawa's concerns over the potentially anti-competitive consequences of domestic mergers.[9] But there was a problem with this strategy: foreign subsidiaries had been losing market share in Canada throughout the 1990s.

Given the level of US foreign direct investment in other industries and Canada's proximity to the United States, one would have expected US banks to have the highest percentage of claims of any of the foreign banks in the Canadian market. In fact, however, foreign financial institutions – which participate in the Canadian market primarily in such niches as commercial banking, credit-card operations, Internet banking, and small-business lending – are more trans-Atlantic than continental. As a result of the considerable presence of the London-based Hong

Kong and Shanghai Banking Corporation (HSBC) – the world's third-largest bank by market capitalization and in 2006 the seventh-ranked bank in Canada, holding US$46 billion in Canadian assets[10] – the United Kingdom has the leading amount of consolidated claims for foreign banks in the country (US$70 billion), followed by the United States (US$50 billion).[11] While a number of US banks operate in Canada, their individual shares of Canadian financial assets remained below 5 per cent between 1988 and 1998.[12] Allowing cross-border branching has increased US investment in Canada – with the overwhelming majority of foreign bank branches being US-owned – but the market continues to be dominated by Canada's domestic banks, and structural integration has been modest.

In 2001 Ottawa moved to liberalize the industry by raising the widely held ownership cap from 10 to 20 per cent for voting shares and 30 per cent for non-voting shares of domestic banks and foreign bank subsidiaries. While foreign governments and their investors welcomed the legislation, the impetus behind it lay in the Canadian banking industry's desire to raise more capital to boost their international competitiveness.[13] Although pressure from foreign governments played a role in these legislative changes, domestic factors and interests were decisive.

Despite their home market's small size, Canadian banks' loans in the United States exceeded those of US banks in Canada by over $280 billion in 2006 because – much like firms in other industries – Canadian banks' principal foreign market is the United States.[14] Apart from their domestic operations, the US market has been the principal source of revenue for each of Canada's 'big six' chartered banks over the past decade, since opportunities for growth have been much greater there than in the smaller and saturated Canadian market. Recent deregulation added to the attractiveness of the US market, which Canadian banks have sought to penetrate by acquiring niche service providers and large subregional banks. Toronto-Dominion, for example, focused on developing its US discount brokerage business, primarily through its acquisition of Waterhouse. Meanwhile the Royal Bank of Canada aggressively acquired a variety of financial-service providers in the United States totalling $5.3 billion in 2000, including the $2.2-billion purchase of Centura Banks of North Carolina. The Bank of Montreal developed its primary US holding, Harris Trust and Savings Bank, as a retail and commercial bank based in Chicago and serving the midwestern states. The Canadian Imperial Bank of Commerce focused on expansion in US investment banking by acquiring Oppenheimer.

The only exception to this preoccupation with the US market is the Bank of Nova Scotia, which has concentrated on Mexico, parts of Latin America, and the Caribbean. Scotiabank's purchase of a minority (but controlling) stake in Inverlat, one of Mexico's six largest banks, and its subsequent acquisition of full ownership underlines this unique strategy. Canadian banks continue to expand outward, and, according to the Canadian Bankers Association (CBA), Canada's six largest banks made 18 per cent of their earnings outside Canada in 2005.[15] Overall, the United Kingdom and continental Europe are the secondary and tertiary destinations of Canadian banks' claims, with Mexico coming a distant fourth.

Mexico

Mexico's banking sector has experienced a quarter-century roller-coaster ride of major policy reversals. After a decade of nationalization and government-orchestrated consolidation in the 1980s, President Salinas de Gortari started reprivatizing banks in 1991. These efforts were part of the broader process of selling off major public enterprises in order to shrink the state sector and reactivate private enterprise. Of 61 billion pesos obtained from selling 409 state-owned enterprises, close to 38 billion came from the sale of eighteen banks.[16]

During the NAFTA negotiations, Mexico assumed a defensive position vis-à-vis financial services. Rather than envisaging expansion into the other two NAFTA countries, Mexico City accepted a significant but staged loosening of its highly restrictive regulations in order to permit a gradual increase of US and Canadian participation in its nationally owned banking sector through mergers and acquisitions.[17]

Salinas's efforts did nothing to prevent financial disaster from recurring at the end of his mandate. The huge economic crisis of 1994-5 led to high levels of corporate and personal indebtedness to the banks and then to the debtors' incapacity to pay. Another collapse of the banking system would have cut access to credit and shut down the productive infrastructure, so President Ernesto Zedillo drew on a deposit-guarantee fund to rescue most of the banks from bankruptcy. Of 552 billion pesos in overdue loans, only 30 per cent was recoverable, resulting in the assumption of 387 billion pesos as public debt by the National Congress, with the banks assuming responsibility for only 82 billion pesos.[18] Of the eighteen banks remaining under government control, thirteen went bankrupt.

Zedillo's bailout of the banking system clearly put the interests of the bank owners first, increasing the burden on the taxpayers by over 10 per cent of GDP over several years.[19] In the context of a rapid growth of consumer and mortgage credit that preceded the crisis, individuals and small businesses suffered from much higher interest rates in the early 1990s than they had during previous economic setbacks. Yet the government did not respond to the pleas of the middle and lower-middle classes in the same way that it did to those of the big financial conglomerates. Most individuals and small businesses were left to face bankruptcy and endure destitution.

The crisis had external ramifications as well. Fearing a 'Tequila effect' – an international financial collapse following a Mexican meltdown – the Clinton administration put together a $50-billion multilateral rescue package but demanded that the government immediately drop all barriers to foreign ownership of its banks. In effect, the staged opening negotiated in NAFTA was abandoned in favour of a sudden foreign takeover.[20] Following this bailout, the sector's ownership structure changed drastically through the acquisition of all but one of the banks by foreign corporations, which thereby acquired the capacity to determine Mexican banking policy. Subsequently, a series of reforms strengthened the regulatory system and attracted more foreign investment to bail out an industry devastated by widespread failures and deposit runs. To lure foreign capital, the Mexican government offered to buy two pesos' worth of the bad loans for each peso of fresh capital injected by investors. Most foreign banks approached the offer cautiously, but the Spanish ones headed by Banco Santander Central Hispano (BSCH) used their subsidiaries in Puerto Rico to take advantage of NAFTA's rights in order to establish themselves in the Mexican market. In the case of Grupo Financiero Inverlat, which suffered a tremendous financial deterioration during the crisis, the Mexican government actually had to pursue Scotiabank, offering significant concessions in order to persuade it to invest. After intense negotiations, Scotiabank acquired 10 per cent of Grupo Financiero Inverlat's stocks and the right to administer both Grupo Financiero and Banco Inverlat.

In 2001 direct foreign investment in the Mexican banking sector amounted to more than $16 billion. This increased to over $27 billion as a result of the tax-free selling of Banco Nacional de Mexico (Banamex) to Citigroup for $15.5 billion.[21] By 2004, foreign financial institutions controlled more than 80 per cent of Mexican banking assets and five of Mexico's six largest banks,[22] whose profitability doubled in the first five years of Vicente Fox's administration.[23] In less than two decades, Mexico shifted from being the most autarchic of the three North American systems to becoming the most exposed to external control.

Since most acquisitions were done through partnerships or mergers with banks whose headquarters were located in Europe and the United States, Mexican banks increasingly denominated their debt portfolios in foreign currency. As subsidiaries of foreign companies, their money operations became subject to overseas economic policy considerations. The transfer of the money market into the hands of international conglomerates radically undermined Mexico's economic and policy-making autonomy: any rise in the interest rate by the US Federal Reserve or some other foreign jurisdiction could raise local lending costs significantly and so contract economic activity in the country. The new foreign bankers were at first mainly interested in doing business with the corporate sector, although they gradually expanded their retail activities.[24] Nevertheless, the banks' predominantly foreign-currency portfolios reduced the availability of credits in pesos, on which smaller domestic companies depend.[25]

Mexico's constant search for external capital makes its policy makers keenly aware that their regulatory system must satisfy foreign investors, lest they pick up their investment and move it elsewhere. Accordingly, complaints by international banks[26] led to further investor protections via a new Ley de Sistema de Bancos (Bank System Law) and to a strengthening of the Leyes de Garantía (Bankruptcy Laws). These amendments speeded up the process of repossession in case of loan default, giving banks direct recourse to repossess without having to go through the court system. Some argue that, by making this process faster, the new arrangements mean that loans do not lose their value as quickly as they would if there were a long trial, companies do not incur in-court costs, and borrowers with good credit standing do not have to pay for bad borrowers in the form of higher bank charges. According to this rationale, credit will be cheaper in the long run because interest rates will be lower, response periods for loan requests will be shorter, and collateral requirements will be more flexible.

Although government officials deny any lobbying on the part of international banks concerning these laws, their passage was vital for making the Mexican banking system appear sounder and therefore a more attractive investment.[27] The laws, however, also responded to the need for less expensive credit for those medium- and small-size entrepreneurs who do not have the capacity to seek credit abroad.

In 2005 Spanish banks had total assets of US$20 billion in Mexico, while US banks had US$14 billion, having been latecomers in the Mexican market despite the benefits afforded to them under NAFTA. This can largely be attributed to the perceived risk associated with the Mexican market following the peso crisis and previous decades' volatility. According to one official, 'Citibank did not see enough regulation being implemented to protect its interests and preferred the status quo over the risk of acquiring one of these problematic banks. Only when it saw its Spanish and Canadian competitors had acquired Mexican banks and actually succeeded, did it decide to expand its business there.'[28]

The drain of profits from the Mexican economy by the foreign banks has been challenged by some public regulators, who point out that these banks lend much less than do banks in Brazil, Chile, and Argentina. At the same time, their service charges are higher than in the industrialized world, in effect denying most of the population access to the banking system.[29] The bank takeovers also made the financial-services market a foreign-investment recipient. There was little incentive for these branches to extend beyond the domestic market. Recent expansions by Spanish subsidiaries into money- transfer services from the United States, however, suggest that this trend is slowly changing.

The volume of money transfers by Mexican émigrés in the United States has risen dramatically: a Mexican debit card allows users in Mexico to access money transferred from the United States and some Latin American countries.[30] The tactic used by the BSCH for expanding into the money-transfer market has been to collaborate with the Bank of America through their joint ownership of Banco Santander Serfin – BSCH owns 75 per cent of shares in Santander Serfin, while Bank of America owns 25 per cent – to make inroads into the Hispanic market in the United States. For example, clients of Santander Serfin and Bank of America can now use the other bank's ATMs in the other country free of charge.[31]

Banorte, the only Mexican bank that survived after the economic crisis of 1995, is also looking for Mexican clients in the United States to create a 'bi-national financial culture.' Immigrants will be able to open an account, get a debit card, and use ATMs there while paying no commissions. More important, they will be able to make transfers from the United States to Mexico via telephone, Internet, or at the bank free of charge. The challenge is to convince undocumented workers that the bank will not transmit any information to US authorities about their legal status.[32]

Nevertheless, Mexican banking leaves much to be desired. The commissions that customers must pay are higher than in developed countries, and the services, even if improved in the last fifteen years, are not the best. New local banks like Banco Azteca or Coppel are profiting from this situation by reducing their prices and improving their services.

The Banking Sector under NAFTA

Although the 1988 free-trade agreement between Canada and the United States broke new ground in international trade law by including a specific chapter on financial services, its provisions were not of great moment. Since NAFTA's negotiators recognized that this sector was decisive 'not only in channelling resources, but also in promoting the institutional changes necessary for the signatory countries to respond effectively to the challenges posed by deregulation, competition, and liberalization in the globalized world of the end of the century'[33] they were keen to strengthen the agreement's governance provisions by introducing dispute-settlement mechanisms.

To deal with possible conflicts in the financial sector, NAFTA's Articles 1412 to 1414 provide for the settlement of disputes through the procedures specified by Chapter 20 for government-to-government cases and Chapter 11 for investor-state suits. Either way, NAFTA's Financial Services Committee (FSC) would come into its own, determining whether an alleged violation of the treaty is justiciable.[34] Because an offending party is obliged to make changes to its policies based on the NAFTA tribunal's ruling, this arbitration could therefore be considered a potential form of supranational government. In the event that a private financial-services investor invokes dispute-settlement procedures under Chapter 11, the FSC could play an important role, since it can issue a report on the validity of a defending party's claim, a decision that is binding on the tribunal hearing the case.[35] Although Chapter 11 arbitration rulings on private-sector actions are binding, tribunal decisions on inter-governmental disputes through Chapter 20 are not binding on administrative agencies or national courts. A successful complainant's final recourse is retaliatory action through Articles 1414 and 1415. However, since Chapter 14's procedure is not tailored to the fast-paced realities of the financial-services sector, it could take several years for an arbitration to take place. By that time, the original claim may have lost its relevance, given that the dynamics of the financial sector change significantly from day to day.[36]

In addition, NAFTA's Chapter 14 commits the three governments to grant each other's firms the right to establish premises in their respective territories (Article 1403) and to engage in cross-border trade (Article 1404), meaning that a bank in one country can sell its financial services in another.

All these provisions notwithstanding, the ability of the dispute-settlement mechanisms to affect domestic banking policy in each country and promote a common North American governance is dubious. NAFTA created nothing in the way of inter-governmental decision making in financial services apart from its FSC, which has not become a vehicle for expanding the agreement's scope in practice. The FSC was also intended to be a forum for officials from Canada's Department of Finance, the US departments of the Treasury and Commerce, and the Secretaría de Hacienda y Crédito Público to share information about proposed regulatory changes in each jurisdiction and other issues related to Chapter 14's stipulations. The annual day-long meetings mandated under Article 1412(3) have been little more than a congenial forum for discussion. Mexican financial system administrators take these meetings more seriously than their colleagues, because they consider them indispensable for keeping up to date with regulatory developments in the United States and Canada,[37] but US and Canadian officials see the annual meetings as little more than an opportunity to network and resolve minor irritants.

To date, there have been no disputes presented before the FSC, which is therefore moribund as a judicial instrument. With no headquarters, bureaucratic apparatus, or decision-making power, the FSC cannot be said to be a site for significant transborder governance. While it remains a forum for inter-governmental decision making on paper, it has been ineffectual so far and shows no signs of strengthening over time given that transnational financial-services regulatory issues are dealt with increasingly through such global governance institutions as the International Organization of Securities Commissions, which brings financial system regulators together annually and has the technical capacity to propose regulatory changes.[38]

Under Chapter 14, the parties must extend to their two partners' trading or investing firms' most-favoured nation (MFN) treatment (Article 1406) and national treatment (Article 1405). MFN treatment requires a party to extend 'treatment no less favourable' than it accords investors or traders from other countries. National treatment requires a party to accord investors and traders of financial services 'treatment no less favourable' than what it gives its domestic financial institutions. In other words, the parties agreed in Chapter 14 to refrain from discriminatory behaviour against financial institutions based in other NAFTA countries, whether they are investing in actual foreign premises or providing cross-border services from their home countries. But this apparent abandonment of each signatory's financial-sector protectionism was contradicted by another norm entrenched in the agreement, the prudential principle.

Because the liberalization of trade in financial services would have been unacceptable to any country were it to restrict its ability 'to adopt and maintain laws and regulations for such purposes as the protection of investors and depositors in its territory,'[39] Article 1410(1) states that NAFTA's obligations will not prevent a party from using 'reasonable measures' to maintain the 'integrity and stability of a Party's financial system.' This prudential clause – a massive exclusion that allows a country to exempt itself from rules pertaining to the international regulation of financial services if it is to protect the interests of depositors and establish domestic economic stability – allows signatories to breach the agreement without much to fear from a potential dispute panel. In global economic governance, a similar exemption in the Annex on Financial Services to the WTO's General Agreement on Trade in Services allows members not to be 'prevented from taking measures for [prudential] reasons.'[40] Such 'prudential carve-outs' cover the protection of depositors, investors, policyholders, and policy claimants. They also include the maintenance of the financial system's overall integrity and stability through rules governing, for example, the ratio of a bank's capital to its risk-weighted credit exposure, the treatment of conflicts of interest, and the handling of certain liquidity and risk-management issues, as well as through other rules prohibiting self-dealing and setting out disclosure requirements designed to constrain the risk exposure of banks.

Although the inclusion of a dispute-settlement mechanism in both GATS and NAFTA's Chapter 14 appeared to herald a new level of intrusive supranational governance, prudential carve-outs have largely negated this potential. If a country can simply cite financial security as a reason to ignore NAFTA rules, then a coherent trilateral agenda in North America is unlikely to emerge, and prospects for continental governance – let alone continental government – are slim. In effect, each country has retained most of its policy-making autonomy, although, in an obvious reference to Mexico, NAFTA requires that, should a country run into macroeconomic troubles which threaten the overall integrity of its financial system, it must remedy the situation by seeking *and taking* the advice of the International Monetary Fund and such other relevant bodies as the World Bank.

Another reason for Chapter 14's irrelevance can be found in global governance. The provisions of the GATS Annex on Financial Services delineates strictly defined measures to ensure the stability of the financial system. GATS calls for a Council on Services if there are difficulties with a country's adherence to the appropriate schedules for the liberalization of trade in services.[41] This option for legal recourse through arbitrations and appeals makes the more muscular WTO the preferred alternative (for those wanting strong multilateral disciplines) to NAFTA, whose dispute settlement in financial services becomes ipso facto moot.

Both the NAFTA and the WTO Agreement on Financial Services contain provisions that acknowledge the coexistence of the continental and global levels of governance. The WTO recognizes the existence of regional trade agreements, and NAFTA's dispute-settlement provisions permit a complaining party to have recourse to either NAFTA or the WTO in cases covered by both sets of rules. NAFTA's negotiators did not accord legal priority to one or the other. The uncertainty surrounding the relationship between NAFTA and the WTO opens the door to 'forum shopping,' whereby states and individuals seek the legal regime more favourable to their cause.

The WTO Agreement on Financial Services contains provisions similar to NAFTA's on cross-border trading and has similar investment rights subject to MFN and national treatment. With NAFTA and WTO rules for banking being essentially the same, member nations can choose between either dispute-settlement mechanism in the event of an alleged violation in this sector unless the dispute involves environmental, sanitary/phytosanitary, and technical standards, in which case the parties can demand that the case be brought in front of a NAFTA panel. Because the privileges afforded to cross-border financial-service investors and traders in the WTO agreement and its dispute-settlement mechanism are superior to NAFTA's, global economic governance further marginalizes continental governance in North American banking.

International Banking Standards and Regulatory Bodies

The domestic rationale for regulating financial institutions sees banks as inherently unstable and prone to crises of confidence because their liabilities (the deposits they take in) are usually fixed in value and payable on demand, whereas their assets (the loans they give out and the securities in which they invest) are of variable value and not collectible on demand.[42] Stiff global competition exacerbates the pressure to make perilous investments in an unregulated international arena where credit risk is not aligned with a bank's capital reserves. Because banks invest and operate globally, a bank failure in any part of the world has the potential for triggering a domino effect that can devastate the whole international banking system, as was seen following the August 2007 burst of the United States' subprime market's bubble. This interlinking of financial markets, as well as the growth of such profitable but destabilizing activities as derivatives, currency speculation, and the securitization of mortgages, has led bank regulators to cooperate more at the global than the continental level.

After the Asian and Russian financial crises of 1997, the Financial Stability Forum (FSF) was created under the leadership of the G7 countries, with a small secretariat at the Bank of International Settlements (BIS) to improve transparency and supervision and thereby promote international systemic stability. To foster these goals, the FSF coordinated a number of institutional actors, including the G7 finance ministers, central bank presidents, national supervisors, the BIS, the World Bank, the IMF, and the OECD.

No trilateral decision-making organization formulates banking standards specific to North America. In contrast, various institutions at the global level are charged with oversight and standard setting in the financial arena. Under the umbrella of the BIS, the Basel Committee on Banking Supervision is one such standard-setting organization. Although the Basel committee does not possess any formal supervisory authority (its recommendations were never intended to have legal force), it formulates broad supervisory standards and recommends best practices – in the expectation that individual authorities will take steps to implement them in ways appropriate to their national systems. Despite the non-binding nature of the Basel Accords, countries generally do observe them because they participate in making the rules in order to strengthen the hegemony and integrity of the international banking system.[43] One major area of influence is capital-adequacy standards – the amount of liquid reserves a bank is required to maintain to protect itself against risks. The International Monetary Fund and the World Bank also play a significant role in ensuring implementation of the Basel rules as well as other internationally agreed principles for financial-sector regulation and supervision.[44] Another instance of continuous global regulatory development that has no equivalent in North America is IOSCO's issuing of proposals for tougher oversight of credit-rating agencies in the aftermath of the global market turmoil triggered by the subprime crisis of August 2007.[45]

Banks with global investments operate under a set of rules and standards designed to protect investors, consumers, and financial systems from potential irregularities or imperfections in the international market. Prime among these are the Basel Committee's 1997 Core Principles for Effective Banking Supervision, which specify the fundamental authority that bank supervisors need in order to do their job and recommend appropriate methods of supervision and the basic elements of prudential regulations. This system represents a form of supranational governance resulting from negotiations and consultations between governments, international organizations, and banking institutions at the global level that generate international standards in the banking arena. These non-binding rules have become mandatory in practice in some contexts, not only because they appear in the reform packages that international organizations prescribe for failing countries, but also because investors have increasingly become accustomed to judging the safety of their capital by whether a financial institution adheres to these standards.

In sum, standards and trade rules are being generated more at the global level than at the continental one. As the United States, Canada, and Mexico adhere to a system that operates outside North America, they participate in a form of global governance that shunts aside the continental governance once promised by NAFTA.

Unlike the European Union, NAFTA does not possess its own set of standards for the banking industry that go beyond the minimum rules set in Basel. The European Committee for Banking Standards works in association with the International Organization for Standardization, the European Commission's Enterprise Directorate-General, the European Central Bank, and the European Bankers' Association to set standards for such banking-related transactions as credit cards, automated cross-border payments, security, and electronic services. In contrast, North America approaches banking standards in a less intrusive manner. Indeed, critics of Basel refer to North America's stance towards banking standards when they describe their vision of an alternative approach that 'allows free entry for foreign-owned subsidiaries, national standards, and a territorial rule [rather than] an international capital standard that prevents regulatory competition among countries.'[46]

For Canada, the United States, and Mexico, therefore, the institutional framework for multilateral regulatory cooperation is international, rather than continental, which aptly reflects the global channels of capital movement. This circumstance may actually improve the North American periphery's regulatory capacity: lacking formal North American channels for coordinating financial regulation, Canada and Mexico find that they enjoy relatively more capacity at the global (as the tenth-largest economies among 150 others) than they do at the continental level (as middle powers over ten times smaller than their neighbouring colossus).[47]

The United States, in contrast, finds itself less dominant in the global arena than it is continentally. Before 1971, it was *itself* the pre-eminent regulatory structure in the international political economy. Afterwards, it became the dominant influence in the Basel Committee because it wanted to bolster the capacity of its large, multinational banks to enter foreign markets and compete internationally.[48] But, over time, US enthusiasm for Basel initiatives has cooled. In the 1990s, the United States resisted further standard-setting in order to free up capital for its banks. In the 2000s, Washington even applied Basel's general standards selectively. For example, the Securities and Exchange Commission decided to apply Basel II standards – which set minimum capital requirements, provide guidelines for supervisory review processes, and mandate market discipline – only to the ten largest US investment banks. This decision raised serious concerns in the European Union that Washington had set up an uneven playing field for European banks operating in the United States.[49]

Washington's inability to tailor the emerging Basel II regime to its own preferences points to some decline in its capacity to shape the international regulatory environment now that the Basel Committee can proceed without it. This suggests that the United States has retreated from its hegemonic leadership of a whole system in order to sustain dominance within its own bailiwick. Even in the continental periphery, which enjoys considerable local autonomy owing to its participation in genuinely multilateral institutions of governance, Washington does not dominate policy making in the banking sector.

Market Governance: Firm Lobbying and Strategies

Transnational financial integration has changed both the nature of cooperation between governments and the manner in which the banking sector promotes its interests. Not only have foreign firms created their own lobby committees within existing associations in host jurisdictions, but they have also become increasingly engaged in directly lobbying foreign governments. Lobbying in the North American banking industry, however, has not occurred around specifically North American issues. In fact, little lobbying collaboration occurs among banking associations in the three countries or among banks with significant investments in North America. Sector representatives from the three countries meet at the annual summits of banking associations from OECD countries, but no meetings specific to North American banking associations are held. The global nature of individual banks' investments also leads them to form lobbying alliances with other banks based on individual issues, not on the geographical position of their headquarters.

Banking Sector Associations

As firms increasingly venture beyond their national boundaries, be it through cross-border transactions or direct investment, the regulatory frameworks of the countries in which they operate take on greater significance. Not surprisingly, transnational banks are making renewed efforts to influence the decision-making process in foreign jurisdictions using multiple channels, including the home government's trade representatives and other officials, their own national banking associations, associations of foreign banks, and international financial institutions. Collaboration among national banking associations is virtually nonexistent, apart from the two meetings per year among the heads of bankers' associations from OECD countries to exchange papers on such issues of common concern as the Basel II negotiations and money laundering.[50] No real decision making takes place at these meetings, which serve only as a forum to share views on issues of mutual concern.

North America's three banking associations' diverse membership explains why they make no coordinated efforts to affect the continental market: they represent banks from all over the world. In fact, no association represents only domestic banks. In the United States, the Institute of International Bankers (IIB) is the foreign banks' leading association. Although these banks are also members of the American Bankers Association, the IIB – whose mission is 'to ensure that federal and state banking laws and regulations provide international banks operating in the United States with the same competitive opportunities as domestic banking organizations'[51] – plays the principal role in promoting their interests in the United States. Through letters, frequent testimony, briefings, and informal discussions, the IIB defends foreign banks' interests on pending legislative and regulatory issues before such governmental bodies as the Treasury Department, the House and Senate banking committees, the Federal Reserve Board, the Office of the Comptroller of the Currency, state banking agencies, and various other governmental bodies responsible for financial-services regulation and supervision. Although the IIB strongly advocated reform of Glass-Steagall, the ultimate legislative change, as we have seen, resulted less from foreign pressure than from years of intense lobbying by the domestic banking industry.

Canada's most influential association, the Canadian Bankers Association, has several executive committees that represent the interests of different parts of the sector. Foreign banks from a wide variety of countries constitute the Foreign Bank Executive Committee, in which British HSBC, Canada's largest foreign bank subsidiary, is the most influential member. In the lead-up to the 1999 branching legislation, the committee approached the Department of Finance on the question of foreign branching and made submissions to the finance committee in Parliament. The committee also engaged some of the larger Canadian banks that belong to the CBA's Executive Council to put the branching issue on the agenda. These lobbying efforts nevertheless were not a key factor in the 1999 legislation allowing branching.

The CBA closely monitors US regulatory developments that might affect its members and also engages in direct lobbying. When the Sarbanes-Oxley legislation was being drafted, for example, the CBA directly lobbied members of Congress and the Securities and Exchange Commission to obtain exemptions for Canadian firms. Individual banks prefer to exert pressure on policy through their home governments, whose officials enjoy better access to policy makers abroad.

In Mexico, bank executives tend to approach officials directly in the three agencies in charge of banking regulation – the Secretaría de Hacienda, the Banco de México, and the Comisión Nacional Bancaria y de Valores – concerning regulatory burdens and other procedural and legislative issues that affect their operations. Banks prefer to act independently, approaching government officials about specific issues rather than about legislation. For example, executives from large banks met officials in the Secretaría de Hacienda in order to complain about having to file separate financial statements with the three regulatory agencies. The procedure, they said, was cumbersome and unnecessary because the financial reports had to be tailored to the particular requests of each agency. As a result, in May 2003, the Secretaría introduced a new online reporting system for banks' financial statements.

Petitions for permission to introduce new services have also become a de facto form of lobbying for international banks, since executives must meet regulators in order to ensure that their banks will receive proper clearance. For example, after signing the agreement whereby BSCH and Bank of America would share ownership of Santander Serfin, Bank of America had to petition for clearance from the Secretaría de Hacienda for quite some time before being able to offer its new money-transfer systems. Mexican regulators wanted to ensure that, if they granted this permission, Banco Santander Serfin would gain as much from the transaction in the United States as the Bank of America did in Mexico.[52]

Conclusion

NAFTA's financial-services chapter notwithstanding, the continentalization of North America's banking sector remains undeveloped. Institutionally, the policies and norms formulated by the institutions and agreements that regulate global financial services determine domestic banking regulations more than does NAFTA. Structurally, the pattern of monetary flows and regulation has not taken on a particularly continental character. Indeed, regulatory harmonization and standardization in banking have been more intense among the larger OECD countries than among NAFTA partners. Despite its usefulness as an information-sharing network, NAFTA's Financial Services Committee – the only relevant trilateral decision-making body at the continental level – has been largely ineffectual. Inter-governmental financial negotiations in North America have taken the form of bilateral dialogue between regulators and supervisors and periodic lobbying by governments in other jurisdictions on behalf of their banks, but no continentally concentrated lobbying effort has emerged among firms or their sector representatives from the three countries.

Patterns of investment in banking within each country form diffuse networks that extend beyond the geographic boundaries of North America and obey a commercial logic in which the benefits and advantages granted by NAFTA play only a small role in motivating banks to invest in North American countries. Given the trans-Atlantic – and increasingly trans-Pacific – nature of the international financial market, inter-governmental decision making takes place at the global level in institutions heavily influenced by the interests of the G7 countries.

Weakness in continental governance structures also derives from the huge asymmetries among the three NAFTA countries. In order to construct a viable multilateral institution, a rough equality among the key participants in the process is required. This reality explains the United States' reluctance to support multilateralism the way middle powers do. It is also consistent with Canada's and Mexico's sensitivities about the neighbouring giant's political and economic influence in their countries. Indeed, a group of states that are non-hegemonic and roughly equal in size are much more likely to engage in multilateralism both because they pose less of a threat to one another and because they have a greater need for the efficiencies that come with pooling resources. A case in point is the highly developed government structures found in the European Union, where there is much greater equality of power among the major member countries. In North America, where power asymmetries are far greater, the costs involved in operating a highly developed governance structure do not favour its creation. Indeed, for the United States, entering into such an arrangement would constrain its ability to exercise its power. For Mexico and Canada, such an arrangement would probably institutionalize their subservience.[53]

Despite periodic public-policy proposals, the prospects for a North American community with a common currency, a central bank, and an integrated monetary policy remain dim. The erection of a monetary union would be impractical because economic conditions in one country are often markedly different from those in the others: if inflation rates are different in each market they warrant different monetary policy responses. In both Canada and the United States, provincial and state governments have been reluctant to cede any decision-making power to their respective federal governments, so it would be unlikely that they would agree to cede their authority to a supranational entity. These are just two of the myriad practical considerations that impede the emergence of a continental structure for financial services. Given the economic asymmetries among the NAFTA countries, the impediments to structural integration, and the nature of North America's financial markets, NAFTA has no chance of becoming capable of regulating the North American banking sector.

In the next chapter, we turn to a sector that presents a different picture. In sharp contrast with banking, in which American companies are not the dominant players driving change in North America, US biotechnology corporations continue to lead efforts at both the global and continentl levels to force acceptance of genetically modifued organisms in the agriculture sector.

XIV Labelling Genetically Modified Food

The banking sector showed that the European banks played a larger role in Canada and Mexico than US banks, but it also demonstrated that, apart from NAFTA's financial-services dispute-settlement rules that would turn out to be of little moment, transborder governance in this sector was global, not North American.

Despite North America's lack of governance structures, significant policy harmonization between the three countries has occurred informally in related policy areas, but not necessarily because they are members of the same continent. The three governments' common posture on genetically modified (GM) food labelling is an excellent example of this informal process, being a product of a government-corporate partnership functioning in opposition to civil-society pressure. With biotechnology transforming agriculture, transborder governance issues involve a new industry battling singly and successfully for supremacy over its opponents inside each domestic jurisdiction. The conflicted story of genetically modified foods is about a rising giant using its power independently of any continental institutions to have NAFTA's members adopt a largely uniform stance against labelling GM products.

In order to assess what kind of governance exists on this issue, this chapter examines how industry and civil society shaped the legislative debates about GM food labelling in the United States, Canada, and Mexico. In all three countries, there is evidence of transnational influences swaying the policy debate. In fact, the US biotech industry played a significant role in pressuring both the Canadian and Mexican governments to reject mandatory labelling, but not in a way that was unique to North America. Following a brief introduction to the GM food debate, an individual examination of each country suggests how a quiet alliance between national governments and the biotech industry constitutes North America's participation in transnational global governance in this sector.

Issues at Hand and the Debates

The debate over the genetic modification of food revolves around a contested understanding of the benefits and costs of biotechnology. The scientific consensus in North America paints biotechnology as critical to its future prosperity. In contrast, the scientific community in the European Union has been more sceptical about the long-term human-health consequences of genetic manipulation. Understandably, the majority of GM food supporters tend to come from within the industry itself, although endorsements of biotechnology are often echoed by government. For their part, consumer, environmental, and social groups are the main critics of GM technology and urge mandatory labelling. Because genetic manipulation is a relatively young practice, there is little solid evidence that can conclusively assess the safety of biotech food. There is, however, widespread speculation about the unforeseen long-term impacts on human health and the environment. Fear of 'Frankenfoods' has been mounting for years, particularly in France and the United Kingdom. In the aftermath of the outbreak of mad cow disease in Britain in 1996 along with the discovery of dioxin-polluted chickens in Belgium in 1999, the question of food safety became a highly emotive issue throughout Europe, encompassing the specific issue of genetic modification.

Proponents of GM foods argue that new plant varieties offer significant benefits to both producers and consumers. For example, they claim that an increase in crop yields through genetically enhanced resistance to insects can cut costs for farmers, who will then pass on the savings to consumers. GM technology supporters further claim that the environment also gains by an overall reduction in the use of pesticides, herbicides, and other chemical sprays, and that this technology can benefit human health through the addition of nutrients, vitamins, and other enrichment to foods.[1]

According to the United Nations' Cartagena Protocol on Biosafety, the 'precautionary principle' allows countries to refuse the importation of any genetically modified food or commodity that they fear may cause harm to public health or the environment, even if there is not yet sufficient scientific evidence to substantiate this concern convincingly. The principle has become the target of much criticism resulting from the vagueness of the norm. For example, the US Department of Agriculture criticized the EU's 2000 Communication on the precautionary principle for being 'strikingly vague in some areas' and 'rais[ing] questions in others.'[2] The USDA also pointed out the omission of any concrete definition of the precautionary principle within the Cartagena Protocol. On the other side of the debate, activists and some scientists are sceptical of claims that the consumption of GM food is safe. Other concerns include the spectre of GM food resistance to herbicides and pesticides, the potential for new allergens, and the possible creation of novel human toxins.

Some direct environmental effects of GM foods have already occurred. The contamination of the corn supply for human consumption by unapproved GM technology in StarLink corn products resulted in a massive North American recall. In this case, a maize variety with a genetically built-in toxin, *Bacillus thuringiensis* (Bt), designed to kill particular insects, accidentally entered the food supply in 2000, causing the contamination of non-Bt maize. This case has been much cited by NGO groups to highlight the perceived dangers of GM foods and the lack of adequate governance to manage the new technology. Similarly, in Mexico, genetically modified elements have been found in native Mexican maize, prompting concerns that GM food is risking the country's genetic diversity. Speculation linked the contamination to the import of Bt maize from the United States, cross-pollination by wind or insects, or illegal testing.[3]

In addition to a cost-benefit analysis of genetic technology, GM foods have raised ethical issues in public-policy debates. Polls suggest that overwhelming majorities of North American consumers would prefer products containing GM food to be so labelled. The public's 'right to know' constitutes one of civil society's most powerful pressures for the establishment of a labelling system.

The creation of an accurate and accountable labelling system would involve the complete segregation of GM crops from conventional crops at all levels of production and transportation. While the burden of this system of segregation would fall primarily on producers and consumers, the government would bear the costs involved in enforcing and regulating the system. Industry, in particular, has appealed to this 'unneeded' increase in production costs as an argument against the establishment of a mandatory labelling system. Biotech firms and their supporters (for example, the Grocery Manufacturers of America [GMA], the National Food Processors Association, the Canadian Council of

Grocery Distributors, and AgroBIO Mexico) oppose mandatory GM labelling schemes, citing the lack of proof that there has been any detrimental impact on health. As a compromise, industry representatives have pushed for a voluntary labelling system, which would put the onus on the corporation not using GM food either to inform the consumer of its benefits or to create a niche market of products labelled as GM-free.

Labelling requirements can violate international trade commitments, which allow countries to require food labels only for health and safety reasons. Any other forms of labelling may be considered a non-tariff barrier to trade and so sanctionable by economic retaliation. According to the least-trade-restrictive rule of the WTO's Agreement on Technical Barriers to Trade, governments are required to minimize the negative impacts on trade in setting domestic product standards, and GM food labelling risks violating this rule. This uncertainty has not been resolved by the Codex Alimentarius Commission Committee on Food Labelling, which is divided between those nations that believe mandatory labelling should be product-based only (led by the United States) and those that believe it should identify differences in the process of production such as the use of GM technology (led by the EU).[4] At the Codex's 35th session, the US delegate argued that, because GM foods had already been found to be safe, there was no need to label them. She further suggested that, because no consensus was reached, the committee should drop the issue. Mexico and Canada supported the US position along with New Zealand and Australia.

In North America, an ongoing struggle pits biotech corporations, which want to keep GM labelling off the political agenda, against consumer and health organizations, which want to practise precaution. The industry is composed of the dozens of US agribusinesses that have developed GM seeds, the thousands of farmers who grow and market genetically modified produce, and the hundreds of food-processing companies that make and distribute the final product. All members of the biotech industry have reasons for opposing mandatory GM labelling, such as the costs labelling would entail and the potential loss in sales owing to possible consumer aversion to these products once their contents are identified. Whenever and wherever the issue is raised in public debate, the biotech industry has poured millions of dollars into lobbying campaigns to pressure domestic and foreign governments to suppress it. Health and consumer groups, on the other hand, struggle to keep the issue on the political docket, their attempts limited both by a lack of financial resources and by difficulties in organizing across borders.

The corporate dominance of the food process has been a result of governments' interest in encouraging economic growth through increased trade. Instead of concerns for the public good, profit-driven corporate interests have prevailed in policy making. The lack of public input into the process of food and biotechnology regulation is creating a pattern of covert governance in which the biotech industry is entrusted with its self-regulation. Furthermore, the United States' supremacy in the field of biotechnology is forcing Canada and Mexico to harmonize their policies accordingly.

The important paradigm shift in North America's farm science over the last twenty-five years can be seen in the move from a state-led to a market-oriented approach, forcing the three countries' publicly funded agricultural research networks to rely increasingly on corporate funding. In the area of biotechnology, Canada moved away from having its own experimental farms generate publicly available knowledge towards the US model, in which corporate-initiated research generates privately developed knowledge that becomes proprietary information protected by copyright.[5] This shift was reflected in Ottawa's food-labelling policies.[6] Governments with the dual responsibility of responding to popular concerns and promoting corporate interests are left in the uncomfortable space between adamant citizens and demanding industry. As the next sections show, all three national governments have chosen to side with the biotech industry.

The United States

The United States, which is the largest producer and exporter of GM foods in the world, dominated the biotech field at its inception, and, as the industry matured, US scientists and companies continued to innovate and commercialize new GM technologies and products. Consequently, the US government has aggressively promoted GM technology and defended the industry's interest abroad.

Washington pays close attention to changes in foreign labelling regimes but has left domestic regulation almost entirely in the hands of the industry itself. Daniel Glickman, secretary of the USDA under the Clinton administration, once remarked that, given the industry's overwhelming power, he did not know whether his role should be the promotion or the regulation of biotechnology. [7]

Through their political contributions and lobbying, corporations such as Monsanto and business organizations such as the Grocery Manufacturers of America and the National Food Processors Association pressure the US government to maintain a regulatory environment conducive to biotech food production and marketing. These lobbies declare biotechnology an integral part of the US economy, which must be protected from the unfounded attacks of NGOs.

The effective exercise of corporate power by the biotech industry is evidenced in the fact that the US government has given up its role in conducting third-party food-safety tests, instead letting the biotech corporations self-administer these assessments.[8] Though the Food and Drug Administration (FDA), the Environmental Protection Agency, and the USDA ultimately approve test results, this has become a formality since these agencies have largely abandoned any autonomous public process to verify industry claims.

The biotech industry's right to write its own playbook was won during the Reagan years, when Monsanto effectively wrote the rules to administer biotechnology.[9] Although the USDA and the EPA wanted a special regulatory apparatus for approving new biotechnology products, the FDA resisted this demand and called for 'voluntary conciliation' as a compromise.[10] This meant that the biotech corporations themselves could announce when a new product would be released. Written in 1992 by several members of the biotech industry, the FDA's official policy statement on biotech regulations accepted the reasoning that, because the evaluation of a foodstuff should be based on the end-product rather than on the process that produced it, biotech food should not require specific regulations. Labels would be mandatory only if there were a change in the food's normal nutritional content or if the product could cause allergies.[11] This position is in direct opposition to the European position on biotechnology regulation, whereby the Novel Foods Regulations ensure that foodstuffs in which genetically modified organisms (GMOs) constitute anything higher than 1 per cent of the total are labelled.[12]

A clear government-industry consensus on the benefits of biotechnology at the state and the federal level has led to increased public-private cooperation both domestically and abroad. This corporate-government combine has created a significant barrier to grass-roots consumer and environmental groups' demands for GM food labelling in the United States.

Despite the NGOs' failure in their quest for mandatory GM food labelling, national polls indicate that US consumers do want foods derived from GM technology to be so labelled. For example, the North Carolina State University food survey, conducted in February 2003, showed that 92 per cent of those polled wanted GM food to be labelled.[13] At the same time, since very few consumers are going to answer 'no' to the option of more information, these results overstate the intensity of the public's position; American public support for GM food has been described as 'a mile wide, but an inch deep.'[14]

In May 2002, and then again in July 2003, Congressman Dennis Kucinich (D. Ohio) introduced 'The Genetically Engineered Food Right to Know Act' to require food companies to label all food that contains or is produced with GM material. Although heavily supported by many NGOs, this federal bill had no chance of success.[15] Yet, despite its failure, similar bills continue to be proposed: Kucinich introduced six more in May 2006.[16]

There have been significant attempts to establish mandatory GM labelling in several states, including California, Colorado, Maine, Oregon, and Vermont.[17] In the fall of 2002, the state of Oregon proposed Measure 27, a GM labelling initiative that, according to polls, two-thirds of the public favoured. Fearing a precedent, corporate giants, including chemical makers Monsanto and DuPont and food producers General Mills, H.J. Heinz, and Kraft, set up the 'Coalition against the Costly Labelling Law,' which spent over $5.5 million to defeat the measure. With its supporters having a mere $200,000 at their disposal, the industry's campaign flooded Oregon airwaves and mailboxes with its claim that GM food labels would grossly increase the cost of food for Oregon residents. Measure 27 was defeated by over a two-thirds margin. [18]

Outside North America, the US government and the biotech industry also maintain active international lobbying campaigns to persuade foreign countries to accept GM foods without restrictions. For example, Greg Conko, the director of food safety policy for the Competitive Enterprise Institute, has been employed by various food corporations to discuss the labelling issue with foreign countries, especially in Europe.[19]

Canada

Ottawa has a two-step process for approving a new biotech product's commercial launch. The product must first meet the health and safety requirements of the Canadian Food Inspection Agency (CFIA), the governing body responsible for regulating food labelling, which reports to Agriculture Canada. But the CFIA does not do any independent research, relying instead on industry-sponsored test results. Next, the product is approved by Health Canada, which again performs no testing of its own. Canadian corporations are not required to provide information about their products' environmental impact. Without any independent, third-party testing, the government has to rely on the industry's testing integrity. This minimal approval process does not require the CFIA to inform the public that an application has been made and leaves no room for scientific peer review or public input. There is no mechanism to stop an approval, even if Parliament or the majority of Canadian citizens do not want the product to be released commercially.

The CFIA is widely criticized for a clear conflict of mandates since it has the double duty of consumer protection and industry promotion. Environmental groups like Greenpeace have asserted that, with regard to GM foods, the Canadian government favours corporate interests over private citizens and allows the industry to function in a 'virtually unregulated manner.'[20] In this framework, biotechnology is perceived to be an economic engine of growth, and, consequently, regulations are made to facilitate the approval of biotechnology products' arrival on the market.

Charles Caccia, the late Liberal Member of Parliament who sponsored a private member's bill that proposed mandatory GM food labelling, argued that the conflicting mandates should be 'both exposed and modified.'[21] A 2001 government-commissioned Royal Society of Canada report, 'Elements of Precaution: Recommendations for the Regulation of Food Biotechnology in Canada,' expressed serious concerns about the Canadian regulatory process and the safety of GM food.[22] Dr Spencer Barrett, a member of the Royal Society's expert panel, also identified the CFIA as having a direct conflict of interest because of its dual role of promoting and regulating biotechnology.[23] In addition to these incompatible mandates, Barrett believed that the entire regulatory process of biotechnology was 'too in-house.' He pointed to a relationship of informality between CFIA scientists, who have the responsibility to verify and analyse the biotech industry's results, and the biotech scientists, with many approvals occurring during friendly phone conversations. Both Caccia and Barrett advocated increased transparency of the Canadian regulation process via third-party participation in data analysis and approval.

The lack of public input and civil-society participation became especially evident to Canadians when Monsanto's application for introducing GM wheat was considered by the CFIA. Experts on agricultural trade predicted that the likely approval of Monsanto's application for 'Roundup Ready Wheat' for commercial release in Canada would have adverse effects on the export of Canadian wheat. Despite the possibility of losing market share in the EU, Japan, South Korea, and other countries that embargo imports of foodstuffs grown with GM technology, there was no mechanism within the CFIA or Health Canada processes for input from farmers, citizens, or even politicians. The lack of democratic participation in the regulatory process forced wheat farmers to air their concerns over GM wheat directly with the biotech industry. On May 22, 2003 the Canadian Wheat Board sent a letter to Monsanto asking the company to withdraw its application for approval to grow genetically engineered wheat in Canada. The CWB chair warned that the economic harm resulting from the approval of Monsanto's Roundup Ready Wheat could include 'lost access to premium markets, penalties caused by rejected shipments, and increased farm-management and grain-handling costs.'[24] Monsanto rejected the CWB's request and, despite a growing apprehension among North American wheat farmers, argued that its bid to win approval in Canada and the United States had 'tremendous support.'[25]

On October 17, 2001 the House of Commons defeated, by 126 to 91 votes, Bill C-287, which would have amended the Canada Food and Drug Act to require the labelling of GM food. There had been extensive lobbying efforts on both sides of the issue. On the one hand, corporate and agricultural interests worked for its defeat, claiming that mandatory labelling would make Canadian farmers lose their domestic market and so hurt them and their families, increase food prices, and 'unduly undermine Canadians' confidence in Canada's food supply and regulatory system.'[26] Consumer and environmental groups supported the bill, because it protected the consumer's 'right to know' and 'right to choice.' The contested nature of this bill and the intense lobbying efforts from both sides leading to its defeat was uncharacteristic. The fear that mandatory labelling in Canada would set a precedent for the global biotech industry led to a powerful TNC campaign to defeat the proposed legislation.

The climax of the industry's lobbying effort was a pamphlet placed on the desk of every Member of Parliament on the morning of the vote, asking the MPs to 'vote against Bill C-287 and support Canada's Agri-food Business.' Funded by the 'Task Force on Foods from Biotechnology in Canada,' this brochure was considered extremely effective in swaying the vote. Members of the task force included the Canadian Federation of Agriculture, the Food and Consumer Products Manufacturers of Canada, the Canadian Council of Grocery Distributors, and the Canadian Federation of Independent Grocers. The brochure claimed that Bill C-287 was unworkable for Canada's agri-food industry and urged MPs to support this industry by defeating the measure. In the end, the bill was defeated in spite of an eighty-group coalition supporting it, including the Council of Canadians and the Sierra Club of Canada, as well as several polls showing that an overwhelming majority of Canadians approved mandatory GM food labelling.

The third dimension in this issue was trade. During the debates over Bill C-287, there was a consistent emphasis on how labelling would affect trade with other nations. Although current trade agreements allow countries to require labelling for reasons of health and safety, labelling for other reasons, as already noted, could be considered a non-tariff barrier to trade and leave Canada open to a WTO or NAFTA challenge.[27] A report to the Government of Canada Biotechnology Ministerial Co-ordination Committee by the Canadian Biotechnology Advisory Committee argued that, even without a trade action, Canada's trading partners might 'choose to bypass the relatively small Canadian market, rather than bear the increased costs associated with labelling.'[28] The report made the case that the establishment of mandatory labelling in Canada could disturb the highly integrated nature of Canada-US agricultural and food-processing sectors, resulting in a reduction of both trade and consumer choice. Only a negligible portion of this report raised the potential for enhanced trade opportunities for Canadian producers in foreign markets hostile to GM foods, such as the EU, Japan, Australia, and New Zealand.

In November 2002 Agriculture Canada once again rejected mandatory labelling of GM food, citing 'commercial factors' and 'trade agreements' for the decision.[29] This position was in response to a request from the House of Commons's standing committee on agriculture and agri-food for an assessment of the trade implications of labelling GM food. The government's reply also alluded to US hostility to the idea of mandatory labelling as an influence on its decision. All of this suggested that the government gave trade and good relations with the United States a higher priority than domestic civil-society concerns. Canadian policy makers had strived to harmonize their policies with their neighbour's stance; domestic agricultural and corporate lobbies succeeded in pressuring the Canadian government into following the US labelling lead while building a shared ideological acceptance of GM food safety as beyond question. This evidence of bilateral market governance between Canada and the United States, in which Canadian policy appears to be harmonizing with the official US government's position because of pressure from Canadian branches of US biotech TNCs, contrasts with the success of activists and some scientists in Europe to construct alternative ideologies within EU food governance.

Mexico

Like Canada, Mexico relies on large exchanges of agricultural products with the United States and is reluctant to offend either the US government or the powerful US biotech industry, whose influence in Mexico is far more overt than it is in Canada. Between 1999 and 2003, the Mexican Congress considered four separate GM food-labelling bills. All were controversial and heavily criticized by the biotech industry, the scientific community, and foreign governments, whose lobbying efforts revealed the nature of transborder biotechnology governance in Mexico. Dramatically, when the Chamber of Deputies was reviewing a GM labelling bill in 2000, the US manufacturers went directly to the deputies arguing that labelling would increase their per-product pricing. This effectively blocked the new regulation.[30]

On March 30, 2000 the Mexican Senate voted unanimously to require that all foods containing GM substances be labelled as 'food made with genetically modified products.'[31] Before becoming law, the bill needed approval from both the Chamber of Deputies and the president. The bill, which was an amendment to the General Health Law, received no ruling from the Chamber of Deputies and was left to the Health Commission, which in turn decided that the policy was simply too controversial.[32] It ultimately became buried in bureaucracy shuttling between several inconclusive legislative commissions. Civil-society observers reported that the various bills on GM food labelling were stalled because of the biotech industry's pressure and the Mexican scientific community's dependence on commercial funds for its research.[33]

One of the main problems associated with the mandatory labelling legislation was its vague wording. For example, the legislation suggested that biotech products must be labelled according to the 'norms per product.' Although the vagueness of 'norms' would allow the law to be manipulated, the biotech industry still vehemently resisted any such changes. The largest opponent to GM food labelling is a powerful consortium of biotech companies called AgroBIO Mexico A.C., an influential international agribusiness lobby that is composed of multinational biotech corporations such as Monsanto, Syngenta, and Grupo Pulsar.

The Mexican government's self-defined need to keep multinational corporations working within its borders has greatly limited its policy options. In March 2003 one Senate aide told Liza Covantes of Greenpeace, 'The companies are saying that if we impose mandatory labelling, then they will take their investments outside of Mexico.'[34] This industry power demonstrates a clear shift in governance authority away from domestic stakeholders.

Besides direct US-controlled industrial lobbying about legislation, an informal group on biotechnology brings the other NAFTA governments' influence to bear. The Grupo Informal de Biotecnología (Informal Group on Biotechnology) was led by the US Grains Council and included the biotech industry in Mexico, AgroBIO, the US and Canadian embassies, Monsanto, and other biotech companies. Meetings were scheduled every three months or so to discuss legislation in Congress in order to give voice 'to the position of the companies regarding different issues'[35] and lobby government officials.

An element complicating the governance of Mexican GM food policy is the role played by science. Because the leaders of the scientific community have allied themselves with the biotech industry, critics charge that science has lost its independence and turned into a force very much wrapped up in both business and politics. José Luis Solleiro is a prime example of the revolving door linking the biotech industry, science, and government. An AgroBIO representative, Solleiro is also a researcher at the Universidad Nacional Autónoma de México as well as a member of the Comisión Intersecretarial de Bioseguridad y Organismos Transgénicos (Interministerial Commission on Biosecurity and Transgenic Organisms), a government body that oversees biotechnology policy. Despite working for a biotech corporation, doing research at a university, and sitting on an influential government panel, Solleiro has denied any conflict of interest.[36] Critics, however, see a major problem with the increasing number of under-funded and under-resourced scientists who are forced to work for the biotech industry to supplement their income. Because scientists who receive industry support must refrain from publishing their research, the arrangement 'generates many conflicts of interest that prevent them from speaking out freely.'[37] Such a combination of corporate and scientific pressure on biotechnology policies significantly limits the Mexican government's authority in the area of GM food labelling.

Beyond having to deal with extremely effective domestic biotech lobbying, the Mexican government must maintain trade and business with its continental partners. The United States, in turn, is also intensely interested in any foreign legislation that would adversely affect US exports. In February 2001 twenty different US agricultural groups sent a letter to Secretary of State Colin Powell asking him to urge President Bush to air the biotech industry's concerns over Mexican draft legislation on GM labelling with President Fox during his March visit.[38] The Canadian biotech industry also joined in to pressure Mexican policy makers to stall the legislation. The 'First Trinational Forum on Agricultural Biotechnology' meeting in May 2001 was widely regarded as an attempt by the US and Canadian biotech industries to constrain Mexico's policy manoeuvrability regarding GM crops.[39] Canada's dual role in absorbing and exerting external pressure is just one aspect of the dynamic and contested structure of North American governance relating to biotechnology. While it is impossible to measure any one factor's effectiveness in paralysing the legislation, the combination of domestic and foreign opposition to GM labelling clearly made the bill too controversial to pass.

Foreign governments also influence domestic decisions through informal processes of policy collaboration, which in this case produced a common North American posture on GM labelling.[40] In the related matter of bio-security, institutional mechanisms encouraged Mexican collaboration with foreign agriculture agencies like the USDA and Agriculture Canada. The broadening of Mexican governance to include the position of foreign governments and agencies naturally induces a proclivity to harmonize policies.

For their part, environmental and consumer NGOs played a very limited role in the debate over Mexican GM food labelling. Compared to the highly organized US and Canadian NGOs, the organization of Mexican civil society and the formulation of its demands are still in their infancy. Nevertheless, there is a strong segment of the Mexican population that is concerned about transgenic foods.[41] A poll in August 2001 by Sigma Dos showed that 88 per cent of Mexicans support their labelling.[42]

NGOs' relatively insignificant role in the Mexican debate is partly

explained by the policy makers' and the biotech industry's hostile attitude. One of the NGOs' liabilities is the widely held perception that
these groups are hard-line environmentalists with unrealistic goals. For
example, civil-society groups such as Grupo Informal de Tecnología
were excluded from the labelling debate because their arguments were
seen as too radical.[43] Similarly, researchers have indicated that becoming too involved with NGOs could compromise their public standing.[44]

NGOs may become a more legitimate force in affecting the outcomes
of GM food policy debates if they are seen to represent the will of Mexican citizens. The case of maize contamination helped provide a critical
link between angered citizens and NGOs and, in turn, raised major concerns over GM food. This 'genetic pollution' had severe implications
for Mexico's biodiversity, environment, trade, and the local economy,
sparking a civil-society backlash against biotechnology. In January 2002
over four hundred representatives from different NGO groups gath-
ered in Mexico City for the 'Defence of Maize' in order to organize a
common struggle against corn contamination. The GM issue is politically explosive because it is so closely linked to the NAFTA-induced
flood of US imported corn, which is pushing small farmers out of Mexico's internal market. Since only a few US corporations hold the patents
for GM crops, the biotechnology issue can trigger raw nationalist
nerves sensitive to any new evidence of US domination and help shift
the perception of NGOs in Mexico from being radical to representing
mainstream public attitudes. [45]

The case of GM labelling in Mexico demonstrates a significant degree
of both internal and external corporate governance. The highly effective
pro-biotech lobbying campaigns have systematically limited the scope
of domestic policy choices regarding GM food. However, the market
governance that does exist is best described as bilateral rather than continental. While the Mexican government is aware of Canadian interests,
it is US policy and industry interests that predominate, with the Canadian business-government partnership present on the sidelines.

The North American Continent as a Force in Global GM Food Policy

Despite North America's lack of a formal political infrastructure to harmonize policies across borders, the governments of the United States,
Canada, and Mexico have demonstrated remarkable convergence by
consistently resisting pressures to require GM food to be so labelled. In
fact, the three governments have embraced biotechnology companies

as allies and pursued an aggressive campaign to challenge not just GM food labelling but more general regulations controlling what products may be admitted into the food system. In the wake of the bitter schism between the 'Miami Group' (United States, Canada, Argentina, Uruguay, and Australia) and the 'Like-Minded Group' (over one hundred developing nations, led by the EU) in Montreal in 2000 during the negotiation of the Cartagena Protocol on Biosafety, the NAFTA countries continue to band together on the issue. While the Miami Group pushed for the supremacy of the WTO's narrow, trade-enhancing construction of scientific safety, the Like-Minded Group wanted the Cartagena Protocol's trade-restricting, broader approach to scientific innovation based on the precautionary principle to enjoy legal equality with WTO norms.

Pursuing the goals of the Miami Group since the turn of the new millennium, the three North American governments have formed a business-friendly bloc to oppose stringent global regulations of GM food shipments. This tacit regional agreement suggests the existence in North America of an informal governance consisting of interactions among various political, social, and economic actors outside or on the boundary of the three governments' structures. North American resistance to GM food labelling offers a striking contrast with the ethos prevailing in Europe, where distrust of science was widespread following the mad cow and foot-and-mouth-disease scares of the 1990s.[46]

This joint position has been particularly prominent in trade policy, where anxiety surrounding trade retaliation over GM foods has contributed to an informal consensus among policy makers in the United States, Canada, and Mexico on policies that affect North America as a whole. Subsequent to the negotiation of the Cartagena Protocol, Canada and Mexico, alongside Argentina and a few other third parties, supported the United States in its 2003 WTO challenge of the EU's GM food moratorium. This challenge represented both an explicit agreement among North American policy makers over GM food and a corporate-governance victory over civil society. While Article 5, Paragraph 7 of the WTO's Agreement on the Application of Sanitary and Phytosanitary Measures does allow for precaution where relevant scientific information does not exist, as the EU argued was the case with GM foods, it does stipulate that 'members shall seek to obtain the additional information necessary for a more objective assessment of risk and review the sanitary or phytosanitary measure accordingly within a reasonable period of time.'[47]

It was on this basis that Canada, Argentina, and the United States sought to attack the EU's delay in approving North American GM food imports. On February 7, 2006 the WTO panel ruled that 'bans on EU approved GE crops in six EU member countries violated WTO rules and that the EU failed to ensure that its approval procedures were conducted without undue delay.'[48] Two years before, the EU had approved a genetically engineered corn variety (Syngenta Bt-11) for human consumption, in effect ending the moratorium. Subsequently, the EU approved genetically engineered corn varieties (Monsanto's NK603) for both human and animal consumption, corn for feed use (Pioneer's 1570), and seventeen strains of genetically engineered corn seed for commercial use.[49] The WTO appellate body's rejection of the EU's right to rely on the precautionary principle indefinitely, without seeking scientific support for the moratorium within a reasonable period of time, means that any country banning GM food imports in the absence of convincing scientific justification could be vulnerable to retaliatory trade measures. Although Trade Representative Robert Zoellick insisted that this action by the US government was focused on lifting the moratorium, he did leave the door open to other challenges involving labelling. The United States' enlistment of its two neighbours at the global level foreshadows further harmonization of the three North American governments regarding biotechnology policy. The WTO challenge may have planted the seeds of a public-private continental hegemony, with the US biotech industry dominant in all three markets and the United States government calling the shots in public.

Conclusion

The struggle over GM food labelling in North America reveals a situation in which, having identified a key industry as a driver of future economic growth, the three governments allied with it to make public policy. This sector's informal transborder governance cannot be described as balanced or trilateral. Instead, it is primarily two sets of asymmetrical, but skewed, bilateral relations in which both Canada and Mexico (with other countries like Brazil) are subordinates within the US-led hegemony. However, as the middle power in biotech agriculture, Canada plays a junior-partner role helping the United States strong-arm a weaker Mexico.

This is not to say that the outcome of the biotech struggle is predetermined. Part of the success of the biotech industry's lobbying efforts on policy decisions comes from the alliance it makes with farmers in all countries. Aware of the detrimental impacts that GM wheat could have on world exports, many wheat farmers have begun an active resistance to the introduction of Monsanto's GM wheat. This resistance could spill over onto other crops: if GM wheat is introduced despite farmer disapproval, it might spark the departure of farmers from the pro-biotech coalition. Either way, global sentiment towards GM food technology will be a substantial factor in determining the fate of the biotech industry's influence over domestic policies.

North America's successful WTO challenge of the EU's moratorium on approving new biotech products also indicated corporate biotechnology's predominance over civil society in its solidarity with government. Although the action was not explicitly against labelling, it still demonstrated the level of commitment of the United States, Canada, and even Mexico to promote the biotech industry abroad. The WTO finding in favour of the hemisphere's claim that the EU's policies on biotech products violated several trade rules will likely stimulate even greater cooperation between corporate interests and government policy makers within North America.

In the decade following NAFTA's implementation, increased levels of continental economic integration resulted from cross-border TNC expansion and greater trade flows among the three countries. This new continental reality has, in turn, affected each state's policy making. Reluctant to jeopardize trade, all three countries have protected transnational corporate interests. In particular, Canada and Mexico have ceded domestic policy autonomy in order to avoid confronting a US-dominated industry.

The process of policy harmonization has brought GM policies in North America to a point of convergence. With the cooperation of each government, the biotech industry in each country successfully kept GM food labelling off the policy agenda. The new continental reality has diluted domestic policy autonomy. Beyond having to balance domestic desires, policy makers in the periphery had to take into account how their continental neighbours were addressing the GM labelling issue. It is clear that, if one country were to adopt a mandatory labelling system, it would cause a significant disturbance in the agricultural sectors in the other two economies of North America. As a result, the highly integrated nature of the North American economy has created a pattern of external forces affecting domestic legislation that might appear to have generated a muscular form of continental governance. But, in fact, these aggressive TNCs have pursued the same goals in many other countries using the same tactics so that, while there is governance of the GM food-labelling question *in* North America, it is not strictly speaking continental governance *of* North America

The same can be said of another sector. North America's legal drugs industry is anything but a wallflower, but its transnational governing activities appear, like GM food labelling, to be more a matter of global than of continental governance. US pharmaceutical TNCs, exerting their power both in North America and on the world stage, are constantly pushing the continental periphery to make major concessions to the intellectual property interests of 'Big Pharma.'

XV Intellectual Property Rights and Big Pharma

The global economic governance promoted by the General Agreement on Tariffs and Trade was all about reducing the commercial barriers erected by states at their territorial borders. GATT focused on reducing the tariffs and quantitative restrictions that raised the prices or limited the volumes of goods that exporting countries tried to sell in other markets. While some of the thousands of rules contained in the World Trade Organization's agreements still deal with border barriers affecting the trade of physical goods, this landmark agreement represented a revolution in global economic governance because it also included rules directing national governments to alter their treatment of foreign providers of services and foreign-controlled corporations operating within their national borders. If the WTO ushered in a new era of 'deep integration,' it was because of these intrusive norms dealing with TNCs' conditions for doing business in host countries. The goal was to equalize those conditions between foreign and domestic corporations in order to eliminate the advantages from which a country's national firms may benefit. Intellectual property rights (IPRs) are an example of the kind of legal issue that used to be the sole prerogative of the sovereign state but became a supra-constitutional norm trumping national policy.

This chapter explores North America's transborder governance in a policy area of intense concern to all knowledge-intensive sectors, such as biotech, mass entertainment, or information technology, which rely on intellectual property rights to recoup through extended sales the huge investments needed to produce new products that can then be reproduced at very low cost. It was from the late 1970s debate over how to reverse the United States' apparent hegemonic decline that its new global IPR strategy emerged. It had already developed a substantial comparative advantage in knowledge-based industries and, hoping that these sectors could help it consolidate and retain the same economic dominance as the automobile had done for it in the twentieth century, Washington decided it needed to universalize the IPRs that had already turned these sectors at home into powerhouses. Monsanto, Disney, and IBM had exploited a regulatory system that let them achieve near-monopoly control over their home markets. Universalizing these rules would allow them and other US corporations in these fields to compete and profit as freely abroad as they had done at home.

The problem was one of degree. Disney and IBM already had a dominant position in most economies outside the socialist bloc. Nevertheless, the evolution of the Keynesian welfare state both in the West and in the South had fostered public sectors which excluded foreign investment through domestic regulations favouring national producers. A further problem was the piracy that reproduced and widely distributed proprietary information – movies, music, software – without paying the copyright owners any royalties.

While piracy was not a significant issue in the global pharmaceutical economy, the clash between enforcing strong, monopolistic IPR protections for 'Big Pharma' – the transnational corporate oligopoly based in the United States, Europe, and Japan – and guaranteeing a supply of reasonably priced 'generic' drugs to promote the health of a country's citizenry is the issue that roils North America's transborder governance of pharmaceuticals as a regional reality within the broader global scene.

In and of themselves, global IPRs do not protect against imitators. It is still necessary that each country's administrative and judicial systems be able to detect and prosecute violations.[1] In developing countries, patients who cannot afford the cost of an original patent medicine demand drugs at affordable prices. Outside the United States, most public-health systems in developed countries regulate drug prices, producing the counter-intuitive result that Canada (where costs of treatments are controlled) has lower prices in pharmaceuticals than Mexico (where there are no price controls and legislation is not necessarily enforced).[2]

Pharmaceuticals and Intellectual Property Rights

Because of its population's health having an overwhelming economic, social, and political salience, every government evolved its own mix of medical services provided through a public sector and a private market. Each country's IPR legislation largely reflected whether its medicines were developed domestically or abroad and determined whether they were marketed by their creators as 'brand-name' or as generic drugs manufactured under 'compulsory licences' which authorize competing companies to copy the formulae without having invested in the research.

Estimates claimed that the average cost of developing a new brand-name drug is $1 billion compared to $1 million required to produce a generic drug. To recover their research and development costs, brand-name pharmaceutical companies benefit from IPR legislation, which grants them as proprietors an effective monopoly on the production and sale of the medicine, thus guaranteeing the patent holder exclusive marketing privileges for a specified number of years. High earnings in this period allow the investors to recoup their money and make substantial profits. Pharmaceutical companies lobby their governments for stronger and longer IPR protection, claiming that weak laws hinder R&D by limiting monetary incentives. Opponents of stricter IPR laws argue that long patent protections give Big Pharma excessive market power, encourage wasteful advertising, and make drugs unaffordable. They lobby for weaker IPRs so that more people can buy generic medicines at lower prices.

This basic conflict between corporate profit and public access becomes even more complicated when pharmaceutical companies operate across state boundaries. Although national legal and medical systems' unique characteristics have deepened over the decades, Big Pharma has pushed its home governments either to negotiate international rights that supersede domestic standards or directly to persuade individual governments to adopt IPRs that allow it to reduce its transaction costs and maximize its overall profits.

Since the policies regulating the pharmaceutical industries of the United States, Canada, and Mexico have become more similar since NAFTA incorporated powerful IPRs, students of North America might well think that transborder governance has been effective at the continental level. This chapter argues to the contrary that North America's continental governance in this domain is illusory. Instead, the harmonization that has taken place on the continent is a product of a dual political strategy orchestrated in Washington. First, the US government has exerted unilateral coercive power directly over its periphery on Big Pharma's behalf. More indirectly, it has been the prime mover in generating a universal economic hegemony through the WTO's tough agreement on Trade-Related Aspects of Intellectual Property Rights (TRIPs), whose rules Canada and Mexico agreed in 1994 to adopt – along with over a hundred other countries which embraced the trade-liberalization hegemony.

Despite NAFTA containing a special chapter on IPRs, we will see that Washington's combination of unilateral and multilateral pressuring makes the idea of North American governance irrelevant. Further, while the WTO's IPR protections yielded an increase in external capacity for the United States and the EU, this chapter nevertheless shows that Canada and Mexico have managed to maintain some autonomy in this area of their decision making. Before I pursue this analysis, I need first to establish the context within which the pharmaceutical issues presented themselves in each country by the early 1980s, when a neoconservative Washington committed itself to making the world safe for its pharmaceutical giants.

The Three Medical Worlds within North America

For all the common influences they had experienced, it is remarkable how substantially the health-care systems in the United States, Canada, and Mexico differ from each other. We will look at them in turn.

The United States

Large (297 million people in 2004) and rich ($40,000 per-capita GDP) though it may be, the United States is a public-health outrider in the industrialized world. With its weak public sector, its huge insurance industry, and the free rein it accords Big Pharma, the American system is extraordinarily inefficient, consuming 15 per cent of the economy's GDP while providing no medical insurance to some 15 per cent of the public and achieving inferior levels of infant mortality and longevity. Yet, with brand-name pharmaceutical sales valued at US$270 billion per year, the American market is the most lucrative in the world.[3] Of the top ten global pharmaceutical companies, five are American and five are European, but the United States is the major profit centre for all ten.[4]

In a key counterattack in 1957 that forestalled the United States from developing a Canadian-style health-care system, massive lobbying by brand-name pharmaceutical manufacturers defeated Senator Estes Kefauver's Senate Subcommittee on Antitrust and Monopoly in its attempt to address rising drug prices. Particularly objectionable to the brand-drug manufacturers was the subcommittee's recommendation calling for compulsory licensing, which would have allowed regulators to issue a licence to a generic drug manufacturer so that it could produce and market a drug within three years of its being licensed.[5]

Lobbying efforts by the newly created Pharmaceutical Manufacturers Association (PMA) and a dearth of effective response from generic drug manufacturers resulted in Congress' rejecting the subcommittee's recommendations. The Drug Price Competition Act and Patent Term Restoration Act favoured the interests of the brand-name pharmaceutical manufacturers vis-à-vis those of their generic counterparts,[6] which had to content themselves with the act's recognition of drugs that were bioequivalent – that is, whose effects and composition were identical – to brand-name counterparts.[7] The political wind was in Big Pharma's sails. At home, amendments in the 1980s extended the effective protection period for brand-name manufacturers of between seven and ten years to fourteen.[8] At the same time, the brand-name pharmaceutical companies began to transform global economic governance through their ability to orchestrate the US government's campaign to make the world safe for themselves.

Not every US industry can direct American foreign economic policy. One reason for the brand-name pharmaceutical companies' influence is their close personal connections with the government. For example, Donald Rumsfeld, twice the secretary of defense, had worked for two US pharmaceutical companies, Gilead and G.D. Searle. Deborah Steelman, the White House budget adviser to George W. Bush and the chair of his Quadrennial Advisory Council on Social Security and Medicare, was also employed by Eli Lilly and had represented Aetna, Bristol Myers Squibb, Johnson and Johnson, Pfizer, and the main drug lobby.[9]

Many elected politicians, having made high-level connections in the Administration, leave the legislature to join the pharmaceutical industry. Billy Tauzin, president of Pharmaceutical Researchers and Manufacturers of America (PRMA), was once a Louisiana congressman; James C. Greenwood, president of the Biotechnology Industry Organization, was once a congressman in Pennsylvania.[10] This revolving door between government and industry allows pharmaceutical leaders to entrench the brand-name industry's power over policy both at home through their influence in the Food and Drug Administration and abroad through their sway over the Office of the United States Trade Representative.

Canada

Small in size (population of 32 million in 2004), rich in revenue ($31,000 per-capita GDP),[11] and social-democratic in political culture, Canada had developed a much-admired medical system by the time that Keynesianism fell into disrepute. An uneasy and complex compromise between socialized health care (free treatment in hospital and free access to doctors) and capitalist principles (many services available only in the private sector, and drug costs outside hospital covered only for seniors and those with employment-based insurance policies), the Canadian medical system was one of the most efficient in the OECD countries (health expenditures accounting for only 9.9 per cent of GDP) and most successful (in terms of lowest infant mortality and longest longevity).

Accounting for approximately 3 per cent of the global pharmaceutical economy,[12] the medical drug market in Canada is dominated by brand-name American companies that set up domestic subsidiaries and branch plants to avoid regulatory barriers and engage in more effective local marketing. These subsidiaries primarily serve the domestic market, importing raw materials and exporting only 10 per cent of their output. This results in a pharmaceutical trade deficit, more than 60 per cent of which is accounted for by the in-house exports of the US parent companies to their subsidiaries.[13] Parents of subsidiaries also receive patent royalties on products sold in Canada, which further contribute to the current-account deficit within the industry.

Domestic ownership is higher in the relatively robust generic drug industry, which has survived international pressure as a result of the country's constitutional division of powers. Although the federal government administers the granting of patents (which puts Ottawa under the direct aegis of global and continental IPR norms), the provincial governments are responsible for determining what drug coverage is provided by their public health-insurance programs, which account for some 40 to 45 per cent of drug expenditures. As a result, the federal government deals primarily with brand-name companies, whereas the provinces' interest in affordable medicines bolsters the generic industry. Although generic drugs filled more than 40 per cent of all retail prescriptions, they accounted for only 16 per cent of the CD$15.4 billion spent annually on prescription drugs in Canada at the beginning of the twenty-first century. More than 40 per cent of generic-drug production is exported.[14]

Mexico

Three times larger than Canada in population, with 103 million inhabitants, and five times poorer with a per-capita GDP of $6,500, Mexico spends only one-tenth of its neighbours' expenditures on public health – $270 per person. This public-sector spending is so low that personal, out-of-pocket expenditures amount to 94 per cent of the country's total health budget.

Mexico's pharmaceutical industry structure is complex. During the protectionist decades of state-led development following the Second World War, the Secretaría de Comercio y Fomento Industrial (Ministry for Trade and Industrial Development) instituted strict price controls and the Instituto Mexicano del Seguro Social (IMSS, Mexican Institute of Social Security) enforced stringent supervision over the commercializing and marketing of pharmaceuticals. These requirements resulted in prices one-third of those obtaining in more industrialized countries. Given US Big Pharma's low penetration of the market, domestic Mexican manufacturers have been opposed to stringent patent controls. Since their members carried out only limited R&D, senior officials of the Federación Mexicana de Químicos y Farmacéuticas (FMQF, Association of Latin Pharmaceutical Companies) and the Asociación Latinoamericana de Empresas Farmacéuticas (ALEF, Federation of Mexican Chemists and Pharmacists) argued that providing more stringent patent protection would push the domestic industry into bankruptcy. Drugs were considered to be public goods and only a few select manufacturers were granted licences to produce each product. Most governmental research institutes imported chemicals without providing them patent protection. Transnational corporations and Mexican laboratories acquired drug technologies from abroad, frequently obtaining a licence from the foreign manufacturer. Yet, despite the lax intellectual property standards, US drug companies already accounted for one-quarter of Mexican pharmaceutical manufacturers by the mid-1980s.[15]

The initial pressure for stronger IPR laws resulted from the debt crisis of the early 1980s. By then, the rising, US-trained generation of Mexican leaders had come to believe that economic growth would be achieved most effectively through market liberalization. Because the United States was already providing two-thirds of Mexico's incoming direct foreign investment, the PRI's leadership gambled that trade liberalization would increase the US investment which it so desperately wanted.[16] In other words, to encourage US investment, the Mexican government believed it had to introduce better protection for patents. The liberalization of Mexico's intellectual property rights followed as soon as direct pressure was exerted by Washington.

Under the 'Super 301' Section of the 1988 Trade and Competitiveness Act, the USTR had the right to investigate countries that have 'a history of violating existing laws and agreements dealing with intellectual property rights.'[17] Threatened by being placed on the USTR's priority watch list under Super 301, which could lead to adverse repercussions on foreign investment, the Mexican government rapidly overhauled its IPR system.[18] Domestic lobby groups – particularly the Cámara Nacional de la Industria Farmacéutica (CNIF, National Pharmaceutical Industry Chamber, 20 per cent of whose members were foreign manufacturers), the ALEF, and the FMQF – were at first resistant to changing the patent laws but gradually acquiesced because of an influx of foreign investment for R&D.[19]

Global Intellectual Property Rights in the Continent

The United States

In 1987 over one hundred of the largest firms in research-intensive industries, including pharmaceuticals, formed the Intellectual Property Owners to lobby for strengthened IPRs.[20] To defend their place on the agenda, twelve US pharmaceutical companies including Bristol-Myers, Dupont, Merck, and Pfizer formed their own Intellectual Property Committee[21] whose close links to the USTR helped brand-name manufacturers ensure that strengthened intellectual property rights were at the forefront of trade-liberalization negotiations. Their position was bolstered by claims that intellectual property piracy contributed to an estimated loss of $4 billion in 1991.[22]

Once US corporations had convinced their national government about the importance of strict IPR laws, they worked with business associations abroad to obtain foreign support for tougher IPR law at the international level. Critics have called GATT's Uruguay Round IPR negotiations an 'asymmetric, non-transparent and autocratic process,' dominated by brand-name pharmaceutical representatives and lawyers who were everywhere, even in negotiators' hotels at night after the day of negotiations had concluded.[23]

Clear as was Big Pharma that its global future depended on strong intellectual property rights, rising countries in the South were equally clear-minded about the threat that such IPRs presented to their own industrial development. Brazil and India led the resistance in GATT's long Uruguay Round, causing a bottleneck in the trade-rule negotiations that led Washington to consider its Plan B – bilateral negotiations with compliant partners to set the precedents it would then try to universalize at the global level.

Canada

Enter Prime Minister Brian Mulroney in 1985, when, for lack of a political agenda after one year in office, he adopted the Macdonald Report's grim analysis that the Canadian economy was headed for disaster unless it secured a free-trade deal with the United States. With Canada as *demandeur* and its prime minister signalling his desperation for a deal, Ottawa made concession after concession to the tough American negotiators for whom stronger IPRs were a top priority[24] – even though the evidence showed that Big Pharma was already doing extremely well in Canada.

Despite the US brand-name subsidiaries' claims to the contrary, the government-appointed Commission of Inquiry on the Pharmaceutical Industry found that pharmaceutical firms had continued to be highly profitable after 1969, when the Trudeau government had allowed the import of generic drugs.[25] Moreover, the profitability of multinational firms was higher in Canada than in most industrialized countries. The commission's report calculated that, since 1969, TNCs had lost only 3.1 per cent of the Canadian market to generic firms,which took in only 14 per cent of the total revenue of the Canadian market. Nevertheless, compulsory licences saved consumers $211 million in 1983 alone. Because the commission concluded that the compulsory licensing system was working well, it recommended only minor changes – a four-year period of market exclusivity would provide a sufficient profit incentive to encourage patent-holding firms to introduce new drugs to the Canadian market.[26]

The political efforts of the association representing the interests of domestic brand-name manufacturers – Research Based Pharmaceutical Companies (Rx&D) – demonstrated superior lobbying abilities by defeating domestic interests when bilateral free trade was being negotiated. Rx&D called for national treatment for international enterprises, transparency in IPRs, and the abolition of compulsory licences – not coincidentally, the negotiating position of the US government.[27]

During the negotiations, Washington pressed Canada for intellectual property rights to be included in CUFTA, but ultimately it settled for a side deal. The Mulroney government did not want to be seen to be caving in to US demands that would weaken the public health-care system by undermining generic-drug production and raising drug costs, so it introduced separate legislation – first Bill C-22 (1987) and then Bill C-91 (1993). These statutes limited the use of compulsory licences and incorporated in domestic legislation the United States' IPR demands, which were later embodied in NAFTA's Chapter 17 and the WTO's TRIPs.[28] To comfort the generic manufacturers in the face of their defeat, Bill C-22 created the Patented Medicines Prices Review Board to monitor price increases, act as a quasi-judicial tribunal to remedy price gouging, and report R&D patterns.[29]

Mexico

Meanwhile, Washington, which wanted the rules changed globally, was still facing a logjam in the Uruguay Round. By the end of the 1980s, an impasse in the IPR negotiations prompted Arthur Dunkel, GATT's director general, to circulate a draft that was accepted by the United States, Europe, and Japan without contention because it incorporated the provisions for which their industries had been pressing.[30] When Mexico came knocking on its door to negotiate a border-lowering economic agreement, Washington seized the occasion to move the IPR agenda forward on a bilateral basis. For his part, the newly elected Mexican president, Salinas de Gortari, was determined to transform Mexico's political economy by shifting it onto a neoconservative development path. Only when he ran out of options by failing to interest the European Union in a free-trade arrangement did he accept the necessity of such an agreement with the United States.

In the resulting bilateral negotiations into which Mulroney inserted Canada, Washington made the Dunkel Draft the basis of NAFTA's Chapter 17. Under intense US pressure, Mexico accepted significant concessions to obtain its entry into NAFTA. Although the Mexican government wanted to protect its domestic industry by forbidding Canadian and US companies from bidding on pharmaceutical contracts, the final text mandated the phasing in of such bidding within eight years of NAFTA's implementation.[31] While Mexico sought a fifteen-year phasing-in period for other Chapter 17 provisions, it had to settle for ten.[32]

The Mexican government's willingness to strengthen its IPRs was supported by the Consejo Empresarial Mexicano para Asuntos Inter-nacionales (Mexican Business Council for International Affairs), an umbrella association of Mexican business associations involved in inter-national trade issues, and the CNIF, representing forty-eight pharma-ceutical TNCs.[33] Since TNCs did not have protection for their R&D, they pressed Mexico to endorse NAFTA's draft Chapter 17.

With NAFTA entering into force on January 1, 1994, its Chapter 17 established basic standards for IPR protection and enforcement in the United States, Canada, and Mexico. It also provided protection for a term of twenty years from the date a patent application was filed or sev-enteen years from the date a patent was granted, although a party could extend the protection term to compensate for delays in regulatory-approval processes. Even though there were no specific enforcement mechanisms for the IPR provisions, NAFTA specified that enforcement procedures should be available under domestic law and be used to pre-vent barriers to trade. NAFTA did not take into account disparities among the enforcement procedures in the three countries.

As far as Canada was concerned, Big Pharma pledged between C$200 and $400 million in R&D spending in exchange for the Canadian government's compliance with the text. The generic drug makers' cam-paign against the elimination of compulsory licensing proved futile. Having abandoned compulsory licensing in the 1980s round of bilat-eral negotiations, the Mulroney government had little problem with adopting Chapter 17's stipulations on intellectual property.[34] The US generic manufacturers made no documented resistance to Chapter 17.

Having signed off on Chapter 17's IPR clauses, Mexico then con-sented to similar provisions in the WTO's TRIPs agreement, which left the Dunkel Draft largely intact. A number of similarities and some identical clauses appear in both documents, although TRIPs require-ments were more comprehensive, encouraging technology transfer, promoting public health, and providing for dispute settlement under the WTO's procedures.[35] Departing slightly from NAFTA, TRIPs sets out a protection of twenty years from the date of a patent's grant.

Continental versus Global Intellectual Property Rights

NAFTA's Chapter 17 seemed to herald a new phase of deep integration for North America, but, in the end, it was not to be. Once TRIPs was in place, Geneva became the capital of transborder IPR governance for North America.

Mexico

It is difficult to evaluate the impact on Mexico of the IPR regimes introduced by NAFTA and TRIPs because they have only had time partly to
transform the pharmaceutical industry. Reported increases in R&D
expenditures cannot be verified because of administrative obstacles,
the reluctance of Mexican company officials to discuss their business,
and the unavailability of data, including the tendency of TNCs to
aggregate public financial statements about all their foreign subsidiaries in a single figure. Interviews with key experts confirmed that the
lack of significant R&D activity in the Mexican pharmaceutical industry is the result of policies that continue to favour government procurement of unpatented drugs and the weakness of judicial institutions for
enforcing IPR.

The IMSS makes massive purchases of drugs from the pharmaceutical companies, which, in turn, constantly lobby its administrative personnel in charge of purchasing.[36] In 1984 the Comisión Permanente de
Farmacopea (Permanent Pharmacopeia Commission) was created to
monitor the quality of the drugs that the IMSS is buying. Its labs
depend directly on the Secretaría de Salubridad y Asistencia (Ministry
of Health) and collaborate with such institutions as UNAM, the Instituto Politécnico National (National Polytechnic Institute), the Academia Nacional de Medicina (National Academy of Medicine), and the
Centro Mexicano de Desarollo e Investigación Farmacéutica (Mexican
Centre of Pharmaceutical Development and Research). Patients covered by the IMSS receive all the medicines that they need free of charge
so the IMSS prefers purchasing generic drugs instead of branded pharmaceuticals.[37]

Acquisitions of Mexican public-sector companies by transnational
companies have caused significant changes in the industry's structure.
As well, the United States has pressured the Mexican Ministry of
Health to require that the IMSS and the Instituto de Seguridad y Ser-
vicios de los Trabajadores del Estado (Social Security Institute for
Government Workers) purchase only patented drugs[38] instead of exclusively buying domestically produced generic drugs. In fact, they
buy both: as required by NAFTA, these agencies had to open their bidding processes to US and Canadian firms in 1992.

Strengthened IPRs in Mexico have resulted in an influx of foreign
subsidiaries into the pharmaceutical market and an increase in that
industry's share of the Mexican economy. According to the Cámara

Nacional de la Industria Farmacéutica (National Chamber of the Pharmaceutical Industry), at the turn of the century, government purchases accounted for 50 per cent of total drug sales – with the IMSS alone representing close to $US1,500 million[39] – while the private sector accounted for 45 per cent of the volume and 87 per cent of total sales.[40] By 2006, pharmaceutical sales in Mexico were around $9.3 billion.[41]

Big Pharma's growth in Mexico has been accompanied by its increased lobbying to protect itself from policies favouring easier access to drugs for HIV/AIDS treatment.[42] Under pressure from HIV/AIDS activists and in order to protect their public image, some pharmaceuticals firms have reduced their prices.[43]

Pharmaceutical subsidiaries in Mexico used their new patent rights to increase prices by 385 per cent between 1991 and 1997.[44] This abrupt price increase was accompanied by a 23 per cent growth in sales, as restrictions on exports were removed and Mexican manufacturers began to sell their drugs in South America.[45] Despite the more favourable IPR provisions, some companies remained cautious about entering the Mexican market, expressing particular concerns about corruption, bureaucratic impediments, and lower prices.[46]

Mexico's domestic pharmaceutical firms have already felt the strain of increased international competition. Although domestic generic manufacturers have retained 80 per cent of the market share, 20 per cent of medicines are now imported (compared to complete self-sufficiency prior to trade liberalization). Industry restructuring was reflected in significant consolidation. In 1992, 350 domestic Mexican manufacturers were operational. By 1997, 218 were in business, forty of them subsidiaries of transnational companies.[47] By 2006, there were 224 medicine laboratories run by 200 companies, forty-six of which were majority-owned foreign TNCs.[48]

The foreign pharmaceutical industry has enjoyed strong support within the Mexican government. Under President Zedillo (1994–2000), for example, during the Congressional debate concerning drug patents and the authorization of generic drugs, high-level officials from the secretariat of health were in permanent contact with members of the pharmaceutical industry in order to keep them informed of developments.[49] When the Green Party caucus in the National Congress introduced legislation to authorize new generic medicines and reduce the length of patent protections, direct representation of the brand-name industry's interests and diplomatic pressure exerted on Zedillo's administration to prevent the initiative from being passed were not enough. With support from the HIV/AIDS policy community, the Greens managed to get the generic-drugs legislation authorized by Congress and confirmed by Zedillo's secretary of health, but their attempt to reduce patent rights from twenty to ten years failed.[50] Meanwhile, as a result of the decision to commercialize new generic drugs, Victor González Torres, a relative of the Green Party's founder, established in 1997 a national chain of drugstores called 'Farmacías Similares' (copycat drugs), offering prices on average 57 per cent cheaper than those of the brand-name equivalents. The chain rapidly gained a market share of almost 10 per cent, and by 2007 it had 3,576 pharmacies throughout Latin America.[51] Apotex, a Canadian manufacturer of generics, has been operating in Mexico since 1996.[52] Its marketing in Mexico is small, but little by little it is winning customers, selling through Wal-Mart and other popular chains like Farmacía del Ahorro or Farmacías Benavides.

Canada

Both through NAFTA and TRIPs, judicial rulings in the tussle between branded drugs and patient rights have heavily favoured Big Pharma. Although NAFTA offers means of redress for non-compliance with the new IPRs – namely through Chapter 11 (for investor-state disputes) and Chapter 20 (for disputes between states) – the USTR and the PRMA are reluctant to use them, preferring the more muscular venue offered by the WTO.[53]

Two cases have been brought before the WTO alleging that the Canadian government failed to comply with TRIPs. In 1998 the European Union challenged the Canadian Patent Act's Bolar provisions (which allow generic manufacturers to engage in R&D and apply for regulatory approval prior to the expiration of a branded drug's patent term), stating that they were not fully compatible with TRIPs. The WTO dispute settlement board, however, ruled that the Bolar provisions did comply with Canada's obligations.

In 2000 the United States lodged a complaint at the WTO alleging that Canada's Patent Act provided only seventeen years of patent protection from the date of grant for patents issued before October 1, 1989 – which was in accord with its NAFTA obligations.[54] This time, the WTO panel ruled against Canada, finding Canadian practices inconsistent with TRIPs, which provides twenty years' protection from the date of filing. After a failed appeal, Ottawa amended the Patent Act accordingly.[55] Under pressure from Pfizer and Bristol-Myers Squibb, which were facing the expiration in Canada of patents on two drugs, Washington lodged another complaint at the WTO. Again, Canada lost the case but appealed the WTO ruling, winning time until the Pfizer patent had expired. Bristol-Myers Squibb continued lobbying intensively to get the Canadian government to comply.[56]

These cases show how pharmaceutical TNCs attempt to achieve changes in policy and practice in Canada and Mexico using the arbitration procedures of transnational governance. They also show the mix of hegemonic and imperial governance in North America, with the United States using its globally and continentally established norms along with direct-pressure tactics to strong-arm its two neighbours into compliance with its pharmaceutical industry's seemingly insatiable demands. Nevertheless, the periphery retains considerable autonomy. It has not lost all its battles at the WTO, and it, like Washington, knows how to use the rules in order to stall when it helps.

Drug Wars without End

Notwithstanding the United States' long campaign to universalize its intellectual property norms in continental- and global-governance instruments, the US pharmaceutical industry's pressure on the periphery never relaxes. The market clout of American brand-name pharmaceutical manufacturers provides them with opportunities to exert direct control over the Canadian and Mexican pharmaceutical industries through their subsidiaries. American head offices determine the location of branch plants according to the relative advantages of particular countries in specific activities. For some industries, these advantages include resource abundance and low wage levels. For brand-name pharmaceuticals, strong IPR protection and a fiscal environment offering tax relief for R&D expenditures help determine their manufacturing location decisions. Brand-name manufacturers exert pressure on national governments to comply with their demands by offering the carrot of allocating R&D expenditures to the governments' jurisdictions.[57]

The reason subsidiaries stay in Canada despite Big Pharma's complaints are its favourable tax conditions for R&D. Canada has particularly favourable incentives, effectively decreasing the cost of R&D by 60 per cent and providing a faster lead time into the market through less extensive requirements for drug testing and production. Still, US manufacturers view Canada as a restricted market which they claim is constrained by high overhead costs and stringent marketing regulation for pharmaceuticals (for example, pharmaceutical companies are not allowed to advertise on television).[58]

Other issues trouble transborder relations within the industry. US drug prices were still 170 per cent higher than those in Canada in 2005.[59] Health Canada cited four particularly important reasons for the price differentiation – lower national income, bulk purchases by public-health agencies, exchange-rate fluctuations, and limits on direct-to-consumer advertising. Across the border, exceedingly high drug prices have led over a million US citizens to look abroad for lower-priced supplies. Even though these medicines may be made in the United States and exported to Canadian wholesalers, they can ultimately be purchased by Americans more cheaply via the Internet from Canadian pharmacies and reimported.[60] Senior citizens groups such as the Minnesota Seniors Federation and the American Association of Retired Persons represent the broad spectrum of grass-roots and national organizations favouring reimportation as a temporary solution to health-policy shortcomings. Because public opinion supported reimportation initiatives,[61] the issue garnered bipartisan backing.[62] Yet, since the Canadian market is far too small to satisfy the demands of the US consumers, this can provide only a short-term solution.

Embarrassed by this indirect proof of its price gouging in the American market, GlaxoSmithKline lobbied Ottawa to curtail Internet exports, alleging that the safety of US citizens was at risk. In March 2003 the Canadian Competition Bureau validated this claim by permitting the company to stop supplying drugs to Canadian Internet pharmacies. The brand-name industry's concerns about the reimportation of prescription drugs from Canada led the US FDA to threaten several states and municipal governments with prosecution under the Food and Drug Act if they engaged in such practices. Brand-name manufacturers also exerted similar pressure on Congress. In 2004 Dennis Hastert (R-Ill.), one of the top ten recipients of pharmaceutical funding,[63] pressed the US trade representative, Robert Zoellick, to consider 'forcing Canada to level the drug-price playing field.'[64]

The periphery's conformity to NAFTA and WTO rules is not necessarily enough to satisfy Washington, which uses its Super 301 powers to keep up the pressure. When Mexico appeared on the USTR watch list in 2003 for the production of copycat versions of US patented drugs, Washington threatened to pursue Mexico using the procedures of TRIPs or NAFTA.[65] Mexico's Federal Commission for Protection against Health Risks rejected these claims as false, claiming that pharmaceutical companies were exerting too much influence on the US government.[66] Canada appeared on the USTR Super 301 watch list in 2006 for failing 'to protect against unfair commercial use of undisclosed test and other data submitted by pharmaceutical companies seeking marketing approval for their products.'[67]

Far from participating in an equitable decision-making system, the Mexican and Canadian governments still find themselves yielding to US pressure to change their rules. With their governments led by conti- nentalist parties, and their domestic pharmaceutical space increasingly occupied by US-owned subsidiaries, Canadians and Mexicans are liv- ing with a limited but persistent autonomy in the face of continuing US pressure.[68]

Prospects for a change of North America's pharmaceutical gover- nance seem uncertain. In the United States, the Pharmaceutical Re- searchers and Manufacturers of America continues to dominate the US government's IPR agenda, publishing industry position papers, partic- ipating in government consultations, and, of course, making massive political contributions. Although the industry has contributed heavily to both major parties, it has channelled twice as much of its lobby funds to the Republican Party as to the Democratic Party since 1996.[69] In 2006 the industry spent $11 million on lobby efforts, with 69 per cent of the funding directed to the Republicans.[70]

Generic pharmaceutical manufacturers have generally remained on the sidelines in terms of their market presence and lobby efforts and seem incapable of shifting the balance of power. The Generic Pharma- ceutical Association lobbies for shorter patent terms, compulsory licens- ing, and the stockpiling of generic drugs prior to a branded drug's patent expiration.[71] Expenditures on lobby efforts by the generic indus- try and trade groups amounted to $7 million in 2001, a mere 10 per cent of the $75 million spent by Big Pharma.[72]

Even American civil society seems an unlikely candidate as a force for change. Although vocal and active patient groups are raising aware- ness about diseases, designing clinical trials, and leading high-profile campaigns,[73] and although patient associations' contributions to politi- cal campaigns through Public Action Committees totalled US$6 million in 2002,[74] their loyalties are divided. On one side of the conflict, senior citizens, who constituted 17 per cent of the US population in 2004, side with generic manufacturers in lobbying for low-cost, accessible medi- cines. Many patient groups, however, support the brand-name phar- maceutical manufacturers in lobbying for increased R&D.[75] The HIV/ AIDS patient network has been particularly successfully at working with brand-name pharmaceutical companies to raise public awareness about issues related to the treatment of the illness. The groups usually call for further investment in R&D of new drugs and indirectly support strong IPR laws. Intensive lobby efforts by the HIV/AIDS patient groups resulted in the enactment of the 1983 Orphan Drug Act, which granted drugs treating diseases that affect less than one out of a thousand people fast-track approval and seven-year market exclusivity – a landmark achievement that paved the way for strengthened lobby efforts by all patient groups.[76]

Nevertheless, it is common practice for US pharmacies to substitute generic for brand-name pharmaceuticals when filling prescriptions. Doctors have the option of indicating whether substitutes are allowed, and many health-care plans cover only the generic versions of drugs, if such versions are available. Thus, pressure exerted by insurance companies may play a role in boosting the generics' power vis-à-vis Big Pharma.

In the periphery, prospects for change are equally bleak. In Canada, the entrenched position of US brand-name subsidiaries gives them enormous clout in the political system. While Mexico has demonstrated more autonomy than Canada, the NAFTA/WTO norm of national treatment will favour the further expansion of foreign pharmaceutical capital and the resulting extension of its political influence.

Conclusion

What policy coordination does take place in North America results more from unilateral pressure than movement towards a trilateral consensus, and it favours global over continental judicial institutions. Even though TRIPs and NAFTA's Chapter 17 enhanced the influence of American pharmaceutical companies on IPR policies in Canada and Mexico, these agreements did not institutionalize this influence. NAFTA remains too institutionally weak to provide governance from above. On the other hand, TRIPs has become the normative arm of Big Pharma. Without trilateral consultation or continental working groups seeking to coordinate the IPR systems or standardize practices in the pharmaceutical industry, transborder governance is still limited to market actors influencing foreign governments' policy indirectly through lobbying in each national polity.

At the grass-roots level, action by patient groups takes place at the national or global but not the continental level. The Consumer Project on Technology, a unique online compendium of information about IPRs, does not focus its activities on North America. Instead, its lobby efforts are directed either to the global level or within the United States, where the organization is headquartered.

NAFTA and TRIPs failed fully to harmonize IPR provisions in Canada, the United States, and Mexico because of the disparate approaches to health care taken by each country. US companies with significant market power continue to coordinate their own practices across borders to meet predefined corporate objectives in each country. Simultaneously, they lobby national governments for policy change. With their policies heavily influenced by foreign non-state actors, Mexico's and Canada's limited capacity to act autonomously and their negligible influence in Washington do not produce a sufficiently coherent system of governance in the North American pharmaceutical industry for it to be called a hegemony.

Under the auspices of TRIPs, US pharmaceutical companies' government lobbying efforts have gone global. The proximity to the United States of the Canadian and Mexican economies and their extensive corporate interrelationships do not mean that the pharmaceutical industries of the three countries are linked more closely to each other than US Pharma is connected to countries in the rest of the world. But, regardless of whether one examines the issues at the continental level or at the more effective global level, the dominance of EU- and US-based companies and their attempts to influence both policies and practices of the national pharmaceutical industries everywhere remains this economically and medically significant sector's emerging reality.

Ottawa's and Mexico City's geographic proximity to Washington may make access easier for Big Pharma, but the growing transnational corporate control experienced in Canada and Mexico could have happened anywhere. In a word, transborder pharmaceutical governance in North America is not what meets the eye. We are dealing not with a continental governance in which North America has a meaningful 'existence' but with two medium-sized powers that are coping with a new global imperium in which they have felt obliged to participate while offering rearguard resistance to the demands of international Big Pharma.

In another area of continental relationships, centre-periphery tension is less the norm than is intergovernmental cooperation. It is now time to turn our attention away from specific economic sectors and towards two related sets of issues: first security and defence, then a strengthened Mexican-Canadian bilateralism and its attendant new trilateralism – the subjects of Part Five.

PART FIVE

Just What It Used To Be:

Persistent State Dominance

So far, this text has offered four answers to our question about North America's existence. In institutional terms, North America was anti-climactic – given all the attention paid to the negotiation and signing of NAFTA – when we saw how little it created. Approached in terms of specific economic sectors for which geographical propinquity matters, here North American governance turned out to be more than meets the eye. As for those economic sectors more connected to global than continental governance regimes, there are two categories. Some sectors are in a state of transition, moving from significant continental governance to more globalized systems. Others are already firmly global, so not at all what meets the eye when apparent continental harmonization is actually an aspect of global regulatory governance.

The reader will have noticed that the issues considered in the last three parts primarily involved non-state actors, mainly from the corporate community but also from some social movements, interacting with the three governments. I now come to what changed following the catastrophe of September 11, 2001, when NAFTA's institutions proved impotent in dissuading the United States from asserting autarchic control over its own space by unilaterally closing down its borders and so upending its previous continental-integration project. Although Washington brought continental trade to a temporary standstill in response to its tragedy, no special meeting of NAFTA's executive, the Free Trade Commission, was convened to address the crisis. Even though the toughening of US national security had a direct – and negative – impact on the management of Mexico's and Canada's airports, seaports, and borders, the heads of government of the three North American states did not hold a special trinational summit or even set up a working group to develop a trilateral approach to the three governments' interdependent security problems. Instead, North American governance reverted to what it had previously been – formal relationships between the three states.

This final section argues that North America is just what it used to be when we look at the inter-governmental regulatory activities that have taken place under Washington's insistence since September 11, 2001. Following that national trauma, the United States proceeded unilaterally to rewrite the continental rulebook, imposing on its two neighbours a radical paradigm shift from trade liberalization and economic-border disarmament to anti-terrorist security and political-border rearmament. This change meant that pressure from Washington on its two neighbours to lower their economic barriers to US investment and expand the domain of transborder market governance switched into pressure on them to raise their political barriers to terrorists by reasserting the power of the Mexican and Canadian governments over their borders. What had been an exercise to generate a participatory continental economic hege-

*mony became an imperial, government-to-government effort to strong-arm –
using the threat of restricted access to the US market – the periphery into supplying security services that buttressed US homeland defence.*

*Chapter XVI details the centrality of government as the prime agency of
border management. With inter-governmental policy making driven by its
obsession with terrorism, the US government's security concerns about both of
its land borders had the effect of reducing the skewed nature of its two bilateral
relationships. Having once applied a different approach to its northern border
with Canada (open, easy, informal, and designed to increase demographic
flows) from its approach to its southern border with Mexico (militarized,
walled off, and aimed to decrease migration flows), Washington moved towards applying a common, anti-terrorist approach to both its territorial frontiers. The much touted 'undefended' US border with Canada was armed, while
border security with Mexico went beyond controlling narco-traffic and undocumented immigrants to include enforced cooperation on visa policies and
infrastructure surveillance.*

*Although border management reduced the skewed nature of the two bilater-
als, revamping US territorial defence under a new Northern Command reaffirmed the historical imbalance between Canada's intimate military relations
with the Pentagon and Mexico's persistent disconnect. Chapter XVII records
how, although the United States redefined continental defence to include Mexico in the wake of the attacks on New York and Washington, Mexico City was
much more reluctant than Ottawa to fall into step.*

*A top political priority in both Canada and Mexico has always been the for-
mal relationship with their once belligerent, still dominant, and at times overwhelming neighbour. Over the decades, their respective bilateral relationship
with the United States established rules and norms that produced regularized
methods of addressing new issues and resolving conflicts. Government also
predominates in North America's third bilateral relationship. While Mexico's
and Canada's relations with each other do not approach the same intensity as
their relations with the United States, one of NAFTA's side effects has been to
initiate a relationship where nothing much existed before. And one of September 11's side effects was to intensify this relationship because dealing with
Washington's border preoccupations provided a common agenda for Ottawa
and Mexico City. While the private sector and civil society are involved in
some Mexico-Canadian governance, the state is in the driver's seat. As chapter
XVIII makes clear, even the economic phenomenon of Mexican campesinos
coming as seasonal, low-cost labour to work for the Ontario tomato industry is
a product of the two federal governments' formal agreement.*

We are left with the paradox that, even if NAFTA turned North America into a 'world region,' its political existence as a distinct mode of regulation remains as tenuous as its ill-defined but largely fractured economic identity. The success of efforts to strengthen its continental governance through the 2005 Security and Prosperity Partnership of North America and its business counterpart, the North American Competitiveness Council, still remains to be demonstrated, as chapter XIX explains. In sum, North America remains what it used to be in matters of security, namely, traditional inter-governmental cooperation driven by Washington's coercive persuasion.

XVI Border Security and the Continental Perimeter

The US government's immediate circling-the-wagons response to the terrorist attacks of September 11, 2001 produced enormous blockages at the two American borders' crossing points. Trucks lined up for many kilometres. Commuters could not get to work. Automobile assembly plants designed for just-in-time production closed down, costing them daily hundreds of millions of dollars.[1] The borderless world of the 1990s had suddenly been overcome by an instinctually territorial and autarchic response as Washington looked global terrorism in the face.

The central challenge of the new security environment was an intensified version of the ancient border-management dilemma – how to facilitate the flows of legitimate people and goods while preventing the entry of dangerous people (terrorists and criminals) and dangerous goods (weapons and contraband). The answer to this challenge in North America was not found through trilateral continental governance – as one could have expected since so much political capital had been expended on promoting an integrated continental political economy – but by separate border agreements negotiated between a United States obsessed about its military security and its two hapless neighbours obsessed about their economic security. While the two agreements had many similarities, their differences would underline the imbalance of the two distinct bilateral relationships and their security histories.

This chapter begins by tracing the notion of continental security through its recent iterations, which reveal how the United States had expanded its notion of security to include Mexico and, by the 1990s, had already moved towards an anti-terrorist approach with Canada. It then examines the US-Canada and US-Mexico border agreements, paying attention to both the formal and informal aspects of governance, relative asymmetries, and policy autonomy. The analysis concludes with some reflections on the future of trilateral security arrangements. Ultimately, while the United States made its own security a continental concern, North American border management was bereft of much meaningful trilateral governance. What resulted was two bilateral relationships directed on a hub-and-spokes basis. Curiously, while Washington initially reverted to a coercive approach to its periphery in response to its primal cry of pain, it then responded to the realization that, to the extent that its national security depended on its neighbours' collaboration, it had to construct a new continental hegemony in which Canada and Mexico accepted the necessity of dealing with the United States' needs by participating more equally.

The Evolution of Continental Security: Towards a De Facto Perimeter?

North American border-security relations have oscillated between two dominant visions. The first conceives of the border as two land lines separating the United States from its neighbours to the north and to the south – formal frontiers requiring levels of autonomous policing commensurate with the policy priorities and security issues of the time. The second view relocates the border to the continent's perimeter, within which the three national spaces must be defended against common external threats and which require some level of joint monitoring. Today, the two conceptions coexist in a not necessarily coherent tension in which the North American perimeter is the forward line for American, Canadian, and Mexican security, while the internal borders remain the basic barricade guarding against the deficiencies of the neighbours' defences.[2]

Towards the end of the Cold War, US national security concerns expanded from an anti-Soviet defence to embrace such transnational threats as the traffic of illegal narcotics. In 1986, when the Reagan administration officially declared its 'War on Drugs,' it had already extended its security perimeter southward to include Mexico. Three years later, President George H.W. Bush launched a second anti-drug policy that gave the American armed forces increased drug-control powers both along the US-Mexico border and deeper into Central and South America. In effect, an anti-drug trafficking campaign to combat the problem at the supply and delivery stages replaced anti-communism as the driving force of US security policy in Latin America.[3] Just as the Cold War had created an aerial perimeter around the United States and Canada, this War on Drugs attempted to push the US frontier away to Mexico's southern border. For Mexico, this shift had strategic implications of a different kind: meeting US demands on narco-trafficking was an essential prepayment to Washington for entry into its economic fold. Militarizing its drug-enforcement efforts helped create the prerequisite consent in Congress for opening the US-Mexico border to freer trade and investment.[4]

The incineration of New York's World Trade Center, the destruction at the Pentagon, and the apparent near miss on Congress or the White House on September 11, 2001 set the stage for a paradigm shift based on the Americans' realization that, despite their unchallengeable military might, they were vulnerable to non-state warriors at home. Opinion leaders insisted that the level of security analysis and the monitoring of goods and people crossing the relevant borders needed to be significantly reconceived and increased. While the national leaders in the peripheral states made appropriate gestures of support, it initially appeared that responses to the crisis would be made-in-the-USA alone. The George W. Bush administration went into an autarchic mode, making it clear that the United States would decide what counted as its territorial security needs. Canada and Mexico would only be left to decide how to conform to Washington's demands.

While no country trading with the United States was unaffected, nowhere was the impact of the US paradigm shift more immediate and powerful than on its two immediate neighbours. In their new thinking, Americans saw the continental periphery as the prime source of their security risk. But the new approach in which 'security trumps trade' directly jeopardized the previous decade's project of building an integrated North American market. NAFTA's two peripheral states had reconfigured their own policy systems in response to Washington's demands that they deregulate and further open their already highly exposed economies to US investment. Having paid a high price in foregone autonomy for easier entry to its market, they found themselves having to make new commitments in order to regain the now militarily denied access.

Given the difference between the threats it perceived coming from Canada and Mexico, their different institutional capacities, and the discrepancy in their commercial relations with the United States, Washington chose to deal with its two neighbours separately. This created a paradox: in an effort to protect its indivisible security in North America, the United States grounded its new continental policy framework in two distinct bilateral agreements, the US-Canada Smart Border Declaration (December 2001) and the US-Mexico Border Partnership Agreement (March 2002), to whose analysis I now turn.

US-Canada Border Relations and the Smart Border Declaration

Throughout the nineteenth century, the governments' presence along the shared border was generally restricted to the collection of customs duties, but the First World War led to the tightening of both Canadian and American immigration policy. Even within the heightened security context of the Second World War and the Cold War, the United States remained relatively unconcerned about its northern border, focusing instead on building a military perimeter around itself and Canada as protection against possible German, Japanese, and ultimately Soviet attack. The attention paid by Washington to its northern border was nowhere near as thorough as the later efforts it made to secure its southern border against drug trafficking and unwanted immigration. This imbalance was evident in the fact that, before September 11, 2001, there were almost thirty times more US border officials along the Mexican border than along its much longer northern frontier.[5]

Anti-terrorist cooperation on US-Canada border issues began in 1993, when the Royal Canadian Mounted Police (RCMP) joined the Federal Bureau of Investigation (FBI) in investigating the World Trade Center bombing. In 1995 the US-Canada Shared Border Accord was signed to enhance collaboration on smuggling and immigration issues. The following year, Congress gave the Immigration and Naturalization Service (INS) a mandate to develop an entry-exit system to track all aliens, but it neglected to provide sufficient funding until 2000. In 1997 a Border Vision Initiative was set up between Citizenship and Immigration Canada and the INS to increase cooperation and intelligence exchanges for combating illegal migration. In the same year, the Cross-Border Crime Forum was established to facilitate cooperation between law- enforcement agencies at the various levels of government in fighting transnational crime. Included in this initiative was an experimental Integrated Border Enforcement Team (IBET) along the British Columbia-Washington border.[6]

American anxiety about terrorism in the 1990s raised counterpart concerns in corporate Canada. With support from the Canadian government and its US allies, the Canadian business community lobbied against Section 110 of the 1996 Illegal Immigration Reform and Immigration Responsibiity Act (IIRIRA), which would require the electronic documentation of travellers entering and exiting the United States. Business argued that it would restrict the flow of people and goods and produce costly bottlenecks.[7] Through the support of large transnational US business interests, the act was replaced with the Immigration and Naturalization Service Data Management Improvement Act of 2000, which required improvements to cross-border tracking but without increasing the documentary burden on importers/exporters and travellers.[8] This cross-border corporate-government coalition demonstrated the importance of American business support to Canadian lobbies wishing to influence US policy.[9]

While business made recommendations through organizations it supported financially, governments actively sought private-sector input through other consultative fora. During the period between 1995 and 1997, a number of border agreements were signed by the Canadian and US governments but subsequently ignored.[10] Most important for our purposes was the creation of the Canada-US Partnership (CUSP), established by Prime Minister Jean Chrétien and President Bill Clinton in 1999 to promote high-level dialogue among governments, border communities, and stakeholders on border management. CUSP was the product of a joint, public-private-sector effort to take a more holistic look at border issues and mobilize the political will necessary to consider innovative solutions to the border dilemma – how to reconcile the twin goals of free movement with public security.

The CUSP process brought together various societal stakeholders – mostly from business and government – who set seamless transactions as the objective. A perimeter approach was recommended in order both to facilitate trade and to increase security where human resources were limited and where existing border infrastructure was incapable of managing the 'exponential' growth in the flow of people and goods since the implementation of CUFTA and NAFTA. Indeed, since CUFTA's signing, US-Canada trade in goods and services had grown from US$174 billion in 1988 to US$447 billion in 1999, amounting to roughly $1.9 billion in daily two-way trade.[11] In other words, bilateral trade had more than doubled since the FTA came into effect, much of it carried by 18,000 trucks which mostly crossed at a handful of gateways each day.[12]

Participants in the CUSP process felt that the border was administratively overstressed – the various border-inspection agencies were responsible to over fifty government agencies[13] – and felt that border governance was actually trying to do too much.[14]

In response to pressure for more public-private-sector collaboration, a number of pilot projects were undertaken by the Canadian government, primarily between the Canada Customs and Revenue Agency (CCRA) and the Canadian Manufacturers and Exporters. Guided by the concepts of 'risk management' and 'pre-release/pre-clearance,' the CCRA's Customs Action Plan proposed a risk-based strategy to improve import/export processes by streamlining transit for pre-approved, low-risk goods and travellers which would not require increasing border resources.[15] The plan set guidelines for unilateral initiatives like fast lanes for low-risk goods and travellers – Customs Self-Assessment (CSA) for cargo and CANPASS or NEXUS for people. Concurrently, the CCRA planned to intensify the processing for traffic of high and unknown risk.[16] On the other side of the border, the INS created INSPASS for travellers while US Customs created the National Customs Automation Prototype to clear cargo electronically through pre-arrival processing.[17] These programs existed alongside C-TRAP, a US customs program in which business voluntarily underwent a self-assessment of supply-chain security. Once businesses entered the CSA and C-TRAP programs, they could then be eligible for membership in the bilateral Free and Secure Trade Lanes (FAST) program, allowing for expedited truck-border crossings through designated lanes.[18]

The beginning of acute US concern that its northern border was a security risk came two years before September 11, when Ahmed Ressam, a radical Islamist with connections to al-Qaeda, was apprehended by US Customs officials while driving from the province of British Columbia to the state of Washington with a trunk full of explosives which could have been used in an attack on the Los Angeles airport. Although it was Canadian intelligence that had alerted Washington, the US media spin on this incident heightened the perception that Canada's immigration and refugee laws were so weak that its porous external border put American citizens at risk.

Canadian business was also active through its associations and in its funding of research undertaken by favoured think tanks. For instance, in a publication entitled *The Views of Canadian Industry and Business Associations on Canada-United States Economic Integration*, the Public Policy Forum identified the US-Canada border as a 'nuisance'[19] which intersected production lines and represented a significant transaction cost for just-in-time delivery systems. From interviewing over fifty top-ranking executives, the Public Policy Forum found that many business associations shared the objective of 'creating a *seamless* movement of goods and people between Canada and [the] United States.'[20] Six months later, and well before the September 11 attacks, the Forum identified a 'perimeter' approach to managing the US-Canada border as 'an efficient and safe solution to decrease congestion at the border' and suggested that government should 'let the private sector lead.'[21] The perimeter approach involved a redefinition of the role of the border that would call for the joint US-Canada inspection of incoming people and goods to occur at offshore points of origin (Rotterdam, Hong Kong), at continental points of entry (airports and seaports), and at points in transit (using biometric technologies at the border or constant monitoring with sophisticated global-positioning systems).[22]

For Canada, the shock of September 11 was less the loss of twenty-three fellow citizens in the World Trade Center's wreckage than the shutting down of the 49th parallel, which jeopardized its economic access to the US market. In part because of the immediate but erroneous allegation, given credence by Senator Hillary Clinton, that all nineteen al-Qaeda terrorists had crossed the land border from the north, Canada was again perceived as a country whose liberal immigration and refugee system made it a haven for terrorists. To restore unhindered commerce, Canadians had to convince the United States that their shared border was reliable enough to meet its homeland-security concerns. Ottawa did this in the weeks following September 11 by elevating counter-terrorism to the top of its policy hierarchy, which meant tightening immigration policy, passing extensive anti-terrorism legislation, enhancing border controls, and stepping up law enforcement and intelligence integration with Washington. Canada put its entry ports on higher alert, tightened airport security, allocated $176 million for personnel and inspection technology, and passed legislation to restrict financial flows to terrorists, freeze presumed terrorist organizations' assets, and tighten immigration controls.[23]

The continental economic integration boosted by NAFTA – and the corporate relationships it had engendered – infused the three governments' actions. Business associations with an interest in the unhindered flow of goods, services, investment, and specialized personnel across North America's borders hurriedly met and desperately called on the three governments to guarantee free but more secure flows across the two US boundaries. Because the voices of business were heard loud and clear, the Bush administration ultimately responded to its northern border-security problems by using more economic than military means. The same was true in Ottawa, where business virtually dictated the government's proposals for action. In a situation where Washington realized that its security now depended on its neighbour's cooperation, Ottawa became actively involved in working out the nature and scope of enhanced bilateral-security measures.

Ottawa's fiscal commitment to US counter-terrorism efforts was reflected in the $7.7 billion that Finance Minister Paul Martin allocated in a special December budget over the next five years for enhancing intelligence capacity, improving interagency coordination and maritime surveillance, strengthening infrastructure protection, extending the military's anti-terrorist resources, and preparing for possible chemical, biological, or nuclear attacks.

In the period after September 11, Washington and Ottawa engaged in intense negotiations in order to come to grips with a host of specific questions, many of which had been promised in the agreements signed in the 1990s but subsequently ignored – including the Canada-US Border Vision Initiative, the cross-border Crime Forum, and the Canada-US Partnership. Business associations lobbied desperately for the implementation of these previously proposed measures in the hope that they would preserve their project of economic liberalization by simultaneously speeding up border traffic and enhancing surveillance. As a result, Canadian diplomats in Washington claimed that the bulk of the proposals forming the 30-Point Smart Border Plan signed by Homeland Security Adviser Tom Ridge and Deputy Prime Minister John Manley in Ottawa on December 12 had been made in Canada.

As plenipotentiaries in charge of their two governments' security policy, Ridge and Manley quickly developed an excellent personal rapport, so that Canada quietly managed to be included within the Americans' anti-terrorist security thinking rather than be condemned to exclusion outside an enclosure consisting of the forty-eight continental states only. But once the US administration restructured its machinery of government around a new Department of Homeland Security (DHS) – a massive reorganization that involved bringing twenty-two agencies with more than 170,000 officials under one bureaucratic roof – considerable confusion ensued.

In addition to US government measures implementing the established Customs-Trade Partnership Against Terrorism (C-TPAT), Canadian trade-facilitating initiatives included the Canada Customs and Revenue Agency's Customs Self-Assessment, which was implemented on December 6, 2001 after several years of planning. At a Bush-Chrétien meeting in September 2002, the two leaders jointly announced the launch of FAST – a program whose purpose was to facilitate commercial flows and which was built on the two earlier initiatives, CSA and C-TPAT. Under another program, NEXUS, fast lanes for low-risk pre-cleared travellers were opened in June 2002 at two border crossings.

In spite of significant pressure from certain sectors of government and the business community, Canada and the United States did not ever envisage the full integration that a continental-security perimeter would have entailed, complete with a disarmed bilateral border. Rather, the Smart Border Declaration tried to create a 'zone of confidence' which would use risk-management assessment to reconcile the opposing needs of closing borders to terrorists and opening them to economic flows. The declaration brought together four main border-security themes previously addressed separately by the two governments: the secure flow of people, the secure flow of goods, secure infrastructure, and policy coordination and information sharing in the enforcement of the plan's objectives.

Secure Flow of People

Nearly half of the agreement's thirty points addressed the movement of people, since dangerous individuals who might or might not be residents or citizens of North America had to be detected while not obstructing the more than 300,000 people who daily crossed the US-Canada border for business and tourism. The combination of new technology, risk assessment, and policy coordination in the agreement's people 'pillar' was designed to enable border officials to make this distinction. To identify falsified or duplicated identities by non-citizens, Canada issued new permanent-residence cards containing such biometric information as fingerprints and irises.[24] Although the United States did not plan to follow suit, both countries agreed to common standards and interoperable technology for scanning and interpreting biometrics.

This application of advanced technology helped support risk assessment and procedures to facilitate legitimate travel. One of the most visible manifestations of the Smart Border Declaration was the expansion of NEXUS to expedite low-risk travellers' crossings while allowing border officials to concentrate on high-risk movements. Applicants had to submit to security checks, meet admissibility requirements for both Canada and the United States, and be reviewed and approved by both governments. The pre-clearance of in-transit air passengers arriving in North America, the collection of air-passenger information for customs and intelligence use, and the stationing of American and Canadian immigration officers overseas helped manage the risks of cross-border travel.

In the area of policy coordination and bilateral cooperation, joint passenger-analysis units were established on a trial basis at the Vancouver and Miami international airports where co-located Canadian and American customs and immigration officials cooperated in analysing passenger information. These pilot programs concluded in 2004, when Canada's National Risk Assessment Centre and the United States' National Targeting Center assumed responsibility for sharing passenger information. Both countries also undertook to make their immigration processes' technological infrastructure more compatible in order to share more security data.[25]

As part of the border plan, the two states pledged to coordinate their visa policies and consult each other in reviewing third countries for visa exemption or restriction. In 2001, of the fifty countries from which nationals could enter Canada without visas, twenty were excluded from the US list of visa-exempt states.[26] Afterwards, Canada changed its visa regulations to require residents of such countries as Saudi Arabia and Malaysia to obtain visas, bringing its list more in line with its American counterpart. This substantial coordination on visa policy, though, fell short of full harmonization.[27]

Although Canada had been trying to eliminate the large number of asylum claims filed from the United States – over one-third of Canada's refugee applicants in 2000[28] – its attempt in the mid-1990s to negotiate a safe third-country agreement had not borne fruit. September 11, 2001 generated the requisite US political interest, and the Smart Border Declaration gave the two governments a green light to tighten policies on migration and refugees. The bilateral Safe Third Country Agreement of December 5, 2002,[29] requiring refugees to 'claim protection in the first safe country they arrive in,'[30] was designed to prevent asylum shopping and economize the resources needed to deal with applications by those in genuine need of refugee protection.[31] In this way, the mantra of anti-terrorist security allowed both countries to achieve their prior policy goal of imposing stricter controls on general flows of people over the border.

Canada took the lead on many of the Smart Border Declaration's other points. Beyond the smart permanent-resident card and changed visa policies, it implemented a new advance passenger-information and name-recognition tracking system within a year and a half of September 11. The United States' progress was slower. In order to meet some of the requirements of the border agreement, the United States sought to modernize its Computer Assisted Passenger Pre-screening program by developing a successor model, but these changes were scrapped owing to privacy concerns by civil-liberties organizations and the Government Accounting Office.

Ignoring Canada's proven capacity for measured action and its own security-perimeter rhetoric, Washington proposed tripling the number of American customs officers at its northern border. While these officials never materialized, the proposal underlined the US government's lingering, uninformed distrust of its neighbour. Its related proclivity for unilateral action was exemplified by US-VISIT, an entry-exit system at most US airports and numerous seaports that collected biometric and personal information from all entrants to the United States except US citizens, American immigrants, and citizens of such visa-waiver countries as Canada.[32] Cross-checked against lists of criminals, illegal aliens, immigration offenders, outstanding warrants, and terrorist watch lists, the information was collected for use by the DHS and could be shared with local, national, or foreign law-enforcement agencies.[33] This system, which did not extend to the Canadian or Mexican perimeters, effectively fortified the United States' internal borders against its neighbours.

Secure Flow of Goods

These US actions to secure the border demonstrated how national security could become a new kind of protectionist barrier. Immediately following the terrorist attacks, US border officials were put on high alert, leading to a substantial slowdown in cross-border commerce. Previously, truckers hauling cargo could expect a one- to two-minute wait at the border. In the days following the terrorist attacks, the wait time for these same trucks was ten to fifteen hours.[34] The North American automobile industry was especially hard hit. Fearing that this commercial bottleneck would not be temporary, many Canadian business leaders began lobbying once again for a joint-security perimeter. Shortly after September 11, the CEO of Canadian Pacific made his case: 'Canada will have to adopt US-style immigration policies if it doesn't want the border between the two countries to become almost impossible to cross ... We have to make North America secure from the outside. We're going to lose our sovereignty increasingly, but necessarily so.'[35]

Backed by the Canadian government and its American corporate allies, the Canadian business community lobbied against Section 110 of IIRIRA, arguing that it jeopardized NAFTA-expanded commercial flows.[36] Owing to pressure from large US TNCs, the act was replaced, as we have seen, with the Immigration and Naturalization Service Data Management Improvement Act of 2000. This cross-border business-government cooperation showed how powerful US economic interests will fight back if security measures impose a disproportionate cost.[37]

The Smart Border Declaration also harmonized commercial processing procedures through FAST. Equivalent in many ways to NEXUS, and built on previous practices for expediting cargo shipments, FAST allowed 'pre-approved importers, carriers, and drivers to expedite the movement of low-risk shipments across the border.'[38] Those who qualified for the program received a range of benefits including quicker clearance at the border, dedicated lanes, and time-related cost reductions. Despite FAST's high security, Canada was required to notify the US government of all outgoing shipments twenty-four hours in advance. Canada and the United States also agreed to share more information on cargo shipments and to participate in joint enforcement and cargo-searching initiatives. Options discussed included privately operated pre-processing centres, international federal-inspection zones, and reverse inspections where authorities from each country switch places and conduct physical investigations on the other side of the border. Framing border issues in terms of national security allowed each government to justify to its taxpayers spending billions of dollars on improved border infrastructure.

Implementing an efficient method for allowing goods to cross the border also had significant implications for private-sector governance. Designing the FAST program and such policies as the pre-clearance of shipments involved close consultation with the business community, which wanted to achieve faster transit but had to create its own security safeguards, police its staff and manufacturers, and implement more efficient, better-monitored practices in order to minimize transit time at the border.

The remaining points in the goods pillar of the Smart Border Declaration consisted of combined US-Canada initiatives and information exchanges. Joint facilities for Canadian and US customs officials and immigration agents had been proposed before 2001, but progress had been slow because of differing laws and policies. By 2004, six joint facilities existed along the US-Canada border.[39] However, numerous problems, such as 'the legal and operational issues associated with the establishment of international zones and joint facilities, including ... the arming of law enforcement officers in such zones and facilities,' had to be resolved.[40] American customs officials could be found at stations in Vancouver, Halifax, and Montreal, while Canadian officials were present at the Seattle-Tacoma and Newark stations. The role of the out-of-country customs officials was merely to assist, since neither state could apply its laws in the other country.[41] The Harper government's $1-billion, multi-year program for arming Canadian border guards settled one of the most contentious disputes regarding the operation of joint facilities, while moving Canada closer to the US template of making the border a militarized space.

Secure Infrastructure

The changes outlined in the people and goods pillars of the Smart Border Declaration would not be possible without substantial improvements in infrastructure. Before 2001, American authorities had neglected their northern border, leading to congestion, outdated technologies, and inadequate monitoring. More aware of these shortcomings than their American counterparts, Canadian officials responded quickly to the new US security interest.[42] As with measures designed to secure the flow of people and goods, upgrades to the border's infrastructure needed to be translated into a security language to extract the requisite financial resources. Canada committed C$665 million through the Border Infrastructure Fund to 'reduce congestion, improve flow of goods and services, and expand infrastructure capacity.'[43] The United States made contributions to similar initiatives through a previously established Transportation Equity Act for the 21st Century.

Other initiatives under the infrastructure pillar included the expanded use of Intelligent Transportation Systems, an application of technology to procedures such as customs clearance that was first developed by Canada in 1999, the creation of a binational committee to cooperate on critical infrastructure protection, and the two countries' recognition of one another's standards for airport and flight security.

Coordination and Information Sharing

Securing movements of goods and people across the border required substantial mutual trust, so the measures in the 'co-ordination and information' pillar were underpinned by a formal commitment to mutual support. As with the agreement's three other pillars, the provisions for coordination and information sharing relied heavily on prior joint enforcement efforts. Building on the 1996 Washington-British Columbia experiment, Integrated Border-Enforcement Teams were installed at several other points along the US-Canada boundary. The 1997 Cross-border Crime Forum continued to deal with issues like cross-border radio cooperation and human trafficking.[44] Other joint enforcement efforts concentrated on the removal of deportees and counter-terrorism training.

These enforcement efforts were supported, at least in theory, by the sharing of intelligence information. On this point, Canada and the United States built on each country's existing national intelligence institutions. Canada established Integrated National Security Enforcement Teams composed of national law-enforcement and intelligence agencies as well as foreign partners including US agencies.[45] On the other side of the border, Canada participated in the US Foreign Terrorist Tracking Task Force, which sought to 'detect, interdict, and remove foreign terrorists.'[46] The capacity of the RCMP and the FBI to share fingerprint information increased greatly as a result of the Smart Border Declaration.

The most controversial component of the 'co-ordination and information' pillar of the border agreement concerned counter-terrorism. Within months of September 11, both Canada and the United States enacted anti-terrorism laws, which were criticized for the speed with which they were passed, the lack of debate over important issues, their expansion of law-enforcement powers, and their potential to erode civil liberties.

Canada's Anti-Terrorism Act inserted a definition of terrorist activity into the Canadian Criminal Code, mandated preventive arrests and detention without charges, and allowed the government to withhold information classified as 'sensitive to international relations, national security, or defence.' Critics maintained that the bill was unnecessary, particularly since murder was already punishable under the Criminal Code and the Privacy Act allowed for sensitive information to remain classified. Human-rights and civil-liberty activists argued that the lawful suspension of civil liberties permitted police to target unpopular groups, restrict freedom of the press, and stigmatize those participating in strikes and protests.[47]

Passed six weeks after the terrorist attacks, the United States' Uniting and Strengthening America by Providing Appropriate Tools Required to Intercept and Obstruct Terrorism (PATRIOT) Act gave law-enforcement agencies unprecedented powers to engage in a range of draconian practices – surveillance, secret hearings, deportation, detention without charges, denial of legal representation to detainees – and generally to reduce government transparency and openness.[48]

As a result of all these measures, the Smart Border Declaration signalled a significant change in the understanding of 'security,' which had previously become defined largely in individual terms. With the mistrust of government that neoconservatism had propagated in the 1990s, the state had been perceived as the greatest threat to an individual's security. Roles reversed after September 11, as governments recognized their own vulnerability to the actions of individuals and non-state actors, and citizens again turned to their state for one of the most basic of public goods – security.[49] The Smart Border Declaration demonstrated a renewed faith in the state as the protector of individual and collective security and an acceptance that personal liberties should be sacrificed for the safety of the whole country. While power asymmetries remained between Canada and the United States, the Smart Border Declaration tended to foster coordination rather than coercion between the two neighbours. The US tendency to unilateralism persisted, but Canada played a leading role in drafting the agreement and suggesting its provisions. Although border-security measures would not have been toughened without the September catastrophe, it remains the case that – because so many of the changes had been advocated in Ottawa and resisted in Washington – the Smart Border episode demonstrated an increase in Canadian capacity within the US-defined imperium-turned-hegemony without much decrease in Ottawa's autonomy.

US-Mexican Border Relations and the Border Partnership Action Plan

Very different from the factors just considered, US-Mexican border relations had been shaped by conflictual issues such as drug traffic and illegal immigration which prompted the United States to solve its southern border problems more through unilateral law enforcement within its own autarchy than by bilateral cooperation. The War on Drugs provided several American administrations with the rationale and the funds to extend US enforcement powers across the border and beyond.[50] During the Clinton era, considerable domestic pressure was exerted on the Administration to deter would-be Mexican migrants from entering the United States. The 1996 IIRIRA called for doubling the border-patrol staff by 2001, increased the penalties for illegal immigrants and their smugglers, invested in new technologies and border infrastructure, and authorized the building of a large fence along the Tijuana-San Diego border.[51] Eventually the whole 3,200-km US-Mexico border was staffed with armed guards. As a result, apprehension regarding migrants dropped, and the policy of 'prevention through deterrence' was deemed a success.[52] But tensions mounted as mortality rates increased for migrants being smuggled into the United States through dangerous desert and mountainous regions[53] which were less patrolled by the INS.[54]

The interconnected problems of drugs and immigrants were virtually insoluble for two sets of reasons. On the northern side of the border, the US government saw no way to decrease its own market's apparently insatiable dual demand for illegal drugs and cheap labour. To the south, the Mexican government did not have the capacity to resist the social and economic forces that were driving contraband and undocumented workers northward. Meanwhile, NAFTA gave economic integration a new legal framework for the freer movement of goods between Mexico and the United States by lowering economic barriers, increasing rates of US direct investment, and so multiplying business partnerships between Mexican and American firms.

Owing to the ongoing process of rural-urban migration, agrarian reforms, and population growth, migration from rural Mexico to the United States had become deeply rooted well before NAFTA, but the new political-economy conjuncture accelerated the trend.[55] Burgeoning social and economic linkages enhanced by NAFTA promoted the illegal movement of people into the United States, as business partners and families expanded ties across the border.[56] Both the US and Mexican governments promoted these economic and social linkages through programs such as the TIES Exchange of the US Agency for International Development, which fostered large-scale academic exchanges between the two countries. The resulting integration of transborder social networks caused problems of border security to overlap with issues of domestic security in such cities as Tijuana, Juárez, and Matamoras where the drug cartels had established secure houses and had corrupted police forces at the local level.[57]

In the period preceding September 11, both governments sought to formalize and manage these links. Signed in June 2001, the Action Plan for Border Security Cooperation aimed to lower the risks experienced by would-be migrants trying to cross over. The Alliance for the Mexican-American Frontier's action plan to establish a 'smart border for the 21st century' was signed in 2002 to bring security and efficiency to the zone.[58]

Newly elected presidents Bush and Fox met under the auspices of the recently formed Partnership for Prosperity, a bilateral initiative aimed to strengthen the Mexican economy so that would-be migrants would have less incentive to come to the United States. Both Bush and Fox had aspirations for greater bilateral cooperation and deeper integration, and both saw that the border could be secured effectively from narco-traffic only if the issue of illegal migration was tackled cooperatively. Accordingly, both sides agreed in principle on the need for an expanded temporary-worker program, the granting of legal status to undocumented Mexicans in the United States, an increased US visa quota for Mexicans, stronger border security, and investment in those Mexican regions that produced the most migrants.[59]

Prior to September 2001, President Fox created the Centro de Investigación y Seguridad Nacional (CISEN, Centre for Intelligence and National Security) to encourage information sharing among the Mexican government's various intelligence services (police, navy, army, and the government's justice department, the Procuraduría General de la República [PGR]), each of which had its own intelligence service and institutional interests.[60] After September 11, significant reforms were undertaken in the PGR and the new CISEN.[61] Special efforts were made through the Secretaría de la Defensa Nacional (to strengthen airport security and monitor the frontier); the Mexican navy and the PGR (to intensify collaboration with the FBI and the US Drug Enforcement Administration); CISEN and the Instituto Nacional de Migración (National Immigration Institute) (to provide stricter vigilance in migratory areas and information sharing between intelligence services, improved border vigilance, and bus-station security); the Commission for Northern Frontier Affairs, a binational council of border-state governors (to promote a culture of legality along the frontier); the Secretaría de Turismo (Secretariat of Tourism), which was connected to CISEN (to secure the safety of domestic and foreign tourists); and the

Secretaría de Comunicaciones y Transportes (Secretariat of Communications and Transport) (to improve communication with US customs in the interests of toughening the surveillance of people and speed the control of goods).[62]

Despite these efforts, the United States remained suspicious about Mexico's security agencies, which, for lack of structural reform and adequate funds, were inefficient, restricted to domestic affairs, and without either international networks or intelligence agreements with other countries.[63] Lacking a central bureau to coordinate the many secretariats and institutions with which it connected, CISEN's management was still perceived as weak at best and, at worst, a corrupted new institution quickly infiltrated by narco-traffickers.[64] (Fox dismantled the drug cartels, not realizing that they could work individually in small groups, out of his control. The special force he set up to control narco-traffic was itself taken over by the drug lords.) Quietly but effectively, US agencies cooperated with Mexican intelligence agencies at the local level – bus stations, car rental offices, airports, and ports.

September 11 transformed the Bush administration's approach to its Mexican immigration problem. That the terrorists had entered the United States legally led the American public and administration officials to reverse their favourable disposition towards legalizing Mexican migrants. An embittered President Fox eventually abandoned his attempt to get the United States to sign an immigration agreement.[65]

As it had done with Canada, Washington opted for a policy that embraced technology in an attempt to combine open trade with screening high-risk crossings. On March 22, 2002 US Secretary of State Colin Powell and Mexican Secretary of State Santiago Creel signed the Border Partnership Agreement, whose twenty-two points were finalized after a lengthy inter-governmental process in which the Department of State, the DHS, other federal agencies, and the Mexican government wrestled with budgetary constraints.

When the United States signed the Smart Border Declaration with Canada and somebody asked Tom Ridge if it would do the same with Mexico, he said: 'No, Mexico is a developing country.' The Partnership had only seven points about the security of border infrastructure; the rest were about people crossing. Congress sanctioned $25 million for Mexico in order to fund security projects, including improvements to Mexican technology infrastructure and the training of Mexican customs officials. Because the DHS cannot fund international security projects, the funds authorized by Congress were channelled to the Mexican government through the Department of State's Bureau of Narcotic

Affairs (NAS), which can fund projects overseas. After the DHS decided on a border-security project, the NAS office in Mexico City supplied Mexico with the funds to implement it.[66]

The Border Partnership Agreement represented the formal roadmap for strengthening Mexican and American border technology and infrastructure. The agreement, which contained a set of goals that stressed greater bilateral institutional cooperation and policy harmonization, had only three pillars: the secure flow of people, the secure flow of goods, and secure infrastructure.

Secure Flow of People

Approximately one million people cross the United States' southern border every day. Indeed, 'the flow is so enormous that at just one of the crossings – Laredo-Nuevo Laredo – the equivalent of more than half the population of the United States transits in a year.'[67] Since migrants remained the US government's central concern, the people pillar occupied pride of place in the border agreement. Like the US-Canada Smart Border Declaration, the US-Mexico agreement proposed a combination of technology, risk management, and joint initiatives to manage this huge flow.

One of the people pillar's most important initiatives was the expansion of the Secure Electronic Network for Travellers Rapid Inspection (SENTRI) system. Initiated in 1994 for the Otay Mesa, California's port of entry, the program was expanded to include two additional crossings. Like NEXUS, SENTRI expedited border crossings for travellers who, after extensive background checks, have been categorized as low-risk. In January 2004 close to 70,000 border crossers were enrolled in the system.[68] However, 'wait times of up to six months to register in the program and a cost of US$129 annually have deterred potential users.'[69] The DHS made a commitment to integrate SENTRI with the more advanced NEXUS program. While it was vehicle-based – requiring registered individuals to use the same vehicle at each crossing – the NEXUS system allowed specific individuals to pass through border crossings, thus expediting cross-border movement of both cars and people.[70]

Another technology-driven initiative was a joint advance passenger-information exchange mechanism for flights between Mexico and the United States.[71] On the Mexican side, the implementation of this component of the border agreement was difficult, mostly because of the absence of a sufficient computer infrastructure at Mexican airports. In order to deal with this technological deficit, 'Mexico received funding and assistance from the United States to acquire [computer and data sharing] capabilities, and in November 2003, Mexican customs began collecting and, as of February 2004, actually exchanging these data with US counterparts.'[72]

Other people measures included enhancing bilateral anti-smuggling efforts and joint training operations, continuing consultations on the possibility of visa policy coordination, and improving database compatibility to facilitate sharing intelligence information. Cooperating in the detection and management of 'dangerous third-country nationals'[73] reportedly took the form of the United States taking over the background checks on everyone wanting to enter Mexico on a visa. Mexican consulates, it is said, have to send all visa applications – whether from tourists, students, or workers – to Washington.[74]

The North American security perimeter cannot be watertight because Mexico City cannot control the smuggling of people and drugs from Central America across its southern border.[75] For instance, the Maratruchas gang, which started in Los Angeles, moved to El Salvador when it was expelled from the United States and found its way back into the United States through drug and prostitution rings in Mexico.[76]

Uncontrolled criminal activity in Mexico helped generate the view in the United States that the Mexican government was not doing enough to secure its own borders. Under attack for his weak leadership on this issue, President Bush dispatched 6,000 members of the National Guard to strengthen the southern border's defences. At the same time, he proposed a plan that would 'treat people with dignity' by legalizing the status of the five to seven million undocumented Mexicans who had resided in the United States for five years and allowing the three million who had been there two to five years to apply to emigrate. Mexicans who had arrived within two years were to be deported and would be able to return only under a temporary-workers plan.[77] Hispanics across the United States mobilized against these proposals, staging a one-day work and school stoppage on May 1, 2006 and launching a symbolic boycott of US goods in Mexico.[78] Although President Fox's criticism of Bush's plan was applauded in Mexico, his passivity in the face of the United States' further unilateral militarization at the border was denounced as an excessive concession for which he received nothing in return.

The substantial differences in the two governments' capacities affected their abilities to implement the Border Partnership's provisions.

Mexico demonstrated a genuine willingness to cooperate, partly to increase security at the border and partly to improve relations with Washington (particularly between the customs and immigration agencies). Its willingness notwithstanding, most of the work on these issues fell on US shoulders, since Mexico lacked the budget and resources.[79]

While a $25-million contribution from the United States went some way to dealing with this problem, the money did not come close to what would be required to achieve significant improvements. Yet the sum is substantial enough to raise questions about Mexico's ability to implement an autonomous security policy. In any event, one of Mexico's major concerns about the border agreement is that it focuses too much on US priorities. Whereas the United States has concentrated almost solely on *security*, Mexico would like to see more policy attention directed towards *safety* at the border. In Spanish, *seguridad* means not only security but also safety, and for Mexico, the two issues are of equal importance.[80]

Secure Flow of Goods

Significantly more progress has been made on the goods pillar. In fact, the two countries' cooperation 'was cited as a model for the type of cooperation possible in other arenas.' As with the US-Canada Smart Border Declaration, the main reason for the progress is that the initiatives in this pillar built on previous programs. The agreement was therefore 'perceived as a joint effort consistent with previous ones, rather than an initiative imposed upon one party' by the other.[81] Success in this component of the agreement was crucial, given the growing importance of US-Mexico trade, which had more than trebled from US$80 billion in 1994 to $270 billion in 2002.[82]

Many of the initiatives in the goods pillar mirrored those in its US-Canada counterpart, including a commitment to electronic-information exchange, the development of a means for tracking and securing in-transit shipments, technology exchange, and anti-fraud and anti-contraband measures. However, the Border Partnership Agreement was more explicit that public-private-sector cooperation would be needed to ensure a secure flow of commercial goods. Central was a commitment to 'expand partnerships with private sector trade groups and importers/exporters to increase security and compliance of commercial shipments, while expediting clearance processes.' Several measures have been implemented that are consistent with this goal. For instance, US Customs and Border Protection and the General Customs Administration of Mexico have expanded operations with the Business Anti-Smuggling Coalition, an international private-sector coalition with offices in Mexico that aims to address the problem of concealing contraband in commercial trade.[83]

FAST lanes combined with the Customs-Trade Partnership against Terrorism represented a similar public-private-sector effort allowing Mexican and American customs agents to focus their energy on higher-risk border crossings. C-TPAT was a 'joint government-business initiative to enact procedures that expedite customs processing at points of entry by shifting some of the responsibility of secure shipments to the private sector.'[84] Businesses voluntarily went through a self-assessment of supply-chain security, adhering to a set of guidelines prepared by US Customs and the trade community. Once businesses became members of the C-TPAT program, they then had to communicate its guidelines to other businesses within their supply chain so that the program became ingrained at every stage of production.[85] After all businesses within a given supply chain had entered the C-TPAT program, they could then become eligible for FAST's expedition of border crossings through dedicated lanes.

Cooperating with the United States on DHS-led initiatives, Mexico also created its own public-private-sector programs for southbound trade called Empresas Certificadas (Certified Enterprises) and Expres, which paralleled C-TPAT and FAST, respectively. For the government of Mexico, these programs served a double purpose: they ensured the secure movement of goods while allowing Mexican Customs to tax imports correctly – a long-standing difficulty in a historically under-staffed, underfunded, and corrupt Mexican customs agency.[86]

As in the US-Canada agreement, Washington retained its autonomy to control the flow of goods across its borders. Technological measures in the goods pillar strengthened both the Mexican and US governments' capacity to cross-reference electronic information and images from a common database regarding the northbound shipments of goods.[87] Gamma ray machines to detect weapons of mass destruction and con-traband, installed by Mexico along railroad and truck border crossings, revealed a second facet of this transborder governance – imperium.[88] Mexican officials did not see cross-border movements of weapons of mass destruction as a primary – or even tertiary – security concern, so obliging Washington on this issue came closer to coerced cooperation than consensual participation in a common hegemonic project.

Secure Infrastructure

With NAFTA's stimulus of increased cross-border trade, both Mexico and the United States recognized that the border needed more adequate security infrastructure. Bottlenecks had increased as customs officials instituted heavier security at already overcrowded border crossings. The infrastructure pillar of the US-Mexico border agreement addressed these problems directly by creating and monitoring new points of entry in order to reduce traffic density. In addition, both the US and Mexican governments shared the longer-term goal of securing critical energy infrastructure from a possible terrorist attack. The destruction of natural gas production facilities and oil pipelines in Mexico could affect the economies of both countries. Thus, the infrastructure pillar also served a dual purpose – it formally guided long-term development projects for new points of entry while creating a documentation and assessment system that could help determine which security concerns were most urgent.

At its 2003 meeting, the US-Mexico Binational Commission's Working Group on Homeland Security and Border Co-operation announced the harmonization of the hours of service for the US Customs and Border Protection and the General Customs Administration of Mexico.[89] This decision was a small manifestation of bilateral government, since the inter-governmental decision had direct effect.

Many of the points in the US-Mexico Border Partnership Agreement resembled those in the Canada-US Smart Border Declaration, even though the imbalance between the two security relationships was significant. Of the agreement's twenty-two points, those that were funded by the US government to increase Mexican security technology infrastructure have been instituted with more vigour than those that reiterated the older cooperative efforts dealing with Mexico's concerns about migration. In other words, the components of the agreement that were best implemented were those materially supported by the United States. These themes will be explored further in chapter XIX's analysis of the Security and Prosperity Partnership of North America.

Narco-traffic is one area where the imbalance between Canada and Mexico's relations with the United States appears to be increasing. A DHS report in October 2006 claimed that drug lords were not only smuggling narcotics over the Texas-Mexico border but were establishing alliances with and thus strengthening US criminal gangs. It showed that there was increasing evidence of illegal immigrants from the Middle East lingering in Mexico before they enter Canada. Further, US military and intelligence officials believed that Venezuela was emerging as a potential hub of terrorism in the Western Hemisphere and that terrorists – including members of Hezbollah – had entered the United States through its southern border. In Texas, a state border-security strategy included four key areas of focus: increasing patrols and law-enforcement presence; centralizing command, control, and intelligence operations; increasing state resources deployed for border security; and making better use of technology to fight border crime.[90] Since its southern border remained a conduit for legal commercial activity, the United States faced the old challenge of cracking down on illegal behaviour while trying to keep legitimate goods and people flowing.

Conclusion

In the first phase of the US 'War on Terror,' Washington extended its security border to North America's perimeter by pressuring its two neighbours to adopt immigration and counter-terrorism measures that were the functional equivalent of its own. Transborder governance had reverted to the two bilateral relationships being tailored to Washington's perceived needs – in this case, remediating Canada's and Mexico's differing anti-terrorist capabilities. Canada's administrative strength and focused political will enabled it both to maintain some autonomy on security issues and to exert greater capacity in Washington in order to resolve its border problems over technology and infrastructure, re-creating a bilateral inter-governmental cooperation similar to what had existed before.

In the meantime, the US perception of Mexico as a country with an out-of-control emigration problem and a drug trade potentially connected with global terrorism meant that the United States continued its much less symmetrical security relationship in which it exerted considerable muscle while nevertheless having to rely on Mexico's frail governing resources. The United States' awareness that its border security depended on Mexico's own internal security – as well as Mexico's realization that it could not achieve its domestic security against the drug cartels without US help – was dramatically expressed by the negotiation and signature in 2007 of the Plan Merida, in which Washington undertook to supply $1.4 billion of military aid whether in the shape of helicopters and other military hardware or anti-terrorist training and intelligence software. The Plan Merida represented a giant step towards

Mexico's acceptance of the realities of its security interdependence with the United States: its security autarchy, like its economic autarchy, had become a thing of the past.

In one respect, US pressure had paradoxical effects. The demands from Washington that Canada and Mexico strengthen their border vigilance, which compelled the two countries to beef up their own security apparatus, served to increase their autonomy – that is, their ability to implement domestic policy measures – in order to participate in the new continental security hegemony.

Unlike land-based border security, where Washington's need for the periphery's cooperation reduced the continent's normal asymmetries and where common problems, policies, and technologies levelled the imbalance between Mexico's and Canada's US relationships, defence against military threats from overseas heightened both the asymmetry and the imbalance that had characterized the continent's military governance during the Cold War. This is the subject of chapter XVII.

XVII North American Defence

For most countries, border security and military defence merge seamlessly one into the other. But for Canada and Mexico, living as they do on the glacis of the world's most powerful military machine, the issues remained largely distinct until global terrorism conflated the two.

As recently as the 1990s, when the world's trouble spots were far from the Western Hemisphere, students of North America would have had little reason to analyse the continent's transborder military relations. But President George W. Bush's declaration of a War on Terror, his administration's publication of a new security doctrine, the government's commitment to national missile defence, and the Pentagon's organization of a regional command for North America precipitated the return of defence to the agenda of North American governance.

To comprehend the current imbalance of North America's military polity, in which Canada has been an intimate participant with the United States for seventy years and Mexico a principled abstainer, this chapter examines the restructuring of defence in North America after September 11, 2001. In order to assess the military's significance for transborder governance, it shows how the inter-governmental character of North American military decision making is distinct from the transborder governance in which the interactions of non-governmental actors – primarily business lobbies but also civil-society organizations – tend to drive government action.

The United States and Canada: A History of Expanding Cooperation

When it comes to the United States' territorial defence, Canada has occupied a very important piece of real estate since the republic's first days, when the constitutional fathers counted (in vain) on North America's remaining British colonies rallying in solidarity with the American Revolution. Following two unsuccessful invasions of Canada, Washington reconciled itself to a continuing British presence along its northern border, but it made clear that the Western Hemisphere was off-limits to other imperial rivals. In 1823 President James Monroe declared: 'The American continents … are henceforth not to be considered as subjects for future colonization by any European powers.'[1]

No longer a target for US military expansion once the Americans and the British achieved a rapprochement in 1906, Canada ultimately became a geographical partner when the old North America found itself facing common overseas enemies and, later, transpolar threats. With the clouds of war gathering on the horizon of both the United States' oceans in 1938, President Franklin Delano Roosevelt set out the first principle of what was to become the North American security-perimeter concept when he pledged in Kingston, Ontario, that 'the people of the United States would not stand idly by if Canadian soil is threatened by any other empire.' Prime Minister Mackenzie King, who presumably recognized Roosevelt's implicit threat of unilateral intervention should Canada not defend itself satisfactorily, immediately responded that Canada would make itself 'immune from attack or possible invasion' so that 'enemy forces should not be able to pursue their way either by land, sea, or air to the United States across Canadian territory.'[2] By agreeing to defend itself against a commonly identified enemy, Canada promised to protect the United States' northern flank and Washington similarly guaranteed – in its own self-interest – Canada's security against foreign threats.

Since this 'Kingston dispensation' was first proclaimed, the continent's northern defence collaboration has evolved through a variety of binational institutional mechanisms.[3] The 1940 Ogdensburg Agreement institutionalized these reciprocal pledges by establishing the Permanent Joint Board on Defence (PJBD), a binational strategic policy-making group made up of equal numbers of senior American and Canadian military and diplomatic personnel who make joint recommendations to their two governments on defence matters.[4] The 1941 Hyde Park Agreement, designed to mobilize the economic resources of the two countries for the war effort, led to the creation of numerous joint committees and boards dedicated to the production of military materiel.[5]

Following the Second World War, the PJBD dealt primarily with broad political and strategic questions inspired by the Soviet threat and was supplemented by a Military Cooperation Committee (MCC) to manage the tactical and operational aspects of defence planning. With the PJBD and the MCC reporting through their national chains of command, Canada and the United States brokered over 80 treaty-level defence agreements, 150 bilateral forums, and 250 memoranda of understanding, the most important of which remains the North American Air Defence Command (NORAD) – all with a considerable degree of symmetry.[6]

Since its establishment in May 1958, NORAD has been led by an American commander-in-chief (CINC NORAD) with a Canadian deputy. Originally assigned the job of detecting and responding to the Soviet bomber threat, the organization was reoriented in the 1960s towards threat-assessment intelligence on the launches and trajectories of intercontinental ballistic missiles (ICBMs). Rechristened in 1981 the North American Aerospace Command to reflect its space-based surveillance capabilities, NORAD had its importance enhanced by the Pentagon's decisions to adopt the Strategic Defense Initiative (SDI) in 1983 and to create a US Space Command in 1985. CINC NORAD concurrently commanded US Space Command, under which SDI was developed.

More recently, NORAD played a central role in the aftermath of the September 11 attacks when, in conjunction with civilian authorities, 142 flights heading for US destinations were redirected to Canadian airports.[7] It also organized combat air patrols to guard against possible attacks, coordinated over 34,000 sorties, and scrambled or diverted fighters more than 1,700 times in response to potential threats. Since September 11, NORAD has been assigned to work with the Federal Aviation Administration and Navigation Canada, monitoring internal flight activity and enforcing both nations' aerospace sovereignty.[8]

Mexico and the United States: A History of Fits and Starts

When the United States entered the Second World War, Mexico temporarily altered its strategic thinking on account of US fears that the Japanese could land in Baja California or the Germans could attack through Mexico's northeastern states.[9] Accordingly, the only exception to Mexico's absence from the defence of the old North America occurred in 1942, when Washington and Mexico City formed the Joint Defence Commission (JDC), a binational consultative body for coordinating the defence of the two countries' Pacific approaches. The United States assigned a permanent military attaché to Mexico and financed the erection of three radar stations that were manned by Mexican soldiers.[10] Mexico's contribution of Escuadrón de Pelea 201 (Fighting Squadron 201) to the joint defence constituted its first participation in a multinational war and required making military service obligatory for all male citizens. In recognition of Mexico's military collaboration, and to resolve its labour shortage, the United States agreed to admit its seasonal agricultural workers under the Bracero program.

Following the Second World War, Mexico again receded from Washington's geo-political consciousness. Preoccupied with containing communism globally, bolstering the North Atlantic alliance regionally, and planning the anti-Soviet defence of their northern approaches with Canada bilaterally, American officials were satisfied by Mexico's stance. Its participation in the Organization of American States (OAS) and other Latin American security initiatives such as the Inter-American Defence Board and the Rio Treaty of 1947 (which sought to provide collective security for the hemisphere against what was perceived as an expansionary communism) allayed US concern about its 'backyard' during an ex-tended period of high anxiety.

This US-Mexico defence relationship lay dormant until 1989, when the first Bush administration sought Mexico's military cooperation in its war on drugs. In an attempt to reactivate the JDC, a special office was opened in San Diego and numerous high-level meetings were held, but Mexican army brass resisted the initiative, which managed only to develop training programs and recommend sales of used military equipment.[11]

Owing in large part to the Mexican constitution,[12] whose principle of non-intervention prohibits the participation of armed forces in external – even multilateral or humanitarian operations – without the consent of Congress, the Mexican military had a limited operational relationship with its American counterparts. And, with the exception of officer participation in training programs – especially peacekeeping – and even more sporadic staff talks, the Mexican military also had minimal contact with Canadian forces.

Budgets and the Military

The United States is investing aggressively in digital defence technologies – 'smart' bombs guided by global-positioning systems, aerial, marine, terrestrial, submersible, and satellite surveillance systems, unmanned aerial vehicles – and is making rapid advances in communications technology. This obliges its allies either to follow suit in order to remain 'interoperable' or risk being unable to conduct combined operations. Most Canadian air and sea forces such as the Halifax-class frigates are fully interoperable with their American counterparts. Mexico's armed services are decidedly not.[13]

The United States outspends Canada, Mexico, and the rest of the world in defence appropriations, the gap having widened drastically after September 2001. Compared to the US$335 billion in fiscal year 2001, military spending in 2003 increased to US$447 billion or around 4 per cent of the country's GDP and now exceeds all other national military budgets combined.[14]

Consequently, extreme asymmetry characterizes the NAFTA partners' military capabilities. The United States currently maintains approximately 1.5 million soldiers and their related civilians. Mexico fields a total force of 240,000 regulars, the majority of whom are in an army whose prime mission is to control domestic instability.[15] Although the Canadian Armed Forces have a comparatively low 60,000 men and women in uniform, their force-projection capabilities surpass Mexico's by virtue of their superior equipment, training, and interoperability with US systems.[16] Canadian defence spending is modest. In 2003 it was US$9.5 billion, a significant portion of which covered the Canadian contribution to the International Security Assistance Force deployment in Afghanistan. At 1.2 per cent of GDP, Canada ties Spain for the second-lowest level of military spending among NATO signatories.[17] Figures on Mexican defence expenditures are still lower. Its US$3.5 billion in 2001 represented 0.60 per cent of domestic GDP.[18]

Terrorism, the Bush Doctrine, and North American Defence

Despite their near monopoly on conventional military force around the world, Americans felt vulnerable at home following the terrorist attacks of September 11, 2001. Washington's subsequent adoption of a new security paradigm aimed at forestalling further attacks on US territory forced Canada and Mexico to accept their neighbour's preoccupation with the terrorist threat. The 2002 National Security Strategy put special emphasis on the military's role in American security and outlined four strategic elements to this end: 'assure our allies and friends; dissuade future military competition; deter threats against US interests, allies, and friends; and decisively defeat any adversary if deterrence fails.' The United States was not to be eclipsed: 'Our forces will be strong enough to dissuade potential adversaries from pursuing a military build-up in hopes of surpassing, or equalling, the power of the United States.'[19]

Following the September attacks, the Bush administration ordered the largest reorganization of the executive branch since the Second World War. Having previously assumed that their military mandate was an 'away game,' US defence planners now had a 'home game' component, requiring significant changes to 'deter, prevent, defeat, or mitigate' the terrorist threat.[20] Accordingly, the Pentagon created a new Northern Command, with responsibility over the greater North American geographic region.[21]

In theory, homeland defence was the military subset of homeland security, but overlap existed with the Department of Homeland Security's twenty-two agencies dealing with the civilian element of security. Northern Command was responsible for preparing the five armed services (including the Coast Guard and the National Guard when federalized) for missions with both the DHS and non-DHS civil agencies. In effect, the DHS and Northern Command shared responsibility for security, with the DHS leading in most civil contingencies and Northern Command responsible for homeland defence.

Northern Command became fully operational on October 1, 2003, with geographic responsibility for continental North America, the Caribbean, and parts of Central America as well as the contiguous area 800 kilometres miles off each coast. Its mandate was to direct, plan, and conduct defence and civil-military support operations within the United States and in conjunction with those countries falling under its area of responsibility, that is, Mexico and Canada in particular. Like the other US regional commands, Northern Command had jurisdiction over only US forces. Few personnel were permanently assigned, most being seconded on an ad hoc basis by US Joint Forces Command.

Command and control were streamlined under one commander-in-chief, who was authorized in times of emergency, subject to approval by the president or secretary of defense, to command the US military's total force within Northern Command's area of responsibility. By centralizing the chain of command, this reorganized increased US capacity for effective oversight and response in the event of emergency or external attack.

Northern Command had formal jurisdiction over the land and sea elements of homeland defence, while NORAD retained responsibility for air surveillance and air defence. This distinction was theoretical, since both were commanded by the same dual-hatted commander-in-chief. The two commands also shared facilities and staff at Peterson Air Force Base in Colorado Springs. They worked together to develop a continental operational picture, incorporating data from air, land, sea, and space-based surveillance platforms – as well as information from intelligence, law enforcement, and civil sources – to provide the 'situational awareness' (real-time knowledge of all activity in a given theatre) necessary for effective defence.

Unlike the other regional commands (excepting Pacific Command, with responsibility for Hawaii), Northern Command was assigned an additional civil-support role in order to give aid to civil authorities when dealing with natural or man-made disasters. However, its mandate to operate within the United States is limited by Posse Commitatus, a federal statute dating back to the post-Civil War period, when stringent limitations were placed on the degree and type of military operations that could be deployed in the absence of a direct military threat.[22]

Northern Command's 'Strategic Vision' acknowledged that a close relationship with Canada and Mexico was critical to the effective defence of the United States and suggested it might require expansion in future years.[23] The vision document also confirmed a close cooperative relationship with NORAD, which could later involve Mexico: 'Ongoing efforts and future discussions to expand defense cooperation with NORAD will depend upon the mutual interests of the United States, Canada, and Mexico.'[24] But as the Plan Merida for security cooperation, explained in chapter XVI, suggests, the war on drugs will remain the US priority for security on its southern border.

While the Pentagon was interested in a trilateral defence arrangement for an augmented NORAD,[25] Northern Command nevertheless re-mained a US-only command, which would 'maintain and improve its capabilities to defend the United States and North America unilaterally or in concert with its allies' and 'continue to serve as the single US-only organization solely focused on homeland defense.'[26] It was conceived as an administrative change; coordinating the continent's defence with Canada and Mexico was only a secondary priority.[27] The Strategic Vision reiterated that, while homeland security involved passive defence, Northern Command constituted the active kind: 'US Northern Command will prepare and defend the homeland via a layered defence in order for the US Department of Defense to conduct the "away game" successfully – to fight terrorism and threats overseas rather than on US territory. The global war on terrorism places a premium on protecting the homeland as a launch platform for power projection forces.'[28]

A secure North America would allow the United States to deploy its defence capabilities overseas – against state-supported terrorism and rogue states such as North Korea. This implied that Canadian/Mexican participation in continental defence would indirectly support the active aspect of US military policy.

The North American Security Perimeter and Canada's Response to NORTHCOM

Immediately following September 11, 2001, the PJBD met to exchange information about each nation's response to the attacks, but no concrete developments followed.[29] Dwight Mason, chair of the US section, nonetheless tabled a proposal to expand NORAD to include land and sea elements and centralize all North America's defence planning.[30] Various other analysts in the US defence-policy community had reached a similar position.[31] The Canadian chair apparently conveyed his government's misgivings about NORAD's institutional expansion, while accepting increased 'cooperation' in principle.[32]

Informal talks addressing areas for greater military cooperation continued between high-level civilian and military officials in the Canadian Department of National Defence (DND) and their US counterparts through the fall of 2001. In January 2002 US officials met in Ottawa formally to discuss deepening defence ties with their Canadian counterparts, who had not achieved an inter-departmental consensus. With US representatives present, a verbal disagreement erupted between representatives from DND and Canada's Department of Foreign Affairs and International Trade, an incident characterized as 'embarrassing' by one witness.[33] DFAIT was perturbed by what was seen as 'ambitious planning' undertaken by DND and the US Department of Defense (DOD) without DFAIT representation.[34]

A week after the announcement of Northern Command, the former secretary of state for foreign affairs, Lloyd Axworthy, and Michael Byers (then at Duke University, now at the University of British Columbia) issued a report that raised numerous questions about the implications for Canadian sovereignty of deeper military cooperation: 'Operational control or command is a de facto form of sovereignty switch.'[35] They worried that Canadian participation in the new command might constrain Canada's ability to abide by its international commitments, affect internal Canadian military policy, and put pressure on the military to fight abroad in the event of US overstretch overseas.[36] This 2002 report, along with the fallout from the 'friendly fire' accident that killed four Canadian soldiers in Afghanistan earlier in April, delayed a joint presentation to cabinet scheduled for later that month by the ministers of defence and foreign affairs. Residual anti-Americanism and the time requirements necessary to find answers to the report's questions persuaded DND officials to delay the presentation.

Binational Planning Group

By June, the Chrétien cabinet had authorized DND and DFAIT to begin negotiations with the United States. In December, Minister of Foreign Affairs Bill Graham exchanged notes with US Secretary of State Colin Powell agreeing to 'enhance Canada-US security cooperation.'[37] The product of this agreement was the Binational Planning Group (BPG), which was mandated to investigate specific ways to strengthen North America's defences. DFAIT's misgivings and a hesitant prime minister appear to have prolonged negotiations by six months, during which time high-level discussions continued both inside Ottawa and with the US government.

The BPG consisted of Canadian and American officers, defence contractors, and civilian representatives specializing in emergency management. Canadian Lieutenant-General E.A. Findley, deputy commander of NORAD, headed the group, which was co-located in Colorado Springs with NORAD and Northern Command.[38] Though the BPG shared personnel and facilities with NORAD/Northern Command, it was not formally integrated into either command. It was commissioned to prepare contingency plans to ensure a cooperative, well-coordinated response to national requests for military assistance in the event of a threat, attack, or civil emergency in Canada and/or the United States; to coordinate maritime surveillance and intelligence cooperation so as to enhance overall awareness of potential maritime threats; to assess maritime threats, incidents, and emergencies; to establish appropriate planning and liaison mechanisms with such civilian authorities involved in crisis response as police, firefighters, and other first responders; to design and participate in exercises; to conduct joint training programs; and to validate the practicality and effectiveness of plans prior to their approval.[39]

The most controversial element in the BPG's mandate concerned transborder emergency operations involving American and/or Canadian land forces in the other's territory. Recognizing public apprehensions about sovereignty, the Chrétien government emphasized that these cross-border cooperative missions would occur only 'under conditions approved by both governments, on a case-by-case basis.' Moreover, should American forces 'ever be required to help respond to an emergency across the border, these forces would come under operational control of the home country.'[40] This meant that American troops operating in Canada would fall under the jurisdiction of the Canadian military/political authorities (albeit with American 'rules of engagement' – i.e., rules for when a soldier may utilize coercive force).

Since US Northern Command's Strategic Vision insists that it 'be structured and capable of defeating national security threats to the United States on a unilateral basis,'[41] combined land operations are highly improbable,[42] although the Canadian navy sent units to lend assistance after the Hurricane Katrina disaster in New Orleans 2005. National forces and existing civil-security agencies already possess the resources to handle most foreseeable contingencies. In addition, Posse Commitatus constrains the US military's ability to train and operate in the domestic sphere and thus limits the US army's capacity to interact with its Canadian and/or Mexican counterparts.

The Binational Planning Group focused on enhancing cooperation in the maritime theatre. Indeed, US Admiral Vernon E. Clark, chief of naval operations (USN), and General Ralph E. Eberhart suggested that the BPG could evolve into something of a 'naval NORAD' that would concentrate on maritime warning and assessment in parallel with the space functions performed by NORAD.[43] Military logic implies, however, that the BPG may develop into something significantly more substantial than a mere binational naval command. An institutional division between NORAD proper and a naval-NORAD would merely complicate defence planning with an operationally meaningless, legalistic distinction, which may nevertheless be judged necessary for political reasons in Canada.

In 2005 the Canadian government announced the creation of a Canada Command, paralleling the structure and functions assigned to Northern Command. By unifying domestic operations under one chief commander, Canada Command was to allow for a more rapid and responsive domestic application of Canadian military resources. For the first time, Canada possessed an integrated chain of command at the national level, along with the authority to deploy maritime, land, and air power in their regional areas of responsibility in support of domestic operations. Once operational, Canada Command would work closely with Northern Command, although it, too, is a national-forces-only command.

The BPG's final report, published in 2006, exemplified political sensitivity: each chapter's recommendations were followed by 'possible impediments to change' under political, cultural, as well as structural headings. Among the BPG's concrete achievements were the drafting of a new Canada-US Basic Defence document, the development of a Combined Defence Plan, a Civil Assistance plan and a binational document library, enhanced strategic maritime cooperation, a redefined relationship among NORAD, Northern Command, and Canada Command, and improved inter-agency cooperation.[44]

It may take years to reveal what this document means in practice. Meanwhile, Canada took an immediately significant step marking its deepening integration within the US military machinery by permanently extending NORAD. Reducing the possibility for democratic oversight, the previous parliamentary review needed for the quadrennial renewal was replaced with a withdrawal option for both countries pending one year's notice.[45] Further, NORAD's 'aerospace control' role was expanded to include 'all domain' warning, which meant that its remit included the satellite surveillance necessary for the United States' ballistic missile program to function.[46]

The Canadian Response to Ballistic Missile Defence (BMD)

The United States had toyed with the missile-defence idea since the 1940s, even deploying a modest, though ineffective, system in the mid-1970s. President Reagan's SDI revived interest in the project, which lost momentum as technological difficulties, high cost-estimates, and a diminishing Soviet threat showed it to be not just unfeasible but superfluous. Motivated by concerns about the changed security environment, the continuing proliferation of ballistic missiles, and increased pressure from a jingoistic Republican Congress, President Clinton signed the National Missile Defense Act, authorizing the US DOD to commence work on a 'reasonably' sized ground-based anti-missile system once the technology allowed.[47]

Despite the tenuous connection between terrorists and ballistic technology, the shock of September 2001 gave the Bush administration the chance to infuse the BMD program with new urgency. In December,

President Bush declared his intention to withdraw from the Anti-Ballistic Missile treaty. Arguing that the doctrine of mutually assured destruction no longer applied, he announced the planned deployment of an initial BMD system by the fall of 2004. Many defence analysts,[48] including forty-nine retired US generals and admirals, lobbied the president to delay what they felt was an untested and deficient system.[49]

The rationale for an operational BMD system was to expand the United States' freedom of action by preventing such rogue nations as North Korea from using the threat of nuclear attack to hold American foreign policy hostage. It was also to protect US citizens and key facilities in the event of either hostile or accidentally launched missiles – in other words, an insurance policy. It was related to terrorism only as a long-term potentiality.

The accelerated rate of BMD development forced Ottawa to reassess its position, because of the feared effects non-participation could have both on Canada's role in NORAD and on Canadian-American relations more generally. The fundamental problem was the overlap between the functions performed by NORAD and those needed for BMD. The Pentagon required NORAD's Integrated Tactical Warning and Attack Assessment (IT/WAA) capability for BMD battle management. In the event of a missile attack, tracking and other information provided by the IT/WAA would be necessary before the BMD system could send up an interceptor missile to attack the incoming weapon. Canadian non-participation in BMD would have required this capability to be transferred to NORTHCOM,[50] with NORAD consequently relegated to responding to hostile threats originating from North America's own airspace.

After an extended period of temporizing, the ministers of national defence and foreign affairs announced an amendment to the NORAD agreement in August 2004, authorizing NORAD to make all missile-warning information available to those regional and functional commands conducting ballistic missile defence. Pierre Pettigrew, the minister of foreign affairs, insisted that the 'amendment safeguards and sustains NORAD regardless of what decision the Government of Canada eventually takes on ballistic missile defence.'[51] With this amendment, Canada effectively maintained its position within NORAD, supporting BMD in practice even if it decided not to endorse it in theory. Canadian officers would thus participate in BMD battle management, albeit in a passive capacity, through NORAD's IT/WAA working seamlessly with Northern Command. In effect, BMD expanded NORAD's mission, blurring the functional – albeit not the institutional – division between the two commands.[52]

Prime Minister Paul Martin's February 2005 decision not to participate in BMD was largely meaningless. Had Canada officially signed on to the program, Canadian NORAD officers would have sat at BMD computer consoles in addition to IT/WAA consoles, located just steps away. In either scenario, launching authority remained within the US chain of command. Minister of National Defence Bill Graham made much of the distinction between NORAD's gathering and evaluating data about a threat and making the decision to launch a missile, as if such decision-making power was ever a possibility for Canada. Canadian anti-BMD opinion was distracted by the Liberals' equivocation, and the August 2004 amendment was enshrined in the 2006 NORAD renewal.[53]

The Mexican Response: Delaying the Inevitable?

Although logic favours the United States cooperating with Mexico in order to extend its defence perimeter away from its homeland, forging a military relationship with Mexico City was a far more difficult challenge for Washington than deepening a historically entrenched relationship with Ottawa. General Eberhart confirmed the Pentagon's efforts to increase cooperation with its southern neighbour by 'leveraging existing relationships with the Mexican military and pursuing efforts to expand assistance to Mexico using counterterrorism and counter-drug funding. In addition, we are working with the National Guard to develop new training opportunities with the Mexican military in a variety of areas.'[54]

The Department of Homeland Security cooperates with Mexico's Centro de Investigación y Seguridad Nacional. In 2003 six inter-agency working groups, each chaired by a bilateral committee, were dedicated to safeguard critical infrastructure in border regions in the energy, transportation, health, agriculture, water, and telecommunications sectors.[55]

With the exception of the Second World War, Mexico had maintained a posture of non-intervention in foreign relations and never collaborated internationally in a military capacity, whether in combat or peacekeeping missions – even under the auspices of the United Nations. When rescuing the civil population after natural catastrophes such as earthquakes and hurricanes – a military mission that was executed successfully in various Central American countries after Hurricane Mitch in 1998 and again in 1999 during flooding in Venezuela[56] – command and control was passed to civilians at the Interior Ministry.[57] The effectiveness of Mexican humanitarian disaster relief was demonstrated after Hurricane Katrina in September 2005, when troops were dispatched to help in the storm's aftermath. Directed by General Francisco Ortiz, Mexican aid took the form of 195 soldiers, physicians, and nurses; 200 tons of food and medicines; mobile kitchens to feed 21,000 people a day; mobile plants for water treatment; and 15 trailers of bottled water. They were received in Laredo, Texas, and directed to San Antonio, where people who had lost their homes in New Orleans had been sent. Twelve other vehicles and rescue helicopters were also sent to the Mississippi coasts.[58]

After President Fox's election victory in 2000, it seemed that the Mexican military's traditional orientation towards internal security might change. His new foreign minister, Jorge Castañeda, signalled a new internationalism by talking about Mexican participation in overseas security initiatives. Fox supported Castañeda's activist foreign-policy inclinations by committing Mexico to entertain invitations for troops to take part in international peacekeeping missions.[59]

After 2001, when the Bush administration lobbied for Mexican involvement in its plans for North America's defence, General Gerardo Clemente Vega Garcia, Mexico's minister of defence, flew to Washington for talks about a new joint agenda in the context of Northern Command. This apparent rapprochement coincided with Castañeda's criticism of Cuba's human-rights record and accompanied Mexico's unprecedented abstention from a vote condemning Cuba at the 57th UN Human Rights Commission, a move that abruptly terminated four decades of close relations with Cuba. The Mexican press criticized both decisions; the PRI opposition in the Senate even claimed that the UN vote on Cuba violated the principle of non-intervention enshrined in Article 89 of the Mexican constitution.[60] Fox's handling of Cuba and Garcia's visit provoked the Senate's refusal to grant him permission to travel to the United States and Canada – punishment for what was considered an overly pro-American line.

Whether the Senate was indulging in partisan posturing or was acting out of genuine concern about respecting the constitution, discomfort over the prospect of defence collaboration with Northern Command was widespread. Both congressional chambers' defence commissions demanded that the presidency supply detailed information about the command's possible impact on Mexico. Going further, the Senate initiated a challenge to the constitutionality of military cooperation with the United States, basing its case on Article 76 of the constitution, which obliges the executive to obtain Congressional approval before deploying Mexican troops overseas.[61] Traditionally anti-American public opinion opposed greater military collaboration, moving US Ambassador Jeffrey Davidow to pen a letter to the newspaper *El Universal* in an attempt to mollify Mexican fears about the new command.[62]

Mexican analysis of the security threat was affected very little by September 11th. That US disagreement with Mexican defence policy derived from differing conceptions of security was underlined by President Fox's withdrawal from the Rio Treaty, which theoretically committed countries to a principle similar to NATO's Article 5 – 'an attack against one is an attack against all.'[63] Just days before September 11, 2001, in a speech at the Organization of American States' headquarters in Washington, President Fox questioned the Rio Treaty's value in the new globalized system, where the hemisphere does not face an extracontinental enemy requiring self-defence through a military alliance. Fox favoured the United Nations (where US influence is substantially lower) to the OAS as the multilateral forum for the Mexican military.

Criticism of Fox's management of the Cuba and Northern Command dossiers and the backlash against his generally pro-American position impelled him to announce Mexico's intended withdrawal from the Rio Treaty. When, in its place, Fox proposed a new regional-security agenda to combat poverty, defend democracy and human rights, promote environmental protection, and continue the fight against transnational organized crime, he made no mention of terrorism, defence, or military solutions.

Fox's signalled exit from the Rio Treaty on the eve of the first anniversary of the September 11 attacks sent a message that was completely at odds with US thinking: a strong rejection of military solutions to the threat posed by global terrorism. Mexican policy makers were more concerned with advancing a broader conception of human security than in supporting Washington's narrower focus on terrorism. Official Washington was not amused.

Officers, not civilians, oversee the Mexican armed forces. Although both answer to the president, the army and navy are independent of each other, with separate chains of command and separate representatives in the president's cabinet. The secretary of defence commands both the army and air force, while the secretary of the navy controls the naval forces. While heading a government institution, each remains an active officer and chief of his respective service. Allocations of the defence budget provide a rough guide to the relative importance of each branch: approximately 75 per cent goes to the army, 5 per cent to the air force, and the remaining 20 per cent to the navy. The departments are constantly fighting over limited funding, the army retaining a dominant position in the deliberative and budgetary process by virtue of Mexico's security concerns, which are primarily internal.

The army is essentially a constabulary force, its domestic responsibilities having expanded after law-enforcement agencies were found either incapable or too corrupt to assure Mexico's internal security. This policing is at odds with most armies' orthodox function to meet external threats. Indeed, the Mexican high military command resists contact with the United States because it does not consider itself able to carry out joint operations with a genuine army. It is better equipped to help civilians in emergencies than to fight real battles. The navy is more professional and so has carried out joint exercises with the American fleet in the Caribbean.[64] Younger, mid-level military officers of the NAFTA-generation, with diplomas from training courses taken in the United States or overseas, exhibit more openness to the prospect of collaborative defence ventures. Like their navy counterparts, they want to modernize, professionalize, and take what they consider their rightful place in the international defence community.[65]

The Mexican armed forces enjoy a greater degree of internal autonomy than their American or Canadian counterparts. This stems from the one-party political system that evolved out of the Mexican revolution when chronic insecurity created the conditions leading to a civil-military pact, wherein the army pledged loyalty to the government party and non-interference in political/governmental matters on condition that the political leadership not intervene in internal military matters and missions. This arrangement persisted until the army's brutal handling of counter-insurgency operations in Chiapas, Guerrero, Oaxaca, and other areas of the south in the 1990s. The inclusion of senior military officers in corruption charges related to narcotics trafficking in the north further sullied the army's reputation, leading to domestic and international demands for greater civilian oversight.

Because of the Mexican military establishment's tremendous influence in the defence decision-making process,[66] US officials have targeted its officers and not the president in their efforts to extend the American defence perimeter into Mexico. Nevertheless, the Mexican military establishment appears content with its domestic focus. Institutional hostility even to the possibility of participating in multilateral peacekeeping was demonstrated by a very senior-ranking Mexican officer. When asked during the Fox presidency if the Mexican armed forces were going to take on peacekeeping duties, his quick and emphatic reply was 'Impossible!'[67]

While not at all impossible, Mexico's military participation in combined operations would require an attitudinal revolution. Mexicans are deeply averse to using 'hard power' to solve international conflict, as was clearly reflected in Mexico's 2003 opposition at the Security Council to the United States' attempt to get UN support for its military attack on Iraq. Having suffered grievously in the nineteenth century from US militarism, Mexicans resist the American tendency to view the world in Manichean terms and to translate problems into some sort of war, whether the 'War on Poverty,' the 'War on Drugs,' the 'First Persian Gulf War,' the 'War on Terror,' or the 'Iraq War.' Their international sensibilities are reflected in the principles endorsing, respect for sovereignty and self-determination that are enshrined in their constitution. A high premium is placed on avoiding involvement in American wars, whether in an active or passive role. The same is true of the desire to inhibit the spread of bellicose American attitudes, especially among officers in the military.[68]

The Mexican navy is more interested in bolstering defence collaboration with the United States than is the army. The secretary of the navy, Admiral Marco Antonio Pierot, and other senior officers have visited the Pentagon and NORAD/Northern Command headquarters in Colorado Springs for briefings and meetings. The navy hopes to leverage its force-projection capabilities through closer cooperation with the United States and so satisfy long-held ambitions to build a blue-water navy (perhaps with outdated US equipment at discounted prices) in exchange for integrating maritime surveillance (financed by US funding) and coordinating naval-response measures.[69]

Except for the 2007 Merida initiative, there are no official plans on Mexico's part to increase defence cooperation with the United States. Most discussions regarding continental defence are conducted behind closed doors, hidden from an unsupportive Mexican public. Secretary Pierot had to tread lightly, especially following a controversy in 2002 when naval exercises involved a multinational consortium of Latin American navies under US sponsorship and using US ships organized by US Southern Command. The PRI-dominated Congress was shocked to learn that the navy had contributed a frigate to the exercises. Pierot subsequently appeared before Congress, where he fought and won a bitter debate similar to the one held in Ottawa some months earlier over Northern Command.[70] This outcome established the precedent that extra-territorial combined military exercises do not constitute a violation of the constitution, even if they use live ammunition. Combined exercises remain one of the most immediate of the Pentagon's wishes, but cooperation between the two navies beyond the new norm will undoubtedly require substantial attitudinal, political, and even constitutional change.[71]

The Mexican army's attitude towards enhanced military cooperation is complicated. By all accounts, the two sides are talking at a higher level and tempo than ever before, but they remain cautious. High- and mid-level meetings between the two countries accelerated after 2001. General Vega's trip to Washington in April 2002 responded to Pentagon officials' visit a few months earlier, when an invitation to participate in Northern Command was extended. He has subsequently revisited the American capital periodically.[72]

Recognizing the Mexican army's hesitancy (and/or hostility), the US DOD has adopted a two-pronged strategy, encouraging confidence-building measures at high levels and accelerating military sales and training.[73] The Pentagon wants to create and maintain favourable relations with the army leadership, while making it more dependent on US equipment, doctrines, and information. But, even if the Mexican government was more disposed towards greater defence cooperation, it would take concerted political will to make the army change its traditionally domestic mission orientation.[74]

Government with Governance

Analysing North American defence cooperation necessarily focuses on the three governments and their officialdoms' manoeuvrings. Defence relations among the NAFTA partners remain a top-down process, fully in keeping with orthodox models of international relations. This section broadens the analysis by considering the contributions of non-state actors to defence governance in North America.

The testimony of numerous officials and academics from the North American defence/security community indicates that governance is a marginal element in the defence policy-making process in North America. While business organizations, academia, and citizens' groups engage in small amounts of transnational politicking, the impact of these contributions is minimal. NORTHCOM's creation has not altered this fundamental reality in Canada-US defence relations, which remain predominantly inter-governmental.

In the United States, the defence industry has shown itself far more preoccupied with winning contracts for armament manufacturing and reconstruction in Iraq and Afghanistan than for homeland defence. Northern Command has generated little increased funding, with the exception of BMD, which is only tangentially part of its mission. Crudely put, the profit trail does not lead to Colorado Springs, although the American defence industry's presence there has increased. US personnel shortages have required the increased use of retired military officers employed and paid by US defence manufacturers but working for the US Department of Defense to fill positions on the BPG.[75] This makes business indirectly involved in continental defence planning, consolidating relations between the Pentagon and the US defence industry and freeing up scarce resources in return for preferred status when contracts relating to other missions are awarded.

Overt transborder US lobbying of Canadian officials is superfluous, since the horizontal integration of the North American defence industry's base allows American TNCs to lobby less conspicuously through their Canadian branch-plant offices.[76] As a result of low Canadian defence expenditures and limited trade in armaments, the political clout of the Canadian defence lobby remains small, so that US transnational corporate influence on governmental decision makers seems incidental. More generally, US business has expressed little concern about enhancing military cooperation with Canada.

In contrast, Canadian business has exhibited decidedly greater interest in defence relations between the two nations, adopting an aggressive strategy to ingratiate itself with the Bush administration. Articulated by the C.D. Howe Institute following September 11, the 'Big Idea' – which supported committing Canadian troops to the Iraq war and recommended that Ottawa negotiate a comprehensive trade, security, and even monetary policy package to deepen the bilateral relationship – gained currency within the Canadian business community. Calls for a Fortress North America were made to pre-empt the erection of a Fortress United States, a scenario that would have spelled disaster for Canadian business's quest for unhindered access to the American market. At the vanguard of this pro-continentalist initiative was the Canadian Council of Chief Executives, an organization representing over

150 of Canada's most powerful companies. With the passage of time and the evident disaster in Iraq, the CCCE exhibited greater moderation. By 2004, its paper *New Frontiers: Building a 21st Century Canada-United States Partnership in North America* merely suggested that the expansion of NORAD should include land and sea forces and immediate involvement in BMD.[77]

Although Canadian big business has a tremendous amount invested in deepening continent integration, the Canadian defence-industry lobby lacks clout within it. Total Canadian exports of defence-related articles to the United States amounts to $2 billion dollars annually[78] – a meagre figure compared to the almost $400 billion worth of exports shipped from Canada in 2003. Still, Canadian corporate elites are known to adopt their US counterparts' attitudes and priorities. Given the weakness of Canada's military-industrial complex, the Martin and Harper governments' repeated increases of their military budgets and their extraordinary commitment to deadly counter-insurgency operations in Afghanistan in the mid-2000s were undoubtedly promoted by the business community's commitment to placating Washington by reshaping Canada's defence policy.

In Canada, such organizations as the Institute for Research on Public Policy, the Canadian Institute of International Affairs, and the Polaris Institute have published numerous articles and held various colloquia on North American defence/security issues, as has the US Center for Strategic and International Studies and the Center for Defense Information. Academics, officials, and interested citizens from Canada, the United States, and Mexico have also met at various fora to exchange information and ideas.[79] The impact of academic contributions on governance is oblique; it facilitates ideas, which sometimes are translated into policy.

Of the non-state actors surveyed here, citizen's groups make the most marginal contribution to continental defence governance. No known US groups are against increased military cooperation with Canada, although such opponents of BMD as the Global Network against Weapons and Nuclear Power in Space[80] and Spacewar.com[81] are vocal dissidents. In Canada, the Canadian Peace Alliance,[82] People against the Weaponization of Space,[83] Science for Peace,[84] and the Council of Canadians[85] rallied in opposition to increased ties with the US military in general and BMD in particular. The general Canadian public tends to be evenly divided on military issues outside a distinctly less militaristic Quebec.

This is not the case in Mexico, where anti-American public opinion is deep-rooted, rejecting subordinate status with its neighbour and very sensitive to the danger of Mexico losing sovereignty in its relations with the United States. These perceptions are strongest relating to security and defence, which explains Mexico's minimal military cooperation with the neighbours. Given Vicente Fox's own pro-American proclivities, Mexican civil society has to be considered a significant element of military governance, since it deflected the government from its preferred trajectory.

Armed forces' structures and actors have legitimacy through the authority delegated to them by their respective national governments. Ultimate authority resides with these politicians, even though they are only partially involved in the ongoing deliberative process. Because members of the military in NORAD operate with delegated authority to function on behalf of the state with representatives of another state, they can be considered as participating in transborder military government. The United States' preponderance creates asymmetries, which have to be factored into any analysis of hemispheric defence. Its search for maximum security and total collaboration in the war against terrorism leads it to press for multilateral coordination at all levels. To achieve this, it employs all the available instruments – military, intelligence, legal, diplomatic – as the basis for seeking optimal cooperation with allies through revitalizing existing agreements.[86]

For its part, Mexico has no foreign military policy, its international military stance being determined by the foreign policy of the Secretaría de Relaciones Exteriores. In this respect, the military is subordinated to the president and the traditional diplomatic elite.[87]

So we can see that, in North American defence, governments matter. Authoritative testimony suggests that governance plays almost no role in shaping Canadian defence policy.[88] The Canadian government retains formal sovereignty over its decision-making process, wielding de jure control over the armed forces. Its military capacity abroad is low, and it has little autonomy when it comes to continental defence matters within NORAD. The Mexican government retains formal sovereignty over its decision-making process and wields de jure but not de facto control over its armed forces, which continue to exercise a traditional veto right. It has negligible military capacity abroad but has complete autonomy when it comes to defence matters because of its non-participation in NORAD or other joint military institutions.

Bilateral Canadian-American institutional integration is highly advanced within NORAD and expanded strategic cooperation is high on the US list of defence priorities. The Pentagon has forged deepened links with Canada, and could do the same with Mexico in the future. A trilateral defence architecture is possible, but it will be contingent on US leadership, its sensitivity to Mexican (and Canadian) concerns, and the degree to which Mexico and Canada are willing to cooperate. However, the United States remains essentially imperial in military matters: it will never allow itself to be seriously constrained by any junior partner. Trilateral cooperation would essentially mean two bilateral defence arrangements developing at different speeds and associated in some way with NORTHCOM as the dominant and decisive agency in North American defence.

Conclusion

At the political level, broad questions of strategy will remain the prerogative of each government, although common policies could be implemented at the tactical and operational level. Divergences in strategic-defence policy will continue to be settled as they are now – politically. Closer ties with the United States on defence will lead to the continued adoption of US equipment and doctrines, while convergence in the values and attitudes of officers will likely continue as well. The means of doing business will become harmonized, but not necessarily the ends. Whether such harmonization will place upward pressure on politicians in the periphery to adopt unwanted policies remains to be seen, though NORAD's relative success suggests that tactical and operational integration in passive defence does not necessarily translate into common active defence – a case in point being the war in Iraq. Absent a possible clash between government policy and public opinion over military operations in Afghanistan, civil society in Canada will remain on the sidelines. In sum, present trends indicate the continued existence of three distinct national defence polities in North America, despite enhanced defence ties. Such enhanced cooperation notwithstanding, the United States will continue to take the lead in defining defence relations in North America, and Canada and Mexico will continue to respond in their distinct and opposite ways.

Although Northern Command's decisions have an impact on the defence of the whole continent, one cannot speak of defence governance in the new North America without Mexico's participation. In the old North America, a more comprehensive institutional mechanism in the shape of a super-NORAD has been realized only very partially. The Binational Planning Group merely recommended various options. In sum, the revival of the United States' military machine following September 2001 has recreated a transborder governance profile familiar during the Cold War. Within an overwhelming asymmetry in fighting capacity, Canada reactivated its willing junior-partner role by integrating itself into the United States' global military strategy. Still faithful to its revolutionary credo, a militarily weak Mexico remained autarchic, while its officers contemplated the temptations of partnering with the Pentagon and joining the continental hegemony. Transborder military governance in North America remains just what it has always seemed – traditional inter-governmental relations that are highly asymmetrical and deeply skewed.

There would be a stronger case to be made that the new North America has developed trinational governance if its governmental relations amounted to more than just the two asymmetric dyads made up of the US hub's individual dealings with its northern and southern neighbours. For this reason, I cannot end my examination of the continent's existence without a glance at North America's third, if lesser, relationship, the one linking the two periphery states themselves. This is the task of chapter XVIII.

XVIII The Third Bilateral: The Mexico-Canada Relationship

A remarkable feature of the old North America was Canada's manifest disinclination – in terms of both economic self-interest and intellectual curiosity – to connect with Mexico. The opposite was equally true: even though Mexico's exports to Canada were considerable, its political and cultural connections were minimal. This chapter first reports how Canada and Mexico gradually developed a bilateral relationship of their own once NAFTA linked them within a formal economic arrangement, helping to stimulate increased commercial interrelations. It was not a matter of love at first sight when senior trade officials came to know each other during the NAFTA negotiations. On the contrary, Ottawa was at first wary lest becoming involved with Mexico City might somehow contaminate its historically cosy relationship with Washington. By the 2000s, however, the two capitals found growing reasons to collaborate in the face of their common problem – the Americans' paranoia about terrorism and their resulting obsession with its security.[1]

The second part of this analysis examines the seasonal farm-migration program between Canada and Mexico which, though small in numbers and profile, has long linked together the two peripheral countries of NAFTA in a mutually beneficial fashion. Despite the inequities inherent in this program, it shows that Canada and Mexico are able, despite the overbearing presence of the United States in North America, to partner independently in some small but mutually supportive ways.

1990s: Negotiating and Implementing NAFTA

The NAFTA negotiations marked a watershed from which the new bilateral relationship flowed, tentatively at first when negative factors predominated but then with greater assurance as more positive forces started to prevail over the course of the decade. Having always been marginal to Canada, Mexico had suddenly impinged alarmingly on Ottawa's vital relationship with Washington. This happened in 1991, when Prime Minister Brian Mulroney persuaded the American and Mexican presidents to let him intrude on their impending economic-integration negotiations. He feared that his southern rival might obtain competitive advantages that would make it more attractive to foreign investment or gain it superior access to the US market, thereby jeopardizing something for which he knew he had paid a very high price in negotiating CUFTA just four years previously.

Inklings of future collaboration were present from the beginning. Mexican trade officials sought their Canadian counterparts' advice about how to involve the business community in the negotiating process (as discussed in chapter VII). Civil-society connections briefly blossomed as Mexican labour and environmentalist leaders, along with some academics and policy experts, turned to their Canadian counterparts in order to learn what lessons they might garner from Canada's experience with CUFTA (chapters IV and V).

Having a seat at the negotiating table, Canadian officials came to know their Mexican interlocutors. In cases such as the energy negotiations, the Canadians abstained: CUFTA's energy provisions were retained while Washington went toe to toe with Mexico City, unsuccessfully trying to crack open the Mexican petroleum market for US participation. In reworking CUFTA's dispute-settlement mechanism, Canada was fully engaged. Although the Canadian team resisted Washington's attempt to introduce investor-state arbitration, Mexico declared it a deal breaker since it wanted to assure foreign investors that they would be fully protected. Canada gave way, as recorded in chapter III.

The ensuing years of NAFTA implementation gradually increased interactions and mutual knowledge among the two periphery governments' senior officials. In some situations, their collaboration took the form of further hands-on participation in such NAFTA-spawned committees as the trilateral working group to negotiate accelerated tariff reductions that took place in July 1997 and August 1998. In other situations, the officials representing one government watched with interest as their counterparts struggled with the United States. The Canadians took note of Washington's foot dragging in Mexico's Chapter 20 trucking case; Mexicans kept a watching brief on Canada's interminable vicissitudes with Washington in the Chapter 19 softwood-lumber case.

Thereafter, economic relations strengthened. From 1990 to 2000, Mexico's exports to Canada rose 242 per cent, and, from 2000 to 2006, they rose a further 69 per cent, keeping Canada as Mexico's second-largest market. Although Canada's exports to Mexico grew 73 per cent from 1990 to 2000, they remained a minuscule 0.5 per cent of its international market. From 2000 to 2006, they grew a relatively insignificant 54 per cent more. For its part, Mexican investment in Canada was negligible, growing by one-third, from a tiny $161 million in 1995 to a mere $215 million in 2000 and $277 million in 2006, but Canadian direct investment in Mexico multiplied thirteen times in five years, from $294 million to $3.9 billion in 2000 and a not insignificant $4.4 billion in 2006.[2]

As bilateral economic relations developed between the two countries – particularly through transborder production chains in the auto sector – their respective embassy officials had more work to do. But bilateral cooperation did not follow a steadily climbing curve. The two diplomatic machines continued to compete with each other for Washington's favours, since each country's relationship with the United States remained its overwhelming priority. As well, both Canada and Mexico continued to negotiate their own free-trade agreements with other states, confirming the marginality of the still-weak third NAFTA bilateral.

Some related multilateral issues supported the growing relationship. In the ultimately failed project to negotiate a Free Trade Area of the Americas, Canada and Mexico shared both a common commitment to strengthening international trade rules and a common interest in sustaining (on Mexico's part) and generating (on Canada's) relationships with the rest of Latin America that could help offset the two countries' hyperdependence on the US market.

Other multilateral endeavours were cause for tension. Ottawa's efforts in the late 1990s to deepen international human-rights norms were threatening to a Mexico City which, still under PRI rule, resisted expanded notions of human security that might legitimize other countries' right to question its own democratic deficits. And some economic issues proved contentious. A serious direct dispute erupted over the Quebec company Bombardier's bid for a contract to renew the rolling stock in Mexico City's subway system.

The United States remained the elephant in the room. Nothing either government contemplated doing with the other would be allowed to compromise its relationship with its main export market, its main supplier of imports, its main source of foreign investment, and its main locus of technology. Washington remained contested territory. Engulfed with nostalgia for the significant special relationship of earlier times – when Canada had been an indispensable military ally in the Second World War and played a valuable Cold War role in the North Atlantic alliance – Canadian diplomats resisted being associated in US politicians' minds with a Mexico that translated politically as illegal immigration and narco-traffic. At the same time, Ottawa and Mexico City were attracted to each other as partners who could increase their leverage in Washington when their positions coincided on such issues as US agricultural subsidies.

Meanwhile, other types of bilateral collaboration developed in domestic affairs. Following a memorandum of understanding signed in 1996, Elections Canada assisted enthusiastically in the establishment of the Instituto Federal Electoral, which became one of the world's best-rated electoral institutions.[3] On the economic front, considerable promotional efforts climaxed in 1996 with a blitz visit by the Chrétien government's Team Canada to court contacts and sign contracts. But results were not spectacular.

While the economic links grew, the political relationship became more noteworthy. The two foreign services recognized each other's importance. DFAIT established a special division dealing with Mexico and beefed up its embassy in Mexico City. The Mexican foreign office created an undersecretariat for North American affairs and expanded its embassy in Ottawa. Visits back and forth multiplied between senior officials in various departments and secretariats. Summit meetings between the two heads of government increased in frequency and substance. President Zedillo's visit to Ottawa in 1996 prompted the signing of a Declaration of Objectives for the Mexico-Canada Relationship. Its Action Plan was extended at the 13th Joint Ministerial Committee meeting of February 1999.[4] In short, the two governments had developed a viable working relationship by the end of the millennium.

But distrust and disconnect lingered below the surface. When a former governor of the state of Chihuahua was triumphantly elected president of Mexico in July 2000 and when the former governor of Texas was declared president of the United States five months later, Canadian diplomats in Washington were far from delighted. Since Vicente Fox and George Bush were territorial neighbours, fellow conservatives, wear-it-on-their-sleeve Christians, and political friends, the embassy staff worried that it would not be able to get attention paid to Canadian issues by an Administration that more automatically looked south than north. When Fox reiterated his campaign proposal to refashion NAFTA with more effective institutions that could transfer funding from the two rich partners to help develop desperately needed infrastructure in Mexico, Prime Minister Jean Chrétien was notably cool. The government of Canada had nourished amicable diplomatic relations with Mexico, but it was not about to endorse European-style practices of economic equalization and social solidarity in order to promote a competitor economy.

Still, it was not saying a great deal to affirm that, by the time the Summit of the Americas convened in Quebec City in April 2001, Mexico had become Canada's main partner in Latin America. The focal point of the gathering – the Free Trade Area of the Americas – turned out to be doomed but, by this point, Canada and Mexico had at least become familiar, though not intimate, associates in the new North America. This hesitant bilateral relationship would end up helping both countries through the crisis in continental governance that followed from what seemed to them to be the United States' extreme reaction to the terrorist attacks perpetrated on September 11, 2001.

2000s: Continuing Crisis after September 11, 2001

While it may be excessive to claim that September 11, 2001 changed the world forever, it certainly changed North America. This was because of four notable effects that Washington's reaction had on the bilateral relationship between Canada and Mexico.

Border Blockade

The United States' virtual blockade of its own confirmed first that NAFTA had not, after all, guaranteed secure access for the periphery to the US market. That Canada and Mexico did not even call an emergency meeting of NAFTA's' Free Trade Commission to challenge Washington's unilateral behaviour indicated how inconsequential they considered NAFTA's institutions to be. Nor was a trinational summit convened to consider how North America's economic intercourse should continue under the terrorist spectre.

Afghanistan

Mexico's cool official response to the al-Qaeda attack instantly chilled the once-effusive Fox-Bush friendship. By contrast, Canada was inti-

mately involved in the crisis: a Canadian was acting commander of
NORAD on that day, directing air force surveillance. Skilled air-traffic
professionals guided 1,500 aircraft to safe landings on the 11th, including 239 diverted aircraft – most of which had been en route from
Europe for the United States – to Canadian airports across the country
where they were offered warm hospitality in makeshift circumstances.[5]

The second US response to the September attacks – the invasion of
Afghanistan – confirmed how alien the Canadian and Mexican military
cultures were from each other. Mexico's constitution forbade troops
being sent abroad, and Mexico's public opinion constrained President
Fox or his staff from expressing even moral support for the US operation to oust the Taliban. Though Ottawa's commitment of troops on the
ground was delayed, 750 soldiers were eventually sent in February
2002 to fight under American command in Afghanistan. On this issue
there was no solidarity between Canada and Mexico.

'Smart Borders'

The next US response to 9/11 – Washington's negotiating 'Smart Border' agreements with Canada and Mexico – showed how inconsequential was the third bilateral relationship in issues of concern to the
United States, which still dealt with Ottawa and Mexico City as if they
were completely separate spokes emanating from its control hub. Even
when the periphery acceded to American pressure for increased security along the two borders, the trilateral relationship was nowhere to be
seen. Washington first negotiated its thirty-point deal with Ottawa in
the autumn of 2001; no direct consideration was given to Mexico's
stance on security issues. Instead of working out a trilateral agreement
on security, the US administration bound its two neighbours in separate agreements. Using the Canadian deal as a template – the Canadian
government had informally communicated the agreement's contents to
its Mexican counterpart – the United States reached a twenty-two-point
border agreement with Mexico City, which was signed the following
February.

Iraq

Washington's fourth response, its invasion of Iraq, showed how Canada
and Mexico could transcend Washington's divide-and-rule approach
by cooperating in the multilateral arena. Seventeen months after Sep-

tember 11, Prime Minister Chrétien visited President Fox in Mexico City as part of a coalition of the unwilling states which were trying to delay or divert the impending US blunder. Although the Liberal prime minister had refused to consider deepening NAFTA's trilateral governance, he enthusiastically supported Mexico, then occupying one of the non-permanent seats of the United Nations' Security Council, in its opposition to the US position. Ottawa and Mexico had chosen to bowl alone before when dealing with US domestic security concerns. They had bowled separately in Afghanistan, despite the international consensus supporting US military action there. But they bowled together with a multilateral community that was strongly opposed to the United States' pre-emptive war against Iraq.

Developing Ties, Post-September 11

In addition to their federal governments, other players in Mexico and Canada had become more interactive. The government of Quebec had operated an autonomous delegation in Mexico City for two decades, leading the way for Ontario and then Alberta to send representatives who were housed in the Canadian Embassy. Canadian and Mexican activists in environmental, labour, educational, and religious organizations had maintained some, albeit more distant, communications in the decade following their intense cooperation in opposition to the NAFTA negotiations. Some cities twinned. Some Canadian provinces connected with counterpart Mexican states.

During these ten years, while the relationship between Canada and Mexico slowly became more complex, the two economies also grew closer. By 2004, bilateral trade had tripled – admittedly from a small base – reaching US$12 billion.[6] For Canada, Mexico was its fourth export market but its first in Latin America. Aroused by the sense that NAFTA had made business possibilities more secure in this foreign setting, some 1,400 Canadian companies, many of small and medium size, had invested $3.2 billion there. For Mexico, Canada had become its third foreign investor and fourth trading partner after the United States, Japan, and the entire European Union.[7]

With its war in Iraq diverting the US Administration's attention from its continental relations and with Congress' and the Department of Homeland Security's concerns causing continuing tensions along the borders, the two periphery states started to reframe their relationship. Once again, the initiative came from the south and was initially resisted in Ottawa. President Fox called for a new strategic partnership with Canada on the day he was elected in 2000. Paul Martin, who had become Canada's prime minister in January 2004, confirmed his predecessor's disinterest in deepening NAFTA's institutions by repeatedly emphasizing his commitment to a reactivated US relationship. By setting up and chairing a special cabinet committee to handle US relations, he reaffirmed Ottawa's historic concentration on achieving – and nostalgia for nurturing – intimate relations with Washington.

Never shy about embracing contradictory positions, Martin nevertheless committed himself to enhancing Ottawa's connection with Mexico City. And, as a second-best position when actual relations with Washington deteriorated – which they quickly did when the prime minister resisted President Bush's pressure to support the US Ballistic Missile Defense program – it did make sense to coordinate positions with Mexico. There was a natural convergence of interests when the two governments both differed from Washington (NAFTA dispute settlement), when they defended common positions (opposing US proposals requiring American citizens to have passports at the border), or when they wanted to avoid being isolated and played off against each other by the United States. It also made sense to raise the third bilateral relationship to a new level for its own sake.

Modelled on the quadripartite Partnership for Prosperity, which the United States and Mexico signed in 2003 to bring business into closer coordination with government on specific bilateral issues, the Canada-Mexico Partnership (CMP) was announced to considerable fanfare in October 2004. The CMP consisted of five working groups – urban housing, sustainable cities, human capital, competitiveness, and agribusiness. Four-headed in its leadership, each was to be chaired by representatives from each government and a representative from civil society or the private sector in each country. The working group on competitiveness, for example, was chaired on the Canadian side by an official from Industry Canada and Thomas d'Aquino, chairman of the Canadian Council of Chief Executives, and, on the Mexican side, by an official from the Secretaría de la Economía and Roberto Newell, president of the Mexican Institute for Competitiveness.

Three years after their establishment, it was difficult to assess these groups' accomplishments. The working group on sustainable cities closed down once Industry Canada terminated the funding which had supported Canadian developers trying to export their technology for landfill sites and water systems.[8] The human-capital working group involved the Association of Universities and Colleges of Canada with the Canadian Education Centre – a marketing arm in Mexico for post-secondary educational institutions. But the scope of these committees seemed small. For all the good intentions expressed about facilitating academic exchanges, the government of Canada offered a mere four-teen scholarships for Mexican university students in 2006; also in that year, only 2,658 visas were issued for Mexican students, half of whom went to learn English in Canadian high schools.[9] Of DFAIT's interna-tional academic program budget, the $540,000 allocated that year for Mexico represented 5 per cent of its global expenditures and 24 per cent of its outlays for North America.[10]

The working groups' meetings were closed to observers and they published no reports of their activities or recommendations. Interviews suggested that the structure was stumbling under its own weight, with the chief players spending inordinate amounts of time attending meet-ings of committees with overlapping mandates. The diplomats in charge were driven by the process, spending their time getting meet-ings organized. Excessively bureaucratic and largely dependent on Canadian government funding, the groups appeared oriented to do lit-tle more than help the Canadian private sector drum up some business in Mexico.

Modest though they may have been in policy production, the value added by the Partnership appeared to be its contribution to sustaining a high level of interaction between the two countries' federal gov-ernments and selected members of their civil societies. Ottawa felt supported when Vicente Fox, attending a bilateral summit meeting in Vancouver in October 2005, endorsed the Canadian position on NAFTA's dispute-settlement processes, even though the softwood-lumber case was an entirely US-Canada issue. For its part, the Mexican government appreciated Prime Minister Stephen Harper's attendance at Felipe Calderón's contested inauguration.

By 2007, George W. Bush was worse than a lame duck. His foreign policy had proven an unmitigated disaster, making collaboration on multilateral issues impossible. As far as his domestic agenda affected Mexico, he had failed to improve the treatment of immigrants at the border, where vigilantism and wall-building prevailed. With no hope for serious relations being re-established with Washington until the change of administration in January 2009, the new Canadian prime minister and the even newer Mexican president realized that they could push ahead on some common continental issues by having their two governments work with each other.

There was much to work on. Calderón was recalibrating Mexico's relationship with Latin America in general and Cuba in particular, trying to fix the damage done by his predecessor. For Harper's part, having signalled his disinterest in Africa, he had affirmed that Latin America was to have a special priority. With Mexico its prime Latin relationship, this implied that Canada was interested in further developing that relationship inside or outside NAFTA. On the level of personal relations, President Calderón spent family time at the prime minister's summer residence before the 2007 Montebello meeting of the Security and Prosperity Partnership of North America. A necessary item on their agenda for discussion was the long-standing, generally amicable relationship that the two countries had developed in labour-market relations.

The Special Bilateral Labour Relationship: SAWP

If North America existed as a genuine common market in the way Europe does, there would be free movement of labour across its national boundaries. In the case of Mexico and the United States, if labour flows are the criterion by which international integration is measured, then integration may be seen as impressively high, despite Washington's efforts to blockade and suppress the inflow of Mexican immigrants. For the other two bilateral relationships, however, the situation is much different. With the exception of the TN visa discussed in chapter I, labour integration between Canada and the United States is surprisingly low. As for the third bilateral relationship, which connects two countries that are separated by a great physical and psychic distance, labour integration remains minimal, again with one exception – the agricultural sector.

While the massive and illegal movement of Mexican labour into the United States is widely discussed,[11] much less is known about the governance of Mexican migrant labour in Canada. There is one aspect of this subject, however, that has attracted the attention of sociologists, lawyers, and civil-society organizations: the Seasonal Agricultural Workers Program (SAWP), an initiative that started over four decades ago and now brings some 13,000 migrant farmhands from Mexico to work in Canada every year. Although the workers moving back and forth from Mexico to Canada are relatively few in number, the governance of this legal human traffic offers a revealing glimpse into how the government of Canada exercises its autonomy (control at home) and capacity (power abroad) within North America's third dyad.

In this bilateral arrangement between the two peripheral states in North America, the Canadian government has been able to set the terms, little constrained by global norms or NAFTA and only slightly limited by concerns over human rights. Pressures from globalization notwithstanding, the Canadian state has retained substantial control over guest-worker flows, as can be seen in the following examination of the policy's origins, the federal government's managerial role, and the entrance of civil-society into its governance.

Origins

SAWP's Canadian origins lie in the broad socio-economic changes following the Second World War, when family farms consolidated and agricultural labour left for other, more industrialized sectors of the economy.[12] From 29 per cent of the Canadian workforce in 1941, agricultural labour had dropped to 8 per cent by 1966.[13] Nevertheless, the need for farmhands persisted because growers had difficulty obtaining reliable workers – a particularly acute problem in the horticultural sector, where growing vegetables and fruits continued to be labour-intensive and time-sensitive. Even labourers willing to remain on the land often had outside jobs that took them away from the farms during the harvest season, when produce cannot wait and much of a crop can be lost if not picked at the right moment.[14] Foreign workers, with no social or family ties in Canada and restricted labour-market mobility within the domestic market, came to be seen as the only viable solution to this problem.

As the labour shortage and growers' demands persisted, the federal government eventually arranged the organized importation of seasonal workers from the Caribbean. The 1966 Seasonal Agricultural Workers Program was designed to provide growers with the reliable workforce they needed because contracts would bind workers to a single employer, thus eliminating the risk of their being lured away by better conditions offered in other sectors. A flexible and responsive system, SAWP would import workers for the periods in which they were required and return them home when they were no longer needed. The restrictions on the labour mobility of workers imported through SAWP and the provision that these workers would not have citizenship rights meant that the rural labour shortage could be alleviated without leading to the then perceived dangers of widespread Black immigration to Canada.[15]

By 1974, the Non-Immigrant Employment Authorization Program (NIEAP) had established the legal category of 'foreign worker' – a non-citizen whose mobility can be restricted without violating the constitutional rights guaranteed to Canadian citizens. NIEAP provided the statutory umbrella under which SAWP was expanded to include Mexico.[16] During the period in which the program was being designed, Ontario farmers had been paying brokers to import Mexican Mennonites to work in their fields with their wives and their children. The Department of Manpower and Immigration reported that the workers were kept in deplorable conditions and recommended a formal agreement with Mexico.[17]

As a result of increasing demand, a program that in its first year admitted 264 Jamaican workers came to process close to 20,000 workers annually from Mexico and the Caribbean, 85 per cent being employed in Ontario and concentrated in areas that specialized in fruit, vegetables, and tobacco.[18] Mexican participation in the program grew steadily over the years: from one-fifth in 1987 to half of all arrivals in 2006.[19] More than 98 per cent are men.[20]

The Canadian Government's Dominant Role

SAWP's labour-recruitment process starts in Canada, where growers communicate their needs to local Human Resources and Skills Development Canada (HRSDC) offices at least eight weeks prior to the employment period. Once approved by HRSDC, a grower's request for foreign labour is transferred to Foreign Agriculture Resource Management Services (FARMS), a private-sector, grower-run, user-fee-funded organization to which many of SAWP's administrative functions were downloaded in 1987. FARMS notifies officials in Mexico's Secretaría del Trabajo y Previsión Social (STPS, Ministry of Work and Social Security) of its requirements and makes travel arrangements for the workers. After STPS recruits the workers, the Secretaría de Relaciones Exteriores administers further documentation. Subsequently, the Canadian Embassy reviews the relevant paperwork and issues work permits.[21]

The Canadian growers provide workers with housing and pay them the prevailing rates, generally the minimum wage. They also pay for the workers' travel expenses, which may be partially recuperated from their pay. Other deductions include contributions to the Canada Pension Plan, Employment Insurance (EI), and workers' compensation.[22] The provincial governments are responsible for ensuring that the relevant labour, health, and employment statutes are upheld. Mexican officials in Canada meet workers at the airport, inform them of their rights and responsibilities, and deliver them to the growers or their representatives.[23]

The contract that the recruits sign at the STPS affirms that their Canadian employers will provide all the basic services, but compliance remains problematic.[24] While Mexican consular officials are tasked with monitoring living and working conditions on farms, the consulates do not have sufficient staff to carry out this function. For instance, in 2002 there were only five Mexican officers to service 7,633 Mexican workers in Ontario. Moreover, these same officials are assigned conflicting responsibilities. In resolving disputes that arise between workers and growers, they are not merely responsible for representing workers; they must also act as mediators and propitiate the growers by preventing the escalation of troubles and helping repatriate 'troublesome' workers.[25]

SAWP makes a Third World labour supply the linchpin in Canada's internationally competitive horticultural sector.[26] The agriculture and agri-food industry accounted for 8.3 per cent of Canada's gross domestic product in 2003, when its exports were valued at $24.4 billion.[27] Since the early 1990s, Canada has substantially increased its export of tomatoes and cucumbers to the United States and even to Mexico, shifting from being a net importer to a net exporter of that vegetable. While the total number of Canadian workers in sectors using SAWP labour declined by more than 27 per cent between 1983 and 2000, the number of SAWP workers increased by 72 per cent in the same period.[28] Migrant workers have become a crucial structural component of Canada's export-oriented agricultural sector.

Premised on the importation of a flexible, temporary, and vulnerable migrant labour force that can be deployed as needed, Canada's strategy for becoming internationally competitive in the export of labour-intensive agricultural produce illustrates how the Canadian government can exercise its autonomy within the confines of its external constitution.[29] For, in managing this transborder flow of labour, Canada has partly avoided coming under the norms of global governance. When signing their memorandum of understanding, Human Resources and Skills Development Canada and Mexico's Secretaría de Relaciones Exteriores insisted that this 'administrative arrangement' was neither an inter-governmental agreement nor an international treaty and so not subject to the international law pertaining to treaties.[30] As a result, Canadian governance of migrant agricultural workers may be reviewed only under such instruments of domestic law as the Canadian Charter of Rights and Freedoms and general principles of administrative law, leaving the Canadian political system in effective control.[31]

Nor was the Canadian state's autonomy reduced by either NAFTA or its labour side agreement. While NAFTA's extensive set of rules included the movement of skilled professionals within North America, it did not address the transnational movement of unskilled labourers. As chapter IV explained, in response to vocal agitation on the part of NAFTA opponents concerned about workers' rights and the potential for the movement of US jobs to Mexico, the United States, Canada, and Mexico negotiated the North American Agreement on Labour Cooperation, which gave a new commission the mandate to promote high standards for the treatment of non-professional workers within North America.

In actual practice, each North American government continued to determine its own labour standards. Since only those sectors of the labour market that come under federal jurisdiction are bound by the NAALC in any case and since agriculture falls under provincial jurisdiction in Canada, SAWP escapes NAALC's aegis.[32] The right to collective bargaining does not exist for agricultural workers in Ontario, and NAFTA provides no remedies for this situation. Besides, even if the rights of migrant agricultural workers could be addressed via the NAALC, its weak enforcement procedures would frustrate any effort to constrain the power of the Canadian government to manage the program on its own terms.

Another set of international instruments that might be thought to constrain Ottawa is the body of international conventions dealing with the rights of migrant workers, but Canada has not ratified the four important International Labour Organization conventions and the UN Convention on the Protection of the Rights of Migrant Workers and Members of their Families. Two aspects of SAWP that maintain the vulnerability of Mexican migrant workers – the denial of a right to collective bargaining and the inability to circulate in the labour market – would violate these conventions.[33] Ultimately, the Canada-Mexico memorandum of understanding's form, NAALC's ineffectiveness, and Canada's disengagement from international labour norms and refusal to legislate migrant-worker rights buttressed the domestic regulatory system's disregard for this transborder issue.

That SAWP's exemption from international law is not complete became clear when Ottawa was unable to expand the program in response to requests by the Mexican government, which seeks to increase the flow of remittances that Mexicans working abroad can generate by extending SAWP to the construction and energy industries and services as well.[34] In the Uruguay Round, Canada had SAWP grandfathered so that the Most Favoured Nation norm in the WTO's General Agreement on Trade in Services would not compel it to extend the agreement to other countries. Now Ottawa maintains that it cannot substantially expand the program lest it be considered a new instrument and so subject to GATS' prohibitions of preferential deals.

Enter Civil-Society Governance

Reinforcing the migrant workers' inability to circulate in the labour market,[35] an informal mechanism lets employers and Mexican officials determine whether a worker – who is without access to independent representation – has breached the employment agreement and should be sent home.[36] By institutionalizing relations of unfreedom in the workers' contracts, the Canadian government has effectively eliminated the workers' power to resist the conditions under which they work and live. Those who object are subject to early and often arbitrary repatriation without any formal right of appeal or the ability to enforce their rights under the terms of their contract or Canadian law. For example, when four workers in Leamington's tomato greenhouses expressed dissatisfaction with their living conditions, they were repatriated within two days. There was no indication that the accommodations over which they had objected were ever inspected.[37] This lack of transparency creates an atmosphere of fear among the workers, who are subject to conditions that they cannot affect through input, compromise, or negotiation.

Fear of repatriation and the possibility of being barred from future participation in the program make workers accept long hours and poor living conditions.[38] By managing the global process of migration in a way that meets the country's economic needs while not threatening domestic workers, the Canadian government has, with Mexico's participation, carved out a role for itself as a buffer between global economic processes and local commercial imperatives.

The migrant workers' plight must be understood in the context that they voluntarily come to Canada to earn higher wages than they would receive at home. For instance, in 2002 Mexican migrant agricultural workers earned a net average of $9,100. In Mexico, they would have earned $900 for comparable seasonal work. The average remittance by Mexican seasonal workers in Canada was $4,800 in 2002.[39]

Organizations such as the United Food and Commercial Workers (UFCW) of Canada and Justicia for Migrant Workers have been actively fighting for the recognition of a right to collective bargaining for migrant agricultural workers. Since advocacy organizations can invoke no effective international instruments in order to uphold and strengthen the rights of migrant workers, they must work within the domestic Canadian legal system, in which even Canadian farm workers have consistently been denied collective-bargaining rights by courts and legislatures. Although the Supreme Court of Canada ruled in *Dunmore v. Ontario* (2001, SCC 94) that farm workers have the right to organize and form associations, Ontario still denies them this right to bargain collectively and unionize.

These organizations have also argued that migrant agricultural workers should be permitted to collect from the Employment Insurance program, to which they contribute through payroll deductions. In March 2006 the UFCW won the right to challenge the constitutionality of the Canadian EI program's discrimination against migrant workers.[40] Showing how the monopoly of government in this domain has been diminished by governance, Ontario brought migrant agricultural labourers under the protection of the province's Occupational Health and Safety Act in June 2006.

In conjunction with other labour organizations, the United Farm Workers of Americas' Canadian office launched the Global Justice Care Van Project 'to document working and living conditions of the seasonal guest workers in Ontario and to formulate policy recommendations to the Canadian government.'[41] The project opened a migrant-worker support centre in Leamington in 2002. Similar offices opened subsequently in other regions of Ontario, indicating that non-state actors have considerable potential for civil-society governance. For instance, in response to growing public attention sparked by a powerful National Film Board of Canada documentary, *El Contrato*, Mexico opened a consulate in Leamington in order to provide greater support for the many Mexicans labouring in this area's booming greenhouse industry.

Although much analysis of North American integration describes the erosion of governments' policy-making ability, SAWP shows how the Canadian government tapped into a global process to meet its own economic needs, a situation not unusual in the area of labour migration.[42] While most industrialized migrant-receiving states have sacrificed a portion of their sovereignty and increased their rates of immigrant naturalization,[43] they have developed institutional tools to fit labour migration to their needs. Most fundamentally, the nation-state retains the power to withhold citizenship status and to set the conditions of entry and residence for foreigners in its territory. Such state-regulated labour initiatives as the US H2A program, the European 'guest-worker' programs, and the Canadian SAWP represent strong institutional responses on the part of migrant-receiving countries which have demonstrated a remarkable capacity to assert their power to control global migratory processes. At the same time, migrant-sending countries have also developed mechanisms to expand the movement of their nationals to other countries in order to increase the transmission of foreign remittances.

Antedating NAFTA by almost three decades, the SAWP program created the template for North America's third bilateral relationship. In essence, it is a secondary relationship in which the two governments play the primary role only when responding to and steering pressures from the marketplace and civil society.

Conclusion

North America's third bilateral relationship dwarfs Ottawa's relations with all other Latin American countries and has become Mexico's most important foreign connection after the United States and the European Union as a whole. Nevertheless, it is overshadowed by the two states' primary North American relationship, their connection with Washington. SAWP and the two capitals' efforts to build a separate bilateral relationship implicitly confirm that NAFTA's direct or indirect consequences did not include a genuine trilateralism. With no overall vision or programmatic substance, the Canada-Mexico Partnership can hardly be considered a transformative addition to North American governance.

Nevertheless, the two countries' cooperation has broadened, deepened, and strengthened. SAWP is seen as a positive program by both governments and is used by Mexico as a model when pressing Washington to regularize the status of undocumented Mexican immigrants in the United States. Canada has become Mexico's fourth-largest supplier of foreign direct investment. As a member of the OECD, Mexico is ineligible for Canadian aid, but assistance happens in other ways. Mexican officials came to Canada to find out about software systems for processing government information. Mexico's new law on government transparency was based on the Canadian Access to Information Act. Establishing a more professional, less politicized civil service was accomplished by a reform based on the Canadian Public Service Act. The Canada Health Act was a model for reforms made in Mexico's public health system. Mexican military leaders have participated in workshops organized by their Canadian counterparts. As expressed by the Martin government's International Policy Statement, Mexico has taken on a far greater significance in Canadian foreign policy than it had ever enjoyed before NAFTA.

A more equitable and mutual modus operandi with Canada has helped Mexico reduce the asymmetry of its relationship with the United States and so diminish the imbalance of the two prime North American bilaterals. With North America's peripheral members having developed an independent relationship of their own, it is clear that the continent's governance is more than just a sum of their two relationships with the system's hegemon.

The nuances of this picture are further revealed when we turn our attention to the 2005 Security and Prosperity Partnership and the 2006 North American Competitiveness Council. With the advent of these instruments, as the next chapter shows, North American governance entered a new, if conflicted, phase.

XIX The Security and Prosperity Partnership

The immediate institutional lesson taught by Washington's unilateral border blockade on September 11, 2001 was confirmation that NAFTA had not provided Canada or Mexico with new capacity to affect issues of overriding North American importance. NAFTA's Free Trade Commission did not meet to review the US government's actions. No Chapter 20 dispute panel was convened to determine whether the United States had appropriately applied the national-security rationale for violating its NAFTA obligations not to constrict trade flows. No North American summit was called to address the United States' unnegotiated shift to a new policy paradigm in which, as immortalized by the American ambassador to Canada, 'security trumps trade.' But in a matter of days, once the realities of interdependence had American TNCs beating on Washington's door about the interruption of their production chains, the United States found itself negotiating with the periphery to establish new modalities for the secure passage of goods and people across its two land borders.

As chapter XVI showed, the thirty-point Smart Border Agreement signed in December 2001 restored a government-led but strictly bilateral substance to the Canada-US component of North America's transborder governance. Parallel but separate measures resulting from the subsequent twenty-two-point Smart Border Agreement between Washington and Mexico City reinforced the dual-bilateral character of continental governance. When the foreign ministers of Mexico and Canada met in the Mexican Embassy in Washington to discuss the border-security crisis a few weeks after September 2001, the Canadian foreign minister, John Manley, told his Mexican counterpart that Canada's relationship with the United States was 'different' from Mexico's. Officially, security and intelligence cooperation under NATO and other military agreements were cited as the official reasons for Ottawa's decision to negotiate directly with Washington. However, there was also a perception that the issues of illegal immigration, drug trafficking, and organized crime at the Mexican-US border impeded a trilateral approach to transborder governance.[1]

The cumulative impact of this new border-security paradigm being to stem the forces of economic integration, it took a surprisingly trilateral initiative to start to rebalance the three governments' differing security and economic priorities. Ironically, the move to trilateralize cooperation in North America was born in the White House at the very moment – March 2003 – when the Bush administration's public anger with its neighbours was at its hottest. The election of Vicente Fox and George Bush had stimulated an unusual blooming of Mexico-US friendship, but the bonhomie had rapidly chilled when Mexico expressed scant solidarity with the Americans after the terrorist attacks of September 11, 2001 and failed, even rhetorically, to support their retaliation against the Taliban in Afghanistan. Nor had Washington expected the Mexicans to stymie its military plans in Iraq by opposing it in the Security Council, where they held a temporary seat. It was equally disappointed by Canada's parallel efforts within the UN General Assembly to delay the American attack on Baghdad by negotiating a new international consensus for further negotiations.

Notwithstanding the open trilateral discord resulting from the periphery's resistance to the US determination to achieve regime change in Iraq, the March meeting at 1600 Pennsylvania Avenue with senior officials from the Fox and Chrétien governments came to the conclusion that border bottlenecks caused by US security measures should no longer be allowed to jeopardize the transboundary flows of goods and people that were crucial to the three economies and therefore crucial to their hopes for future global competitiveness.[2] Security might trump trade in theory but should not jeopardize prosperity in practice.

The formalization of this executive consensus took two years to gestate, largely because of the United States' 2004 elections. In mid-2005 a task force of continentally leaning persons, sponsored by the Council of Foreign Relations collaborating with its counterpart, the Mexican Council of Foreign Relations, and the corporate Canadian Council of Chief Executives, was assigned the task of developing specific recommendations for a trinational integration agenda.[3] Subsequently, the continent's three heads of government met in Waco, Texas, for the first time in over a decade and formally proposed launching a new North American governance agenda. There, on March 23, 2005, Presidents Bush and Fox and Prime Minister Paul Martin signed a document of uncertain legal status called the Security and Prosperity Partnership of North America.[4]

Galvanized by their leaders' commitment and by a tight, three-month deadline to produce an action plan, officials in the three governments dealing with border security, transportation, agriculture, energy, and economic policy started a process of trilateral consultation in order to insert policy content into the Partnership. Content did not necessarily mean coherence. The measures proposed for the transportation sector were cobbled together on the telephone and by e-mail without their authors in the three capitals ever getting together for a meeting. The provisions envisaged for food safety required intervention by the US trade representative, Robert Zoellick, to induce a reluctant Food and Drug Administration to agree to negotiate explicit criteria governing the entry of Mexican food products into the United States. In the hope that inclusion under the SPP umbrella might extract government funding, officials took projects off their shelves and bulked up the text. As a result, when ministers from the three countries met in Ottawa in June 2005 to announce the SPP's work plan, their shiny trilingual (English, Spanish, French) document looked something like an intergovernmental version of a Sear's catalogue but without the Barbie-doll illustrations modelling the lingerie. It detailed some three hundred proposals for regulatory changes that were to square the familiar post-September 11 circle: achieve the highest possible level of border security for North America while facilitating the smoothest possible transboundary flows of people and commerce.[5]

Understandably, there was little public discussion of these proposals and still less general comprehension of their significance. For one thing, outsiders had no way of telling the difference between meaningless verbiage (initiate dialogue to identify issues in moving towards a trilateral agreement on expanding air transportation), trivial projects (improve transparency and coordination in energy information, statistics, and projections), and powerful proposals (greater economic production from oil sands). For another, there was no obvious institutional motor through which each federal government could credibly administer the Partnership's targets, let alone a trinational authority that could monitor progress on a continental basis. Nor was there any indication where money would come from to pay for these initiatives. Disinterested observers were not the only ones to voice their doubts. Highly interested businesses whose production chains traversed the Canadian-US and/or Mexican-US border were happier that action was being promised than with the actual program or the all-bureaucrat-all-the-time process by which it had been cobbled together.

North American Competitiveness Council

Dismayed that a wide range of regulatory issues were being discussed without their being consulted, business representatives from the three countries decided they needed to reconnect with the politics of continental integration, an issue to which they had only twice paid serious attention – during the negotiation of the free-trade agreements (as we saw in chapter IV) and in the immediate aftermath of September 11 (chapter XVI). Early in 2006, United Parcel Services invited some fifty government officials and business leaders from Canada, Mexico, and the United States to its transportation hub in Louisville, Kentucky, to demonstrate how border delays had created huge problems for its courier business and to discuss what should be done. Under the spectre of growing competition from China, many American businesses were reconsidering how to reduce their production costs within North America. It was one thing for small-and medium-sized Canadian businesses to suffer serious losses from the border obstructions.[6] It was quite another for the giant TNCs to feel the pinch. Transborder shipment delays caused by the highly intrusive security demands of US border controls and inadequate highway and customs-clearance infrastructure had created significant transaction costs for many US TNCs which had dispersed entities of their production chains around the continent. They were ready to consider getting directly involved in the SPP.

One meeting led to another. Sixty business leaders met two months later in Washington under the joint auspices of the Council of the Americas and the US Chamber of Commerce. By then, an idea had emerged that the SPP should not just be monitored but also activated by business participation through an independent but connected body.

When, on March 31, 2006, newly elected Canadian Prime Minister Stephen Harper managed to get himself invited to what had been scheduled as a Mexico-US summit in Cancún, the trilateral conclave was able to mark the SPP's first anniversary by announcing three further decisions. The leaders accepted one of the Council of Foreign Relations task force's recommendations by agreeing to meet on an annual basis. Next, they simplified the 'Sear's catalogue' action plan from the previous June into five more manageable priorities: strengthening competitiveness, emergency management, avian and human pandemic influenza, energy security, and smart, secure borders. Then, with a handful of big businessmen whom they had brought along to Cancún to dress up the event, the leaders announced the creation of a North American Competitiveness Council, which was to insert the three corporate communities directly into their governments' trilateral decision-making process.

Institutionally speaking, these three innovations promised to change the face of North American governance. Whereas there had been no meeting of the three countries' leaders between September 2001 and March 2005, there was now to be a yearly North American summit that would address common concerns. While easy to dismiss as yet another occasion for photo opportunities, such get-togethers had substantial potential. For one thing, a regular trilateral gathering would put the US president temporarily on a par with the periphery's two heads of government, symbolically reducing the power asymmetry between the former and the latter, who, ipso facto, would enjoy greater access to the White House. For another, each impending trinational summit would energize the senior reaches of each country's executive, impelling them to insist that, lower down the bureaucratic hierarchy, their own officials cooperate with their counterparts in the other two countries in order to put together an agenda. The meetings' decisions would produce a new action program that would drive subsequent governmental actions and foster further bilateral or trilateral cooperation among officials and business. Their resulting achievements would, in turn, have to be evaluated as the basis for their next meeting's agenda.

More intriguing by far was the NACC's insertion into the three countries' institutional order. Its first meeting in Washington in August 2006 was attended by Mexican and Canadian business representatives appointed by the respective president and the prime minister, the US business representatives having been recruited through the US Chamber of Commerce and the Council of the Americas. The thirty-member parity structure of the NACC was idiosyncratic: each country appointed ten members at its own discretion. On the Canadian side, a group of ten business representatives was announced by Prime Minister Harper on June 13, 2006,[7] consisting of the five CEOs who had accompanied him to the Cancún meeting in March plus another five members from the Canadian Council of Chief Executives.[8] The Mexican representatives were appointed through a similarly arbitrary process by President Fox, with the majority coming from the Consejo Mexicano de Hombres de Negocios (Mexican Council of Businessmen), a counterpart to the CCCE.[9]

Unlike its neighbours, the United States could not appoint an advisory body without Congressional approval. As a result, the selection of NACC's American members was entrusted to the US Chamber of Commerce and the Council of the Americas, which – determined to keep the process as open as possible – had invited any member company which desired to take a seat at NACC's advisory table. The result was a dual structure in NACC's American section: its executive committee was chosen from fifteen big US corporations that were formally meant to 'represent the sectors in which their business operates' rather than 'simply the interests of their individual companies.'[10] From these, ten senior management people were selected to attend NACC's trilateral meetings. The US advisory committee was made up of over two hundred companies, sectoral associations, lobbies, and local chambers of commerce.

During the August session, the governments' participants asked the continental corporate leaders to tell them what they were doing wrong. US Secretary of Commerce Carlos Gutierrez urged the newborn council to stimulate visible and rapid government action by focusing its advice on the short term. Picking the low-hanging fruit, they should produce recommendations that the three governments could implement quickly and easily without having to involve their legislatures. The goal was not to open the Pandora's box otherwise known as representative democracy: the in-volvement of their elected politicians in debating these measures, ob-taining legislative authorization, or voting budgetary allocations. Three priority areas were selected and responsibility for proposing solutions was delegated to one country's business leadership – Canada for border security, Mexico for energy integration, and the United States for regulatory harmonization.

By then, all ten business leaders whom Harper had invited to be the Canadian members of the NACC were members of the Canadian Council of Chief Executives – Annette Verschuren of Home Depot had been the exception, but she subsequently joined the CCCE – so it was hardly surprising that the CCCE's head, the veteran free-trade lobbyist Thomas d'Aquino, was asked to provide the Canadian secretariat for the NACC. In effect, d'Aquino had pushed aside Canada's other big business associations to seize control of the process and take over the drafting of its recommendations for border-security and trade-facilitation measures.

Mexico City's business participation was almost as predictable. The voice of Mexican capitalism was offered to those business associations that were most involved with exports. Not having the policy-analysis capacity of Canadian or American business groupings, these associations lodged the secretariat for the Mexican side of the NACC in a recently established, economically very conservative, and small but dynamic think tank dedicated to promoting economic competitiveness, the Instituto Mexicano para la Competitividad. IMCO's task for the NACC was to propose measures to bolster North American competitiveness and security in the energy sector.

Intense discussions involving American CEOs with their US competitors and Mexican or Canadian counterparts were orchestrated jointly by the US Chamber of Commerce and the Council of the Americas. By November, the three national business secretariats had produced draft proposals which were circulated to their corporate cousins for comment and revision. In contrast with their neighbours' corporate interlocutors, who worked hand in glove with their governments, the NACC's American participants kept their distance from the Bush administration, then rapidly losing credibility, and organized their own participatory process. The US Chamber of Commerce communicated its mandate – proposals for transborder regulatory harmonization – to its entire membership, inviting any company that so desired to take a seat at its NACC advisory table.

The results of these negotiations were made public at NACC's next formal gathering, which took place in Ottawa on February 23, 2007. On that day, representatives from each country's business community presented their fifty-one detailed recommendations to an impressive trinational ninesome: the US secretaries of state, Condoleezza Rice; commerce, Carlos Gutierrez; and homeland security, Michael Chertoff; the Mexican secretaries of external relations, Patricia Espinosa; economy, Eduardo Sojo; and interior, Francisco Ramírez Acuña; and the Canadian ministers of public safety, Stockwell Day; industry, Maxime Bernier; and foreign affairs, Peter MacKay. Curiously absent from a group mandated to boost cross-border trade was the US trade representative.

The NACC report, *Enhancing Competitiveness in Canada, Mexico and the United States*: *Private Sector Priorities for the Security and Prosperity Partnership of North America*, was an amalgam of recommendations for the three key areas of border security, regulatory harmonization, and energy integration that was meant to streamline trilateral cooperation and improve the 'efficiency of commercial exchanges within North America.'[11] NACC's proposals were clearly circumscribed by its instructions to produce short-term goals that would not have to involve legislative authorization, particularly on the US side, where extremist groups were denouncing the program as a threat to American sovereignty. The report adopted the same timelines as those of the Council of Foreign Relations: short-term recommendations were set for implementation by 2008, longer-term goals by 2010.[12]

Not only had NACC created a continental business trialogue at the highest level, it had given this three-headed corporate powerhouse direct access to a new trinational North American cabinet subcommittee. It was of slight import that this step towards more formalized continental governance had given the Canadian, Mexican, or American business communities more privileged access to their own national executive and bureaucracy, since this was an intimacy each had long enjoyed. More significant, the NACC presented the corporate and political leadership from Canada, Mexico, and the United States with similar access to the other two capitals. This could have major effects on the Mexican and Canadian governments' autonomy in areas where the three business communities and the other two governments agree on what actions should be taken in the periphery.

Looking at the other side of the same coin, the quasi-cabinet structure of NACC's institutionalized access within the Washington beltway should increase Canadian and Mexican governments' capacity in Washington. It was a still more dramatic innovation to give corporate Canada and corporatist Mexico greater capacity there as well. On issues where Ottawa, Mexico City, and their two business communities are in agreement, the continental periphery might gain new purchase in the American capital. Regularized interactions with Mexican officials have also animated the Canada-Mexico relationship, which had been activated by NAFTA, revivified after September 2001, and, following some years on life support, formalized in 2004 with the establishment of the Canada-Mexico Partnership – an instrument that, as we saw in chapter XVIII, was designed to give more content to this still tentative third continental bilateral.

At a time when neoconservatism is fighting a rearguard action globally and hemispherically, NACC's creation represented continued movement in the old direction because it shifted more economic power from the reach of legislators to that of transnational corporations and strengthened their isolation from environmental-, labour-, and social-policy concerns. Should this corporate forum survive and grow, it will mark a notable addition to North America's constitution, empowering a muscular form of transborder governance in which big business has greatly increased rights of political access. In its present form, this new continental institution is carefully insulated from the United States, Mexico, and Canada's civil-society organizations and the democratically elected institutions defined by the three countries' internal constitutions – the two Congresses, the Parliament, and the state and provincial governments – and can be amended at the pleasure of the participating leaders.

Beyond its institutional novelty, the SPP's impact in creating new norms and rules for each country's legal order is likely to be modest for the immediate future. Its normative banner could be inscribed with such slogans as 'Security Shall Not Trump Trade' or 'Trialogue Beats Dialogue.' Since its programmatic thrust focuses on measures that can be implemented quickly and without legislative involvement – the preparation for handling medical emergencies and natural disasters and the harmonization of certain minor standards in the periphery with those of the United States – immediate changes in each country's rules will be limited.

Continuing engagement in the NACC by the three business communities will depend on their evaluation of the governments' response to the February 2007 action program. Should the experiment be deemed a success so that the Partnership subsequently becomes more ambitious, its longer-term impact on the domestic legal order in the three countries could become more intrusive as trilateral continental governance becomes more effective. In the medium term, SPP remains an uneasy relationship within and between the three member states. Within each federal government, the fit between security and economic agencies remains awkward.

In Mexico City on the security side, the Centro de Investigación y Seguridad Nacional is a young institution with little power to do much more than try to get the federal government's various agencies with security and intelligence operations to pull together. The prosperity dossier is far more securely rooted in the governmental structure, since the same generation of technocrats that had negotiated NAFTA is still staffing the working groups and driving the process of economic-policy development. Having initially refused to sign off on the Security and

Prosperity Partnership, the Secretariat for External Relations is now taking back the role of lead department in overall charge of the SPP.

In Ottawa, the shift from the narrow focus of the Smart Border Agreement to the multi-dimensional Security and Prosperity Partnership was accompanied by a parallel institutional evolution. The former had been negotiated and implemented on the Canadian side by John Manley when he was deputy prime minister operating in the Privy Council Office, from where he was able to interact personally and continually with his American alter ego, Tom Ridge, then in the White House. Political and administrative control of the SPP then moved down the bureaucratic ladder to two associate deputy ministers, one in the Department of Public Safety, the other in the Department of Industry, with the Department of Foreign Affairs and International Trade having an overall coordinating function – hardly a structure guaranteeing dynamic and effective interaction with the Partnership's US and Mexican interlocutors.

Much worse, in Washington, the bureaucratic nightmare otherwise known as the Department of Homeland Security remained in control of security issues. Unlike Ottawa, where the centralization characteristic of parliamentary government ensured close collaboration between the assistant deputy ministers responsible for the prosperity and security portfolios, little could be done to have the DHS compromise its goal of impermeable American land borders by making concessions on the altar of economic competitiveness.

This tension broke into the open in May 2007, when DHS Secretary Michael Chertoff cut off talks to establish a pilot project on land pre-clearance at the Fort Erie-Buffalo crossing. Although the two-year-long negotiations had been premised on the principle that the agreement would respect the laws of the country hosting the pre-clearance area, and although fingerprinting is mandatory in Canada only for those charged with a crime, Chertoff insisted on US officials in Fort Erie being able to fingerprint even those US-bound travellers who got cold feet and decided at the last minute not to cross the border. Despite tremendous political and corporate support for a land pre-clearance system similar to the long-established pre-clearance facilities in major Canadian airports, Chertoff's decision showed how difficult it was to pass from the SPP's prosperity rhetoric to the practical problem of getting Homeland Security to temper its security obsession. Despite endorsement by the Council of Foreign Relations 2005 task force and enthusiastic support in the NACC's February 2007 report, the pilot pre-clearance project's failure brought into question the SPP's ability to prevail over the DHS.

Unlike land pre-clearance, regulatory harmonization has actually proceeded. By May 2007, Ottawa had agreed to harmonize Canadian and US pesticide rules on the grounds that the difference in residue limits on domestic and imported food had long been a barrier to trade. In practice, regulatory harmonization meant that the Canadian Pest Management Regulatory Agency brought its standards into line with US regulations, which allowed higher residue levels for 40 per cent of the pesticides used, compared to only 10 per cent of cases where Canadian limits were higher.[13] Another case of Canadian standards being brought into compliance with US rules became public in June 2007, when Canada's 'Passenger Protect' program introduced a no-fly list managed by the RCMP and the Canadian Security and Intelligence Service. Although the roster had been compiled by the federal government, it was also revealed that Canadian airlines would continue to use the much broader US list compiled by Washington, even on domestic Canadian flights.[14]

Such concrete moves towards regulatory harmonization may be credited to the trilateral SPP, but they can also be seen as the maturation of the unilateral 'Smart-Regulation' initiative that was launched by Jean Chrétien in May 2003, when he struck the External Advisory Committee on Smart Regulation (EACSR) to be the government's main vehicle for advice on how to redesign the Canadian regulatory system.[15] With six of its ten members being senior corporate executives and one a leader of the OECD's regulatory reform program, the group had an obvious interest in relaxing regulations. Indeed, as critics quickly pointed out, the initiative placed a premium on economic competitiveness and industrial promotion at the expense of the environment and public health and safety. The claim that the Canadian regulatory system was bloated, unsustainable, overlapping, and unduly burdensome was not supported by proof. In the area of environmental assessment, for instance, there was little evidence of needless duplication of regulatory requirement even before a 1998 agreement to harmonize federal and provincial environment-assessment regimes.[16] Characterizing the existing framework of federal regulation as unsustainable in the face of global market dynamics, increasingly complex policy issues, and rising public expectations for empowerment and accountability, the EACSR's 2004 report called for increased regulatory cooperation among governments. Apart from stressing the need for harmonization between federal, provincial, and territorial governments (which would have required inter-governmental agreement), it went on to recommend greater harmonization of regulatory standards and product approvals with the United States (which Ottawa could implement unilaterally).[17]

For Ottawa and Mexico City's prime political concern – their relationship with Washington – the SPP created a potentially important consultative process with which they hoped to supersede the institutionally moribund NAFTA. Between Canada and Mexico, a growing commonality of interest was bridging a long history of mutual ignorance. The difficulty each government continued to experience when dealing with Washington had made it easier working with the other peripheral state on the many different SPP agenda items.

For the Canadian, American, and Mexican publics, however, it remained difficult to decipher the concrete significance of the Security and Prosperity Partnership. The official document, published as the annual 'Report to Leaders,' presented security and prosperity initiatives as being either 'completed,' 'on track,' or 'delayed.' Irrespective of the initiative's status, the reports provided inadequate information about each initiative for even a skilled analyst to understand what the SPP might be expected to achieve. The hundreds of proposed initiatives, ranging from the mundane (such as efforts to develop a trilateral inventory of chemicals in commerce) to those with potential for far-reaching impact on the rules and norms of Canada, Mexico, and the United States (formalizing a framework for trilateral regulatory cooperation by 2007), were treated with equal but Delphic brevity in these documents.[18]

The published reports of the SPP's nineteen working groups, corresponding to the partnership's nineteen original areas, were skimpy – if they could be located at all.[19] As of July 2007, only six of the nineteen working groups had released reports pertaining to their short- and long-term goals. Whereas the annual Report to Leaders comprehensively outlined the ongoing initiatives of the security and prosperity mandates, reports put out by the working groups have been lumped under the general headings of 'SPP Documents' and 'SPP Reports' on the Canadian and American SPP websites. With the exception of fragmentary information from the Bio-Protection, Environment, Financial Services, Manufactured Goods and Sectoral Regional Competitiveness, E-Commerce and Information and Communications and Technologies, and Energy[20] working groups, the inner workings of the SPP are opaque.

The working group reports that have been made available show little congruence with the annual Report to Leaders, revealing the difficulty of making sense of the policy impact of the Security and Prosperity initiatives. The North American Energy Working Group, a previously constituted forum for trilateral discussion predating the SPP and discussed in chapter VIII, is one of the few groups to have consistently made its policy proposals available to the public. A comparison of the initiatives listed in the 2006 Report to Leaders with published reports demonstrates the gap between the policy proposals ongoing within SPP working groups and the comprehensive summaries being made available to the public. Oil-sands discussion in the 2006 Report is limited to a brief description of three policy papers published between January 2006 and June 2007 that 'discuss the mid- to long-term aspects of the oil sands ... market development ... and infrastructure.'[21] On the other hand, the *Oil Sands Workshop SPP Report* of January 2006[22] discusses 'pipeline expansion plans that are already in place to meet ... the doubling of oil sands production ... by 2010 to 2012' as well as policy in the areas of labour, external markets for oil-sands products, natural gas, and upgrading of refineries in Canada – all of which, in effect, suggests a much more developed policy process than is evident in the Report to Leaders.

Reports from the remaining five groups are even less comprehensive. Only two policy papers have been released by the working groups addressing the SPP prosperity agenda: *North American Steel Strategy* and *Framework of Common Principles for Electronic Commerce*, by the Manufactured Goods and Sectoral and Regional Competitiveness Working Group, and the E-Commerce and Information Communications Technologies Working Group, respectively. The remaining reports deal with information sharing and agency cooperation in the fields of environment, financial services (consumer products in particular), and bio-protection, none of which is of assistance to Canadian, US, and Mexican publics in deciphering the implications of the SPP for the future of North American governance.

The lack of concrete information about the Security and Prosperity Partnership or its working groups poses a challenge to the perceived legitimacy of the fledgling continental institution. Particularly, the unavailability of information has contributed to a deep apprehension about the SPP's power on the part of several citizens' groups, activist organizations, and the general public in Canada, the United States, and Mexico. Council of Canadians and Canadian Peace Alliance activists mobilized under the banner of 'Take Back Canada!' to release several publications that attempt to decipher the inner workings of the SPP, and paint the partnership as a forerunner of deep integration with the United States.[23] In the United States itself, the transparency and openness of the SPP to public scrutiny have been questioned by the activist group Stop the Security and Prosperity Partnership and the civil-society group Judicial Watch. Both have cited concerns that the Freedom of Information Act was necessary in order to gain access to SPP documents.[24]

Absence of direct, legitimate access to the policy-making process of the SPP has prompted some citizen's groups to hold 'teach-ins' and protests that challenge the partnership's legitimacy. But even reactive methods of this kind have been frustrated by the security obsessions of the trilateral SPP meetings – which in large part have been closed both to the press and to the public. During what became the trilateral March 30, 2006 Cancún meeting, a zone of the city was locked down and access was denied to Mexico police services and residents.[25] Similar security precautions and corresponding anger by civil-society organizations at Montebello (July 2007) and New Orleans (April 2008) have given an anti-globalization gloss to these trilateral summits.

A glimpse of what a successful SPP might deliver was offered by the vision of North American governance projected in the *North American Future 2025 Project*. Run by Washington's Center for Strategic and International Studies, the Centro de Investigación y Educación (CIDE, Centre for Research and Education), and the Conference Board of Canada on behalf of the three governments, this project was generated by closed-door roundtables with 'pertinent government officials from Canada, United States, and Mexico ... groups of experts, the private sector, and academia' on six broad issues: labour mobility, energy, the environment, security, competitiveness, and border infrastructure and logistics. While bulk-water diversion did not figure among the many short- and medium-term initiatives addressed in the Prosperity Annex of the 2007 Report to Leaders, an early draft of the *North American Future 2025* proposed looking at 'regional agreements between Canada, the United States, and Mexico on issues such as water consumption, water transfers, [and] artificial diversions of fresh water'[26] between 2007 and 2025. The implication of *Future 2025* was that, should the SPP and NACC reach their potential as new institutions of North American governance, this vision would likely help form their agenda – and would be highly contested, particularly the idea of large-scale water shipments out of Canada, which we discussed in chapter VI.

Conclusion

Notwithstanding the rhetoric of 'partnership,' 'partenariat,' or 'alianza,' relations between the three capitals remain precarious. To begin with, the three electoral cycles never coincide and constantly breed uncertainties. During 2006, the almost winning campaign, and subsequent near uprising, orchestrated by Andrés Manuel López Obrador left the United States and Canada uncertain whether they would be dealing with a Mexican Hugo Chávez or a clone of Vicente Fox. In 2007 a politically wounded and electorally lame George Bush made the United States an unreliable interlocutor. The next year was somewhat worse, since the presidential primaries and subsequent election campaign consumed most of Washington's scattered political energies. Although Canada might appear the least unstable polity of the three, the uncertainty generated by Paul Martin's erratic behaviour and minority position outlasted him until Prime Minister Harper clarified that he would endorse his Liberal foe's legacy and support the SPP, albeit with muted enthusiasm.

Relations between Mexico and the United States remain vulnerable to tensions on either side of the border over immigration, provocative political acts, inflammatory rhetoric, and criminal violence – any of which can sabotage advances in regulatory cooperation. Harmonious collaboration between the two northern right-wing governments, which share decidedly militaristic and security-state propensities, is nevertheless remarkably elusive since the DHS remains deeply distrustful of its northern neighbour's anti-terrorist integrity.

The Canada-Mexico relationship is still constrained by Ottawa's reluctance to invest significant sums in solidarity with its much poorer and frailer partner. In May 2007 Minister of Foreign Affairs Peter MacKay met his Mexican counterpart, Patricia Espinosa, to discuss a 'full bilateral agenda' and 'opportunities for hemispheric collaboration' leading up to a visit to Canada by President Calderón – potentially a sign of growth in the third bilateral.[27] For Mexico City's and Ottawa's prime concerns – their relationship with Washington – SPP has introduced an important consultative process they hope will transcend the institutionally moribund NAFTA on which both had pinned so many of their economic hopes.

Mexico and Canada operate simultaneously in two interacting worlds. In their multilateral sphere, they are located in the mid-to higher ranks of the global hierarchy – neither so weak that they can exert no capacity abroad nor so strong as to operate without regard for international pressures.[28] As middle powers with a necessary interest in a liberal multilateral order, they must take their participation in international institutions very seriously, not the least because this multilateralism may offer each government some room for manoeuvre outside the direct control of their dominant neighbour.

In their continental sphere, they have to confront the reality of their location in the United States' backyard and defence perimeter. Given that the major constraints in Mexico City's and Ottawa's operating systems are the multifarious interests of their generally dominant, sometimes imperialistic, often isolationist neighbour, the new Security and Prosperity Partnership of North America needs to be understood in the context of two long-standing relationships which have altered significantly over the decades, sometimes in harmony, other times not. Each change affects Ottawa's and Mexico City's room for manoeuvre. Hence the SPP creates a double-edged operating framework.

On the one hand, it gives official recognition to the continent's basic political reality: nothing proceeds that the United States does not want to see happen. Mexico City and Ottawa can pursue their own economic objectives only by first meeting US security requirements. Accepting the United States' security fixation as its point of departure, the SPP provides a framework within which, at the most, US pressure can be managed and perhaps mitigated. On the other hand, the SPP's annual heads-of-government summits create new capacity for the Canadian and Mexican governments by legitimizing their voice in a number of key Washington agencies whose policies affect the periphery's interests.

Trilateralizing formerly bilateral issues will also affect the continent's power dynamic. Mexico has historically preferred a more formalized relationship with Washington than Canada's more informal approach. For its part, Ottawa has long resisted being identified with the United States' other territorial neighbour, lest its relationship with Washington be contaminated by Congressional fears of illegal immigrants and narco-traffickers. The SPP and NACC seriously challenge North America as two disconnected dyadic relationships – for better or for worse. The Western Hemispheric Travel Initiative, requiring American travellers to have secure identity documents when returning to the United States, has caused both Mexico and Canada to lobby together and with their American business allies on this issue. To the extent that American policies designed to counteract the problems of illegal immigration at the Mexican border apply to Canada, Canadians will be affected. To the extent that American policies designed to counteract the infiltration of terrorists across the Canadian border apply to Mexico, Mexicans will be affected. To the extent that Canada and Mexico together exert more power over the continental giant, their capacity is increased, their power asymmetry is offset, and the skewed quality of the two bilaterals is reduced as the northern state and its southern partner learn to act together.

If a country's external capacity is subjectively determined by its leadership's will to act, only time can tell how capable the Mexican presidency and the Canadian Prime Minister's Office turn out to be in exploiting the SPP, which at present remains flimsy to put it mildly. In the meantime, we can conclude with some certainty that Mexican and Canadian big business representatives have pulled off a coup by inserting themselves into the government processes of all three countries, while their elected politicians and civil societies are pushed farther to the political sidelines.

Conclusion: Framing the Answer

I am starting to draft these concluding words in Mexico City at the beginning of 2008, just as the North American Free Trade Agreement has brought the last Mexican duties on food imports down to zero and the local media are full of portentous news concerning the country's position in the same North America that has been the subject of this book.

Rural organizations are seizing highway tollbooths and threatening to close down US branch plants to protest the implementation of NAFTA's final cuts of the tariffs on corn and beans. They are calling for the renegotiation of its agricultural chapter, which they claim has caused 2 million rural jobs to be lost, leaving 70 per cent of campesinos in poverty and forcing 300,000 to emigrate to the United States every year. Protest leaders recognize that annual agricultural exports have increased since NAFTA to a value of 11 billion pesos but point out that imports have grown to 13 billion pesos. Worse, the real trade deficit of corn[1] actually amounts to 4 billion pesos because all the country's fertilizers are now being imported.[2] Meanwhile, frequent government-sponsored spots on FM radio sing NAFTA's praises.

Much international expertise is cited in the Mexican capital's press to highlight Mexico's various economic conundrums. A report by IMD World Competitiveness Surveys places the country a disconcerting 55th out of 104 economies in terms of its competitiveness,[3] with the cost of living having increased well over 400 per cent since 1994 while the minimum salary grew well under 200 per cent.[4] Meanwhile, Standard and Poor is pointing out another distortion: 15 per cent of Mexico's working-age population has moved to the United States, while the economy has become dependent on the remittances that these exiles send home.[5] A report by the United Nations Conference on Trade and Development has declared Mexico's economy to be the most vulnerable in the world in the face of the United States' impending recession.[6] To substantiate this point, the Consejo Nacional de la Industria Maquiladora y Manufacturera de Exportación (National Council for the Maquiladora and Export Manufacturing Industries) has warned that this same recession threatens the survival of the country's 8,900 maquiladora plants along with their 2.4 million employees.[7]

On the petroleum front, the former governing party, the PRI, has just fallen in line with President Calderón's Partido Acción Nacional to support Pemex's increased collaboration with foreign investors. Dramatizing the country's polarization over this further step towards the conservatives' goal of full energy-sector privatization, the presidential candidate of the left-wing Partido de la Revolución Democrática (PRD) in 2006, Andrés Manual López Obrador, has just announced that he is heading up a new popular movement to keep petroleum in the public sector and wants to debate the president over the energy dossier, a challenge the government has dismissed as mischief making.[8]

For lack of spectacular avalanches in the Rocky Mountains or murdered tourists in Cancún, Canada is seldom mentioned in the local media (except for three solid reports in as many days on Canada's harsh treatment of Mexican refugee claimants), but I don't need Mexican reportage to tell me that free trade is a politically dead issue in the continent's attic. Some modest mobilization has occurred in Canada around the Security and Prosperity Partnership, which has given the sorely weakened bearers of the nationalist torch an issue on which to concentrate their concerns about the country's beleaguered sovereignty. But opposition to the SPP has little to do with Mexico, from which Canadians' consciousness remains largely disconnected. Activists' anxieties are focused on the slippery slope of further 'deep integration' with the United States that regulatory harmonization implies for them. Otherwise, Canadians are more concerned with the high price of oil, which boosts Alberta's petroleum industry profits; the high exchange rate for the Canadian dollar, which prices Ontario's manufacturing industry out of export competition; and the US economic recession, which spreads the gloom to every other province's export sector.

These are themes completely absent from Mexico's media, which, always preoccupied by the colossus to the north, have their collective nose pressed against the observation-deck window of the US pre-presidential campaign. A New York correspondent notes that, according to polls, the American public believes by a margin of two to one that free trade has been bad for the US economy.[9] The same reporter, reviewing the primaries, reports that every Democratic candidate has taken a position against free trade, with even Hillary Clinton – the wife of the president who signed NAFTA in 1993 – vowing to renegotiate the agreement, which has become the symbol of and scapegoat for globalization's threat to working-class Americans' job prospects.

Events and issues in early 2008 may well have faded from our memories by the time this book appears, but they can help us reflect on what existence North America really enjoys. What, in fact, is this North America, if not an entity with many different faces beyond the one called NAFTA? I believe that it is, and is not, the following:

- It is an identifiable *geographical entity*, although Hawaii seems an incongruous extension, and Russia may be challenging the exact location of the continent's legal margins in the Arctic.
- It is not a *community* in the sense that Mexicans, Americans, and Canadians think of themselves primarily as members of their continent. Among civil-society organizations, trinational continental activism is a rarity compared to the much more common global engagement of internationally oriented non-governmental organizations.
- It is a new, if weak, *legal-institutional reality* which has thousands of powerful norms and rules whose long-term effectiveness is being vitiated by institutions too ineffectual to adapt the continent's collectively to changing circumstances.
- It has some coherence as a market, particularly in those economic sectors that are strongly integrated within the region owing to the expansion of US transnational corporations for which the continent is a meaningful production and marketing zone. Otherwise, it is generally more integrated in the global economy than an identifiably continental regime of accumulation. Trade and investment have increased substantially but separately along the US-Mexico and US-Canada axes, with trinational automobile supply chains providing a notable exception.

In other words, North America is not a self-contained region *of* the world. Rather, it is one region *in* the world, particularly in those sectors such as banking and pharmaceuticals whose North American constituents operate as parts of other global systems. Observers who interpret the trend towards the consolidation of multi-state regional groupings as a territorial manifestation of globalization's dynamic must pause when they come to North America. On the one hand, they can find support for their thesis in the fact that NAFTA was negotiated as a response to the three economic elites' fear of competitive pressures from overseas. This evidence was buttressed in March 2005 when, in response to China's looming competitive threat, the three heads of government committed themselves to promote a new Security and Prosperity Partnership of North America, and also in March 2006, when the same leadership trio institutionalized big corporations' participation in trilateral governance by giving the new North American Competitiveness Council regular access to their three cabinets.

On the other hand, NAFTA's institutions were patently incapable ab initio of generating a continental mode of regulation. By 2008, it was also clear that the SPP was not delivering anything of regulatory substance. It did what it could (not much), but not what it should (a great deal), to address the social, environmental, and migratory problems generated by North America's integration. The continental leaders' rhetorical affirmation of their commitment to the spirit of regional economic integration has been continually contradicted by the United States' propensity to take unilateral and protectionist action. Mexico's call for strengthening NAFTA's institutions along EU lines fell on deaf ears in both Washington and Ottawa. In short, there is some transborder governance *in* North America but precious little governance *of* North America.

Thus, North America's apparent participation in globalization's trend towards regional governance turns out to be misleading. A site that generates both integration and fragmentation internationally, it has itself no separate political centre, no governance locus equivalent to that played by Brussels for the European Union. Designed on the Canadian and Mexican sides by negotiators who were ideologically committed to the double proposition that North America's federal governments should reduce, not refine, their controls over the economy and that the European model of intrusive supranational government should be avoided, NAFTA's institutions were too weak to give the periphery any meaningful role in a new kind of continental governance, let alone prevent the United States from violating the new rules when it saw fit. This makes the prospects for transborder cooperation largely contingent on the Americans' perception of the problem, a perception that their neighbours best influence if their voices are amplified through the regular channels of US politics. But the institutions located in Washington's imperially columned palaces enfranchise US citizens just as clearly as they disenfranchise Mexicans and Canadians, whose fates they determine almost as directly, much as they did before the era of trade liberalization.

These last pages will now reflect *analytically* on North American governance in order then to reprise *synthetically* the general questions posed in the Introduction about the scope and character of transborder governance in North America. Since every field studied in this volume is constantly changing, these thoughts should be read as an intellectual photograph summing up a seven-year investigation into North America that began in 2001 and came to an end in the midst of the American presidential campaign of 2008.

Analytical Perspectives on North America

Whether objectively or subjectively, North America did not look very different in 2008 from the way it had appeared in 1993. After living fourteen years with NAFTA and three years with the SPP, the three states of North America were showing by their behaviour that they were still operating separately, not hanging together.

Three Separate States

Earlier apprehensions in the periphery notwithstanding, the United States had not absorbed either of its neighbours. US corporations had extended their domain in such sectors as agri-food, retail, and manufacturing. Washington had been fortunate that like-minded conservative governments had been elected in the periphery – in Canada favourable to its military agenda and in Mexico supportive of its economic agenda. Otherwise, direct American political influence had not spread either in Mexico, where anger over US treatment of Mexican immigrants remained simmering, or in Canada, where hostility to the George Bush administration prevented the Stephen Harper government from adopting overtly pro-American policies. Having created a more mutually accessible trading and investment area with its neighbours around the principles of neoconservative economic integration, Washington had then stymied the NAFTA forces that it had originally unleashed. First, it pursued its own trade policy both multilaterally and bilaterally with other countries, while paying little heed to the cause of North America's collective development.[10] Then, by imposing on its partners an extreme

definition of the non-state threat from Islamic terrorism, it heavy-hand-
edly superimposed a security imperium over its economic hegemony.
Overall, although its global supremacy may have declined following its
misadventure in Iraq, its dominance over the continent had increased.

Canada had intensified but not radically reordered its relationship
with Washington, which had refused to give up enough sovereignty to
concede to Ottawa its hoped-for exemption from US trade-protection
legislation. The Security and Prosperity Partnership of North America
had provided the continental periphery with a vehicle for gaining more
access to the White House, but Washington's focus on its southern border's narcotics and immigration nightmares diverted its attention from
Canada's bilateral priorities. Sending troops to the most dangerous
area in Afghanistan was the card that Ottawa played to distinguish
itself from Mexico and generate a positive image with which to ingratiate itself with the Administration, which nevertheless continued to
refuse compliance with NAFTA and WTO rulings against its punitive
duties on Canadian softwood lumber.

For its part, Mexico had missed the chance which it thought NAFTA
and its locational advantages had offered it in order to generate a specially prosperous position within the United States' sphere of influence.
Its corporate sector remained hamstrung by rigid monopolies and
corporatist associations – *camaras* – which resisted change rather than
helping move their members into a more dynamic capitalist model. To
underline this failure, China displaced it as the largest source of the
United States' low-labour-cost imports. Mexico remained stuck: having
joined the OECD, it was not yet fully inside the United States' domain;
having left the G-77's Third World regime, it still looked southward to
Latin America for its feeling of community.

Internationally, each country looked out for itself in the trade world.
Except for annual trilateral summitry, there was no evidence of any
capacity for collective action or any sentiment of community solidarity,
certainly not to the point that the two rich countries might effectively
act to bolster the poor, beleaguered state to the south.

The three countries' differing levels of nationalist feeling – ambivalent, but still reflecting an anti-US consciousness in a still somewhat isolationist Mexico; protectionist, and persistently inward-looking in the
globally dominant United States; and largely quiescent in a still liberal-
internationalist Canada – lead us to reconsider our first question:
whether North America has developed a subjective sense of continental
identity.

Only within the transnational corporate elite in the North American periphery does the devotion to continental integration come close to trumping all other concerns. Mexican and Canadian big business leaders are still pursuing the pot of gold they thought they had found in the original free-trade negotiations: enhanced and secure access to the world's biggest market, whether through a North American style multimodal transportation corridor or through regulatory harmonization. Their American counterparts are not so much opposed to more North American integration as they are focused on the world overseas, since the biggest US transnationals' continental plans are only derivative of their global vision. If a positive North American self-identity is not shared even at the summit of each country's corporate hierarchy, continental consciousness can be only weaker farther down the socio-economic ladder.

At the level of the average Mexican or average American or average Canadian, the multiplication of US franchises could lead one to infer that Canadians and Mexicans are becoming more like Americans. Continentally integrated merchandising systems and consumer patterns, which have Canadians and Mexicans alike sporting New York Yankees baseball caps, might suggest that consumerism under US logo dominance is producing homogenized identities across the continent. Certainly, some movement has taken place in this direction. The proliferation of Wal-Marts throughout Mexico also brought US-style, if China-made, consumer goods to the Mexican public. With Starbucks outlets spreading equally fast despite their outrageous prices, historians have been talking about Mexico's new American generation. With the collapse or takeover of Eaton's, Simpsons, and the Hudson's Bay Company, Canada experienced free trade as the similar replacement of its domestic east-to-west retail system by US brand-name chains extending their territorial market northward.

Rigorous survey research has documented how the values of Mexicans, Americans, and Canadians are converging along capitalist, post-materialist, and cosmopolitan lines.[11] But it is dangerous to infer that a greater attitudinal convergence among Mexicans, Americans, and Canadians proves that a *North* American identity is emerging, since the consumer behaviour of burgeoning lower and middle classes in other countries has become similarly Americanized. In any case, a slowly changing *socio-cultural* consciousness must be assessed against the corresponding national *political* consciousness. Whatever their official rhetoric concerning the glories of continental integration may be,[12] and however ideologically sympathetic to each other were George Bush, Stephen Harper, and Felipe Calderón, Washington spent the 2000s building ever longer and ever higher walls to keep out unwanted Mexicans, and Ottawa has been toughening its immigration officials' handling of would-be Mexican refugees in order to impede their influx. The point is that, in North America, each state's political consciousness continues to be generated primarily at the local, regional, and federal level through its own unique political processes. Simply put, NAFTA has brought North America no nearer to a public consciousness of itself as a community in any way approaching Europeans' consciousness of themselves as citizens in an entity transcending their own nation-states. An exception proves the rule. 'North American' enters US discourse only when Americans verbally appropriate Canada's and Mexico's resources and markets, as in 'North American energy.'

This lack of continental consciousness coexists with a weakly integrated continental political economy whose three separate governments and various economic sectors turn out to be connected by five different forms of governance.

LOW INSTITUTIONALIZATION

NAFTA's negotiators believed in negative, not positive integration. Their mission was to bring down political barriers to trade and investment flows, not to construct institutions or create programs that would address such common problems in the three countries as the environmental degradation or social distress resulting from economic expansion. As a result, it was a mark of the NAFTA designers' success that its institutions turned out to be so much less than met the eye, whether these were for executive, legislative, administrative, or judicial government functions. As for NAFTA's labour and environmental institutions, much ink has been spilled to confirm their general impotence, some positive by-products notwithstanding. Looking at an area not addressed by NAFTA – the governance of transboundary waters – reminded us that significant bilateral institutionalization had long existed when tensions between interests on different sides of the border had to be addressed by the federal governments or within particular border regions by civil society, business, and state, provincial, or municipal governments.

SIGNIFICANT TRANSBORDER CORPORATE GOVERNANCE

In terms of economic governance, where interests lobbied government for the programs they wanted, North America was more than met the eye when big business participated actively in writing the new continent's general rules or in certain sectors where the three economies' contiguity mattered. The governance of the largely integrated US-Canada relationship in the oil, natural gas, and electricity markets is largely invisible to the average citizen in either country. Much more attention is paid by Mexicans to the governance of their energy relationship with the United States since it involves their business, government, and expert communities coming up against a still fierce, popular demand to keep energy in the Mexican public sector. The beef, wheat, and corn sectors have been restructured continentally by the major US transnationals with contradictory effects. Given their interests in easy cross-border flows of animals and grain, these TNCs ultimately prevail over US farmers' demands for autarchy. With corn, we could see the dramatic impact of Mexico's concessions in NAFTA, whose radical tariff cuts and massive consequent imports of US corn sowed disaster through the ranks of literally millions of small-scale, subsistence-economy campesinos.

TRANSBORDER GOVERNANCE UNDER GLOBALIZING PRESSURES
With the passage of time, some economic sectors where geographical proximity mattered appeared to be in transition. In 2005, steel, the textile and apparel industries, and North America's three capital markets were governed continentally. However, NAFTA's rules were insufficiently institutionalized to offer shelter against the pressures of globalization, which were turning steel and textiles from being centripetally focused on the region to being centrifugally connected with markets and head offices around the world. Steel is an industry that has been globalized by mergers and acquisitions although it produces and trades continentally. Textiles and apparel lost its regional coherence through simple trade pressures from lower cost competitors. The asymmetrical intimacy between the periphery's capital markets and the United States, which used to be a close continental dependence, is now becoming part of a globally interconnected network of stock exchanges.

NORTH AMERICAN PARTICIPATION IN GLOBALIZED GOVERNANCE
North America was not at all what it seemed when instances of policy harmonization among the three countries turned out to be participation in forms of global governance. From above, the three governments participate in the G7 Financial Stability Forum and the committees of the Bank of International Settlements, where they decide the global norms by which they will regulate their own banking institutions. From below, in some issues such as strengthening intellectual property rights for pharmaceuticals, governmental policies are dictated by trans-

national corporate interests which are powerful enough to get global governance institutions to discipline the periphery. When this phe-nome-non can be observed in the three countries of North America, it is not an index of specifically continental governance, because the same corporate giants lobby just as insistently for the same policies to be adopted by other countries around the globe, as we saw with the US producers of GM food technologies.

STATE-DOMINANT INTER-GOVERNMENTALISM

Lastly, North America turned out to be just what it used to be in areas where traditional inter-governmental relations prevailed. The United States' radical paradigm shift from a border-flattening economic liberalization to a barrier-constructing security priority was equally decisive in turning transborder governance in North America back to a more state-led praxis. Defence, which had not been a continental issue in North America since the Second World War, returned as a policy priority when Washington chose to respond to the threat of global terrorism by military means. Given the vast territory that separates Canada and Mexico, it is not surprising that inter-governmental relations have driven the continent's third bilateral relationship ever since the Prime Minister's Office in Ottawa and the presidential office, Los Pinos, in Mexico City negotiated their first agreement on temporary labour migration.

Synthetic Review of North America's Transborder Governance

This medley of governance forms produces conflicting messages for us as we stand back from the individual studies in order to put together a composite picture of North America's power relationships, whether among governments or within individual economic sectors. Three main trends can be identified: deepened asymmetry, substantial resid-ual autonomy, and spreading hegemony with shrinking autarchy.

Deepened Asymmetry

As the European Community matured into the European Union, inter-governmental relations there became more complex and less formal. This has been true to a markedly lesser extent in North America, in part because the continent has only three members and in part because NAFTA created little in the way of a structural forum for increased interaction among governmental, market, and societal actors.

An intensified bilateral relationship between the governments of Mexico and Canada was the product first of NAFTA and later of the Security and Prosperity Partnership. With relatively low levels of economic, social, and cultural exchanges between the two countries, the relationship remains focused on such formal, government-to-government programs as the Canada-Mexico Partnership and the long-standing Seasonal Agricultural Workers Program. Nevertheless, most of North America's transborder relations still focus on the US-Canada or the US-Mexico dyads, which have remained the continent's overwhelmingly dominant relationships despite NAFTA.

North America has developed less trilateralism than might have been expected. Certainly, there is much more communication among the governments' officials at senior levels than existed before NAFTA. Notwithstanding the much-heralded SPP's three-way approach to many issues of North American governance, the United States' proposal to reinforce Mexican efforts to suppress its narco-traffic cartels was negotiated bilaterally as the completely separate Merida Plan of 2007, which demonstrated that, while security could be talked about in trilateral forums, concrete action was still a matter for bilateral cooperation. Given the three executives' reluctance to involve their legislatures and given the heated resistance of the three states' nationalist forces, the SPP's managers and their corporate counterpart, the North American Competitiveness Council, have been leery about moving towards a genuinely muscular trilateralism.

Astonishingly, steel was the only sector where some significant corporate continentalization was found. It was only regarding steel that the three governments collaborated with the three industry associations in order to generate a common international negotiating position, but steel is now losing its North American coherence because of global corporate restructuring.

While NAFTA's rules of origin presupposed some North American identity for the textile industry, its continental coherence broke down under massive trade pressures from China and the US government's subsequent disregard for its continental neighbours' interests. Transnational corporate structures vary enormously from company to company, but the typical American TNC still includes Canada as part of its US operations while Mexico remains organizationally part of Latin America.

Though the neoconservative governments of Canada and Mexico must have believed that trade liberalization would enhance their position within their own political systems, North America has not followed in the European Union's footsteps by mitigating the huge power discrepancy between its strongest and weakest state members. On paper, the NAFTA and WTO dispute-settlement regime promised Canada and Mexico a more level playing field, which they did obtain on minor issues. But, in such major conflicts as transborder trucking for Mexico and softwood-lumber exports for Canada, prolonged US refusal to comply with panel rulings revealed that North America's basic power asymmetry had not been offset by the new institutions. Indeed, the *Sports Illustrated* case discussed in chapter III showed that Washington remained the master at exploiting dispute-settlement processes by using the WTO's US-modelled international economic norms to increase its cultural industries' market power in Canada.

Transborder corporate governance was more than met the eye in capital-market regulation and the beef and corn sectors. Resisting that trend, the still-robust Canadian Wheat Board maintained considerable symmetry in US-Canada grain relations. The expansion of tar-sands mining and refining in Alberta allowed the Stephen Harper government to brag that Canada had become an 'energy super-power.' However, the US transnationals' dominant role in the old North America's petroleum sector along with CUFTA's constraints on Canada's policy autonomy make it sensible to consider Alberta as a largely autonomous subfederal political economy integrated in a US-led system.

In industries where transborder corporate governance was in transition, changes in asymmetry varied considerably. The steel sector's experience during NAFTA's first decade showed that the Canadian and Mexican players were integrating under US corporate leadership mediated through the American Iron and Steel Institute. The subsequent takeover of Canada's principal steel corporations suggested a substantial loss of that country's economic power, but more in a global than a continental context. A similar fracturing within the textile and apparel industry left the Mexican and Canadian sectors more integrated continentally while simultaneously being more exposed to global pressures. Asymmetries may have increased between the centre and periphery of North America, but they did so within the global context of a declining United States and a fragmenting continental coherence.

Banking revealed an unusual situation. Canada continued to maintain considerable symmetry within the old North America. Meanwhile, Mexico's near-total loss of ownership of its own sector, now characterized by very considerable non-US corporate control, left its power asymmetry aggravated but diversified rather than concentrated in a US dependency. In contrast, the astonishing success of US Big Pharma in internationalizing its intellectual property rights through NAFTA and the WTO, combined with the industry's ability to get Washington to exert unilateral pressure on its behalf, clearly enhanced the asymmetry within both of the pharmaceutical industry's US-Canada and US-Mexico dyads.

Inter-governmental relations in North America since 2001 demonstrated quite a different rebalancing of previous power discrepancies. Defending itself against global terrorism required the United States to abandon attempts at achieving total security through autarchy. It was not a question of either to have a secure US border or not. Where massive cross-border traffic of goods and humans required the national border to be supplemented by a secure continental periphery, Washington dealt inter-governmentally with Ottawa and Mexico City. A strong argument could be made that, while the periphery's *autonomy* declined and the central state's *capacity* increased in matters of border security, continental *asymmetries* decreased, because Washington had to rely on Mexico City and Ottawa delivering on their numerous commitments to 'smarten' their borders. Similarly, where the SPP and NACC have developed meaningful trilateral discourse – particularly in the annual summits that bring the Mexican president and Canadian prime minister face to face with their US homologue – we can see further institutional decrease in continental asymmetry.

While significant, these details distract from the big picture originally painted during the CUFTA and NAFTA negotiations, when Canada and Mexico negotiated their qualified inclusion in the US market on conditions of increased governmental symmetry. As it turned out, though the neighbour states disarmed many of their economic defences, the United States retained both its economically offensive capacity to subsidize its producers and its defensive capacity for protection through trade remediation.

Consistent with other themes in this analysis, changes in the imbalance between a generally harmonious US-Canada and a generally conflictual US-Mexico relationship varied considerably from issue to issue. Where developments in Mexico – for instance, in environmental policy – have reduced US-Mexican asymmetry, they are likely to have reduced the imbalance between this dyad and the US-Canada relationship. As the two US neighbours become more similar in their regulatory regimes – harmonizing, for instance, with US standards concerning genetically modified food or intellectual property rights – the imbalance between their two relationships with Washington has also declined. To the extent that a more symmetrical relationship between Canada and Mexico has helped the latter to make institutional progress in, for instance, electoral reform or modernizing governmental norms on transparency, the third bilateral relationship helps reduce the imbalance between North America's two other dyads.

Substantial Residual Autonomy

How developments in North America have affected its three states' ability to do what they want within their territory and without is clearly linked to the previous themes. For this analysis, I have been interested less in what sovereignty each has retained or given up de jure than in what (internal) autonomy and (external) capacity they enjoy de facto in the new North America.

Given the nature of the trade-liberalization process – both Canada and Mexico having negotiated their free-trade agreements from positions of political and economic weakness with a United States very clearly focused on the bilateral 'irritants' it wanted to eliminate and the precedents it wanted to achieve in new international economic norms – it is clear that the United States' neighbours accepted major reductions in their autonomy in exchange for what they believed would be greater capacity, that is, enhanced and secure access to the US market for their exporters. What little autonomy the United States gave up de jure – primarily binational panels to review its trade-remedy determinations – it ignored de facto when major domestic interests flexed their protectionist muscles. The United States' resistance to the erosion of its own autonomy has necessarily affected its neighbours. In the dominant state, established institutions that are anchored in constitutional and democratic legitimacy still determine – while ceding minimal sovereignty to continental governance – how adaptations are made to globalization, whether these be in the name of economic prosperity or anti-terrorist security.

Evidence of some independence in Mexico's and Canada's diplomacy does not mean that these middle-sized powers can recapture their autonomy over domestic policy as easily as Washington can refuse to give up its own. On the contrary, the structural changes in the continental periphery resulting from deepened integration make it extremely difficult to turn back the clock. Efforts to re-establish federal government control over agriculture in Mexico or the petroleum industry in Canada would encounter massive resistance from domestic interests that have become dependent on or acquired by their American partners. Mexico's rural depopulation and impoverished suburbanization, accelerated by the devastation of the its corn economy, cannot be reversed by re-establishing the tariff on corn as the campesino protesters obviously hope.

Being related to political will, autonomy lies partly in the eye of the beholder. Canadian and Mexican neoconservatives *felt* little loss of autonomy since reducing the powers of their state in order to unleash the energies of their corporate players was integral to their ideological agendas. Losses of autonomy would be put to an empirical test only if a newly elected government tried to exert a power that its predecessor had given up. This is the concern of nationalists in both countries who see losses of autonomy aggravating power asymmetries which force each state into a pattern of continual compliance. Nationalism does indeed inspire some resistance in the periphery, particularly among Canadians for certain highly symbolic issues such as the US war in Iraq or, for Mexicans, threats to their constitution's sacrosanct Article 27.

But looking at the US neighbours from a broader vantage point shows the same two governments to be complicit in constraining their own autonomy. They negotiated their way into economic globalization through multiple channels and have sustained their own relationships with weaker economic partners by signing free-trade agreements. Mexico has done so with its Central American neighbours, and Canada has negotiated a trade deal with South Africa that imposes the very same state-autonomy-reducing, TNC-enhancing investor-state dispute arbitration on that country that many of its citizens had objected to in NAFTA's Chapter 11. The North American periphery's powerful corporations in petroleum and the information media participate in worldwide TNC networks, and their elites – including many of their academics and NGO leaders – circulate globally in their own specialized groupings.

Even if the Mexican and Canadian governments resisted joining Washington in its Iraq war, they have also resisted building their own bilateral axis in solidarity against Washington. They may declaim against American perfidies, but the context for their ire is as likely to be the desire for greater access to the US market than Washington will permit as it is dismay about US demands that they change their own policies.

In the normal play of treaty-based transnational relations, when a state sacrifices its autonomy by giving up some sovereignty, it can expect to increase its capacity internationally. As we saw, the United States' unusual concessions on grain policy led to greater Canadian capacity in the US market. Yet there is little other evidence to indicate that Mexico, Canada, or their business communities have increased their capacity in the United States. Treaty-violating assertions of US autonomy have come at the cost of reduced Mexican or Canadian capacity in the United States to influence the resolution there of problems caused by US-generated externalities in such areas as water management in Mexico's case or air-pollution control in Canada's.

Although autonomy is generally sacrificed to increase capacity, in some cases autonomy and capacity are directly related. In US-Canada border-water management, the Great Lakes example showed that, where Canada enjoyed enough autonomy that it could inflict potential damage to US interests (by licensing bulk-water exports from Lake Superior), it had greater capacity to influence the outcome of major inter-governmental negotiations (in this case, rules governing water diversion).

Spreading Hegemony with Shrinking Autarchy

Because of its enormous complexities, the centre-periphery relationship in North America shows simultaneous indications of imperium, hegemony, and autarchy. With the exception of post 9/11 border-security issues, there is little public evidence that the United States government imposes its will on its neighbours on general issues of public policy through the use of coercion, whether through threats to use physical force or to apply severe economic penalties. What imperial power the United States does exert as a government happens more through big business insisting that Washington defend its specific corporate interests. As we saw, if the biotechnology or pharmaceuticals industry has enough lobby power to direct the international actions of the US government, Washington demonstrates imperial power when its exercise of coercion – in the form of threats of economic retaliation – leaves the periphery government believing it has no option but to comply.

Otherwise, if a hegemon is understood as the leader of a regime in which the weaker partners participate on the basis of a willing consensus, we have witnessed a general increase of hegemony in North America's political economy through the periphery's adjusting to and adopting common, US-made norms and rules. Of course, the successful exercise of coercive power can also generate a hegemony once the weaker partners bend to the dominant party's threats, adjust to the new reality, and ultimately embrace the new regime. In the public sector, we observed how this happened when an imperial exercise of power by the Federal Energy Regulatory Commission (Canadian power utilities were forced to privatize if they wanted to continue to export electricity) turned into a hegemony as FERC's regulatory and administrative counterparts in Canada fell into line with the new US system.

Given the extraordinarily close interconnections between North America's centre and its periphery, we could see in the cases of GM foods and brand-name drugs how imperially driven sectors gradually became hegemonic. The more these powerful US transnationals deepen their roots in a neighbour's economy, the more they co-opt local business and political elites, so that the Mexican or Canadian governments ultimately ingest their interests, defending rather than resisting what they had originally seen as external American threats. Ultimately, we can see how North America's political economy facilitates the entrenchment of a decentralized corporate hegemony through public-private cooperation in which the peripheral governments fend off civil-society resistance in favour of transnational enterprise.

It is consistent with the notion of hegemony that the weaker partners exert some influence over the dominant power. We have seen that the Canadian Wheat Board extended Canadian grain growers' export presence in the US market, that Ontario affirmed its right to participate in determining Great Lakes water-diversion policy, and that Mexico developed some leverage over US immigration policy through its legal and undocumented workers' presence in the United States.

More paradoxically, if consensus has been achieved through external pressure such as FERC's or by the domestic dominance of foreign-controlled corporations, transborder governance may be simultaneously hegemonic for consenting domestic elites and imperial for a protesting civil society marginalized from the continent's political process. Depending on which network is being considered, the question of Mexico's corn tariffs can be seen either as a hegemony (because of the integrationist PAN government's belief that future progress lies in supporting Mexico's industrial agri-exporters through the NAFTA regime to which they fully subscribe) or as an imperium (because the PRD insists that NAFTA's agricultural chapter, which has devastated the campesinos' economy, be renegotiated). Equally, the Security and Prosperity Partnership of North America can be understood either as an evolution of the North American neoconservative hegemony (with the Canadian Council of Chief Executives happily taking the lead) or as the latest manifestation of the US imperium (with defeated presidential candidate López Obrador bitterly protesting the further sapping of his country's sovereignty).

In North America, autarchy is generally identified with revolutionary Mexico's attempt to cut itself free of its pre-First World War economic, cultural, and social dependency on the United States and with its post-Second World War experience of import-substitution industrialization, when high barriers to trade and investment were put in place to foster a national economic space reserved for a domestically owned and oriented national capitalism. But what may be autarchic in one hub-to-spoke relationship can be hegemonic in the other. In defence, we saw how Washington's shift to a security paradigm reactivated the Cold War's two distinct bilateral relationships, with Mexico maintaining the maximum autarchy demanded by a public opinion that remained hyper-sensitive to any suggestion of military entanglements abroad or US interventions at home, while the Canadian military enthusiastically participated as a junior partner in a Pentagon-led hegemony. With energy, we saw a variation on this pattern: enthusiastic Canadian participation in Washington's energy-security hegemony, while cross-border integration with Mexico was resisted by a governing elite reluctantly having to pay heed to a public still committed to maintaining Pemex as the country's last corporate symbol of its tenuous sovereignty. With the exception of energy, Mexico's conservative counter-revolution has broken down its autarchic capacity. NAFTA's supra-constitutional power has become all too evident to protesting campesinos and clergy as they vainly call for a reassertion of Mexico's agricultural autarchy.

Autarchy may represent a vestige from Mexican history, but it is still a luxury that the United States can afford, particularly in traditionally protected industries. Curiously, it is the globally dominant superpower that showed it can shift to autarchic positions at will, blocking its borders when terrorists struck in 2001 or closing them to trade in beef when a mad cow was discovered in Canada a little later. Yet, while autarchy may be the US protectionists' default position, the forces of US-led corporate restructuring make it a short-term stance that has few prospects for long-term success. As we saw with the beef and wheat sectors, even fierce western-farmer protectionism is no longer a political match for globally oriented US food corporations which require open but well-regulated borders.

On occasion, the United States asserts autarchy territorially as a defensive posture while nevertheless insisting that its partners continue to play by the regime's rules. Excessive cheating of this kind may undermine the leader's legitimacy and cause its partners to withdraw their consent to its hegemony, although, within North America's trilateral regime, Washington's neighbours are generally too weak or too timid to exercise this option.

Last Words

I began this study asking whether North America existed by using the European Union as the comparator for the multi-state world regions of the late twentieth century. Unlike the EU, North American forms of transnational governance do not constitute a system of 'multi-level governance,' defined by European scholars as effective regulation with satisfactory compliance rates in which each level enjoys its own autonomy, identity, and understanding of the common good.[13]

If the North American world region's nature is very different from that of its counterpart across the Atlantic, we could conclude by looking elsewhere. Perhaps its asymmetrical power system will set the standard for the regionalism emerging in the twenty-first century in other areas of the world – a regionalism characterized by

- few institutional constraints on the regional leader;
- new forms of private authority reducing the autonomy of constitutionally established national authorities;
- increased autonomy and capacity for transnational businesses liberated from national control; and
- diminished access for a polarized and de-democratized civil society to these dispersed, ever-more inaccessible centres of power.

But the forces of change are relentless, and it would be rash to predict what patterns will appear as the century proceeds. Will the sudden decline of US hard and soft power in the world cause Canada and Mexico to intensify their integration, for instance, by Mexico restructuring Pemex with private investors and Canada promoting tar-sands development regardless of the environmental consequences? Or will the periphery try to reverse what was until recently thought to be the unstoppable process of integration, with Mexico again deciding to reserve its energy resources for its own use and with Canada determining to achieve its own energy security by constructing a trans-Canada energy corridor?

The collapse of the George W. Bush administration's popularity could signal the end of neoconservativism's three-decades-long affair with an idealized market. The 2006 elections of very conservative governments in both Canada and Mexico did not herald either ecologically or socially liberal government in the continental periphery, but the probable victory of Barack Obama in the United States in 2008 heralded an ideological watershed after three decades of right-leaning republicanism. Meanwhile, as the three political systems, their economic actors, and roiling political movements interact, it seems safe to predict that, while many forms of transborder governance will persist in North America, this world region will remain a contested space whose existence remains economically precarious, politically unstable, and institutionally impotent.

In the European Union, such periodic crises as the Irish rejection of the Lisbon Treaty in 2008 have not prevented the region's persistent development as a self-governing, multi-state community. For better or worse, by the autumn of the same year, if North America existed it was still more as geography than as governance.

Notes

INTRODUCTION

1 Harold A. Innis, 'Economic Trends in Canadian-American Relations' (1938), in Mary Q. Innis, ed., *Essays in Canadian Economic History* (Toronto: University of Toronto Press, 1956), 238.

2 John Redekop, 'A Reinterpretation of Canadian-American Relations,' *Canadian Journal of Political Science* 9 (1976): 227–43.

3 Stephen Clarkson, 'Continentalism: The Conceptual Challenge for Canadian Social Science,' in *The John Porter Memorial Lectures: 1984–1987* (Montreal: Canadian Sociology and Anthropology Association, 1988), 23–43.

4 Stephen D. Krasner used the notion of 'regime' to address a similar reality: a set of 'implicit or explicit principles, norms, rules, and decision-making procedures around which actors' expectations converge in a given area of international relations.' See his edited volume *International Regimes* (Ithaca, N.Y.: Cornell University Press, 1983), 2.

5 Livingston T. Merchant and A.D.P. Heeney, 'Canada and the United States – Principles of Partnership,' *Department of State Bulletin*, Aug. 2, 1965.

6 Canada, Foreign Investment Division, Department of Industry, Trade and Commerce, *Foreign Direct Investment in Canada since the Second World War* (Ottawa: Government Printer, Statistics Canada, 1970); George Hoberg, 'Canada and North American Integration,' *Canadian Public Policy* 26, no. 2 (2000): 39.

7 John J. Kirton and David DeWitt, 'Canada as a Principal Power,' *Canadian Journal of Political Science*, 17, no. 1 (1984): 193, 194.

8 Maria Teresa Gutiérrez-Haces, *Procesos de integración económica en México y Canadá: una perspectiva histórica comparada* (México: Universidad Nacional Autónoma de México, 2002).

9 Manuel Garcia y Griego. 'The Importance of Mexican Contract Laborers to the United States, 1942–1964,' in David Gutierrez, ed., *Between Two Worlds: Mexican Immigrants in the United States* (Wilmington, Del.: Jaguar Publications, 1996).

10 Josefina Z. Vázquez and Lorenzo Meyer, *The United States and Mexico* (Chicago and London: University of Chicago Press, 1985), 66–71.

11 Raymond Vernon, 'Multinationals and Governments: Key Actors in the NAFTA,' in Lorraine Eden, ed., *Multinationals in North America* (Calgary: University of Calgary Press, 1994), 31.

12 D. Held et al., 'The Globalization of Economic Activity,' *New Political Economy*, 2, no. 2 (1997): 257–77. See also D. Held et al., *Global Transformations: Politics, Economics and Culture* (Cambridge, U.K.: Polity Press, 1999); and Anthony Giddens, *The Consequences of Modernity* (Cambridge, U.K.: Polity Press, 1990), 64.

13 Robert A. Pastor, *Toward a North American Community* (Washington, D.C.: Institute of International Economics, 2001), 34–6.

14 Ibid.

15 Michel Aglietta, *Theory of Capitalist Regulation* (London: New Left Books, 1979).

16 Julian Castro-Rea, 'Are US Business Priorities Driving Continental Integration?' *Edmonton Journal*, March 27, 2006.

17 Following four decades of social-science research on European integration, a second, more comparative political-economy literature has analysed the new generation of continental-integration projects such as MERCOSUR and ASEAN that were negotiated following the disintegration of the Soviet bloc and the intensification of globalization. Shaun Breslin, Richard Higgott, and Ben Rosamund, 'Regions in Comparative Perspective,' in Shaun Breslin et al., *New Regionalisms in the Global Political Economy* (New York: Routledge, 2000).

18 Robert A. Pastor, 'A North American Community,' *Norte América*, 1, no. 1 (2006): 209–21.

19 The World Bank, Key Development: Data and Statistics (2005), http://devdata.worldbank.org/external/CPProfile.asp?PTYPE=CP&CCODE=LVA (accessed on April 10, 2008).

20 Here, I am referring to various works such as Robert Dahl's *Polyarchy: Participation and Opposition* (New Haven, Conn.: Yale University Press, 1971), or his *Dilemmas of Pluralist Democracy: Autonomy vs. Control* (New Haven, Conn.: Yale University Press, 1982); James Bohman's *Public Deliberation: Pluralism, Complexity, and Democracy* (Cambridge, Mass.: MIT Press, 1996); and Paul Gottfried's *After Liberalism: Mass Democracy in the Managerial State* (Princeton, N.J.: Princeton University Press, 1999). It is also worth mention-

ing some works with a more national focus: Paul Herrson, *The Interest Group Connection: Electioneering, Lobbying, and Policymaking in Washington* (Washington, D.C.: P.C.Q. Press, 2005); Sebastián Lerdo de Tejada Covarrubias and Luis Antonio Godina Herrera, *El lobbying en México* (Mexico City: Miguel Angel Porrúa, 2004); and Pierre B. Meurier, *Lobbying in Canada* (Toronto: Carswell, 2003).

21 For a discussion on the various roles of UN institutions, see Bruce Cronin, 'The Two Faces of the United Nations: The Tension between Intergovernmentalism and Transnationalism,' *Global Governance*, 8, no. 1 (2002): 53–71. For the increasing engagement between civil society and international governmental organizations, see Gabriel Casaburi and Diana Tussie, 'From Global to Local Governance: Civil Society and the Multilateral Development Banks,' *Global Governance: A Review of Multilateralism and International Organizations*, 6, no. 4 (2000): 399–403, as well as Paul Cerny, 'Globalization and the Changing Logic of Collective Action,' *International Organization*, 48 (1995): 595–625.

22 Sandford Borins et al., *Change, Governance and Public Management: Alternative Service Delivery and Information Technology* (Ottawa: Public Policy Forum and KPMG, 2000), 25.

23 See Elisabeth J. Friedman, ed., *Sovereignty, Democracy, and Global Civil Society: State-Society Relations at UN World Conference* (New York: State University of New York Press, 2005).

24 K. Buse, S. Fustukian, and K. Lee, eds., *Health Policy in a Globalising World* (Cambridge: Cambridge University Press, 2002), 713.

25 For the analogies between government and the corporate sector, see James Q. Wilson's *Bureaucracy: What Government Agencies Do and Why They Do It* (New York: Basic Books, 1989).

I. NORTH AMERICA AS MARKET AND COMMUNITY

1 This is GDP at the 2005 exchange rate. It was chosen, instead of GDP at Purchasing Power Parity (PPP), to make it more comparable to the North American GDP figure quoted in current US dollars. Central Intelligence Agency (CIA), 'The World Factbook – European Union,' https://www.cia.gov/library/publications/the-world-factbook/geos/ee.html (accessed on April 8, 2008).

2 World Trade Organization (WTO), 'World Trade Statistics 2005. Chapter 3 Trade by Region,' http://www.wto.org/english/res_e/statis_e/its2005_e/its05_to c_e.htm (accessed on April 8, 2008).

3 GDP is measured in current US dollars. Data taken from World Bank, 'Key

Development Data and Statistics 2007,' http://web.worldbank.org/WBSITE/EXTERNAL/DATASTATISTICS/0,co ntentMDK:20535285~menuPK:1192694~pagePK:64133150~piPK:641331 75~theSitePK:239419,00 .html (accessed on April 8, 2008).

4 WTO, 'World Trade Statistics 2005' (accessed on April 8, 2008).

5 In terms of GDP at PPP. Data taken and calculated from the WTO, 'World Trade Statistics 2005' (accessed on April 8, 2008).

6 International Monetary Fund (IMF), 'World Investment Reports 2000 and 2004,' UNCTAD and IMF, www.unctad.org/en/docs/wir2004_en.pdf (accessed on April 8, 2008).

7 World Bank, 'Key Development Data and Statistics (2006),' http://web.worldbank.org/WBSITE/EXTERNAL/DATASTATISTICS/0,content-MDK:20535285~menuPK:1192694~pagePK:64133150~piPK:64133175 ~theSitePK:239419,00.html (accessed on April 8, 2008).

8 WTO, 'International Trade and Tariff Data 2001–2006,' http://www .wto.org/english/res_e/statis_e/statis_e.htm (accessed on April 8, 2008).

9 Walter Nugent, 'Crossing Borders, Countering Exceptionalism,' in Marc Rodriguez, ed., *Repositioning North American Migration History: New Directions in Modern Continental Migration, Citizenship, and Community* (Rochester N.Y.: University of Rochester Press, 2004), 7.

10 Bruno Ramirez, 'Borderland Studies and Migration: The Canada/United States Case,' in Rodriguez, ed., *Repositioning North American Migration History,* 16–26.

11 Ibid., 17–21.

12 Ibid., 21.

13 Stephen Easton, 'Who Goes There? Canadian Emigration to the United States in the Twenty-First Century,' in Richard Harris, Stephen Easton, and Nicholas Schmitt, eds., *Brains on the Move: Essays on Human Capital Mobility in a Globalizing World and Implications for the Canadian Economy* (Toronto: C.D. Howe Institute, 2005), 1–12, 3.

14 Sister Mary Colette Standard, 'The Sonoran Migration to California 1848–1856: A Study in Prejudice,' in David Gutierrez, ed., *Between Two Worlds: Mexican Immigrants in the United States* (Wilmington, Del.: Jaguar Publications, 1996), 3–22.

15 Gary Freeman and Frank Bean, 'Mexico and US Immigration Policy,' in Frank Bean et al., *At the Crossroads: Mexico and US Immigration Policy* (Lanham, Md.: Rowman and Littlefield, 1997), 23.

16 Ibid., 25.

17 Mae Ngai, 'Braceros, Wetbacks, and the National Boundaries of Class,' in Rodriguez, ed., *Repositioning North American Migration History,* 206–64.

18 Ibid., 234–5.

19 Ibid.
20 CIA, 'The World Factbook,' https://www.cia.gov/cia/publications/fact-book/rankorder/2095 rank.html (accessed on April 8, 2008).
21 Easton, *Who Goes There?* 10.
22 John Zhao, Doug Drew, and Scott Murray, 'Brain Drain and Brain Gain: The Migration of Knowledge Workers to and from Canada,' *Education Quarterly Review* 6, no. 3 (2000): 8–35.
23 Jeffrey Passel, Jennifer Van Hook, and Frank Bean, 'Estimates of the Legal and Unauthorized Foreign-Born Populations of the United States, based on Census 2000,' Sabre Systems and Census Bureau, June 1, 2004, http://members.aol.com/copafs/Passel.pdf (accessed on April 8, 2008).
24 Migration Policy Institute, 'Migration Information Source,' December 2007, http://www.migrationinformation.org/issue_dec07.cfm (accessed on April 8, 2008).
25 Freeman and Bean, *Mexico and US Immigration Policy,* 27.
26 Alene Gelbard and Marion Carter, 'Mexican Immigration and US Population,' in Bean et al., *At the Crossroads*, 120.
27 Gerlbard and Carter, *Mexican Immigration and US Population*, 122.
28 Tamara Woroby, 'North American Immigration: The Search for Positive-Sum Returns,' in Isabel Studer and Carol Wise, eds., *Requiem or Revival: The Promise of North American Integration* (Washington, D.C.: Brookings Institution Press, 2007), 252.
29 Gelbard and Carter, *Mexico and US Immigration Policy,* 120.
30 Rogelio Sanchez, Maria Morales, and Janie Filotea, 'The Demography of Mexicans in the United States,' in Roberto de Anda, ed., *Chicanas and Chicanos in Contemporary Society* (Lanham, Md.: Rowman and Littlefield, 2004), 3–20.
31 Freeman and Bean, *Mexico and US Immigration Policy,* 3, 35.
32 Sanchez, Morales, and Filotea, *The Demography of Mexicans in the United States*, 6.
33 US-Mexico Binational Council, *Managing Mexican Migration to the United States: Recommendations for Policymakers*, Report of the US-Mexico Binational Council (Washington, D.C.: Center for Strategic and International Studies and Instituto Tecnológico Autónomo de Mexico, 2004), 1.
34 Jacob Hornberger, 'Dejen a los Americanos en México Ser,' *Nuevas Raíces*, April 11, 2007, http://www.nuevasraices.com/content/templates/articulosnr.as p?articleid=3713&zoneid=36 (accessed on April 8, 2008).
35 Mariana Martínez, 'Del norte al sur,' *BCC Mundo*, Dec. 19, 2005, http://news.bbc.co.uk/hi/spanish/business/barometro_economic o/newsid_4541000/4541476.stm (accessed on April 8, 2008).
36 Douglas Massey and Audrey Singer, 'Immigration and Its Consequences:

New Estimates of Undocumented Mexican Migration and the Probability of Apprehension,' *Demography* 32, no. 2 (1995): 203–13.

37 Jeffrey Passel, 'Unauthorized Migrants: Numbers and Characteristics. Background Briefing Prepared for Taskforce on Immigration and America's Future' (Pew Hispanic Center, 2005), 6, http://pewhispanic.org/files/reports/46.pdf (accessed on April 8, 2008).

38 Ibid., 16.

39 Pia Orrenius, 'The Effect of US Border Enforcement on the Crossing Behavior of Mexican Migrants,' in Jorge Durand and Douglas Massey, eds., *Crossing the Border: Research from the Mexican Migration Project* (New York: Russell Sage Foundation, 2004), 318–19.

40 Philip Martin, Richard Chen, and Mark Madamba, 'United States Policies for Admission of Professional and Technical Workers: Objectives and Outcomes,' *International Migration Paper* 35 (Geneva: International Labour Office, 2004), 3.

41 Maia Jachimowicz and Deborah W. Meyers, 'Temporary High-Skilled Migration,' Migration Policy Institute, November 2002, http://www.migrationinformation.org/feature/display.cfm?ID=69 (accessed on April 8, 2008).

42 Don DeVoretz and Diane Coulombe, 'Labour Mobility between Canada and the United States: Quo Vadis?' Paper presented at the Social and Labour Market Aspects of North American Linkages Workshop and Industry Canada-Human Resource Development Workshop, Ottawa, Nov. 21, 2002.

43 Doris Meissner et al., eds., *Immigration and America's Future: A New Chapter.* Report of the Independent Taskforce on Immigration and America's Future, 2006, Co-chairs Spencer Abraham and Lee Hamilton, 97.

44 DeVoretz and Coulombe, *Labour Mobility between Canada and the United States*, 2.

45 Jachimowicz and Meyers, 'Temporary High-Skilled Migration' (accessed on April 8, 2008).

46 Katherine Richardson, 'Sieve or Shield: Cascadia and High Tech Labour Mobility under Nafta,' in D. Wolfish and R. Roberge, eds., *Rethinking the Line: The Canada-US Border* (Vancouver: University of British Columbia Press, 2002), 2–21; DeVoretz and Coulombe, *Labour Mobility between Canada and the United States*, 4.

47 Richard Harris and Nicholas Schmitt, 'Labour Mobility and a North American Common Market: Implications for Canada,' in Harris, Easton, and Schmitt, eds., *Brains on the Move*, 138.

48 James Vazquez-Azpiri, 'Through the Eye of a Needle: Canadian Information

Technology Professionals and the TN Category of the NAFTA,' *Canada Immigration and Citizen News*, June 26, 2000, http://www.canadaimmigrationlaw .net/WorkVisas/Articles/Artic le5/itprofessionals1.htm (accessed on April 8, 2008).

49 Woroby, 'North American Immigration,' 257.

50 Pia Orrenius and Daniel Streitfield, 'TN Visas: A Stepping Stone towards a NAFTA Labour Market,' *Federal Reserve Bank of Dallas* (November–December 2006): 6.

51 Karl Deutsch, *Political Community at the International Level: Problems of Definition and Measurement* (New York: Doubleday, 1954); Ernst B. Haas, 'International Integration: The European and the Universal Process,' *International Organization* 15, no. 3 (1961): 366–92.

52 Robert O'Brien, 'North American Integration and International Relations Theory,' *Canadian Journal of Political Science* 28, no. 4 (1995): 693–724.

53 Robert A. Pastor, 'North America and the Americas: Integration among Unequal Partners,' in Mary Farrell, Björn Hettne, and Luk Van Langenhove, eds., *Global Politics of Regionalism: Theory and Practice* (London: Pluto Press, 2005), 203.

54 Mauricio Tenorio Trillo, 'On the Limits of Historical Imagination: North America as a Historical Essay,' *International Journal* 61, no. 3 (2006): 567–87.

55 Sidney Weintraub, 'The Fence as a Metaphor for How the United States Views Its Relations with Mexico,' *Issues in International Political Economy* (Washington, D.C.: Center for Strategic and International Studies, October 2006), 82.

56 Samuel P. Huntington, *Who Are We?* (New York: Simon and Schuster, 2004).

57 Allan Gotlieb, *Romanticism and Realism in Canadian Foreign Policy* (Toronto: C.D. Howe Institute's Benefactors Lecture, 2004).

58 Robert A. Pastor, 'A North American Community,' *Nortéamerica* 1, no. 1 (2006): 213.

59 White House, 'Remarks by President Bush and President Fox of Mexico at Arrival Ceremony,' Sept. 5, 2001; William Walker, 'Bush Woos – Most Important – Mexico; Canada Gets a Brief Mention as U.S. Bids to Mend Relations,' *Toronto Star*, Sept. 6, 2001.

60 Pastor, *A North American Community*.

61 Ronald Inglehart, Neil Nevitte, and Miguel Basáñez, *The North American Trajectory.* (New York: Aldine de Gruyter, 1996).

62 Miguel Basáñez, Ronald Inglehart, and Neil Nevitte, 'North American Convergence, Revisited,' *Nortéamerica* 2, no. 2 (2007): 21–62.

63 Michael Adams, *Fire and Ice: The United States, Canada and the Myth of Converging Values* (Toronto: Penguin, 2003).

64 Edward Grabb and James Curtis, *Regions Apart: The Four Societies of Canada and the United States* (Toronto: Oxford University Press, 2004), cited in James Bristow, 'Advancing the Values Debate,' *Literary Review of Canada* (March 2006): 26–8.

65 Inglehart, Nevitte, and Basáñez, *North American Trajectory.*

66 Basáñez, Inglehart, and Nevitte, *Convergence Revisited.*

67 Earl Fry, 'The Role of Subnational Governments in the Governance of North America,' Institute for Public Policy, *Mapping the New North American Reality Series* (Montreal: September 2004), 5.

68 Jeff Heynen and John Higginbotham, 'Advancing Canadian Interests in the United States: A Practical Guide for Canadian Public Officials,' CSPS Action-Research Roundtable on Managing Canada-US Relations, 2004, 40, http://www.csps-efpc.gc.ca/Research/publications/html/p127/1_e.html (accessed on April 8, 2008).

69 Ibid., 6.

70 European Commission, 'How Europeans See Themselves' (Brussels: European Communities, 2001), http://ec.europa.eu/publications/booklets/eu_documentation/0 5/txt_en.pdf (accessed on April 8, 2008).

71 O'Brien, *North American Integration*, 714.

72 Stephen Clarkson, 'The Joy of Flux: What Europe May Learn from North America's Preference for National Currency Sovereignty,' in Colin Crouch, ed., *After the Euro: Shaping Institutions for Governance in the Wake of European Monetary Union* (Oxford: Oxford University Press, 2000), 140–61.

73 Herbert G. Grubel, *The Case for the Amero: The Economics and Politics of a North American Monetary Union*, Critical Issues Bulletin (Vancouver: Fraser Institute, 1999), http://oldfraser.lexi.net/publications/critical_issues/1999/ amero/ (accessed on April 8, 2008); Canadian Council of Chief Executives, *Security and Prosperity: Toward a New Canada-United States Partnership in North America*, January 2003, www.ceocouncil.ca/publications/pdf/716af13644402901250657d4c 418a12e/presentations_2003_01_01.pdf (accessed on April 8, 2008).

74 John P. Manley, Pedro Aspe, and William Weld, *Building a North American Community* (New York: Council on Foreign Relations, 2005).

75 Murray Dobbin, 'Zip Locking North America: Can Canada Survive Continental Integration?' (Council of Canadians, October 2002), http://www.canadians.org/DI/issues/ZipLockingNA.html (accessed on April 8, 2008).

76 Minuteman Project, *Stop the SPP*, www.stopspp.com, North American Union, (accessed on April 8, 2008).

77 In perhaps an apt metaphor for North American integration, the Security

and Prosperity Partnership website does not have an author displayed on it, giving it a supranational air, but all of the privacy policy and disclaimers belong to the US government. US Department of Commerce, 'SPP Myths vs. Facts,' www.spp.gov/myths_vs_facts.asp, SPP.GOV (accessed on April 8, 2008).

78 Tony Judt, *Postwar: A History of Europe since 1945* (New York: Penguin, 2005), 156–9, 275.

79 Sidney Weintraub, 'A North American Community: Pros and Cons,' *Issues in International Political Economy* (Washington, D.C.: Center for Strategic and International Studies, January 2005), 61.

80 Jeff Faux, 'The Global Class War.' Paper presented at the Week of International Relations Universidad Iberoamericana, Mexico City, Sept. 28, 2007.

81 Morten Boas 'The Trade-Environment Nexus and the Potential for Trade Institutions,' in Breslin et al., eds., *New Regionalisms in the Global Political Economy* (New York: Routledge, 2000), 63.

82 Peter Katzenstein makes the definitive case for a conception of the post-Cold War world rooted in regions embedded within his proposed 'American imperium.' Peter Katzenstein, *A World of Regions: Asia and Europe in the American Imperium* (New York: Cornell University Press, 2005).

II. NAFTA'S INSTITUTIONAL VACUUM

1 Stephen Clarkson, 'Canada's External Constitution under Global Trade Governance,' in Ysolde Gendreau, ed., *Dessiner la société par le droit/Mapping Society through Law* (Montreal: Les Éditions Thémis, CRDP, Université de Montréal, 2004). For a more general analysis, see David Schneiderman, *Constitutionalizing Economic Globalization: Investment Rules and Democracy's Promise* (Cambridge: Cambridge University Press, 2008).

2 Beatriz Leycegui and Mario Ruiz Cornejo, 'Trading Remedies to Remedy Trade: The NAFTA Experience,' *Southwestern Journal of Law and Trade in the Americas* 10, no. 1 (2003–4): 25.

3 Anthony De Palma, 'The Reluctant Trinity: Canada, Mexico and the United States.' Lecture delivered at Carleton University, Ottawa, Jan. 24, 2002.

4 Robert Pastor, *Toward a North American Community: Lessons from the Old World for the New* (Washington, D.C.: Institute for International Economics, 2001), 73–4.

5 Larry Herman, 'Comments on the NAFTA Chapter 19 Dispute Settlement Process.' Testimony to the Sub-committee on International Trade, House of Commons, Ottawa, March 1, 2005, 8.

6 Gary H. Sampliner, 'Arbitration or Expropriation Cases under US Investment Treaties – A Threat to Democracy or the Dog that Didn't Bark?' *ICSID Review – Foreign Investment Law Journal* (2003): 32.

7 This section borrows from Stephen Clarkson, Sarah Davidson Ladly, and Carlton Thorne, 'A North American "Community of Law" with Minimal Institutions: NAFTA's Committees and Working Groups,' in John Kirton and Peter Haynal, eds., *Sustainability, Civil Society, and International Governance: Local, North American and Global Perspectives* (New York: Ashgate, 2006); and Stephen Clarkson et al., 'The Primitive Realities of Continental Governance in North America,' in Edgar Grande and Louis W. Pauly, eds., *Complex Sovereignty: Reconstituting Political Authority in the Twenty-first Century* (Toronto: University of Toronto Press, 2005).

8 Although NAFTA's Annex 2001.2 lists twenty CWGs, it is virtually impossible to establish a finite number for these entities because some have generated further ad hoc working groups as needed.

9 Joseph McKinney, 'Related Institutions in the Context of Theory,' in Joseph McKinney, ed., *Created from NAFTA: The Structure, Function, and Significance of the Treaty's Related Institutions* (Armonk, N.Y.: M.E. Sharpe, 2000), 17.

10 Interview with Claude Carrière, director general, Canadian Embassy, Trade Policy Bureau, Washington, D.C. April 10, 2002.

11 McKinney, 'Related Institutions,' 22.

12 Carrière interview.

13 McKinney, 'Related Institutions,' 14.

14 Interview with Kent Shigetomi, director for Mexico and NAFTA affairs, Office of the United States Trade Representative, Washington, D.C., April 10, 2002.

15 The Organization of American States (OAS), Foreign Trade Information System (SICE), 'Documents Relating to the Free Trade Commission,' http://www.sice.oas.org/TPD/NAFTA/NAFTA_e.ASP (accessed on April 9, 2008).

16 Ibid.

17 Ibid.

18 Shigetomi interview.

19 Confidential communication from a Canadian civil servant via questionnaire.

20 Ibid.

21 Shigetomi interview.

22 Ibid.

23 Interview with Charles Doran, Johns Hopkins University, Washington, D.C., April 11, 2002.

24 Shigetomi interview.
25 Interview with Carl Hartill, Economic and Trade Policy Division, Canadian Embassy, Washington, D.C., April 12, 2002.
26 The North American Energy Working Group, 'North America – The Energy Picture,' June 2002, http://www2.nrcan.gc.ca/es/es/energypicture/main_e.cfm (accessed on April 9, 2008).
27 Hartill interview.
28 Ibid. Equivalent data for the United States and Mexico not given.
29 Hartill interview.
30 Bradly Condon and Tapen Sinha, 'An Analysis of an Alliance: NAFTA Trucking and the US Insurance Industry,' *Estey Center Journal of International Law and Trade Policy* 2, no. 2 (2001): 238.
31 Ibid., 237.
32 Ibid., 235–6, 240.
33 Ibid., 238.
34 Foreign Affairs and International Trade (DFAIT), 'Meeting of the NAFTA Land Transportation Standards Subcommittee – Joint Statements of Accomplishments,' Oct. 25–28, 1999, http://www.dfait-maeci.gc.ca/nafta-ALENA/report13–en.asp (accessed on April 9, 2008).
35 Ibid.
36 NAFTA, Ch. 9, Annex 913.5.a-1, 2(a)iii.
37 Interview with David Decarme, chief, Surface, Maritime and Facilitation Division, United States Department of Transportation, Washington, D.C., April 11, 2002.
38 Shigetomi interview.
39 Pastor, *North American Community*.
40 United States, Department of Commerce, Bureau of Economic Analysis, 'International Transactions' (1990), http://www.bea.gov/methodologies/ (accessed on April 9, 2008).
41 United States, Department of Commerce, Bureau of Economic Analysis, 'Direct Investment Positions for 2006,' 33, http://www.bea.gov/bea/ARTICLES/2006/07July/0706_DIP_WEB.pdf (accessed on April 13, 2008).
42 DFAIT, 'Stock Outward by Country 2006 Data,' http://www.international.gc.ca/eet/pdf/FDI-stock-outward-by-country-2006–data-en.pdf, DFAIT (accessed on April 9, 2008).
43 DFAIT, 'FDI Stock Inward by Country,' http://www.dfait-maeci.gc.ca/eet/excel/FDI-stocks-Inward-by-Country-2006–data-en.xls (accessed on April 9, 2008).
44 Wendy Dobson, 'Shaping the Future of the North American Economic

Space: A Framework for Action,' Commentary – Border Papers (C.D. Howe Institute, April 2002).

III. NAFTA'S UNEVEN JUDICIAL CAPACITY

1 Stephen Handelman, 'The Rise of North America Inc.: A Perspective from the United States,' *ISUMA* 1, no. 1 (2000): 17–23.
2 Rodney Grey, cited in Stephen Clarkson, *Canada and the Reagan Challenge: Crisis and Adjustment, 1981–85* (Toronto: Lorimer, 1985), 122–3.
3 Stephen Clarkson, 'NAFTA and the WTO in the Transformation of Mexico's Economic System,' in Joseph S. Tulchin and Andrew D. Selee, eds., *Mexico's Politics and Society in Transition* (Boulder Colo.: Lynne Rienner Publishers, 2002), 215–54.
4 Modesto Seara Vázquez, *Política Exterior de México* (Mexico City: Harla, 1985), 198.
5 Beatriz Leycegui and Luz Elena Reyes de la Torre, 'The 10 Major Problems with the Anti-Dumping Instrument in Mexico,' *Journal of World Trade* 39 (2005): 137.
6 Rodolfo Cruz Miramontes, *El TLC: controversias, soluciones y otros temas conexos*, 2nd ed. (Mexico City: Porrúa, 2002), 11.
7 Jeffrey P. Bialos and Deborah E. Siegel, 'Dispute Resolution under the NAFTA: The Newer and Improved Model,' *International Lawyer* 27, no. 3 (1993): 25.
8 Gary C. Hufbauer and Jeffrey J. Schott, *NAFTA Dispute Settlement Systems* (Washington, D.C.: Institute for International Economics, November 2004), 52.
9 Arbitral Panel Established Pursuant to Article 2008, in the Matter of Tariffs Applied by Canada to Certain U.S.-Origin Agricultural Products, Final Report of the Panel, Case no. CDA-95-2008-01 (Dec. 2, 1996).
10 Panel Established under Chapter Twenty of the North American Free Trade Agreement, Matter of the U.S. Safeguard Action taken on Broom Corn Brooms from Mexico, Case no. USA-97-2008-01 (Jan. 30, 1998). Citing NAFTA Annex 803.3(12)
11 David Gantz, 'Tariffs: Clinton Removes Safeguard Tariffs on Broom Corn Brooms,' Arizona Legal Studies Discussion Paper no. 06–26 (University of Arizona, July 2006), http://ssrn.com/abstract=918542 (accessed on April 9, 2008).
12 Bradly Condon and Tapen Sinha, 'An Analysis of an Alliance: NAFTA Trucking and the US Insurance Industry,' *Estey Center Journal of International Law and Trade Policy* 2, no. 2 (2001): 240.

13 Interview with Jon Huenemann, vice-president, Fleischman-Hilliard Government Relations, April 1, 2004.

14 Final Report of the Panel, in the Matter of Cross-Border Trucking Services, Case no. USA-MEX-98–2008–01 (Feb. 6, 2001). See also Condon and Sinha, 'An Analysis of an Alliance,' 238.

15 Jorge Witker, 'Controversia del autotransporte de carga en el TLCAN,' in Jorge Witker, coord., *El Tratado de Libre Comercio de América del Norte. Evaluación jurídica: diez años después* (Mexico City: UNAM, 2005), 435–6.

16 Paul Blustein, 'High Court Opens US Roads to Mexican Trucks,' *Washington Post*, June 8, 2004.

17 La Jornada, 'En abril abren la frontera de EU al transporte de carga mexicano,' *La Jornada*, Feb. 26, 2007, 18.

18 Huenemann interview, April 1, 2004.

19 Interview with Hugo Perezcano, Secretaría de la Economía, Mexico City, March 10, 2006.

20 Huenemann interview, April 1, 2004.

21 Foreign Affairs and International Trade Canada (DFAIT), 'Softwood Lumber Agreement between the Government of Canada and the Government of the United States,' Sept. 12, 2006, http://www.international.gc.ca/eicb/softwood/SLA-main-en.asp, Article XIV.8 (accessed on April 9, 2008).

22 NAFTA Article 1904(1).

23 Data for January 1994 to March 2005 in Beatriz Leycegui, 'Trading Remedies to Remedy Trade: The NAFTA Experience.' Presentation to District of Columbia Bar, Washington, D.C., May 2005. Author's archive.

24 Bialos and Siegel, 'Dispute Resolution under the NAFTA,' 620.

25 Ibid.

26 Notimex Reuters, 'Final conflicto de cemento México-EU; hoy firman acuerdo,' *El Financiero*, March 6, 2006.

27 Robert Howse, 'Settling Trade Remedy Disputes: When the WTO Forum Is Better than the NAFTA,' *Commentary* 111 (C.D. Howe Institute, June 1998).

28 Hufbauer and Schott, 'NAFTA Dispute Settlement Systems,' 47.

29 World Trade Organization (WTO), 'United States – Continued Dumping and Subsidy Offset Act of 2000,' Report of the Appellate Body AB-2002–7 (Jan. 16, 2003).

30 DFAIT, 'Canada Takes Action on Byrd Amendment,' Press Release no. 75, April 29, 2005, http/www.international.gc.ca (accessed on April 9, 2008).

31 CTV.ca News Staff, 'PM Strikes Deal with US to End Lumber Dispute,' Canadian Television Network (CTV), April 28, 2006, http://www.ctv.ca/servlet/ArticleNews/story/CTVNews/20060426 /softwood_folo_060427/20060427?hub=TopStories (accessed on April 9, 2008).

32 Huenemann interview, April 1, 2004.

33 Of the huge literature on the softwood-lumber dispute, the most comprehensive and comprehensible is Joseph A. McKinney, 'Political Economy of the US-Canada Softwood Lumber Dispute,' *Canadian-American Public Policy* (August 2004): 57.

34 Elliot J. Feldman, 'Deal or no Deal: Snatching Defeat from the Jaws of Victory,' *Journal of International Trade Law and Regulation* 5 (2007): 91–7.

35 Lawrence L. Herman, 'American Corn and Canadian Trade Actions: One Step Forward, Two Status Steps Back,' C.D. Howe Institute e-brief, April 5, 2007, http://goliath.ecnext.com/coms2/gi_0199–6722049/Recent-C-D-Howe-Institute.html (accessed on April 9, 2008).

36 Todd Weiler, 'NAFTA Investment Arbitration and the Growth of International Economic Law,' *Canadian Business Law Journal* 12, Abstract 4 (2002): 406.

37 Stephen Clarkson, 'Systemic or Surgical? Possible Cures for NAFTA's Investor-State Dispute Process,' *Canadian Business Law Journal* 36 (2002): 376.

38 Ann Capling and Kim Richard Nossal, 'Blowback: Investor-State Dispute Mechanisms in International Trade Agreements,' *Governance* 19, no. 2 (2006): 151–72.

39 Alejandro Posadas Urtusuástegui and Gustavo Vega Cánovas, 'El capítulo 11 del TLCAN,' in Witker, coord., *El Tratado de Libre Comercio de América del Norte*, 126.

40 NAFTA, Article 1105.

41 Elizabeth May, 'Fighting the MAI,' in Andrew Jackson and Matthew Sanger, eds., *Dismantling Democracy: The Multilateral Agreement on Investment and Its Impact* (Toronto: CCPA and Lorimer, 1998), 32–47.

42 Myers Press, 'NAFTA Tribunal Awards Damages in S.D. Myers Case,' Government of Canada Press Release, Oct. 21, 2002, www.appletonlaw.com/cases/S.D. Myers Press Release – Oct21–02.pdf (accessed on April 9, 2008).

43 International Center for Settlement of Investment Disputes, Final Award in the Matter of Arbitration under Chapter 11 of the North American Free Trade Agreement, 'Metalclad Corporation v. the United Mexican States,' Case no. ARB(AF)/00/3 (Aug. 25, 2000), 36.

44 Perezcano interview, March 10, 2006.

45 Gus van Harten, 'Chapter 11 and the Francovich Doctrine: Comparing State Liability under NAFTA and EC Law.' Paper presented at CERLAC Conference, York University, Sept. 14, 2003, 17.

46 Stephen Clarkson, 'Hijacking the Canadian Constitution: NAFTA's Investor-State Dispute Arbitration,' in Alan S. Alexandroff, ed., *Investor Protection in the NAFTA and Beyond: Private Interest and Public Purpose*, Policy

Study 44 (Ottawa: C.D. Howe Institute, March 2006). On the claims for damages current to March 1, 2007, see Scott Sinclair, comp., 'NAFTA Chapter 11 Investor-State Disputes,' Canadian Centre for Policy Alternatives, http://policyalternatives.ca/documents/National_Office_Pubs/2007/NAFTA_Dispute_Table_March2007.pdf (accessed on April 9, 2008).

47 Stephen Clarkson 'Systemic or Surgical?' 386.

48 Guillermo Aguilar Alvarez and William W. Park, 'The New Phase of Investment Arbitration: NAFTA Chapter 11,' *Yale Journal of International Law* 28 (2003): 357–82.

49 Ibid., 356.

50 US Department of State, 'Methanex Corp. v United States,' Final Award of the Tribunal on Jurisdiction and Merits, US Department of State, Aug. 3, 2005, http://www.state.gov/s/l/c5818.htm (accessed on April 9, 2008).

51 Steven Chase, 'Canada Post NAFTA Win Sets Precedent,' *Globe and Mail*, June 14, 2007.

52 Scott Sinclair, 'NAFTA Chapter 11 Investor-State Disputes to March 1, 2007' (Ottawa: Canadian Centre for Policy Alternatives, 2007).

53 Gus Van Harten, 'Private Authority and Transnational Governance: The Contours of the International System of Investor Protection,' *Review of International Political Economy* 12, no. 4 (2005): 608.

54 Steven Shrybman, 'How NAFTA Overrides National Sovereignty: Recent Cases Show Dangers of Letting Investors Sue Governments,' *CCPA Monitor* 7, no. 9 (Ottawa: Canada Centre for Policy Alternatives, March 2001): 7.

55 Yves Dezalay and Bryant T. Garth, *Dealing in Virtue: International Commercial Arbitration and the Construction of a Transnational Legal Order* (Chicago: University of Chicago Press, 1996), 117.

56 Claire A. Cutler, *Private Power and Global Authority: Transnational Merchant Law in the Global Political Economy* (Cambridge: Cambridge University Press, 2003), 226.

57 Frederick M. Abbott, 'The North American Integration Regime and Its Implications for the World Trading System,' in J.H.H. Weiler, ed., *The EU, the WTO and the NAFTA: Towards a Common Law of International Trade* (Oxford: Oxford University Press, 2000).

58 Rodolfo Oscar Cruz Barney and Cruz Miramontes, 'Diez años del capítulo XX,' in Witker, coord., *El Tratado de Libre Comercio de América del Norte*, 160.

59 Hufbauer and Schott, 'NAFTA Dispute Settlement Systems,' 23.

60 Interview with Lawrence Herman, Cassels Brock and Blackwell LLP, Toronto, Feb. 20, 2004.

61 Howse, 'Settling Trade Remedy Disputes,' 16.

62 Interview with Anthony Giles, research director of NAFTA's Commission on Labour Cooperation, April 1, 2004.
63 Rodolfo Cruz Miramontes, 'Seminario del TLCAN: Una evaluación jurídica.' Paper presented at UNAM, Instituto de Investigaciones Jurídicas, Mexico City, Feb. 16, 2006.
64 NAFTA Annex 302.2, Article 1.
65 Centro de Estudios para América Latina (CEPAL), 'Matter of Tariffs Applied by Canada,' CEPAL, December 2, 1996, www.cepal.org/publicaciones/xml/8/9098/nafta-cn.html – 83k (accessed on April 9, 2008).
66 Verónica Martínez, 'Dejan IEPS en fructuosa,' Reforma Negocios, May 26, 2006.
67 Appellate Body Report, 'Mexico – Tax Measures on Soft Drinks and Other Beverages,' WT/DS308/AB/R, adopted March 24, 2006, para.10.
68 David A. Gantz, 'The United States and NAFTA Dispute Settlement: Ambivalence, Frustration and Occasional Defiance,' Arizona Legal Studies, Discussion Paper no. 06–26, July 2006, http://www.law.arizona.edu/faculty/FacultyPubs/Documents/Gan tz/ALS0626.pdf (accessed on April 9, 2008).
69 WTO, Report of the Appellate Body: Canada, 'Certain Measures concerning Periodicals,' Case no. WT/DS31/AB/R, AB-1997–2 (June 23, 1997).
70 CUFTA Article 2005(2) is incorporated into NAFTA by Article 2106, Annex 2106.
71 Robert Pastor, Toward a North American Community: Lessons from the Old World to the New (Washington, D.C.: Institute for International Economics, 2001), 103.
72 Interview with David Schneiderman, University of Toronto, Faculty of Law, March 17, 2004.

IV. TRANSBORDER LABOUR GOVERNANCE

1 W. Olle and W. Schoeller make a similar argument. See 'World Market Competition and Restrictions on International Trade Union Policies,' Capital and Class 2 (1977): 56–75.
2 Mexican Federal Law of Labour, Federal Law of Public Workers, Federal Law of Social Security, the Law of the Institute of Social Security and Services of the Public Workers (ISSSTE), and the Law of the National Fund for the Workers' Housing.
3 Leoncio Lara, Cuestiones Laborales (Mexico City: Secretaría del Trabajo y Previsión Social, Procuraduría Federal de la Defensa del Trabajo, 1984), 18.

4 Interview with Leoncio Lara Sáenz, Instituto para Investigaciones Jurídicas, Universidad Nacional Autónoma de México (UNAM), Mexico City,
   Feb. 1 2006.

5 Robert H. Babcock, *Gompers in Canada: A Study of American Continentalism
   before the First World War* (Toronto: University of Toronto Press, 1974).

6 Irving Abella, *Nationalism, Communism and Canadian Labour: The CIO, the
   Communist Party and the Canadian Congress of Labour* (Toronto: University of
   Toronto Press, 1973).

7 Nelson Lichtenstein, *State of the Union* (Princeton, N.J.: Princeton University
   Press, 2002), 35.

8 Ibid., 118.

9 Craig Heron, *The Canadian Labour Movement* (Toronto: James Lorimer, 1996),
   72.

10 Andrew Jackson and Bob Baldwin, 'Policy Analysis by the Labour Movement in a Hostile Environment.' Working Paper presented at Ontario
   School of Policy Studies, Queen's University, Kingston, Ont., March 14,
   2005, 4.

11 Leo Panitch and Donald Swartz, *From Consent to Coercion: The Attack on
   Trade Union Rights* (Toronto: Garamond, 1993).

12 Ian MacDonald, 'NAFTA and the Emergence of Continental Labor Cooperation,' *American Review of Canadian Studies* 33, no. 2 (2003): 173.

13 Leoncio Lara, 'El Acuerdo de Cooperación Laboral en América del
   Norte,' in Jorge Witker, coord., *El Tratado de Libre Comercio de América del
   Norte. Evaluación jurídica: diez años después* (Mexico City: UNAM, 2005),
   445–6.

14 For a review of this literature, see Raul Hinojosa Ojeda, 'The Theory and
   Practice of Regional Integration: Trans-Atlantic Lessons for the New
   World.' Paper presented for the seminar 'Confronting Challenges of
   Regional Development in Latin America and the Caribbean,' Milan, Italy,
   March 22, 2003.

15 Peter Dungan and Steve Murphy, 'The Changing Industry and Skill Mix of
   Canada's International Trade,' in *Perspectives on North American Free Trade*,
   paper no. 4, http://www.ic.gc.ca/epic/site/eas-aes.nsf/en/ra01771e.html
   (accessed on May 25, 2008).

16 Bruce Campbell, 'False Promise: Canada in the Free Trade Era,' in *NAFTA
   at Seven* (Economic Policy Institute, April 2001).

17 Daniel Trefler, 'The Long and Short of the Canada-US Free Trade Agreement,' in *Perspectives on North American Free Trade*, paper no. 5, 35, http://
   www.ic.gc.ca/epic/site/eas-aes.nsf/en/ra01772e.html (accessed on April
   9, 2008).

18 Robert E. Scott, 'NAFTA's Legacy: Rising Trade Deficits Lead to Significant Job Displacement and Declining Job Quality for the United States,' in Robert E. Scott, Carlos Salas, and Bruce Campbell, 'Revisiting NAFTA: Still Not Working for North America's Workers,' *Economic Policy Institute Briefing Paper*, no. 173 (September 28, 2006): 3–32.

19 Kim Moody, 'Nafta and the Corporate Redesign of North America,' *Latin American Persepctives* 22, no. 1 (1995): 102.

20 Figure cited in Alejandro Alvarez Bejar, 'Mexico's 2006 Elections: The Rise of Populism and the End of Neo-Liberalism?' *Latin American Perspectives* 147, no. 33 (2006): 17–32.

21 Carlos Salas, 'Mexico Labor Report: 2001–2006,' *Global Policy Network Report*, www.gpn.org (accessed on April 9, 2008).

22 Ibid.

23 Philippe Masse, 'Trade Employment and Wages: A Review of the Literature,' in *Trade Policy Research 2001* (Ottawa: Government of Canada, 2001), 216.

24 René Morissette and Anick Johnson, 'Are Good Jobs Disappearing in Canada?' *Economic Policy Review* 11, no. 1 (2005), http://ssrn.com/abstract =784645 (accessed on April 9, 2008).

25 Andrew Jackson, *Work and Labour in Canada: Critical Issues* (Toronto: Canadian Scholars' Press, 2005).

26 Robert E. Scott, 'Broken Promises: NAFTA Cost US Jobs and Reduced Wages,' Economic Snapshots Economic Policy Institute, Oct. 4, 2006, http://www.epi.org/content.cfm/webfeatures_snapshots_20061004 (accessed on April 9, 2008).

27 Alejandro Alvarez, 'Mexico Eleven Years on from NAFTA: A Ripe Neo-colony of Youth without a Future?' Paper presented at the conference 'NAFTA and the Future of North America: Trilateral Perspectives on Governance, Economic Development and Labour,' University of Toronto, Feb. 7, 2005.

28 International Relationships Center, 'Seven Myths about NAFTA and Three Lessons for Latin America,' Americas Program, Interhemispheric Resource Program, 2, http://americas.irc-online.org/articles/2003/0311_7–myths .html (accessed on 13 April 2008).

29 Carlos Salas, 'Between Unemployment and Insecurity in Mexico: NAFTA Enters Its Second Decade,' in Scott, Salas, and Campbell, 'Revisiting NAFTA,' 48.

30 Sandra Polaski, 'Jobs, Wages, and Family Income,' in John Audley et al., *NAFTA's Promise and Reality: Lessons from Mexico for the Hemisphere* (Washington, D.C.: Carnegie Endowment for Peace, 2003), 48.

31 Kim Moody, *Workers in a Lean World* (New York: Verso, 1997), 71.

32 Morley Gunderson, *Ten Key Ingredients of Labour Policy in the New World of Work* (Ottawa: Human Resources and Skills Development Canada, February 2003), http://www110.hrdc-drhc.gc.ca/psait_spila/ntipt_ndlp/dic_tki/index-en.html#2 (accessed on April 9, 2008).

33 Mandatory elections give employers time to exercise their considerable economic leverage over employees. Chris Riddell, 'Union Certification Success under Voting Versus Card-Check Procedures: Evidence from British Columbia,' *Industrial and Labor Relations Review* 57, no. 4 (2004): 509.

34 Lance Compa, *Unfair Advantage: Workers Freedom of Association in the United States under International Human Rights Standards* (Washington, D.C.: Human Rights Watch, 2001), 10.

35 Ibid., 10.

36 Kate Bronfenbrenner, 'We'll Close! Plant Closings, Plant-Closing Threats, Union Organizing and NAFTA,' *Multinational Monitor* 18, no. 3 (1997): 8; Kate Bronfenbrenner, 'Uneasy Terrain: The Impact of Capital Mobility on Workers, Wages, and Union Organizing, Part II: First Contract Supplement,' submitted to the U.S. Trade Deficit Review Commission, June 1, 2001.

37 The draft bill has not yet been approved by Congress. For details, see Ian Thomas MacDonald, 'Negotiating Mexico's Labour Law Reform: Corporatism, Neo-Liberalism and Democratic Opening,' *Studies in Political Economy* 73 (spring/summer 2004): 139–58.

38 Andrew Jackson, 'Solidarity Forever? An Analysis of Changes in Union Density,' *Canadian Labour Congress Research Paper #25* (Ottawa: CLC, 2003), 14.

39 Statistics Canada, 'Number of Unionized Workers, Employees and Union Density, by Sex and Province; Both Sexes; Union Density' (Ottawa: Statistics Canada, 2005).

40 Bureau of Labor Statistics figures available at www.bls.gov (accessed on April 13, 2007).

41 Enrique de la Garza Toledo, 'La Polémica acerca de la tasa de sindicalización en Mexico,' *Trabajo. Cambio en las Relaciones Laborales*, 2 (2006) (Mexico City: UAM, OIT, Plaza y Valdez).

42 MacDonald, 'NAFTA and the Emergence,' 173.

43 Afef Benessaieh, 'Les États-Unis, la clause sociale et l'art de la vertu démocratique,' *Continental: cahiers de recherches* (September 1998), http://www.unites.uqam.ca/gric/cahiers.html (accessed on April 9, 2008).

44 North American Agreement on Labour Cooperation (NAALC), 'Objectives,' http://www.naalcosh.org/index_e.htm (accessed on April 9, 2008).

45 MacDonald, 'NAFTA and the Emergence,' 180.

46 Ibid., 181.

47 This paragraph is a summary of a similar point made in ibid., 181–2.

48 David Bacon. 'Testing NAFTA's Labor Side Agreement,' North American Commission for Labour Cooperation (NACLA), *Report on the Americas* (May/June 1998): 7.

49 Ibid., 8.

50 Quoted in 'Deals for NAFTA Votes II: Bait and Switch,' Public Citizen, www.citisen.org/publications/release.cfm?ID=6825 (accessed on April 9, 2008).

51 Jim Stanford, *Social Dumping under North American Free Trade* (Ottawa: Canadian Centre for Policy Alternatives, 1993).

52 International Solidarity, 'Mexican Labor News and Analysis Articles,' http://www.ueinternational.org/Mexico_info/mlna_articles.php ?id=83 (accessed on April 9, 2008).

53 Dale Hathaway, *Allies across the Border* (Cambridge, Mass.: Southend Press, 2000), 173.

54 Barry Carr, 'Globalization from Below: Labour Internalism under NAFTA,' *International Social Science Journal* 59 (1999): 53.

55 Hathaway, *Allies across the Border*, 176.

56 Ibid.

57 BorderLines, 'Post-NAFTA Labor Solidarity Advances Shakily,' *BorderLines* 25, 4, no. 6 (1996), http://americas.irc-online.org/borderlines/1996/bl25/bl25fta_body.html (accessed on April 9, 2008).

58 Canadian Labour Congress (CLC), 'The Social Dimension of NAFTA,' *CLC Policy Paper*, 81.

59 Maria de la Luz Arriaga Lemus, 'NAFTA and the Trinational Coalition to Defend Public Education,' *Social Justice* 26, no. 3 (1999): 154, http://www.questia.com/googleScholar.qst?docId=5001869591 (accessed on April 9, 2008).

60 Interview with Eduardo Torres, editor, STRM, Mexico City, Feb. 16, 2002.

61 Ibid.

62 Richard Roman and Edur Velasco Arregui, 'Solidarity or Competition: Mexican Workers, NAFTA, and the North American Working Class.' Paper presented at the conference 'NAFTA and the Future of North America'; David Brooks and Jonathan Fox, 'NAFTA: Ten Years of Cross-border Dialogue,' *IRC Americas Program Special Report* (March 2004).

63 Interview with Salvador Medina, Mexico City, June 17, 2003.

64 Hathaway, *Allies across the Border*, 207.

65 Michael Yates, '"Workers of All Countries, Unite": Will This Include the US Labor Movement?' *Monthly Review* (July/August 2000), http://

www.monthlyreview.org/700yates.htm (accessed on April 9, 2008); Kim Scipes, 'The AFL-CIO in Venezuela: Déjà Vu All Over Again,' *Labor Notes* (April 2004), http://www.counterpunch.org/scipes03292004.html (accessed on April 9, 2008).

66 Greg Albo and Dan Crow, 'Under Pressure: The Impasses of North American Labour Movements.' Paper presented to the conference 'NAFTA and the Future of North America.'

67 Sam Gindin, 'The Auto Industry: Concretizing Working Class Solidarity: Internationalism beyond Slogans,' *Socialist Project* (Apri, 2004), http://www.socialistproject.ca/documents/the_auto_industry.h tml (accessed April 9, 2008).

V. TRANSBORDER ENVIRONMENTAL GOVERNANCE

1 André Beaulieu and Pierre-Marc Johnson, *The Environment and NAFTA* (Washington, D.C.: Island Press, 1996), 22.

2 'Command and Control Instruments (CAC),' United Nations ESCAP Virtual Conference (Dec. 10, 2003), http://www.unescap.org/drpad/vc/orientation/M5_2.htm (accessed on April 15, 2008).

3 US Environmental Protection Agency (EPA), 'An Environmental Revolution,' http://www.epa.gov/history/publications/origins5.htm (accessed on April 10, 2008).

4 EPA, 'Looking Backward: A Historical Perspective on Environmental Regulation,' and 'The Guardian: Origins of the EPA,' http://www.epa.gov/history/publications/origins.htm (accessed on April 10, 2008).

5 Samuel P. Hays, *Explorations in Environmental History* (Pittsburgh, Penn.: University of Pittsburgh Press, 1998), 246.

6 Jack Lewis, 'Looking Backward: A Historical Perspective on Environmental Regulation,' EPA, http://epa.gov/history/topics/regulate/01.htm (accessed on April 10, 2008). The important role of the federal government in regulating environmental compliance across states is institutionalized through the interstate-commerce clause in the US constitution.

7 George Hoberg and Kathryn Harrison, 'It's Not Easy Being Green,' *Canadian Public Policy* 20 (1994): 119–37.

8 F.L. Morton, 'The Constitutional Division of Powers with Respect to the Environment in Canada,' in Kenneth M. Holland, F.L. Morton, and Brian Galligan, eds., *Federalism and the Environment: Environmental Policy-making in Australia, Canada, and the United States* (Westport, Conn.: Greenwood Press, 1996), 37–54.

9 Cesar Nava Escudero, *Urban Environmental Governance: Comparing Air Quality Management in London and Mexico City* (Burlington, Vt.: Ashgate, 2001), 1–267.

10 Jan Gilbreath, *Environment and Development in Mexico* (Washington, D.C.: Center for Strategic and International Studies, 2003), 12–13.

11 Jordi Díez, 'Political Change and Environmental Policymaking in Mexico,' PhD thesis, University of Toronto, 2004, 67; Barbara Hogenboom, *Mexico and the NAFTA Environment Debate* (Amsterdam: International Books, 1998), 76.

12 Gilbreath, *Environment and Development in Mexico*, 13.

13 Díez, *Political Change and Environmental Policymaking in Mexico*, 62.

14 Ibid., 93.

15 Discussed in Hogenboom, *Mexico and the NAFTA Environment Debate*, 100.

16 Gilbreath, *Environment and Development in Mexico*, 14.

17 Díez, *Political Change and Environmental Policymaking in Mexico*, 62.

18 Hogenboom, *Mexico and the NAFTA Environment Debate*, 143–5.

19 Gilbreath, *Environment and Development in Mexico*, 21.

20 Blanca Torres, 'A Diez Años de la Firma de los Acuerdos Ambientales Paralelos al Tratado de Libre Comercio de América del Norte,' *Foro internacional* 44, no. 3 (2004): 337.

21 Leslie R. Alm, 'Scientists and Environmental Policy: A Canadian-US Perspective,' *Canadian American Public Policy* 37 (February 1999).

22 EPA, 'Border 2012: US-Mexico Environmental Program' (May 5, 2003), http://www.epa.gov/usmexicoborder/pdf/2012_english.pdf (Sept. 4, 2006).

23 Bryan Husted and Jeanne M. Logsdon, 'Impact of NAFTA on Mexico's Environmental Policy,' *Growth and Change* 28, no. 1 (1997): 3–5.

24 Gary Hufbauer et al., eds., *NAFTA and the Environment: Seven Years Later* (Washington D.C.: Peterson Institute, 2000), 40.

25 Gilbreath, *Environment and Development in Mexico*, 40.

26 Hufbauer et al., eds., *NAFTA and the Environment*, 39; Beaulieu and Johnson, *The Environment and NAFTA*, 19.

27 Gilbreath, *Environment and Development in Mexico*, 20.

28 US Department of Commerce, International Trade Administration, 'NAFTA Facts Document #1125: Mexico's Environmental Market,' http://www.mac.doc.gov/NAFTA/1125.htm (accessed on Feb. 13, 2005).

29 Richard H. Steinberg, 'Trade-Environment Negotiations in the EU, NAFTA, and WTO: Regional Trajectories of Rule Development,' *American Journal of International Law* 9, no. 2 (1997): 251.

30 Mark J. Spalding, 'Improving Institutional Response to Environmental

Problems,' in *Both Sides of the Border*, vol. 2 (Amsterdam: Springer Netherlands, 2003), 20.

31 Gareth Porter et al., *Global Environmental Politics. 3rd Edition* (Oxford: Westview Press, 2000).

32 Beaulieu and Johnson, *The Environment and NAFTA*, 29.

33 Patricia Marchak, 'Environment and Resource Protection: Does NAFTA Make a Difference?' *Organization and Environment* 11, no. 2 (1998): 148.

34 Alejandro Nadal Egea, 'Technology, Trade, and NAFTA's Environmental Regime,' UNU/INTECH Working Paper no.15 (January 1995).

35 Frederick W. Mayer, *Interpreting NAFTA: The Science and Art of Political Analysis* (New York: Columbia University Press, 1998), 4.

36 Hufbauer et al., eds., *NAFTA and the Environment*, 5.

37 Michael Dreiling, *Solidarity and Contention: The Politics of Security and Sustainability in the NAFTA Conflict* (New York: Garland, 2000), 23.

38 Luc Juillet, 'Regional Models of Environmental Governance in the Context of Market Integration,' in Edward O Parsons, ed., *Governing the Environment: Persistent Challenges, Uncertain Innovations* (Toronto: University of Toronto Press, 2000); Anita Kranjc, 'In Defence of the Environmental State: NGO Strategies and Tactics in Canada.' Paper presented at the annual conference of the Canadian Political Science Association, Toronto, May 29–31, 2002.

39 Steven Shrybman, *Selling the Environment Short: An Environmental Assessment of the First Two Years of Free Trade between Canada and the United States* (Ottawa: Canadian Centre for Policy Alternatives, 1991), 10.

40 Husted and Logsdon, 'Impact of NAFTA on Mexico's Environmental Policy,' 6.

41 Hogenboom, *Mexico and the NAFTA Environment Debate*, 152.

42 Beaulieu and Johnson, *The Environment and NAFTA*, 34.

43 Hogenboom, *Mexico and the NAFTA Environment Debate*, 147.

44 Frederick W. Mayer, 'Negotiating the NAFTA,' in Carolyn L. Deere and Daniel C. Esty, eds., *Greening the Americas: NAFTA's Lessons for Hemispheric Trade* (Cambridge, Mass.: MIT Press, 2002), 97–116.

45 Gustavo Alanis-Ortega and Ana Karina González-Lutzenkirchen, 'No Room for the Environment: The NAFTA Negotiations and the Mexican Perspective on Trade and the Environment,' in Deere and Esty, eds., *Greening the Americas*, 41–60; Monica Araya, 'Mexico's NAFTA Trauma: Myth and Reality,' in ibid., 61–78.

46 Stanton Kibel, *The Earth on Trial: Environmental Law on the International Stage* (New York: Routledge, 1999).

47 Beaulieu and Johnson, *The Environment and NAFTA*, 34.

48 Pierre-Marc Johnson, 'From Trade Liberalization to Sustainable Develop-
ment: The Challenges of Integrated Global Governance,' in John Kirton and
Virginia W. Maclaren, eds., *Linking Trade, Environment, and Social Cohesion:
NAFTA Experiences, Global Challenges* (Burlington, Vt.: Ashgate, 2002), 33.

49 Beaulieu and Johnson. *The Environment and NAFTA*, 22.

50 Commission for Environmental Cooperation of North America (CEC),
'North American Agenda for Action: 2003–2005,' December 2002, http://
www.cec.org/files/PDF/PUBLICATIONS/3yp03–05_en.pdf (accessed on
April 15, 2008), 97.

51 Marisa Jacott, 'Environmental Recommendations Insufficient to Offset
Trade Priorities,' Americas Program, Interhemispheric Resource Center
(October 2004), http://americas.irc-online.org/am/1026 (accessed on April
15, 2008).

52 Beaulieu and Johnson. *The Environment and NAFTA*, 137.

53 Stephen P. Mumme and Pamela Duncan, 'The Commission on Environmental Co-operation and the US-Mexico Border Environment,' *Journal of
Environment and Development* 5, no. 2 (1996): 201.

54 Johnson, 'From Trade Liberalization to Sustainable Development,' 33.

55 Christopher Tollefson, 'Stormy Weather: The Recent History of the Citizen
Submission Process of the North American Agreement on Environmental
Co-operation,' in Kirton and Maclaren, eds., *Linking Trade*, 163.

56 Robert A. Sanchez, 'Governance, Trade, and the Environment in the Context of NAFTA,' *American Behavioral Scientist* 45, no. 9 (2002): 1369–93.

57 Laura Carlsen and Hilda Salazar, 'Limits to Co-operation: A Mexican Perspective on the NAFTA's Environmental Side Agreement and Institutions,'
in Deere and Esty, eds., *Greening the Americas*, 221–44.

58 Jeffrey Ayers, 'Contentious Politics in North America.' Paper presented at
the annual conference of the Canadian Political Science Association, Toronto, May 29–31, 2002.

59 John D. Wirth, 'Perspectives on the Joint Public Advisory Committee,' in
David L. Markell and John H. Knox, eds., *Greening NAFTA: The North Amer-
ican Commission for Environmental Co-operation* (Stanford, Calif.: Stanford
University Press, 2003), 205.

60 Díez, "Political Change and Environmental Policymaking in Mexico,' 56–7.

61 Gloria Soto and Diana Ponce, Presentation at the Conference on North
America's New Environmental Agenda: Legislative and Institutional
Responses, Universidad Iberoamericana, Mexico, March 6, 2006.

62 For example, the United Nations Environment Program: www.unep.org.

63 Sierra Club of Canada, 'International Trade and the Environment,' http://
www.sierraclub.ca/national/programs/sustainable-economy/
trade-environment/index.shtml (accessed on April 10, 2008).

64 Hogenboom, *Mexico and the NAFTA Environment Debate*, 147.
65 Díez, *Political Change and Environmental Policymaking in Mexico*, 67.
66 Ibid., 73.
67 Ibid., 76.
68 Alan M. Rugman, and John Kirton. 'Multinational Enterprise Strategy and the NAFTA Trade and Environmental Regime,' *Journal of World Business* 33 (1998): 438–54.
69 Gilbreath, *Environment and Development in Mexico*, 48.
70 Torres, 'A Diez Años de la Firma de los Acuerdos Ambientales Paralelos,' 337.
71 Ibid., 352.
72 Gilbreath, *Environment and Development in Mexico*, 41.
73 Debora L. Van Nijnatten and W. Henry Lambright, 'North American Smog: Science-Policy Linkages across Multiple Boundaries,' *Canadian-American Public Policy* 45 (April 2001).
74 United States-Mexico Chamber of Commerce, 'Environmental Issues under NAFTA,' http://www.usmcoc.org/b-nafta10.html (accessed on April 10, 2008).
75 US International Trade Administration, 'NAFTA Facts Document #1125: Mexico's Environmental Market.'
76 Gilbreath, *Environment and Development in Mexico*, 48.
77 John Knox and David Markell, 'The Innovative North American Commission for Environmental Cooperation,' in Markell and Knox, eds., *Greening NAFTA*, 8.
78 John J. Kirton, 'Winning Together: The NAFTA Trade-Environment Record,' in Kirton and Maclaren, eds., *Linking Trade*, 79.
79 Sierra Club of Canada, 'US-Mexico Border: Taking Aim at Toxic Pollution from ASARCO Factory,' http://www.sierraclub.org/beyondtheborders/mexico/ (accessed on April 10, 2008).
80 Díez, *Political Change and Environmental Policymaking in Mexico*, 67, 73.
81 Soto and Ponce, Presentation at the Conference on North America's New Environmental Agenda.
82 Harrison and Hoberg, 'It's Not Easy Being Green,' 180–3.
83 Glen Toner, 'Environment Canada's Continuing Roller Coaster Ride,' in Gene Swimmer, ed., *How Ottawa Spends 1996–97: Life under the Knife* (Ottawa: Carleton University Press, 1997), 99–132.
84 Emmanuel Brunet-Jailly, Susan Clarke, and Debora VanNijnatten, 'An Emerging North American Model of Cross-border Regional Cooperation.' Paper prepared for the Government of Canada, Policy Research Initiative, North American Linkages: Leader Survey on Canada-US Cross-Border Regions, February 2006, 2.

85 Christopher Sands. 'Getting to Know the North American Century,' *CSIS North American Integration Monitor* 3 (October 2005).
86 Randy Widdis, 'Migration, Borderlands and National Identity,' in John Bukiwczyk, ed., *Permeable Borders* (Calgary: University of Calgary Press, 1997), 154.
87 Debora VanNijnatten. 'Building a North American Environmental Régime … from Below?' Paper prepared for Raul Pacehgo-Vega, ed., 'North American Environmental Policy: NACEC and the North American Environmental Regime at the 10+ mark,' unpublished manuscript, 2006, 2–3, 16.
88 Committee on the Environment and the Northeast International Committee on Energy of the Conference of New England Governors and Eastern Canadian Premiers, 'Climate Change Action Plans 2001,' http://www .negc.org/documents/NEG-ECP%20CCAP.PDF (accessed on April 10, 2008).
89 Office of the Premier, British Columbia, 'B.C. Joins Western Regional Climate Action Initiative,' April 24, 2007, http://www2.news.gov.bc.ca/ news_releases_2005–2009/2007OTP00 53–000509.htm (accessed on April 10, 2008).
90 VanNijnatten, *Building a North American Environmental regime*, 27.
91 Governments of Manitoba and California, 'Memorandum of Understanding between the Province of Manitoba, Ca., and the State of California, USA,' December 2006, http://www.gov.mb.ca/asset_library/en/premier/ mou_california .pdf (accessed on April. 10, 2008).
92 Office of the Premier, Ontario, 'Ontario and California Sign Historic Accord on the Low-Carbon Fuel Standards, Collaborate on Cancer Research,' May 30, 2007, http://www.premier.gov.on.ca/news/Product.asp?ProductID =1281 (accessed on April 10, 2008).
93 Debora VanNijnatten. 'Towards Cross-border Environmental Policy Spaces in North America: Province-State Linkages on the Canada-US Border,' *AmeriQuests* 3, no. 1 (2006): 1, 13.
94 Victor Konrad and Heather Nicol, 'Boundaries and Corridors: Rethinking the Canada-United States Borderlands in the Post-9/11 Era,' *Canadian-American Public Policy* 60 (December 2004).
95 Soto and Ponce, Presentation at the Conference on North America's New Environmental Agenda.

VI. TRANSBOUNDARY WATER GOVERNANCE

1 Joachim Blatter, 'Debordering the World of States: Towards a Multi-Level System in Europe and a Multi-Polity System in North America? Insights

from Border Regions,' *European Journal of International Relations* 7, no. 2 (2001): 175.

2 Ibid.

3 Jutta Brunée and Stephen Toope, 'Environmental Security and Freshwater Resources: Ecosystem Regime Building,' *American Journal of International Law* 91 (1997).

4 Javier Delgado et al., 'The Environment,' in Laura Randall, ed., *Changing Structure of Mexico: Political, Social, and Economic Prospects* (Armonk, N.Y.: M.E. Sharpe, 2006), 312–13.

5 International Joint Commission, *Pollution of Lake Erie, Lake Ontario and the International Section of the St. Lawrence River* (Ottawa: Information Canada, 1970).

6 Marcia Valiente, Paul Muldoon, and Lee Botts, 'Ecosystem Governance: Lessons from the Great Lakes,' in Oran Young, ed., *Global Governance: Drawing Insight from the Environmental Experience* (Tullamore, Ireland: Massachusetts Institute of Technology, 1997).

7 David Schindler and Adele Hurley, 'Potential Problems with Cross-Border Water Issues: The US and Canada in the 21st Century,' unpublished paper from the Canada and the New American Empire Conference, University of Victoria, November 2004.

8 George Francis, 'Great Lakes Governance and the Ecosystem Approach: Where Next?' in Lynton K. Caldwell, ed., *Perspectives on Ecosystem Management for the Great Lakes: A Reader* (Albany: State University of New York Press, 1988); also, Alan H. Hicory and Tracy G. Mehan, 'Watershed Approach to Water Quality Management in the USA,' unpublished paper presented to the International Water Association, Cardiff, Wales, Jan. 28, 2005.

9 Reid Kreutzwiser and Rob de Loë, 'Water Security: From Exports to Contamination of Local Water Supplies,' in Bruce Mitchell, ed., *Resource and Environmental Management in Canada: Addressing Conflict and Uncertainty* (Don Mills, Ont.: Oxford University Press, 2004), 172.

10 Elizabeth Brubaker, 'Property Rights in the Defence of Nature' (Toronto: Environment Probe, 1995), 79.

11 A. Dan Tarlock, 'Inter and Intrastate Usage of Great Lakes Waters: A Legal Overview,' *Case Western Reserve Journal of International Law* 18 (1986): 71.

12 US Supreme Court, *Ogden v. Gibbons*, 22 U.S. (9 Wheat), http://supreme.justia.com/us/22/1/case.html (accessed on April 10, 2008).

13 Peter V. MacAvoy, 'The Great Lakes Charter: Toward a Basin-wide Strategy for Managing the Great Lakes,' *Case Western Reserve Journal of International Law* 18 (1986): 56.

14 Council of Great Lakes Governors, 'The Great Lakes Charter,' 1985, http://www.cglg.org/projects/water/legal.asp (accessed on April 15, 2008).

15 Chris Shafer, 'Great Lakes Diversions Revisited: Legal Constraints and Opportunities for State Regulation,' *T.M. Cooley Law Review* 17 (2000): 483.

16 James P. Hill, 'The New Politics of Great Lakes Diversion: A Canada-Michigan Interface,' *Toledo Journal of Great Lakes Science and Policy* 2 (1999–2000): 80.

17 Government of Canada, 'Comments from the Government of Canada on Annex 2001 to the Council of Great Lakes Governors,' 2005, Sierra Club Canada, http://www.sierraclub.ca/national/postings/goc-comments-proposed-annex.pdf (accessed on April 10, 2008).

18 Council of Great Lakes Governors, 'Great Lakes Basin Water Resources Compact,' June 30, 2005; Council of Great Lakes Governors, 'Great Lakes Basin Sustainable Water Resources Agreement – Entente sur les ressources durables en eaux du basin des grands lacs,' June 30, 2005. Documents available from the Canadian Environmental Law Association, Toronto, Canada.

19 Carmen Maganda, 'Collateral Damage: How the San Diego Imperial Valley Water Agreement Affects the Mexican Side of the Border,' *Environment and Development* 14 (2005): 493.

20 Ibid., 490.

21 It should be noted here that, owing to its allocative responsibilities, the IBWC has exercised a much greater level of influence on transboundary water governance than the IJC.

22 Interview with Jesús Román Calleros, researcher at the Universidad Autónoma de Baja California, cited by Benito Jiménez, 'Reprochan a EU pagar agua sucia,' *Reforma*, Feb. 22, 2006.

23 Ibid.

24 Interview with Gloria Soto, Universidad Iberoamericana, Santa Fe, Mexico, June 14, 2006.

25 Mark Spalding, 'A Synthesis of Institutional Activities and Practices,' in *The Mexico-US Border Environment and Economy: A Call to Action to Make the Mexico-US Border Region a Model of Binational Cooperation for Sustainability* (Washington, D.C.: Aspen Institute, 2000), 15–142.

26 Ibid.

27 Marburg Wilder and Scott Whiteford, 'Flowing Uphill toward Money: Groundwater Management and Ejidal Producers in Mexico's Free Trade Environment,' in Randal, ed., *Changing Structure of Mexico*, 344.

28 Valerie J. Assetto, Eva Hajba, and Stephen Mumme, 'Democratization, Decentralization, and Local Environmental Policy Capacity: Hungary and Mexico,' *Social Science Journal* 40 (2003): 249–68.

29 An action made possible by previous amendments to Article 27 of the constitution.

30 Soto interview.

31 Edit Antal, 'Cross-Border Relations of Mexican Environmental NGOs in Tijuana-San Diego,' in Barbara Hogenboom, Miriam Alfie Cohen, and Edit Antal, eds., *Cross-border Activism and Its Limits: Mexican Environmental Organizations and the United States* (Amsterdam: Centre for Latin American Research and Documentation, 2003), 66.

32 Francisco Lara, 'Transboundary Networks for Environmental Management in the San Diego-Tijuana Border Region,' in Lawrence Herzog, ed., *Shared Space: Rethinking the US-Mexico Border Environment* (San Diego: University of California-Center for US-Mexican Studies, 2000), 155–81.

33 Soto interview.

34 Stephen Mumme, 'Environmental Politics and Policy in US-Mexican Border Studies: Developments, Achievements, Trends,' *Social Science Journal* 40 (2004): 593–606.

35 John Knox and David Markell, 'The Innovative North American Commission for Environmental Cooperation,' in John Knox and David Markell, eds., *Greening NAFTA: The North American Commission for Environmental Cooperation* (Stanford, Calif.: Stanford University Press, 2003), 8.

36 Linda Fernandez, 'Revealed Preferences of an International Trade and Environmental Institution,' *Land Economics* 80, no. 2 (2004): 232.

37 Ibid., 233.

38 Patricia Muñoz Ríos, 'ONG buscan revertir privatización silenciosa de los recursos hidráulicos,' *La Jornada*, Feb. 9, 2006.

39 Stephen P. Mumme, 'Reinventing the International Boundary and Water Commission,' http://americas.irc-online.org/briefs/2001/bl79.html (accessed on April 13, 2008).

40 Christopher Brown and Stephen Mumme, 'Applied and Theoretical Aspects of Binational Watershed Councils (Consejos de Cuencas) in the US-Mexico Borderlands,' *Natural Resources Journal* 40 (2000): 895–929.

41 Hicory and Mehan, 'Watershed Approach to Water Quality Management in the USA.'

42 Javier Delgado et al., 'The Environment,' 313.

43 Maganda, 'Collateral Damage,' 499–500; J. Jesús Esquivel, 'Robbery Beginning,' *Proceso* 1493 (June 12, 2005).

44 Staff Reforma, 'Temen desabasto en la frontera. Enfrentan sequía ganaderos,' in *Reforma*, Feb. 22, 2006.

45 Ostrom Elinor et al., 'Revisiting the Commons: Local Lessons, Global Challenges,' *Science* 284, no. 5412 (1999): 278.

46 Joachim Blatter and Helen Ingram, 'States, Markets and Beyond: Governance of Transboundary Water Resources,' *Natural Resources Journal* 40 (2000): 439–74.

VII. THE ROLE OF BIG BUSINESS IN NEGOTIATING FREE TRADE

1 Richard Lehne identifies three types of business associations: leadership, trade, and specialized. *Government and Business: American Political Economy in Comparative Perspective* (Washington, D.C., CQ Press, 2006), 119–26.
2 For classic accounts of business's power in politics, see Theodore J. Lowi, 'American Business, Public Policy, Case-Studies, and Political Theory,' *World Politics* 16 (1964): 677–715; Charles E. Lindblom, *Politics and Markets: The Worlds Political-Economic Systems* (New York: Basic Books, 1977).
3 Gilbert R. Winham, 'NAFTA and the Trade Policy Revolution of the 1980s: A Canadian Perspective,' *International Journal* 99 (summer 1994): 475–8; Stephen Blank et al., 'US Firms in North America: Redefining Structure and Strategy,' *North American Outlook* 5, no. 2 (1995), makes a similar point at page 9.
4 Stephen Blank and Jerry Haar, *Making NAFTA Work: US Firms and the New North American Business Environment* (Boulder, Colo.: North-South Center Press, 1998).
5 Ibid., 22.
6 Robert Gilpin, *Global Political Economy: Understanding the International Economic Order* (Princeton, N.J.: Princeton University Press, 2001), 292.
7 Alan Rugman and Micahel Gestrin, 'NAFTA's Treatment of Foreign Investment,' in Alan Rugman, ed., *Foreign Investment and NAFTA* (Columbia: University of South Carolina Press, 1994), 48–50.
8 John Knubley, Marc Legault, and Someshwar Rao, 'TNCs and Foreign Direct Investment in North America,' in Lorraine Eden, ed., *Multinationals in North America* (Calgary: University of Calgary Press, 1994), 145–6.
9 Donald Barry and Ronald C. Keith, eds., *Regionalism, Multilateralism, and the Politics of Global Trade* (Vancouver: University of British Columbia Press, 1999), 12; also, Strom C. Thacker, *Big Business, the State, and Free Trade* (New York: Cambridge University Press, 2000), 4.
10 Brian W. Tomlin 'The Stages of Pre-negotiation: The Decision to Negotiate North American Free Trade,' *International Journal* 44 (spring 1989): 268; and Robert Pastor and Carol Wise, 'The Origins and Sustainability of Mexico's Free Trade Policy,' *International Organization* 48, no. 3 (1994): 459.

11 Bruce Doern and Brian Tomlin, *Faith and Fear: The Free Trade Story* (Toronto: Stoddart, 1992), 23.

12 Blank and Haar, *Making NAFTA Work*, 13.

13 W.T. Stanbury, *Business-Government Relations in Canada* (Toronto: Methuen, 1988); Ruth Spalding, 'The Mexican Variant of Corporatism,' *Comparative Political Studies* (July 1981): 139–61; D. Wayne Taylor, *Business and Government Relations: Partners in the 1990s* (Toronto: Gage, 1991), 117–18; and Martin Needler, 'The Consent of the Governed? Coercion, Co-optation, and Compromise in Mexican Politics,' *Mexican Studies / Estudios Mexicanos* 10 (1994): 383–90.

14 David Langille, 'The Business Council on National Issues and the Canadian State,' *Studies in Political Economy* 24 (autumn 1987): 41–85; Doern and Tomlin, *Faith and Fear*, 48 and 217–19; Neil Bradford 'The Policy Influence of Economic Ideas: Interests, Institutions and Innovation in Canada,' in Mike Burke et al., eds., *Restructuring and Resistance* (Halifax: Fernwood Publishing, 2000), 67, 72; and Henry J. Jacek, 'Public Policy and NAFTA: The Role of Organized Business Interests and the Labour Movement,' *Canadian-American Public Policy* 19 (1994).

15 Tomlin, 'The Stages of Pre-negotiation,' 265.

16 Business Council on National Issues, 'Reflections on a Quarter Century of Business Leadership on Behalf of Enterprise and Country,' 4, http://www.ceocouncil.ca/publications/pdf/6c02dee3d5adc4361c dc96cf51846d14/speeches_2001_05_09.pdf (accessed on April 10, 2008).

17 Langille, 'The Business Council on National Issues and the Canadian State,' 65–9.

18 Doern and Tomlin, *Faith and Fear*, 48.

19 Duncan Cameron, 'The Dealers,' *This Magazine* 21, no. 8 (1988): 18.

20 Bruce Campbell and David Macdonald, 'Straight Talk: Big Business and the Canada-US Free Trade Agreement Fifteen Years Later,' *Behind the Numbers* 5, no. 2 (Dec. 22, 2003): 1–4.

21 Duncan Cameron, ed., *The Free Trade Papers* (Toronto: James Lorimer, 1986), xv.

22 John W. Warnock, *Free Trade and the New Right Agenda* (Vancouver: New Star Books, 1988), 115.

23 Richard Simeon, 'Inside the Macdonald Commission,' *Studies in Political Economy* 22 (spring 1987): 170. The definitive work showing majority business opposition to free trade is Greg Inwood, *Continentalizing Canada: The Policy and Legacy of the Macdonald Royal Commission* (Toronto: University of Toronto Press, 2006).

24 Winham, 'NAFTA and the Trade Policy Revolution of the 1980s,' 490.

25 Jayson Myers, 'Canada: Meeting the Challenges of North American Inte-

gration.' Paper submitted to the House of Commons Standing Committee on Foreign Affairs and International Trade, Feb. 5, 2002, 2.

26 Warnock, *Free Trade and the New Right Agenda*, 115.

27 Doern and Tomlin, *Faith and Fear*, 49.

28 Stephanie Golob, 'Beyond the Policy Frontier: Canada, Mexico, and the Ideological Origins of NAFTA,' *World Politics* 55 (2003): 389.

29 Stephen Haggard, 'Regionalism in Asia and the Americas,' in E.D.Mansfield and H.V. Milner, eds., *The Political Economy of Regionalism* (New York: Columbia University Press, 1997), 36. See also Bruce Doern and Brian Tomlin et al., *Decision at Midnight: Inside the Canada-US Free Trade Negotiations* (Vancouver: University of British Columbia Press, 1994); Gordon Ritchie, *Wrestling with the Elephant: The Inside Story of the Canada-US Trade Wars* (Toronto: Macfarlane Walter and Ross, 1997).

30 Pastor and Wise, 'The Origins and Sustainability of Mexico's Free Trade Policy'; Blanca Heredia, 'Contested State: The Politics of Trade Liberalization in Mexico,' PhD thesis, Columbia University, 1996.

31 Henry Jacek, 'The Role of Business in the Formulation and Implementation of Regional Trade Agreements in North America,' in Justin Greenwood and Henry Jacek, eds., *Organized Business and the New Global Order* (London: Macmillan, 2000), 5–6.

32 Aldo R. Flores Quiroga, *Proteccionismo Versus Librecambio: La Economia Politica de la Protección en México, 1970–1994* (Mexico City: Fondo de Cultura Económica, 1998), Table 7.14, 320.

33 Deborah L. Riner and John V. Sweeney, 'The Effects of NAFTA on Mexico's Private Sector and Foreign Trade and Investment,' in R. Roett, ed., *Mexico's Private Sector: Recent History, Future Challenges* (Boulder, Colo.: Lynne Rienner, 1998), 165.

34 Thacker, *Big Business, the State, and Free Trade*, 13–14 and 82.

35 Pastor and Wise, 'The Origins and Sustainability of Mexico's Free Trade Policy,' 479.

36 Flores, *Proteccionismo Versus Librecambio*, chapter 7. On the more assertive, increasingly activist Mexican private sector, see also Pastor and Wise, 'The Origins and Sustainability of Mexico's Free Trade Policy,' 479.

37 John Warnock, *The Other Mexico: The North American Triangle Completed* (Montreal: Black Rose, 1995), 86.

38 Pastor and Wise, 'The Origins and Sustainability of Mexico's Free Trade Policy,' 479.

39 Warnock, *The Other Mexico*, 86.

40 Gil Winham, *International Trade and the Tokyo Round Negotiation* (Princeton, N.J.: Princeton University Press, 1986), 307.

41 Winham, *International Trade and the Tokyo Round Negotiation*, 308–9.

42 Gustavo del Castillo, 'Private Sector Trade Advisory Groups in North America: A Comparative Perspective,' in del Castillo, ed., *The Politics of Free Trade in North America* (Ottawa: Centre for Trade Policy and Law, 1999), 36–42.

43 Doern and Tomlin, *Faith and Fear*, 109.

44 Ibid., 110.

45 Ibid. See also Judith Bello and Gil Winham, 'The Canada-USA Free Trade Agreement: Issues of Process,' in L. Waverman, ed., *Negotiating and Implementing a North American Free Trade Agreement* (Vancouver: Fraser Institute, 1992), 45–6.

46 Bello and Winham, 'The Canada-USA Free Trade Agreement: Issues of Process,' 47.

47 Doern and Tomlin, *Faith and Fear*, 114–20.

48 Del Castillo, 'Private Sector Trade Advisory Groups in North America,' Table 1, 36.

49 Winham and Bello, 'The Canada-USA Free Trade Agreement: Issues of Process,' 46–7.

50 Éric Montpetit, 'Can Québec Neo-Corporatist Networks Withstand Canadian Federalism and Institutionalization?' in A.G. Gagnon, ed., *Quebec State and Society*, 3rd ed. (Peterborough, Ont.: Broadview, 2004), 172, 176–7.

51 Doern and Tomlin, *Faith and Fear*, 106–8.

52 Thacker, *Big Business, the State, and Free Trade*, 87–8.

53 Martha Lara de Sterlini, 'The Participation of the Private Sector in International Trade Negotiations,' unpublished paper, 2–3.

54 Thacker, *Big Business, the State, and Free Trade*, 142.

55 Martha Lara de Sterlini, 'The Participation of the Private Sector in International Trade Negotations,' 5.

56 Del Castillo, 'Private Sector Trade Advisory Groups in North America,' 41.

57 Thacker, *Big Business, the State, and Free Trade*, 166–7; and Kristin Johnson Ceva, 'Business-Government Relations in Mexico since 1990: NAFTA, Economic Crisis, and the Reorganization of Business Interests,' in Riordan Brett, *Mexico's Private Sector: Recent History, Future Challenges* (Boulder, Colo.: Lynne Rienner, 1998), 129.

58 Johnson Ceva, 'Business-Government Relations in Mexico since 1990,' 128.

59 Del Castillo, 'Private Sector Trade Advisory Groups in North America,' 42.

60 Pastor and Wise, 'The Origins and Sustainability of Mexico's Free Trade Policy,' 480. See also Johnson Ceva, 'Business-Government Relations in Mexico since 1990,' 126.

61 Thacker, *Big Business, the State, and Free Trade*, 163.

62 Ibid., 144.

63 Ibid. See also Johnson Ceva, 'Business-Government Relations in Mexico since 1990,' 129; and Martha Lara de Sterlini, 'The Participation of the Private Sector in International Trade Negotiations,' 9.
64 Del Castillo, 'Private Sector Trade Advisory Groups in North America,' 42.
65 Helen Milner, *Resisting Protectionism: Global Industries and the Politics of International Trade* (Princeton, N.J.: Princeton University Press, 1988).

VIII. CONTINENTAL ENERGY (IN)SECURITY

1 North American Energy Working Group (NAEWG), 'North America – The Energy Picture: 2002,' as discussed in Monica Gattinger, 'From Government to Governance in the Energy Sector: The States of the Canada-US Energy Relationship,' *American Review of Canadian Studies* 35, no. 2 (2005): 321–52.
2 Larry Pratt and John Richards, *Prairie Capitalism: Power and Influence in the New West* (Toronto: McClelland and Stewart, 1979), 80.
3 Carmen Dybwad, 'Energy Trade and Transportation: Conscious Parallelism.' Speech at the IAEE North American Conference, Mexico City, Oct. 20, 2003.
4 Paul Bradley and G.C. Watkins, 'Canada and the US: A Seamless Energy Border?' *The Border Papers* (April 1, 2003): 5.
5 Stephen Clarkson, *Canada and the Reagan Challenge: Crisis and Adjustment 1981–1985* (Toronto: James Lorimer, 1985), 57, 75.
6 Ibid., 82.
7 Gattinger, 'From Government to Governance in the Energy Sector,' CBC web archives, http://archives.cbc.ca/IDC-1–73–378–2139/politics_economy/alberta_oil/clip5 (accessed on April 10, 2008), 326; interview with Larry Pratt, University of Alberta, Edmonton, June 1979.
8 Gattinger, 'From Government to Governance in the Energy Sector,' 326.
9 G.C. Watkins, 'NAFTA and Energy: A Bridge Not Far Enough?' in Steven Globerman and Michael Walker, eds., *Assessing NAFTA: A Trinational Analysis* (Vancouver: Fraser Institute, 1993), 207.
10 Naturalgas.org, 'The Market under Regulation,' http://www.naturalgas.org/regulation/market.asp (accessed on April 10, 2008).
11 International Energy Agency (IEA), 'Energy Policies of IEA Countries: Canada 2000 Review,' IEA/OECD Publication (2000).
12 NAFTA, 609.1
13 Watkins, 'NAFTA and Energy: A Bridge Not Far Enough?' 209.
14 IEA, 'Energy Policies, 11.

15 Ibid.
16 Pietro S. Nivola, 'Energy Independence or Interdependence? Integrating the North American Energy Market,' *Brookings Review* (Washington: Brookings Institute, spring 2002): 20–2.
17 Interview with Rob Cupina, deputy director, and Jeff Wright, chief of Energy Infrastructure Policy Group, Federal Energy Regulatory Commission, Washington, D.C., April 1, 2004.
18 Donald F. Santa, 'New Challenges in the Integrated North American Energy Market.' Speech at the Energy in the North American Market Conference, June 12, 2003, available at: http://www.canadianembassy.org/trade/santa-en.asp (accessed on Aug. 26, 2006).
19 NAEWG, 'North America – The Energy Picture: 2002,' 17.
20 Gattinger, 'From Government to Governance in the Energy Sector,' 337.
21 Federal Energy Regulatory Commission (FERC), 'Gas – Memorandum of Understanding (MOU),' May 10, 2004, http://www.ferc.gov/industries/gas/gen-info/mou.asp (accessed on April 10, 2008).
22 Santa, 'New Challenges,' quoting Chairman Wood.
23 United States Energy Association (USEA), 'Towards an International Energy Trade and Development Strategy,' USEA Publications, October 2001, http://www.usea.org/T&Dreport.pdf (accessed on Dec. 12, 2005).
24 Marjorie Cohen, 'International Forces Driving Electricity Deregulation in the Semi-periphery: The Case of Canada,' in Stephen Clarkson and Marjorie Cohen, eds., *Governing under Stress: Middle Powers and the Challenge of Globalization* (London: Zed Books, 2004), 177.
25 Ibid., 222.
26 Ibid., 224.
27 IEA, 'Energy Policies,' 9.
28 Cohen, 'International Forces,' 230.
29 Bradley and Watkins, *Canada and the US: A Seamless Energy Border?* 18.
30 Ibid.
31 Cohen, 'International Forces,' 223.
32 Cupina and Wright interview.
33 John Grant, 'Electricity Restructuring: Is Ontario Getting It Right?' *International Association for Energy Economics Newsletter* (Fourth Quarter 2002): 14–16.
34 IEA, 'Energy Policies,' 10.
35 Cohen, 'International Forces,' 230; and IEA, 'Energy Policies,' 10.
36 Bradley and Watkins, *Canada and the US: A Seamless Energy Border?* 19.
37 Ibid.
38 Ibid., 23.

39 Interview with Neil McCrank, chairman, Alberta Energy and Utilities Board, Edmonton, March 2, 2004.

40 US National Energy Policy Development Group (NEPDG), *The National Energy Policy* (Washington, D.C.: US Government Printing Office, 2001), 3.

41 (NAEWG), 'North America -The Energy Picture: 2002,' 17.

42 Bradley and Watkins, *Canada and the US: A Seamless Energy Border?* 19.

43 Interview with John Grant, board member, Independent Electricity Market Operator (of Ontario), Toronto, March 9, 2004.

44 NEPDG, *The National Energy Policy*, 3.

45 Marjorie Cohen, 'Imperialist Regulation: US Electricity Market Designs and Their Problems for Canada and Mexico.' Paper presented at conference on 'Neo-Liberal Globalism and Its Challengers: Reclaiming the Commons in the Semi-periphery. A Comparative Study of Mexico, Norway, Australia and Canada,' Bergen, Norway, October 4–7, 2003.

46 NEPDG, *The National Energy Policy*, 9.

47 The language in the Cheney Report suggests that whoever becomes the Electricity Reliability Operator (ERO) should seek consultation and coordination with Canada and Mexico, following the precedent set by the continental NERC and in keeping with the reality of the North American grid.

48 NEPDG, *The National Energy Policy*, 3.

49 Ibid.

50 Gary Clyde Hufbauer and Ben Goodrich, 'Toward One Continent of Energy,' *Electric Perspectives* 28 (May/June 2003): 115.

51 CBC, 'Blackout Report Blames Ohio Utility,' *CBC News*, Nov. 19, 2003, www.cbc.ca/news/story/2003/11/19/blackout031119.html (accessed on April 10, 2008).

52 US-Canada Power System Outage Task Force, 'Interim Report: Causes of the August 14th Blackout in the United States and Canada,' November 2003, 8.

53 CBC, 'Blackout Report Blames Ohio Utility.'

54 Cohen, 'International Forces,' 228.

55 McCrank interview.

56 George Roland and Paul Mortensen, *Towards a Continental Natural Gas Market: The Integration of Mexico* (Calgary: Canadian Energy Research Institute, 1995), 36.

57 Roland and Mortensen, *Towards a Continental Natural Gas Market*. Official figures suggest that Pemex supplied 37 per cent of government revenues in 2002, but unofficial estimates are as high as 70 per cent.

58 Victor Rodríguez-Padilla, 'La estrategia oficial para privatizar la industria

petrolera mexicana y Pemex.' Paper presented at the International Seminar of Natural and Strategic Resources: Hydrocarbons and Water, UNAM, Mexico City, May 27–28, 2004.

59 CBC, 'Blackout Report Blames Ohio Utility.'
60 Roland and Mortensen, *Towards Continental Natural Gas Markets*, 36.
61 Interview with Sarahí Angeles, UNAM, Mexico City, March 14, 2006.
62 Roland and Mortensen, *Towards Continental Natural Gas Markets*, 36.
63 Opalín, 'México precisa una reforma energética amplia,' 45.
64 Ibid., 35.
65 NAFTA, 601.1.
66 Sidney Weintraub, 'The North American Free Trade Agreement as Negotiated: A US Perspective,' in Globerman and Walker, eds., *Assessing NAFTA*, 3.
67 Watkins, 'NAFTA and Energy: A Bridge Not Far Enough?' 210.
68 Ibid.
69 Ibid.
70 Ibid.
71 'Natural Gas Import and Export Point Database – as of August 2006 – Ordered by US State (Column A) and US Entry/Exit Point Name (Column B)'; provided by Jim Tobin, Energy Information Administration, Office of Oil and Gas.
72 Energy Information Administration, Office of Oil and Gas, 'Additions to Capacity on the U.S. Natural Gas Pipeline Network: 2005,' August 2006, http://tonto.eia.doe.gov/FTPROOT/features/ngpipeline.pdf (accessed on April 9, 2008).
73 Joseph. M Dukert, 'North American Energy Interdependence -A Critical Survey,' *USAEE Dialogue* 10, no. 1 (2002): 16.
74 Alejandro Álvarez and Nora Lina Montes, '¿Cuál cambio estructural requiere el sector energético en México?' *MACROeconomía* 147 (Nov. 1, 2005): 10–20.
75 Associated Press, 'Pemex Chief Says Company Needs Boost,' Washington *Post* (Feb. 2, 2004), http://ww.washingtonpost.com/wp-dyn/articles/A6806–2004Feb2.html (accessed on April 16, 2008).
76 Rodríguez-Padilla, 'La estrategia oficial para privatizar la industria petrolera mexicana y Pemex.'
77 Alejandra Palma Gutiérrez, 'Acaparan firmas extranjeras jugosos contratos de Pemex,' *El Financiero*, Feb. 21, 2006.
78 Cupina and Wright Interview.
79 Ibid.
80 Ibid.

81 Nelson Antoush, 'Marathon Cancels Tijuana Project,' Houston *Chronicle*, March 1, 2004.
82 Interview with Jorge Witker, Instituto de Investigaciones Jurídicas, UNAM, Mexico City, Feb. 19, 2006.
83 León Opalín, 'México precisa una reforma energética amplia,' *El Financiero*, March 6, 2006, 41.
84 Alejandro Álvarez and Nora Lina Montes, '¿Cuál cambio estructural requiere el sector energético mexicano?' 9.
85 'Brasil y México se disputan la IED,' *El Economista*, October 17, 2007.
86 Enrique Andrade Gonzalez, 'Mexico Still Hopes for Energy Reform,' *Mexidata.info*, March 14, 2005), http://www.mexidata.info/id420.html (accessed on April 11, 2008).
87 Sidney Weintraub, 'Mexico's Oil, Gas, and Energy Policy Options,' *Issues in International Political Economy* 68 (August 2005), 1–2.
88 Roland and Mortensen, *Towards Continental Natural Gas Markets*, 38.
89 Ibid.
90 Ibid.
91 Fossil Energy International, 'An Energy Overview of Mexico,' October 2002, http://www.geni.org/globalenergy/library/national_energy_grid/mexico/LatinAmericanPowerGuide.shtml (accessed on April 15, 2008).
92 Ibid.
93 NAEWG, 'North America, Subsection Electricity Infrastructure.'
94 Fossil Energy International, 'An Energy Overview of Mexico.'
95 EIA, 'International Energy Outlook 2006,' June 2006, http://www.eia.doe.gov/oiaf/ieo/electricity.html (accessed on April 11, 2008).
96 Armando Llamas et al., 'La gasificación como alternativa al gas natural en las plantas de ciclo combinado,' *Energía en Transferencia*, Instituto Tecnológico de Estudios Superiores de Monterrey, Feb. 26, 2007.
97 Angeles interview.
98 Reforma Staff, 'Ven viable dos plantas nucleares,' *Reforma*, April 21, 2006.
99 Interview with Rocío Vargas, UNAM, Mexico City, March 14, 2006.
100 Ibid.
101 Joseph M. Dukert, 'North American Energy Interdependence – A Critical Survey,' *USAEE Dialogue* 10, no. 1 (2002).
102 NEPDG, *The National Energy Policy*, 3, 14.
103 Ibid., 8.
104 Interview with Paul Connors, first secretary of Energy, and Christine Hanson, second secretary of Trade Policy and of Congressional and Legal Affairs, Canadian Embassy, Washington, D.C., April 1, 2004.

105 Ibid.
106 NAEWG, 'North America – The Energy Picture: 2002.'
107 For a more detailed overview of energy supply and demand in North America, see North American Energy Working Group / Security and Prosperity Partnership Energy Picture Experts Group, 'North America: The Energy Picture II,' http://www.pi.energy.gov/documents/ NorthAmericaEnergyPicture II.pdf (accessed on 15 April 2008).
108 Ibid., appendix 2.
109 *Security and Prosperity Partnership of North America: Report to Leaders*, June 2005, 28–33.
110 Interview with Roberto Newell, director, Instituto Mexicano para la Competitividad, Mexico City, March 5, 2007.
111 Cupina and Wright interview.
112 NAESB, 'About NAESB,' www.naesb.org/aboutus.asp (accessed on April 11, 2008).

IX. AGRICULTURE: BEEF, WHEAT, AND CORN

 1 José Luis Calva Tellez, 'Efectos del TLCAN en la economía mexicana y algunas reflexiones sobre el sector agrícola,' Instituto de Investigaciones Jurídicas, 230–1, www.bibliojuridica.org/libros/4/1667/12.pdf (accessed on April 11, 2008).
 2 Ibid.
 3 Giovanni Anania, Colin A. Carter, and Alex F. McCalla, 'The U.S.-E.C. Agricultural Trade Conflict,' in Giovanni Anania, ed., *Agricultural Trade Conflicts and GATT* (Boulder, Col.: Westview Press, 1994), 6.
 4 Ibid.
 5 Calva, 'Efectos del TLCAN en la economía mexicana,' 228–9.
 6 Anania, Carter, and McCalla, 'The U.S.-E.C. Agricultural Trade Conflict,' 7.
 7 EU agriculture had also benefited from heavy subsidization via the Common Agricultural Policy (CAP), which transformed the EU from an importer of grains to a significant exporter.
 8 Jimmye S. Hillman, 'The US Perspective,' in K.A. Ingersent, A.J. Rayner, and R.C. Hine, eds., *Agriculture in the Uruguay Round* (New York: St Martin's Press, 1994), 28.
 9 J. Bruce Bullock, 'What Is the 1985 Farm Problem?' CATA Institute, *Policy Analysis* 55 (1985).
10 Linda M. Young and John M. Marsh, 'Integration and Interdependence in

the US and Canadian Live Cattle and Beef Sectors,' in Gregory P. Mar-
childon, ed., *Agriculture at the Border: Canada-US Trade Relations in the Global Food Regime* (Regina: Canadian Plains Research Centre, 2000), 113.

11 Ibid., 104–8.

12 Ibid., 115–16.

13 This has not removed all controversy around these measures but it has influenced national positions as the two countries anticipate having to defend themselves in trade disputes.

14 USDA Animal and Plant Health Inspection Service, Foreign Animal and Poultry Disease Advisory Committee's Subcommittee, 'Report on Measures Relating to Bovine Spongiform Encephalopathy (BSE) in the United States,' 1, Feb. 2, 2004. Emphasis added.

15 US Court of Appeals for the Ninth Circuit, no. 05–35264

16 Interview with Barbara Spangler, executive director of farm policy for the National Association of Wheat Growers, Washington, D.C., March 31, 2004.

17 USDA Animal and Plant Health Inspection Service, 'Response to R-CALF Fact Sheet,' Feb. 2, 2005, http://www.aphis.usda.gov/dpa/pubs/fsheet_faq_notice/r-calfstatement.pdf (accessed on April 11, 2008).

18 Gregory P. Marchildon, 'The Grain Trade in Contemporary Canada-US regulations,' in Marchildon, ed., *Agriculture at the Border*, 13–16.

19 Ibid., 17.

20 Canada's chief negotiator, John Weekes, stated: 'We had absolutely no flexibility on that at all': Frederick W. Mayer, *Interpreting NAFTA: The Science and Art of Political Analysis* (New York: Columbia University Press, 1998), 122.

21 Richard Gray and Mel Annand, 'The Grain Trade in Contemporary Canada-US Relations,' in Marchildon, ed., *Agriculture at the Border*, 27–8.

22 W.H. Furtan and K.R. Baylis, 'State Trading in Wheat: Perceptions and Reality in Canada-U.S. Relations,' in Marchildon, ed., *Agriculture at the Border*, 66–77.

23 USDA Economic Research Service, 'Effects of NAFTA on Agriculture and the Rural Economy,' WRS-02–01, 2002, 24.

24 Gray and Annand, 'The Grain Trade in Contemporary Canada-US Relations,' 22–4.

25 Ibid.

26 William W. Wilson and Bruce Dahl, 'Pressures and Challenges in Integrating the US-Canada Grains Sector,' in Marchildon, ed., *Agriculture at the Border*, 135–8.

27 Compiled from information in ibid. and National Farmers Union website, www.nfu.ca (accessed on April 11, 2008).

28 Sergio Sarmiento, 'Mexico Alert: NAFTA and Mexico's Agriculture,' *Center for Strategic and International Studies* 11, no. 7 (2003): 6.
29 Jonathan Fox, *The Politics of Food in Mexico* (Ithaca, N.Y.: Cornell University Press, 1993), 48.
30 Gloria M Delgado de Cantú, *Historia de México 2. Estado moderno y crisis en el México del siglo XX* (Mexico City: Alhambra Mexicana,1996), 175.
31 Richard Snyder, 'Introduction,' in Richard Snyder and Gabriel Torres, eds., *The Future Role of the Ejido in Rural Mexico* (San Diego: Center for US Mexico Studies, University of California, 1998), 1–7.
32 Alejandro Nadal, 'Corn in NAFTA: Eight Years After.' Report prepared for the North American Commission for Environmental Cooperation, May 2002.
33 Fox, *The Politics of Food in Mexico*, 61–3.
34 Aldo R. Flores Quiroga, *Proteccionismo versus Libre Cambio. La economía política de la protección comercial en México, 1970–1994* (Mexico City: Fondo de Cultura Económica, 1998), 332–3.
35 Ricardo Dominguez, *The Transformation of the Maize Subsidies in Mexico: From Generalized to Targeted* (Buenos Aires: Centro de Investigaciones Europeo-Latinoamericanas, Serie Documentos de Trabajo Eural [57] 1993), 3–13.
36 Ibid., 13.
37 Delgado de Cantú, *Historia de México*, 478–9.
38 Ibid., 523; various authors, *Todo México 1995* (Mexico City: *Enciclopedia de México*, April 1995), 321–2.
39 Alejandro Nadal, 'The Environmental and Social Impacts of Economic Liberalization on Corn Production in Mexico.' Study commissioned by Oxfam GB and WWF International, October 2000, 5.
40 Mayer, *Interpreting NAFTA*, 122–3.
41 Frank Ackerman et al., *Free Trade, Corn and the Environment: Environmental Impacts of US-Mexico Corn Trade under NAFTA* (Medord, Me.: Tufts University, Global Development and Environment Institute, Working Paper 03–06, 2000), 3.
42 Santiago Levy and Sweder van Wijnbergen's 1992 study figured prominently in the mind of Salinas negotiators: 'Transition Problems in Economic Reform: Agriculture in the North American Free Trade Agreement,' *American Economic Review* 85, no. 4 1995): 738–54.
43 Mayer, *Interpreting NAFTA*, 123.
44 Ibid.
45 Nadal, 'The Environmental and Social Impacts,' 10–11.
46 Ibid., 37–9.
47 Ibid., 12–21.

48 Nadal, 'Corn in NAFTA,'section II.4.
49 Alejandro Nadal, 'Cesiones Procampo,' *Jornada UNAM*, sección Economía (Mexico City: UNAM, Jan. 3, 2001).
50 Nadal, 'The Environmental and Social Impacts,' 23–4.
51 Ibid., 15.
52 Ackerman et al., 'Free Trade, Corn and the Environment,' 15–16.
53 Nadal, 'The Environmental and Social Impacts,' 8.
54 Gisele Henriques and Raj Patel, 'NAFTA, Corn, and Mexico's Agricultural Trade Liberalization,' in Americas Program Special Report (Americas IRC, Feb. 13, 2004), 1–8.
55 Nadal, 'Corn in NAFTA,' section I.2.
56 Steven Zahniser and William Coyle, 'US-Mexico Corn Trade during the NAFTA Era: New Twists to an Old Story' (USDA FDS-04D-01, May 2004), 6–7.
57 Alejandro Nadal, Francisco Aguayo, and Marcos Chavez, 'Seven Myths about NAFTA and Three Lessons for Latin America,' Americas Program, Interhemispheric Resource Center, Washington, D.C., www.americaspolicy .org/articles/2003/0311_7–myths.html (accessed on April 11, 2008).
58 Instituto Nacional de Estadística Geografía e Informática (INEGI), www.inegi.gob.mx. 2003 (accessed on April 11, 2008).
59 Mayer, *Implementing NAFTA*, 115.
60 Nadal, 'The Environmental and Social Impacts,' 34–5.
61 Ibid.
62 Ibid.
63 Ackerman et al., 'Free Trade, Corn and the Environment,' 12–13.
64 Including the processing of HFCS and meat-processing facilities.
65 Miles Kahler, 'Conclusion: The Causes and Consequences of Legalization,' *International Organization* 54, no. 3 (2000): 663.
66 Magda Kornis, 'Mexican Farmers Demand Protection against Imports of US Agricultural Products,' *International Economic Review* (May/June 2003): 2.

X. THE STEEL INDUSTRY

1 United Steelworkers of America (USWA), 'Major Milestones in USW History,' http://www.usw.org/usw/program/content/3779.php#1940 (accessed on 15 April 2008).
2 William E. Scheuerman, 'Joint Ventures in the U.S. Steel Industry: Steel's Restructuring Includes Efforts to Achieve Tighter Control over Raw Materi-

als and Markets,' *American Journal of Economics and Sociology* 4, no. 49 (1990): 417.

3 Anthony P. D'Costa, *The Global Restructuring of the Steel Industry* (New York: Routledge, 1999).

4 Department of Foreign Affairs and International Trade (DFAIT), 'Dispute Settlement: US Trade Remedy Law: The Canadian Experience,' June 2002, http://www.dfait-maeci.gc.ca/tna-nac/disp/menu-en.asp (accessed on April 13, 2008).

5 Gerardo Espinosa Vega, 'Transformación y Perspectivas de la Industria del Acero,' in Nadima Simón Domínguez and Isabel Rueda Peiro, eds., *Globalización y competitividad de la industria siderúrgica en México* (Mexico City: UNAM, 2002), 57–9, Figure 1.

6 Ibid., 55–6.

7 Ibid., 44–5.

8 Interview with Isabel Rueda Peiro, UNAM, Mexico City, Feb. 20, 2006.

9 Ibid.

10 SteelNews, 'Steel Industry Bankruptcies: Bankruptcy Filings and Other Major Events, 1998–2003,' Steel News.com, http://www.steelnews.com/companies/steel_bankruptcies.htm (accessed on April 13, 2008).

11 Statistical data compiled by the Canadian Steel Producers Association (CSPA) using information from StatsCan, Natural Resources Canada, Industry Canada, and the American Iron and Steel Institute (AISI), http://www.canadiansteel.ca (accessed on April 13, 2008).

12 DFAIT, 'Dispute Settlement.'

13 Dofasco website, http://www.Dofasco.com, and Stelco website, http://www.Stelco.com (accessed on April 13, 2008).

14 CSPA, , 'Industry Snapshot,' http://www.canadiansteel.ca/index.php/en/facts#snapshot (accessed on April 13, 2008).

15 CSPA, 'International Trade in Steel: An Overview,' http://www.canadiansteel.ca/industry/factsheets/intertradeov er.htm (accessed on Aug. 16, 2006).

16 Espinosa Vega, 'Transformación,' 66–7.

17 Ma. de Lourdes Álvarez, 'Cambios en la industria automotriz frente a la globalización: el sector de autopartes en México,' *Contaduría y Administración* 206 (July-September 2002): 37.

18 Isabel Rueda Peiro, 'La globalización de la industria siderúrgica,' in Domínguez and Rueda, eds., *Globalización*, 30.

19 'Fiebre por el acero,' CNNExpansion, Aug. 2, 2007, http://www.cnnexpansion.com/obras/fiebre-por-el-acero/print (accessed on May 29, 2008).

20 Alenka Guzmán, *Las Fuentes del crecimiento en la siderúrgia mexicana: innovación, productividad y competitividad* (Mexico City: Universidad Autónoma Metropolitana and Grupo Editorial Miguel Angel Porrúa, 2002).

21 José Antonio Fernández Carbajal, at conference organized by the Mexico Institute at the Woodrow Wilson International Center for Scholars and Letras Libres Magazine (Perceptions and Miconceptions: How We See Each Other in Mexico-US Relations), Washington D.C., Feb. 27, 2004.

22 Luis Antonio Cruz Soto y Francisco Javier Vargas, 'Las prácticas antidumping,' in Domínguez and Rueda, eds., *Globalización*, 78.

23 Guzmán, *Las Fuentes del crecimiento*, 112.

24 Organization for Economic Cooperation and Development (OECD), 'NAFTA: A North American Perspective on Global Steel Developments,' OECD Steel Workshop Presentation, May 16–17, 2006, New Delhi, http://www.steel.org/AM/Template.cfm?Section=Trade2&TEMPLATE =/CM/ContentDisplay.cfm&CONTENTID=14889 (accessed on April 13, 2008).

25 Ibid.

26 NASTC, 'The NAFTA Steel Industry Pulse,' http://www.steelnet.org/new/20040500.htm (accessed on April 13, 2008).

27 United States Office of Public Affairs, 'Commerce Department on Steel Trade Strategy,' Department of Commerce, July 26, 2000, http://www.useu.be/issues/steel0726.html (accessed on Aug. 16, 2006).

28 AISI, CANACERO, and CSPA, 'Common NAFTA-wide Draft Positions and Principles for the 4th WTO Ministerial and a New Round of Trade Negotiations Affecting Steel,' Nov. 8, 2001.

29 AISI, CANACERO, and CSPA, 'Common NAFTA-wide Positions and Principles for the 5th WTO Ministerial and Other Trade Negotiations Affecting Steel,' Sept. 3, 2003.

30 'Joint Statement of NAFTA Steel Producers on Major Principles for the FTAA,' Sept. 23, 2003.

31 See discussion in OECD, 'The OECD High-Level Steel Initiative, Oct. 16, 2003, 1, http://www.oecdwash.org/PDFILES/schlogl_statement_on_steel.pdf (accessed on April 18, 2008).

32 John Herd Thompson, 'Playing by the New Washington Rules: The US-Canada Relationship 1994–2003,' *American Review of Canadian Studies* 33, no. 1 (2003): 12.

33 DFAIT, 'Joint Statement of NAFTA Governments on the Establishment, Operation and Initial Agenda of a North American Steel Trade Committee,' Feb. 23, 2004, http://www.dfait-maeci.gc.ca/nafta-alena/nafta-govern-en.asp (accessed on April 13, 2008).

34 AISI, 'The Capitol Line Newsletter, June 2004, 2, http://www.steel.org/

AM/Template.cfm?Section=Newsletters2&CO NTENTID=7402&TEM-
PLATE=/CM/ContentDisplay.cfm (accessed on April 18, 2008).

35 CSPA, 'Proposed Mission Statement for NAFTA Steel Industry Efforts in
the NASTC,' May 20, 2004, http://www.canadiansteel.ca/newsroom/
reports/NAFTA%20Prop%20 Miss%20Statement.pdf (accessed on Aug. 16,
2006).

36 Letter from the North American Steel Association chairmen and presidents
to Minister David Emerson, Secretary Fernando Canales Clariond, and Secretary Carlos Guttierez, http://www.stopspp.com/stopspp/docs/
American_Steel_proposal_ 5_05.pdf (accessed on April 13, 2006).

37 OECD, 'India/North American Steel Strategy.' Presentation by Kenneth P.
Smith Ramos, director general for International Trade Negotiations, Ministry of the Economy, Mexico, at Directorate Joint India/OECD/IISI Workshop, New Delhi, May 16–17, 2006, 2, http://www.oecd.org/dataoecd/48/
16/36889025.pdf (accessed on 18 April 2008).

38 Nancy E. Kelly, 'Steel Subsidy Blueprint Called Seriously Flawed,' *American
Metal Market* (June 7, 2005). Emphasis added.

39 NASTC, http://www.nastc.org (accessed on 18 April 2008).

40 OECD, 'India/North American Steel Strategy,' 3.

41 Greg Keenan, 'A Canadian Dream That Melted Away,' *Globe and Mail*, 26
Oct. 2007.

42 International Iron and Steel Institute, *World Steel in Figures: 2006* (Brussels:
IISI, 2006), 2.

43 Rueda Peiro, *La globalización de la industria siderúrgica*, 25.

44 Vivian Patroni, 'The Decline and Fall of Corporatism? Labour Law Reform
in Mexico and Argentina in the 1990s,' *Canadian Journal of Political Science*
34, no. 2 (2001).

45 Arturio Alcalde and Graciela Bensusan, 'El regimen juridico del trabajo
asalariado,' in Graciela Bensusan and Teresa Rendon, eds., *Trabajo e trabajadores en el México contemporeana* (Mexico City: D.F.: Porrua, 2000), 127–
61.

46 Testimony by Bill Klinefelter, assistant to the president of the USWA, to the
House Subcommittee on Commerce, Trade, and Consumer Protection
(Committee on Energy and Commerce), Sept. 10, 2002.

47 USWA, Press release by Canadian section of the USWA, Feb. 10, 2005,
http://www.uswa.ca (accessed on April 5, 2005).

48 USWA, 'Reform Canada's Bankruptcy Laws,' www.uswa.ca (accessed on
April 5, 2008).

49 Greg Keenan, 'Union Favours Russian Stelco Bid,' *Globe and Mail*, Feb. 14,
2005.

XI. TEXTILES AND APPAREL

1 Gary Gereffi, 'The Organization of Buyer-Driven Global Commodity Chains: How US Retailers Shape Overseas Production Networks,' in Gary Gereffi and Miguel Korzeniewicz, eds., *Commodity Chains and Global Capitalism* (Westport, Conn.: Praeger, 1994), 95–122.
2 Ibid., 102.
3 Frederick H. Abernathy, *A Stitch in Time: Lean Retailing and the Transformation of Manufacturing – Lessons from the Apparel and Textile Industries* (New York: Oxford University Press, 1999), 33–5.
4 Ibid., 26.
5 Ellen Israel Rosen, *Making Sweatshops: The Globalization of the US Apparel Industry* (Berkeley: University of California Press, 2002), 98.
6 J. Michael Finger and Ann Harrison, 'The MFA Paradox: More Protection and More Trade?' in Anne O. Krueger, ed., *The Political Economy of American Trade Policy* (Chicago: University of Chicago Press, 1996), 206.
7 Ibid., 218–26.
8 William R. Cline, *The Future of World Trade in Textiles and Apparel* (Washington, D.C.: Institute for International Economics, 1987), 155.
9 Ibid., 116.
10 Aurora Gómez-Galvarriato, 'The Political Economy of Protectionism: The Mexican Textile Industry, 1900–1950,' in Sebastián Edwards, ed., *Growth, Institutions and Crises: Latin America from a Historic Perspective* (Chicago: University of Chicago Press, 2007), 4.
11 Ibid., 30–1.
12 Ibid., 49.
13 Jennifer Bair, 'Beyond the Maquila Model? NAFTA and the Mexican Apparel Industry,' *Industry and Innovation* 9 (2002): 205.
14 Maria Luisa González Marín, 'Efectos del TLCAN en la industria textil y de la confección mexicana,' in Isabel Rueda Peiro, Nadima Simón, and María Luisa Gonzáles Marín, eds., *La industria de la confección en México y China ante la globalización* (Mexico City: UNAM, 2004), 94.
15 Ibid., 92.
16 Ibid., 93.
17 Ibid., 206.
18 Gómez-Galvarriato, 'The Political Economy of Protectionism,' 2.
19 Alan B. McCullough, *The Primary Textile Industry in Canada: History and Heritage* (Ottawa: Parks Services, 1992), 49.
20 Caroline Pestieau, *The Canadian Textile Policy: A Sectoral Trade Adjustment Strategy?* (Montreal: C.D. Howe Research Institute, 1976), 5; McCullough, *The Primary Textile Industry in Canada*, 75.

21 Donald Kelly, 'The Development of a New Textile Policy for Canada' Graduate thesis, Harvard University, Graduate School of Business Administration, 1974, appendix A.

22 Pestieau, *The Canadian Textile Policy*, 6.

23 Ibid., 13.

24 Maryse Robert, 'Textiles and Apparel: Canada the Odd Man Out,' in *Negotiating NAFTA: Explaining the Outcome in Culture, Textiles, Autos, and Pharmaceuticals* (Toronto: University of Toronto Press, 2000), 128.

25 Leah F. Vosko, 'Fabric Friends and Clothing Foes: A Comparative Analysis of Textile and Apparel Industries under the NAFTA,' *Review of Radical Political Economics* 25 (1993): 45–58; Robert, 'Textiles and Apparel,' 144.

26 Robert, 'Textiles and Apparel,' 142.

27 Ibid., 112–14.

28 Ibid.

29 Foreign Trade Information Service (SICE), 'Report on NAFTA Committee on Trade in Worn Clothing,' http://www.sice.oas.org/trade/nafta/naftatce.asp (accessed on April 14, 2008).

30 Jennifer Bair and Gary Gereffi, 'NAFTA and the Apparel Commodity Chain: Corporate Strategies, Interfirm Networks, and Industrial Upgrading,' in Gary Gereffi, David Spener, and Jennifer Bair, eds., *Free Trade and Uneven Development: The North American Apparel Industry after NAFTA* (Philadelphia: Temple University Press, 2002), 39.

31 United States Department of Labor, Bureau of Labor Statistics, 'Career Guide to Industries, 2006–07 Edition, Textile, Textile Product, and Apparel Manufacturing,' http://www.bls.gov/oco/cg/cgs015.htm, Feb. 21, 2006 (accessed on April 14, 2008).

32 Working Group on Textiles and Apparel, 'Report from the Trilateral Working Group on Textiles and Apparel to the NAFTA Free Trade Commission,' http://www.ustr.gov/assets/Document_Library/Reports_Publicat ions/2005/asset_upload_file597_8153.pdf, 7 March 2005 (accessed on April 28, 2008).

33 Ibid., 9.

34 Bureau of Labor Statistics, 'Career Guide to Industries.'

35 American Apparel and Footwear Association, 'Trends Annual 2003,' http://www.apparelandfootwear.org/UserFiles/File/Statistics/Trends2003Annual.pdf, 16; 'Trends Annual 2005,' ibid.,16 (both accessed on April 14, 2008).

36 American Apparel and Footwear Association, 'Trends Annual 2003,' 16.

37 Working Group on Textiles and Apparel, 8.

38 Ibid., 12.

39 Bair and Gereffi, 'NAFTA and the Apparel Commodity Chain,' 46.

40 Working Group on Textiles and Apparel, 'Report,' 4.
41 Ibid., 12.
42 Bair, 'Beyond the Maquila Model?' 206.
43 Working Group on Textiles and Apparel, 'Report,' 12.
44 American Apparel and Footwear Association, 'Trends Annual 2003,' 2.
45 Marín, 'Efectos del TLCAN en la industria textil,' 99–100.
46 Industry Canada, 'Canadian Textiles,' http://www.ic.gc.ca/epic/site/
    textiles-textiles.nsf/en/tx03216e.html (accessed on April 14, 2008).
47 Industry Canada, 'Apparel Industry of Canada.'
48 Ibid.
49 Working Group on Textiles and Apparel, 'Report,' 3.
50 Ibid.
51 Ibid.,
52 Interview with Isabel Rueda Peiro, UNAM, Mexico City, Feb. 20, 2006.
53 Kathleen Rees and Jan Hathcote, 'The US Textile and Apparel Industry in
    the Age of Globalization,' Global Economy Journal 4 (2004): 15.
54 Bernard A. Gelb, 'Textile and Apparel Quota Phase-out: Some Economic
    Implications,' CRS Report for Congress, CRS Report RS20229 (2005), 5.
55 U.S. Census Bureau, 'Special Report on Textile Imports,' Foreign Trade Sta-
    tistics, http://www.census.gov/foreign-trade/statistics/country/sreport/
    textile.html (accessed on Nov. 23, 2007).
56 Interview with Cass Johnson, president, National Council of Textile Orga-
    nizations, Washington, D.C., April 6, 2006.
57 Vivian C. Jones, 'Safeguards on Textile and Apparel Imports from China,'
    CRS Report for Congress, RL32168 (2005), 3.
58 Ibid., 7–9.
59 'CANAINTEX Demands to Keep Compensatory Dues of 533% to Chinese
    Textiles,' Corporate Mexico, Via Factiva, June 17, 2005, http://www.factiva
    .com (accessed on April 14, 2008).
60 Cass Johnson, 'NCTO Testimony on China Threat before the US-China Eco-
    nomic and Security Review Commission,' National Council of Textile
    Organizations (NCTO), http://www.ncto.org/threat/index.asp (accessed
    on April 14, 2008).
61 Randy Rotchin, Testimony before the Standing Committee on Industry,
    Natural Resources, Science and Technology, 38th Parliament, 1st Session,
    7 March 2005.
62 Harvey Penner, Testimony before the Subcommittee on International Trade,
    Trade Disputes and Investment of the Standing Committee on Foreign Af-
    fairs and International Trade, 38th Parliament, 1st Session, Nov. 30, 2004.
63 Elliot Lifson, Testimony before the Subcommittee on International Trade,
    Trade Disputes and Investment of the Standing Committee on Foreign

Affairs and International Trade, 38 Parliament, 1st Session, Nov. 30, 2004.

64 Scott Malone and Kristi Ellis, 'WTO Textile Issues Create a Marriage of Convenience,' *Women's Wear Daily* (Jan. 25, 2002), 2.

65 Johnson interview.

66 'Fifth Western Hemisphere Trade Ministerial and Business Forum Toronto, Canada – Nov. 1999,' SICE, http://ctrc.sice.oas.org/FTAA/toronto/forum/papers/gpwks_e.asp (accessed on 16 April 2008).

67 Adolfo Kalach, 'The Mexican Textile Industry.' Presentation at Sourcing USA Summit, Scottsdale, Arizona, Nov. 14–17, 2002.

68 CANAINTEX, 'Statement of Camara Nacional de la Industria Textil, Ciudad, Mexico,' *Hearing Archvies, Committee on Ways & Means, US House of Representatives*, http://waysandmeans.house.gov/hearings.asp?formmode=printfri endly&id=2307 (accessed on April 14, 2008).

69 Harvey Penner, chairman of Canadian Textiles Institute (CTI), Testimony before the Subcommittee on International Trade, Trade Disputes and Investment of the Standing Committee on Foreign Affairs and International Trade, 38th Parliament, 1st Session, Nov. 30, 2004.

70 Allen Gant, 'NCTO Board Votes to Support DR-CAFTA,' NCTO News Release, May 9, 2005, http://www.ncto.org/newsroom/pr200518.asp (accessed on April 14, 2008).

71 Interview with Tommy Sevier, legislative director, Office of Representative Robin Hayes (R-NC), Washington, D.C., April 6, 2006.

72 Johnson interview.

73 Working Group on Textiles and Apparel, 2.

74 The three governments have now passed these amendments.

75 Interview with Catherine McClymont, industry officer, Industry Canada, and Canadian chair, NAFTA Working Group on Textiles and Apparel, Ottawa, March 23, 2006, and Carol Miller, deputy textile negotiator, Office of the United States Trade Representative, Washington, D.C., April 5, 2006.

76 Norman Caulfield, 'Labor Relations in Mexico: Historical Legacies and Some Recent Trends,' *Labor History* 45 (2004): 455.

77 Lynda Yanz, 'Testimony to the Canadian National Administrative Office (NAO) – Public Communication CAN 2003–1 (Puebla),' Maquila Solidarity Network, http://www.maquilasolidarity.org/campaigns/NAO/Toronto%20Eng lish/MSN_Presentation.pdf (accessed on Nov. 24, 2005).

78 Huberto Juarez Nuñez, 'Maquila Workers in Mexico: The Prospects for Organ and International Solidarity,' *Labor History* 43 (2002): 444.

79 María Teresa Mendoza Fernández, 'La industria maquiladora de la confección en Yucatán,' in Rueda, Simón, and Gonzáles Marín, eds., *La industria de la confección*, 197.

80 Marín, 'Efectos del TLCAN en la industria textil,' 97.

81 Interview with Isabel Rueda Peiro, UNAM, Mexico City, Feb. 20, 2006.

82 Robert J.S. Ross, 'The New Sweatshops in the United States: How New, How Real, How Many, and Why?' in Gereffi, Spener, and Bair, eds., Free Trade and Uneven Development, 101.

83 Roxanna Ng, 'Homeworking: Home Office or Home Sweatshop?' NALL Working Paper #06–1999, http://www.oise.utoronto.ca/depts/sese/csew/nall/res/06homew orkers.htm (accessed on April 14, 2008).

84 Ross, 'The New Sweatshops in the United States,' 111.

85 North American Commission for Labour Cooperation (NACLC), 'Mexican NAO 2001–1,' http://www.naalc.org/english/summary_mexico.shtml (accessed on April 14, 2008).

86 NACLC, 'US NAO 2003–1,' http://www.naalc.org/english/summary_usa.shtml, and 'Canadian NAO 2003–1,' http://www.naalc.org/english/summary_canada.shtml (both accessed on April 17, 2008).

87 Lance Compa, Justice for All: The Struggle for Worker Rights in Mexico (Washington, D.C.: American Center for International Labor Solidarity, 2003), 11.

88 Interview with Samantha Tate, Senior Program Officer, Americas AFL-CIO Solidary Center, Washington, D.C., April 6, 2006.

89 Benjamin Cashore, 'Legitimacy and the Privatization of Environmental Governance: How Non-State Market-Driven Governance Systems Gain Rule-Making Authority,' Governance 15 (2002): 503–29; Dara O'Rourke, 'Outsourcing Regulation: Analyzing Nongovernmental System of Labor Standards and Monitoring,' Policy Studies Journal 31 (2003): 1–27.

90 Cashore, 'Legitimacy and the Privatization of Environmental Governance,' 504.

91 O'Rourke, 'Outsourcing Regulation,' 1–27.

92 David Bacon, Children of NAFTA: Labor Wars on the US/Mexico Border (Berkeley: University of California Press, 2004), 208–14.

93 Ibid., 212.

XII. THE GOVERNANCE OF CAPITAL MARKETS

1 For a comprehensive overview of corporate-governance issues, see Andrei Shleifer and Robert Vishny, 'A Survey of Corporate Governance,' Journal of Finance 52, no. 2 (1997): 737–83.

2 Rafael La Porta et al., 'Investor Protection and Corporate Governance,' Journal of Financial Economics 58 (2000): 7.

3 Kerry Shannon Burke, 'Regulating Corporate Governance through the Market: Comparing the Approaches of the United States, Canada and the United Kingdom,' Journal of Corporation Law 27 (spring 2002): 342. Taken

from Paul Coombes amd Mark Watson, 'Three Surveys on Corporate Governance,' *McKinsey Quarterly* (summer 2000): 74–6. The study revealed that investors are willing to pay 18 per cent more for the equity of an American or a British company.

4 J. Thain, 'Sarbanes-Oxley: Is the Price Too High?' *Wall Street Journal*, May 27, 2004.

5 United Nations Statistics Division, Statistical database (GDP at market prices, 1990), http://unstats.un.org/unsd/databases.htm (accessed on 17 April 2008).

6 World Federation of Exchanges, 'Total Value of Share Trading (Secretariat),' http://www.world-exchanges.org/WFE/home.asp?menu=378& document=3556 (accessed on April 11, 2008).

7 Ibid.

8 'Datos Generales del Mercado,' *Bolsa Mexicana de Valores*, Nov. 24, 2003, http://www.bmv.com.mx/wb3/wb/BMV/BMV_resumen_del_mercado/ _ri d/194/_mto/3/_url/BMVAPP/resumenMercado.jsf (accessed on April 11, 2008).

9 El Universal, 'Guillermo Prieto Trevino: Entrevista Exclusive Online,' http://estadis.eluniversal.com.mx/graficos/entrevistas/bmv/h ome.htm (accessed on April 11, 2008).

10 Market segmentation is the most traditional explanation for cross-listing. See, for example, Robert Merton, 'A Simple Model of Capital Market Equilibrium with Incomplete Information,' *Journal of Finance* 42 (1987).

11 John Coffee is a main proponent of this explanation, which he refers to as the 'bonding hypothesis.' See John C. Coffee, Jr, 'Racing towards the Top? The Impact of Cross Listings and Stock Market Competition on International Corporate Governance,' Columbia Law School, May 25, 2001, 1767.

12 In 1990 there were approximately 200 cross-listings compared to over 750 in 2000.

13 NYSE Group, 'About NYSE Group > Listed Companies > Listed Company Directory,' Dec. 15, 2006, http://www.nyse.com/about/listed/ listed.html?ListedComp=All (accessed on April 11, 2008).

14 Usha R. Mittoo, 'Globalization and the Value of US Listing: Revisiting Canadian Evidence,' *Journal of Banking and Finance* 27 (2003): 1632.

15 Ibid., 1634.

16 Éric Choéuinard and Chris D'Souza, 'The Rationale for Cross-Border Listings,' Bank of Canada Review (winter 2003–4), http://www.bankofcanada .ca/en/review/winter03–04/chouinarde. pdf, Dec. 28, 2006 (accessed on April 11, 2008). Calculation based on data from the TSX Review.

17 Mittoo, 'Globalization and the Value of US Listing,' 1631.

18 Michael King and Dan Segal, 'International Cross-Listing and the Bonding Hypothesis,' Bank of Canada Working Paper no. 2004–17, 2.
19 Ibid., 159.
20 Christopher Nicholls, 'The Characteristics of Canada's Capital Markets and the Illustrative Case of Canada's Legislative Regulatory Response to *Sarbanes-Oxley*,' *Canada Steps Up: Volume 4 Research Studies – Maintaing a Competitive Capital Market in Canada*, June 15, 2006, 154, http://www.tfmsl.ca/docs/Volume4_en.pdf (accessed on April 18, 2008).
21 Andrew Willis, 'Bay Street Keeps a Keen Eye on Interlisted Stock Trade Action,' *Globe and Mail*, Dec. 10, 2003.
22 Jean-Marc Suret and Cecile Carpentier, 'Securities Regulation in Canada,' Working paper for CIRANO, July 29, 2003, http://www.cirano.qc.ca/pdf/publication/2003RP-12.pdf, 14 (accessed on April 18, 2008).
23 Ibid.
24 Harry Arthurs, 'The Hollowing Out of Corporate Canada?' in Jane Jenson and B. Santos, eds., *Globalizing Institutions: Case Studies in Social Regulation and Innovation* (London: Ashgate Press, 2001), 29–51.
25 Jagoda Pike, 'Foreign Takovers Deserve Scrutiny,' Toronto *Star*, Dec. 2, 2006.
26 Bertrand Marotte, 'Head Office Loss "Alarming": Hollowing Out Threatens Sovereignty,' *Globe and Mail*, May, 2002.
27 Chris Hewat and Craig Thorburn, 'Mergers & Acquisitions: Blakes Survey Shows M&A Activity to Reach New Heights in Canada,' Business with Canada, Nov. 2, 2006, http://www.blakes.com/english/publications/businesswithcanada/bwc/html/article.asp?article=411 (accessed on Dec. 29, 2006). This article summarizes a longer report on a survey of Canadian corporate executives, Canadian investment bankers, and US and European investment bankers: Blake, Cassels and Graydon LLP, 'Canadian M&A Spotlight, September 2006, http://www.blakes.com/mergersandacquisitions/CanadianM&ASpot lightfinal.pdf (accessed on April 15, 2008).
28 La Porta et al., 'Investor Protection and Corporate Governance,' 3–27.
29 Edgar Ortiz and Jonathan Torres, 'Optimal Financial Structure: A Modigliani and Miller Dynamic Model for Mexican Corporations,' in D. Ghosh and Mohamed Ariff, eds., *Regional Financial Markets* (London: Praeger, 2004), 138.
30 Antonio Sandoval, 'Generaron emisoras de la BMV,' *El Financiero*, April 26, 2006.
31 Isabel Mayoral Jiménez, 'BMV, a 20 años del crac bursátil,' *El Economista*, Oct. 19, 2007.
32 Coffee, 'Racing towards the Top?' 1770.

33 Kent Hargis, 'International Cross-listing and Stock Market Development in Emerging Economies,' *International Review of Economics and Finance* 9, no. 101 (2000).

34 Lorenza Martinez and Alejandro Werner, 'Capital Markets in Mexico: Recent Developments and Future Challenges' (Mexico: Banco de México, November 2002), http://www.banxico.org.mx/siteBanxicoINGLES/ gPublicaciones/s eminarios/ing/dgie/estamacromer/CapitalMarkets .pdf, 32 (accessed on Aug. 26, 2006).

35 'Non-US Historical Dollar Value of Trading, by Geographical Region' (New York: NYSE, 2002).

36 'Unlisting Issuers Are Much More Than Listing Ones in the Stock Market,' *Corporate Mexico*, May 9, 2005.

37 'Non US Historical Dollar Value of Trading.'

38 This figure includes foreign firms trading. 'Datos Generales del Mercado' (Mexico City: Bolsa Mexicana de Valores, Nov. 24, 2003), http://www.bmv .com.mx/BMV/JSP/sec2_capitales.jsp (accessed on Aug. 26, 2006).

39 Coffee, Jr, 'Racing towards the Top?' 1773.

40 Interview with Mauricio Basila (vice-president, stock-market supervision), Miguel Ángel Garza (vice-president, financial institutions supervision), and Carlos Quevedo (stock markets supervision) at CNBV, Mexico City, March 13, 2006.

41 E-mail exchange with Mauricio Basila, CNBV, April 19, 2006.

42 Jorge Calderón Familiar, 'Gobierno Corporativo en México,' in *Evolución, avances y retos* (Washington, D.C.: Interamerican Development Bank, 2003), 18–28.

43 Ferdinand Banks, *Global Finance and Financial Markets* (London: World Scientific Publishing , 2001), 83.

44 Gerald Davis and Tracey Thompson, 'A Social Movement Perspective on Corporate Control,' *Administrative Science Quarterly* 39 (1994): 141–73.

45 'The United States,' *Handbook of International Corporate Governance* (2004), 180.

46 Shleifer and Vishny, 'A Survey of Corporate Governance,' 770.

47 *International Handbook of Corporate Governance* (2004), chapter 9.

48 Pierre-Marie Boury and C. Spruce, 'Auditors at the Gate: Section 404 of the Sarbanes-Oxley Act and the Increased Role of Auditors in Corporate Governance,' *International Journal of Disclosure and Governance* 2 (February 2005): 27–52. See also 'Special Report: A Price Worth Paying? – Auditing Sarbanes-Oxley,' *The Economist*, May 21, 2005.

49 'The United States,' in *International* Handbook of *Corporate Governance*.

50 'Special Report: A Price Worth Paying,' 83.

51 Ibid., 84; R. Barker, 'When Companies "Go Dark" Investors Can Lose: Sarbanes-Oxley Is Raising the Cost of Being Public,' *Business Week*, May 24, 2004, 120; C. Murphy, 'Keeping Small Business off the Street,' *Fortune Small Business* 13 (Nov. 18, 2003): 18.

52 Karen Howlett, 'Critics Fear US Regulations Will Deter Risk-taking and Hurt the Economy,' *Globe and Mail*, Sept. 9, 2003.

53 'Battle of the Bourses,' *The Economist* (May 25, 2006).

54 Publicaciones del Instituto Mexicano de Contadores Públicos, 'Ley Sarbanes-Oxley, principales aspectos e implicaciones para la empresa mexicana,' Centro de Investigación de la Contaduría Pública (IMCP), Mexico City, 2005.

55 Alberto Barranco Chavarría, 'Batalla Final,' in *Síntesis*, April 3, 2006, http://puebla.sintesisdigital.net/index.php?mod=article&cat= Posdata&article =4173.

56 David Simchi-Levi, Phil Kamisnsky, and Edith Simchi-Levi, *Designing and Managing the Supply Chain* (New York: McGraw-Hill/Irwin, 2002).

57 DataSec, 'Sarbanes Oxley e Informe Coso,' Nov. 15, 2004, http://www .datasec.com.uy/archivos/SARBANES_OXLEY_E_INFORME_ COSO.pdf (accessed on Sept. 4, 2006).

58 Noel Hernández Ayala, '¿Porqué afecta la Sarbanes Oxley Act a las empresas mexicanas?' *Gestiopolis*, November 2004, http://www.gestiopolis.com/ canales3/ger/oxley.htm.

59 International Organization for Standarization, 'SO ISO/IEC 17799:2000 Information technology – Code of Practice for Information Security M,' cited in '¿Porqué afecta la Sarbanes Oxley Act a las empresas mexicanas?' *Monografías*, Nov. 4, 2004.

60 Geoffrey E. Hale, 'Canadian Federalism and the Challenge of North American Integration,' *Canadian Public Administration* 47, no. 4 (2004): 497.

61 John Partridge, 'Market Has Image Problem: Dodge Warns Canadian Regulatory Environment Seen Abroad as a "Bit More of a Wild West,"' *Globe and Mail*, Dec. 10, 2004.

62 Ibid.

63 See Karen Howlett, 'Appetite for Regulatory Reforms Lacking, Former OSC Boss Says,' *Globe and Mail*, Feb. 17, 2003.

64 Sinclair Stewart, 'Head of TSX Seeks to End Turf Wars, Stymiest Challenges "Feuding" Regulators to Work Together,' *Globe and Mail*, Nov. 28, 2002.

65 The Association of Canadian Securities Administrators formed a permanent secretariat in September 2003 through which provincial regulators are able to harmonize their policies, and the body has proposed reforms, such as the passport system based on mutual recognition. Hale, 'Canadian Federalism and the Challenge of North American Integration,' 13.

66 Lori Verstegen Ryan, 'Corporate Governance and Business Ethics in North America: The State of the Art,' *Business and Society* 44, no.1 (2005): 61.

67 Hale, 'Canadian Federalism and the Challenge of North American Integration,' 12.

68 An Act respecting Nasdaq Stock Exchange Activities in Québec, RSQ c. E-20.01; Bertrand Marotte, 'Nasdaq Reducing Canadian Operations,' *Globe and Mail*, July 10, 2004.

69 Janet McFarland, 'BCSC to Allow Direct Trading on NASDAQ,' *Globe and Mail*, Nov. 13, 2003.

70 'Nasdaq Announces Changes in Canada,' *Nasdaq Newsroom*, July 9, 2004.

71 Derek DeCloet, 'Tough Enough: Long Criticized as Too Timid to Make the Difficult Decisions, Royal Bank CEO Gord Nixon Just Engineered a Bold Executive Shakeup. Now Comes the Hard Part,' *Globe and Mail*, Oct. 29, 2004; Derek DeCloet, 'Barbara Stymiest's Legacy at TSX – Modernizing a Financial Dinosaur,' *Globe and Mail*, Sept. 10, 2004.

72 'Nasdaq Canada Closing Montreal Office; to Be Operated from New York, Chicago,' *Canadian Press*, July 9, 2004.

73 Ibid.

74 Ibid.

75 B. Husted and C. Serrano, 'Corporate Governance in Mexico,' *Journal of Business Ethics* (May 2002): 37, 3.

76 David Luhnow, 'New Static: A Mexican Billionaire Now Faces Investigation in US,' *Wall Street Journal*, Feb. 27, 2004.

77 Comissión Nacional Bancaria y de Valores, 'Nueva Ley del Mercado de Valores,' January 2006, 14.

78 David Hernandez and Juan Carlos Conejo, 'Mexico Takes on Corporate Governance Challenge,' *International Financial Law Review* 22, no. 9 (2003): 62–5.

79 Ritch Grande Ampudia, 'Corporate Governance in Mexico,' *International Financial Law Review* 21 (2002): 159–62.

80 Ibid., 160.

81 Interview with Carlos Martínez, Mexican Embassy, Office of Economic Affairs, Washington, D.C., March 30, 2004.

82 John Authers, 'Mexico Moves to End Share Class Warfare: New Rules on Tender Offers Will Boost the Voting Rights of Minority Stockholders,' *Financial Times*, May 2, 2002, 24.

83 Hernandez and Conejo, 'Mexico Takes on Corporate Governance Challenge.'

84 John Authers, 'Mexico Moves to End Share Class Warfare,' 24.

85 La Porta et al., 'Investor Protection and Corporate Governance,' 21.

86 Luhnow, 'New Static.'

87 Martinez interview.
88 Luhnow, 'New Static.'
89 Ampudia, 'Corporate Governance in Mexico.'
90 'Battle of the Bourses.'
91 Anuj Gangahar, 'NYSE Vote Approves Euronext Deal,' *Financial Times*, Dec. 21, 2006.
92 Gaston Ceron, 'Moving the Market: NYSE Group's Shareholders Approve Takeover of Euronext,' *Wall Street Journal*, Dec. 21, 2006 ('More exchange consolidation is expected. NYSE Chief Executive John Thain again said that Asia remains the next logical place for NYSE Euronext to expand, but that a deal there may not take the form of a full-blown merger').
93 Joe Gawronski, 'Much Ado about Nothing – Sarbanes-Oxley Is Only Partly to Blame for the Decline in Foreign Companies Listing Their Stock on U.S. Markets,' *Wall Street and Technology*, Dec. 1, 2006; and Jeremy Grant, 'Regulators and Companies Fight Legislative Creep,' *Financial Times*, Oct. 31, 2006.
94 Jeremy Grant, 'Regulators Rush to Keep up with Mergers,' *Financial Times*, July 12, 2006 ('Stephen Cutler, a former SEC enforcement head and now co-chairman of the securities department at WilmerHale, a US law firm, argues that the time has come for "some level of [global] regulatory convergence, otherwise there will be a race to the bottom" in standards').

XIII. THE BANKING SECTOR

1 United Nations Statistics Division, 'Statistical Database, Common Database,' GDP at market prices, 2000 prices in US dollars, http://unstats.un.org/unsd/cdb/cdb_advanced_data_extract.asp (accessed on April 14, 2008).
2 Interview with Miguel Ángel Garza, vice-president, financial institutions supervision, Comisión Nacional Bancaria y de Valores (CNBV), March 13, 2006.
3 Bank of International Settlements, 'Consolidated Banking Statistics, Dec 2006,' Table 9B: Foreign claims by nationality of reporting banks, immediate borrower basis,' http://www.bis.org/publ/qtrpdf/r_qa0612.pdf#page=62 (accessed on April 14, 2008).
4 Joseph Iteiney and Ann Matasar, *The Impact of Geographic Deregulation on the American Banking Industry* (Westport, Conn.: Quorum Books, 2002), 3.
5 Jill M. Hendrickson, 'The Long and Bumpy Road to Glass-Steagall Reform: A Historical and Evolutionary Analysis of Banking Legislation,' *American Journal of Economics and Sociology* 60, no. 4 (2001): 862.

6 Department of Finance, 'Canada's Banks,' http://www.fin.gc.ca/toce/ 2002/bank_e.html (accessed on April 14, 2008).

7 In 2003 Canada had one of the lowest interest-rate spreads in the OECD. Canadian Bankers Association, 'Taking a Closer Look: Competition in the Canadian Financial Services Sector,' May 2005, http://www.cba.ca/en/ viewDocument.asp?fl=5&sl=111&tl=&docid= 451&pg=1 (accessed on April 14, 2008).

8 Stephen Harris, 'Canadian Financial Services Regulation: An International Perspective,' in G. Bruce Doern et al., *Changing the Rules: Regulatory Institutions and Regimes* (Toronto: University of Toronto Press, 1999); Stephen Harris, 'Financial Sector Reform in Canada: Interests and the Policy Process,' *Canadian Journal of Political Science* 37, no. 1 (2004): 161–84.

9 Harris, 'Canadian Financial Services Regulation,' 383.

10 Peter Hadekel, 'We May Be Foreign Territory, but HSBC Feels Right at Home,' *Montreal Gazette*, Sept. 27, 2006.

11 Bank of International Settlements, 'Table 9B: Foreign claims by nationality of reporting banks.'

12 Heather McKeen, Tony Porter, and Ian Roberge, 'The Rise of Private Governance: NAFTA and Integration in the Financial Sector.' Paper prepared for presentation at the Conference on Federalism and Trans-Border Integration in North America, 2003, 11.

13 Canadian Banking Association, 'Banking on Both Sides of the 49th Parallel: Risks and Rewards of an Integrated Market.' Speech by Raymond Protti, president and chief executive officer, Sept. 25, 2001, http://cba.ca/en/ viewDocument.asp?fl=5&sl=69&tl=80&docid=199 &pg=1 (accessed on April 14, 2008).

14 Bank for International Settlements, 'Table 9B: Foreign claims by nationality of reporting banks.'

15 Canadian Bankers Association, 'The Banking Industry in Canada: Taking a Closer Look 2006,' August 2006, 39, http://www.cba.ca/en/content/ publications/2006_TakingACloser Look_Full_English.pdf (accessed on April 14, 2008).

16 Mexican Congress, 'Fobaproa: Paso a Paso.' Official website of the Mexican House of Representatives, http://www.cddhcu.gob.mx/cronica57/contenido/cont2/fobapro1. htm (accessed on April 14, 2008).

17 Interview with Mario Tamez, president of International and Special Juridical Affairs, Banco de México, May 14, 2003.

18 Garza interview.

19 Stephen Fidler, 'Mexico: What Kind of Transition?' *International Affairs* 72, no. 4 (1996): 713–25.

20 Manuel Pastor and Carol Wise, 'A Long View of Mexico's Political Economy: What's Changed? What Are the Challenges?' in Joseph Tulchin and Andrew Selee, eds., *Mexico's Politics and Society in Transition* (Boulder, Colo.: Lynne Rienner, 2003).

21 Jorge Torres, 'La Nomenclatura del Poder,' *Revista Fortuna*, Portada, http://revistafortuna.com.mx/opciones/archivo/2006/noviembre/htm/Carstens_nomenclatura_del_poder.htm (accessed on April 14, 2008).

22 Heiner Schulz, 'Foreign Banks in Mexico: New Conquistadors or Agents of Change?' Wharton Financial Institutions Center Working Paper no. 06-11, April 22, 2006, http://ssrn.com/abstract=917149 (accessed on April 14, 2008).

23 Laura Carrillo and Gabriela Cabrera, 'Duplican bancos su rentabilidad,' *Reforma*, March 23, 2006.

24 Garza interview.

25 Gregoria Vidal, 'Bancos, fortunas y poder: una lectura de la economía en el México del 2000,' in Eugenia Correa and E. Girón, eds., *Crisis y futuro de la banca en México* (Mexico City: Miguel Ángel Porrúa, 2002).

26 Adolfo Navarro, Moisés Ramírez, and Veronica Galán, 'Divide Opiniones Ley de Garantias,' *Mural* online, 28 July 2003, http://www.mural.com/negocios/articulo/285558/ (accessed on 29 July 2003).

27 Interview with Moises Schwartz, president of Comisión Nacional del Sistema de Ahorro para el Retiro (CONSAR, National Commission for the Retirement Saving System), Secretaría de Hacienda, Mexico City, May 8, 2003.

28 Interview with Federico Abarca Reyes, adjunct-director of values, Secretaría de Hacienda, Mexico City, May 20, 2003.

29 John Lyons and Tom Barkley, 'López Obrador ladra (pero no muerde) a los bancos de México, dicen asesores y analistas,' *Wall Street Journal Americas*, March 29, 2006.

30 BBVA Bancomer, 'BBVA Bancomer Líder del Mercado de Remesas Familiares de Dinero Enviadas de EUA a México, July 2, 2003, http://www.bancomer.com.mx/salaprensa/corn_comup_0207A.html (accessed on April 14, 2008).

31 Financial Times, 'Expansion: SCH Buys Bank of America Assets,' *European Intelligence Wire*, Oct. 24, 2006; 'Santander Serfin y Bank of America dan avances concretos en su alianza,' *PR Line Espāna*, June 18, 2003.

32 Roberto González, 'Impulsa Banorte un sistema financiero binacional con EU,' *La Jornada*, March 26, 2007.

33 Alicia Girón, 'La banca comercial en Canadá, Estados Unidos y México,' in

Alicia Girón, Edgar Ortiz, and Eugenia Correa, eds., *Integración Financiera y TLC: Retos y Perspectivas* (Mexico City: Siglo XXI, 1995), 251.

34 K.N. Schefer, *International Trade in Financial Services* (London: Kluwer Law International, 1999), 133.

35 See NAFTA Articles 1412(2)(c) and 1415(2).

36 Interview with Lawrence Herman, Cassels Brock and Blackwell LLP, Toronto, Feb. 20, 2004.

37 Confidential interviews with officials at the Secretaría de Hacienda, Mexico City, May 20, 2003.

38 Author's notes, 33rd annual conference of the International Organization of Securities Commissions, Paris, May 28–29, 2008.

39 Eric Leroux, 'Trade in Financial Services under the World Trade Organization,' *Journal of World Trade* 36, no. 3 (2002): 430.

40 General Agreement on Trade in Services (GATS), Annex on Financial Services 2(a).

41 World Trade Organization (WTO), 'WTO Legal Texts – A Summary of the Final Act of the Uruguay Round,' http://www.wto.org/english/docs_e/legal_e/ursum_e.htm#Unders tanding (accessed on April 14, 2008).

42 L. Jacobo Rodriguez, 'Banking Stability and the Basel Capital Standards,' *Cato Journal* 23, no. 1 (2003): 116.

43 Ibid., 115.

44 Sydney Key, 'Trade Liberalization and Prudential Regulation: The International Framework for Financial Services,' *International Affairs* 75, no. 1 (1999): 71.

45 Jennifer Hughes, 'Watchdogs Eye Rating Agencies,' *Financial Times*, May 28, 2008. Michel Prada, 'Le régulateur de marché face à la crise du *subprime*,' *Rapport moral sur l'argent dans le monde 2008* (Paris : Asssociation d'économie financière, 2008), 63–70.

46 Rodriguez, 'Banking Stability and the Basel Capital Standards,' 119.

47 Duncan Wood, *Governing Global Banking: The Basel Committee and the Politics of Financial Globalisation* (Aldershot, U.K.: Ashgate, 2005), 32, 163.

48 Ibid., 163.

49 Thomas Atkins, 'EU Seeks Common Ground with US on Banking Rules,' *Forbes.com*, Nov. 13, 2003, http://www.forbes.com/home_europe/newswire/2003/11/13/rtr114 6762.html (accessed on Aug. 9, 2003).

50 Beatrice Weder and Michael Weden, 'Will Basel II Affect International Capital Flows to Emerging Markets?' OECD Development Centre, Technical papers no. 199 (October 2002).

51 The IIB's mission statement can be found on its website: http://www.iib.org/.

52 Interview with Manuel Acevedo Guadiana, director of international links, Department of Banks and Savings in Secretaria de Hacienda, Mexico City, May 13, 2003.
53 McKeen, Porter, and Roberge, 'The Rise of Private Governance: NAFTA and Integration in the Financial Sector,' 7.

XIV. LABELLING GENETICALLY MODIFIED FOOD

1 Mark A. Pollack and Gregory C. Shaffer, 'Biotechnology: The Next Transatlantic Trade War,' *Washington Quarterly* 23 (autumn 2000): 42.
2 Doug Palmer; 'U.S. Sees Faults in EU Precautionary Principle Paper,' *Reuters*, March 22, 2000.
3 Global Exchange, 'Background and Information about Mexican Maize and the Contamination,' Global Exchange Website, http://www.globalexchange.org/campaigns/mexico/news/gmo10010 1.html (accessed on April 11, 2008).
4 Royal Society of Canada, 'Elements of Precaution: Recommendations for Regulation of Food Biotechnology in Canada' (Ottawa: January 2001).
5 Louise Moore, 'Science, Internationalization, and Policy Networks: Regulating Genetically-Engineered Food Crops in Canada and the United States, 1973 to 1998,' PhD thesis, University of Toronto, 2000, 27.
6 Ibid., 30.
7 Interview with Julia Moore, public-policy expert, Woodrow Wilson International Center for Scholars, Washington, D.C., April 7, 2003.
8 Ibid.
9 Lawrence Busch, Institute for Food and Agricultural Standards, 'The Politics of GM Food.' Presentation at GM Workshop, University of Toronto, Jan. 17, 2003.
10 Interview with Greg Conko, director of Food Safety Policy, Competitive Enterprise Institute, Washington, D.C., April 10, 2003.
11 Ibid.
12 European Commission, 'Commission Proposes de Minimis Threshold and Labelling Rules for GMOs,' Oct. 22, 1999, http://www.foodlaw.rdg.ac.uk/news/eu-99-67.htm (accessed on April 11, 2008).
13 15 Ronald C. Wimberley et al., 'Food from Our World: The Globalization of Food and How Americans Feel about it,' Feb. 24, 2003, http://sasw.chass.ncsu.edu/global-food/foodglobal.pdf (accessed on April 11, 2008).

14 Interview with Michael Khoo, representative, Union of Concerned Scientists, Washington, D.C., April 11, 2003.

15 Interview with Charles Margulis, genetic-engineering campaigner, Greenpeace, Washington, D.C., April 9, 2003.

16 Press Release, 'Kucinich to Introduce Bills to Label Genetically Engineered Food and Protect Consumers,' http://kucinich.house.gov/News/DocumentSingle.aspx?DocumentI D=42904 (accessed on April 11, 2008).

17 Alaska, California, Colorado, Hawaii, Maine, Massachusetts, Michigan, Minnesota, New York, Ohio, Oregon, Pennsylvania, Texas, Vermont, and West Virginia comprise the states that have attempted to legislate some sort of mandatory GM labelling system.

18 Craig Winters, 'Statement from the Campaign to Label Genetically Engineered Foods,' Campaign to Label Genetically Engineered Foods, http://www.voteyeson27.com/campaign_statement.htm (accessed on April 11, 2008).

19 Conko interview.

20 Interview with Pat Venditti, Greenpeace campaigner, Toronto, March 5, 2003.

21 Interview with Charles Caccia, Member of Parliament, Liberal Party, Toronto, Feb. 21, 2003.

22 Clayton Ruby, 'Forget about Labels, Just Eat What Ottawa Puts in Front of You,' *Globe and Mail*, Feb. 13, 2001.

23 Interview with Dr Spencer Barrett, member of the Royal Society of Canada's expert panel, Toronto, Feb. 2, 2003.

24 Letter to Peter Turner, president of Monsanto Canada, from Ken Ritter, dated May 22, 2003. Found at http://www.cwb.ca/public/en/newsroom/releases/2003/052703.jsp (accessed on April 11, 2008).

25 Carey Gillam, 'Monsanto Undeterred as Biotech Wheat Debate Persists,' Reuters, May 27, 2003, http://www.agobservatory.org/agribusiness_records.cfm?nID=74 (accessed on April 11, 2008).

26 The position of the Canadian Federation of Agriculture on Bill C-287 can be found at http://www.cfa-fca.ca/upload/fact_sheets_CFA_C-287.pdf (accessed on April 18, 2008).

27 Canadian Biotechnology Advisory Committee, 'Improving the Regulation of Genetically Modified Foods and Other Novel Foods in Canada,' Report to the Government of Canada Biotechnology Ministerial Co-ordination Committee, August 2002, 41–2, _www.cbac.report.pdf (accessed on April 19, 2008).

28 Ibid., 42.

29 Council of Canadians, 'GM Labelling: Canada Is Crawling before Industry and USA,' Nov. 13, 2002, http://www.canadians.org/display_document .htm?COC_token=4@@a ebffb944c6f955af42b9c818744b976&id=483 &isdoc=1&catid=67 (accessed on April 11, 2008).

30 Interview with Liza Covantes, Greenpeace, Mexico City, May 27, 2003.

31 Reuters, 'Mexican Senate Passes Bill on Genetic Food Labels,' May 31, 2000, *Reuters World Report.*

32 Covantes interview.

33 Interview with Maria Colin, Greenpeace, Mexico City, May 27, 2003.

34 Covantes interview.

35 Interview with Adriana Carrillo, trade-system specialist, Canadian Embassy, Mexico City, May 29, 2003.

36 Interview with José Luis Solleiro, AgroBIO Mexico representative, Mexico City, May 14, 2003.

37 Covantes interview.

38 Cropchoice News, 'Industry Mobilizes to Modify Mexico's Labelling Measures,' CropChoice.com, Feb. 12, 2002, http://www.biotech-info.net/ industry_mobilizes.html (accessed on April 11, 2008).

39 For an example of the reaction of civil society: 'US and Canada Threaten Mexico's Corn Biodiversity,' Food Safety Network, May 31, 2001, http:// archives.foodsafetynetwork.ca/agnet/2001/6–2001/ag-06–03–0of1–01.txt (accessed on April 11, 2008).

40 Solleiro interview.

41 Interview with Karen Antebi, economic counsellor, Trade and NAFTA Office, Mexican Embassy, Washington, D.C., April 8, 2003.

42 Global Exchange, 'Background and Information about Mexican Maize and the Contamination.'

43 Carrillo interview.

44 Covantes interview.

45 Solleiro interview.

46 Christoph Strunck, 'Why Is There No Mad Cow Disease in the United States?' Institute of European Studies, University of California at Berkeley, http://ies.berkeley.edu/enews/articles/old/madcow.html (accessed on April 11, 2008).

47 World Trade Organization, 'The WTO Agreement on the Application of Sanitary and Phytosanitary Measures (SPS agreement),' http://www.wto .org/English/tratop_e/sps_e/spsagr_e.htm (accessed on April 11, 2008).

48 Charles E. Hanrahan, 'Agricultural Biotechnology: The US-EU Dispute,' Congressional Research Service, http://www.usembassy.it/pdf/other/ RS21556.pdf (accessed on April 11, 2008).

49 Ibid.

XV. INTELLECTUAL PROPERTY RIGHTS AND BIG PHARMA

1   Emmanuel Combe and Etienne Pfister, 'Patentes y acceso a medicamentos,' in Alenka Guzman and Gustavo Viniegra, eds., *Industria farmacéutica y propiedad intelectual* (Mexico City: Miguel Angel Porrua, UNAM, 2005), 83.

2   Ibid., 88–9.

3   P.A. Francis, 'World Pharma at 602 BN,' Pharmabiz.com, March 29, 2006, http://www.pharmabiz.com/article/detnews.asp?articleid=32584 &sectionid=47 (accessed on April 14, 2008).

4   Marcia Angell, 'Over and Above: Excesses in the Pharmaceutical Industry,' *Canadian Medical Association Journal* (Dec. 7, 2004).

5   Ronald W. Lang, *The Politics of Change: A Comparative Pressure-Group Study of the Canadian Pharmaceutical Manufacturers Association and the Association of the British Pharmaceutical Industry, 1930–1970* (Lexington, Mass.: Lexington Books, 1974), 13.

6   The Independent Institute, *History of Federal Regulation: 1902–Present*, Nov. 15, 2002, FDA Review.org, http://www.fdareview.org/history.shtml# sixteenth (accessed on April 14, 2008).

7   Henry G. Grabowski and John M. Vernon, 'Longer Patents for Increased Generic Competition in the US: The Waxman-Hatch Act after One Decade,' *PharmacoEconomics* 10, no. 2 (1996): 112.

8   Ibid.

9   Consumer Project on Technology, 'Revolving Door between the US Government and Industry: Version 2.0,' January 2002, http://www.cptech.org/ ip/health/politics/revolvingdoor.html (accessed on April 14, 2008).

10   Robert Pear, 'Drug Industry Is on the Defensive as Power Shifts,' *New York Times*, Nov. 24, 2006.

11   Source for these statistics on each country: World Health Organization Core Health Indicators Database, http://www3.who.int/whosis/core/core _select.cfm (accessed on April 14, 2008).

12   Patented Medicines Prices Review Board (PMPRB), *PMPRB Annual Report* (2005).

13   Human Resources and Social Development Canada, 'Pharmaceutical and Medicine Industry,' http://www.hrsdc.gc.ca/en/hip/hrp/sp/ industry _profiles/pharm aceutical_medicine.shtml (accessed on April 14, 2008).

14   Ibid.

15   Gustavo Burachik, Joan Brodovsky, and Sergio Queiroz, 'La industria mexicana en los años 90,' in Jorge M. Katz, ed., *Apertura económica y desregulación en el Mercado de medicamentos: la industria farmacéutica y farmoquímica*

de Argentina, Brasil y México en los años 90 (Buenos Aires: Alianza, 1997), 170–1.

16 United States Department of State Dispatch, 'Fact Sheet: Mexico' 2, no. 38 (Sept. 23, 1991): 713.

17 M. Destler, *American Trade Politics* (Washington, D.C.: Institute for International Economics, 1995), 318.

18 Malcolm D. Rowat, 'An Assessment of Intellectual Property Protection in LDCs from both a Legal and Economic Perspective – Case Studies of Mexico, Chile, and Argentina,' *Denver Journal of International Law and Policy* 21, no. 2 (1993): 414–15.

19 Rosemary E. Gwynn, 'Mexico,' in R. Michael Gadbaw and Timothy J. Richards, eds., *Intellectual Property Rights: Global Consensus, Global Conflict?* (London: Westview Press, 1998), 239.

20 Helena Stalson, *Intellectual Property Rights and US Competitiveness in Trade* (Washington, D.C.: National Planning Association, 1987), 38.

21 Ibid., 37.

22 Peggy E. Chaudhry and Michael G. Walsh, 'International Property Rights: Changing Levels of Protection under GATT, NAFTA and the EU,' *Columbia Journal of World Business* 30, no. 2 (1995): 80–92.

23 The South Centre, 'Trade-Related Intellectual Property Rights: A New Regime,' the TRIPS Agreement: A Guide for the South, the Uruguay Round Agreement on Trade-Related Intellectual Property Rights, http://www.southcentre.org/publications/TRIPS/TRIPSmaintextt rans-01.htm (accessed on April 14, 2008).

24 Linda McQuaig, *The Quick and the Dead* (Toronto: Viking, 1991), 136.

25 H.C. Eastman, 'The Report of the Commission of Inquiry,' Can. Cat. No. CA CP32–46/1985E (Ottawa, 1985).

26 Eric Wolfhard, *The Mote in GATT's Eye: Intellectual Property Rights and International Trade in the Uruguay Round* (Toronto: Ontario Centre for International Business, 1990), 83.

27 Ibid.

28 Wayne D. Critchley, 'Drug Patents and Drug Prices: The Role of the PMPRB.' Notes for an Address at the Patented Medicines Prices Review Board to Drug Patents Conference, Toronto, March 4, 2002, 3.

29 Ibid.

30 Abraham Rotstein, 'Intellectual Property and the Canada-US Free Trade Agreement: The Case of Pharmaceuticals,' in K.R.G. Nair and Ashok Kumar, eds., *Intellectual Property Rights* (New Delhi: Allied Publishers , 1994), 230–2.

31 M.A. Valencia, 'Tratado de Libre Comercio México, Estados Unidos y

Canadá – Posición del Sector Farmacéutico' (Mexico City: CANIFARMA, 1993).

32 Ibid.

33 Gwynn, 'Mexico,' 239.

34 Rotstein, 'Intellectual Property,' 230.

35 Keith E. Maskus, *Intellectual Property Rights in the Global Economy* (Washington, D.C.: Institute for International Economics, 2000), 192.

36 Interview with Héctor Gómez, chief of acquisitions, 24th Hospital of IMSS, Mexico City, Oct. 30, 2007.

37 Interview with Dr Santiago Martínez, former director of several IMSS hospitals, Mexico City, Oct. 23, 2007.

38 Office of the United States Trade Representative (USTR), '2003 National Trade Estimate Report on Foreign Trade Barriers: Mexico,' 2003.

39 Staff Rumbo de México, 'Fantasma de la privatización,' *Rumbo de México*, Dec. 14, 2005, http://www.industria-farmaceutica.com/index.php (accessed on Jan. 28, 2008).

40 Gustavo Leal y Carolina Martínez, 'Puntos de vista sobre la industria químico-farmacéutica. Un parpadeo sobre un actor de la arena de la política pública de salud y seguridad social,' *El Cotidiano*, UNAM, 17, no. 106 (2000): 92.

41 Jorge Kuri, 'El mercado farmacéutico en México, patentes, similares y genéricos,' *Marketing Global* 9, no. 55 (2006), http://www.mktglobal .iteso.mx/numanteriores/2006/septiembre06/septiembre063.htm (accessed on April 14, 2008).

42 Antonio Torres-Ruiz, 'An Elusive Quest for Democracy and Development in a Globalized World: The Politics of HIV/AIDS in Mexico,' PhD thesis, University of Toronto, 2005.

43 Rocío Sánchez, 'Colaboración regional, logros ampliados,' *Notiese* (Feb. 16, 2006), http://www.notiese.org/interior.shtml?sh_itm=5bc3a40c14c39e7 236c5b8c3bdc2a4c3 (accessed on April 14, 2008).

44 Burachik, Brodovsky, and Queiroz, 'Apertura económica y desregulación en el mercado de medicamentos,' 183–4.

45 Canadian Embassy, Mexico City, Trade and Business Development Division, 'Priority Sector Action Plan 2000–2001: Opportunities and Challenges,' *Pharmaceuticals and Biotechnology*, http://www.dfait-maeci.gc.ca/ mexico-city/trade/priorsectorpharmacet-en.asp (accessed on Feb. 16, 2003).

46 Burachik, Brodovsky, and Queiroz, 'Apertura económica y desregulación en el mercado de medicamentos,' 189.

47 Maryse Robert, *Negotiating NAFTA: Explaining the Outcome in Culture, Tex-

tiles, Autos, and Pharmaceuticals (Toronto: University of Toronto Press., 2000), 219.

48 KPMG en Mexico, 'The Pharmaceutical Industry in Mexico: 60 Years in Mexico' (Mexico City: Programa de Industrias, 2006), www.kpmg.com.mx/publicaciones/libreria/mexico/st-farmaceutico(06).pdf (accessed on April 14, 2008).

49 Torres-Ruiz, *An Elusive Quest for Democracy*, 201.

50 Ibid., 201–2.

51 Farmacias Similares website, http://www.farmaciasdesimilares.com.mx/historia.html (accessed on April 14, 2008).

52 Apotex Mexico website, http://www.apotex.com.mx/preguntas.htm (accessed on April 14, 2008).

53 Interview with David A. Balto, White and Case LLP, Washington, D.C., May 7, 2003.

54 Canadian Generic Pharmaceutical Association, 'The Impact of the World Trade Organization Rulings on Canada's Prescription Drug Costs,' http://www.cdma-acfpp.org/en/issues_international/wto.html (accessed on April 14, 2008).

55 Staff Techlawjournal, 'WTO Appellate Body Rules That Canada's 17 Year Patent Term Violates TRIPs,' *Techlawjournal*, http://www.techlawjournal.com/trade/20000919.asp (accessed on April 14, 2008).

56 Jacqueline D. Krikorian, 'Planes, Magazines, and Automobiles: The Impact of WTO Decisions on Canadian Law and Policy, 1995–2002,' Working Paper, University of Toronto, Sept. 18, 2002.

57 J.H. Dunning, *Multinational Enterprise and the Global Corporation* (New York: Addison Wesley, 1993).

58 Industry Canada, 'Changing Conditions and Industry Response,' *Sector Competitiveness Framework Series – Pharmaceutical Industry* (Jan. 19, 2001).

59 PMPRB, *PMPRB Annual Report*, 2005.

60 'Local Government in US Buy Cheaper Prescription Drugs in Canada,' *British Medical Journal* 323, no. 7424 (Nov. 15, 2003): 1126.

61 'GOP Can't Ignore Push for Importing Cheaper Drugs,' *Washington Post*, March 13, 2004, http://seattletimes.nwsource.com/html/nationalpolitics/20018 78106_canadadrugs13.html (accessed on April 14, 2008).

62 Donald L. Barlett and James Steele, 'Why We Pay So Much for Drugs,' *Time International*, Jan. 27, 2004.

63 Open Secrets.org, Center for Responsive Politics, www.Opensecrets.org (accessed on April 14, 2008).

64 Lynn Sweet, 'Following the Leaders: Hastert Talks Trade,' *The Hill*, Feb. 5, 2004.

65 USTR, *2003 Special 301 Report: Watch List*, http://www.ustr.gov/Document

_Library/Reports_Publications/20 03/2003_Special_301_Report/Section
_Index.html (accessed on April 23, 2008).

66 Juan Ramon Nava, Antonio Sanchez, and Daniel Millan, 'Difiere diagnós-
tico de medicina pirata,' *Reforma*, May 15, 2003.

67 USTR, *2006 Special 301 Report: Watch List*, http://www.ustr.gov/Document
_Library/Reports_Publications/2006/2006_Special_301_ Review/Section_
Index.html (accessed on April 23, 2008).

68 Human Resources and Social Development Canada, 'Pharmaceutical and
Medicine Industry.'

69 In the 2004 election cycle, 66 per cent of campaign contributions went to the
Republican Party. Open Secrets.org, Center for Responsive Politics, http://
www.opensecrets.org (accessed on April 14, 2008).

70 Open Secrets.org, Center for Responsive Politics, 'Pharmaceutical/Health
Products: Long-Term Contribution Trends,' http://www.opensecrets.org/
industries/indus.asp?Ind=H04 (accessed on April 14, 2008).

71 Generic Pharmaceutical Association Web Site, http://www.gphaonline.org
(accessed on April 14, 2008).

72 Public Citizen Publication, 'Brand-name Drug Companies versus Generics:
Lobbying and Campaign Contributions,' http://www.citizen.org/
documents/brand%20vs%20generic.pdf (accessed on April 14, 2008).

73 Dwijen Rangnekar, 'Innovations in Ethical Drugs: A Framework for Analysis of the Role of Patient Groups,' School of Public Policy, University College, London, Working Paper, July 2001, 197.

74 Public Citizen Publication, 'Brand-name Drug Companies.'

75 Rangnekar, 'Innovations in Ethical Drugs,' 196.

76 Ibid., 197.

XVI. BORDER SECURITY AND THE CONTINENTAL
    PERIMETER

1 Deborah Waller Meyers, 'Does "Smarter" Lead to Safer? An Assessment of
the US Border Accords with Canada and Mexico,' *International Migration*
41, no. 4 (2003): 6.

2 Daniel Drache, *Borders Matter: Homeland Security and the Search for North
America* (Toronto: Fernwood, 2004).

3 Peter Andreas, 'Redrawing the Line: Borders and Security in the Twenty-
first Century,' *International Security* 28, no. 2 (2003): 87.

4 Ibid.

5 Ibid., 86–92.

6 Christopher Sands, 'Terrorism, Border Reform, and Canada-United States

Relations: Learning the Lessons from Section 110.' Keynote address at Linkages across the Border: The Great Lakes Economy Conference, Detroit,
April 4, 2002, 3–9.

7 Christopher Sands, 'Fading Power or Rising Power: 11 Sept. and Lessons
from the Section 110 Experience,' in N. Hillmer and M. Appel Molot, eds.,
Canada among Nations: A Fading Power (Toronto: Oxford University Press,
2002), 49–73; Department of Foreign Affairs and International Trade
(DFAIT), *Building a Border for the 21st Century: CUSP Forum Report* (Ottawa:
DFAIT, December 2000), 14–15.

8 DFAIT, *Building a Border for the 21st Century*, 15.

9 Sands, 'Fading Power or Rising Power,' 65.

10 DFAIT, *Building a Border for the 21st Century*, 15–177; Sands, 'Fading Power
or Rising Power,' 51–64.

11 DFAIT, *Building a Border for the 21st Century*, 3–12.

12 Yves Poisson, *Background Report: The Views of Canadian Industry and Business
Associations on Canada-United States Economic Integration* (Ottawa: Public
Policy Forum, October 2000), 12.

13 DFAIT, *Building a Border for the 21st Century*, 11.

14 George Haynal, presentation given to the Public Policy Conference on Can-
ada's Policy Choices. Summarized in Erick Lachapelle, ed., *Canada's Policy
Choices: Managing Our Border with the United States* (Ottawa: Public Policy
Forum, 2001), 18.

15 For nearly two years, the CCRA consulted with staff, the trading and travellers communities, and other stakeholders across the country to create a
'comprehensive plan for the future customs program over the next five
years.' The result was a publication, 'Investing in the Future: The Customs
Action Plan 2000–2004,' which Minister Martin Cauchon launched on April
7, 2000 at the Canadian Importers Association's Spring conference in Toronto (Sept. 7, 2006).

16 Rachelle Cloutier, 'Making the "Northern" Border Work in an Integrated
North America.' Conference Report for the Public Policy Forum Roundtable on Borders, Transportation and Trade, April 10–11, 2001, 13.

17 DFAIT, *Building a Border for the 21st Century*, 36, 38.

18 Canadian Border Services Agency, 'FAST,' http://canadaonline.about
.com/od/customs/Canada_Customs_and_ Border_Services.htm (accessed
on April 14, 2008).

19 Poisson, *Background Report*, 39.

20 Ibid. Emphasis added.

21 Cloutier, 'Making the "Northern" Border Work in an Integrated North
America,' 6.

22 George Haynal, 'Interdependence, Globalization and North American Borders,' *Policy Options* (September 2002): 20–6.

23 Cited by Raúl Benítez, 'A Tale of Two Borders: The US-Canada and US Mexico Lines after 9/11,' in Peter Andreas and Thomas Biersteker, eds., *The Rebordering of North America: Integration and Exclusion in a New Security Context* (New York: Routledge, 2003).

24 DFAIT, 'Smart Border Action Plan Status Report,' Dec. 17, 2004, http://www.dfait-maeci.gc.ca/can-am/menu-en.asp?act=v&mid=1&cat=10&did=2465 (accessed on Sept. 3, 2006).

25 Ibid.

26 Stephen Brill, *After: How America Confronted the September 12 Era* (New York: Simon and Schuster, 2003), 219.

27 Kent Roach, *September 11: Consequences for Canada* (Montreal and Kingston: McGill-Queen's University Press, 2003), 137.

28 Ambassador Michael Kergin, *Cold Shoulder to Terrorism* (Dec. 21, 2001), Canadian Embassy, Washington, D.C., http://www.canadianembassy.org/ambassador/011224–en.asp?form at=print (accessed on April 14, 2008).

29 DFAIT, 'Latest Status Report on the Smart Border Action Plan,' Oct. 3, 2003.

30 Citizenship and Immigration Canada (CIC), *News Release: Safe Third Country Agreement: Proposed Regulations Pre-Published*, Oct. 25, 2002, http://www.tbs-sct.gc.ca/rma/dpr/02–03/CIC-CIC/CIC-CIC03D-PR_e.asp?printable=True (accessed on April 14, 2008).

31 Ibid.

32 Privacy Commission of Ontario, *US-VISIT System Overview, Staff Briefing Note* (Feb. 3, 2004).

33 Ibid.

34 Andreas, 'Redrawing the Line,' 93.

35 M. Campbell, as quoted in Roach, *September 11*, 135.

36 Sands, 'Fading Power or Rising Power,' 49–73; DFAIT, *Building a Border for the 21st Century*, 14–15.

37 Sands, 'Fading Power or Rising Power,' 65.

38 DFAIT, 'Smart Border Action Plan Status Report,' Dec. 17, 2004.

39 Ibid.

40 Canadian Embassy, Washington, D.C., 'Canada-US Customs Co-operation,' April 26, 2005, http://www.canadianembassy.org/border/customs-en.asp (accessed on April 14, 2008).

41 DFAIT, 'Smart Border Action Plan Status Report,' Dec. 17, 2004; Canada Border Services Agency, *In-transit Container Targeting at Seaports*, September 2002, http://www.cbsa.gc.ca/media/facts-faits/015–eng.html (accessed on April 18, 2002).

42 Public Policy Forum, *Canada's Policy Choices: Managing our Border with the United States* (Toronto: Public Policy Forum, 2001), 3.
43 DFAIT, *Canada's Border Infrastructure Fund: Promoting Economic Growth, Prosperity and Security* (2005), http://www.dfait-maeci.gc.ca/can-am/menu-en.asp?act=v&mid=1&cat=1&did=2099 (accessed on Sept. 5, 2006).
44 Ibid.
45 DFAIT, 'Latest Status Report on the Smart Border Action Plan,' Oct. 3, 2003.
46 Department of Homeland Security (DHS), 'US-Canada Smart Border/30-Point Action Plan Update,' White House, Dec. 6, 2002, http://www.whitehouse.gov/news/releases/2002/12/20021206–1.h tml (accessed on April 14, 2008).
47 Canadian Centre for Policy Alternatives 'Analysis of Bill C-36: An Act to Combat Terrorism.'
48 Drache, *Borders Matter*, 7.
49 Public Policy Forum, *Canada's Policy Choices: Managing our Border with the United States*, 47.
50 Mónica Serrano, 'Bordering on the Impossible,' in Thomas Biersterker, ed., *The Rebordering of North America: Integration and Exclusion in a New Security Context* (New York: Routledge, 2003), 55.
51 Peter Andreas, 'The Escalation of US Immigration Control in the Post-NAFTA Era,' *Political Science Quarterly* 113, no. 4 (1998/1999): 2.
52 Ibid., 4.
53 US Commission on Civil Rights (USCCR), 'Summary of Migrant Civil Rights along the Southwest Border,' April 2003, http://www.usccr.gov/pubs/migrant/summary.htm (accessed on April 14, 2008).
54 Ibid.
55 Demetrios G. Papademetriou, 'The Shifting Expectations of Free Trade and Migration,' in Papademetriou et al., eds., *NAFTA's Promise and Reality: Lessons from Mexico for the Hemisphere* (Washington, D.C.: Carnegie Endowment for International Peace, 2003), 52.
56 Andreas, 'The Escalation of US Immigration Control,' 8.
57 Benítez, 'A Tale of Two Borders,' 8.
58 Secretaría de Relaciones Exteriores, *La política exterior mexicana en la transición* (Mexico City: Secretaría de Relaciones Exteriores, 2005), 21.
59 Jorge Castañeda, 'The Forgotten Relationship,' *Foreign Affairs* (May/June 2003): 3.
60 Interview with Professor Imtiaz Hussain, Universidad Iberoamericana, Santa Fe, Mexico, April 27, 2006.
61 John Bailey, 'México-EU: el potencial de la quinta canasta,' *El Universal*, May 17, 2002.

62 José María Ramos García, *La gestión de la cooperación transfronteriza México-Estados Unidos en un marco de inseguridad global: problemas y desafíos* (Mexico City: Consejo Mexicano de Asuntos Internacionales [COMEXI]-Porrúa, 2004), cited by Benítez, 'A Tale of Two Borders,' 10.

63 Interview with Raúl Benítez, CISAN, UNAM, Mexico City, Feb. 21, 2006.

64 Hussain interview.

65 Ibid.

66 Confidential interview with senior Mexican government official, Mexico City, March 2007.

67 US-Mexico Binational Council, *US-Mexico Border Security and the Evolving Security Relationship: Recommendations for Policymakers* (Washington, D.C.: Centre for Strategic and International Studies, April 2004), 3.

68 Ibid., 8.

69 Ibid., 9.

70 Office of the Press Secretary, the White House, *Smart Border 22–Point Agreement – US-Mexico Border Partnership Action Plan*, March 21, 2002, http://www.state.gov/p/wha/rls/fs/8909.htm (accessed on April 14, 2008).

71 Ibid.

72 US-Mexico Binational Council, *US-Mexico Border Security*, 11.

73 Office of the Press Secretary, *Smart Border 22–Point Agreement*.

74 Benítez interview. This information was firmly denied by a senior Mexican government official in a confidential interview in March 2007.

75 Interview with Senador Jeffrey Jones, Mexican Congress, Mexico City, February 2006.

76 Hussain interview.

77 David Brooks, 'Bush busca militarizar la frontera en apoyo a su plan migratorio,' *La Jornada*, May 13, 2006.

78 Reforma/Staff, 'Resiente el boicot comercio fronterizo,' *Reforma*, May 3, 2006.

79 Meyers, 'Does "Smarter" Lead to Safer?' 20.

80 Ibid., 20–2.

81 Ibid., 20.

82 US-Mexico Binational Council, *US-Mexico Border Security*, 3.

83 Office of the Press Secretary, *Smart Border 22–Point Agreement*.

84 US-Mexico Binational Council, *US-Mexico Border Security*, 12.

85 US Customs and Border Security, *DHS, C-TPAT Fact Sheet and Frequently Asked Questions*, http://www.customs.gov.xp/cgov/import/commercial_enforcement /ctpat/fact_sheet.xml (accessed on March 30, 2004).

86 US-Mexico Binational Council, *US-Mexico Border Security*, 14.

87 Ibid., 13.

88 Ibid., 14–15.
89 US Department of State, Bureau of Western Hemisphere Affairs, 'US-Mexico Binational Commission Working Group on Homeland Security and Border Security,' Washington, D.C., Nov. 12, 2003.
90 US House Committee on Homeland Security, 'A Line in the Sand: Confronting the Threat of the Southwest Border,' 38, http://www.house.gov/mccaul/pdf/Investigaions-Border-Report.pdf (accessed on April 14, 2008).

XVII. NORTH AMERICAN DEFENCE

1 The Monroe Doctrine, Address to US Congress by President James Monroe, Dec. 2, 1823.
2 Dwight N. Mason, 'US-Canada Defence Relations: A View from Washington,' in David Carment et al., eds., *Canada among Nations 2003: Coping with the American Colossus* (Don Mills, Ont.: Oxford Tech University Press, 2003), 137.
3 Phillipe Lagasse, 'NORAD, NORTHCOM, and the Binational Planning Group: The Evolution of Canada-US Defense Relations,' *Canadian-American Strategic Review*, part 1, www.sfu.ca/casr/ft-lagasse1.htm (accessed on April 15, 2008).
4 Dwight N. Mason, 'The Future of Canadian-US Defense Relations,' *American Review of Canadian Studies* (spring 2003): 64.
5 William R. Willoughby, 'Canadian-American Defense Co-operation,' *Journal of Politics* 13, no. 4 (1951): 675–6.
6 Kenneth Calder and Colonel Rick Williams, Statements to House of Commons, Standing Committee on National Defence and Veterans Affairs, Feb. 13, 2003, http://www.parl.gc.ca/InfoComDoc/37/2/NDVA/Meetings/Evidence/NDVAEV10–E.htm#Int-417841 (accessed on Sept. 3, 2006).
7 Lt.-Gen. George Macdonald, 'Canada-US Defence Relations, Asymmetric Threats and the US Unified Plan.' Presentation to Senate Standing Senate Committee on National Security and Defence, May 6, 2002.
8 Adam J. Hebert, 'The Return of NORAD,' *Air Force Magazine* (February 2002): 50–4, http://www.afa.org/magazine/feb2002/0202norad.pdf (accessed on April 15, 2008).
9 See Stephen R. Niblo, 'Allied Policy towards Axis Interests in Mexico during World War II,' *Mexican Studies* 17, no. 2 (2001): 351–73.
10 Monica Serrano, 'The Armed Branch of the State: Civil-Military Relations in Mexico,' *Journal of Latin America Studies* 27, no. 2 (1995): 435.
11 Ibid., 437.

12 David Rudd and Nicholas Furneaux, *Fortress North America? What Continental Security Means for Canada* (Toronto: Canadian Institute of Strategic Studies, 2002), 58.

13 Vice-Admiral Ron Buck and Commodore Jean-Yves Forcier, Evidence Presented to House of Commons, Standing Committee on National Defence and Veterans Affairs, March 18, 2003, http://www.parl.gc.ca/InfoComDoc/37/2/NDVA/Meetings/Evidence /NDVAEV14–E.htm (accessed on April 15, 2008).

14 Center for Defense Information (CDI), *US Military Spending*, *Fiscal Years 1945–2008*, http://www.cdi.org/news/mrp/us-military-spending-graph.pdf (accessed on April 15, 2008).

15 Joseph Nuñez, 'A 21st Century Security Architecture for the Americas: Multilateral Cooperation, Liberal Peace, and Soft Power,' *Strategic Studies Institute Publication* (August 2002), http://www.isn.ethz.ch/pubs/ph/list.cfm?lng=en&v21=106841&cl ick53=106841 (accessed on April 15, 2008).

16 NATO, 'NATO/OTAN. Financial and Economic Data relating to NATO Defence: Defence Expenditures of NATO Countries (1980–2003),' http://www.nato.int/docu/pr/2003/p03–146e.htm (accessed on April 15, 2008).

17 Canadian figures are in USD at current prices and exchange rates; calculations are based on information tables provided in ibid.

18 Janes Information Group, 'Defence Spending: Mexico,' www.janes.com (accessed on April 15, 2008).

19 United States, White House, 'The National Security Strategy of the United States of America, 2002,' 1, 18, http://www.whitehouse.gov/nsc/print/nssall.html (accessed on April 15, 2008).

20 Ibid.

21 United States, Department of Defense (DOD), 'US Northern Command's Strategic Vision,' Sept. 11, 2003.

22 Bonnie Baker, 'The Origins of the Posse Comitatus,' *Air Space and Power Journal* online, Nov. 1, 1999, http://www.uscg.mil/hq/g-cp/comrel/factfile/Factcards/PosseComitatus.html (accessed on April 15, 2008).

23 United States, DOD, 'US Northern Command's Strategic Vision,'14.

24 Ibid., 9–10.

25 Interview with Dwight Mason, Center for Strategic and International Studies, Americas Program – Canada Project, Washington, D.C., March 31, 2004.

26 United States, DOD, 'US Northern Command's Strategic Vision,' 4–5.

27 Interview with Amanda J. Dory, Planning and Integration, Pentagon, Office of the Assistant Secretary of Defense Homeland Defense, Washington, D.C., April 1, 2004.

28 United States, DOD, 'US Northern Command's Strategic Vision,' 5.

29 Interview with Rear-Admiral Ian Mack, Canadian defence attaché, Canadian Embassy, Washington, D.C., April 2, 2004.
30 Mason interview.
31 Dory interview.
32 Mason, 'US-Canada Defence Relations: A View from Washington,' 147.
33 Mack interview.
34 Interview with Patricia Fortier, minister counsellor and head of section, Canadian Embassy, Washington, D.C., April 2, 2004.
35 Mike Trickey, 'Military Officials Fear NorthCom Backlash; Anti-Americanism Delays Pitch to Cabinet on Joining Continental Defence Scheme,' Ottawa *Citizen*, April 30, 2002.
36 Michael Byers, 'Canadian Armed Forces under United States Command,' *International Journal* (winter 2002–3).
37 Canada, Department of National Defence (DND), 'Enhanced Canada-US Security Cooperation: Backgrounder' (Ottawa: Department of National Defence, Dec. 9, 2002), http://www.forces.gc.ca/site/newsroom/view_news_e.asp?id=509 (accessed on April 15, 2008).
38 Canada, DND, 'Sorting through 50 Years of Military Agreements: US-Canadian Planning Group Eyes Enhanced Defense Cooperation,' *Inside the Pentagon*, Aug. 14, 2003, http://www.forces.gc.ca/site/focus/canada-us/pentagon2_e.asp (accessed on April 15, 2008).
39 Canada, DND, 'US-Canada Planning Group Eyes Enhanced Defence Cooperation,' Aug. 3, 2006, http://www.forces.gc.ca/site/focus/canada-us/pentagon2_e.asp (accessed on April 15, 2008).
40 Canada, DND, 'Enhanced Canada-US Security Cooperation.'
41 United States, DOD, 'US Northern Command's Strategic Vision.'
42 Lt.-Gen. Mike Jeffrey, Evidence, House of Commons, Standing Committee on National Defence and Veterans Affairs, April 1, 2003.
43 Lagasse, 'NORAD, NORTHCOM, and the Binational Planning Group.'
44 Binational Planning Group (BPG), *The Final Report on Canada and the United States Enhanced Military Cooperation*, March 13, 2006, http://www.queensu.ca/csd/conferences/BiNational_Planning_Gr p.pdf (accessed on April 15, 2008).
45 *Agreement between the Government of Canada and the Government of the United States of America on the North American Aerospace Defense Command*, April 2006, http://www.treaty-accord.gc.ca/ViewTreaty.asp?Treaty_ID=105060 (accessed on April 15, 2008); Ernie Regehr, 'NORAD Renewal: Further down the Slippery Slope?' *Ploughshares Monitor* 27, no. 3 (2006): 2.
46 BPG, *Final Report*.
47 Ibid.

48 Center for Arms Control and Non-Proliferation, 'Briefing Book on Ballistic Missile Defense – May 2004,' in cooperation with the Center for Defense Information and Union of Concerned Scientists, http://64.177.207.201/static/nmd/pdf/ briefing_book_nmd_2004.pdf (accessed on Aug. 9, 2004).

49 Mary Gordon, 'Retired General Scorns Missile Shield,' *Toronto Star*, Aug. 11, 2004.

50 Statement of General Ralph E. Eberhart, Senate Armed Services Committee, March 25, 2004.

51 Canada, DND, 'Canada and the United States Amend NORAD Agreement,' National Defence News Release, Aug. 5, 2004, http://www.forces.gc.ca/site/Newsroom/view_news_e.asp?id=1422 (accessed on April 15, 2008).

52 CBC, 'Ka-boom or Bust: The US Missile Defence System,' *CBC News Online*, Dec. 6, 2004, http://www.cbc.ca/news/background/us_missiledefence/ (accessed on April 15, 2008).

53 Regehr, 'NORAD Renewal: Further down the Slippery Slope?' 3.

54 Statement of General Ralph E. Eberhart.

55 Raúl Benítez Manaut and Carlos Rodríguez, 'US-Mexico Border Security and the Evolving Security Relationship: Recommendations for Policymakers' (Center for Strategic and International Studies and Instituto Tecnológico Autónomo de México, April 2004), 9.

56 Raúl Benítez Manaut, 'Seguridad Hemisférica,' *Debates y desafíos* (Mexico City: CISAN, UNAM, Cuadernos de América del Norte, 2005), 51.

57 Raul Benitez Manaut, 'Security and Governance: The Urgent Need for State Reform,' in Joseph S. Tulchin and Andrew P. Selee, eds., *Mexico's Politics and Society in Transition* (Boulder Colo.: L. Rienner, 2003), 62.

58 Abe Levy, 'Mexican Troops Arrive for Katrina Relief,' *Washington Post*, Sept. 9, 2005.

59 Nunez, 'A 21st Century Security Architecture for the Americas.'

60 Serrano, 'Bordering on the Impossible: US-Mexico Security Relations after 9–11,' 60.

61 Ibid., 61.

62 Jeffrey Davidow, 'EU no busca subordinación de las Fuerzas Armadas de México,' *El Universal*, April 15, 2002, 5.

63 Gary Clyde Hufbauer and Gustavo Vega-Cánovas, 'Whither NAFTA: A Common Frontier,' in Peter Andreas and Thomas Biersteker, eds., *The Rebordering of North America? Integration and Exclusion in a New Security Context* (New York: Routledge, 2003); Organization of American States, 'Inter-American Treaty of Reciprocal Assistance,' http://www.oas.org/juridico/english/Treaties/b-29.html (accessed on April 15, 2008).

64 Interview with former Mexican ambassador Andrés Rozental, Mexico City, March 14, 2006.

65 Interview with Raúl Benítez Manaut, Centro de Investigaciones sobre America del Norte, UNAM, Mexico City, March 31, 2004.

66 Roderic Ai Camp, *Generals in the Palacio: The Military in Modern Mexico* (New York: Oxford University Press, 1992).

67 Nunez, 'A 21st Century Security Architecture for the Americas.'

68 Interview with John Bailey, director of the Mexico Project at the Center for Latin American Studies, Georgetown University, Washington, D.C., March 31, 2004.

69 Interview with Commander David Steele, vice-director, NORAD Plans and Policy, Ottawa, March 5, 2004.

70 Benítez Manaut interview.

71 Ibid.

72 Dory interview.

73 Interview with Brian Vickers, retired US officer formerly seconded to NORAD, Washington, D.C., March 26, 2004.

74 Benítez Manaut interview; Camp, *Generals in the Palacio: The Military in Modern Mexico.*

75 Vickers interview.

76 John Leggat, assistant deputy minister, Science and Technology, DND, and Ingar Moen, director, Science and Technology, DND, Evidence Presented to House of Commons Standing Committee on National Defence and Veterans Affairs, March 27, 2003.

77 Canadian Council of Chief Executives, 'New Frontiers: Building a 21st Century Canada-United States Partnership in North America,' April 2004, http://www.ceocouncil.ca/publications/pdf/8502a13cf417d09eab13468e 2a7c9f65/New_Frontiers_NASPI_Discussion_Paper_April_20 04.pdf (accessed on April 15, 2008).

78 Interview with Paul Mitchell, Canadian Forces College, Toronto, Feb. 10, 2004.

79 Commander Robert H. Edwards, 'Maritime Security Conference Report: Continental Security and Canada-US Relations: Maritime Perspectives, Challenges, and Opportunities,' Centre for Foreign Policy Studies (2003); 'Northern Command, Ballistic Missile Defence, Homeland Security: Quels choix pour le Canada/Where Does Canada Fit?' Conference, March 26, 2004. Jointly hosted by Institut d'Études Internationales, Université du Québec á Montréal (UQAM), and Woodrow Wilson International Center for Scholars, Montreal. http://www.er.uqam.ca/nobel/ieim/article .php3?id_article=1416 (accessed on April 15, 2008).

80 Global Network against Weapons and Nuclear Power in Space, http://www.space4peace.org (accessed on April 15, 2008).
81 Space War, http://www.spacewar.com (accessed on April 15, 2008).
82 Canadian Peace Alliance, http://www.acp-cpa.ca/en/index.html (accessed on April 15, 2008).
83 People Against Weapons in Space, http://www.pawscanada.ca/ (accessed on April 15, 2008).
84 Science for Peace, http://scienceforpeace.sa.utoronto.ca (accessed on April 15, 2008).
85 Council of Canadians, http://www.canadians.org (accessed on April 15, 2008).
86 Benítez Manaut, 'Seguridad Hemisférica,' 18.
87 Ibid., 50.
88 Kenneth Calder and Colonel Rick Williams, Evidence Presented to House of Commons Standing Committee on National Defence and Veterans Affairs, Feb. 13, 2003, http://www.parl.gc.ca/InfoComDoc/37/2/NDVA/Meetings/Evidence /NDVAEV10–E.htm#Int-417841 (accessed on Aug. 20, 2006).

XVIII. THE THIRD BILATERAL: THE MEXICO-CANADA RELATIONSHIP

1 The first part of this chapter is based on off-the-record interviews with government officials in Mexico City, Washington, and Ottawa in the winters of 2006 and 2007.
2 Mexican Ministry of Economy, Underministry of International Trade Negotiations, http://www.nafta-mexico.org/ls23al.php?s=24&p=3&l=2# (accessed on April 15, 2008); Department of Foreign Affairs and International Trade Canada (DFAIT), Office of the Chief Economist, 'Trade, Investment and Economic Statistics: Foreign Direct Investment Statistics,' http://www.international.gc.ca/eet/foreign-statements-en.asp (accessed on April 15, 2008).
3 Olga Abizaid Bucio, *The Canada-Mexico Relationship: The Unfinished Highway* (Ottawa: FOCAL Policy Paper, October 2004), 5.
4 Ibid., 6.
5 NAVCanada, 'Nav Canada and the 9/11 Crisis,' 29, http://www.navcanada.ca/NavCanada.asp?Language=en&Content=Co ntentDefinitionFiles%5CNewsroom%5CBackgrounders%5C911crisis. xml (accessed on April 15, 2008).

6 Bucio, *The Canada-Mexico Relationship*, 5.
7 Noemi Gal-Or, 'The Future of Canada-Mexico Relations according to Canada's International Policy Statement,' *Nueva época* 11 (summer 2006): 2.
8 Confidential interview, Ministry of External Relations, Mexico City, March 13, 2007.
9 Interview with Marguerite Pajot, Canadian Education Centre, Mexico City, March 13, 2007.
10 E-mail communications from Jean Labrie, DFAIT, March 21, 2007.
11 United States, White House, 'President Bush Proposes New Temporary Worker Program.' Remarks by the President on Immigration Policy, Jan. 7, 2004, www.whitehouse.gov (accessed on April 15, 2008); CNN, 'Bush Pushes Guest-worker Program, March 31, 2006, http://edition.cnn.com/2006/POLITICS/03/31/bush.cancun/index .html (accessed on April 15, 2008).
12 Tanya Basok, *Tortillas and Tomatoes: Transmigrant Mexican Harvesters in Canada* (Montreal and Kingston: McGill-Queen's University Press, 2002), 25–9.
13 Veena Verma, *The Mexican and Caribbean Seasonal Agricultural Workers Program: Regulatory and Policy Framework, Farm Industry Level Employment Practices, and the Future of the Program under Unionization* (Ottawa: North-South Institute, 2003), 5.
14 Basok, *Tortillas and Tomatoes*, 17.
15 Memo from the deputy minister of the Department of Citizenship and Immigration (Dec. 10, 1966), quoted in V. Satzewich, 'Rethinking Post-1945 Migration to Canada: Towards a Political Economy of Labour Migration,' *International Migration* 28, no. 3 (1990): 335.
16 Nandita Sharma, *Home Economics: Nationalism and the Making of "Migrant Workers" in Canada* (Toronto: University of Toronto Press, 2006), 19.
17 Basok, *Tortillas and Tomatoes*, 33.
18 Ibid., 27.
19 Ibid., 33; Foreign Agricultural Resource Management Services (FARMS), http://www.farmsontario.ca (accessed on April 15, 2008).
20 Ibid.
21 Basok, *Tortillas and Tomatoes*, 38–50.
22 Kerry Preibisch, *Social Practices between Seasonal Agricultural Workers, Their Employers and the Residents of Rural Ontario, Report for the North-South Institute – Executive Summary* (Ottawa: North-South Institute, 2003), 4.
23 Basok, *Tortillas and Tomatoes*, 39.
24 Blanche Petrich, 'Trabajadores temporales viven en pésimas condiciones,' *La Jornada* Oct. 1, 2005, 1.
25 Verma, *The Mexican and Caribbean Seasonal Agricultural Workers Program*, iv.

26 Ann Weston and Luigi Scarpa de Masellis, *Hemispheric Integration and Trade Relations – Implications for Canada's Seasonal Agricultural Workers Program*, Report for the North-South Institute – Executive Summary (Ottawa: North-South Institute, 2003), 4.

27 Agriculture and Agri-Food Canada, *An Overview of the Canadian Agriculture and Agri-Food System* (Ottawa: Queen's Printers, 2005), 6, 12.

28 Weston and Masellis, *Hemispheric Integration and Trade Relations*, 4.

29 Sharma, *Home Economics*, 8.

30 Ibid., 14.

31 Ibid., 5.

32 Ibid.

33 Verma, *The Mexican and Caribbean Seasonal Agricultural Workers Program*, 86.

34 José Antonio Román, 'Canadá y México ampliarán el programa de trabajo temporal,' *La Jornada*, Feb. 12, 2007.

35 Robert Miles, *Capitalism and Unfree Labour: Anomaly or Necessity?* (London: Tavistock Publications, 1987), 32–3.

36 Verma, *The Mexican and Caribbean Seasonal Agricultural Workers Program*, viii.

37 United Food and Commercial Workers (UFCW) Canada, 'National Report: Status of Migrant Farm Workers in Canada,' December 2002.

38 Monica Boyd, Chris Taylor, and Paul Delaney, 'Temporary Workers in Canada: A Multifaceted Program,' *International Migration Review* 20, no. 4 (1986): 929–50.

39 Rural Migration News, 'Mexico-Canada Guest Workers,' *Rural Migration News* (n.d.), http://migration.ucdavis.edu/rmn (accessed on April 15, 2008).

40 National Union of Public and General Employees, 'UFCW Canada Wins Right to Represent Migrant Farm Workers,' March 15, 2006, www.nupge.ca (accessed on April 15, 2008).

41 Tanya Basok, 'Post-national Citizenship, Social Exclusion and Migrants' Rights: Mexican Seasonal Workers in Canada,' *Citizenship Studies* 8, no. 1 (2004): 60.

42 Tanya Basok, 'Refugee Policy: Globalization, Radical Challenge, or State Control?' *Studies in Political Economy* 50 (1996): 136.

43 Stephen Castles, *Ethnicity and Globalization: From Migrant Worker to Transnational Citizen* (London: Sage, 2002).

XIX. THE SECURITY AND PROSPERITY PARTNERSHIP

 1 Andrés Rozental, 'The Security and Prosperity Partnership: An Overview,' *International Journal* 61, no. 3 (2006): 541.

2 This analysis is based on confidential interviews carried out in Mexico City in 2006 and 2007 (primarily in the secretariats of External Relations, Agriculture, Transport, and the Economy) and in Washington in 2006 and 2007 (in the Mexican and Canadian embassies, the National Security Council, and the Department of Commerce, as well as with officers in the US Chamber of Commerce, the Council of the Americas, and the Canada-US Business Council).

3 Council on Foreign Relations, *Building a North American Community: Report of an Independent Task Force* (Washington, D.C.: 2005).

4 United States, Office of the White House Press Secretary, 'Joint Statement by President Bush, President Fox, and Prime Minister Martin: Security and Prosperity Partnership of North America,' March 23, 2005.

5 Security and Prosperity Partnership of North America, 'Report to Leaders' (June 2005).

6 Alan D. MacPherson and James E. McConnell, 'A Survey of Cross-border Trade at a Time of Heightened Security: The Case of the Niagara Binational Region,' *American Review of Canadian Studies* 37, no. 3 (2007): 301–21.

7 Prime Minister of Canada, 'Prime Minister Announces Canadian Membership of North American Competitiveness Council,' 13 June 2006, http://www.pm.gc.ca/eng/media.asp?id=1200 (accessed on April 15, 2008).

8 The five accompanying Prime Minister Harper were Paul Desmarais, Jr, chairman and Co-CEO, Power Corporation of Canada; David A. Ganong, president, Ganong Bros.; Richard L. George, president and CEO, Suncor Energy; Richard E. Waugh, president and CEO, Bank of Nova Scotia; and Annette Verschuren, president, Home Depot Canada; the extra five were: Dominic D'Alessandro, president and CEO, Manulife Financial; E. Hunter Harrison, president and CEO, Canadian National Railways; Linda Hasenfratz, CEO, Linamar Corporation; Michael Sabia, president and CEO, Bell Canada Enterprises; and James A. Shepherd, president and CEO, Canfor Corporation.

9 Membership of the Mexican NACC executive has varied but in 2007 was made up of: José Luís Barraza, president, Consejo Coordinador Empresarial (CCE), and CEO of Grupo Impulso, Realiza y Asociados, Inmobiliaria Realiza, and Optima; Gastón Azcárraga, president, Consejo Mexicano de Hombres de Negocios (CMHN), and CEO of Mexicana de Aviación and Grupo Posadas; León Halkin, president, Confederación de Cámaras Industriales (CONCAMIN), and chairman of the board and CEO of four companies in the industrial and real estate markets; Valentín Díez, president, Consejo Mexicano de Comercio Exterior (COMCE); Jaime Yesaki, presi-

dent, Consejo Nacional Agropecuario (CNA); Claudio X. González, president, Centro de Estudios Económicos del Sector Privado (CEESP), and chairman of the board and CEO of Kimberly-Clark de México; Guillermo Vogel, vice-president, TAMSA (Tubos de Acero de México); César de Anda Molina, president and CEO, Avicar de Occidente; Tomás González Sada, president and CEO, Grupo CYDSA; and Alfredo Moisés Ceja, president, Finca Montegrande. North American Competitiveness Council, *NACC Members* (July 17, 2007).

10 North American Competitiveness Council, 'Enhancing Competitiveness in Canada, Mexico, and the United States. Private-Sector Priorities for the Security and Prosperity Partnership of North America. Initial Recommendations of the North American Competitiveness Council' 4 (February 2007).

11 Ibid.

12 Ibid.

13 Kelly Patterson, 'Canada Raising Limits on Pesticide Residues,' *CanWest News Service*, Ottawa *Citizen*, May 8, 2007, http://www.canada.com/montrealgazette/news/story.html?id=2fa 3e7f8–9c83–4ea9–ad60–c13b548fe688&k=6929 (accessed on April 15, 2008).

14 Canadian Press, 'Canadian Airlines to Keep Using U.S. No-fly List,' *CTV*, May 23, 2007, http://www.ctv.ca/servlet/ArticleNews/story/CTVNews/20070523 /nofly_list_070523 (accessed on April 15, 2008).

15 External Advisory Committee on Smart Regulation (EACSR), *Smart Regulation*, from Natural Resources Canada website, http://www.cela.ca/coreprograms/detail.shtml?x=2017 (accessed on April 15, 2008).

16 Stephen Hazell, *Canada v. The Environment: Federal Environment Assessment 1984–1998* (Toronto: Canadian Environmental Defence Fund, 1999).

17 EASCSR, *Overview of the EASCSR Report on Smart Regulation: A Regulatory Strategy for Canada* (2004).

18 Security and Prosperity Partnership (SPP), *Prosperity Annex: Report to Leaders* (August 2006).

19 This assessment is the result of examining all the documents published on the US and Canadian governments' SPP websites, as of July 7, 2007.

20 The North American Energy Working Group (NAEWG) has made a number of its reports available to the public, including *North American Energy Working Group* (March 23, 2005); *North America – The Energy Picture II* (January 2006); *Oil Sands Experts Group Workshop, SPP of North America, Houston, Texas* (January 24–25 2006); *North American Natural Gas Vision* (January 2005); and *Natural Gas Workshop Report* (June 28, 2006). But the NAEWG had been established in 2001 as a free-standing trilateral organ that was simply given another hat under the SPP.

21 SPP, *Prosperity Annex: Report to Leaders*, August 2006.
22 Natural Resources Canada, 'Oil Sands Experts Group Workshop: Security and Prosperity Partnership of North America' (January 24–25, 2006).
23 Teresa Healy, 'Deep Integration in North America: Security and Prosperity for Whom?' Canadian Labour Congress (February 20, 2007), 1–22; Jillian Skeet, 'Notes on Responding to the Security and Prosperity Partnership or Integration Agenda' (July 12, 2007).
24 Judicial Watch Press Office, 'Newly Uncovered Commerce Department Documents Detail "Security and Prosperity Partnership of North America" (September 2006), http://www.judicialwatch.org/5979.shtml (accessed on April 15, 2008).
25 Thanhnien News, 'Cancún in Security Lockdown for Bush Visit,' March 30, 2006, http://www.thanhniennews.com/worlds/?catid=9&newsid=13983 (accessed on April 15, 2008).
26 Armand B. Perschard-Sverdrup et al., *North American Future 2025 Project* (Washington, D.C.: Center for Strategic International Studies, 2007), 1–25.
27 Foreign Affairs and International Trade Canada, 'Minister MacKay Meets with Mexican Secretary of External Affairs in Halifax, Nova Scotia' (May 23, 2007).
28 Stephen Clarkson and Marjorie Griffin Cohen, 'Introduction: States under Siege,' in Clarkson and Cohen, eds., *Governing under Stress: Middle Powers and the Challenge of Globalization* (London: Zed Books, 2004), 1–11.

CONCLUSION

1 El siglo de Torreón, 'Niegan alza en maíz por TLCAN,' *El siglo de Torreón*, Jan. 11, 2008, http://www.elsiglodetorreon.com.mx/noticia/323817.niegan-alza-en-maiz-por-tlcan.siglo (accessed on April 15, 2008).
2 Emir Olivares Alonso, 'Toma El Barzón caseta de peaje de la México-Toluca,' *La Jornada*, Jan. 11, 2008, 5.
3 Organization for Economic Cooperation and Development (OECD), *OECD Economic Surveys: Mexico* (Paris: OECD), 29.
4 Enrique Mendez, 'Critica el PRD beneficios parciales con el TLCAN,' *La Jornada*, Jan. 12, 2008, 6.
5 Rogelio Gasca Neri y Raúl Fuentes Samaniego, 'Petro-globalización sin paridad: la tormenta perfecta,' *Energía a Debate*, no. 16 (2006): 7–13, http://www.energiaadebate.com.mx/Articulos/articulos_anterio res.htm (accessed on April 15, 2008).
6 Reuters, 'EU, el timón de la economía mundial,' *El Universal, Finanzas*, Sept.

2, 2006, http://www.eluniversal.com.mx/finanzas/53254.html (accessed on April 15, 2008).

7 Victor Cardoso, 'Cerrarán maquiladoras en México por la desaceleración económica en EU,' *La Jornada*, Jan. 17, 2008, 25.

8 Alma Muñoz, 'Constituyó AMLO el Movimiento Nacional en Defensa del Petróleo,' *La Jornada*, Jan. 10, 2008, 13.

9 David Brooks, 'El TLCAN, bajo escrutinio en proceso electoral de EU,' *La Jornada*, Jan. 12, 2008, 23.

10 Isidro Morales, *Post-NAFTA North America: Reshaping the Economic and Political Governance of a Changing Region* (New York: Palgrave, 2008), 180.

11 Miguel Basáñez, Ronald Inglehart, and Neil Nevitte, 'North American Convergence Revisited,' *Norte América* 2, no. 2 (2007): 21–61.

12 Wilson Center, *NAFTA at 10: Progress, Potential, and Precedents. Volume II: Remarks by President George Bush, President Carlos Salinas, and Prime Minister Brian Mulroney* (Washington, D.C.: Woodrow Wilson International Center for Scholars, 2005).

13 Henrik Enderlein, Sonja Wälti, and Michael Zürn, eds., 'Introduction,' in their *Handbook on Multilevel Governance* (Cheltenham, U.K.: Edward Elgar, forthcoming).

Acknowledgments

No sensible scholar would have undertaken this book.

Sensible would have been to organize a conference or three on transborder governance in North America. The problem was that very few experts were knowledgeable about any policy issues in all three countries and the interconnections among them. With the exception of analysts working on NAFTA and its institutions (in particular, its dispute-settlement processes) and a handful of prescient scholars with an unusually broad research agenda such as Stephen Blank, Daniel Drache, Teresina Gutiérrez-Haces, Julian Castro-Rea, Isabel Studer, Sidney Weintraub, and Carol Wise, and apart from energy – an issue driven by the United States' persistent quest for secure supplies of oil and natural gas – there are still very few researchers whose expertise embraces the two complex fields of the US-Canada and US-Mexico relationships, let alone emerging trilateral relations.

A decade ago, I was such a sensible person. Having had a long-standing interest in the relationship between my country, Canada, and its overpowering neighbour to the south, I realized in 1994 that the advent of NAFTA and then the World Trade Organization would require me to broaden my field of study. While I set about learning Spanish, I had no illusion that I could be an expert knowledgeable about all the policies and problems of the new North America and had no ambition to become one. It was my dean and my students who pushed me in that direction, so the blame and – should there be any, the credit and so the thanks – for the creation of this book must fall, first of all, on them.

It is the dean of the Faculty of Arts of the University of Toronto, Carl Amrhein, whom I first need to credit for originally giving me the means in the academic year 2001–2 to take half a dozen of our best undergraduates to finish their research on a North American issue of their choice by enjoying the luxury of a week's work in Washington. Dean Amrhein renewed this grant when the first experiment turned out to have been surprisingly productive. When his successor, Pekka Sinervo, saw our list of academic achievements (several papers for conferences and chapters accepted for peer-reviewed books), he generously supported two more years (2003–4 and 2005–6) of my continuing to take six top students under my wing with the objective of bringing their year's intensive work with me to a climax with a mind-opening research trip to the District of Columbia.

The second dose of blame and/or thanks falls on the shoulders of these students, particularly the first dozen, since it was at the end of our second year that their work on the various issues they had chosen to investigate led us to believe that, perhaps, there was reason to pursue this project more strategically. Accordingly, in 2003–4 and 2005–6, I was more directive, recruiting students to take on specific issues needed to fill in obvious gaps in our accumulating coverage in order to put together what came to be known among my nearest and dearest as my 'big, boring book.' *Boring* it was likely to be for the great mass of humanity – barring those intrepid readers who might have a burning interest in the policy face of a continent that had come to the fore as a new 'world region' with the signing of the North American Free Trade Agreement. *Big* it needed to be since, if we were to probe the reality of North America as a political-economic entity, we had to make a sufficiently large number of probes over a sufficiently broad spectrum of issues that a reader could feel we had investigated the subject fairly if not encyclopedically. To be *fair* we needed to look at issues where NAFTA played a major role and issues where it did not. Not trying to be *encyclopaedic*, we omitted some crucial issues such as transportation and, sadly, ignored the Monarch butterfly, the one true North American citizen.

Our four, week-long visits to Washington would not have produced the information and understanding that they did without the generous collaboration of a number of institutions each year. As first among equals, our stays would have been lesser experiences had we not been hosted by the Woodrow Wilson International Center for Scholars, thanks to its inspiring director, Lee Hamilton, David Biette, the founding director of its Canada Institute, and Andrew Selee, the director of its Mexico Institute. The embassies of Mexico and Canada to the United States were unfailing in their welcome each year and in their willingness to direct individual students to the appropriate colleague for further information. Under the warm guidance of Carl Ek, the Congressional Research Service made many specialists available for our group consultations. Depending on the year and the issues involved, we also profited from meetings at the Center for Strategic and International Studies, the Institute for International Economics, the School for Advanced International Studies at Johns Hopkins University, and the Office of the United States Trade Representative. Many individuals also gave us their time and shared their knowledge with us, in particular Jon Huenemann, the late Bill Merkin, Christopher Sands, Sidney Weintraub, and Tamare Woroby.

Beyond learning with my students in Washington, I also profited from my own discussions there each year with colleagues and with officials – most of whom required anonymity – in the Department of Commerce, the Canadian Embassy, and the National Security Council where I learned most about the Bush administration's attitude to the Security and Prosperity Partnership. On the North American Competitiveness Council, I had very helpful meetings with officials at the Council of the Americas and the US Chamber of Commerce.

The following are the most important student-colleagues and the chapters to which they contributed: II – NAFTA's institutional vacuum (Sarah Davidson-Ladly and Carlton Thorne); III – NAFTA's judicial capacity (Roopa Rangaswami); IV – transborder labour governance (Ian MacDonald, who, while still a third-year undergraduate, published his first term's essay for me in the *American Review of Canadian Studies*); V – transborder environmental governance (Stefanie Bowles with help from Nicholas Brandon); VI – transboundary water governance (Christiane Buie, who presented her work as 'The (Dis)integration of North American Transboundary Water Governance' to the annual meeting of the Canadian Political Science Association, University of Western Ontario, June 2, 2005); VII – big business's role in negotiating free trade (this leaned on work I had done with Maria Banda for a chapter in Ricardo Grinspun's *Whose Canada?* [2007] but was researched anew and drafted by Erick Lachapelle, who presented his analysis as 'Business' Role in North American Governance: Free Trade, Smart Borders and other Big Ideas' to the annual meeting of the Canadian Political Science Association, University of Western Ontario, June 2, 2005); VIII – energy (Kate Fischer); IX – agriculture (Rick Russo); X – steel (Christina Kish and Chris Pigott); XI – textiles and apparel (Nicholas Van Exan); XII – capital markets (Emily Tang); XIII – banking (Jesse Sherrett); XIV – genetically modified food (Kristen Brown); XV –

pharmaceuticals (Anne Swift, who presented her work as 'Discerning Manifestations of Continental Governance in the North American Pharmaceutical Industry in the Context of Intellectual Property Rights' to the annual meeting of the Canadian Political Science Association, York University, June 2, 2006; XVI – border security (Ben Hyman, Lanchanie Dias, and Alison McQueen); XVII – defence (Ben Hutchinson); XVIII – seasonal agricultural workers (Alison McQueen, who presented her work as 'Canadian Hegemony in the Continental Periphery: An Analysis of the Role of the Canadian State in the Seasonal Agricultural Workers Program' to the annual meeting of the Canadian Political Science Association, York University, June 2, 2006).

From 2001 onward, I involved these students in presenting their work to various scholarly conferences with papers that in many cases became chapters in this book or in co-authoring chapters for publications to which I had been invited to contribute. Not only did the students learn about the delights and drudgery of academic research, I sharpened my understanding of these issues by this continuous interaction between their work and my colleagues' projects.

For all its groundbreaking value, these undergraduates' work just got the process moving. Over the next several years, each study had to be reworked, sometimes drastically restructured, in some instances completely rewritten, and in every case – as time passed – constantly updated and substantially supplemented with information about the Mexican side of the problem. I employed other young colleagues, mainly MA and doctoral students, to work on correcting or improving information, harmonizing footnotes, and reworking the weaker texts. Particularly helpful were Daniella Aburto, Wendy Hicks-Casey, Dina Khorasanee, Artiom Komarov, Kim Lawton, Regina Martyn (who re-researched the daunting capital-markets problem), Alanna Krolikowski, Gemma Oberth, and Nadiya Sultan. For much of the summers of 2006 and 2007, my friends Carolyn McIntyre and Harley Smyth offered me editorial asylum in their sea captain's cottage on Amherst Island in Lake Ontario, whose waters provided a context of calm as I reworked, sometimes completely rewriting, what seemed to be endless drafts.

More challenging a problem for a project carried out in Toronto was achieving adequate information about Mexico. To this end, my greatest debt of gratitude goes to my colleague Maria Teresa Gutiérrez-Haces, the founding president of the Mexican Association of Canadian Studies, who introduced me to her country's political economy by inviting me to a number of conferences in Mexico before and after NAFTA was negotiated. Among many other collegial interconnections, she offered me space in her office in the Instituto para Investigaciones Económicas (IIE) at the Universidad Nacional Autónoma de México (UNAM) in my first full research trip to Mexico in the winter of 2006 and, with the support of the IIE's director, Jorge Basave, my own office there the next year. She also found me the perfect and indispensable assistant, Blanca Martínez López, who helped me organize and record discussions about my many draft chapters with several dozen government officials and academic researchers in 2006. A year later, Blanca came back to the manuscript, systematically upgrading and updating the Mexican part of the various chapters' analysis.

Given the impossibility of researching almost twenty policy fields from scratch, Blanca and I had conversations with many experts based on their having agreed to read the relevant draft chapter of my manuscript. I was saved from serious errors about the Tijuana River Basin by Gabriela Angeles, who sent me fresh documentation on the basis of which I recast the Mexican part of that analysis, and by Adriana Alvarez Andrade at the Colegio de la Frontera Norte in Tijuana. I am indebted to Michel Prada, president of the Autorité des Marchés Financiers in Paris for the introduction that led to the outstanding contributions to my banking and capital-markets chapters by Mauricio Basila (vice-president of Stock-market Supervision), Miguel Ángel Garza (vice-president of Financial Institutions Supervision), and Carlos Quevedo (Stock-market Supervision) at the Comisión Nacional Bancaria y de Valores. I gained important insights that led me to improve other chapters from conversations with Alejandro Álvarez (agriculture and genetically modified food), Isabel Studer (labour), Blanca Torres and Edit Antal (environment), Gustavo Vega and Jorge Witker (dispute settlement), Rocío Vargas (energy), Alejandro Villamar (pharmaceuticals), Don Brean (banking), Peter Warrian (steel), Isabel Rueda Peiro (textiles), and Raúl Benitez, Imtiaz Hussain, and Marcela Cenorio (security). At the Secretaría de la Economía I learned from Luz Maria de la Mora, Hugo Perezcano, and Ken Smith; at the Secretaría de Relaciones Exteriores, from Mayomi de la Cid Rencón, Isabel Studer, and Gerónimo Gutiérrez. Formal and informal discussions with Ambassador Gaëtan Lavertu and several associates at the Canadian Embassy in Mexico City were valuable in themselves; completely invaluable were the embassy's introductions to senior Mexican officials, which led to otherwise impossible-to-secure appointments yielding unattributable revelations about the Fox government's attitude towards and participation in the Security and Prosperity Program of North America.

In a broad synthesis such as this, much of its value comes from the accuracy of the information it provides. But facts have relevance only when linked to their interpretation. Although this study engages with hundreds of facts, its crucial ingredients are balance and perspective. It will be for readers to judge whether I have achieved these qualities, but in my quest for global perspective I benefited immeasurably from participating in a number of large research endeavours which gave me the chance to interact over this seven-year period with colleagues in several disciplines and various countries.

As an executive member of the Social Sciences and Humanities Research Council (SSHRC)-funded Major Collaborative Research Initiative on Neoliberal Globalism, under the leadership of Gordon Laxer of the University of Alberta, I was able to present my analysis and have it critiqued while being exposed to the views of colleagues during conferences in Mexico, Norway, and Australia. My work on North America was integrated with my co-editor Marjorie Cohen in *Governing under Stress: Middle Powers and the Challenge of Globalization* (London: Zed Books, 2004).

Within the even larger SSHRC-funded program on Globalization and Autonomy, under the rigorous direction of McMaster University's William D. Coleman, I developed a chapter about North America for the book that Louis Pauly edited with Coleman, *Global Ordering: Institutions and Autonomy in a Changing World* (Vancouver: University of British Columbia Press, 2008).

As a senior fellow at the Centre for International Governance Innovation (CIGI), my participation in the management group establishing an electronic bibliographical Portal on North America helped keep me in touch with research being done throughout the continent about the continent. CIGI also generously supported the indexing of this book.

I had a mind-expanding year in 2004–5 spent as a virtual professor for the now defunct Law Commission of Canada researching and co-authoring with Stepan Wood, a professor of environmental law at Osgoode Hall Law School, a study on how Canadian law should respond to globalization issues: *Governing beyond Borders* (UBC Press, forthcoming).

I mentioned my profiting from participation in SSHRC-funded programs. This book would simply not have happened at all without the financial support that came from two of SSHRC's three-year, peer-reviewed standard research grants.

Beyond raising the quality of the individual texts, much effort was needed to achieve their coherence as chapters in a monograph. Crucial in identifying inconsistencies in the various texts' approach or in their use of a particular concept was the contribution of two MA classes in 2006 and 2007 which workshopped successive drafts of the complete manuscript. A number of these students worked on individual chapters in order to refine their analysis or update their data: Héloíse Apestéguy-Rioux, Iona Hancas, Josh Kurtzer, Stella Luk, Patrick McConnell, Stevie O'Brien, and Francisco Obando. A week-long workshop with Edgar Grande's doctoral students at the University of Munich in 2007 was a major help in giving me a more comparative perspective on North America as seen by young researchers studying transborder policy regimes in the European Union.

Further assistance in testing my overall thesis came from the chance to present its general themes – and get my audiences' reactions – at various venues: the Freie Universität in Berlin; the University of Alberta in Edmonton; the Colegio de México, the Centro para Investigaciones sobre América del Norte, and the Faculdad de Relaciones Internacionales at UNAM, and the Universidad Iberoamericana in Mexico City; the Universidad Autónoma de Queretaro, the Instituto Tecnológico de Monterrey, and the Colegio de la Frontera Norte outside Mexico City; and, in Washington, American University and the School of Advanced International Studies at Johns Hopkins University's Washington campus.

A handful of individuals deserve singling out. In 2003 I was fortunate to have the help of Anna Maria Cuenca, a Woodrow Wilson Center intern, who helped some of my students by undertaking a research trip to Mexico on their behalf. First as my post-doctoral student, later as departmental colleague, Antonio Torres-Ruiz gave my manuscript his careful attention, notably contributing to its explication of 'governance' and to its treatment of intellectual property rights in Mexico concerning pharmaceuticals. In 2006 and 2007 Mary Albino devoted her extraordinary editorial sense and critical mind to help improve and even restructure many of the chapters. Finally, as the manuscript entered its final phase, Matto Mildenberger worked tirelessly and intimately with me throughout 2007–8 to fine-tune the ultimate draft and prepare it for copy editing.

Although not a 'sensible' book, I hope that this product of many years' collaboration with many students and colleagues finally makes sense. Any and all remaining errors of fact and interpretation remain my responsibility so that, while I have many to thank for their contributions to its quality, I have only myself to blame for its shortcomings.

Index

OTHER PUBLICATIONS BY STEPHEN CLARKSON

Monographs

The Big Red Machine: How the Liberal Party Dominates Canadian Politics (2005)

Uncle Sam and Us: Globalization, Neoconservatism, and the Canadian State (2002)

Trudeau and Our Times. Volume 2: The Heroic Delusion (1994) trans. as *Trudeau: L'illusion héroique* (1995) (with Christina McCall)

Trudeau and Our Times. Volume 1: The Magnificent Obsession trans. as *Trudeau: l'homme, l'utopie, l'histoire* (1990) (with Christina McCall)

Canada and the Reagan Challenge: Crisis in the Canadian-American Relationship (1982)

The Soviet Theory of Development: India and the Third World in Marxist-Leninist Scholarship (1978)

City Lib: Parties and Reform (1972)

L'analyse soviétique des problèmes indiens du sous-développement (1955–64) (1971)

Edited Books

My Life as a Dame: The Personal and the Political in the Writings of Christina McCall (2008)

Governing under Stress: Middle Powers and the Challenge of Globalization (2004) (with Marjorie Griffin Cohen)

Visions 2020: Fifty Canadians in Search of a Future (1970)

An Independent Foreign Policy for Canada? (1968)